Research in Criminology

Series Editors
Alfred Blumstein
David P. Farrington

Research in Criminology

Understanding and Controlling Crime: Toward A New Research Strategy
David P. Farrington, Lloyd E. Ohlin and James Q. Wilson

The Social Ecology of Crime
J.M. Byrne and R.J. Sampson (Eds.)

The Reasoning Criminal: Rational Choice Perspectives on Offending
Derek B. Cornish and Ronald V. Clarke (Eds.)

The Social Contexts of Criminal Sentencing
Martha A. Myers and Susette M. Talarico

Predicting Recidivism Using Survival Models
Peter Schmidt and Ann Dryden Witte

Coping, Behavior, and Adaptation in Prison Inmates
Edward Zamble and Frank J. Porporino

Prison Crowding: A Psychological Perspective
Paul B. Paulus

Off School, In Court: An Experimental and Psychiatric Investigation of Severe School Attendance Problems
I. Berg, I. Brown and R. Hullin

Policing and Punishing the Drinking Driver: A Study of General and Specific Deterrence
Ross Homel

Judicial Decision Making, Sentencing Policy, and Numerical Guidance
Austin Lovegrove

Criminal Behavior and the Justice System: Psychological Perspectives
Hermann Wegener, Friedrich Lösel and Jochen Haisch (Eds.)

Male Criminal Activity from Childhood Through Youth: Multilevel and Developmental Perspectives
Marc Le Blanc and Marcel Fréchette

continued after index

Minoru Shikita Shinichi Tsuchiya

Crime and Criminal Policy in Japan

Analysis and Evaluation of the Showa Era, 1926–1988

Springer-Verlag
New York Berlin Heidelberg London Paris
Tokyo Hong Kong Barcelona Budapest

Minoru Shikita
President, Research and Training Institute, Ministry of Justice, Chiyoda-ku, Tokyo, Japan

Shinichi Tsuchiya
Director, Research Department, Research and Training Institute, Ministry of Justice, Chiyoda-ku, Tokyo, Japan; formerly Chairman, United Nations Committee on Crime Prevention and Control

Series Editors:

Alfred Blumstein
School of Urban and Public Affairs, Carnegie-Mellon University, Pittsburgh, PA 15213, USA

David P. Farrington
Institute of Criminology, University of Cambridge, Cambridge CB3 9DT, United Kingdom

Printed on acid-free paper.

Production managed by Linda H. Hwang.
Printed and bound by Edward Brothers, Inc., Ann Arbor, MI.
Printed in the United States of America.

9 8 7 6 5 4 3 2 1

ISBN 0-387-97647-7 Springer-Verlag New York Berlin Heidelberg
ISBN 3-540-97647-7 Springer-Verlag Berlin Heidelberg New York

PREFACE

The Showa Era in Japan commenced in December 1926, when Emperor Showa ascended the Throne, and came to an end in January 1989, when His Majesty passed away, ushering in the new Heisei Era. The Showa Era was marked by drastic changes in the economy, society, and political and legal systems, which brought about an ebb and flow in criminality and precipitated various criminal policies. From an economical, political, and criminological perspective, the Showa Era stands out as a remarkable period in Japanese history.

The Research and Training Institute of the Ministry of Justice, which has annually published the White Paper on Crime in Japan since 1960, received Cabinet approval to introduce a special topic section, "Criminal Policy in Showa" in the White Paper for 1989, which was published in October the same year. This White Paper is the first comprehensive publication that deals not only with the crime situation but also with the various activities of the criminal justice system, including the police, public prosecutors' offices, courts, correctional institutions, and probation and parole supervision organisations for 63 years. Preparing for the Paper involved a difficult task to analyse various statistical data and to look for appropriate materials regarding legislation and administration from the archives of the Ministry of Justice, the Supreme Court, and the Diet. Since the categories, methodologies, and standards of statistics have changed somewhat over time, it was also a troublesome task to adjust, equate, and recalculate relevant data so as to analyse them in a consecutive and consistent manner.

After the Paper had been widely circulated and well received in Japan, it was strongly felt that this very unique compilation and analysis of the 63-year history of the crime and criminal justice system in Japan would also be useful and interesting for officials and scholars in other parts of the world. Thus, it was decided to publish the relevant part of the Paper in English. It was therefore edited, compiled, and supplemented further in order to facilitate a better understanding among readers who are unfamiliar with the Japanese legal system.

A review of the Showa Era reveals that it may be roughly divided into three periods, namely the prewar and war period from 1926 to 1945, the postwar period from 1945 to 1960, and the recent period from 1960 to 1989.

In the beginning of the prewar period, the democratic principles of government were an inherited legacy from the preceding Taisho Era, in which two large political parties emerged. The acute economic conditions surrounding the Great Depression, including bankruptcies and food shortages, aggravated people's living standards in the late 1920s and early 1930s. The worsening social conditions bolstered the military power in politics, and the resulting shift in mood and political structure became dominated by fascism and militarism. The military-oriented government waged the Manchurian Incident in 1931; the China-Japan Incident in 1937; and finally entered World War II in 1941. The atomic bombing of Hiroshima and Nagasaki signaled Japanese defeat in the war in which nearly 3 million Japanese had perished.

The incidence of crime had fluctuated in accordance with the changes occurring in socio-economic conditions. Almost all categories of crime rose during the period of economic depression and political instability in the mid-1930s. Crime, however, decreased during wartime, 1937–1945, as the population was preoccupied with the war effort.

With regard to the postwar period, almost all the metropolitan areas had burnt to the ground and many industries that had fueled the prewar economy had been destroyed at the end of war. Japan was restored to life as a peace-loving, democratic nation from the ashes of devastation after the war. In the early postwar years, most Japanese were absorbed in overcoming the chronic shortages of food and daily necessities and fighting spiraling inflation. During this period of confusion and chronic shortage, crime was rampant and the social order eroded. The Japanese economy recovered gradually through the reconstruction. Social order was likewise restored with improvements in standards of living and reinforcement of law. After the Peace Treaty was concluded in San Francisco in 1951, Japan rejoined the international community in 1956, when United Nations membership was approved.

Crimes, especially robbery, larceny and violent crimes, increased dramatically during the chaotic period immediately after the war. Reported crime, however, gradually decreased as industry recovered and social order was restored in the 1950s.

With respect to the recent period, from the 1950s onward, Japan's economy has achieved rapid progress through the development of new industries and expansion of international trade. Although economic recessions have occurred during the two "oil shocks," the economy swiftly recovered and developed till the present stage.

During this period, rapid industrialization and urbanization have brought about a rise in certain offences, such as traffic-related infractions, minor property crime, and more recently, stimulant drug offences. Japan is considered to be one of the safest countries in the world, where most crimes, including serious and violent crimes and sex offences, are declining. Yet Japan still faces the persistent problems of juvenile delinquency, gang-related crime, stimulant drug abuse, and criminal recidivism.

Criminal policies throughout the Showa Era changed in accordance with the conditions of crime, the legal system, fundamental philosophies concerning crime prevention, and the treatment of offenders. From the beginning of the war period, the particular emphasis has been placed on the suppression of crime and the maintenance of social order, through the wide use of summary proceedings of disposition for minor offences by the chiefs of police stations, punishment of political offenders under the Maintenance of Public Order Law, and severe punishment imposed through summary trial procedures under the Special Wartime Criminal Law.

After the war, many of these extraordinary legislations and practises were eradicated as old ordinances were abolished and new statutes were enacted under the new Constitution. Adequate measures have been taken to maintain social order and at the same time to protect the human rights of the accused. In the postwar period, criminal policies have been significantly improved, the treatment measures of offenders in the community have been widely expanded, and institutional treatment of offenders has become more humane and scientific.

Thus, throughout the Showa Era the pendulum has swung widely between extremes of totalitarianism and democracy, war and peace, poverty and affluence, and social disorder and order. During the Showa Era, society experienced numerous and diverse forms of criminality and implemented effective countermeasures to overcome them. Although the rapid social change precipitated by industrialization and urbanization has widely been believed to be criminogenic, Japan has realized one of the safest societies in the world despite its rapid economic development.

The overall criminal policies in the Showa Era, especially after the war, may be considered to be successful. An analysis of crime and criminal policies in the Showa Era may therefore reveal the significant factors that had contributed to the low crime rate in Japanese society. Since Japan has experienced various stages of socio-economic development with diversified criminality, countries at different stages of development may find positive or negative examples fit for their respective criminal policies from some parts of Japanese experience. This text describes, analyses, and considers the crime phenomena with regard to the treatment of offenders, criminal law, organisation of criminal justice systems, correctional programmes, etc., during the 63 years of the Showa Era. It is our sincere hope that this publication would prove useful to criminal justice personnel, criminologists, and other persons concerned with crime prevention and the treatment of offenders throughout the world community.

By way of our acknowledgement, we would like to express our most sincere appreciation to the Miyazawa Foundation for Criminal Policy and Victim Study, Professor Koichi Miyazawa of Keio University and the Asia Crime Prevention Foundation for their financial support and encouragement given for the publication of this book. We also wish to extend our most cordial thanks to the Japan Criminal Policy Society for its undertaking concerning the publication of this book heartily. Our grateful acknowledgement is tendered to the Honourable Atsushi Nagashima, former justice of the Supreme Court, who is currently the Executive Director of the Asia Crime Prevention Foundation, for his valuable contribution in giving precise advice to the staff of *The Daily Yomiuri* on legal matters concerning procedures, terminology, and the law itself. Without their invaluable contributions this publication would not have been realized. Finally, we express our deep gratitude to the staff members of *The Daily Yomiuri* for their difficult and time-consuming work of translating the Japanese draft into English.

For the convenience of those readers who are not familiar with the Japanese criminal justice system, the Introduction contains an overview. We gratefully acknowledge the valuable contribution of Professor B.J. George of New York Law School in this regard.

Minoru Shikita
Shinichi Tsuchiya

NOTES

1. The term Penal Code offence means offence prescribed in the following laws:
   a) Penal Code;
   b) Explosives Control Law;
   c) Law on Duelling;
   d) Law for the Punishment of Acts of Violence, etc.;
   e) Law Concerning the Prevention and Punishment of Burglary, Theft, etc.;
   f) Law for the Punishment of Crimes of Tax Stamps;
   g) Law Concerning Punishment of Unlawful Seizure of Aircraft;
   h) Law for the Punishment of Crimes Relating to Environment; Pollution Which Adversely Affects the Health of Persons;
   i) Law Concerning Punishment of Acts Endangering Air Navigation;
   j) Law for the Punishment of Compulsion and other Related Acts Committed by Those Having Taken Hostages
2. The term Special Law offence means an offence prescribed in penal provisions other than the laws given above.
3. The term professional negligence means professional or gross negligence causing death or bodily injury.
4. The term traffic professional negligence means professional or gross negligence causing death or bodily injury by traffic accident.
5. The term road-traffic violation means violation of the Road Traffic Law or the Law Concerning Places to Keep Automobiles, etc.;
6. The basic Penal Code offence categories enumerated in note 1 include the following types of offence variations:
   a) attempt;
   b) preparation;
   c) instigation and assistance;
   d) offences resulting in death or bodily injury;
   e) aggravated forms of offences prescribed in the Law Concerning the Prevention and Punishment of Burglary, Theft, etc.

   For example, robbery includes attempted robbery (Art.243), preparation for robbery (Art.237), instigation of robbery (Articles 61 and 236), assistance in robbery (Articles 62 and 236), robbery resulting in injury (Art.240), and robbery resulting in death (Art.240), unless noted otherwise in figures or tables.

7. The following Penal Code offence categories include the specific offence categories given below:
    a) homicide: participation in suicide (Art.202);
    b) robbery: murder in the course of robbery (Art.240) and rape in the course of robbery (Art.241);
    c) bodily injury: encouragement of bodily injury (Art.206);
    d) intimidation: compulsion (Art.223);
    e) obstruction of the performance of an official duty: compelling of the performance of an official duty (Art.95, Para, II) and destruction of seals, etc. (Art.96); and
    f) forgery and counterfeiting: forgery of various documents, making a false entry in an officially authenticated instrument, etc., and the uttering of these forged documents, etc. (Articles 154 through 161).

    (The articles enumerated in notes 6 and 7 are those of the Penal Code.)
8. – in Tables means zero in number or not applicable, ··· in Tables means unknown.
9. Abbreviations used in figures and tables:

Cannabis	Cannabis Control Law
Firearms and swords	Law Regulating the Possession of Guns, Swords, etc.
J.T.S.	Juvenile Training School
Narcotics	Narcotics Drugs Control Law
Poisonous substances	Poisonous and Injurious Substances Control Law
Professional negligence	Professional or gross negligence causing death or bodily injury
Prostitution	Anti-Prostitution Law
Public morals	Law to Control Business Affecting Public Morals
Stimulant drugs	Stimulant Drugs Control Law
Violent acts	Law Concerning the Punishment of Acts of Violence, etc.

CONTENTS

INTRODUCTION: AN OVERVIEW OF THE CRIMINAL JUSTICE SYSTEM IN JAPAN

Section 1. *Introduction*

The following overview of the current organisation and administration of Japan's criminal justice system is offered to facilitate an understanding on the part of persons in other countries about the circumstances of crime and the administration of criminal justice throughout the Showa Era. The Japanese criminal justice system, like those of other nations, consists of five interrelated segments: police, prosecution, courts, correctional institutions, and aftercare services.

As one would have expected, Japan's criminal justice system has undergone considerable change during the past 63 years, particularly in the aftermath of World War II. The present Penal Code has been in force since its enactment in 1907, but has been revised more than ten times to bring it into conformity with Japan's new Constitution of 1945 and to accommodate other pressing needs. The Code of Criminal Procedure and other laws governing the criminal justice system also were substantially amended after the war.

The activities of Japan's police were under strict central governmental control until the war ended. However, under the present Constitution, police administration is the responsibility of prefectural governments. In the prewar period, public prosecutors offices and courts functioned within the Ministry of Justice, even though with considerable autonomy. Under the 1945 Constitution, in contrast, the courts have become an independent branch of the national government, while public prosecutors offices remain within the Ministry of Justice.

Since their establishment in 1890, Japanese courts have functioned in three tiers: a single court at the highest level, originally called the *Daishin'in*, or Great Court of Adjudication, and now designated as the Supreme Court under the Constitution; intermediate courts of appeal, now called high courts; and courts of first instance, now designated as district, family, and summary courts. The judicial structure and the powers of the courts were revised under the present Constitution; the most notable change lay in the creation in the Supreme Court of the power to decide the constitutionality of laws invoked in specific cases.

Until 1947, trials in courts of first instance were inquisitorial in character, patterned on Continental European legal systems. Since 1947, however, criminal trial proceedings have become much more adversarial, under the influence of the Anglo-American legal system.

There have been few changes in the statutes and ordinances governing correctional administration in Japan. Nevertheless, prisons and other correctional institutions, and their facilities, have been remarkably improved in recent decades. Moreover, the treatment of offenders has become greatly enhanced by the use of advanced scientific and humane methodologies.

Japan introduced for the first time after the Pacific War community-based treatment and aftercare services for adult offenders. It had made use of such treatment and services in prewar years, primarily for juvenile delinquents, but extended their coverage to adult offenders only after the war had ended.

This introduction, of course, offers only a general overview of Japan's present system. Readers will find, in many portions of the main body of this book, more precise and detailed descriptions of these changes in the organisation and operation of the Japanese criminal justice system.

Section 2. Organisation of the Criminal Justice System

1. *THE POLICE*

The two cardinal principles that govern police organisation and activities in Japan today are the rule of law and local autonomy. The Police Law, enacted in 1945 in conformity with these two principles, aimed at providing a more efficient police structure consisting of the national police and prefectural police within each prefecture.

A National Police Agency, headed by a Director-General, was established under the control of the National Public Safety Commission. The Commission is responsible for administering police activities relating to national security. To that end, it establishes standards and controls relating to police training, police communications, police vehicle and equipment standards, and forensic laboratory administration; it also coordinates police administration at both the national and prefectural levels. The Agency implements Commission policies at the operational level. The Director-General directs and supervises the activities of each prefectural police agency falling within the scope of responsibilities of the National Police Agency.

The National Police Agency's organisation comprehends the Director-General's Secretariat and five bureaus: Police Administration Bureau, Criminal Investigation Bureau, Traffic Bureau, Security Bureau, and Commission Bureau. In addition, three specialised entities are attached to the Agency: the Police College, the National Research Institute of Police Science, and the Imperial Guard Headquarters. Seven regional police bureaus have been established as local offices of the National Police Agency, the jurisdiction of which extends to all regions other than the Tokyo Metropolitan Region and Hokkaido.

A prefectural police agency generally has jurisdiction only within the geographical limits of the particular prefecture. Forty-seven prefectural police agencies have been established in Japan.

The authorised personnel strength of a prefectural police agency is determined by prefectural ordinance, but the total number of police officers must conform to standards fixed by cabinet order. Prefectural police officers with a rank higher than senior superintendent are designated as "local senior police officials," and enjoy the same status as national police officials. They are appointed and may be dismissed by the National Public Safety Commission, with the consent of the responsible prefectural public safety commission.

The total number of police personnel authorized by law as of 1989 approximated 257,000. At present, the National Police Agency comprises about 7,600 people, consisting of about 1,200 police officers and officials, about 900 Imperial Guards, and 5,500 civilian personnel. The 47 prefectural police agencies have a total strength of 250,000, of which 220,000 are police officers and officials, and 30,000 are civilian personnel. The total ratio of police to the general population, therefore, is about 1 : 555, which represents a considerably smaller police establishment than is to be found in many western countries.

2. *PUBLIC PROSECUTORS*

Public prosecutors offices are organised into the Supreme Public Prosecutors Office, eight high public prosecutors offices, 50 district public prosecutors offices, and 810 local public prosecutors offices. These correspond to the Supreme Court, high courts, district courts, and summary courts, the structure of which is described below.

The Supreme Public Prosecutors Office consists of the Prosecutor General, Deputy Prosecutor General, and a number of public prosecutors. A superintending prosecutor and a number of public prosecutors staff each high public prosecutors office, while district public prosecutors offices are staffed by a chief public prosecutor and public prosecutors primarily, and local public prosecutors offices by a public prosecutor and assistant public prosecutors. All public prosecutors are appointed to office by the Government of Japan.

As of 1990, there were 1,100 public prosecutors and 900 assistant public prosecutors.

Only Japanese public prosecutors can participate at every level of criminal proceedings and the administration of criminal justice. A unique characteristic of the Japanese criminal justice system is that only public prosecutors are empowered to determine the institution of prosecution and to direct the enforcement of criminal sentences.

Article 248 of the Code of Criminal Procedure provides:

> If, after considering the character, age and situation of the offender, the gravity of the offence, the circumstances under which the offence was committed, and conditions subsequent to the commission of the offence, prosecution is deemed unnecessary, prosecution need not be instituted.

Although such a decision should reflect the gravity of the offender's misconduct, a prosecutor always should consider the exercise of the prosecutorial power to suspend the institution of prosecution, as a means of affording offenders an opportunity to rehabilitate themselves without bearing the stigma of being characterised as criminals by the prosecution and receiving judgments of conviction.

Prosecutors make painstaking efforts to determine whether criminals should be prosecuted, or whether institution of prosecution against them should be suspended. The broad power of prosecutors to suspend the institution of prosecution (*kiso yûyo*) appears unique to Japan. A decision to suspend the institution of prosecution will be rendered only after a public prosecutor has examined carefully all the evidence and has determined that it is sufficient to establish guilt by the formal standard of *in dubio pro reo* (all doubts are to be resolved in favor of the accused); prima facie proof of guilt does not suffice.

This quasi-judicial standard governing the disposition of criminal matters in public prosecutors offices, which appears stricter than that invoked in other countries, has resulted in a surprisingly low rate of acquittals after trial. For example, in 1989 the acquittal rate in district courts amounted to a mere 0.01% and in summary courts to 0.28%.

An important characteristic of prosecutorial administration in Japan is the power of public prosecutors to investigate all categories of criminal cases on their own initiative and without assistance from the police and other law enforcement agencies. For example, the special investigation departments of public prosecutors offices in Tokyo and Osaka, which are staffed by substantial numbers of well-trained and well-qualified public prosecutors and their assistants, uncovered and prosecuted in court a number of cases of bribery involving highly placed governmental officials, and instances of corporate crimes like breach of trust by executives, illegal manipulation of financial settlements, and tax evasion.

3. *COURTS*

The Supreme Court, consisting of the Chief Justice and 14 Justices, is Japan's highest court. The Chief Justice is appointed by the Emperor upon designation by the Cabinet; other Justices are appointed by the Cabinet, and the Emperor attests their appointments.

The Supreme Court exercises appellate jurisdiction in the forms of *jôkoku* and special or *tokubetsu jôkoku* appeal, both of which are provided for specifically in the Code of Criminal Procedure. Hearings and adjudications in the Supreme Court are undertaken either by the Grand Bench, consisting of all the Justices sitting *en banc*, or by a petty bench composed of five Justices. A Grand Bench quorum is composed of nine Justices, and a petty bench quorum is made up of three Justices.

High courts are located in eight major cities in Japan: Tokyo, Osaka, Nagoya, Hiroshima, Fukuoka, Sendai, Sapporo, and Takamatsu. Each high court is assigned judicial competence over one of the eight regions into which Japan is divided. There are a total of about 280 high court judges, including 8 presiding judges. As a rule, a high court's judicial competence extends to appeals filed against judgements rendered by district courts, family courts, and summary courts. High courts usually hear cases in three-judge panels.

Japan's 50 district courts possess judicial competence within a judicial district, the geographical area of which corresponds to a given prefecture; the exception is Hokkaido, which is divided into four judicial districts. District courts are subdivided into 201 branch courts; they are staffed by about 910 judges and 460 assistant judges.

District courts are the primary courts of general first-instance or original competence (jurisdiction); only cases heard in family courts and summary courts fall outside their competence. District court cases are handled by either a single judge or a collegial body of three judges, depending on the seriousness of the case.

Family courts are established in each judicial district; in all, about 200 judges and 150 assistant judges staff them, along with about 1,500 family court probation officers. Family courts deal with cases of juvenile delinquency and family concerns.

There are 452 summary courts in cities, towns, and villages throughout the country; the total number of summary court judges approximates 800. Summary courts have original competence in criminal cases involving offences punishable by a fine or a lesser punishment, and other minor offences like theft and embezzlement.

Judges of inferior courts are appointed by the Cabinet. The categories of judges are presiding judges of high courts, judges, assistant judges, and summary court judges. In all, there were in 1989 about 1,400 judges, 610 assistant judges, and 810 summary court judges throughout Japan.

Assistant judges are appointed from among persons who first have passed the National Judicial Examination, and then have completed two years of training at the Legal Training and Research Institute of the Supreme Court and passed the final qualifying examination. After 10 years' experience, they may be appointed as judges.

In addition to judges, courts are staffed with other specialised personnel, including judicial research officials, court clerks, family court probation officers, court stenographers, bailiffs, marshals, and court secretaries; as of 1989, there were in all about 21,800 such functionaries.

Section 3. *Criminal Procedure*

1. *INTRODUCTION*

Procedure in criminal prosecutions is uniform throughout Japan, because there is but a single national governmental system. The principal sources of criminal procedural law are the Code of Criminal Procedure of 1948 and the Rules of Criminal Procedure of 1949. Because Japan is within the civil- or Roman-law tradition, judicial precedents are of only secondary significance.

Modern Japanese criminal procedural law is a blend of European and

Anglo-American legal concepts. The so-called old Code of Criminal Procedure of 1922 was based in its entirety on German law. The Code of Criminal Procedure of 1948, enacted in conformity with the new Constitution of 1946, continues to be based on the 1922 code in its general plan, but it has been substantially modified to reflect Anglo-American legal concepts in contexts important to the protection of human rights.

2. *CONSTITUTIONAL SAFEGUARDS*

The Constitution is the source of most of the rights of individuals in the setting of criminal investigation and trial. Article 31 provides that "no person shall be deprived of life or liberty, nor shall any other penalty be imposed, except according to procedure established by law," while Article 33 states that "no person shall be arrested except upon a warrant issued by a competent judicial official, which specifies the offence with which a person is charged, unless . . . arrested during the commission of offences." In addition, Article 34 establishes that

> No person shall be detained or confined without being at once informed of the charge against him and without the immediate privilege of counsel. Nor shall he be confined without adequate cause and, upon demand of any person concerned, such cause must be immediately shown in open court in his presence and the presence of his counsel.

Again, Article 35 provides protection for persons' residences and property:

> The right of all persons to be secure in their homes, papers, and effects against entries, searches, and seizures shall not be impaired, except upon warrant issued for adequate cause and particularly describing the place to be searched and things to be seized.

Several provisions of the Constitution directly govern trial proceedings. Article 38 establishes that "no person shall be compelled to testify against himself," that "confessions made under compulsion, torture, or threat, or after prolonged detention or confinement shall not be admitted in evidence," and that "no person shall be convicted or punished in cases where the only proof against him is his own confession."

Other basic individual rights are protected in the course of criminal trials by Article 37, which provides that "in all criminal cases, the accused shall enjoy the right to speedy and public trial by an impartial tribunal," that accused persons "shall be permitted full opportunity to examine all witnesses on [their] behalf at public expense," and "at all times . . . shall have the assistance of competent counsel who shall, if the accused is unable to secure the same by personal efforts, be assigned by the State." On that basis, defense counsel are appointed by courts not only for financially unable accused persons, but also for accused persons who, for any reason whatever, are unable to retain counsel. If, following a judgement of conviction, an accused person proves to be financially capable, he or she can be required to reimburse the state for the counsel fees earlier paid by the state.

In addition, Article 39 of the Constitution provides that "no person shall be held criminally liable for an act which was lawful at the time it was committed or of which he has been finally acquitted, nor shall he be placed in double jeopardy."

Finally, if persons have been detained or confined and later acquitted of criminal charges against them, Article 40 provides that they may sue the state for indemnity or redress.

3. *PROCEDURE FROM ARREST TO TRIAL*

(a) Investigative Agencies

The police and public prosecutors constitute the principal investigative agencies; they work cooperatively with one another. Police, who have the primary responsibilities for criminal investigation, usually conduct initial inquiries in criminal matters. When their investigation has been completed, they must refer the matter immediately to a public prosecutor, together with the written or other evidentiary data they have gathered. The recipient public prosecutor then may direct police officers to inquire further into the matter, or may conduct an independent investigation. An investigation continues to the point that the responsible public prosecutor can determine whether to institute public prosecution against the suspect, or to suspend the institution of prosecution.

There are, however, instances in which public prosecutors conduct completely independent investigations of crime without any police involvement, until they are persuaded that there are sufficient evidentiary data to support the filing of an accusatory instrument. Large-scale crimes of official corruption often are dealt with in that way.

There are two categories of crimes: Penal Code offences and special law offences. The former comprise crimes delineated in the Penal Code of 1908, including conventional crimes like homicide, robbery, theft, and bodily injury. The latter embrace offences set forth in a number of special laws; generally they consist of administrative violations like traffic offences, and illegal possession of firearms or explosives. During 1988, the police arrested or investigated about 990,000 persons for Penal Code offences and 1,370,000 persons for special-law offences. Of the suspected Penal Code offenders, 590,000 were under investigation for negligently causing death or bodily injury in traffic accidents.

(b) Arrest

The general principle is that judicial warrants are necessary for arrests to be made. However, any person may arrest, without a warrant, an offender who is committing or has just committed a crime in the presence of the individual who makes the arrest. Investigating officials also may arrest suspects without warrant if they have sufficient grounds to believe that the latter have committed certain types of serious crimes and if, in addition, there is no time to obtain a warrant. In these cases, a warrant must be obtained promptly after an arrest has been made. Arrests without advance judicial authorisation generally comprise about 20% of all arrests.

(c) Procedure After Arrest

Officials (police) who have arrested suspects must inform them immediately of the reason for the arrest and of their right to obtain counsel at their personal expense, and allow them to tender any explanation they wish. The police must release arrested persons immediately if they perceive no urgent need for further detention. If there is such a need, the police must arrange for arrested persons to be transferred to a public prosecutors office, along with all evidentiary data collected to that point, within 48 hours after the arrest. Public prosecutors who receive custody of arrested persons in that way must give the latter an opportunity to offer any explanation they desire. If public prosecutors believe that continued detention of arrested persons is unnecessary, they must release the latter immediately. If further detention appears necessary, they must apply to a judge for a warrant of detention; this must be done within 24 hours of the time the police have transferred custody, or a maximum of 72 hours from the time of arrest.

Applicant public prosecutors must submit to a recipient judge sufficient data, including documents, to support the existence of reasonable grounds supporting detention. If no request for a judicial authorisation of detention is made, and if prosecution is not instituted within the statutory period, a suspect must be released immediately.

A judge who has received a request for a warrant of detention must first examine the materials attached to the request, and then inform the suspect of the charges against him or her and allow the suspect to tender an explanation concerning them. The judge must order the suspect to be released immediately if either there are no grounds for detention or there has been an undue delay in either the transfer of the suspect to the custody of a public prosecutor or an application by a public prosecutor for a warrant of detention. However, if reasonable grounds to detain a suspect have been established, the judge must promptly issue a warrant or order of detention. The term "reasonable grounds" covers cases in which there is a reasonable basis to suspect that the suspect has committed a crime, and that the suspect (1) has no fixed dwelling, (2) may destroy evidence, or (3) may flee the jurisdiction.

The portion of proceedings based on a request for a warrant of detention, during which the judge informs a suspect of the nature of the pending charges and receives any statement the suspect chooses to make in response, is conducted in camera. However, detained suspects and their counsel are entitled to demand an indication by the judge in open court of the reasons for detention.

Detained persons who are dissatisfied with the decision to detain them can apply to a court for the cancellation or amendment of that decision. If a summary court judge has ordered detention, the application is made to the district court having jurisdiction over the summary court; in any other instance the application is made to the court to which the issuing judge is assigned. An application is heard by a three-judge collegial court panel, which determines finally the propriety of the original detention order.

(d) Public Prosecutors' Investigation

Detention for purposes of prosecutorial investigation is generally limited to 10 days' duration. However, the issuing judge may extend the period for no more than 10 additional days upon application of a public prosecutor; in certain exceptional cases, a public prosecutor can apply for a second extension not to exceed 5 days. Public prosecutors must conclude within these periods their investigations into whether there is sufficient evidence to support the institution of public prosecution against suspects. If they are convinced that suspects are guilty, they may file an accusatory instrument with the appropriate court; that serves to commence a formal prosecution.

Accused persons or suspects in detention are allowed to see their defence counsel or attorneys who will become their defence counsel. They also may receive from or hand over to counsel any documents or articles without a guard present.

Japan has no system corresponding to a grand jury in the United States. Since 1948, however, it has established what is called a prosecution investigation committee or inquest of prosecution (*kensatsu shinsakai*), consisting of laypersons chosen by lot from among ordinary citizens. Such a body receives complaints submitted by interested parties, or institutes inquiries *ex officio*, based on noninstitution of prosecution, carries on its own investigation, and determines in an advisory manner the propriety of determinations reached by public prosecutors not to institute prosecution.

(e) Summary Proceedings in Minor Cases

Public prosecutors may institute relatively informal criminal proceedings in summary courts for minor crimes, if accused persons make no objection. Recipient courts consider and decide such cases summarily on the basis of documentary and real evidence submitted by public prosecutors; no public hearings are opened. However, summary proceedings can result in the imposition of no heavier penalties than a fine of ¥200,000. A party dissatisfied with the sentence imposed on the basis of summary proceedings can demand formal trial within 2 weeks after receiving notice of the sentence; the case is then tried in ordinary proceedings.

(f) Disposition

In 1988, 4.6% of all suspects disposed of by public prosecutors offices were prosecuted in formal proceedings, and 54.2% in summary proceedings; 21% were not prosecuted and 20% were referred to family courts for purposes of juvenile delinquency proceedings.

4. *TRIAL*

(a) Trial Courts and Their Organisation

Japan has had a jury trial law since 1923, although it was suspended beginning in 1943 for various practical reasons. Even before the suspension of the Jury Law, accused persons waived their right of jury trial in 99% of all cases. They apparently placed a higher value on the right to a complete factual review of the case by a second-instance court, which would not have been forthcoming after a jury trial. Moreover, the Japanese people have always tended to trust professional judges. Hence, the jury system does not function in Japan today, and factfinding is always done by a court.

Minor cases are tried at the first instance in summary courts, while more serious cases are dealt with at first instance in district courts. High courts, as courts of appeal, usually function as courts of second instance. However, they can serve as courts of first instance for the trial of a small number of serious offences, for example, insurrection.

(b) Trial Procedure

A public prosecutor commences trial proceedings by reading the charges contained in the accusatory instrument. The accused and the accused's counsel next state their opinion concerning the charge, by admitting the charges wholly or partially, or denying them. Japanese procedure does not incorporate the equivalent to a guilty plea at or after arraignment, as in the Anglo-American system. Therefore, even if an accused person acknowledges guilt, the public prosecutor is required to submit evidence establishing guilt.

The public prosecutor makes an opening statement outlining the facts the government intends to prove. This statement serves to acquaint the court, defence counsel, and the accused with the content of the prosecution's allegations against the accused and its plan of presenting its proof. In that way, all present are enabled to follow the evidence as it is presented.

After making an opening statement, the public prosecutor requests the court to examine the prosecution's evidence, which may be produced in the forms of witness testimony, documentary evidence, or real or demonstrative evidence. The accused has a constitutional and statutory right to confront and cross-examine all prosecution witnesses. For that reason, hearsay evidence, including documentary hearsay, is inadmissible as a general statutory principle unless the accused consents to its receipt by the court. Incriminating extrajudicial confessions by the accused cannot be placed in evidence in the early stages of prosecution proof, to avoid prejudicing the court against the accused before the bulk of the prosecution's evidence has been received by the court.

After the prosecution has finished presenting its case, the accused may elect to present evidence refuting the state's case. The court, from time to time, may elect on its own initiative to elicit lawful evidence not presented by the parties. It is usually at this stage that the prosecution will tender statements made by the accused before the institution of prosecution, together with official records showing the prior criminal history of the accused (if any). Defence counsel usually offers at this time documentary evidence tending to establish the good character of the accused and to provide background information about the accused.

At the conclusion of this process, the public prosecutor and defence counsel usually question the accused. Because accused persons are protected by the constitutional right of silence (privilege against self-incrimination), they cannot be required to take an oath before making whatever statements they wish. Nevertheless, responses made by the accused to questions are considered volunteered and so may be admitted as evidence. The court also examines the accused about relevant facts and circumstances. Because Japan's procedural system does not include presentence investigations and reports by probation officers, evidentiary data bearing on sentencing are presented by the parties, supplemented by the court's own inquiries.

Once neither party has additional evidentiary material to present, the court affords both parties an opportunity to make a closing statement, in the course of which they review and analyse the evidence and attempt to persuade the court to render a judgement favorable to the arguing party. The prosecution is required to make its closing argument first. By law, the public prosecutor is required to state an opinion about the facts that should be found and the law that should govern them. He or she also recommends a proper punishment to be assessed by the court. After completion of the closing arguments, the accused is given a final opportunity to submit a personal opinion about the case. The court then announces that the factfinding process has been closed and fixes a later date at which judgement will be pronounced. However, if the case is uncomplicated, the court may pronounce judgement immediately.

(c) Judgement and Sentence

Because Japan has no functioning jury system, the court, consisting of one or more judges, is the exclusive trier of fact; it also is responsible for the application of law to the facts it has determined. On this basis, it renders a judgement of acquittal or conviction and fixes the type and amount of the punishment assessed against a convicted accused. In other than juvenile cases, sentences consist of a specified term of incarceration or amount of a fine.

Facts are to be determined on the basis of evidence received by the court, but the assessment of its probative value rests exclusively in the discretion of the court. If the court is persuaded of guilt after all doubts have been resolved in favor of the accused, it pronounces a judgement of guilt and a sentence. It is required to indicate the facts constituting the offence, to list the evidentiary items supporting the existence of those facts, and to explain the legal norms applicable to the facts that justify the entry of a judgement of guilt.

The reader will recall that, according to the principle of *in dubio pro reo*, all doubts must be resolved in favor of the accused. Because the prosecution carries the burden of persuasion as to guilt, if it fails to persuade the court that the accused has committed an alleged offence, the court must acquit the accused. However, the rate of acquittals is quite low; that minuscule rate constitutes one of the salient characteristics of criminal justice in Japan. As an example, in 1988 only 50 (0.01%) of 57,790 accused persons tried in first-instance courts were found not guilty. The explanation for this probably lies in the fact that public prosecutors ordinarily do not institute public action in criminal matters unless they are quite thoroughly convinced that judgements of conviction can and should be rendered in them.

(d) Compensation for Innocent Persons

Accused persons, subjected to detention or confinement, who are acquitted through a finally binding adjudication, must be compensated by the State, based on the decision of a court. Arrested or detained suspects, against whom no prosecution is instituted, are also entitled to compensation determined through administrative action by a public prosecutor.

5. *PUNISHMENT*

Categories of punishment provided in Japanese penal law are, in descending order of gravity, the death penalty, imprisonment with labour, imprisonment without labour, a fine, penal detention, and a minor fine. Forfeiture of physical objects used in the commission of an offence constitutes a supplementary penalty.

Eighteen Penal Code offences, including homicide, carry the death penalty, but it is invoked by sentencing courts only in a relatively small number of cases involving extremely inhumane and cruel murder, for example, those involving multiple victims committed in a most atrocious manner under circumstances suggesting no irresistible pressures from a victim on a perpetrator.

Imprisonment with labour differs from imprisonment without labour solely in respect of the fact that prisoners sentenced to imprisonment with labour can be forced to perform work assignments; imprisonment without labour carries no such obligation. The term of either can be for life, an indeterminate period, or a specific period of years or months. Fixed terms of imprisonment generally range from 1 month to a maximum of 15 years, but can extend as long as 20 years based on the presence of aggravating circumstances. In contrast, a term may be reduced to less than 1 month if there are mitigating circumstances.

Fines range from ¥4,000 upward, but may be reduced to an amount less than ¥4,000. Minor fines are in an amount from one yen to less than ¥4,000 (¥3,999). Persons sentenced to pay fines or minor fines who are unable to pay in full may be detained in a workhouse pursuant to a court's judgement, for a period of days corresponding to the amount of the unpaid fine, on a prorated basis as calculated by the court to reflect all or a specified portion of the unpaid amount.

Penal detention consists of confinement in a penal detention facility for a period of from 1 day to 29 days. No work assignments may be imposed on prisoners undergoing penal detention.

Depending on circumstances, a sentencing court may suspend the enforcement of a sentence of imprisonment with or without labour for not more than 3 years, or of a fine not exceeding ¥200,000; the period of suspension can range from 1 to 5 years from the date the sentence becomes finally binding. However, only two classes of convicted accused persons are eligible for suspension:

1. Those not previously sentenced to imprisonment without labour or a heavier penalty.

2. Those who, although previously sentenced to imprisonment without labour or a heavier penalty, have not again been sentenced to such a penalty within 5 years from the date the enforcement of the earlier penalty was either completed or remitted.

Persons granted suspension of the enforcement of a sentence may be placed under probationary supervision during the period of suspension. In addition, persons who have been sentenced to imprisonment without labour or a heavier penalty and granted suspension of enforcement of sentence, and who later are sentenced to imprisonment with or without labour for not more than 1 year, may be granted suspension of enforcement of the latter sentence and placed under probationary supervision, provided there are circumstances present especially favourable to them.

If persons granted suspension of enforcement of sentence commit another offence during the period of suspension and are sentenced to imprisonment without labour or a heavier penalty without being granted another suspension of enforcement of sentence, the original pronouncement of suspension of enforcement is revoked and the earlier sentence will be enforced. In contrast, if persons granted suspension of enforcement of sentence remain on good behaviour throughout the period of suspension, the sentence automatically loses its effect upon the expiration of the period of suspension.

In 1989, 4.5% of all offenders convicted in all courts received sentences of imprisonment with labour, 0.3% imprisonment without labour, and 94.3% a fine. Suspension of enforcement of sentence was granted to about 57% of the offenders sentenced to imprisonment.

6. *APPEAL*

Either party dissatisfied with a judgement pronounced by a first-instance court may appeal it to a high court for review, within the period fixed by law. *Kôso* appeal may assert mistakes in factfinding and sentencing and errors on legal issues. One must stress that the prosecution may appeal against a judgement of a trial court which the prosecution believes to be either too lenient or too severe, or against a judgement of acquittal. During 1988, 5,576 appeals were taken against judgements, out of a body of judgements entered affecting an estimated 57,790 accused persons, or an appeal rate of approximately 9.6%.

The reviewing court examines the written records of activities in the trial court and considers the arguments of the defence attorney and public prosecutor. The appellate court either may or must hear additional evidence if it considers that necessary for it to reach a proper judgement. After reviewing both the factual and legal conclusions reached by the lower court, the appellate court renders a written judgement and opinion either affirming or reversing the first-instance judgement; the appellate court must state the reasons underlying its action. An appellate court affirms a lower court's judgement by dismissing the appeal taken against it.

Judgements reversing those of a lower court ordinarily signify that the appellate court has ascertained procedural or substantive irregularities constituting reversible error, or an insufficient factual basis to support the original judgement. At times a reviewing court reverses the original judgement and either remands the case to the original court or transfers it to another first-instance trial court. At other times it reverses the original judgement and enters a plenary judgement of its own. However, if it does the latter, it cannot pronounce a sentence heavier than that originally assessed if the appeal was taken solely by or on behalf of the accused. A first-instance court receiving a case on remand or transfer from an appellate court is bound by the reviewing court's judgement, and cannot render its own judgement inconsistent with it.

A judgement of a reviewing court either reversing or affirming an original judgement does not necessarily constitute a final disposition of the case, however. Under certain conditions prescribed by statute, any of the parties may submit the case to the Supreme Court for further review. For example, if a high court judgement contravenes any provision of the Constitution or conflicts with existing Supreme Court precedents, the Supreme Court may elect to review it. In 1988, 1,623 appeals were taken to the Supreme Court against 5,820 judgements against accused persons in high courts, amounting to an appeal rate to the Supreme Court of about 35%.

7. *EXTRAORDINARY REMEDIES*

Court judgements that have become finally binding can be revised or set aside through extraordinary *de novo* proceedings called *saishin*. A public prosecutor or either an accused person against whom a judgement of conviction has become finally binding, or a relative of the accused within a specified degree of kinship, may request an extraordinary *de novo* proceeding for the benefit of the accused after either a judgement of guilt or a judgement dismissing a *jôso* appeal has become finally binding. Grounds for *saishin*, prescribed by law, include a determination through another finally binding judgement that documentary or real evidence or oral testimony on which the original judgement was based was forged, altered, or false, and the discovery of new evidence supporting a conclusion that a judgement of acquittal ought to have been entered.

A *saishin* request must be submitted to the court that entered the original judgement. If the recipient court determines the request to rest on good cause, it enters a judgement authorising the commencement of *saishin* proceedings. After that judgement approving *saishin* has become finally binding, either a new trial commences or review proceedings are reopened in the court that rendered the original judgement. At the conclusion of *saishin* proceedings, no penalty heavier than that originally assessed may be imposed.

Extraordinary *jôkoku* appeal may be lodged against a finally binding judgement asserting legal error embodied in that judgement. Unless a judgement in an extraordinary *jôkoku* appeal quashes an original judgement disadvantageous to an accused person, it has only a theoretical impact, because it does not change the legal status of the accused in any way; it only serves to correct the judicial records as to questions of legal interpretation.

8. *SPECIAL PROCEEDINGS IN JUVENILE CASES*

The Juvenile Law of 1948 established a family court procedure in juvenile cases, entirely separated from proceedings in regular criminal courts. The law defines "juveniles" as persons younger than 20 years of age. Young persons who commit acts that would be criminal if committed by adults are classified under the law as either juveniles (those 14 through 19 years of age) or children (those 13 years old or younger, denominated "lawbreaking children"). Juvenile proceedings also can be directed at juveniles who are prone to commit crime or violate criminal laws or ordinances, based on their character or environment and their behaviour, such as persistent disobedience to the reasonable dictates of their parents, fleeing from home without good cause, association with criminals or other immoral persons, frequenting places inimical to morals, or evincing a disposition to engage in morally harmful behaviour. All persons meeting any of these prerequisites must be sent by public prosecutors, police, or other officials to a family court for inquiry and hearing, aimed at a determination whether or not the acts of a referred juvenile provide a sufficient basis for further hearings; the inquiry also extends to an examination of the juvenile's temperament and personal environment. On that basis, the family court determines whether there is a need to subject the juvenile to protective measures.

Family courts are staffed with family court presentence investigators trained as social workers. The Juvenile Law provides that, in conducting investigations, every effort must be made to use efficiently medical, psychological, educational, sociological, and other technical knowledge, including, in particular, the results of a classification study conducted by a juvenile classification centre concerning the conduct, life history, disposition, and environment of a delinquent and of the delinquent's guardians and associates. Hearings are closed to the public, including the press and other media, which are prohibited from publishing or disseminating photographs or information that might allow the public to identify the person against whom juvenile proceedings have commenced, either then or at any later time in that person's career.

The controlling philosophy embodied in the Juvenile Law is that juvenile delinquents should not simply be punished, but rather rehabilitated through educative efforts to become responsible citizens. Hence, the protective measures which family courts are authorised to impose are:

1. Placement of juvenile delinquents under supervision of probation officers assigned to a probation office.
2. Commitment to a child education and training home or a home for dependent children.
3. Commitment to a juvenile training school.

The prevailing principle is that criminal prosecution of juveniles is exceptional and to be reserved for instances in which juveniles should receive the death penalty or a sentence of imprisonment. Accordingly, a family court will refer a juvenile offender to a public prosecutor's office only if it finds it reasonable to subject the juvenile to punitive measures, based on an investigation into the juvenile's background and in light of the facts constituting the crime and the circumstances under which it was committed. After juveniles have been transferred to a public prosecutors office for disposition, they are prosecuted in the same manner as adult offenders. However, even in such cases juveniles are usually punished with an indeterminate sentence of imprisonment. No juvenile who was younger than 18 years old at the time of the commission of a capital offence can be sentenced to death. One should note also that no family court referral to a public prosecutors office for punitive measures can be made concerning a juvenile who was younger than 16 years of age at the time of the commission of the offence.

Section 4. *Corrections*

1. *ORGANISATION OF CORRECTIONAL INSTITUTIONS*

The Corrections Bureau of the Ministry of Justice has direct control of correctional administration concerning the institutional treatment of offenders. Noninstitutional treatment of offenders is under the administration of the Rehabilitation Bureau of the Ministry.

There are 59 prisons, 8 juvenile prisons, 3 medical prisons, 7 detention houses, 8 branch prisons, 2 medical branch prisons, and 107 branch detention houses throughout Japan. Juvenile correctional institutions include 54 juvenile training schools, 52 juvenile classification homes, and 1 branch juvenile classification home. There is a single women's guidance home, located in Tokyo. Penal and juvenile correctional institutions and the women's guidance institution are administered through eight regional corrections headquarters which function as intermediate supervisory organs.

In 1989, Japan's penal institutions were staffed by about 17,000 officials and employees, consisting of 823 captains, 1,555 assistant captains, 12,000 guards, and 1,200 specialists. The 2,500 staff members of juvenile training schools included 130 administrators, 2,000 instructors, 90 medical specialists, and 1,200 other staff members, while the 1,200 staff members of juvenile classification homes included 120 administrative officers, 230 classification specialists, and 720 instructors.

Training for correctional personnel is provided by the Ministry of Justice through the Training Institute for Correctional Officials, located in Tokyo, and eight branch training institutes.

During 1989, the average daily inmate census in Japan's penal institutions came to about 45,000 convicted prisoners, 7,500 suspects and accused persons, 4,000 juvenile school trainees, and 1,200 inmates of juvenile classification homes.

The administration of correctional institutions and treatment of prisoners are regulated through such basic laws and regulations as the Prison Law of 1908, the Prison Law Enforcement Regulations, the Ordinance for Prisoners' Progressive Treatment, and the Prisoners Classification Regulations, as well as by directives issued by the Ministry of Justice.

The Juvenile Law of 1948 and the Juvenile Training School Law of 1948 govern the administration of juvenile training schools and juvenile classification homes. The Women's Guidance Home Law of 1958 addresses the administration of the Women's Guidance Home.

2. *TREATMENT OF CONVICTED PRISONERS*

(a) Introduction

The treatment of convicted prisoners in Japan is based on a system of classification and progressive treatment. In principle, the matrix for treatment is a group, but the objective is individualised treatment to correct the criminal inclination of each convicted prisoner.

The system of prisoner classification, in operation since 1949, was revised substantially through new Prisoners Classification Regulations which became effective in 1972, designed to promote a scientific classification of prisoners that will assure a suitable custodial assignment and treatment that takes advantage fully and effectively of the facilities and staffs of prisons, juvenile prisons, and detention houses.

(b) Classification

By designation from the Director-General of the Corrections Bureau, one institution within the geographical area of each of the eight regional correctional headquarters throughout Japan has been constituted a classification centre, with suitable facilities and staff to conduct a classification for each prisoner received for the purpose. Male prisoners under 26 years old sentenced to a term of 1 year or more and who have not served an earlier prison term (other than foreigners in the "F" class discussed below) are committed to a classification centre. Classification procedures require about 55 days at the centre to accomplish, plus perhaps 5 additional days at the correctional institution to which a prisoner is assigned. Prisoners not committed to a centre undergo classification procedures for about 10 days at the facility where they are confined when their sentence becomes finally binding, and an additional 20 days at the correctional institutions where they subsequently are assigned.

Under the Regulations, prisoners are grouped in two ways, one reflecting custodial considerations, and the second treatment considerations:

(i) Grouping based on custodial considerations:
- (I) In terms of gender, nationality, type of sentence, age, and prison term:
  - Class W: Females
  - Class F: Foreigners who require treatment differing from that accorded Japanese
  - Class I: Persons sentenced to imprisonment without labour
  - Class J: Juveniles
  - Class L: Persons sentenced to imprisonment terms of 8 years or more
  - Class Y: Adults under 26 years of age
- (II) By the degree of advanced criminal inclination:
  - Class A: Persons without advanced criminal inclination
  - Class B: Persons with advanced criminal inclination

(III) Based on mental defect or physical illness or defect:
Class M: Mentally defective persons
Class P: Physically ill or disabled persons

(ii) Grouping based on treatment considerations:

(I) By types of required treatment:
Class V: Persons requiring vocational training
Class E: Persons requiring education
Class G: Persons requiring guidance in living
Class T: Persons needing therapeutic treatment provided by experts
Class S: Persons requiring special protection and care

(II) Based on other factors:
Class O: Persons deemed suitable for treatment in open institutions
Class N: Persons considered suitable for assignments to maintenance work

Under this classification system, correctional facilities are authorised to receive only those specific categories of prisoners for whom they can provide appropriate treatment.

(c) The Progressive System

The progressive system is applied to convicted prisoners sentenced to imprisonment with labour under the Ordinance for Prisoners' Progressive Treatment of 1933. There are four grades within the system: Newly received prisoners are placed in the fourth grade, which is the lowest, and then may be promoted sequentially to the first, or highest, grade, where they enjoy considerable self-regulation and privileges.

Persons sentenced to imprisonment without labour are accorded treatment similar to that under the progressive system. This rests on the fact that their numbers have increased significantly in recent years, and a majority of them have elected to engage in prison labour.

(d) Open Institutions

As of March 31, 1989, there were 37 prison labour camps attached to prisons and juvenile prisons throughout Japan. Fourteen of them are open-type "live-in" camps to which prisoners are assigned following classification procedures that take into account an inmate's prison record, the length of the term remaining to be served, and other relevant factors. These camps serve as a form of open intermediate prison for persons whose release is imminent. Innovative forms of institutional treatment have been instituted in every correctional region since 1961, and the experimental approach has been applied throughout the country since 1965.

(e) Prison Labour

As noted, labour is compulsory for convicted prisoners sentenced to imprisonment with labour. As of March 31, 1989, over 93% of all convicted prisoners were engaged in prison employment. In contrast, persons sentenced to imprisonment without labour, under penal detention, or unconvicted and awaiting completion of criminal proceedings against them must apply before they can be given work assignments. A modest and gratuitous compensation is paid to prisoners employed in various prison industries as an incentive for them to work well. Prisoners work 168 hours during each 4-week period, subject to a weekly holiday. Prisoners injured in the course of employment are granted compensation.

(f) Vocational Training

Vocational training is provided chiefly to prisoners who are believed readily amenable to rehabilitation, and to youthful and juvenile offenders. This form of training is provided in addition to regular prison work assignments, and includes such fields as vehicle operation and maintenance, barbering and beauty care, tailoring and dressmaking, laundry operations, printing, and construction work. Training of this sort is designed to enable prisoners to pass governmental licencing and occupational examinations and obtain licences and certificates while they are still in prison, as a means of facilitating their employment upon release.

(g) Educational Opportunities

Juveniles and other inmates in need of basic education are provided with 4 hours a day of classroom instruction. Additional hours of instruction may be provided, however, usually during prisoners' leisure hours.

A branch junior high school was established in 1955 at the Matsumoto Juvenile Prison, to which juvenile prisoners who have not completed their required period of education are transferred from throughout Japan. Two juvenile prisons provide senior high school courses for their inmates.

(h) Correspondence Courses

Both juvenile and adult inmates are encouraged to take correspondence courses to promote their intellectual development. Courses approved for the purpose by the Ministry of Justice include junior and senior high school curricula, selected university-level courses, and vocational courses to qualify inmates as radio technicians, vehicle maintenance workers, electricians, mechanics, bookkeepers, photocopier operators, and maintenance workers. Prisoners may use their free time and holidays for this purpose.

(i) Religious Activities

The Constitution of Japan prohibits the appointment of prison chaplains with status as government officials. However, under the auspices of the Council of Religions, inmates may receive religious guidance under the leadership of religious functionaries of the religious bodies to which prisoners adhere. In that way, the prisoners' freedom to exercise their religion is protected, and prisoners are encouraged and afforded opportunities to cultivate their religious beliefs and to advance their practise of their own religion.

(j) Prison Visitors System

A prison visitors programme, which had its inception in 1953, has achieved remarkable results through providing constructive guidance to prisoners in resolving problems that prisoners face, for example, family difficulties and planning for a livelihood following release. At the end of 1988, 1,100 citizens, including 160 women, were serving the correctional system as volunteer visitors.

(k) Recreational Activities

Recreational activities are encouraged rather than restricted, and take such forms as competitive sports, watching television films, dramatic productions, music, and reading; nonworking hours are devoted to such activities, and the prison system provides needed equipment, books, and supplies. However, censorship is exercised over books and periodicals sent to prisoners from outside.

(l) Diet and Nutrition

Convicted prisoners generally receive their meals through the prison food service, while unconvicted prisoners may purchase their own meals if they wish. The prisoners' nutritional needs are carefully safeguarded in the preparation of meal menus that provide sufficient calories to promote inmates' health and ability to perform work assignments. Standards governing dietary quality and quantity are established through Ministry of Justice directives.

(m) Medical Care

The level of medical care provided to prisoners corresponds to that available to persons in the community at large. Prison clinics are fully equipped with all supplies and equipment appropriate to prisoner health maintenance. Larger institutions have a full-time medical staff. Prisoners are transferred to outside hospitals for needed surgery and special medical treatment. The Corrections Bureau has established three special prisons and two branch prisons to treat inmates suffering from tuberculosis, leprosy, mental illness, and other chronic physical and mental illnesses and conditions. Prisoners also may undergo psychiatric treatment through group therapy, receive orthopedic surgery and prostheses, and be provided with elective surgery of various kinds, including cosmetic surgery to remove tattoo markings.

(n) Prisoner Visitation and Correspondence

Prisoners generally are allowed interview visits with family members, friends, etc., but interviews are always conducted in the presence of a prison official unless they involve unconvicted prisoners and their attorneys. All mail to and from prisoners is subject to censorship.

(o) Programmes Promoting Prisoner Reintegration in the Community

Programmes to promote prisoner rehabilitation go into operation from the time prisoners are admitted to correctional facilities. A probation office, serving as a governmental rehabilitation agency, maintains contact with each prisoner's family, and in that way serves as a liaison between prisoners and their families. Prisoners whose release dates are near are provided systematic educational programmes to help them plan their lives following release and to assist them in finding employment.

(p) Prison Security and Control

Restraining devices like straitjackets, gags to control vocal outbursts, manacles, and restraining cords may be used on inmates who are considered to be escape risks, violently assaultive, or suicidal. Prisoners taken outside prison confines may be handcuffed, but cannot be chained. Firearms, gas-ejecting devices, and batons may be used to quell disorders or riots. However, abuse of any of these weapons is strictly prohibited. In recent years, a substantial number of solitary cells have been built in each correctional facility to serve the same purpose as restraining devices.

(q) Prisoner Incentives and Discipline

Prisoners may be rewarded for exemplary good conduct. Rule violators may be disciplined through suspension of exercise privileges or placement in "minor restricted confinement" status. A sanction of "major restricted confinement" remains an approved disciplinary sanction, but is no longer in actual use.

(r) Prisoner Grievances

Inmates in correctional facilities have a right to submit petitions or complaints, orally or in writing, concerning their treatment to either the Minister of Justice or prison inspection officials.

3. *TREATMENT OF INMATES IN JUVENILE TRAINING SCHOOLS*

(a) Institutional Framework

Juvenile training schools are dedicated to the rehabilitation of juvenile delinquents committed to their custody by family courts as a protective measure authorised in the Juvenile Law of 1948. These schools are categorised as primary, middle, advanced, and medical, and provide correctional education for juvenile delinquents until they reach 20 years of age. However, juveniles may be continued in incarceration at advanced juvenile training schools to age 23 if additional correctional education is needed; if medical care is required, they may be held in a medical juvenile training school until they become 26 years old. Males and females are accommodated in separate institutions.

A single institution is unlikely to achieve multiple correctional educational goals. To advance the effectiveness of juvenile training schools, extensive changes were made in their administration beginning in 1977. Two particularly noteworthy changes have been the authorisation of short-term treatment of juveniles in middle as well as primary juvenile training schools, and the separate administration of courses in living guidance, vocational training, academic education, special education, and medical treatment when long-term custody has been ordered.

(b) Correctional Education

(i) Content

Correctional education, consisting of academic education, vocational guidance, guidance in daily living, other appropriate training, and medical treatment, constitutes the core of juvenile inmate treatment. When necessary, the superintendent of a juvenile training school, with the approval of the superintendent of the regional correctional headquarters, can delegate the responsibility for portions of a correctional educational programme to a school, hospital or private entity, or to an individual.

(ii) Academic Education (E)

The academic education programme extends to primary and junior high courses, but can also embrace senior high school and college-level offerings. The content of academic education conforms to recommendations issued by the Minister of Education. There are, of course, a number of special difficulties in carrying through academic educational programmes in juvenile training schools, in comparison with educational programmes in the community at large: the composition of classes is usually quite different; effective educational guidance is hampered by the low levels of inmate motivation and prior educational attainments; and inmates begin their educational programmes at nonstandard times. Nevertheless, juvenile training schools have achieved a marked improvement in the educational level of their inmates, in significant measure through the use of modern educational techniques like audiovisual aids and group guidance and seminars.

(iii) Vocational Guidance (V)

Vocational guidance is directed at cultivating inmates' willingness to work, and developing the knowledge and skills necessary to qualify inmates for future employment. The latter, in turn, requires an enhancement of their ability to select an occupation appropriate to their personality. Vocational guidance for males includes such fields as woodworking, metalworking, vehicle operation, printing, and agriculture, while that for females includes beauty care, dressmaking, handicraft production, and secretarial work. Inmates receive compensation for participating in vocational training; indemnity is paid as well as for any job-related injuries or death. Vocational training is provided not only within juvenile training schools, but at outside institutions suitable to comprehensive vocational education. If inmates are employed in the community at prevailing wage rates, their earnings are impounded and then paid over to them when they are released.

(iv) Guidance in Daily Living (G)

For a period following their reception at an institution, juveniles are given guidance as to matters of daily living, usually through direction. As juveniles advance through treatment grades, guidance methods are modified in the direction of nondirective methods, for example, group discussions and autonomous living programmes. Juveniles are guided in their daily lives in ways that promote their health and personal hygiene, their cultivation of habits of handling property carefully, leading orderly lives in harmony with others, and of responsibility in general, and the inculcation of a mental attitude necessary for group as well as individual living. These objectives are promoted through club and group recreational activities sponsored under a special guidance programme. In addition, counseling provided by prison visitors has achieved good results; there were 785 volunteer visitors for inmates of juvenile training schools as of the end of 1989.

(c) Medical Care (P, M)

Four juvenile training schools have been established exclusively to accommodate inmates requiring medical treatment for physical diseases and disabilities or psychiatric care, and to provide them with appropriate care and treatment for purposes of rehabilitation. All other juvenile training schools have medical facilities and staff which enable them to serve substantially the same functions as medical clinics in the community at large.

(d) Incentives and Discipline

Treatment at juvenile training schools is measurably more lenient than that in penal institutions. They offer a relatively open environment, and inmates enjoy a number of privileges not allowed to regular prisoners. Inmates in the first treatment grade are allowed home visitation leaves without supervision. Other inmates, whatever their treatment grade, are permitted home visits in the event of the serious illness or death of a close relative. Inmates with good institutional records are rewarded through special leave. Handcuffs may be used to restrain only unruly inmates, and disciplinary action is restricted to reprimand and confinement in a repentance room for a brief period.

(e) Release

Juveniles who have achieved the highest treatment grade may be released by a regional parole board, upon the application of the superintendent of the training school in which they are confined. A regional parole board that has received a release application assigns one of its members to interview the inmate and then decides whether to grant discharge or parole. As a general rule, juvenile inmates who have reached the age of 20 years must be released.

4. *JUVENILE TREATMENT CLASSIFICATION HOMES*

Juvenile classification homes were established in the course of the reorganisation in 1949 of the juvenile justice and correctional system, to conduct classification studies of juveniles for purposes of family court hearings in juvenile cases. A classification home retains custody of juveniles for a period not to exceed 4 weeks, during which it observes their behaviour in various settings and classifies them on the basis of scientific medical, psychiatric, psychological, and sociological evaluations. The resulting data are reported to the competent family court, together with recommendations as to treatment of a juvenile respondent.

Section 5. Rehabilitation of Offenders

1. *ORGANISATION OF PROBATION, PAROLE, AND AFTERCARE SERVICES*

(a) Rehabilitation Bureau

The Rehabilitation Bureau of the Ministry of Justice is responsible for the general administration of rehabilitation services throughout Japan.

(b) Probation Service

Community-based treatment of offenders is the responsibility of probation offices; there are 50 of them located in the same cities as district courts. Their principal responsibilities are:

1. Supervision of probationers and parolees at all age levels.
2. Adjustment of inmates' family relationships and other social circumstances before release from correctional institutions.
3. Aftercare of offenders discharged from correctional institutions.
4. Investigation of prisoners eligible for pardons and submission of applications for pardon on their behalf.
5. Promotion of crime prevention activities within the community.

All these activities are accomplished by probation officers working in close collaboration with volunteer probation officers (VPOs). Japan's 850 probation officers (as of 1989) are salaried, full-time governmental officials assigned to probation offices; they serve essentially as caseworkers. Probation officers must possess appropriate educational qualifications in psychology, education, sociology, or psychiatry, as well as expertise related to the rehabilitation of offenders. They bear principal responsibility for the cases assigned them by the chief of the probation office in which they serve. Rarely, however, do probation officers manage personally all the casework procedures associated with their assigned caseload. Instead, they delegate each case, with appropriate instructions and directions, to a VPO who directly supervises the probationer or parolee.

Ministry of Justice probation officers are not under a duty to conduct presentence investigations. Background inquiries concerning juvenile offenders are conducted by family court probation officers.

At the end of 1989, there were 51,268 juvenile probationers, 17,209 adult probationers, 5,796 juvenile training school parolees, and 7,923 prison parolees.

(c) Volunteer Probation Officer System

As noted, the bulk of parolee and probationer casework is undertaken by VPOs, persons selected from within the community to bring a humanitarian attitude to bear on the rehabilitation of probationers and parolees and their reintegration in the community. VPOs must possess qualifications established by law: (1) confidence and recognition in the community concerning their personality and conduct; (2) enthusiasm and time availability for VPO service; (3) financial stability; and (4) good health and physical ability.

VPOs are appointed by the Minister of Justice for two-year terms, with the possibility of reappointment for additional two-year terms. They receive no salary, but may be reimbursed their actual expenses. At the end of 1989, about 48,000 citizens were serving as VPOs.

(d) Regional Parole Boards

Regional parole boards, of which there are eight in the administrative regions throughout Japan, are responsible for inquiries and determinations concerning parole. Their specific responsibilities, as established by law, are: (1) determination of parole releases from prisons and training schools; (2) revocation of parole; (3) determinations to terminate or provisionally suspend supervision; and (4) extensions of parole periods.

(e) Community-Based Treatment

The legislative basis for community-based treatment is found in: (1) the Offenders Rehabilitation Law of 1949, covering matters of probation and parole supervision; (2) the Law for Probationary Supervision of Persons under Suspension of Execution of Sentence of 1945, authorising courts to assess probationary supervision; (3) the Law for Aftercare of Discharged Offenders of 1950, covering aftercare and rehabilitation aid hostels; and (4) the Volunteer Probation Officer Law of 1950 establishing and regulating the VPO system.

(f) Rehabilitation Aid Hostels

Rehabilitation aid hostels for the accommodation of adult and juvenile offenders are operated by nongovernmental entities under authorisation of the Minister of Justice. However, neither a probation office nor a family court can compulsorily commit a person to a hostel; participation in a hostel programme is voluntary on each offender's part. As of December 1, 1989, the total capacity of the approximately 100 hostels throughout Japan was 2,400 persons; the capacity of individual facilities ranges from 10 to 110.

The principal areas of hostel services are the providing of room and board and consultative guidance in living, to juvenile or adult probationers and parolees, as well as to other discharged offenders. Persons released from imprisonment or detention may be accommodated for up to 6 months following release.

2. *PAROLE AND PROBATIONARY SUPERVISION*

(a) Parole Procedures

In Japan, inmates have no right to submit applications for parole on their own initiative. Instead, only the head of an institution in which an inmate is confined has that power. Screening of inmates for release on parole constitutes the primary responsibility of parole boards. After an application for parole consideration has been received from the superintendent of an institution, one member of the recipient board is assigned to visit and interview the inmate in question. Three parole board members, serving as a panel, then consider the case and decide whether or not parole is to be granted.

(b) Probation and Parole Supervision

Probation and parole casework is accomplished through the cooperative efforts of professional and voluntary probation officers. The following are the procedures routinely followed at the present time:

First, a probation officer in charge of the geographical area interviews a probationer or parolee, who is required to report to the probation office for the purpose. The probation officer then summarises the case record and provides a copy of the summary to the VPO in charge of the case. The VPO maintains frequent contacts with the subject and the subject's family through monthly home visits and office interviews, and is expected to submit regular progress reports to the probation office. If the probation officer believes it necessary to do so, based on the VPO's periodic reports, the probation officer visits the probationer or parolee at home, or requires him or her to appear at the probation office.

(c) Termination of Probation or Parole Supervision

The maximum period of supervision over a juvenile probationer placed by action of a family court is either 2 years or the time until the probationer reaches age 20, whichever is longer. The term of supervision for adult probationers assigned by a court of criminal competence is between 1 and 5 years, corresponding to the period of suspension of enforcement of sentence specified by the sentencing court. The period of supervision for juvenile training school parolees is usually until attainment of age 20, while that for adults paroled from prison corresponds to the portion of the sentence of imprisonment remaining to be served. Persons paroled from life sentences are under supervision for the remainder of their lives unless they are awarded pardons.

Chapter I. INTRODUCTION

The Showa period, which started in 1926, ended on January 7, 1989, ushering in the era of Heisei. Reflection and analysis of the Showa era have started in various sectors in terms of political, social, economic and cultural aspects. The Showa period lasted for more than 60 years, during which time Japan experienced unprecedented changes. The duration of the reign must be interesting in itself. In addition, an analysis of the background behind the turbulent years may provide valuable data for compilation of future policies. These may be motivations behind the reflection and analysis of the Showa era.

Analysis of crimes and measures against criminal offences is no exception in this regard. Criminal cases increased or decreased depending on social, economic and other changes. Take economic changes, for example. The financial depression and economic recession caused by the Great Depression hit Japan in the first six to seven years of the Showa period, followed by the emergence of wartime economic structure based on the munitions industry and economic control from 1937 to 1945, postwar chaos and economic predicaments up until 1950, economic reconstruction in the decade starting in 1955, low-growth economy caused by oil crisis and dollar shock in the first half of 1970s, and stable growth in the years which followed, leading to wealthy economy we enjoy today.

In 1929 and 1934 and in the latter half of 1940s, which saw economic depression and chaos and its repercussions, crimes such as property offences went up. With the development of national economy and the progress in social stability, crime cases started decreasing in many fields from the first half of the 1970s. But as society has become wealthy, minor thefts such as shoplifting, motivated by the material desire or from an impulse of the moment instead of from poverty, have been increasing because opportunities for such crimes increased due to the rise in the number of supermarkets.

The Pacific War also had a big influence on crime trends. As is true of the conventional hypothesis, the number of almost all crimes declined from 1941 to 1945. On the other hand, the postwar progress of automobile traffic has increased the cases of professional negligence sharply. Furthermore, the spread of the liking for drugs led to the rise in the number of crimes caused by stimulants and other drugs. The decline in educational functions in families and regional communities is considered to have something to do with the increase in juvenile delinquency. At any rate, the Showa period saw big changes in social affairs and economic conditions as well as in the people's consciousness and legal systems, which may be reflected in the changes of crime trends in the period.

In accordance with the changes in state fundamental policy against crimes, legal systems and people's consciousness of laws, various measures against crimes and criminal offenders have changed considerably. The Criminal Law, which defines what constitutes crimes, were revised more than 10 times while special criminal laws were established and abolished during the Showa period.

The postwar period saw major changes in the Constitution and legal systems. Above all, the Code of Criminal Procedure, which defines the procedures for investigation, disposition, public trials and court decisions, were revised in its entirety. Also, judicial institutions dealing with criminal affairs have changed greatly in the postwar period. The criminal policies implemented by these institutions have evolved in response to changes in criminal affairs and based on a new concept.

Thus, in the Showa period crime trends swang from extreme to extreme, as it went from an immediate postwar period when public security was the worst to the present when the situation is rather peaceful. In response to the changes in criminal affairs and social conditions, various kinds of effective criminal measures have been implemented.

As a result, Japan has become one of the safest nations in the world, blessed with a favorable public-safety situation. It is no exaggeration to say that crime trends and policies in the Showa period may underscore important points of problems and present solution measures concerning criminal justice. It may be said that there lies a secret to Japan's having created a safe society with fewer crimes and this secret can be used as a model for other countries.

Based on this standpoint, this book delves into criminal trends, treatment of criminals, criminal laws and ordinances, and changes and features of organizations in charge of criminal justice and criminal policy. But this book cannot afford any space for description and qualitative analysis of major incidents because it must contain in limited space an extremely huge data of crime trends and crime policy in the Showa period that lasted for more than 60 years.

It is also difficult to make detailed mention of social changes and crime trends, leaving no alternative but to limit our study to a long-range analysis of various data on police, prosecutor, court trials, correction and rehabilitation of criminal offenders. Even in this instance, it is a painstaking task to make a long-term analysis of old data. As for changes in criminal laws and ordinances, analyses are limited to enactment, revision and abolition of major criminal laws and ordinances without covering all of them.

As regards the description of criminal justice institutions, it puts an emphasis on organizations for prosecution, correction and rehabilitation of criminal offenders which fall under the administration of the Ministry of Justice, as was done in the White Paper in the past. Reference is made to the organizational changes in courts because public prosecutors offices belonged to courts as prosecution bureaus in the prewar period.

Thus, this White Paper is designed to have a bird's-eye view of crime trends and criminal policy in the Showa period mainly through an analysis of various data. This approach of statistical analysis was made possible because, unlike other countries, old and detailed statistical data are available in Japan. But with the changes in the concept, calculation method and analytical standards, it was made unavoidable to recompile the data when necessary as it involved difficulties to make a comprehensive and continual analysis of the entire Showa period. Furthermore, there are discrepancies between available statistics in the concept and compilation standards, posing an obstacle to the comparison of different statistics.

Take the definition of criminal offences, for example. The Ministry of Justice provides the same definition in its statistics on prosecution, correction and protection of criminal offenders, while the definition differs in the similar statistics compiled by police and judicial authorities.

They do not differ as to crimes specified in criminal codes, but they differ with respect to the scope of special law offences to be incorporated. Accordingly, the concept and statistical figures of criminal offenders differ slightly depending on the kind of statistics.

The definition of criminal offences in the White Paper, as mentioned in its introductory remarks, has been changed slightly beginning with this year's edition and kept in line with that adopted by the statistics compiled by the Ministry of Justice. Through the compilation of this special edition, we have discovered various problems that await future studies for elucidation.

To grasp the functions and long-term changes of criminal justice in their right perspectives, it is vital to ensure the continuity, cohesion and comparability of various statistics. After finishing the compilation of this edition, we recognize anew that securing these is one of major problems to be tackled in the future.

Chapter II. CRIME TRENDS

Section 1. *Changes of Penal Laws*

1. PENAL STATUTES IN PREWAR PERIOD

(1) Penal Code and Others

Principal penal statute of the Showa period was the Penal Code promulgated in April 1907 and enforced on October 1, 1908. The Code came into being after major modifications to the old Penal Code of 1880. The new Code made several major revisions; it abolished the distinction of heavy crime (felony), light crime (misdemeanour) and police infractions; it eliminated from the Code such minor offences as defined under police infractions; it also decreased the categories of crimes, namely, in principal punishment; it abolished life or determinate-term reclusion (strict confinement at hard labour in solitary confinement, used for felons), life or determinate-term banishment (penal deportation to an isolated island and imprisonment there, used mainly for political offenders), heavy or light imprisonment with labour, heavy or light imprisonment in penitentiary (used for felons), heavy or light imprisonment in jail (for committing misdemeanours) and simplified the punishments as capital punishment, imprisonment with labour, imprisonment without labour, fines, penal detention and minor fines; and in supplemental punishments, it abolished deprivation of political rights, suspension of political rights, police surveillance and supplemental fines and provided for confiscation.

It stopped minute categorization of crimes and instead defined crimes in simplified, concise and condensed form, extending the scope of application of each provision defining an offence. Also, it gave a wider range of statutory punishments provided for each crime. It increased punishment for attempts of crime as equal to that for consummation of crime.

Other revisions called for: relaxing conditions to grant conditional release from prisons (release on parole) and introduction of the suspension of execution of sentence, abolishing the Law for the Suspension of Execution of Sentence promulgated in 1905.

Cited as penal statutes to supplement the Criminal Law are the Law concerning Punishment of Acts of Violence, etc., promulgated in April 1926 (enforced on April 30 of the same year) and the Law concerning the Prevention and Disposition of Theft etc., promulgated in May 1930 (enforced on June 11 of the same year). The former provided heavier punishment for aggravated crimes of assault, intimidation and destruction committed by a group of offenders and excluded such crimes from those offences subject to prosecution upon complaint (assault and destruction provided in the Penal Code were included herein) as well as introducing such a new offence as forcible interview, strong talk and other threatening conduct committed in a group or habitually. This legislation was designed to control those cases of assault and intimidation, etc., committed through threat under collective force which were rampant during the closing years of Taisho era (1912-1926).

The Law concerning the Prevention and Disposition of Theft, etc., was established to deal with the frequent occurrence of robberies and thefts which caused social unrest from the late Taisho era to the early Showa era. Residents of Tokyo for instance were fearful of a robber called "Preaching Robber" who after committing a robbery lectured his victims on how to prevent housebreaking. The Law introduced special provisions to admit the right of self-defence for the victims of robbery, etc., particularly in disturbing situations which brought about fear, horror and panic.

Concerning prewar revisions of the Penal Code, the Code was partially revised in April 1921 (enforced on May 5 of the same year) to deal with relatively light offences. The lowest limit of statutory penalties for professional embezzlement was lowered. Furthermore, in March 1941, in line with the preparatory work for revision of the Penal Code that had continued since 1921, the Code was partially ammended (the revised law took effect on March 20, 1941) to meet the social changes that ensued after the promulgation of the Code. The revisions were limited to urgently needed amendments.

Illegal evasion of the execution of money judgments, obstruction of auction bidding, bid-rigging (bidding under a secret arrangement), acceptance of bribes in advance of becoming a public officer, a bribe to a third person, aggravated bribery under the promise to do or not to do the specific act requested, acceptance of a bribe after resigning an official post as well as crime concerning the peace and order of society were added to the list of crimes.

During World War II, the Law for Exceptional Punishments of Wartime Crimes was put into effect in December 1941. Provisions were introduced to increase punishments for indecent assault, rape, theft and robbery, etc., committed when the blackout was imposed or when the country was in danger of enemy attack or under other circumstances that would cause unrest among the people. The law was abolished in March of the following year, and was replaced by the Special Wartime Criminal Law. The special law added punishment for arson to the list of severer punishments as had been stipulated in the Law for Exceptional Punishments of Wartime Crimes.

The special law also provided for new crimes such as murder aimed at overthrowing the national government and destruction of public air-defence facilities in wartime, while stipulating exceptional wartime criminal procedures. (See Chapter III-1-1)

In regard to prewar preparation for revision of the Penal Code, the government in 1921 asked the Ad Hoc Legal System Council to work out recommendations on revision of the Code. After five years of deliberations, the council decided on the principles of revision and submitted them to the government. A committee to draft a revised Penal Code was established within the Ministry of Justice in 1927 to put the principles into statutory form and compile a preliminary draft of the revised Penal Code. The preliminary draft was then taken up by a committee set up within the Ministry to study the revision of the Penal Code and the Prison Law. The draft was made public in 1940 but revision was suspended thereafter.

(2) Prewar Special Laws

Of prewar special laws and regulations enforced before the Taisho period (1912-1926), the principal ones are as follows:

The Special Law for the Control of Explosives (enforced in December 1884 as Dajokan Fukoku Decree of Great Council of State, later revised by law) to control the use, manufacture, import and possession of explosives for the purpose of obstructing public security;

The Antique Dealers Control Law (enforced in September 1895) to regulate the antique business through the introduction of a licence system and to punish unlicenced dealers;

The Opium Law (enforced in April 1897) to regulate the manufacture, transaction, transfer and possession of opium;

The Hunting Law (enforced in July 1901; its name was changed to the Law Concerning Protection of Game and Hunting with the revision of the law promulgated in March 1958) forbade the killing and capture of specified wild birds and beasts during cerain seasons, or by certain described means, or in designated areas;

The old Forest Law (enforced in January 1908) to define the kinds of forests and rights of forest owners, as well as to provide for special offences of forest arson and theft of natural forest material, etc.;

The Guns and Explosives Control Law (enforced in May 1911) to regulate the manufacture, transaction, transfer, possession, export and import of guns and explosives;

The Maintenance of the Public Order Law (enforced in May 1925) to punish those who would organize or join associations aimed at toppling the so-called national basic structure, like the Emperor system, or denying the private ownership system; The Ordinance for Punishment of Police Infractions (enforced in October 1908 as an ordinance of the Interior Ministry) to regulate police offences and provide for punishment; and

The Automobile Traffic Control Ordinance (enforced in February 1919 as an ordinance of the Interior Ministry) to provide for regulations on the permissible maximum speed, car inspection and driver's licence and punish violators in terms of the mandatory speed and unlicenced drivers.

Main special laws enforced in the Showa period (1926-1989) are as follows:

The Military Service Law (enforced in December 1927), to provide for regulations on military service, examination for conscription and draft call and punishment for shirkers of military service and the examination for conscription;

The National General Mobilization Law (enforced in May 1938) empowered the government, when considered necessary to mobilize citizens in times of war, to call the people into service and to issue orders on production, repair and rationing of goods, and on prices and freight charges, and provided for punishment against violators; and

The National Defence and Security Law (enforced in May 1941) defined crimes such as leak of state secrets and provided for exceptional criminal procedures for espionage activities.

The Maintenance of Public Order Law was totally revised in March 1941 (enforced in May of the same year) not only to punish the leaders and members of those associations designed to revise the so-called basic structure of the state like the Emperor system, but also provided for provisions whereby those leaders and members of organizations created to support such movements would be punished. Heavier punishments were also provided, on top of special criminal procedures. (See Chapter III-1-1- [2])

The Food Control Law was enforced in July 1942 to strengthen control on the supply of staple foods such as rice and wheat, to improve a rationing system for principal foodstuffs and to provide for punishment against those engaged in transactions of principal foodstuffs with unlicenced dealers.

2. PENAL STATUTES ENACTED IN POSTWAR PERIOD

(1) Abolition of Wartime Special Laws and Others

The National Defence and Security Law, the Maintenance of Public Order Law, the Military Service Law, the National General Mobilization Law and the Special Wartime Criminal Law were abolished from 1945 to 1946 after the end of the Pacific War.

(2) Revision of Penal Code

A. Revision in 1947

With the proclamation of the Constitution, which respects sovereign power residing with the people and fundamental human rights, and renounces war, in November 1946 (enforced on May 3 of the following year), the Penal Code was partially revised in line with the spirit of the new Constitution in October 1947 (enforced on November 15 of the same year).

Major points of revision were: abolition of crimes against the Imperial families, part of crimes concerning foreign aggression and crimes concerning the peace and order of society, and adultery; strengthening statutory penalties against the abuse of authority by public employees and special public employees, violence and humiliation by special public employees, violence, intimidation, libel and slander, indecent acts in public and distribution of obscene publications or other objects; excluding a crime of violence from offences subject to prosecution upon complaint; establishing a crime of gross negligence resulting in death and injury; and providing a new article dealing with the proof of fact as grounds for impunity in libel and slander cases; expanding the scope of application of suspended execution of sentences; and establishing the provision for the extinction of punishments on condition that the specified term elapsed since the completion of the sentence imposed without recurring in new offence.

B. Revisions in 1953 and 1954

A revision proclaimed in August 1953 (enforced on December 1 of the same year) relaxed requirements for suspended execution of sentences to help contribute to reformation and correction of offenders. At the same time, it was made possible to repeat the suspension of the execution of sentences if certain requirements were met and such offenders were made subject to probationary supervision during the period in which the execution of their sentences were repeatedly suspended. A revision promulgated in April 1954 (enforced on July 1 of the same year) provided for the discretionary power of a judge to place under probationary supervision those defendants who are given suspended execution of sentence for the first time.

C. Revision in 1958

To bolster controls on corruption and violent acts, a revision promulgated in April 1958 (enforced on May 20 of the same year) led to creation of regulations and punishment for the following crimes:

Receiving bribes as rewards for the influence which a public officer exerted or is to exert, in response to an entreaty, upon another public officer so as to cause him to improperly perform or fail to properly perform his duties, the regulation of which was considered necessary from the viewpoint of cracking down on bribery by public officers;

Intimidation of witnesses in criminal cases, or "revenge" for damning testimony at court hearings; and

Unlawful assembly by two persons or more with dangerous weapons for the purpose of jointly killing, or inflicting bodily injury upon another person or damaging his property.

Rape and indecent assault, both committed by two or more persons simultaneously at the scene, were excluded from such crimes which shall be prosecuted only upon complaint, because such forms of sexual crimes of a violent, heinous and threatening nature need not wait for complaints of the victims.

D. Revision in 1960

A revision in 1960 led to the establishment of regulations on such crimes as disseisin (unlawfully taking possession of immovable property) and boundary destruction, to deal with illegal infringement on real estate.

E. Revision in 1964

Alarmed by the 1963 kidnapping case in which Yoshinobu, a four-year-old boy, was abducted and killed, a revision of the Penal Code was made to provide for regulations and punishment for kidnapping or abduction for ransom, and preparations made for the purpose of committing such crimes (promulgated in June 1964 and enforced on July 20 of the same year). With the intensification of gang confrontations brought on by the augmentation and spread of underground syndicates, the Law for Punishment of Acts of Violence, etc. was partially revised in June 1964 (enforced on July 14 of the same year) to cope with the situation and to optimize control on and punishment against acts of violence, and to provide for regulations on the crime of injuring with a weapon.

Also, the statutory penalty against habitual acts of violence was strengthened. With the inclusion of Article 204 of the Penal Code in the definition of habitual acts of violence provided in this law, a heavier statutory penalty was established against the overall habitual acts of violence including infliction of bodily injury.

F. Revision in 1968

A revision promulgated in May 1968 (enforced on June 10 of the same year) strengthened the statutory penalty against professional (or gross) negligence resulting in death and injury, for the purpose of imposing more adequate punishment on automobile drivers such as those involved in the most vicious and serious cases, which could elicit a strong public outcry.

G. Revision in 1980

In a revision proclaimed in April 1980 (enforced on April 30 of the same year), the statutory penalty against the crime of bribery, including bribery for arrangement, was bolstered in order to prevent the repetition of such bribery cases as the Lockheed payoff case.

H. Revision in 1987

Partial revisions in June 1987 (one on irregularities related to computers was enforced on June 22 of the same year and the other was necessitated by the conclusion of a treaty-mentioned below-enforced on July 8 of the same year) were made to properly deal with irregularities involving computers and other electronics equipment whose use had become widespread. To this end, regulations were established to control the crimes of illegal creation of electromagnetic records, obstruction of business through such means as destruction of computer machines and the fraudulant use of computers.

Amendments were also made to punish a person who makes a false statement to a public officer and thereby causes an untrue entry to be made on electromagnetic records, being used or to be used as the original of an officially authenticated instrument pertaining to right or duty, and a person who makes use of such electromagnetic records as the officially authenticated instrument. And such an offence has been included in the Penal Code provision to punish untrue entries in an officially authenticated instrument.

Another revision was to include the electromagnetic records in the provisions of Penal Code dealing with destruction of public documents or private documents relating to right or duty and as such, to punish the destruction of public electromagnetic records or private electromagnetic records pertaining to right and duty.

It is required to promptly conclude the "Convention of the Protection and Punishment of Crimes for Internationally Protected Persons, including Diplomatic Agents" in response to the need for building up a stronger international cooperative framework to prevent abduction, killing and other terrorist activities against diplomats. A new provision was introduced in the Penal Code in the same revision, as a measure to cope with the Convention which requires punishment of those offenders who committed the crimes stipulated in the Convention, without giving any consideration to the nationalities of the offenders. Accordingly, the new article (Article 4-2) provided in essence that except those cases covered by the preceding three articles (these articles provided for punishment of the Penal Code offenders who commit such crimes outside Japan, according to the nature and seriousness of the crimes committed), this Code shall also apply to any person who commits the crimes provided for in this Code, in cases when the international convention or treaty requires the offender to be punished, even when the crime has been committed outside Japan.

As a step to implement the "International Convention against the Taking of Hostages," the Law for Punishment of Acts of Coercion, etc., by Taking

Advantage of Hostages was revised, and a general crime of coercive acts by taking advantage of hostages has been introduced, in addition to the aggravated form of such crime which was already mentioned in the Law. And for this new crime, the Penal Code articles mentioned above concerning the application of Penal Code for those crimes committed outside Japan were made applicable.

The Law for Punishment of Acts of Violence, etc. was revised and the crimes stipulated in the Section 1 and 2 of Article 1-2. (the crimes of bodily injury committed with guns or swords in hands and the attempts thereof) were also made to follow the above-mentioned Penal Code provisions considering the application of Penal Code for those crimes committed outside Japan.

I. Raising of Fines

With the postwar economy having experienced accelerated inflation and other economic changes, the value of fines under the Penal Code came to lose its effectiveness. This led to the proclamation in December 1948 of the Law of Temporary Measures concerning Fines, etc. (enforced on February 1, 1949) to raise the maximum value of fines by 50 times against crimes specified under the Penal Code. Further increases in inflation and people's income lowered the effectiveness of monetary penalties, forcing another revision in June 1972 (enforced on July 1 of the same year). The revision called for quadrupling the maximum values of fines to the level equaling 200 times the value of fines stipulated in the Penal Code.

J. Preparation for Total Revision of Penal Code

As mentioned earlier, the current Penal Code was proclaimed in 1907 and enforced in the following year. Given the changes in the social situation and national sentiment, the revision of the Constitution and legal systems, and the development of judicial precedents, academic theories on criminal law and current thought on criminology and criminal policy, it became necessary to study a sweeping revision of the Penal Code in order to meet the requirements of present society. An unofficial committee to study the revision of the law was established in 1956 within the Criminal Affairs Bureau of the Ministry of Justice. The committee published a draft of a revised law in 1961. There were pros and cons on the draft, but a majority of the people concerned supported a plan to launch a total revision of the law based on the draft. The justice minister then asked the Legal System Council to work out recommendations for a comprehensive revision if necessary.

As a result of about 11 years of careful deliberations, the council reached a conclusion in 1974 in favor of a sweeping revision, asserting that an outline of amendments should be in line with a draft revision compiled by the council. The council submitted recommendations to that effect to the justice minister.

Opinion was divided over the advisability of carrying out a sweeping revision of the Penal Code based on the draft compiled by the council. The Ministry of Justice proceeded with a revision after hearing the views of various quarters. It published an interim report in June 1976, and in December 1981 announced a "tentative policy for revision of the Penal Code" and an "outline of protective treatment measures for those offenders discharged on grounds of insanity, etc." (drafted by the Criminal Affairs Bureau). But a sweeping revision of the Penal Code had not been realized by the end of Showa period.

(3) Postwar Special Laws

Special laws enforced in the postwar period are as follows:

A. Special Laws in Immediate Postwar Period

The Price Control Ordinance, enforced in March 1946, enabled the minister in charge to set the levels of control prices in order to secure price stability in the postwar confusion. Provisions were given to ban signing of contracts for commercial transactions at prices beyond the mandatory levels and to punish violators.

The Imperial Ordinance to Ban Possession of Guns, etc. was put into effect in June 1946 to prohibit the possession of guns, explosives and swords. In November 1950, both the ordinance and the Guns and Explosives Control Law promulgated in 1910 were abolished. The law was replaced by the Ordinance Regulating the Possession of Guns, Swords, etc., which bans and regulates the possession, etc. of guns and swords. At the same time, the Explosives Control Law was enforced to regulate the manufacture, sale, storage, transport, purchase etc. of explosives and punish violators.

In April 1958, the Ordinance Regulating the Possession of Guns, Swords, etc. was abolished and the Law Regulating Possession of Guns, Swords, etc. was enforced (the law was partially revised in April 1965 and renamed the Firearms and Swords Control Law). The new law provided for regulations to prevent injuries resulting from the possession of guns, swords, etc. and for punishment for the violators against the prohibitions concerning the possession of guns, swords, etc.

The Ordinance for Punishment of Police Infractions, enforced in 1908, was abolished in May 1948 and replaced by the Minor Offence Law, which regulates minor offences.

B. Road Traffic Law, etc.

The Road Use Control Ordinance and the Automobiles Traffic Control Ordinance, both enforced in 1919, were abolished in January 1948 and replaced by the Road Traffic Control Law, which provided for regulations to prevent danger and ensure traffic safety on roads and to punish violators. The law was replaced by the Road Traffic Law in December 1960, designed to prevent danger under new traffic conditions and to provide regulations aimed at ensuring and facilitating traffic safety, and to punish violators.

In order to meet the changes in traffic conditions, the Road Traffic Law was revised partially, when necessary, in the years to come. A revision, implemented in July 1968, called for establishing the Traffic Infraction Notification System. (See Chapter III-1-1- [2], and 3- [4])

C. Laws on Drugs

The Opium Law, proclaimed in 1897, was abolished in July 1948. The (old) Narcotics Control Law was enforced in that year to ban the handling of narcotics by dealers except those licenced by the health and welfare minister, and to punish violators. Simultaneously, the Cannabis Control Law was enforced to adopt a licence system for cannabis dealers, banning the possession, cultivation, receipt and transfer of cannabis by unlicenced persons, and to punish violators.

The (old) Narcotics Control Law was abolished in April 1953 and the present Narcotics Control Law went into effect. The new law excluded some narcotics, listed as drugs in the old law, from a list of drugs, and also defined the types of narcotics dealers, alleviated obligations for document description by narcotics dealers, etc. It also installed narcotics controllers in each prefecture who were given the power to work as judicial police officers under the Code of Criminal Procedure. The Opium Law was enforced in May 1954 to control the cultivation of opium poppies and the transfer, receipt, possession, etc. of opium and dried opium poppy seeds, and to punish violators.

In December 1947, the Law to Control the Marketing of Poisonous and Injurious Substances was enforced to adopt a licence system for dealers of poisonous and injurious substances and a registration system for manufacturers and importers of such substances, and to punish unlicenced dealers and violators. The law was abolished in December 1950 and was replaced by the Poisonous and Injurious Substances Control Law, which adopted a registration system for the manufacturers, sellers and importers of poisonous and injurious substances, provided for other regulations on such substances and defined the punishment for violators.

With the increase of paint thinner abusers thereafter, the law was revised in June 1972 (enforced in August of the same year) to punish those who inhale thinner or sell thinner knowing it will be inhaled. The law was partially revised in September 1982 (enforced in October of the same year) to include imprisonment with labour, in addition to the conventional punishment of fines, into statutory penalties against the violators.

The number of stimulant drug abusers increased in the postwar period, causing crimes committed by addicts and individuals in a state of illusion and delusion to become a social issue. Given this development, the Stimulant Drugs Control Law was enforced in July 1951, regulating the import, possession, manufacture, transfer, receipt and use of stimulant drugs to prevent health and hygiene damage caused by the abuse of stimulant drugs. The law also provided for punishment and other regulations.

Despite the enactment of the law, the cases of abuse of stimulant drugs rose year after year with the result that the law was revised partially in June 1954 (enforced later in the same month) to raise statutory penalties against those who violated the regulations on the import, possession, manufacture, transfer, receipt and use of the drugs. A new regulation was added to strengthen punishments against profit-taking and habitual offenders.

The law was then revised in August 1955 (enforced in September of the same year) to regulate the material used in stimulant drugs, ban the import of the drugs and increase punishment against traffickers for gains and habitual traffickers for gains.

A revision in October 1973 (enforced in November of the same year) strengthened regulations on the import, export, manufacture, sale, etc. of the material for the drugs, systematized punishment against acts violating the regulations concerning the drug material, raised statutory penalties against violators in this field and abolished the regulations concerning habitual abusers and habitual traffickers for gains.

D. The Law to Control Business Affecting Public Morals

The Law to Control Business Affecting Public Morals was enforced in September 1948 to adopt a licence system for such business and to punish violators. The law was revised for the 13th time in August 1984 (enforced in February 1985), calling for strengthening of the regulations in this area and related business. The name of the law was changed to the Law for Adjusting Business Affecting Public Morals.

E. Other Special Laws

The Imperial Ordinance to Punish Those Who Force Women into Prostitution was enforced in January 1947. The ordinance provided for punishment against those who urged women to engage in prostitution by way of harassment or contractual arrangement. This ordinance was enforced under the authorization of the imperial order of 1945, which had been stipulated in order to promptly cope with the urgent need for responding to the demands of the Supreme Commander of the Allied Forces of occupation, due to the acceptance of the Potsdam Declaration by Japan. At the time of restoration of independence of Japan in 1952, these ordinances promulgated under such authorization were reviewed by the Parliament, and laws were enforced in order either to approve their application in the future or abolish them. One of these laws, which dealt with the ordinances coming under the administrative jurisdiction of the Ministry of Justice (enforced in May 1952), approved the applicabilty of this ordinance in the future as a law.

The ordinance was abolished in April 1958 following the enforcement in April 1957 of the Anti-Prostitution Law (regulations on criminal punishments were enforced on April 1, 1958). The law provides for measures to protect and correct women who are potential prostitutes, and punishment against such acts as inducement for prostitution purposes, offering good offices for prostitution and facilitation of managed prostitution and other kinds of cooperative acts for prostitution.

As the need arose to provide for regulations and punishment against acts which would threaten to cause public hazards to human health during the course of business activities, the Law for Punishment of Crimes of Public Nuisance concerning Public Health was enforced in July 1971. Other regulations concerning pollution include the Air Pollution Control Law enforced in December 1968, the Law concerning Disposal and Cleaning of Waste Matters enforced in September 1971, the Law to Prevent Water Contamination and the Law concerning Prevention of Offshore Pollution and Disasters.

Punishments against the hijacking of aircraft in flight were bolstered while the Law concerning Punishment against Hijacking of Aircraft was put into effect in June 1970 in order to meet the requirements under the international treaty for prevention of hijacking.

As the need arose to streamline domestic laws to punish such acts as destruction of aircraft in service before concluding the Montreal Convention for the Suppression of Unlawful Acts against the Safety of Civil Aviation, the Law concerning Punishment Against Acts Endangering the Safety of Aircraft was enforced in July 1974.

With Molotov cocktails having been used as main weapons by leftist radicals since 1968, it became necessary to punish manufacture, possession and use of Molotov cocktails. As a result, the Law concerning the Punishment against Use of Molotov Cocktails and Other Weapons was enforced in May 1972.

Furthermore, with the intensification and worsening in coercive acts by taking advantage of hostages caught in hijacking or seizure of diplomatic offices, the Law for Punishment of Acts of Coercion, etc. by Taking Advantage of Hostages was enforced in June 1978 to strengthen punishment against such acts of coercion.

In addition to laws and regulations on punishment and treatment of offenders, several laws were established for relief of victims of crime during the Showa period. One such law is the Law concerning State Compensation for the

Victims of Crime, etc., enforced in January 1981. The law provides for regulations on state compensations to the bereaved families of crime victims or persons injured seriously by those offenders who committed crimes against life and body. Other laws intended for relief of crime victims are the Automobile Damage Compensation Security Law enforced in August 1955, the law enforced in October 1952 for provision of compensation to victims in the process of cooperating with police investigation and the law enforced in July 1958 on provision of subsidies for damages incurred by witnesses.

Section 2. TRENDS IN PENAL CODE OFFENCES

1. OUTLINE

How has Japan's crime phenomena developed during the Showa era? Statistical material on the Showa crime phenomena could include police, prosecutors office, court, corrections and probation statistics. Here, however, we shall use police statistics on the number of criminal offences reported and court records on the number of people found guilty at the court of first instance, to discern criminal trends during the Showa era. The former statistics provide figures closest to actual crime phenomena, while the latter, although not actually presenting the actual state of the crime phenomena, allows for statistics on relatively serious criminal acts, which were confirmed through the criminal justice proceedings and penalties paid. By looking at both sets of statistics, we can examine the crime phenomena from the point of view of quantity as well as quality.

(1) Number of Cases Reported, Number of Offenders Cleared by Police and Rate of Criminal Incidents per Population

Fig. 1 and Table 1 in Appendix show trends in the Showa era for the number of criminal offences reported, number of offenders cleared, clearance rates, rates of criminal incidents, etc. According to these graphs, the number of criminal offences reported surpassed the figure of 100,000 cases annually after the prewar year of 1930, and grew continuously until the record high of 1,566,435 cases in 1934. Cases decreased after that time, falling to a low of 711,596 cases reported in 1945. After the war, reported cases reached a peak of 1,603,265 in 1948, after which the figures declined somewhat. In the early 1960 s, however, figures began to increase again, reaching a peak of 1,932,401 cases in 1970. The figures went into a decline after that time, but again began to increase in the late 1970s, breaking 2 million cases in the years after 1982, and reaching 2,207,380 cases in 1988, to become the highest figure reported in the Showa era. The figures for number of cases reported, at the very least, show

Fig.1 Number of Penal Code Offences Reported and Offenders Cleared by the Police (1926—1988)

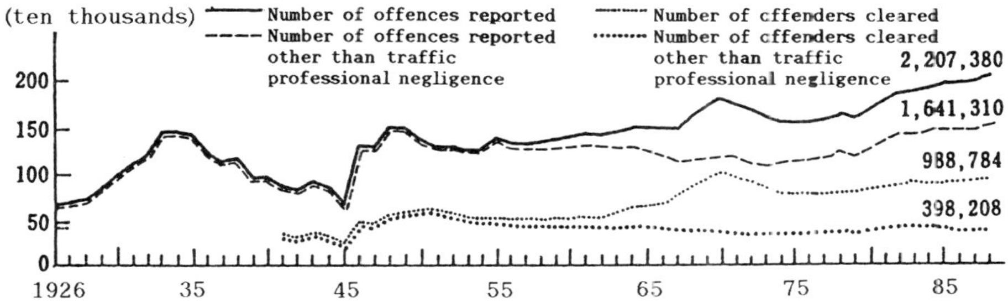

Sources:National Police Agency, Ministry of Home Affairs,etc

that Showa criminal offence trends appeared to consist of (1) Wave No. 1 peaking in 1933 to 1935, (2) Wave No. 2 peaking in 1948 to 1950, (3) Wave No. 3 lasting from around 1955 to about 1970 with a peak in 1970 and (4) Wave No. 4 lasting from about 1975 to the present.

Of course, if we look at the number of cases reported, excluding traffic-related professional negligence (professional negligence before 1965), the pre-war peak came in 1934 at 1,550,645, then declined to a record low of 708,809 cases in 1945. These figures follow virtually the same curve as when professional negligence is included. In the postwar period, however, while the peak was recorded at 1,599,968 cases in 1948, the number floated in the 1.35 million to 1.4 million range in the 1955 to 1965 period, and then began declining in the years starting in 1965, reaching a postwar low of 1,190,549 cases in 1973. Entering the late 1970s, the trend began a continuous increase, reaching 1,641,310 cases in 1988, the highest recorded in the Showa era. This trend differs from the figures when professional negligence is included, showing that Wave No. 3 mentioned earlier was due mainly to an increase in traffic-related professional negligence.

Next, for the number of offenders cleared by the police for Penal Code offences, the figures for the years 1941 to 1945 moved between 200,000 and 300,000. After the war, however, they showed a sudden rise, reaching a peak of 619,035 people in 1951. After that, the numbers decreased somewhat, but then turned around and begin to increase again after 1960, recording an all-time high of 1,073,470 people in 1970. The figures declined slightly into the late 1970s, but then again began a continuous increase, reaching 988,784 people in 1988. Of course, if we look at the number of offenders cleared for Penal Code offences, excluding traffic-related professional negligence, the period after the high wave peaking at 607,769 people in 1950 shows a general declining trend, with some

Table 1 Number of Juvenile and Female Penal Code Offenders Other Than Those of Traffic Professional Negligence (1945～1988)

Year	Total	Juveniles	Females	Juvenile Rate	Female Rate
1945	239,865	…	23,395	(22.6)	9.8
1946	442,579	…	33,819	(25.1)	7.6
1947	455,097	…	35,749	(22.8)	7.9
1948	546,991	…	44,869	(22.7)	8.2
1949	579,897	…	53,605	(22.5)	9.2
1950	607,769	…	54,278	(25.7)	8.9
1951	606,686	…	51,296	(26.9)	8.5
1952	557,521	…	46,918	(24.9)	8.4
1953	519,707	…	43,509	(23.0)	8.4
1954	496,412	…	41,074	(22.3)	8.3
1955	501,429	…	39,667	(21.8)	7.9
1956	470,522	…	31,990	(19.1)	6.8
1957	471,600	…	31,850	(21.0)	6.8
1958	457,212	…	31,995	(22.8)	7.0
1959	454,898	…	31,936	(25.1)	7.0
1960	442,527	…	33,935	(26.3)	7.7
1961	451,586	…	36,711	(27.3)	8.1
1962	430,153	…	42,001	(28.6)	7.8
1963	425,473	…	48,154	(28.7)	11.3
1964	449,842	…	51,183	(28.1)	11.4
1965	440,563	…	49,724	(27.0)	11.3
1966	433,545	148,249	46,471	34.2	10.7
1967	402,738	129,520	44,142	32.2	11.0
1968	393,831	117,125	45,573	29.7	11.6
1969	377,826	107,312	45,057	28.4	11.9
1970	380,850	113,295	47,509	29.7	12.5
1971	361,972	107,107	48,234	29.6	13.3
1972	348,788	100,851	47,408	28.9	13.6
1973	357,738	108,211	51,133	30.2	14.3
1974	363,309	115,453	58,261	31.8	16.0
1975	364,117	116,782	61,432	32.1	16.9
1976	359,360	115,628	67,276	32.2	18.7
1977	363,144	119,199	68,919	32.8	19.0
1978	381,742	136,801	72,986	35.8	19.1
1979	368,126	143,158	69,435	38.9	18.9
1980	392,113	166,073	74,225	42.4	18.9
1981	418,162	184,902	78,946	44.2	18.9
1982	441,963	191,930	79,825	43.4	18.1
1983	438,705	196,783	83,200	44.9	19.0
1984	446,617	192,665	81,784	43.1	18.3
1985	432,250	194,117	78,985	44.9	18.3
1986	399,886	185,373	77,856	46.4	19.5
1987	404,762	187,192	78,062	46.2	19.3
1988	398,208	193,206	82,640	48.5	20.8

Notes : 1 Female Rate $= \frac{\text{Female}}{\text{Total}} \times 100$

2 Juvenile Rate $= \frac{\text{Juvenile}}{\text{Total}} \times 100$

3 Figures in parentheses show the rate where traffic professional negligence is included.

Source: National Police Agency

exceptions, falling to a low figure of 348,788 people in 1972. Entering the late 1970s, the numbers rose somewhat, surpassing 400,000 people in the years 1981 to 1987, but then declined slightly in 1988 to 398,208 people.

In addition, the number of criminal offences reported per 100,000 people (rate of criminal incidents), excluding traffic-related professional negligence, reached a prewar high of 2,282 in 1933, and fell to a low of 984 in 1945. The postwar high was 2,000 in 1948, while the low was 1,091 in 1973. The figure for 1988 was 1,337, a figure similar to those in the first years of the Showa era.

The clearance rate for Penal Code offences in the prewar period up to 1938 stood at high rates, surpassing 90 percent almost every year. After that time, the rate fell steadily, reaching 66.4 percent in 1945. The rate fell to the 50-percent level in 1946 to 1949, and then continued to keep to a 60-percent level, occasionally falling lower up to around 1960. After that time, the rate steadily recovered, moving to around 70 percent.

(2) By Age, Sex, etc.

Now, let's look at the offenders cleared by the police according to adult or juvenile class. Table 1, for offenders cleared for Penal Code offences, excluding traffic-related professional negligence, shows the structural trend of

Fig.2 Rate of Adult and Juvenile Penal Code Offenders Cleared by the Police (1944~1988)

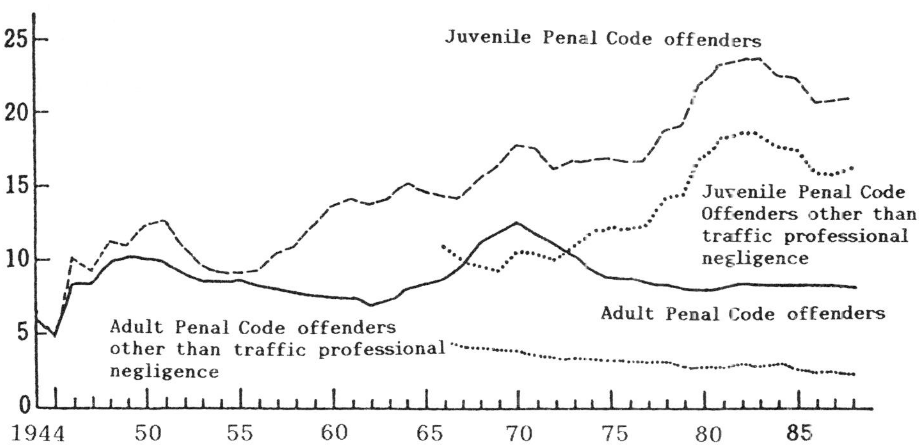

Note: Rate per population means the number of adults aged 20 and over and juveniles aged from 14 to 19 cleared by the police, per 1,000 population.

Sources: National Police Agency and Statistics Bureau, Management and Coordination Agency

adults and juveniles as well as female offenders. The juvenile rates up to 1965 include all offences, including professional negligence. The juvenile rates for the postwar period to 1958 moved at about the 20-percent level, but then began to show an upward trend from 1959, reaching 34.2 percent in 1966. The trend from 1965 and early 1970s moved at around 30 percent. It began again to increase after 1978, reaching 48.5 percent in 1988. In addition, Fig. 2 shows the number of offenders cleared for Penal Code offences per 1,000 population classified by adult and juvenile (called hereafter population ratio).

Fig.3 Percentage of Penal Code Offenders Cleared Other Than Traffic Professional Negligence, by Age Group (1966~1988)

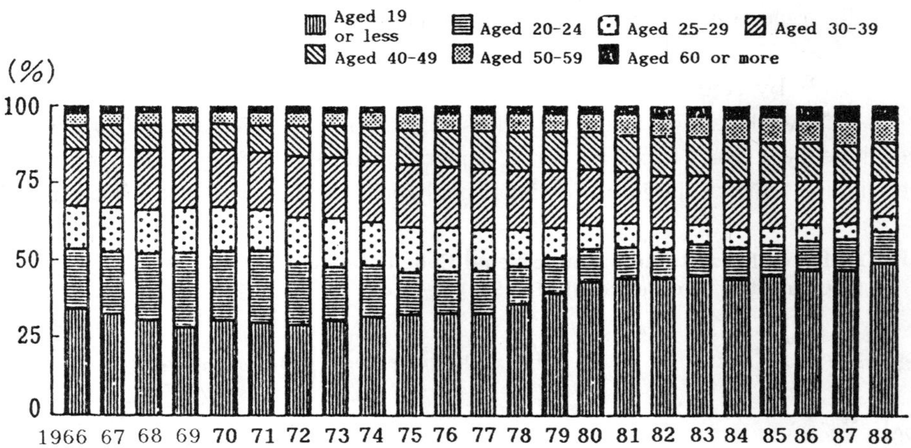

Source: National Police Agency

The period of Wave No. 2 mentioned earlier (1948 to 1950) shows a high wave for both adults and juveniles. In addition, the juvenile population ratio began rising after 1955, surpassing the figure for adults in 1958. After that, the upward trend continued with a few exceptions, and began rising fast after 1980, remaining at a very high figure to the present time. Meanwhile, the population ratio for adults reached a high wave in the late 1960s and early 1970s, with the crest around 1970, but when traffic-related professional negligence was excluded, it is possible to see a generally smooth downward trend. When the graphs are compared for offenders cleared for Penal Code offences as a whole and those cleared for Penal Code offences, excluding traffic-related professional negligence, Wave No. 3 mentioned earlier (from late 1950s to 1970) appeared to be due to the increase in professional negligence, while Wave No. 4 (from late 1970s to present), unlike the earlier wave, can be construed to have been due to the increase in juvenile offences.

Fig. 3 shows the trend in number of offenders cleared by police for Penal Code offences, excluding traffic-related professional negligence, by age group. Notable points seen after 1975 show juveniles increasing, while 20-year-olds declined and over 40-year-olds increased. In addition, reflecting the aging of society, over 60-year-olds showed an increasing trend, reaching 4.5 percent in 1988.

Next, a look at female offenders cleared by police shows an increasing trend after 1970. In the structural ratio for offenders cleared for Penal Code offences, excluding traffic-related professional negligence, a rising trend began after the ratio figure broke through the 10-percent level in 1963, reaching 20.8 percent in 1988.

(3) Repeat Offences among Criminal Offenders

Table 2 Number of Recidivists among Penal Code Offenders Cleared by the Police, by Adults and Juveniles

Year	Total	Recidivists	Adults	Recidivists	Juveniles	Recidivists
1956	524,315	180,059 (34.3)	424,117	149,443 (35.2)	100,198	30,616 (30.6)
1951	580,410	195,228 (33.6)	421,671	151,388 (35.9)	158,739	43,840 (27.6)
1966	…	…	…	…	…	…
1971	353,431	125,928 (35.6)	246,926	93,735 (38.0)	106,505	32,193 (30.2)
1976	359,360	123,007 (34.2)	243,732	90,490 (37.1)	115,628	32,517 (28.1)
1981	318,162	133,230 (31.9)	233,260	83,031 (35.6)	184,902	50,199 (27.1)
1986	399,886	127,872 (32.0)	214,513	70,886 (33.0)	185,373	56,986 (30.7)
1988	398,208	120,598 (30.3)	205,002	66,507 (32.4)	193,206	54,091 (28.0)

Note : Figures in parentheses show the percentage.
Source: National Police Agency

A. Repeat Offenders among Offenders Cleared by the Police

Table 2 shows repeat offenders, for both adults and juveniles, among total offenders cleared for Penal Code offences (excluding professional negligence offences in 1971 and excluding traffic-related professional negligence in and after 1976) from statistics taken in five-year intervals from 1956 onward, and 1988. Repeat offenders listed here include not only those who have been convicted and sentenced to penal sanctions before but also those who have been arrested or investigated before by the police.

The ratio of repeat offenders among total offenders cleared by the police was 34.3 percent in 1956, declining slightly to 33.6 percent in 1961, and rising again to 35.6 percent in 1971. The trend turned down from 1976 onward, to 30.3 percent in 1988. For adult repeat offenders, the ratio was 35.2 percent in 1956 and 35.9 percent in 1961, rising to 38.0 percent in 1971. From 1976, however, the numbers began dropping slightly, reaching 32.4 percent in 1988. For juvenile repeat offenders, the ratio from 1956 to 1988 fluctuated between 27.1

Table 3 Number of Ex-convicts among Those Who Were Prosecuted and Suspended Prosecution for Penal Code Offences Other Than Traffic Professional Negligence

Year	Prosecution and Suspended Prosecution	of whom: Ex-convicts	Prosecution	of whom: Ex-convicts	Suspended Prosecution	of whom: Ex-convicts
1931	289,995	…	97,277	…	192,718	22,491 (11.7)
1936	349,856	…	114,500	…	235,356	25,553 (10.9)
1941	236,835	…	120,066	…	116,769	…
1946	…	…	…	…	…	…
1951	402,184	…	159,546	…	242,638	24,428 (10.1)
1956	392,971	…	194,164	…	198,807	33,976 (17.1)
1961	335,948	121,520 (36.2)	191,329	88,071 (46.0)	144,619	33,449 (23.1)
1966	303,868	122,750 (40.4)	187,506	92,734 (49.5)	116,362	30,016 (25.8)
1971	248,630	98,158 (39.5)	147,550	74,181 (50.3)	101,080	23,977 (23.7)
1976	230,829	102,351 (44.3)	148,594	82,039 (55.2)	82,235	20,312 (24.7)
1981	187,767	90,266 (48.1)	122,268	72,518 (59.3)	65,499	17,748 (27.1)
1986	150,879	76,015 (50.4)	100,022	61,018 (61.0)	50,857	14,997 (29.5)
1988	138,003	67,880 (49.2)	87,109	52,398 (60.2)	50,894	15,482 (30.4

Sources: Annual Report of Criminal Statistics, Annual Report of Statistics on Prosecution, etc.

Table 4 Number and Percentage of the First Time Offenders, Ex-convicts and Recidivists among the Penal Code Offenders in Courts of First Instance

Year	Total Convicted	First time offenders	Ex-convicts	
				Recidivists
1926	104,374 (100.0)	73,064 (70.0)	31,310 (30.0)	8,825 (8.5)
1931	98,431 (100.0)	66,734 (67.8)	31,697 (32.2)	11,813 (12.0)
1936	120,871 (100.0)	76,621 (63.4)	44,250 (36.6)	16,338 (13.5)
1941	116,005 (100.0)	74,649 (64.3)	41,356 (35.7)	11,654 (10.0)
1946	…	…	…	…
1951	105,836 (100.0)	56,302 (53.2)	49,534 (46.8)	20,435 (19.3)
1956	98,059 (100.0)	47,476 (48.4)	50,583 (51.6)	26,372 (26.9)
1961	78,241 (100.0)	33,573 (42.9)	44,668 (57.1)	19,602 (25.1)
1966	73,515 (100.0)	28,150 (38.3)	45,365 (61.7)	16,432 (22.4)
1971	63,610 (100.0)	25,114 (39.5)	38,496 (60.5)	11,922 (18.7)
1976	58,334 (100.0)	20,864 (35.8)	37,470 (64.2)	11,999 (20.6)
1981	49,662 (100.0)	17,109 (34.5)	32,553 (65.5)	11,348 (22.9)
1986	47,493 (100.0)	17,431 (36.7)	30,062 (63.3)	9,955 (21.0)
1987	47,002 (100.0)	17,925 (38.1)	29,077 (61.9)	9,902 (21.1)

Sources: Annual Report of Criminal Statistics, Annual Report of Judicial Statistics

percent and 30.7 percent, for a virtually flat trend. The declining ratio of repeat offenders among total offenders cleared by police is due to the decline in the ratio of repeat offenders among adults.

B. Repeat Offenders among Those Prosecuted or Suspended Prosecution

Table 3 shows the ratio of ex-convicts among the offenders prosecuted or suspended their prosecution for Penal Code offences (excluding professional negligence), in five-year intervals from 1931, and 1988. The ex-convicts listed here differ from repeat offenders among the offenders cleared by police; rather, the term refers to those who have previously been convicted and sentenced to a fine or heavier penalties. In addition, statistics for 1956 and earlier only cover the ratio among those suspended their prosecution.

The ratio of ex-convicts among offenders, including both prosecuted and those suspended their prosecution, was 36.2 percent in 1961. After that time, the trend was generally upward with a few fluctuations, reaching 50.4 percent in 1986. This ratio declined slightly in 1988, to 49.2 percent. A comparison of the ratio of ex-convicts among the offenders, including both prosecuted and those suspended their prosecution, to the ratio of repeat adult offenders among the offenders cleared by the police shows that whereas the two ratios were virtually the same in 1961, the former ratio had become 1.5 percentage points higher in 1971. In 1976 and later, the former ratio showed an upward trend, while the latter ratio trended downward, widening the gap between the two. As was mentioned earlier, the definition of repeat offenders is broader than that of ex-convicts, so that it would appear that the ratio of repeat offenders among the offenders cleared by the police ought to be higher than the ratio of ex-convicts among the offenders, including both prosecuted and those suspended their prosecution. In fact, however, the reverse is the case. The reason for this may be explained by the fact that not a few adult first-time offenders among the offenders cleared by the police for Penal Code offences have been discharged at police stations without their cases being referred to the public prosecutors office under the authorization of the chief public prosecutors for the disposition of minor offences and such dispositions have not been counted in the records of arrests for defining the repeat offenders (Those who were discharged as such at the police stations amounted to 30,635 in 1971, 56,613 in 1976, 82,726 in 1981, 94,166 in 1986 and 89,744 in 1988).

Next, a look at the ratio of ex-convicts among the offenders prosecuted shows 46.0 percent for 1961, rising after that to 61.0 percent in 1986. The ratio declined slightly in 1988 to 60.2 percent. A look at the ratio of ex-convicts among the offenders suspended their prosecution shows a ratio of around 11 percent for the prewar years of 1931 and 1936, while the postwar year of 1951 shows 10.1 percent, a figure virtually unchanged from the prewar years. After that, however, the rate climbed, from 17.1 percent in 1956 to 30.4 percent in 1988. This shows that the ratio of ex-convicts among the offenders both prosecuted and suspended their prosecution has been rising steadily. In addition, when the ratio of ex-convicts among offenders prosecuted is compared to the ratio of ex-convicts among the offenders suspended their prosecution, the former was found to be appreciably higher than the latter. In other words, among the offenders prosecuted, the ratio of ex-convicts is higher while among the offenders suspended their prosecution, the ratio of first offenders is higher.

Fig. 4 Number of Offenders Convicted in Courts of First Instance and Rate of Recidivists

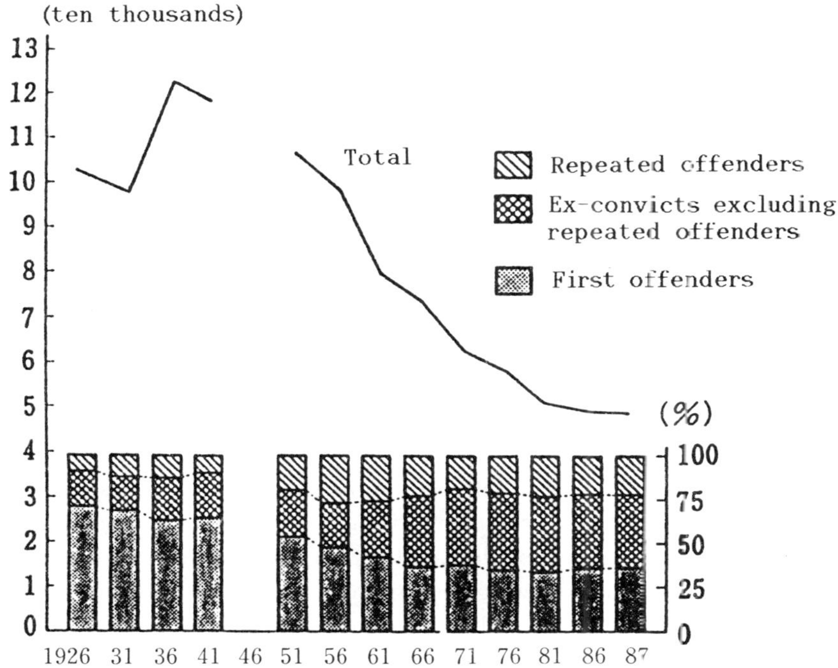

Note: The source is not available in 1946.
Sources: Annual Report of Criminal Statistics and Annual Report of Judicial Statistics

C. Repeat Offenders among the Offenders Found Guilty in the Court of First Instance

Table 4 and Fig. 4 show the ratio of first offenders, ex-convicts and recidivists among offenders found guilty for Penal Code offences in the court of first instance through formal proceedings (figures for those found guilty in the court of first instance for 1941 and earlier include summary proceedings), in five-year intervals from 1926 to 1987. Ex-convicts here, for 1941 and earlier, refer to those who had previously been sentenced to any penal sanctions whatsoever, and for 1951 and later, to people who had previously been sentenced to a fine or heavier punishments.

A look at the prewar ratio of ex-convicts among those found guilty in the court of first instance shows 30.0 percent in 1926, afterward rising to 36.6 percent in 1936, and then falling slightly to 35.7 percent in 1941. The postwar ratio of ex-convicts rose from 46.8 percent in 1951 to reach 65.5 percent in 1981, after which it dropped back to 61.9 percent in 1987. While the prewar and postwar figures cannot readily be compared because of differences in statistical methods as mentioned above, it would appear that the ratio of ex-convicts shows an upward trend from the prewar to the postwar eras. Meanwhile, the ratio of recidivists (the offenders subject to Article 56 of the Penal Code, such as those who have been sentenced to imprisonment with labour, commit a crime again within five years from the day on which the execution of the former sentence was completed or remitted, and are to be sentenced to imprisonment with labour for a determinate term, for a second, third or further time) moved between 8.5 percent and 13.5 percent in the prewar period of 1926 to 1941. In the postwar period, the ratio climbed from 19.3 percent in 1951 to 26.9 percent in 1956, then declined thereafter, to 18.7 percent in 1971. From 1976 to 1987, the ratio moved between 20.6 percent and 22.9 percent. The reason why the ratio of ex-convicts among those found guilty in the court of first instance through formal proceedings rose in the postwar period while the ratio of the recidivists showed a generally flat trend, with some fluctuations, was due to a sudden increase in traffic-related offences in the postwar period, resulting in an increase in ex-convicts sentenced to imprisonment without labour or fines. In addition, it may be explained by the fact that among those sentenced to imprisonment with labour, those who were granted suspended execution of the sentence have been increasing, while those who served in prison, viz., those who meet the conditions to satisfy the recidivists, have been declining.

Fig.5 Number of Penal Code Offenders Convicted in Courts of First Instance (1926～1987)

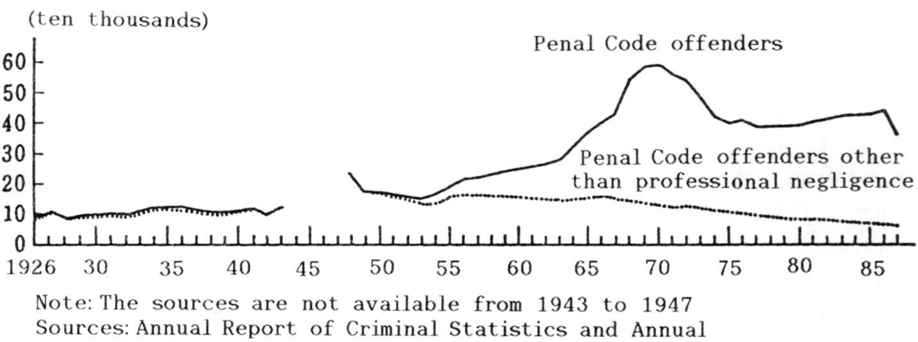

Note: The sources are not available from 1943 to 1947
Sources: Annual Report of Criminal Statistics and Annual Report of Statistics on Prosecution

(4) Offenders Found Guilty in the Court of First Instance

Next, let's look at the Showa crime situation according to trends in the number of offenders found guilty through the formal proceedings at the court of first instance. Fig. 5 and Table 3 in the Appendix show the trends in the number of those found guilty for Penal Code offences in the court of first instance during the Showa era. The numbers during the prewar period showed a wave lasting from 1934 to 1936, peaking at 123,200 people in 1934. Later numbers decreased through 1939, increased slightly in 1940 and 1941, decreased in 1942, but then increased to 125,470 people in 1943, to record a prewar high.

Postwar period data starts from 1948, beginning with a high point of 230,553 people, far higher than the prewar peak. The numbers then steadily declined through the early 1950s. So the curve for those found guilty in the court of first instance followed the same trend of No. 1 and No. 2 Waves as was earlier noted for number of offences reported. Of interest here is the fact that the postwar wave peaking in 1948 was much higher than the prewar wave which peaked in 1934. As the height of the waves for number of offences reported was virtually the same for the prewar and postwar waves, the volume of offences disclosed to police was not all that different. But as the difference in wave heights for those found guilty in the court of first instance shows, postwar offences appear to have differed in quality from prewar offences. In the prewar period, many investigations for light offences took place, which were not prosecuted, while in the postwar period, it can be said that many more serious offences warranting prosecution and the handing down of guilty verdicts were committed. In addition, although police crime investigation capabilities in the postwar period drastically declined in comparison with the prewar period, as the clearance rate depicted in Table 1 in the Appendix shows, the fact that the number of those found guilty in the court of first instance in 1948 nearly doubled the prewar high shows just how bad the crime situation was in the chaotic postwar period.

In addition, a look at the number of those found guilty of Penal Code offences in the court of first instance shows a rising trend from about 1955, peaking at 582,035 people in 1970, after which the trend turned downward. In the late 1970s, the numbers began rising again, however recording 438,309 people in 1986. In 1987, the number was 352,460 people. The large decrease seen in 1987 was due to a revision of the prosecutors office's guideline for handling traffic-related offences, resulting in a sudden drop in the prosecution rate for traffic-related professional negligence and a rise in the suspension of prosecution ratio.

The number of those found guilty of Penal Code offences in the court of first instance, excluding professional negligence, reached a peak of 228,223 people in 1948, after which it declined for some years.

There was a slight increase in the late 1950s, but it was followed by an overall decline, dropping below the 100,000 mark in the late 1970s and recording an all-time low for the Showa era of 61,519 people in 1987. The trend in numbers of those found guilty in the court of first instance implies that Wave No. 3 (from 1955 to 1970) for the previously noted number of cases reported was due to a rapid increase in professional negligence. In addition, a look at the number of those found guilty in the court of first instance shows no evidence of Wave No. 4 (from 1975 to the present) seen in number of cases reported. This is probably due to the increase in juvenile delinquency, which was not reflected in the number of people found guilty in the court of first instance.

(5) Structural Ratio by Type of Penal Code Offences

Table 5 shows the trend in the structural ratio for the top 10 Penal Code offences according to the number of Penal Code offences reported, excluding professional negligence, for the years 1927, 1933, 1941, 1950, 1955, 1960, 1965, 1970, 1975 and 1985. According to the Table, the No. 1 ranking for every year listed was theft. The structural ratio, however, shows a drastic increase for the postwar period. The No. 2 ranking for every year listed was fraud. Embezzlement held the No. 3 ranking for every year except 1960, 1970 and 1975. In those years, embezzlement was replaced by bodily injury, while assault and extortion also rose in the rankings. In addition, while gambling and illegal lotteries ranked high in the prewar period, in the postwar period it was ranked once at the No. 10 ranking in 1950, after which it disappeared from the top 10. By contrast, offences such as assault rose to secure high rankings in the postwar period. These changes no doubt reflect the tenor of each period, but to learn the details it is necessary to look at the trends for each type of crime for the number of cases reported and the number of offenders found guilty in the court of first instance. Hereafter, we shall look at the trends in criminal offences by type of crime, focusing on the changes between the prewar and postwar periods.

2. TRENDS IN MAJOR CRIMINAL OFFENCES

Trends in major Penal Code offences shall be examined in following order: property offences, heinous offences, violent offences, sexual offences and others.

(1) Property Offences

Fig. 6, Table 2 and Table 3 in the Appendix show trends in the number of cases reported and number of people found guilty in the court of first instance for theft, fraud and embezzlement.

A. Theft

For number of cases reported, the prewar peak was 724,986 cases in 1934, while the postwar peak was 1,246,445 cases in 1948. After that, the

Table 5 Number and Rate of the Top Ten Reported Penal Code Offences Excluding Professional Negligence, by Year and in Descending Order

Order	1927			Order	1933		
	Offence	Number of offences reported	Percentage		Offence	Number of offences reported	Percentage
	Total	741,628	100.0		Total	1,538,788	100.0
1	Theft	383,640	51.7	1	Theft	704,913	45.8
2	Fraud	136,934	18.5	2	Fraud	388,666	25.3
3	Embezzlement	91,840	12.4	3	Embezzlement	265,357	17.2
4	Gambling	32,903	4.4	4	Gambling	35,294	2.3
5	Bodily injury	23,448	3.2	5	Bodily injury	26,200	1.7
6	Forgery and Counterfeiting	12,728	1.7	6	Forgery and Counterfeiting	25,640	1.7
7	Fire caused by negligence	11,934	1.6	7	Handling stolen goods	13,681	0.9
8	Handling stolen goods	8,320	1.1	8	Extortion	12,849	0.8
9	Housebreaking	4,858	0.7	9	Fire caused by negligence	12,431	0.8
10	Extortion	3,826	0.5	10	Housebreaking	10,007	0.7

Order	1941			Order	1950		
	Offence	Number of offences reported	Percentage		Offence	Number of offences reported	Percentage
	Total	913,693	100.0		Total	1,461,044	100.0
1	Theft	554,143	60.6	1	Theft	932,341	67.2
2	Fraud	111,629	12.2	2	Fraud	137,528	12.8
3	Embezzlement	97,415	10.7	3	Embezzlement	65,616	4.5
4	Gambling	59,844	6.5	4	Bodily injury	42,769	2.9
5	Bodily injury	17,114	1.9	5	Handling stolen goods	38,234	2.6
6	Handling stolen goods	16,700	1.8	6	Extortion	32,740	2.2
7	Forgeny and Counterfeiting	11,258	1.2	7	Assault	19,730	1.4
8	Fire caused by negligence	9,872	1.1	8	Forgery and Counterfeiting	10,131	0.7
9	Housebreaking	8,833	1.0	9	Housebreaking	10,076	0.7
10	Extortion	6,360	0.7	10	Gambling	9,545	0.7

Order	1960			Order	1970		
	Offence	Number of offences reported	Percentage		Offence	Number of offences reported	Percentage
	Total	1,378,817	100.0		Total	1,277,459	100.0
1	Theft	1,038,418	75.3	1	Theft	1,039,118	81.3
2	Fraud	82,886	6.0	2	Fraud	58,340	4.6
3	Bodily injury	68,304	5.0	3	Bodily injury	50,836	4.0
4	Assault	44,250	3.2	4	Assault	32,028	2.5
5	Extortion	41,060	3.0	5	Extortion	18,775	1.5
6	Embezzle-ment	22,144	1.6	6	House-breaking	10,355	0.8
7	Handling stolen goods	12,282	0.9	7	Embezzle-ment	9,362	0.7
8	House-breaking	9,224	0.7	8	Forgery and Counter-feiting	6,827	0.5
9	Destruction of property	8,393	0.6	9	Fire caused by negligence	5,819	0.5
10	Fire caused by negligence	8,189	0.6	10	Destructuon of property	5,594	0.4

Order	1975			Order	1985		
	Offence	Number of offences reported	Percentage		Offence	Number of offences reported	Percentage
	Total	1,232,381	100.0		Total	1,606,886	100.0
1	Theft	1,037,942	84.2	1	Theft	1,381,237	86.0
2	Fraud	53,647	4.4	2	Fraud	74,424	4.6
3	Bodily injury	34,136	2.8	3	Embezzle-ment	41,567	2.6
4	Assault	21,944	1.8	4	Bodily injury	22,302	1.4
5	Extortion	14,255	1.2	5	Forgery and Counter-feiting	14,843	0.9
6	Embezzle-ment	10,575	0.9	6	Extortion	12,679	0.8
7	House-breaking	10,018	0.8	7	House-breaking	12,675	0.8
8	Forgery and Counter-feiting	7,285	0.6	8	Assault	12,171	0.8
9	Destruction of property	6,125	0.5	9	Destruction of property	10,812	0.7
10	Fire caused by negligence	4,206	0.3	10	Indecent assault	2,645	0.2

Sources: Home Office and National Police Agency

numbers declined somewhat in the early 1950s and later, but remained at very high levels in comparison to the prewar period, hovering at just over one million cases. The numbers began rising again in the early 1980s, recording a postwar record high of 1,422,355 cases in 1988.

For number of people found guilty in the court of first instance, the prewar high was 21,843 people in 1934, in the midst of a high wave of around 20,000 annually from 1933 to 1938. The postwar period began with an exceptionally high wave of 99,632 people in 1948, after which the figures trended downward, reaching the 30,000-range in the early 1960s, and falling to the 20,000-people range in the early 1970s. After that, the figures hovered between 17,000 and 19,000 people, reaching 16,442 people in 1987.

A comparison of the number of cases reported and number of people found guilty in the court of first instance shows a high wave for both categories

Fig.6 Number of Property Offences Reported and Offenders Convicted in Courts of First Instance

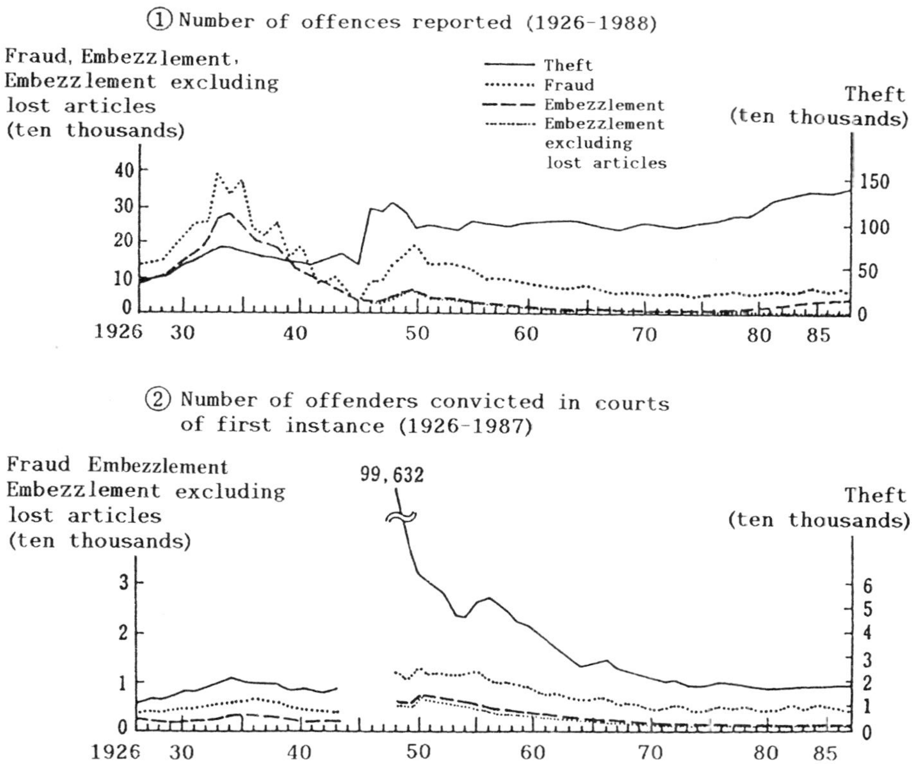

Sources: Annual Report of Criminal Statistics, Annual Report of Judicial Statistics, etc.

in the chaotic postwar period of the late 1940s. Later, however, the high figures seen for number of cases reported, and especially the high wave seen beginning in the early 1980s, is not apparent in the numbers of people found guilty in the court of first instance, demonstrating a great difference between the two categories. This difference can be explained by the following facts. As for the theft offences in the chaotic years after the war, mostly consisting of factory and store burglaries with the aim of stealing production goods or foodstuff, strict measures were taken against these crimes in order to suppress such illegal activities and maintain peace and order in the community facing severe destitution at that time. Later, as the economy began to recover and prosper, motives and modus operandi changed, and relatively light offences such as bicycle theft, shoplifting, etc. were widespread, while serious offences such as pickpocketing and breaking and entering declined. In addition, many of the relatively minor theft offences were committed by juveniles. In particular, the high wave of number of cases reported in the early 1980s was due to a sudden increase in juvenile thefts.

B. Fraud

For number of cases reported, a prewar high wave can be seen from 1933 to 1935 with a peak of 388,666 cases in 1933. The postwar period also has a high wave from 1948 to 1953, peaking in 1950 at 187,528 cases. After that time, however, the figures declined steadily, moving between 50,000 and 70,000 after 1965. There were 65,125 cases in 1988. Meanwhile, for number of people found guilty in the court of first instance, a prewar high wave of between 5,000 and 6,000 people can be seen from 1933 to 1938. In the postwar period, however, high figures of around 10,000 people were recorded annually from 1948 to about 1955, with a peak of 12,391 people in 1950. The figures declined steadily thereafter, reaching a postwar low of 3,932 people in 1974, after which the figures moved in the 4,000 range, with 4,294 people in 1987. So large differences between number of cases reported and number of people found guilty in the court of first instance can be seen for fraud as well. But as has been previously noted, of the number of cases reported, the prewar period included a relatively high proportion of lighter fraud offences. In the postwar period, reports of that kind of fraud offence became relatively unusual, while the kind of fraud offences serious enough to merit prosecution and judgements of guilt became relatively more common.

C. Embezzlement

For number of cases reported, the prewar high wave peaked at 282,595 cases in 1934. In the postwar period, while the high wave lasted from 1948 to 1954, topping out at 65,616 cases in 1950, it was lower than the prewar period and dropped steadily thereafter, falling to less than 10,000 cases annually in the late 1960s and early 1970s. In the late 1970s, however, the numbers began rising again, reaching a high figure of 45,678 cases in 1988. Meanwhile, for number of people found guilty in the court of first instance, the prewar high wave lasted from 1933 to 1936, with a high of 3,169 people in 1935. The postwar period, however, began with a wave higher than the prewar one, lasting from 1948 to 1955, that peaked at 7,150 people in 1951, after which the numbers dropped steadily, reaching 714 people in 1987. As can be seen, embezzlement, like fraud, shows differences between the number of cases reported and number of people found guilty in the courts of first instance. These differences existing in the prewar waves and in the waves in the chaotic postwar period can be explained by the same reasons as were mentioned above for fraud, that is, lighter embezzlement offences were included in the number of reported offences of those years. Concerning the divergence after 1975 in number of cases reported and number of people found guilty in the courts of first instance, most of the increase in number of cases reported is due to the increase in embezzlement of lost property, viz. misappropriation of neglected property. If this category is excluded, the number of embezzlement cases reported tends to follow the same trend as number of people found guilty in the court of first instance, as can be seen in Figure 6, which shows the number of embezzlement cases excluding misappropriation of neglected property. The increase in misappropriation of neglected property after 1975 was due to a sudden increase in misappropriation of neglected bicycles.

(2) Heinous Offences

The trend in number of cases reported and number of people found guilty in the courts of first instance for murder and robbery is shown in Fig. 7, Table 2 and Table 3 in the Appendix.

A. Homicide

For number of cases reported, the prewar period had a high of 2,713 cases in 1933. Nevertheless, every year from 1926 to 1937 had more than 2,000 cases, while the numbers declined slowly from 1938 to 1945. In the postwar period, there was a wave lasting from 1948 to 1955, peaking at 3,081 cases in 1954. The numbers declined somewhat thereafter, but continued to show relatively high figures, in the 2,600 range, until 1961. From the early 1960s, the numbers fluctuated between 2,000 and 2,300 cases, but with a general downward trend, falling through the 2,000 mark in the late 1970s, to 1,441 cases in 1988.

For number of people found guilty in the court of first instance, the prewar period reached its highest point at 1,053 people in 1934, staying in the 800 to 900 range in the 1926 to 1937 period. The numbers declined from 1938. In

Fig.7 Number of Reported Heinous Offences and Offenders Convicted in Courts of First Instance

① Number of offences reported(1926-1988)

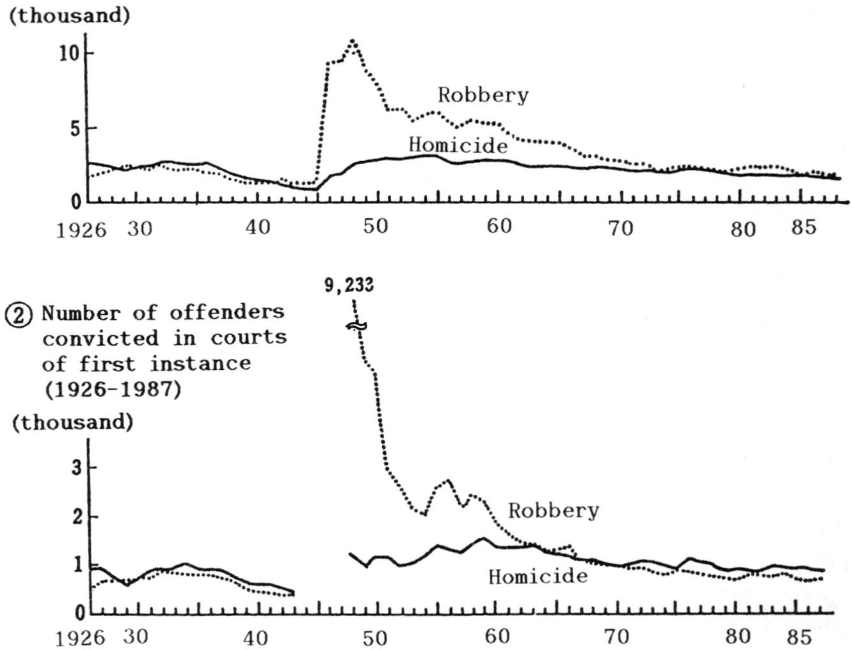

Sources: Annual Report of Criminal Statistics, Annual Report of Judicial Statistics, etc.

the postwar period, a high wave was seen in the late 1950s and early 1960s, peaking at 1,581 people in 1959. Nearly all years from 1948 to 1978 were over 1,000 people, however, after which it declined somewhat, reaching 908 people in 1987. As can be seen, no large changes in homicide trends are noted. In addition, little difference can be seen between the trends for number of people found guilty in the court of first instance and the number of cases reported.

B. Robbery

For number of cases reported, the prewar period had around 2,000 cases annually from 1927 to 1937, peaking at 2,412 cases in 1929 and 2,435 cases in 1932. After that, the trend fluctuated between 1,100 and 1,500 cases. The postwar period began with a high wave from 1946 to 1950, peaking at 10,854 cases in 1948, after which it exhibited a downward trend, reaching the 5,000 range in 1953, the 4,000 range in 1961, the 2,000 range for most years after 1968, and the 1,000 range from 1985, with 1,771 cases in 1988.

For number of people found guilty in the court of first instance, the prewar period moved between the 600 and 800 range from 1927 to 1938, peaking at 862 people in 1932, and then declined thereafter. In the postwar period, a high wave was seen until 1950, peaking at 9,233 people in 1948. The numbers then declined, reaching the 2,000 range in 1952 and the 1,000 range in 1960. It continued declining, with some fluctuations, to 715 people in 1987. As can be seen, robbery also showed very little difference between the trends for number of cases reported and number of people found guilty in the court of first instance.

(3) Violent Offences

Fig. 8, Table 2 and Table 3 in the Appendix show the trends of number of cases reported and number of people found guilty in the court of first instance for assault, bodily injury and extortion.

A. Assault

The number of cases reported was extremely low until 1947. This was due to the fact that assault was treated as indictable upon complaint until a partial revision of the Penal Code became effective Nov. 15, 1947.

Looking at the trend for 1948 and later, the incidence increased steadily through the late 1940s and early 1950s, sketching out a high wave in the late 1950s and early 1960s, with a peak of 46,784 cases reported in 1959. The 40,000 level was held until the late 1960s, after which it began declining, falling through the 20,000 mark in the late 1970s, and reaching 10,004 cases in 1988.

For number of people found guilty in the court of first instance, the numbers increased steadily from 1948, reaching a high wave from 1955 to the late 1960s, with the peak at 20,673 people in 1965. The numbers steadily declined thereafter, falling through the 10,000 mark in the late 1970s, and reaching 3,960 people in 1987. The trend was virtually the same as that shown for number of cases reported.

B. Bodily Injury

For number of cases reported, the prewar period from 1926 to 1939 moved well above 20,000 cases, with a peak of 29,290 in 1935, after which a decline set in. In the postwar period, the numbers increased rapidly from the early 1950s, sketching a high wave from the late 1950s to the late 1960s that surpassed the 60,000 mark, with a peak of 73,985 in 1958. After that, the numbers dropped steadily, falling through the 30,000 mark in the late 1970s and reaching 21,516 cases in 1988.

For number of people found guilty in the court of first instance, the prewar period saw a wave from 1934 to 1937, peaking at 10,391 people in 1934. The trend from 1926 to 1939 showed figures exceeding 7,500 for the entire

Fig.8 Number of Reported Violent Offences and Offenders Convicted in Courts of First Instance

① Number of offences reported(1926-1988)

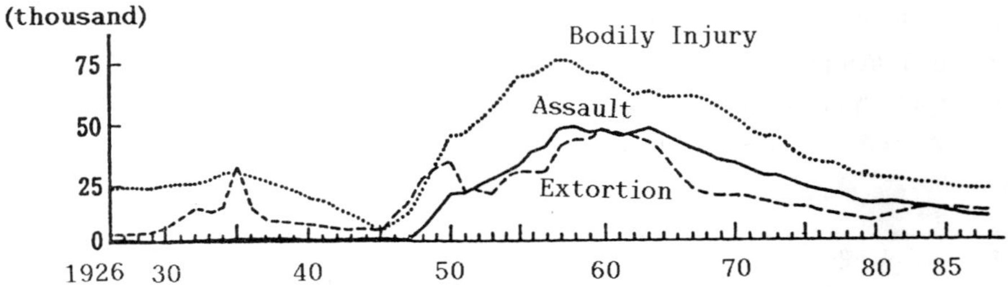

②Number of offenders convicted in courts of first instance(1926-1987)

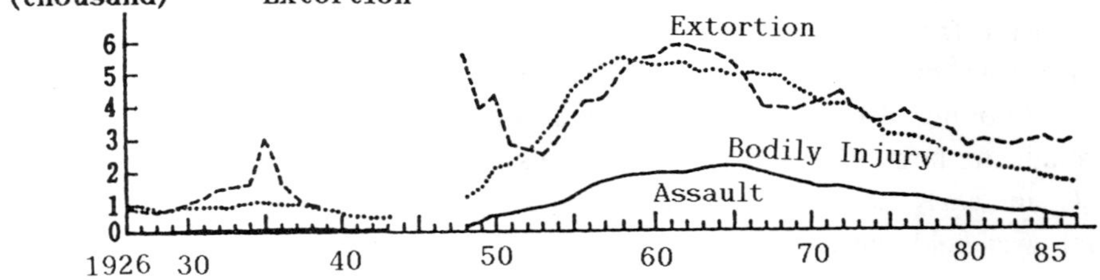

Sources: Annual Report of Criminal Statistics, Annual Report of Judicial Statistics, etc.

period. In the postwar period, as was seen in the figures for number of cases reported, there was a high wave stretching from the late 1950s to the late 1960s in which the numbers easily surpassed 40,000 people, peaking at 53,950 in 1958. The numbers declined steadily thereafter, falling through the 20,000 mark in the early 1980s, and reaching 15,162 people in 1987.

C. Extortion

For number of cases reported, the prewar period saw a high wave from 1932 to 1936, peaking at 32,173 cases in 1935, after which a decline set in. In the postwar period, the numbers increased steadily from the late 1940s, in a wave that peaked at 32,740 cases in 1950. Another increase began from 1955, peaking at 45,306 cases in 1961, and continuing on a high wave through the late 1960s. After that, the numbers declined drastically, falling through the 10,000 mark in the late 1970s. The numbers increased slightly later on, however, to 12,136 cases in 1988.

For number of people found guilty in the court of first instance, the prewar period, as was seen in the number of cases reported, showed a high wave from 1931 to 1937, peaking at 2,998 people in 1935, after which a decline set in. The postwar period began with a high wave in the late 1940s, peaking at 5,561 people in 1948. After that, the numbers declined somewhat, but then entered another high wave lasting from about 1955 and continuing into the late 1960s, with a peak of 5,820 people in 1962. Later, the numbers hovered around the fairly high figure of 3,000, but declined slightly in recent years, reaching 2,892 people in 1987.

(4) Sexual Offences

Fig. 9, Table 2 and Table 3 in the Appendix show the trends for number of cases reported and number of people found guilty in the court of first instance for rape and indecent assault.

A. Rape

For number of cases reported, the prewar period saw a wave from 1933 to 1936, peaking at 1,598 cases in 1935. Unlike other crimes, however, it is interesting to note that high figures continued to be recorded despite the war, reaching 1,589 cases in 1942 and 1,624 cases in 1943.

In the postwar period, cases began increasing from the late 1940s, sketching a high wave from the late 1950s to the late 1960s, and reaching a peak of 6,857 cases in 1964. After that, the numbers declined steadily, falling to 1,741 cases in 1988.

For number of people found guilty in the court of first instance, the prewar period showed figures exceeding 200 people in the period from 1932 to 1940. In the postwar period, much as for the number of cases reported, an increase began in the late 1940s, sketching a high wave from the late 1950s to the late 1960s of over 2,000 people each year, with a peak of 2,733 in 1968. After that, the numbers declined steadily, reaching 661 people in 1987.

B. Indecent Assault

For number of cases reported, a prewar wave continued from a peak of 1,768 cases in 1933 to 1938, with another high wave surpassing 1,000 people From 1941 to 1943. In the pospwar period, numbers began increasing in the late 1940s, sketching out a high wave from the late 1950s to the late 1940s, with a peak of 4,710 in 1965. After that, the numbers declined, falling to the 2,000 level in 1974, and reaching 2,867 cases in 1988.

For number of people found guilty in the court of first instance, the prewar period moved at the very low level of 30 to 60 people. In the postwar period, the numbers began increasing in the early 1960s, surpassing the 400 mark in the late 1960s and early 1970s, but then began declining again after

Fig.9 Number of Reported Sexual Offences and Offenders Convicted in Courts of First Instance

① Number of offences reported(1926-1988)

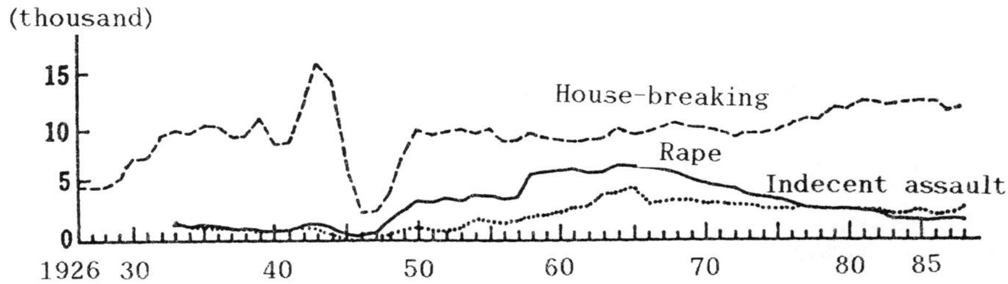

②Number of offenders convicted at first instance courts

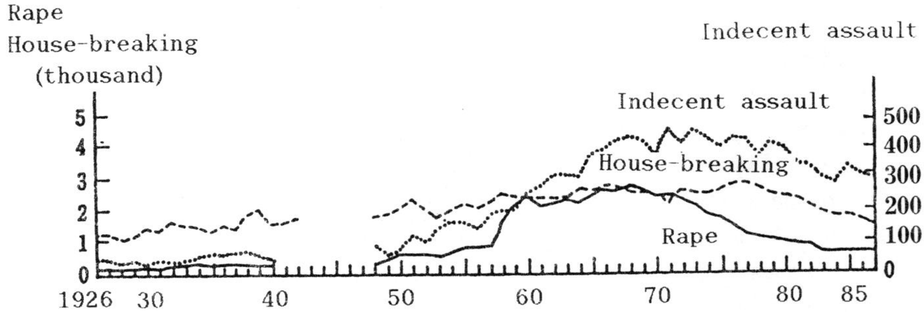

Sources: Annual Report of Criminal Statistics, Annual Report of Judicial Statistics, etc.

1980, with fluctuations falling to 296 people in 1987.

(5) Arson, etc.

Fig. 10, Table 2 and Table 3 in the Appendix show the trends in number of cases reported and number of people found guilty in courts of first instance for arson and negligences causing fire.

A. Arson

For number of cases reported, the figures surpassed 2,000 cases from 1926 to 1935. After that, little change could be discerned through both the prewar and postwar periods, hovering in the 1,000 range. In the late 1970s, the rate moved to about 2,000 cases, after which it declined slightly, to 1,629 cases in 1988.

For number of people found guilty in court of first instance, a high wave in the 800 to 900 range was seen from 1931 to 1935. After that, the trend moved generally in the 200 to 400 range, with no major changes.

B. Negligence Offences Causing Fire

For number of cases reported, the prewar period saw figures in excess of 10,000 cases, while in the postwar period, the figures moved in the 7,000 to 9,000 range. In 1966, the number moved into the 6,000 range, and then continued a downward trend, reaching 1,036 cases in 1988. In addition, for number of people found guilty in court of first instance, the prewar period hovered from the 1,500 to 2,000 range, and in the postwar period, from the 2,000 to 3,000 range until the mid-1970s. After that, the numbers suddenly declined, reaching 326 people in 1987.

(6) Other Offences

Fig. 11, Table 2 and Table 3 in the Appendix show the trends in number of cases reported and number of people found guilty in court of first instance for gambling and lotteries, bribery and kidnapping. All show big differences between prewar and postwar periods.

A. Gambling and Lotteries

For number of cases reported, the prewar period saw a high wave with peaks at 53,594 cases in 1934, 63,396 cases in 1939 and 63,817 cases in 1943. In the postwar period, while figures in the 20,000 range were recorded in the late 1940s, they declined thereafter to the 1,000 level in the late 1950s and early 1960s. A small wave was recorded in the late 1960s and early 1970s, reaching to 4,000 to 5,000 cases. The numbers turned downward again thereafter, recording no more than 1,970 cases in 1988.

For number of people found guilty in court of first instance, the prewar period recorded high figures from 1926 to 1943, in the 40,000 to 80,000 range. In the postwar period, however, while the late 1940s showed high figures similar to the prewar period, they declined sharply after that. Another wave was seen in the 1960s and early 1970s, peaking at 13,288 in 1966, but then another continuous decline began, reaching 4,599 people in 1987.

B. Bribery

For number of cases reported, the prewar period saw a sharp increase after 1933, sketching out a wave which peaked at 4,471 cases in 1936. After that, the figures declined slightly, then began rising again from 1940, sketching out another wave with the peak at 6,166 cases in 1943. In the postwar period, high figures were recorded in the late 1940s, sketching out a high wave which peaked at 8,941 cases in 1949. After that, another wave in the 2,000 range was seen in the 1960s, but no major changes were seen. The figures declined greatly in the late 1970s, to 311 cases in 1988.

For number of people found guilty in court of first instance, the prewar

Fig.10 Number of Arson and Fire Caused by Negligence Reported and Offenders Convicted in Courts of First Instance

① Number of offences reported(1926-1988)

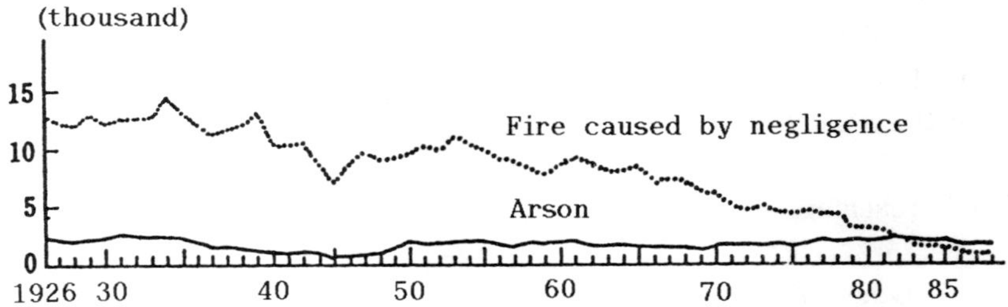

② Number of offenders convicted at first instance courts

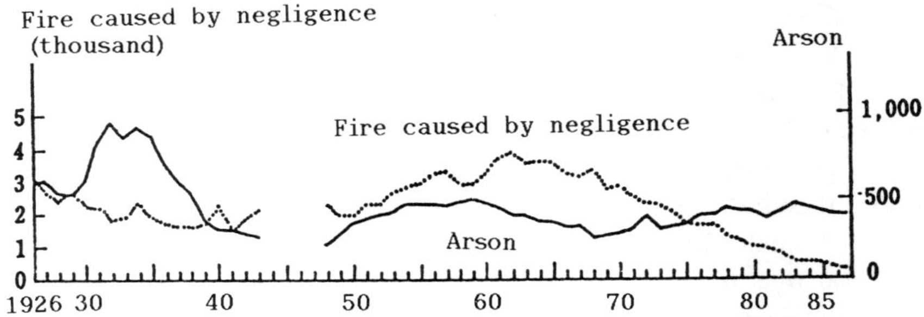

Sources: Annual Report of Criminal Statistics, Annual Report of Judicial Statistics, etc.

period showed a high wave from 1934 to 1936, peaking at 1,492 in 1935. The postwar period showed a high wave in the late 1940s and early 1950s, reaching a peak of 2,286 people in 1949. After that, no major changes were seen, with the exception of 1965, with 1,228 people, and 1968, with 1,144 people, and then continued a declining trend, to 329 people in 1987.

C. Kidnapping

For number of cases reported, the prewar period saw high figures exceeding 1,000 cases until 1936, and then suddenly declined until 1945. In the postwar period, the late 1940s and early 1950s saw a high wave, peaking at 531 cases in 1951, but then showed no major changes thereafter, fluctuating between 150 and 300 cases. Around 1980, the number dropped through the 150 mark, reaching 112 cases in 1988.

For number of people found guilty in courts of first instance, the prewar period moved in the 100 to 200 range. In the postwar period, however, the

Fig.11 Number of Gambling, Kidnapping, etc. Reported and Offenders Convicted in Courts of First Instance

① Number of offences reported(1926-1987)

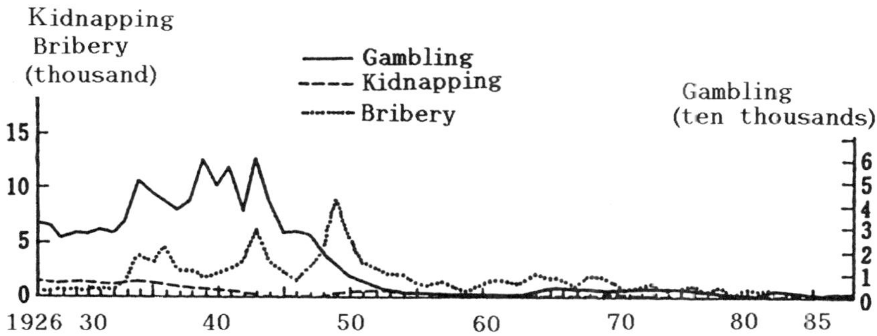

FIG11

② Number of offenders convicted at first instance courts

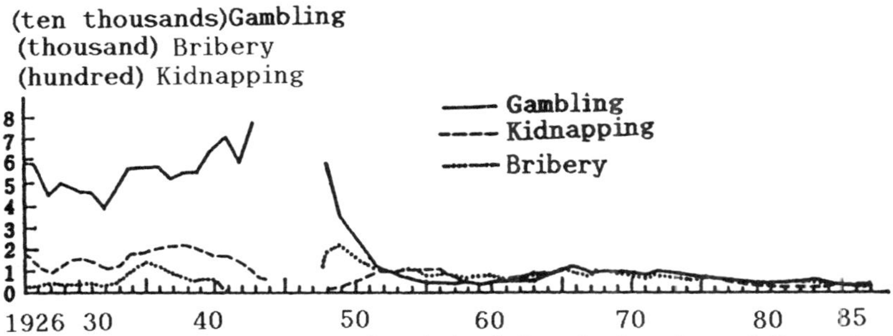

Sources: Annual Report of Criminal Statistics, Annual Report of Judicial Statistics, etc.

numbers dropped drastically. It kept the level of 100 from the early to mid-1950s and from the late 1960s to the early 1970s. The number has been, however, in the 30 to 40 range since the mid-1970s, reaching 42 in 1987.

3. BACKGROUND OF CRIMINAL TRENDS

The foregoing presented criminal offence trends in the Showa era according to changes in the number of reported cases and the number of people found guilty of crimes in courts of the first instance. Now we will turn to the characteristics of each period to delve into the background.

(1) 1933-1935: A Peak Period of Crime Outbreaks

While the number of people found guilty by courts of the first instance was not very high, the number of reported cases reveal a rapid increase in crimes during the period. By type of crime, murders, etc., registered relatively high figures since 1926, but most crimes, particularly crimes involving property such as theft, fraud, embezzlement and extortion, began to rise from 1929 to 1930, and increased rapidly from 1932 to 1933. High figures were recorded in 1935 and 1936, after which they began to decline in the years approaching the war.

After World War I, liberalism and democracy penetrated to some degree and parliamentary government took shape. The worldwide Great Depression struck in 1929, however, seriously influencing Japan's economy as well. On top of financial panic, industrial depression and an impoverished rural economy, a bad harvest in 1934 worsened the situation, along with rising unemployment, frequent outbreaks of labour strife and other problems, aggravating social instability. Socialist parties arose and social movements became active during the period, but were suppressed in quick succession. In addition, a number of scandals occurred which, coupled with the economic depression, led to distrust in government and expanded power for the military. Events progressed toward a military dictatorship with the sudden eruption of the Manchurian Incident in 1931, the assassination of Prime Minister Inukai and others in 1932 by a group of young officers in the 5/15 Incident, and the assassination in 1936 of Home Affairs Minister Saito and others in the 2/26 Incident. In 1937, the full-scale Sino-Japanese War broke out, further strengthening the trend toward a war-time footing.

The increase in crime during this period can be said to have occurred against the backdrop of the people's poverty due to social instability and economic depression. In particular, the economic and agricultural depression led to increased labour and tenant farmer strife, and the people's lives became more difficult not only in metropolitan areas but also in rural villages as well. It cannot be denied that this sort of economic environment stimulated the increase in crimes involving property, in particular.

In addition, it is necessary in any analysis of crimes in this period to note the huge gap between the rate of increase in number of cases reported and the number of people found guilty in courts of the first instance, as mentioned earlier. Regarding the increase in number of cases reported, for example, the total gap reached 250,000 cases from 1932 to 1933 and, whichever category of crime is examined, nearly all crimes showed large increases from the year before. This rapid change is not reflected in the number of persons found guilty in courts of the first instance, with the exception of extortion and a few others. As to why the clearance rate during the period was extremely high, it appears that investigative authorities, when faced with the social situation described above, adopted a strict policy of law enforcement. Cases reported in this period probably included a large number of minor offences compared with other periods.

(2) The War Period: Frequent Incidence of Sexual-Related Crimes

Most crimes declined during the Pacific War period, which lasted from Dec. 8, 1941 to Aug. 15, 1945. But the incidence of rape and indecent assault increased, and gambling, illegal lotteries and bribery registered high figures. The probable reason most crimes declined was that many of the age group most prone to commit crimes, i.e. young adult males, had been drafted and sent off to war fronts overseas.

In considering the increase in rape and indecent assault, it is important to take into account the effects of the investigating authorities' strict wartime policies designed to protect women and girls on the home front. Fig. 9, and Appendix Tables 2 and 3 show breaking and entry into residences increased sharply during the period. Here, too, investigative policy had an effect. At the time, the old provision (repealed after the war) in the Penal Code existed which, in cases of adultery involving a man's wife, punished both the wife and her illicit partner. But these crimes were only indictable on a complaint from the husband, and were in practice difficult to prosecute because it was impossible to get a complaint filed from husbands who were serving on the front lines. So the authorities used the measure of prosecuting illicit partners on charges of residential breaking and entry, on the grounds of violation of the husband's residential rights. This is believed to be the main factor behind the increase in wartime residential breaking and entry cases.

Increases in gambling and illegal lotteries could also be considered to be reflected in strict law enforcement policies designed to protect social order on the home front and prevent tendencies toward idle indulgence. And the increase in bribery should probably be considered, as will be explained below, a characteristic of those societies under a controlled economy.

(3) Chaotic Postwar Period: Frequent Incidence of All Types of Crimes

As has already been seen, crimes increased sharply in the chaotic postwar period from 1945 to about 1950. By type of crime, these included theft, fraud, embezzlement, robbery, extortion, bribery, etc., all showing figures so high as to be incomparable with before the war. But all crimes then showed large drops from about 1950 to 1955. (In the number of reported cases, fraud and embezzlement figures actually fell below prewar levels, but for the actual situation, which requires a survey of the number of people found guilty by courts of the first instance, see 2-(1) above)

During this period, Japan's economy was in a state of devastation, having been completely cut off from raw material supplies while all manufacturing facilities had been destroyed. There were extreme shortages of foodstuffs and other commodities and inflation was racing along at a pace never experienced before. In addition, the population suddenly increased as people returned from the war and the birth rate rose. Streets were filled with vagrants and the unemployed and the people's lives became even more wretched than in the war days. In addition, the sense of values collapsed, moral sense was shaken, unlawful organizations ran rampant, and social instability increased. On top of all that, the government structure, and particularly the police, was weakened. It was a chaotic period from every possible viewpoint. The unprecedented sudden increase in crime could thus be seen as reflecting the social chaos of the period. Among every category of crime increasing during the period, crimes involving property showed the most rapid increase, in particular. It may be said that this fact frankly tells us the story of the economic situation mentioned above.

The frequent occurrence of bribery should be considered as due to the continuance in this period of wartime economic controls. Procurement of nearly all commodities, including foodstuffs, was controlled through a rationing system, and it is easy to surmise that the officials in charge were targeted for bribery by people trying to lay hands on scarce goods.

(4) 1955-1975: Frequent Incidence of Violent Crimes

The rapid increase in crimes during the chaotic postwar period died out in the early 1950s. However, it began to increase again after 1955, reaching relatively high figures by the mid-1960s. By type of crime, assault, bodily injury and extortion saw fast rises. Murder also increased, and robbery, while not reaching the levels of the chaotic postwar period, registered relatively high figures. Following slightly behind these brutal, violent crimes came increases in rape and indecent assault from 1960, reaching a peak in and around the 1970s, after which a decline set in. In addition, this period saw, as mentioned earlier, an increase in juvenile delinquency, as well as a sudden increase in traffic offences involving professional negligence. By contrast, theft increased somewhat in the mid-1950s and then began to decline (with emphasis on the number of convictions by courts of the first instance). Fraud and embezzlement also decreased during the period.

Japan's economy was slowly beginning to revive in the early 1950s. Industry revived, stimulated by demand created by the Korean War, and social order also was restored. With social stability, the number of criminal cases reported also began a slow decline. In the late 1950s and early 1960s, manufacturing development progressed and the economy shifted into high growth. Manufacturing and agricultural output surpassed prewar levels and Japan's economic activity expanded into the international arena as well. Despite this economic development, however, a number of reasons can be offered on why the number of reported crime cases turned upward again after 1955. First, the increase in juvenile delinquency was due to the increase in the late-teen juvenile population, who had spent their formative years in the chaotic wartime and postwar periods. This factor resulted in increased incidents of theft and violent crime, which account for most juvenile offences. Next, the rapid increase in traffic offences involving professional negligence was due to the increase in traffic accidents which accompanied the growth of vehicular traffic.

The early to mid-1950s correspond to the revival period when Japan's new social structure was established, as highlighted by the signing of the San Francisco Peace Treaty in April 1952 and the conclusion of the Japan-U.S. security treaty. It was also a period which saw intensifying socio-philosophical confrontations among the people, as opposition to these treaties intensified with frequent outbreaks of demonstrations and labour strife. The diversification of political doctrines became apparent with the public safety incidents and student demonstrations which arose to oppose revision of the security treaty in 1960, and many cases of violent group crimes occurred. In addition, the economic revival, progress of industrialisation and other factors led to the concentration of population in major metropolises and industrial cities. This created busy new commercial and amusement quarters, and conflict over interests involved therein occurred between new and old gangster organizations. For example, while only 755 gang-affiliated people were placed under criminal investigation for assault or bodily injury in 1952, the two categories reached 4,058 in 1953. The figures showed 10,520 investigated for bodily injury and 3,811 for assault in 1954, 22,451 for bodily injury and 6,310 for violence in 1955, and 34,102 and 11,422, respectively, in 1956. The figures for 1956 represented more than 40 percent of all persons investigated for violence and bodily injury. The rise in crimes, centering around violent crimes, during this period can be assumed to be related to these social factors.

The increase in sexual crimes in the early 1960s can be considered to have occurred in the context of progressive population concentration in the cities, rapid economic growth, fast-changing life-styles, and the rise of leisure and sex-related industries, mainly in the cities. Another factor in the rise in sexual crimes was the partial revision of the Penal Code in May 1958, which did away with the need to file a personal complaint in cases of rape and indecent assault committed by two or more persons. This is believed to have resulted in more such crimes being exposed.

(5) 1975 to the Present: Rapid Rise in Juvenile Delinquency

The period from 1975 to the present saw the highest wave in criminal offences, according to the number of cases reported. But as has already been seen, much of this was due to the rapid increase in juvenile deliquency and the rise in traffic offences involving professional negligence and, in actuality, the number of people found guilty in courts of the first instance showed a declining trend. In addition, by type of Penal Code offence when traffic cases are excluded, the only crimes showing striking increases were theft and embezzlement. Most of the increase in theft was due to relatively light cases such as shoplifting or bicycle thefts, while the increase in embezzlement was due to an increase in misappropriation of properties lost or abandoned temporarily-mostly stealing a ride on such bicycles.

Moreover, juveniles accounted for much of the increase in these types of cases, and most other types of crimes showed a declining trend. The end of the Showa era was thus a period when juvenile delinquency, not really serious in nature, increased rapidly. Overall, it was a period when criminal trends were relatively stabilized.

While this period experienced recessions due to oil crises on two occasions, in 1973 and 1979, and other difficulties, Japan had grown to become one of the world's economic powers after an era of remarkable economic growth, and the period saw the formation of a prosperous society. In addition, it was a period when the social structure and living environment underwent rapid changes, as evidenced by such factors as the rapid growth of the tertiary industries in the share of the overall industrial structure, the accompanying concentration of population in the cities, the growth of automobile traffic, the development of information processing systems through the use of computers and other electronic equipment, the activity of the mass media and other sectors of the information industry, the expansion of consumer life-styles supported by credit systems, etc., and the trend toward smaller families. The environment for youth as well showed change, with 76 percent of all families in 1985 being small units of four people or less, demonstrating the spread of the nuclear family. In addition, expectations for a higher school education for children increased, with the result that the percentage completing mandatory education and advancing to high school broke through the 90-percent level, and the percentage of people going on to college passed 30 percent, with the share rising annually. But the rise of the nuclear family also brought a decline in guidance for some children, and the intensification of competition for a higher school education resulted in the drop-out phenomenon. The rise in juvenile delinquency during this period certainly cannot be completely dissociated from this. In addition, it cannot be ignored that the increase in self-service stores such as supermarkets during this period, and the increased utilization of motorcycles and bicycles, along with their temporary abandonment near train stations and other places, increased the opportunities for shoplifting, bicycle thefts, etc.

4. OTHERS

A review of criminal offence trends in the Showa era reveals that some types of offences underwent great change according to the times, while other types of offences barely changed at all. Criminal offences can be categorized according to the characteristics of these changes, as follows.

(1) Crimes Relatively Unchanged

Crimes where relatively little change has been seen include such offences as arson and fire by negligence. Elsewhere, murder could probably be added, as the change there has not been very remarkable.

(2) Crimes Undergoing Change

Crimes not listed above could be regarded as having changed with the times. These changes can be seen by comparing the prewar with the postwar situation, as follows.

A. Crimes That Declined in the Postwar Period

Crimes that declined in the postwar period include gambling and illegal lotteries. In the immediate postwar period, the figures recorded were close to prewar ones, but then declined rapidly thereafter. Diversification of leisure and nationalized betting operations in the postwar period have had a major influence on these changes.

Another crime which has declined is kidnapping. While high figures were seen in the postwar period particularly around 1955, these figures were still much lower than the prewar period. Behind the enactment of the Child Abuse Prevention Law in the prewar year of 1933 lay many cases of child abuse, exploitation and slave trafficking. In line with the economic growth, etc. of the postwar period, the human traffic disappeared and the allure of kidnapping declined.

B. Crimes That Increased in the Postwar Period

All other crimes not mentioned above increased in the postwar period, but those crimes with unusually steep increases include traffic professional negligence, theft, extortion, robbery, assault, bodily injury, rape, indecent assault, etc.

The rapid rise in the incidence of traffic professional negligence in the postwar period is related to the increase in automobile accidents, a natural outgrowth of the growth in automobile traffic. As has already been mentioned, there were 5,157 cases of professional negligence in 1949, accounting for barely 0.3 percent of all criminal offences reported. Incidents began to increase after the late '50s and early '60s, reaching 654,942 cases in 1970, or 33.9 percent of all cases. After that date, the number of cases declined slightly with implementation of integrated traffic policies, including revision of the Road Traffic Law, but then turned upward again after 1980 in line with the rapid rise in automobile ownership numbers.

The increase in thefts in the postwar period has also been rapid, but unlike the increase in the chaotic period immediately after the war, when cases tended to center around food and manufactured goods typical of a poverty-stricken life, the increase from about 1975 to the present has tended to focus on automobiles, motorcycles, bicycles, shoplifting and other types of cases symptomatic of advancing motorization, the increase in self-service style stores and other changes in the social environment, all of which have broadened the opportunities for theft. Great change in motive and criminal methodology can be seen. The incidence of misappropriation of lost or temporarily abandoned properties has increased since the late '70s and early '80s. This is related to motorcycles and bicycles left parked on roadways, and has contributed to an overall increase in thefts.

Next, the postwar increase in assault, bodily injury and other violent crimes was also notable. The periods of increase showed some divergence, however. Theft, extortion and robbery occurred frequently in the poverty-stricken chaotic period immediately after the war, and economics can be presumed to have been a major factor. (For why the factors behind the recent increase in thefts differ from the one mentioned here, see above.) Assault and bodily injury occurred most frequently in the revival period from the late '40s to about 1965, when the new social system was established, and apparently was influenced by an increased youth population, social unrest and other social factors. Extortion exhibited high figures during the period of chaos, but then occurred even more often in the revival period, probably because it is more characteristic of violent crime than of property-related crime.

Section 3. *Trends in Special Law Offences*

1. OUTLINE

This section examines changing trends in special law offences during the Showa era. In this respect, we have to rely on statistics compiled by the public prosecution and judiciary authorities, but not the police. This is because many special law offences are by nature difficult to clarify until the offenders have been caught, and no statistics have been kept on the incidence of special law violations reported to the police. In addition, the police did not have available a complete record of special law offenders who were either cleared or referred to public prosecutors.

Furthermore, violations of the Road Traffic Law have accounted for the great majority of all special law offences since the end of the war, as is mentioned later in this section. Hence, it would be difficult to clearly identify the changing trends in special law violations if traffic violations were included in the figures. We therefore exclude traffic violations from our analysis of "special law offences" unless specifically mentioned otherwise ("special law offenders" also exclude traffic law violators).

Since the above reason can largely apply to traffic-related professional negligence offences provided in the Penal Code and those offences are also included in overall traffic-related offences, statistical data on Penal Code offences (or Penal Code offenders where applicable) in this section do not include traffic professional negligence provided in Article 211 of the Penal Code.

(1) Changes in the Number of Special Law Offenders Received by the Public Prosecutors Office

Fig. 12 in this section and Table 4 in the Appendix show the changes in the number of Penal Code offenders and special law offenders who were newly received by the public prosecutors office in the Showa era, plus the percentages of special law offenders received as compared with the total number of Penal Code and special law offenders received. The figures for 1948 and earlier, however, are based on the number of cases received since specific numbers of individual offenders before 1948 are not available.

These statistics show that special law offences numbered around 110,000 annually during the 1933-1937 period, but increased sharply in and after 1940, peaking in 1943 at 161,132. The figures of special law offence cases and offenders received by the public prosecutors office after the war were considerably high up until the early 1950s, reaching 971,675 in 1948 and 860,160 in 1949. But the trend showed a remarkable drop in the following years with the annual figures falling mostly below the 150,000 level, though rising to more than 200,000 in 1959, 1960, 1963 and 1967, nearly 190,000 in 1979, then shrinking to 110,562 in 1988.

Of total offenders (or cases up to 1948) received by the public prosecutors office, the percentages of special law offenders (or cases up to 1948) before World War II were relatively low at 20 percent to 25 percent up until 1939. The figure shot up to 37.1 percent in 1940 and further rose during the war in and after 1941, reaching 45.7 percent in 1943. After the war, the percentage in 1946 was roughly the same as the wartime level, but it jumped sharply in 1947 to

Fig.12 Number of Suspects Newly Received by the Public Prosecutors Office (1931~1988)

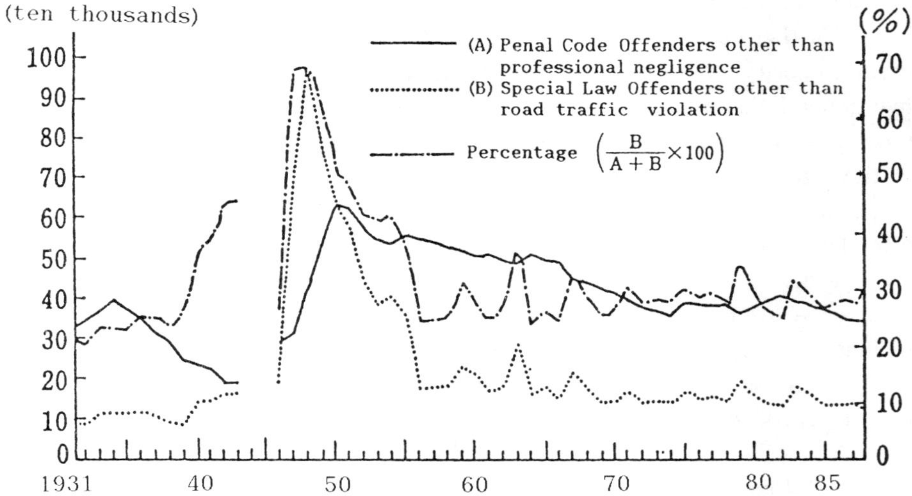

Sources:Annual Report of Criminal Statistics and Annual Report of Statistics on Prosecution

account for 69.7 percent of the total, followed by high figures of 69.3 percent in 1948 and 59.3 percent in 1949. The special law offenders rate remained high till 1955, but declined noticeably thereafter. The figures in and after 1956 were mostly within the 26-29 percent range, though comparatively higher rates in excess of the 30-percent mark were registered in 1959, 1963, 1967, 1975, 1979 and 1983. In 1988, the final year of Showa, the rate stood at 24.3 percent.

(2) Change in the Number of Special Law Offenders Found Guilty in Courts of First Instance

Fig. 13 in this section and Table 5 in the Appendix show the changes in the number of people found guilty for Penal Code offences and special law offences in the courts of first instance in the Showa era, and the percentages of special law offenders to the total offenders both of Penal Code and special law offences.

In the prewar years, the number of special law offenders convicted in the courts of first instance began shooting up in 1940, peaking in 1942 at 85,662. Even after the war, the figures remained high during the period through 1955, registering a peak of 321,495 in 1948. During and after 1956, however, the number of individuals found guilty of special law offences was lower, hovering at around 50,000 to 70,000 a year. The figures for 1959 and 1961 topped the

Fig.13 Number of Offenders Convicted in Courts of First Instance (1931～1987)

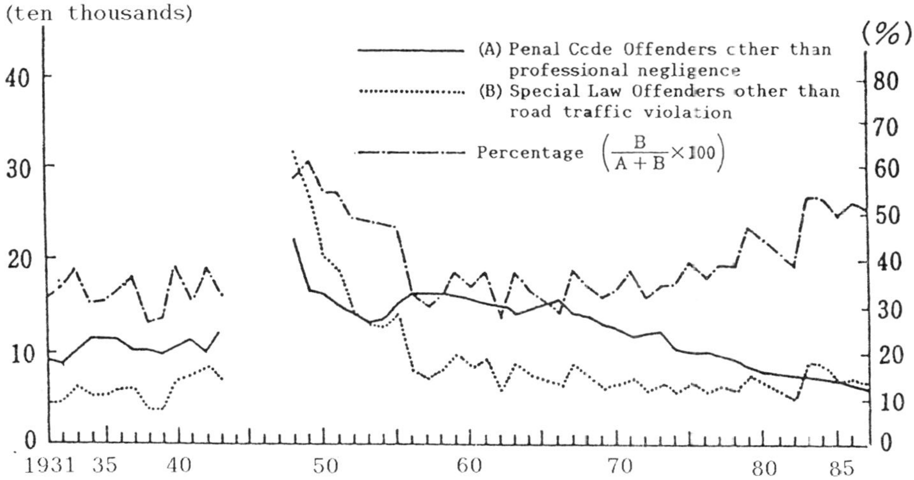

Sources: Annual Report of Criminal Statistics, Annual Report of Judicial Statistics, etc.

90,000 mark, however, and those in 1963, 1967, 1983 and 1984 were above the 80,000 level. The figure for 1987 stood at 66,379.

Through the Showa era, the ratio of special law offenders to the total number of Penal Code and special law offenders found guilty at the courts of first instance was generally higher than that for those offenders newly received by the public prosecutors offices, with the only exceptions being the years 1943 and 1948. This is mainly because of the fact that the prosecution ratio for special law crime suspects is higher in general than that for Penal Code offenders. The figure for 1943 is an exception to this general trend, since many Penal Code offences at that time, as mentioned earlier, were more vicious in nature than during other periods of the Showa era, and the prosecution ratio of the Penal Code offenders as a whole was substantially high. In and after 1965, the percentage of special law offenders to the total number of offenders received by the public prosecutors offices has been approximately 24 percent to 34 percent while the corresponding percentages of those found guilty at the courts of first instance ranged from about 29 percent to about 55 percent. Since about 1983, the figure has remained above 50 percent. The decrease during these years in the number of Penal Code offenders found guilty in the courts of first instance may well explain the reason for the phenomenon.

(3) Changes in the Number of Guilty Offenders

It is not necessarily sufficient for our studies on trends in special law offences to rely only on those special law offenders who were found guilty in the courts of first instance.

The chronological comparisons based on the number of those offenders received by the public prosecutors offices encounter some difficulties regarding the continuity of the statistical data involved. As mentioned earlier, the data on special law violations before 1948 were taken in terms of the number of cases received, while the figures in and after 1949 were given in terms of the number of offenders received. In addition, as for special law offences before the war, it should be remembered that many people were punished under Summary Proceedings for Police Infractions (Proclamation No. 31 of the Meiji Government, issued in the year 1885, the 18th year of the Meiji era). Police station chiefs and their deputies were empowered under the proclamation to impart penal detention or hand down minor fines–after examining evidence–to violators of police infractions. A great majority of those disposed of under the proceedings were special law violators, who numbered more than one million a year during the period between 1934 and around 1936.

The annual figure was more than 10 times the number of those found guilty in the courts of first instance at that time. However, neither the number of offenders received by the public prosecutors office nor the number of offenders found guilty in the courts of first instance included those offenders disposed of under the summary proceedings.

After the war, not only the Summary Proceedings for Police Infractions but also many substantive laws applied through the summary proceedings such as the Imperial Order to Punish Police Infractions were abolished. The remaining law violation cases were referred to the public prosecutors office for their dispositions and included in the number of those offenders received by the public prosecutors office. They were found guilty by the courts of first instance.

In view of the fact that describing the trends in special law offences on the basis of the number of those offenders received by prosecutors offices face the statistical problems mentioned above, the determination shall be made instead on the basis of the number of those offenders who were considered to be guilty of the offence charged at each step of the criminal justice processes. As such, looking at the trends based on the number of guilty offenders, it will become possible to follow the trends in special law offenders with a substantial continuity through all periods of the Showa era.

Hereafter, the trends in special law offenders in comparison with the Penal Code offenders, in the Showa era, shall be examined based upon the number of "realistic" guilty offenders, viz., in prewar years, the total number of those disposed of under the Summary Proceedings for Police Infractions, those granted suspended prosecution by public prosecutors and those found guilty at the courts of first instance. In the postwar period, the trends shall be examined based upon those granted suspended prosecution by public prosecutors and those found guilty at the courts of first instance.

Fig. 14 and Table 6 in the Appendix show the trends in the number of

Fig.14 Number of "Realistic" Guilty Offenders in Courts of First Instance (1931~1987)

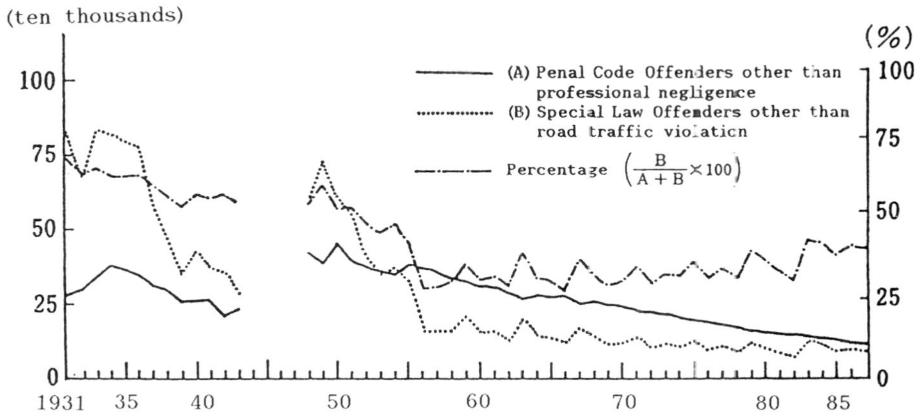

Sources: Annual Report of Criminal Statistics, Annual Report of Judicial Statistics,etc.

special laws and Penal Code "realistic guilty" offenders.

The "realistic guilty" offenders for special law offences before the war registered a peak in 1933 at 845,498, and the figures remained high up until 1936, but turned downward thereafter, reaching a low of 268,899 in 1943. This trend differs from the trend in special law offences that was earlier referred to on the basis of the statistics of offenders received by the public prosecutors office. Instead, the trend disclosed here bears a resemblance to that of the overall Penal Code offenders earlier mentioned in connection with the number of offenders reported to the police.

The high figures for the 1933-1936 period, which fell in an age of high crime rates in Penal Code offences as referred to in 2-3-(1) of this chapter, are also considered attributable mainly to that time's anomalous state of social and economic affairs, which caused higher incidence of crime.

At any rate, special law offences in terms of the realistic guilty offenders before the war showed a sharp decrease toward the start of the war and during the war, contrary to the increases in special law offences in the same period, as seen on the basis of the number of offenders received by the public prosecutors office and the number of those found guilty at the courts of first instance.

The discrepancy in the findings may be partly due to the fact that the incidence of crimes of a less vicious nature decreased markedly in that period, although crimes of a comparatively vicious nature increased to some extent, in addition to the change in law-enforcement policy for special law offences during wartime compared to the prewar years. But further analyses should be conducted in the future to examine in detail the reasons for the contradictory findings.

After the war, the number of "realistic" guilty offenders for special law offences was very high up until 1955, peaking in 1949 at 733,998. Thereafter, however, the figure declined gradually, falling as low as 91,776 in 1987. Comparatively high figures were registered in 1959 and 1963, however, at about 200,000 each, as well as in 1967 at about 170,000, in 1971 at about 130,000 and in 1975, 1979 and 1983 at about 120,000. This pattern is roughly consistent with earlier mentioned findings based on statistics on offenders newly received by the public prosectutors office and those offenders found guilty by the courts of first instance.

The percentages of "realistic" guilty offenders for special law offences compared with the combined number of "realistic" guilty offenders for Penal Code and special law offences were generally high before the war, except for 1939 and 1943, accounting for more than 60 percent, or more than 70 of the total.

It is clearly demonstrated that in the prewar years, the ratio of special law offenders was very high when based on the "realistic" guilty offenders, herein including those found guilty under the Summary Proceedings for Police Infractions, as opposed to the ratio computed by those offenders newly received by the public prosecutors office or found guilty by the courts of first instance. After the war, the ratio of "realistic" guilty offenders for special law offences against the total number of "realistic" offenders remained high at more than 45 percent up until 1955, with the postwar high reaching 65.3 percent in 1949.

The ratio declined more or less in the following years, but it stood fairly high at 38.3 percent in 1959, 42.8 percent in 1963, 39.8 percent in 1967, 38.7 percent in 1975 and 43.1 percent in 1979. From shortly before the middle of the 1980s the figures hovered at the 40 percent level, standing at 44.2 percent in 1987.

The high ratio in the postwar chaos was similar to the ratio computed by those offenders newly received by the public prosecutors office or found guilty by the courts of first instance. The increase in the ratio shortly before the mid-1980s and thereafter, however, showed different patterns, viz., around 30 percent if computed by the offenders newly received by the public prosecutors office, over 50 percent by those found guilty at the courts of first instance, and about 40 percent by the "realistic" guilty offenders.

The rises in Penal Code Offences during the decade preceeding 1984 were due mainly to increases in cases involving juvenile delinquency and comparatively minor property offences. A majority of offenders for these offences were either referred to the Family Court and relieved of penal punishment or suspended from prosecution. As a result, the special law offenders' percentages computed by those found guilty at the courts of first instance and by "realistic" guilty offenders were higher than the corresponding percentages computed by those newly recieved by the public prosectutors offices.

2. TRENDS IN SPECIAL LAW OFFENCES BY CATEGORY OF MAJOR OFFENCES

Table 6 shows changes in the rankings of major special law offences during the prewar period from 1931 through 1943, while Table 7 shows the corresponding statistics for the period after the war, in and after 1949, at an interval of about five years. The figures for the years after the war represent the numbers of suspects received by the public prosecutors office.

Of the major special law offences after the war, the figures for road traffic offenders are given separately at the bottom of the table, above which the 10 most frequent offences are listed.

Regarding the period before the war, the prosecution-provided statistics are not for the number of offenders but that of offence cases, as mentioned earlier, and do not include those who were dealt with under the Summary Proceeding for Police Infractions.

In order to look into the real situation of special law offenders before the war, including those subjected to the above-mentioned proceeding, Table 6 is based on figures of "realistic" guilty offenders.

(1) Special Law Offenders before the War

During the period from 1932 through 1939, as shown by Table 6, three kinds of offences–those of the Ordinance for the Punishment of Police Infractions, the Automobile Traffic Control Ordinance and the Road Use Control Ordinance–were particularly high, as the aggregate of the offenders of these three ordinances accounted for about half the total.

Furthermore, a breakdown of the violators of the Ordinance for the Punishment of Police Infractions shows that about 40 percent of the total were charged with disturbance of road traffic.

When the traffic-related offenders under the ordinance are added to those subjected to the two traffic-related ordinances mentioned above, the overall number of traffic violators come to account for a little more than 40 percent of all special law offenders. The offenders concerning disturbance of road traffic were followed by those dealt with under the Ordinance for the Punishment of Police Inractions for "wandering from place to place without no fixed abode or occupation." Those who were charged with this provision reached as many as one third of the violators reported under the ordinance.

Of the prewar special law offenders other than those who violated the Ordinance for Police Infractions, those in violation of local government ordinances against minor offences accounted for about 30 to 40 percent of the total.

Although the Maintenance of the Public Order Law and others concerning the control of rebellious thought and military-related laws such as the Military Service Law used to have a strong social impact because of heavy penalties meted out against the violators, the actual number of those charged for violation of these laws was rather small.

Taken up below are the offences before the war of economic control laws and ordinances under the government control of the national economy. An age of strict governmental control of the economy began in September, 1937, when the Law for Temporary Measures to Control Imports and Exports of Merchandise, etc., was put into force. The range of the law's application was widened in later years. In addition, the government at that time also placed retail prices of commodities under control. Under the growingly rigid economic control based on the National General Mobilization Law that took effect in May, 1938, the prices of all sorts of goods were frozen at the levels present as of September 18, 1939. As such, the control on commodities both for distribution and sale price came to be fully enforced and the police investigation for the violators of economic control laws and ordinances became quite active.

Under the circumstances, the number of offenders reported for violating the economic control law and ordinances soared sharply in and after 1940, accounting for a large portion of special law offenders.

For example, the National General Mobilization Law which played a central role of the economic control of the nation, the ratio of violators increased markedly, from 11.5 percent of all special law offenders reported in 1940, to 16.4 percent in 1941, 24.4 percent in 1942 and as high as 32.7 percent in 1943.

A majority of those who were investigated and punished, in the prewar years, for the violation of laws and ordinances controlling commodity supply and sale price were targeted as they committed such offences in the course of their business activities, and punishment was rarely inflicted on consumers in general.

As seen above, the trends in special law offences before the war can be

Table 6 Number and Rate of Realistic Guilty Offenders for Major Special Laws in Prewar Period

(1932～1943)

Offence	1932		Offence	1933	
	Number	Rate		Number	Rate
Total	867,966	100.0	Total	1,092,224	100.0
Ordinance for Punishment of Police Infraction	241,749	27.9	Ordinance for Punishment of Police Infraction	293,348	26.9
Road Use Control Ordinance	132,563	15.3	Road Use Control Ordinance	158,333	14.5
Automobile Traffic Control Law	57,293	6.6	Automobile Traffic Control Law	86,848	8.0
Ordinance Regulating the Possession of Guns, Swords, etc.	3,762	0.4	Ordinance Regulating the Possession of Guns, Swords etc.	4,011	0.4
Law concerning the Punishment of Acts of Violence, etc.	2,817	0.3	Maintenance of Public Order Law	3,163	0.3
Maintenance of Public Order Law	1,853	0.2	Law concerning the Punishment of Acts of Violence, etc.	2,687	0.2
Criminal Law for the Control of Explosives	22	0.0	Criminal Law for the Control of Explosives	17	0.0
Government and Local Autonomy Ordinance	358,117	41.3	Government and Local Autonomy Ordinance	443,346	40.6
Others	69,787	8.0	Others	100,471	9.2

Offence	1934		Offence	1935	
	Number	Rate		Number	Rate
Total	1,273,811	100.0	Total	1,298,645	100.0
Ordinance for Punishment of Police Infraction	279,421	21.9	Automobile Traffic Control Law	301,212	23.2
Automobile Traffic Control Law	247,676	19.4	Ordinance for Punishment of Police Infraction	246,757	19.0
Road Use Control Ordinance	194,956	15.3	Road Use Control Ordinance	186,609	14.4
Ordinance Regulating the Possession of Guns, Swords, etc.	4,350	0.3	Ordinance Regulating the Possession of Guns, Swords, etc.	4,292	0.3
Law concerning the Punishment of Acts of Violence, etc.	2,529	0.2	Law concerning the Punishment of Acts of Violence, etc.	2,867	0.2
Maintenance of Public Order Law	2,500	0.2	Maintenance of Public Order Law	1,071	0.1
Criminal Law for the Control of Explosives	39	0.0	Criminal Law for the Control of Explosives	34	0.0
Government and Local Autonomy Ordinance	450,362	35.4	Government and Local Autonomy Ordinance	467,074	36.0
Others	91,978	7.2	Others	88,729	6.8

Offence	1936 Number	1936 Rate
Total	1,246,812	100.0
Automobile Traffic Control Law	281,025	22.5
Ordinance for Punishment of Police Infraction	227,181	18.2
Road Use Control Ordinance	181,508	14.6
Ordinance Regulating the Possession of Guns, Swords, etc.	4,252	0.3
Law concerning the Punishment of Acts of Violence, etc.	2,860	0.2
Maintenance of Public Order Law	609	0.0
Criminal Law for the Control of Explosives	30	0.0
Government and Local Autonomy Ordinance	452,098	36.3
Others	97,249	7.8

Offence	1937 Number	1937 Rate
Total	948,861	100.0
Automobile Traffic Control Law	219,223	23.1
Ordinance for Punishment of Police Infraction	162,123	17.1
Road Use Control Ordinance	141,156	14.9
Ordinance Regulating the Possession of Guns, Swords, etc.	2,873	0.3
Law concerning the Punishment of Acts of Violence, etc.	1,982	0.2
Maintenance of Public Order Law	378	0.0
Criminal Law for the Control of Explosives	26	0.0
Government and Local Autonomy Ordinance	323,746	34.1
Others	97,354	10.3

Offence	1938 Number	1938 Rate
Total	756,131	100.0
Automobile Traffic Control Law	166,136	22.0
Ordinance for Punishment of Police Infraction	136,855	18.1
Road Use Control Ordinance	119,032	15.7
Law for Temporary Measures to Control Import and Export of Merchandises, etc.	6,686	0.9
Ordinance Regulating the Possession of Guns, Swords, etc.	2,508	0.3
Law concerning the Punishment of Acts of Violence, etc.	1,413	0.2
Maintenance of Public Order Law	594	0.1
Criminal Law for the Control of Explosives	10	0.0
Government and Local Autonomy Ordinance	256,158	33.9
Others	66,739	8.8

Offence	1939 Number	1939 Rate
Total	560,844	100.0
Automobile Traffic Control Law	111,412	19.9
Ordinance for Punishment of Police Infraction	104,212	18.6
Road Use Control Ordinance	90,401	16.1
Law for Temporary Measures to Control Import and Export of Merchandises, etc.	16,600	3.0
Ordinance Regulating the Possession of Guns, Swords, etc.	2,201	0.4
Law concerning the Punishment of Acts of Violence, etc.	1,356	0.2
National General Mobilization Law	923	0.2
Maintenance of Public Order Law	640	0.1
Criminal Law for the Control of Explosives	14	0.0
Government and Local Autonomy Ordinance	170,476	30.4
Others	62,609	11.2

Offence	1940	
	Number	Rate
Total	604,042	100.0
Ordinance for Punishment of Police Infraction	102,884	17.0
Road Use Control Ordinance	87,859	14.5
Automobile Traffic Control Law	85,960	14.2
National General Mobilization Law	69,513	11.5
Law for Temporary Measures to Control Import and Export of Merchandises, etc.	12,332	2.0
Ordinance Regulating the Possession of Guns, Swords, etc.	2,089	0.3
Law concerning the Punishment of Acts of Violence, etc.	1,194	0.2
Maintenance of Public Order Law	562	0.1
Criminal Law for the Control of Explosives	19	0.0
Government and Local Autonomy Ordinance	167,015	27.6
Others	74,615	12.4

Offence	1941	
	Number	Rate
Total	537,313	100.0
National General Mobilization Law	87,926	16.4
Ordinance for Punishment of Police Infraction	81,937	15.2
Road Use Control Ordinance	81,480	15.2
Automobile Traffic Control Law	54,341	10.1
Law for Temporary Measures to Control Import and Export of Merchandises, etc.	13,786	2.6
Ordinance Regulating the Possession of Guns, Swords, etc.	1,823	0.3
Law concerning the Punishment of Acts of Violence, etc.	1,068	0.2
Maintenance of Public Order Law	591	0.1
Criminal Law for the Control of Explosives	22	0.0
Government and Local Autonomy Ordinance	139,884	26.0
Others	74,455	13.9

Offence	1942	
	Number	Rate
Total	424,269	100.0
National General Mobilization Law	103,621	24.4
Road Use Control Ordinance	59,526	14.0
Ordinance for Punishment of Police Infraction	55,991	13.2
Automobile Traffic Control Law	22,363	5.3
Law for Temporary Measures to Control Import and Export of Merchandises, etc.	12,154	2.9
Ordinance Regulating the Possession of Guns, Swords, etc.	1,667	0.4
Law concerning the Punishment of Acts of Violence, etc.	1,293	0.3
Maintenance of Public Order Law	958	0.2
Criminal Law for the Control of Explosives	20	0.0
Staple Food Control Law	-	-
Government and Local Autonomy Ordinance	100,859	23.8
Others	65,817	15.5

Offence	1943	
	Number	Rate
Total	297,000	100.0
National General Mobilization Law	97,063	32.7
Ordinance for Punishment of Police Infraction	44,531	15.0
Road Use Control Ordinance	17,329	5.8
Automobile Traffic Control Law	9,703	3.3
Law for Temporary Measures to Control Import and Export of Merchandises, etc.	6,386	2.3
Staple Food Control Law	3,947	1.3
Ordinance Regulating the Possession of Guns, Swords, etc.	1,174	0.4
Law concerning the Punishment of Acts of Violence, etc.	1,064	0.4
Maintenance of Public Order Law	600	0.2
Criminal Law for the Control of Explosives	5	0.0
Government and Local Autonomy Ordinance	71,340	24.0
Others	43,528	14.7

Sources: Annual Report of Criminal Statistics and Summary of Criminal Statistics

Table 7 Number and Rate of Suspects Newly Received by the Public Prosecutors Office for Violation of Special Laws in Postwar Period

(1949, 1954, 1959. 1963, 1967, 1974, 1979, 1984)

1949			1954		
Offence	Number	Rate	Offence	Number	Rate
Staple Food Control Law	523,792	60.9	Staple Food Control Law	221,719	54.9
Price Control Ordinance	137,690	16.0	Stimulant Drugs Control Law	52,820	13.1
Law for the Temporary Adjustment of Supply and Demand of Commodities	98,626	11.5	Liquor Tax Law	17,257	4.3
the Allied Occupation Forces Property Ordinance for Receipt and Possession	10,816	1.3	Aliens Registration Law	17,095	4.2
Firearms and Swords Control Law	8,670	1.0	Forest Law	9,015	2.2
Emergency Ordinance for Eating and Drinking Business	7,151	0.8	Firearms and Swords Control Law	8,702	2.2
Tobacco Monopoly Law	6,805	0.8	Tobacco Monopoly Law	4,307	1.1
Forest Law	5,917	0.7	Vehicles Law	3,792	0.9
Liquor Tax Law	5,711	0.7	Law for Adjusting Business Affecting Public Morals	3,543	0.9
Minor Offece Law	5,563	0.6	Employment Seculity Law	2,373	0.6
Road Traffic Law	199,599	(18.8)	Road Traffic Law	1,243,351	(75.5)

1959			1963		
Offence	Number	Rate	Offence	Number	Rate
Anti-Prostitution Law	18,629	8.1	Firearms and Swords Control Law	20,892	7.6
Staple Food Control Law	15,535	6.8	Automobile Damage Compensation Security Law	20,331	7.4
Firearms and Swords Control Law	12,100	5.3	Aliens Registration Law	18,558	6.7
Aliens Registration Law	11,981	5.2	Anti-Prostitution Law	11,130	4.0
Automobile Damage Compensation Security Law	11,635	5.1	Law for Adjusting Business Affecting Public Morals	10,344	3.7
Law for Adjusting Business Affecting Public Morals	7,738	3.4	Vehicles Law	8,060	2.9
Forest Law	6,761	2.9	Minor Offece Law	5,001	1.8
Forest Law	5,779	2.5	Forest Law	3,603	1.3
Liquor Tax Law	5,416	2.4	Liquor Tax Law	3,419	1.2
Vehicles Law	3,632	1.6	Road Transport Law	3,411	1.2
Road Traffic Law	1,940,701	(89.4)	Road Traffic Law	4,122,095	(93.7)

1967			1974		
Offence	Number	Rate	Offence	Number	Rate
Automobile Damage Compensation Security Law	22,256	10.3	Aliens Registration Law	17,206	12.4
Firearms and Swords Control Law	16,588	7.7	Firearms and Swords Control Law	11,022	7.9
Law for Adjusting Business Affecting Public Morals	16,327	7.6	Law for Adjusting Business Affecting Public Morals	8,883	6.4
Aliens Registration Law	11,662	5.4	Horse Racing Law	8,855	6.4
Anti-Prostitution Law	8,188	3.8	Stimulant Drugs Control Law	7,635	5.5
Labour Standard Law	6,449	3.0	Automobile Damage Compensation Security Law	5,745	4.1
Shipping Officer Law	4,696	2.2	Shipping Seculity Law	4,090	2.9
Minor Offence Law	4,620	2.1	Minor Offence Law	3,528	2.5
Explosive Control Law	2,757	1.3	Poisonous and Injurious Substance Control Law	3,476	2.5
Vehicles Law	2,752	1.3	Anti-Prostitution Law	3,082	2.2
Road Traffic Law	4,597,663	(95.5)	Road Traffic Law	1,868,250	(93.1)

1979			1984		
Offence	Number	Rate	Offence	Number	Rate
Stimulant Drugs Control Law	29,629	15.6	Stimulant Drugs Control Law	32,846	20.5
Law for Adjusting Business Affecting Public Morals	12,664	6.7	Poisonous and Injurious Substance Control Law	28,315	17.7
Aliens Registration Law	8,268	4.4	Law for Adjusting Business Affecting Public Morals	10,462	6.5
Firearms and Swords Control Law	7,703	4.1	Minor Offence Law	6,659	4.2
Poisonous and Injurious Substance Control Law	7,002	3.7	Firearms and Swords Control Law	5,507	3.4
Horse Racing Law	6,007	3.2	Shipping Security Law	4,537	2.8
Automobile Damage Compensation Security Law	5,375	2.8	Aliens Registration Law	3,934	2.5
Law for Managing and Cleaning of Wastes	4,519	2.4	Law for Managing and Cleaning of Wastes	3,831	2.4
Shipping Security Law	4,467	2.4	Anti-Prostitution Law	3,731	2.3
Minor Offence Law	3,427	1.8	Automobile Damage Compensation Security Law	3,627	2.3
Road Traffic Law	1,944,056	(91.1)	Road Traffic Law	2,310,870	(93.5)

Source: Annual Report of Statistics on Prosecution

divided broadly into two periods: the period before 1940, when the violation of the Ordinance for the Punishment of Police Infractions, local government ordinances, the Road Use Control Ordinance and other relatively minor offences constituted a great portion of the entire special law offences, and the period in and after 1940, when violations of economic control laws and ordinances rose drastically, reducing the percentages of the offences that had been dominant in the period before 1940.

(2) Special Law Offences after The War

Table 7 shows that Road Traffic Law violations began increasing drastically early in the 1950s, topping by far the corresponding pre-war figures both in terms of the actual numbers and percentages of all special law offences. Among special law offences other than Road Traffic Law violations, the incidence of Food Control Law offences and other economic control-related offences was high in the mid-1950s through the early 1970s, while offenders of the Anti-Prostitution Law rose conspicuously during the period from the mid-1960s to early in the 1970s, though the number of the offences of the law reported to the police decreased drastically after the middle of the 1960s.

Also on the rise during the period from around 1965 to early in the 1970s were the Fire Arms and Swords Control Law offences and those of the Law for Adjusting Businesses Affecting Public Morals (which was called the Law to Control Business Affecting Public Morals before its revision in February, 1985).

From the early years of the 1970s to early in the 1980s, Stimulant Drug Control Law and other anti-drug law offences jumped markedly.

Figure 15 shows a comparison in the trends in road traffic violations and those of economic control-related offences after the war, which demonstrates a surprisingly rapid pace of increase in road traffic offences. Examined below are trends in major categories of special law offences after the end of the war.

A. Sharp Increases In Road Traffic Law Offences

Although road traffic violations numbered fairly high even in the pre-war days, those after the war have been increasing rapidly with progress in the nation's motorization, surpassing by far the pre-war levels both in actual numbers and ratios to all special law offences.

According to Table 7 and Table 4 in the Appendix, road traffic offenders in 1949, the year after the enforcement of the Road Traffic Control Law, reached 199,599, or 18.8 percent of all special law offenders, and the figure for 1954 rose to 1,243,351, accounting for 75.5 percent of the total.

In 1960, when the current Road Traffic Law was put into effect, road traffic violations stood at 2,571,963, an overwhelmingly large ratio of 92.7

percent of that year's whole special law offenders. The figure continued climbing, registering 4,965,062, or 96.6 percent of all special law offences in 1965.

In 1968, what is called the notification system for traffic infractions was adopted to simplify the fine-collecting procedure for minor offences of traffic rules and exempt a majority of traffic violators from the category of penal punishment. Nevertheless, the number of the other traffic offenders remained high: 1,259,653 in 1988, or 91.9 percent of the special law offenders all told.

Fig.15 Number of Suspects Newly Received by Public Prosecutors Offices for Violation of Road Traffic Law and Economic Control Regulations (1946~1988)

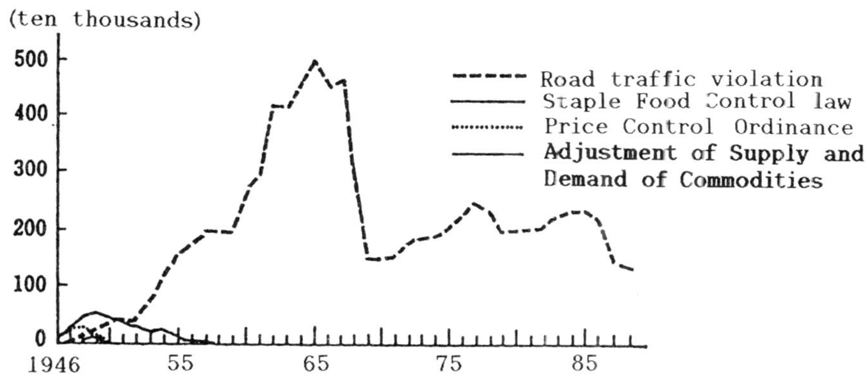

Sources: Annual Report of Criminal Statistics and Annual Report of Statistics on Prosecution

B. Trend In Economic Control Law Offences

Worthy of note regarding trends in special law offences after the war is the sharp rises in the number of violators of economic control regulations during the chaotic period just after the war.

The post-war government control on the economy began with the promulgation in February, 1946, of the Emergency Financial Measure Ordinances and related emergency Imperial decrees.

Also put into force in that month was the revision of the enforcement regulations of the Food Control Law for placing a ban on transportation by anybody other than government agencies of such staple grains as rice and wheat.

Since the Price Control Ordinance was effected the next month and the Temporary Law for the Adjustment of Supply and Demand of Commodities was enforced in October the same year, the nation's post-war government control on prices and rationing of stable foods and other commodities came to be carried out in real earnest. In and after 1947, a full-scale clampdown was conducted on offences of these economic control-related regulations, but they were phased out in and after 1950 as the national economy gradually was restored to stability.

Table 8 Number of Suspects Newly Received by the Public Prosecutors Offices for Violation of Economic Control Regulations (1946~1988)

Year	Food Control Law	Price Control Ordinance	Law of Commodities	Year	Food Control Law	Price Control Ordinance	Law of Commodities
1946	96,119	61,508	629	1968	162	186	–
1947	283,712	248,517	29,151	1969	92	327	–
1948	454,555	270,070	132,510	1970	170	330	–
1949	523,792	137,690	98,626	1971	78	406	–
1950	424,698	40,984	23,949	1972	156	400	–
1951	374,702	6,365	4,875	1973	540	404	–
1952	250,598	2,417	1,151	1974	37	204	–
1953	195,728	842	88	1975	28	207	–
1954	221,719	758	61	1976	34	128	–
1955	111,479	723	18	1977	7	41	–
1956	32,413	845	49	1978	20	21	–
1957	33,992	725	3	1979	6	20	–
1958	24,546	546	–	1980	11	11	–
1959	15,535	438	–	1981	3	16	–
1960	6,179	521	–	1982	–	6	–
1961	3,239	867	–	1983	–	2	–
1962	1,554	823	–	1984	4	10	–
1963	785	407	–	1985	3	4	–
1964	655	273	–	1986	6	6	–
1965	932	288	–	1987	3	6	–
1966	373	331	–	1988	–	14	–
1967	262	345	–				

Sources: Annual Report of Criminal Statistics and Annual Report of Statistics on Prosecution

Table 7 and 8 and Fig. 16 show changes in the number of suspects received by the public prosecutors office for violating either of the Food Control Law, the price control ordinance and the Temporary Law for the Adjustment of Supply and Demand of Commodities.

In 1946, the suspected violators of the Food Control Law numbered 96,119, those of the Price Control Ordinance 61,503, and those of the Temporary Law for the Adjustment of Supply and Demand of Commodities 629. The

Fig.16 Number of Suspects Newly Received by Public Prosecutors Offices for Violation of Economic Control Regulations (1946~1988)

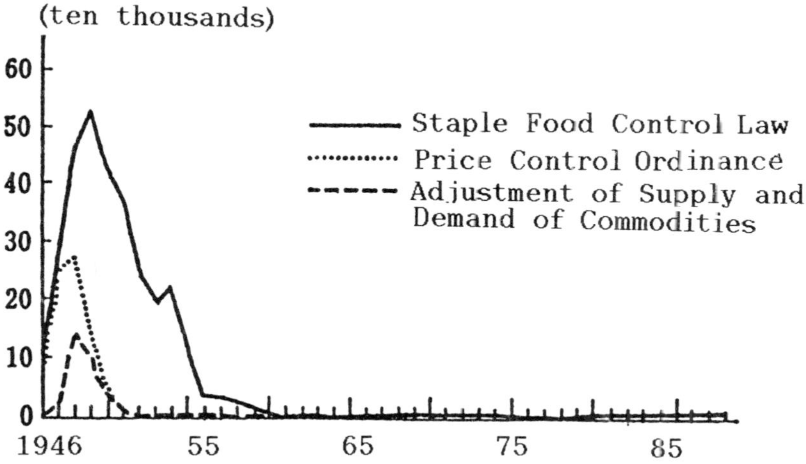

Sources: Annual Report of Criminal Statistics and Annual Report of Statistics on Prosecution

total of the offenders of the three economic control regulations accounted for 78.3 percent of all special law offences except road traffic violators.

The number of the economic control regulation offenders continued rising in the following years, with that of the Food Control Law reaching 523,792 in 1949, when violators of the Price Control Ordinance reached 137,690 and those of the Temporary Law for the Adjustment of Supply and Demand of Commodities stood at 98,626. The offenders of the three regulations amounted to 88.4 percent of all special law offences but road traffic violations in 1949.

In and after 1951, the figure decreased drastically and the total of the violators of the three economic control regulations vanished from the list of the 10 most frequent special law offenders, not including road traffic offences (hereafter simply called "upper 10 special law offenders excluding road traffic offences"), early in the 1960s.

Predominant among offenders of the economic control regulations were those of the Food Control Law, who were mostly consumers arrested on suspicion of transporting such staple grains as rice and wheat. Those offences were attributable to short supplies of food and other daily necessities in the turbulent postwar years, and the incidence of the offences decreased sharply with the progress in the nation's economic rehabilitation.

As referred to at the outset of this section, the prosecution ratios of special law offences in that period were relatively low, probably because consideration was given to the fact that the suspects were mostly ordinary

Table 9 Number of Suspects Newly Received by the Public Prosecutors Office for Violation of Drug Laws (1931～1988)

Year	Cannabis Control Law	Narcotics Control Law	Stimulant Drugs Control Law	Opium Law	Year	Cannabis Control Law	Narcotics Control Law	Stimulant Drugs Control Law	Opium Law
1931	–	67	–	53	1961	25	2,664	512	206
1932	–	55	–	112	1962	46	3,093	621	348
1933	–	68	–	186	1963	136	3,084	1,141	457
1934	–	90	–	157	1964	182	1,070	1,013	560
1935	–	85	–	110	1965	258	1,141	781	917
1936	–	118	–	116	1966	171	992	818	995
1937	–	85	–	37	1967	290	664	753	631
1938	–	57	–	64	1968	398	360	921	967
1939	–	30	–	4	1969	456	263	825	331
1940	–	20	–	19	1970	771	257	1,905	241
1941	–	24	–	37	1971	797	249	3,176	172
1942	–	9	–	44	1972	765	379	6,184	207
1943	–	10	–	68	1973	776	469	11,030	264
1944	…	…	…	…	1974	713	450	7,635	134
1945	…	…	…	…	1975	992	290	13,287	114
1946	–	177	–	19	1976	1,059	207	17,354	152
1947	114	551	–	2	1977	1,318	199	23,711	163
1948	190	1,185	–	7	1978	1,658	191	28,187	124
1949	100	1,447	–	–	1979	1,495	146	29,629	163
1950	63	2,589	–	–	1980	1,607	219	31,464	131
1951	26	2,383	9,841	–	1981	1,474	118	34,170	144
1952	64	1,869	18,359	–	1982	1,391	128	34,431	136
1953	18	1,693	35,115	–	1983	1,409	97	33,088	118
1954	19	2,317	52,820	39	1984	1,760	200	32,846	99
1955	58	2,047	30,935	187	1985	1,427	165	31,520	124
1956	30	1,662	5,607	154	1986	1,516	194	28,699	169
1957	40	1,758	866	184	1987	1,511	154	27,214	156
1958	12	2,327	265	92	1988	1,709	163	26,079	71
1959	32	2,036	361	177					
1960	14	2,561	496	447					

Sources: Annual Report of Criminal Statistics and Annual Report of Statistics on Prosecution

Fig.17 Number of Suspects Newly Received by Public Prosecutors Offices for Violation of Drug Laws (1931～1988)

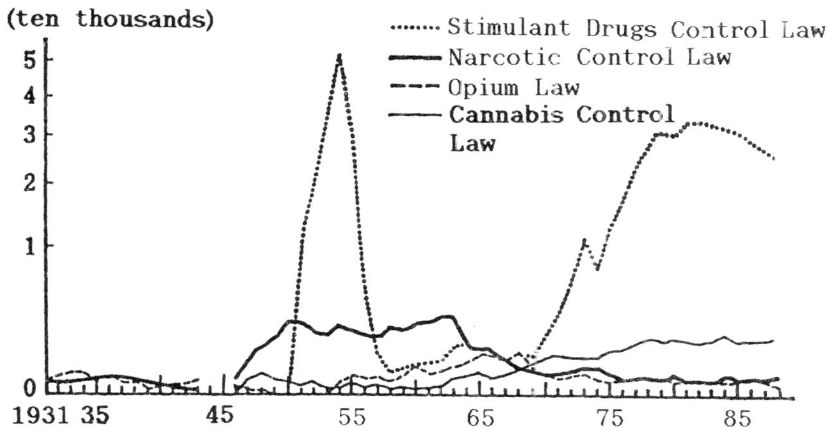

Sources: Annual Report of Criminal Statistics and Annual Report of Statistics on Prosecution

consumers.

C. Trends in Drug Offences

Also worthy of note in special law offences after World War II are the trends in offences of the Stimulant Drugs Control Law and other drug offences.

Table 9 and Fig. 17 show changes in the number of suspects received by the public prosecutors office on suspicion of violating drug laws other than the Poisonous and Injurious Substance Control Law. Table 7 also indicates chronological changes in drug offences.

In the times before the war, there in fact were violators of the Opium Control Law and the Narcotics Control Ordinance, but the cases of drug offences were extremely low, numbering around 100 at the most in a year.

After the war, the use of and trafficking in narcotics and stimulants became prevalent against the backdrop of postwar social disorders, and the laws against narcotics and hemp were enacted in 1948, while an anti-stimulant drug law was laid down in 1951.

The law enforcement authorities' setup for clamping down on drug abuses was strengthened following the enactment of the existing Narcotics Control Law in 1953 and the Opium Control Law in 1954. But the violators of the Stimulant Drugs Control Law and other drug offenders continued increasing sharply. Stimulant Drugs Control Law offenders numbered 52,820 in 1954, accounting for 13.1 percent of all special law offenders not including road

Table 10 Number of Suspects Newly Received by the Public Prosecutors Offices for Violation of Firearms and Swords Control Law, etc. (1946~1988)

Year	Firearms and Swords	Law for Public Morals	Anti-Prostitution Law	Year	Firearms and Swords	Law for Public Morals	Anti-Prostitution Law
1946	2,970	–	–	1968	15,400	18,139	7,757
1947	9,172	–	–	1969	14,055	13,720	6,345
1948	9,826	63	–	1970	12,602	12,344	5,800
1949	8,670	1,124	–	1971	12,217	10,699	5,094
1950	11,389	2,133	–	1972	12,463	9,931	4,367
1951	9,297	2,915	–	1973	10,837	8,969	3,300
1952	7,955	3,570	–	1974	11,022	8,883	3,082
1953	8,058	4,175	–	1975	11,720	8,228	3,074
1954	8,702	3,543	–	1976	11,479	9,695	3,217
1955	7,079	5,463	–	1977	10,905	11,027	2,975
1956	10,068	4,539	–	1978	9,229	12,268	2,608
1957	11,615	4,843	–	1979	7,703	12,664	2,355
1958	12,219	6,039	13,663	1980	7,245	13,583	2,381
1959	12,100	6,761	18,629	1981	7,045	12,130	2,338
1960	15,996	8,939	16,171	1982	6,344	9,976	2,019
1961	15,762	8,738	13,994	1983	5,815	10,255	2,528
1962	17,569	9,751	12,551	1984	5,507	10,462	3,731
1963	20,892	10,344	11,130	1985	5,374	5,924	4,008
1964	21,259	11,061	10,927	1986	5,081	5,128	3,464
1965	21,622	14,687	10,547	1987	4,837	4,471	3,180
1966	19,826	15,713	9,472	1988	4,452	3,877	2,876
1967	16,588	16,327	8,188				

Sources: Annual Report of Criminal Statistics and
Annual Report of Statistics on Prosecution

traffic violators. That year marked the first peak of the drug offences after the war as the number of the Narcotics Control Law offenders in 1954 also rose to a record high at 2,317.

The surges in the stimulant drug offences, however, turned downward markedly in the following years because of the combination of such measures as stiffening of penalties through the revision of the law, thoroughgoing clampdown on offenders, introduction of the system to statutorily hospitalize drug addicts and public relations campaigns for warning the public against the harmful effects of drugs.

The second wave of drug offence prevalence after the war was largely due to increases in the offences of the Narcotics Control Law, in particular the illegal use of heroin.

The number of the law offenders rose as high as 3,093 in 1962 and 3,084 in 1963, but decreased rapidly in the subsequent years because of the conter-measures similar to those taken against the rise in the Stimulant Drugs Control Law offences in 1954.

The third postwar prevalence in drug offences came in and after 1970 due mainly to renewed increases in Stimulant Drugs Control Law offences, which have been continuing even today.

The offenders of the law have long been at the top of the list of the upper 10 special law offenders, excluding road traffic offenders. In 1982, the drug offenders stood at 34,431, or 25.7 percent of all special law offences not including the violations of the Road Traffic Law. The stimulant drug offenders thereafter seem to be on the decline, but the number still stood high at 26,079 in 1988, indicating that the situation does not warrant optimism.

D. Other Special Law Offences

Fig.18 Number of Suspects Newly Received by Prosecutors Offices for Violation of Firearms Control Law, etc. (1946～1988)

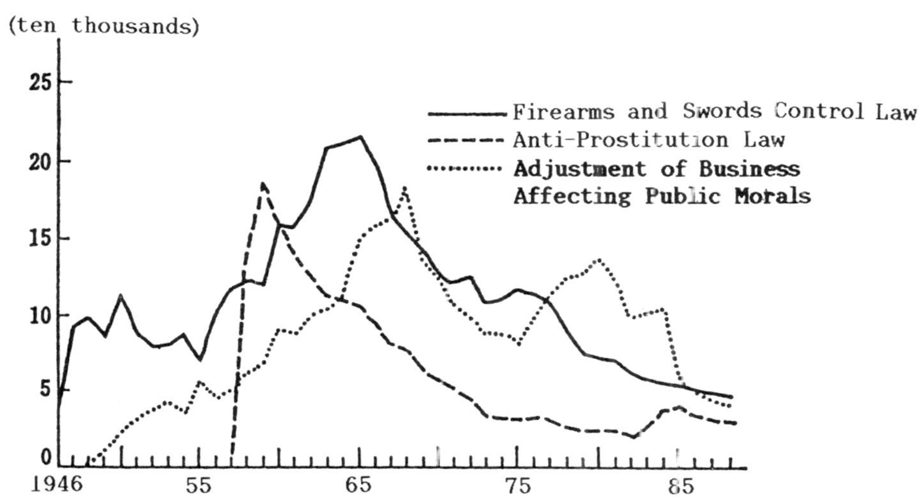

Sources: Annual Report of Criminal Statistics and Annual Report of Statistics on Prosecution

Shown in Table 10 and Fig. 18 are the changes in the number of suspects received by the public prosecutors office for violating the Fire Arms and Swords Control Law, the Law for Adjusting Business Affecting Public Morals, or the Anti-Prostitution Law, which can also be indicated by Table 7.

Offences of the Fire Arms and Swords Control Law began increasing sharply around the middle of the 1950s and showed particularly rapid rises in the 1960s. The pattern generally coincided with that of crimes of violence as referred to earlier in connection with the trends in Penal Code offences, reflecting the social situation peculiar to those days in which the incidence of violent struggles among underworld organizations, "Boryokudan," climbed remarkably.

In 1949, the number of suspects for violating the Fire Arms and Swords Control Law was only 8,670 (or 1.0 percent of all special law offenders excluding road traffic violators) and 8,702 in 1954 (2.2 percent), but the figure shot up to 12,100 (5.3 percent) in 1959, ranking third in the list of the upper 10 special law offenders excluding road traffic offences. In 1963, it further rose to 20,892 (7.6 percent) and topped the list.

The rising trend in the Fire Arms and Swords Control Law offences contined through 1967, but it went down gradually thereafter. The surges in the violators of the law should be considered to have contributed to the high figures of overall special law offences in 1959, 1963 and 1967 as earlier mentioned in the overview of special law offence trends after the war.

Offenders of the Law for Adjusting Business Affecting Public Morals numbered high during the period from the early 1960s to around 1970. Table 7 and Fig. 10 put the figures at only 1,124 (or 0.1 percent of all special law offenders except road traffic violations) for 1949, 3,543 (0.9 percent) for 1954 and 6,761 (2.9 percent) for 1959.

But the figure climbed to 10,344 (3.7 percent) in 1963, placing fifth in the list of upper 10 special law offenders excluding road traffic offences and further to 16,327 (7.6 percent) in 1967, ranking third in the list.

Since the early years of the 1970s, however, the trend began declining gradually, though the figures still were among the list of upper 10 special law offenders excluding road traffic offences.

It can therefore be said that the high figures of the offenders of the Law for Adjusting Business Affecting Public Morals corresponded to the pattern of surges in the number of overall special law offences in 1963 and 1967 as referred to before.

Lastly, trends after the war in the number of offenders of the Anti-Prostitution Law, to which penal privisions were added in April 1958, show that the figures surged significantly during the period from 1959 to 1965, especially high in 1959.

The incidence of the violations of that law went down in the following years but picked up again from early in the 1980s through 1985 before decreasing in 1986 and 1987. As shown by Table 7, suspects of violating the Anti-Prostitution Law reached 18,629 in 1959, or 8.1 percent of all special law offenders but road traffic violaltors, topping the list of that year's upper 10 special law offenders excluding road traffic offences and contributing significantly to the relatively high total of that year's special law offenders.

Subsequently, the Anti-Prostitution Law violators went down gradually to 11,130 in 1963 (4.0 percent of all special law offenders not including road traffic violators) and 8,188 in 1967 (3.8 percent) and vanished from the list of upper 10 special law offenders, but appeared again in the list in 1984 when the prostitution offenders reached 3,731.

Regarding the three kinds of special law offences dealt with above, it can be said that members of underworld organizations, "Boryokudan," often account for high percentages of those who are responsible for these kinds of offences.

Incidentally, all of the three categories of special law offences increased markedly in the period from the mid-1950s through around 1970. Deserving special note is the fact that the mid-1950s-to-1970 period coincided with the time when the incidence of crimes by gangsters, "Boyokudan," rose sharply because of intensified struggles among gangs for their spheres of influence. as earlier referred to in connection with the trends in Penal Code offences.

Section 4. Comparison of Crime Trends in Foreign Countries

Following World War II, not a few countries experienced rapid economic and social changes, such as industrialization and urbanization. The advanced nations of Europe and North America also experienced these changes, but many countries were beset with a simultaneous increase in criminal offences, particularly violent crimes. Worsening security in metropolitan areas in particular has brought much insecurity into the lives of citizens. In Japan, however, as has already been seen, with the exception of the chaotic postwar period and a short while following, Penal Code offences, excluding traffic-related professional negligence, have either declined or increased only moderately despite the rapid economic and social changes, showing a different pattern from the advanced nations of Europe and North America where major crimes have risen relatively fast. Of course, the range and structural condition of offences classified as crimes differs between Japan and these countries, and it is difficult to make strict comparisons because of the different statistical methods used. Nevertheless, to discover where Japan's postwar crime trends stand, it is a profitable exercise to compare the movement in the crime situation from each country's statistical figures.

In this section, we used official records from four Western countries, the United States (called U.S. hereafter), the United Kingdom (called Britain hereafter), the Federal Republic of Germany (called West Germany hereafter) and the French Republic (called France hereafter), and Japan to learn the total number of cases reported for major crimes in each country, and to compare the trends in the number of cases reported per 100,000 population (called occurrence rate hereafter). In addition, we compared the trends in the number of cases reported, occurrence rates and arrest rates for each country for the most serious crime, homicide, the typical sexual crime, rape, and the most common crime, theft.

1. NUMBER OF CASES REPORTED AND OCCURRENCE RATES FOR MAJOR CRIMES

Fig. 19 shows the trends for total number of cases reported for major crimes between 1946 and 1987, in materials released publicly by each country. For statistics of countries other than Japan, however, legal revisions, changes in handling of statistics, material acquisition problems, etc., made it difficult to acquire continuous figures. For this reason, we decided to limit data to those that continuously linked with data as of 1987. As a result, West German figures date from 1951, British figures from 1946, U.S. figures from 1960 and French figures from 1972.

For the total number of cases reported, comparisons with Japanese data for the chaotic period immediately following World War II are possible with West Germany from 1951 and with Britain from 1946. The figures for chaotic, wartorn West Germany and Japan are considerably higher than those for Britain. From the late 1960s, increases are striking in the U.S., Britain and West Germany, and steep rises are seen in the 1970s and later, with France. During this period in Japan, figures in the late 1960s and early 1970s were either declining or flat, after which a rise can be seen in the late 1970s. For this reason, while the number of cases reported in Japan until the early 1960s was smaller than the figures for the U.S. or West Germany, the difference was not all that much, and was larger than the figures for Britain. From the late 1960s, however, Japan's figures fell below those of Britain's, and as those countries' figures accelerated still further, the difference with Japan widened. Setting 1972 equal to 100, the total number of cases reported in each country in 1987 was Britain, 220, France, 189, West Germany, 173, and the U.S., 164. By contrast, Japan reached just 129.

Fig.19 Number of Major Offences Reported (1946~1987)

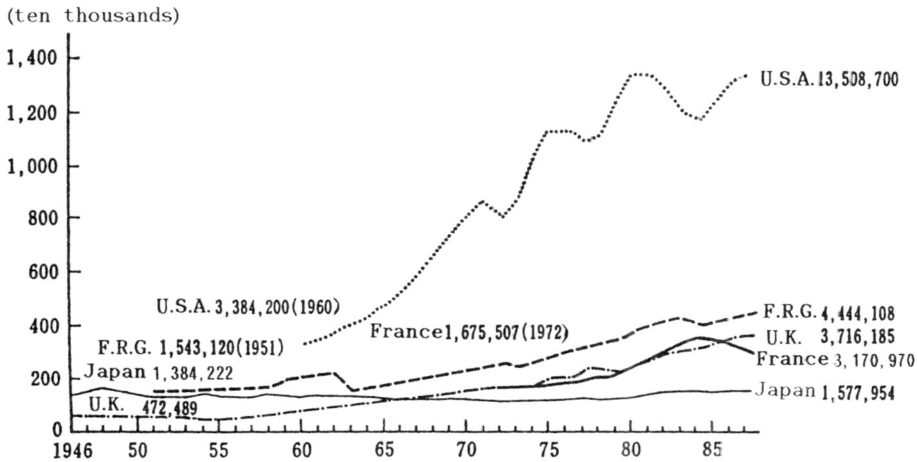

Notes: 1 Based on the following sources:
Crime in the United States, Criminal Statistics England and Wales, Polizeiliche Kriminalstatistik Federal Republic of Germany: La criminalite en France, Annuaire statistique de la justice, Statistics of National Police Agency, Japan.

2 The numbers of reported offences in the respective countries are based on the following criteria:

* United States: Only crime index offences in 1958 (murder, aggravated assault, forcible rape, robbery, burglary, theft and motor vehicle theft) are counted and the figures are estimated.

* United Kingdom: Only indictable offences till 1978 and notifiable offences since 1979 are counted; based on statistics from England and Wales.

* Federal Republic of Germany: The number of Straftat is counted, excluding traffic offences and Staatsschutz-delikte.

* France: The number of crime et délit is counted, excluding traffic offences.

* Japan: Penal Code Offences excluding traffic professional negligence.

Fig. 20 shows the trends in total occurrence rates for major crimes in each country, including Japan. For the occurrence rates for Japan and the other countries, Japan either declines or remains flat from the late 1960s, while other countries show a continuing upward trend from a situation already higher than Japan's, with the gap expanding year-by-year. The occurrence rate for 1987 was Britain, 7,421, West Germany, 7,269, France, 5,712, and United States, 5,550. Japan remained at 1,291.

Fig.20 Occurrence Rate of Major Offences Reported (1946~1987)

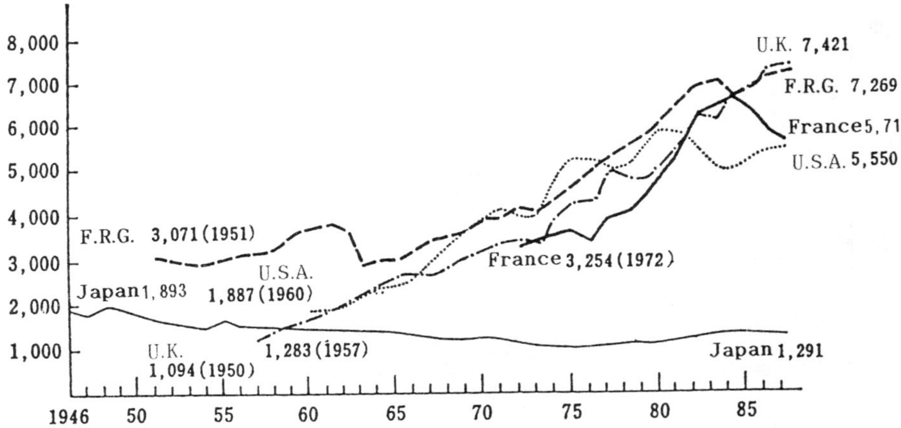

Notes: 1 See notes 1 and 2 of Fig. 19.
2 The occurrence rate means the number of offences reported per 100,000 population.

2. COMPARISON BY CRIME TYPE

Next, we will compare each country's trends for homicide, rape and theft. For each of these crimes, Japan's crime occurrence rate is low in recent years compared to other countries, while the clearance rate is high. Of course,

Fig.21 Occurrence Rate of Homicide Reported (1946~1987)

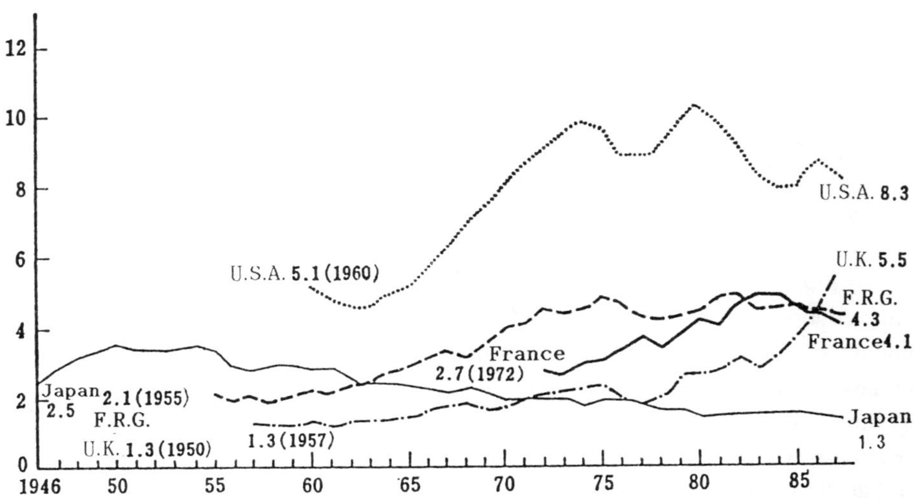

Note: See notes 1 and 2 of Fig.19 and note 2 of Fig.20

Table 11 Number of Homicide Cases Reported, Occurrence Rate and Clearance Rate, by Country (1960～1987)

Year / Item	U. S. A.	U. K.	F. R. G.	France	Japan
1960					
Homicide cases reported	9,110	555	1,215	…	2,784
Occurrence rate	5.1	1.3	2.2	…	3.0
Clearance rate	92.3	95.5	89.5	…	96.7
1965					
Homicide cases reported	9,960	627	1,634	…	2,390
Occurrence rate	5.1	1.4	2.8	…	2.4
Clearance rate	90.5	94.9	95.2	…	97.2
1970					
Homicide cases reported	16,000	823	2,477	…	2,028
Occurrence rate	7.9	1.7	4.0	…	2.0
Clearance rate	86.5	95.0	93.6	…	97.0
1975					
Homicide cases reported	20,510	1,108	2,957	1,576	2,140
Occurrence rate	9.6	2.3	4.8	3.0	1.9
Clearance rate	78.3	…	95.5	82.0	96.0
1980					
Homicide cases reported	23,040	1,303	2,733	2,253	1,729
Occurrence rate	10.2	2.6	4.4	4.2	1.5
Clearance rate	72.3	88.1	95.3	79.4	97.3
1985					
Homicide cases reported	18,980	1,819	2,796	2,497	1,847
Occurrence rate	7.9	3.7	4.6	4.5	1.5
Clearance rate	72.0	79.1	95.0	84.0	96.1
1987					
Homicide cases reported	20,100	2,764	2,651	2,286	1,645
Occurrence rate	8.3	5.5	4.3	4.1	1.3
Clearance rate	70.0	81.5	94.0	93.0	97.6

Note: 1 See Notes 1 and 2 of Figure 19.
2 The number of reported homicide cases in the respective countries are based on the following criteria:
U. S. A. Murder and manslaughter.
U. K. Murder, attempted murder, threat or cospiracy to murder, manslaughter and infanticide.
F. R. G. Murder(Mord), manslaughter(Totschlag), murder on demand(Totung auf Verlagen), and infanticide (Kinderstotung).
France Murder(assasinat), manslaughter(meurtre), parenticide (parricide), infanticide(infanticide) and empoisonment (empoisonnement).
Japan Murder, manslaughter and robbery causing death.
3 Crime rate means the number of reported offences per 100,000 population.

it is impossible to determine the crime trends and security situation in each of these countries based on pure comparisons of these figures alone. Nevertheless, when Japan's figures are compared with those of other countries, the occurrence rates for homicide, rape and theft showed little difference with the other countries' figures until about 1960, with homicide figures higher than Britain's or West Germany's, and rape figures higher than Britain's. After that time, however, while Japan's occurrence rates generally continued on declining or flat trends, the other countries' occurrence rates showed relatively steep increases or otherwise rising trends, so that in recent years, a big gap has appeared between Japan's occurrence rates and other countries' occurrence rates.

(1) Homicide

Table 11 shows the number of cases reported, occurrence and clearance rates for homicide in each country from 1960 to 1987, in five-year intervals. Fig. 21 shows the trends in occurrence rates for each country.

Japan's occurrence rate is lower than figures for the U.S. or France, but until the early 1960s, they were higher than the figures for West Germany and Britain. The figures fell below West Germany's figures in the mid-1960s, and below Britain's figures in the early 1970s. In 1987, the occurrence rate was U.S., 8.3, Britain, 5.5, West Germany, 4.3, and France 4.1. By contrast, Japan was at 1.3.

For the homicide clearance rate, Japan can be said to have maintained fairly high figures compared with other countries. For the clearance rate in 1987, West Germany was 94.0 percent, France, 93.0 percent, Britain, 81.5 percent, and the U.S., 70.0 percent. By contrast Japan was at 97.6 percent.

(2) Rape

Table 12 shows the number of cases reported, occurrence and clearance rates for rape in each country from 1960 to 1987, in five-year intervals. Fig. 22 shows the trends in occurrence rates for each country.

Japan's occurrence rate for rape is lower than figures for West Germany or the U.S., but continued paralleling those two countries at fairly high levels until the mid-1960s, after which a decline began. The figures remained higher

Fig.22 Occurrence Rate of Rape Reported (1946~1987)

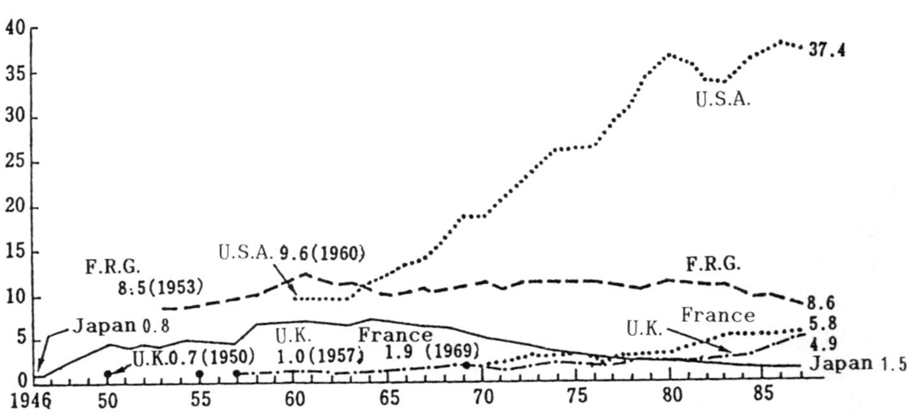

Note: See notes 1 and 2 of Fig.19 and note 2 of Fig.20

Table 12 Number of Rape Reported, Occurrence Rate and Clearance Rate, by Country (1960～1987)

Year/Item	U.S.A.	U.K.	F.R.G.	France	Japan
1960					
Rape cases reported	17,190	515	6,436	…	6,342
Occurrence rate	9.6	1.2	11.6	…	6.8
Clearance rate	72.5	82.5	72.0	…	94.9
1965					
Rape cases reported	23,410	618	5,923	…	5,648
Occurrence rate	12.1	1.4	10.0	…	6.8
Clearance rate	64.0	74.6	71.3	…	95.2
1970					
Rape cases reported	37,990	884	6,889	1,038	5,161
Occurrence rate	18.7	1.8	11.2	2.1	5.0
Clearance rate	56.4	74.5	75.0	…	92.0
1975					
Rape cases reported	56,090	1,040	6,850	1,589	3,704
Occurrence rate	26.3	2.1	11.1	3.0	3.3
Clearance rate	51.3	…	72.4	74.8	91.5
1980					
Rape cases reported	82,990	1,225	6,904	1,886	2,610
Occurrence rate	36.8	2.5	11.2	3.5	2.2
Clearance rate	48.8	73.1	72.3	76.6	89.0
1985					
Rape cases reported	88,670	1,842	5,919	2,823	1,802
Occurrence rate	37.1	3.7	9.7	5.1	1.5
Clearance rate	54.1	63.9	70.6	82.3	90.1
1987					
Rape cases reported	91,110	2,471	5,281	3,196	1,823
Occurrence rate	37.4	4.9	8.6	5.8	1.5
Clearance rate	52.9	70.7	71.2	85.6	87.4

Note: See notes 1 and 2 of Figure 19 and note 3 of Table 11.

than for Britain or France until the mid-1970s, and then declined rapidly in the 1980s, falling below all other countries' figures. The occurrence rate in 1987 was the U.S., 37.4, West Germany, 8.6, France, 5.8, and Britain, 4.9. By contrast, Japan was at 1.5.

For the rape clearance rate, Japan maintained a high rate. For the clearance rate in 1987, France was 85.6 percent, West Germany, 71.2 percent, Britain, 70.7 percent, and the U.S., 52.9 percent. By contrast Japan was at 87.4 percent.

(3) Theft

Table 13 shows the number of cases reported, occurrence and clearance rates for theft in each country from 1960 to 1987, in five-year intervals. Fig. 23 shows the trends in occurrence rates for each country.

Fig.23 Occurrence Rate of Theft Reported (1946~1987)

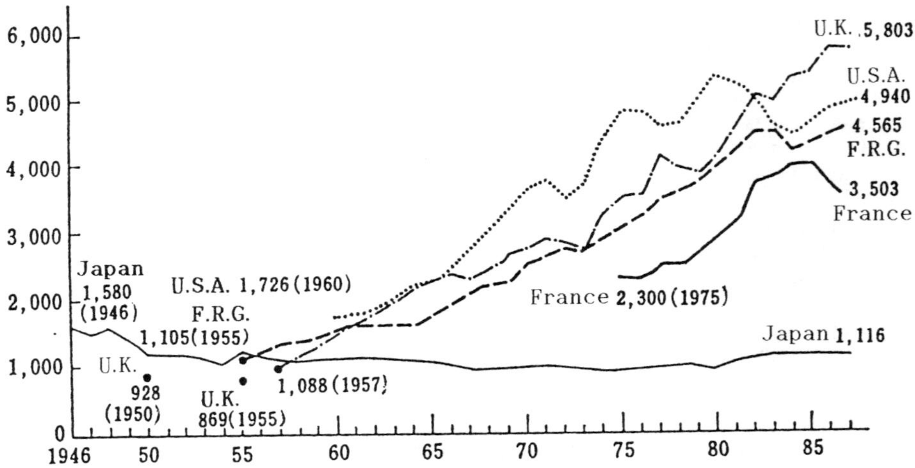

Note: See notes 1 and 2 of Fig.19 and note 2 of Fig.20

Japan's occurrence rate for theft is lower than figures for the U.S. or France, but in the 1950s the figures were relatively high, sometimes higher than for West Germany or Britain. From the 1960s on, however, the numbers declined gradually, even as other countries' figures began to rise, and fell below the figures for West Germany and Britain. In the late 1970s, Japan's figures began to rise again, but the rate of increase in other countries surpassed Japan's rate. The figures for 1987 were Britain, 5,803, the U.S., 4,940, West Germany, 4,565, and France, 3,503. Japan was at 1,116. The trend in the occurrence rate for theft looks similar to the trends for major crime totals as has already been noted. This is probably because theft holds an overwhelming share of the major crimes.

For the theft clearance rate as well, Japan maintained a high rate compared with other countries. For the clearance rate in 1987, Britain was 29.3 percent, West Germany, 27.8 percent, U.S., 17.7 percent, and France, 16.3 percent. By contrast Japan was at 60.2 percent.

Section 5. Trends in Crimes by Gang Organizations

Boryokudan, or gang organization, may be defined in general terms as "an organization or group which collectively and habitually engages or is prepared to engage in criminal activities accompanied by violence." It is quite difficult to comprehend precisely the realities of Boryokudan. A typical gang or gangster includes the categories of professional gamblers, street peddlers,

Table 13 Number of Theft Reported, Occurrence Rate and Clearance Rate, by Country (1960～1987)

Year/Item	U.S.A.	U.K.	F.R.G.	France	Japan
1960					
Theft cases reported	3,095,700	636,605	855,033	…	1,038,418
Occurrence rate	1.726	1.491	1.538	…	1.112
Clearance rate	…	37.2	34.5	…	50.1
1965					
Theft cases reported	4,352,000	989,974	1,034,957	…	1,027,473
Occurrence rate	2.249	2.268	1.753	…	1.046
Clearance rate	…	33.0	32.9	…	50.1
1970					
Theft cases reported	7,359,200	1,338,518	1,549,694	…	1,039,118
Occurrence rate	3.621	2.749	2.519	…	1.002
Clearance rate	18.4	38.7	33.3	…	47.5
1975					
Theft cases reported	10,252,600	1,737,525	1,909,418	1,210,895	1,037,942
Occurrence rate	4.811	3.534	3.088	2.300	927
Clearance rate	18.5	…	28.8	17.5	51.6
1980					
Theft cases reported	12,063,800	2,043,044	2,437,824	1,576,840	1,165,609
Occurrence rate	5.353	4.149	3.960	2.935	996
Clearance rate	16.5	35.3	28.9	17.4	55.0
1985					
Theft cases reported	11,102,600	2,705,430	2,628,933	2,217,344	1,381,237
Occurrence rate	4.651	5.436	4.309	4.027	1.141
Clearance rate	17.8	30.6	30.8	15.2	59.9
1987					
Theft cases reported	12,024,800	2,906,141	2,790,849	1,944,367	1,364,796
Occurrence rate	4.940	5.803	4.565	3.503	1.116
Clearance rate	17.7	29.3	27.8	16.3	60.2

Note: 1 See Notes 1 and 2 of Figure 19 and Note 3 of Table 11.
2 The number of reported theft cases in the respective countries are based on the following criteria:
U.S.A. Larceny theft, motor vehicle theft and burglary
U.K. Theft and burglary
F.R.G. Theft(Disbstahl ohne erschwerende Umstande) and weight theft(Disbstahl unter erschwerenden Umstande)
France Theft(vols)
Japan All kind of theft

delinquent youth groups, stevedore gangs and unscrupulous constructors. Such groups emerged through cracks in the social structure and under the influence of the socio-economic conditions of the time. They repeatedly split and merged among themselves and have survived persistently over the ages. They are true antisocial and malignant elements of a society.

Thanks to better crime statistics kept in the postwar period, it became possible to obtain a comprehensive view of crimes committed in these years by gang members. In the following, the trends of crimes committed by postwar gangs and gangsters will be taken into consideration. The activities of postwar gangs may be classified into five major periods. The characteristic of each period is discussed below.

Table 14 Number of Bōryokudan Members among Penal Code and Special Law Offenders Cleared by the Police (1946～1988)

Year	Total	Penal Code Offence	Special Law Offence	Year	Total	Penal Code Offence	Special Law Offence
1946	…	30,512	…	1968	38,808	32,428	6,380
1947	…	30,116	…	1969	38,180	33,140	5,040
1948	…	12,110	…	1970	42,815	36,524	6,291
1949	…	8,853	…	1971	43,527	35,849	7,678
1950	…	7,400	…	1972	48,177	38,137	10,040
1951	…	2,432	…	1973	52,077	38,004	14,073
1952	…	2,450	…	1974	53,277	39,759	13,518
1953	…	11,175	…	1975	53,058	38,524	14,534
1954	…	34,419	…	1976	56,423	38,491	17,932
1955	…	55,783	…	1977	57,351	38,251	19,100
1956	82,074	80,364	1,740	1978	58,750	37,201	21,549
1957	50,322	47,229	3,093	1979	51,462	32,295	19,167
1958	59,302	54,612	4,612	1980	52,247	32,656	19,591
1959	55,699	51,802	3,897	1981	52,670	32,844	19,826
1960	56,780	51,317	5,463	1982	52,275	33,957	18,318
1961	58,924	52,455	6,469	1983	48,043	29,635	18,408
1962	52,422	46,489	5,933	1984	49,519	29,859	19,660
1963	51,065	44,647	6,418	1985	48,213	28,604	19,609
1964	58,687	51,339	7,348	1986	45,065	26,764	18,301
1965	56,704	47,416	9,288	1987	40,257	24,396	15,861
1966	43,303	34,121	9,182	1988	40,401	24,577	15,824
1967	38,572	31,459	7,113				

Source: National Police Agency

1. PERIOD OF POSTWAR CHAOS (late 1940s)

During this period, a number of new lawless groups, small and large, mushroomed on top of the long-established gangs of gamblers and street peddlers. They advanced into various rackets such as street hawking, black markets, gambling, group robberies and strong-arm protection. The new groups repeatedly battled with the older groups over command of territories and over various interests involved.

Table 14 shows the trends in the number of gang members arraigned on Penal Code and special law offences cleared by the police in the postwar period. Hereafter, those gang members who are involved in Penal Code or special law offences cleared by the police will be referred to as "gangster Penal Code offenders" or "gangster special law offenders." The number of gangster Penal Code offenders was 30,512 in 1946 and 30,116 in 1947. However, the number decreased to 12,110 in 1948, 8,853 in 1949 and 7,400 in 1950. The number further decreased to the 2,400 level in 1951 and 1952.

Unlike the general trends in Penal Code and special law offences, the peak period for the number of gangster Penal Code offenders was not between 1948 and 1950 but instead occurred between 1946 and 1947, immediately after the war. This period was marked by frequent clashes between gangs fighting over their territorial rights and interests such as the running of black markets and other rackets. The fights were frequently large in scale and bloody since the gangs were armed with military weapons and fired on each other indiscriminately, thus causing much public uneasiness. The gangsters became the most important target of the police at that time. After 1948, the number of gangster Penal Code offenders decreased, due primarily to the gradual recovery from the postwar chaos, frequent crackdowns on gangs, and strong police efforts to force the gangs to disband them, including the mandatory dissolution of specific gangs under the Cabinet Order for Controlling Organizations Engaging in Subrersive Activities, Etc. These strict measures against the gangsters criminal activities seem to have worked effectively to reduce the incidence of crime for a while.

2. PERIOD OF GANG WARS (early 1950s to early 1960s)

This was the time when new entertainment quarters arose in major cities and newly industrialized areas along with the nation's rapid social and economic recovery thanks to an economic boom fueled by Korean War procurement. New Gurentai, street gangsters came into power, preying on such quarters, targeting the interests involved in pachinko parlors (a kind of slot-machine), public gambling set-ups (bicycle races, etc.) sex-related business (massage parlors, etc.) prostitution, Philopon (a stimulant drug) and other rackets. The new and

Table 15 Number and Percentage of Bōryokudan Members Cleared by the Police, by Offence

① Penal Code Offence

Year	Total		Homicide		Robbery		Bodily injury		Assault	
	Number	Percentage	Number	Percentage	Number	Percentage	Number	Percentage	Number	Percentage
1958	54,690	100.0	837	1.5	1,606	2.9	10,321	18.9	6,455	11.8
1963	44,647	100.0	778	1.7	937	2.1	14,861	33.3	5,969	13.4
1968	32,428	100.0	444	1.4	334	1.0	9,279	28.6	5,515	17.0
1973	38,004	100.0	538	1.4	344	0.9	11,013	29.0	6,037	15.9
1978	37,201	100.0	495	1.3	386	1.0	10,387	27.9	6,427	17.3
1983	29,635	100.0	577	1.9	379	1.3	8,019	27.1	3,395	11.5
1988	24,577	100.0	356	1.4	310	1.3	6,321	25.7	2,287	9.3

Year	Intimidation		Extortion		Unlawful assembly with weapons		Theft		Fraud	
	Number	Percentage	Number	Percentage	Number	Percentage	Number	Percentage	Number	Percentage
1958	1,566	2.9	10,725	19.6	279	0.5	2,301	4.2	1,020	1.9
1963	885	2.0	7,601	17.0	618	1.4	2,245	5.0	811	1.8
1968	1,109	3.4	4,414	13.6	417	1.3	1,890	5.8	1,026	3.2
1973	1,034	2.7	4,774	12.6	334	0.9	1,583	4.2	1,207	3.2
1978	836	2.2	4,788	12.9	321	0.9	2,208	5.9	1,390	3.7
1983	668	2.3	4,113	13.9	167	0.6	2,445	8.3	1,296	4.4
1988	683	2.8	4,532	18.4	37	0.2	2,407	9.8	1,313	5.3

Year	Rape		Destruction of property		Gambling		Others	
	Number	Percentage	Number	Percentage	Number	Percentage	Number	Percentage
1958	2,042	3.7	…	…	…	…	7,538	13.8
1963	1,347	3.0	707	1.6	1,575	3.5	6,313	14.1
1968	707	2.2	427	1.3	4,456	13.7	2,410	7.4
1973	634	1.7	566	1.5	7,441	19.6	2,499	6.6
1978	429	1.2	714	1.9	5,925	15.9	2,895	7.8
1983	324	1.1	582	2.0	5,237	17.7	2,433	8.2
1988	242	1.0	520	2.1	3,671	14.9	1,898	7.7

② Special Law Offence

Year	Total		Firearms and sword		Narcotics		Stimulant drugs	
	Number	Percentage	Number	Percentage	Number	Percentage	Number	Percentage
1958	4,612	100.0	1,081	23.4	…	…	…	…
1963	6,418	100.0	1,710	26.6	709	11.0	…	…
1968	6,380	100.0	1,440	22.6	16	0.3	335	5.3
1973	14,073	100.0	2,139	15.2	22	0.2	5,092	36.2
1978	21,549	100.0	2,442	11.3	13	0.1	9,234	42.9
1983	18,408	100.0	1,694	9.2	7	0.0	10,668	58.0
1988	15,824	100.0	1,255	7.9	6	0.0	9,221	58.3

Year	Anti-Prostitution Law		Public Morals		Employment Security Law		Child Welfare Law	
	Number	Percentage	Number	Percentage	Number	Percentage	Number	Percentage
1958	…	…	…	…	…	…	…	…
1963	496	7.7	…	…	…	…	…	…
1968	595	9.3	…	…	…	…	…	…
1973	246	1.0	239	1.7	159	1.1	168	1.2
1978	272	1.3	719	3.3	43	0.2	358	1.7
1983	336	1.8	300	1.6	55	0.3	425	2.3
1988	540	3.4	218	1.4	46	0.3	316	2.0

Year	Horse Race Law		Bicycle Race Law		Others	
	Number	Percentage	Number	Percentage	Number	Percentage
1958	…	…	…	…	3,531	76.6
1963	…	…	…	…	3,503	54.6
1968	…	…	…	…	3,994	62.6
1973	2,785	19.8	1,160	8.2	2,061	14.6
1978	4,347	20.2	1,052	4.9	3,069	14.2
1983	1,711	9.3	796	4.3	2,416	13.1
1988	1,280	8.1	460	2.9	2,482	15.7

Source: National Police Agency

old gangs battled incessantly to stake out their territorial claims and there were repeated breakups and mergers to establish the gangs' "division of power" over the nation during the period.

From 1955 to 1965 Japan achieved remarkable economic success, experiencing two historic economic expansion phases, the Jinmu boom from 1955 to 1956 and the Iwato boom from 1959 to 1961. During the decade, roads and housing complexes mushroomed, producing huge profits for the construction industry. The boom also stimulated international trade and multiplied the amount of work at ports. Also, the Cabinet of then Prime Minister Hayato Ikeda came up with a plan to "double the income," which greatly boosted the actual wages of workers. The resulting spending spree proved highly profitable for the entertainment business. This in turn produced huge incomes for gangs which controlled construction and harbor workers and maintained strong-arm men to "protect" the entertainment quarters. During this period, the so-called seven gang syndicates (named as such later by the National Police Agency) achieved great power. The seven syndicates are Yamaguchi-gumi, Honda-kai (later renamed Dainihon Heiwa-kai), Sumiyoshi-kai (currently Sumiyoshi Rengo-kai), Kinsei-kai (currently Inagawa-kai), Nihon Kokusui-kai, Kyokuto Aio Rengo-kai and Matsuba-kai.

(They came to be called "NPA-designated seven syndicates." Later, the term was altered to "eight syndicates" by adding Ichiwa-kai, a gang syndicate which spun out from the Yamaguchi-gumi syndicate.)

The number of gang-associated Penal Code offenders was only 2,450 in 1952 but increased to 11,175 in 1953. It was 34,419 in 1954 and 55,783 in 1955. It rose to 80,364 in 1956. The number then decreased, but hovered at the 40,000 to 50,000 level until 1965. Table 15 shows the number of gang-associated Penal Code and special laws offenders every five years since 1958, classified by offence. The total number of gangsters involved in crimes of violence, bodily injuries and murder in 1968 constitutes 48.4 percent of the total number of gang-associated Penal Code offenders, reflecting the intense inter-gang confrontation and conflicts during the year. Table 16 shows the changes in the number of cases of inter-gang conflicts after 1960, also shown in terms of index. It shows a significant number of such cases in the decade beginning in 1955.

With this situation as the background, the number of gang syndicates and their members drastically increased during the period. Table 17 lists changes in the number of gang organizations and the number of members after 1958. There were 4,192 organizations with 92,860 members in 1958. However, the numbers increased to 4,874 organizations with 105,065 members in 1959, and 5,199 syndicates with 124,763 members in 1960. In 1963, the organizations increased to 5,216, with a record-breaking membership of 184,091.

In 1958, in order to properly cope with the situation, the government proposed in the Diet a bill to introduce in the Penal Code a new article on the crime of intimidation of a witness. The proposal became law.

Also amended was the Code of Criminal Procedure whereby gang-associated inmates were deprived of the right to be released on bail. The amendment placed them under a status in which bail may only be granted at the discretion of the court, if the court deems it likely that they will retaliate against witnesses who testified against gangsters in detention.

In addition, the Law concerning Compensation for Damage Inflicted on the Witness, etc., was promulgated, to provide protection to witnesses.

Besides, with a view to forestalling inter-gang conflicts, the crime of unlawful assembly with dangerous weapons was also introduced in the Penal Code. In the same year, the Firearms and Swords Control Ordinance was revised in a law under which heavier penalties were provided for the use and possession of dangerous weapons, including firearms and swords.

In 1964, the Law for Punishment of Acts of Violence, etc. was amended to introduce an aggravated crime of bodily injury committed with firearms and swords, as well as to provide for heavier penalities for habitual offenders involved in crimes of violence.

From around 1952, local prefec-

Table 16 Number of Inter-Bōryokudan Conflicts (1960～1988)

Year	Total	Index
1960	115	100.0
1961	109	94.8
1962	112	97.4
1963	123	107.0
1964	68	59.1
1965	13	11.3
1966	45	39.1
1967	45	39.1
1968	72	62.6
1969	70	60.9
1970	129	112.2
1971	82	71.3
1972	64	55.7
1973	52	45.2
1974	77	67.0
1975	89	77.4
1976	66	57.4
1977	28	24.3
1978	18	15.7
1979	19	16.5
1980	34	29.6
1981	26	22.6
1982	29	25.2
1983	34	29.6
1984	29	25.2
1985	24	20.9
1986	23	20.0
1987	27	23.5
1988	32	27.8

Source: Criminal Affairs Bureau, National Police Agency

Table 17 Number of Members and Groups of Bōryokudan (1958～1987)
① All groups

Year	Number of groups		Number of members	
	Number	Index	Number	Index
1958	4,192	116.3	92,860	67.1
1959	4,874	135.3	105,065	76.0
1960	5,119	142.1	124,763	90.2
1961	4,970	137.9	162,450	117.5
1962	5,131	142.4	172,711	124.9
1963	5,216	144.8	184,091	133.1
1964	4,573	126.9	177,035	128.0
1965	3,944	109.5	156,293	113.0
1966	3,790	105.2	147,171	106.4
1967	3,752	104.1	142,660	103.2
1968	3,603	100.0	138,288	100.0
1969	3,500	97.1	139,089	100.6
1970	3,481	96.6	138,506	100.2
1971	3,219	89.3	130,407	94.3
1972	2,957	82.1	123,044	89.0
1973	2,723	75.6	114,506	82.8
1974	2,650	73.5	110,819	80.1
1975	2,606	72.3	110,042	79.6
1976	2,555	70.9	109,955	79.5
1977	2,502	69.4	108,266	78.3
1978	2,525	70.1	108,700	78.6
1979	2,517	69.9	106,754	77.2
1980	2,487	69.0	103,955	75.2
1981	2,452	68.1	103,263	74.7
1982	2,395	66.5	100,237	72.5
1983	2,330	64.7	98,771	71.4
1984	2,278	63.2	93,910	67.9
1985	2,226	61.8	93,514	67.6
1986	3,133	87.0	85,935	62.1
1987	3,201	88.8	86,287	62.4

② Wide-area groups, 7 designated groups and 3 designated groups

Year	Number of groups						Number of members					
	Wide-area groups		7 designated groups		3 designated groups		Wide-area groups		7 designated groups		3 designated groups	
	Number	Index	Number	Index	Number	Index	Number	Index	Number	Index	Number	Index
1968	2,285	100.0	767	100.0	490	100.0	69,575	100.0	28,135	100.0	16,561	100.0
1969	2,251	98.5	816	106.4	540	110.2	73,161	105.2	32,225	114.5	19,773	119.4
1970	2,296	100.5	884	155.3	601	122.7	74,909	107.7	34,249	121.7	21,335	128.8
1971	2,213	96.8	883	115.1	607	123.9	71,779	103.2	33,457	118.9	21,105	127.4
1972	2,102	92.0	873	113.8	600	122.4	68,523	98.5	33,002	117.3	20,968	126.6
1973	2,032	88.9	885	115.4	629	128.4	64,506	92.7	32,057	113.9	20,673	124.8
1974	2,032	88.9	945	123.2	680	138.8	63,888	91.8	32,418	115.2	21,161	127.8
1975	2,014	88.1	946	123.3	686	140.0	64,459	92.6	33,071	117.5	21,792	131.6
1976	1,995	87.3	976	127.2	711	145.1	64,844	93.2	34,269	121.8	22,462	135.6
1977	1,939	84.9	906	118.4	650	132.7	62,942	90.5	32,175	114.4	21,051	127.1
1978	2,003	87.7	955	124.5	687	140.2	64,165	92.2	32,614	115.9	21,471	129.6
1979	2,015	88.2	1,035	134.9	754	153.9	63,265	90.9	33,731	119.9	23,255	140.4
1980	1,992	87.2	1,005	131.0	771	157.3	60,990	87.7	32,343	115.0	22,761	137.4
1981	1,957	85.6	1,052	137.2	819	167.1	59,796	85.9	32,960	117.1	23,779	143.6
1982	1,904	83.3	1,033	134.7	805	164.3	58,903	84.7	32,651	116.1	23,958	144.7
1983	1,878	82.2	1,038	135.3	819	167.1	58,490	84.1	32,836	116.7	24,416	147.4
1984	1,825	79.9	1,043	135.9	685	139.8	55,240	79.4	32,146	114.3	21,128	127.6
1985	1,817	79.5	1,055	137.5	722	147.3	56,390	81.0	33,771	120.0	23,198	140.1
1986	2,760	120.8	1,676	218.5	1,154	235.5	70,713	101.6	41,828	148.7	29,879	180.4
1987	2,872	125.7	1,830	238.6	1,294	264.1	71,056	102.1	43,091	153.2	31,107	187.8

Source: Criminal Affairs Bureau, National Police Agency

tural legislatures promulgated the "Public Nuisance Prevention Ordinance" to protect residents from the distasteful, annoying conduct of the gang members, etc. This legislation paved the way for devising nationwide systems to restrain the underworld criminal syndicates.

3. "SUMMIT OPERATION" AND ITS EFFECTS (early 1960s to late 1960s)

With the nationwide campaign for sweeping crackdowns on gang organizations as a background, intensive and comprehensive attempts to control gang members was conducted from 1964 to 1965. The main focus in the policy was strict control of the illegal activities of leaders of gang organizations, crimes related to revenue sources of the syndicates and their weapons. These are called "summit operations," by which police aimed at keeping the activities of gang syndicates in check. The operations were continuously performed, later joined by local governments who banned events sponsored by gangs at public facilities throughout the nation.

Table 14 lists the total number of gangsters cleared by the police for Penal Code offences and special law violations. It reveals that 58,687 gangsters were cleared in 1964 and 56,704 in 1965, which accounted for one-third of the members of the criminal syndicates.

The figure dropped to 43,303 in 1966, and further declined to the 38,000 level between 1967 and 1969, which reflected the concerted "summit operation" and the subsequent reduction in the overall activities of the criminal organizations.

Broken down in terms of offences, heinous crimes and violent offences markedly decreased in 1968 compared with those in the decade from 1955, as Table 14 shows.

The effects of the summit operation were seen in the decrease of gang syndicates and their membership. According to Table 17, the number was 5,216 with 184,091 membership in 1963. However, it decreased by 1,716 organizations to 3,500 in 1969, and membership decreased by 45,002 to 139,089. During the period from 1965 to 1969, major gangs such as Kinsei-kai, Honda-kai and Sumiyoshi-kai, plus the Kanto-kai group, were dissolved.

4. *PERIOD OF REORGANIZATION, EXPANSION OF TERRITORY AND MONOPOLIZATION* (1970 to 1980)

In the early 1970s, gangs managed to revive themselves through reorganization. Major gangs with extensive areas of the nation under their influence absorbed small and medium-sized gangs. A new map of territories governed by such syndicates was made as a result. According to Table 17, the number of gang syndicates was 2,957 in 1972, or the index of 82.1 if the number in 1968 is set as 100. The membership was 123,044, down to 89.0 from 100 in 1968. The number decreased gradually to 2,517 organizations in 1979, 69.9 from 100 of 1968, and the membership was 106,754, down to 77.2 from 100 of 1968. However, the total number of organizations under the NPA-designated seven syndicates was 873 in 1972, with membership at 33,002. The figures showed an increase to 113.8 if the number of organizations under the seven syndicates in 1968 set as 100, whereas the membership was increased to 117.3 from 100 in 1968. Furthermore, the number of organizations under the seven syndicates increased to 1,035 in 1979, or the index of 134.9, and the membership to 33,731, an increase to 119.9 in index.

The power of the gang syndicates, whose influence covered a wide range of areas, did not necessarily decline but was rather reinforced during the period.

The "summit operation" worked effectively on small and medium-sized gang syndicates as a result of a decline in the overall number of organizations and their membership.

However, major gang syndicates placed such damaged small and medium-sized organizations under their umbrellas and thus their power was increased in general.

Because of the economic slump in the period of low economic growth after the oil crisis, it became difficult for gangs to maintain their organizations while depending only on their traditional money sources.

Some gangs disguised themselves into rightist political organizations while others advanced into the field of sokaiya stock racketeers (racketeers to blackmail a company at a general meeting of stockholders). They even intervened in economic transactions and sponsored overseas gambling tours. In this way they promoted multiple business operations, modernization and every possible illegal activity to survive, while trying to hide themselves from police crackdowns.

Small and medium-sized gangs had only traditional illegal money sources, while major syndicates had abundant, diversified money sources, regardless of whether they were illegal or legal, and established the management system by collecting money from organizations under their umbrellas. Because the smaller organizations were vulnerable to invasions of larger organizations and police checks, it was the natural result that smaller organizations were dissolved or merged under major syndicates.

Especially notable were the expansion of the three NPA-designated major syndicates the Yamaguchi-gumi, Inagawa-kai and Sumiyoshi Rengo-kai and the progress of "oligopoly of the gang world" by major syndicates.

Transition in the number of sub-organizations and their membership under the seven major syndicates and the three major syndicates is discussed below. The number of gangs under the umbrella of the NPA-designated seven syndicates and the three syndicates and their membership in 1968 is set at 100. For the seven syndicates, the indicator increased to 134.9 for the number of organizations, and 119.9 for the membership in 1979. For the three major syndicates alone, however, the indicator increased to 153.9 for the number of organizations and 140.4 for the membership in the same year. Therefore, among the seven NPA-designated major syndicates, the increases in the sub-organizations and members of the three syndicates were conspicuous.

According to Table 14, the total number of gangster-related offenders cleared by police on Penal Code and special law violation charges gradually increased after 1970 and the number topped 50,000 from 1973 until around 1975. Although the number of gangsters was decreasing during the period, the number of those cleared by police remained at the high level of the period from 1955 to 1965. From the table we can conclude that the criminal activities by gangsters did not calm down but were rather activated in the new drastic moves including reorganization of the gang world.

Looking at Table 15 in more detail, the number of those cleared increased conspicuously in both Penal Code and special law violations in 1973, compared with the figures of 1968. In Penal Code offences, homicide, bodily injuries and gambling, and special law violations of the Firearms and Swords Control Law and the Stimulant Drug Control Law, showed marked increases.

Compared with the figures in 1973, the number of special law violations increased drastically in 1978. Especially, violations of the Firearms and Swords Control Law, the Stimulant Drugs Control Law, the Law to Control Businesses Affecting Public Morals, the Child Welfare Law and the Horse Racing Law have increased. This trend suggests the progress of gang armamentation and diversification of their money sources. Among them, increases in violations of the Stimulant Drug Control Law suggest that the sale of stimulant drugs is the most convenient and also profitable crime in terms of money sources for major syndicates, which were then rapidly growing during the period, taking advantage of the fact that their influence covered wide areas.

5. *PERIOD OF GENERATION CHANGE AND TRANSITION* (early 1980s to the present)

In the world of gangsters, major generation changes have been going on and the gangland is now experiencing a major transition over a new hegemony. For instance, the third-generation boss of Yamaguchi-gumi died in 1981 and fights over the next boss started. In 1984, those against appointment of the fourth-generation boss spun out from the syndicate and established Ichiwa-kai. In 1985, the fourth-generation boss of Yamaguchi-gumi was shot and killed by members of Ichiwa-kai, triggering a series of fierce battles between the two major syndicates. Ichiwa-kai dissolved in 1989 and the confrontation was finally settled. The fifth-generation boss was appointed to head Yamaguchi-gumi. However, those against the appointment of the fifth boss left the syndicate and declared their independence from Yamaguchi-gumi. The similar problem of succeeding aged bosses is seen in other syndicates which cover major areas. The gangland map is expected to be altered based on the changing of generations hereafter.

Also, criminal syndicates are now expected to face difficulties in trying

Table 18 Percentage of Bōryokudan Members, by Age (1966～1987)

Year	Total		Under 20 years old		20～29 years old	
	Number	Percentage	Number	Percentage	Number	Percentage
1966	147,171	100.0	9,261	6.3	73,259	49.8
1967	142,660	100.0	8,619	6.0	70,834	49.7
1968	138,288	100.0	6,080	4.4	66,009	47.7
1969	139,089	100.0	4,634	3.3	66,512	47.8
1970	138,506	100.0	2,867	2.1	67,487	48.7
1971	129,432	100.0	1,990	1.5	59,981	46.3
1972	123,044	100.0	1,540	1.3	55,258	44.9
1973	114,506	100.0	1,632	1.4	47,776	41.7
1974	110,819	100.0	1,551	1.4	42,754	38.6
1975	110,042	100.0	1,337	1.2	41,381	37.6
1976	109,955	100.0	1,250	1.1	39,614	36.0
1977	108,266	100.0	1,185	1.1	38,352	35.4
1978	108,700	100.0	1,328	1.2	34,097	31.4
1979	106,754	100.0	1,178	1.1	31,579	29.6
1980	103,955	100.0	1,131	1.1	26,982	26.0
1981	103,263	100.0	1,625	1.6	23,852	23.1
1982	100,237	100.0	1,432	1.4	23,037	23.0
1983	98,771	100.0	1,527	1.5	23,584	23.9
1984	93,910	100.0	1,679	1.8	21,205	22.6
1985	93,514	100.0	1,658	1.8	22,594	24.2
1986	85,935	100.0	2,477	2.9	24,402	28.4
1987	86,287	100.0	2,909	3.4	23,236	27.0

30～39 years old		40～49 years old		50 years and over	
Number	Percentage	Number	Percentage	Number	Percentage
43,466	29.5	13,238	9.0	7,947	5.4
42,249	29.6	13,772	9.7	7,186	5.0
43,018	31.1	15,318	11.1	7,863	5.7
43,546	31.3	16,347	11.8	8,050	5.8
43,625	31.5	16,754	12.1	7,773	5.6
43,389	33.5	17,038	13.2	7,031	5.4
41,593	33.8	17,631	14.3	7,022	5.7
40,397	35.3	17,840	15.6	6,861	6.0
40,896	36.9	18,676	16.9	6,942	6.3
40,531	36.8	19,236	17.5	7,557	6.9
41,568	37.8	20,084	18.3	7,439	6.8
42,239	39.0	20,024	18.5	7,466	6.9
43,893	40.4	21,147	19.5	8,243	7.6
45,144	42.3	20,786	19.5	8,067	7.6
45,531	43.8	21,654	20.8	8,657	8.3
43,850	42.5	24,260	23.5	9,666	9.4
42,423	42.3	23,979	23.9	9,366	9.3
40,491	41.0	23,919	24.2	9,250	9.4
36,945	39.3	24,186	25.8	9,895	10.5
34,967	37.4	24,088	25.8	10,207	10.9
28,735	33.4	21,478	25.0	8,843	10.3
26,690	30.9	23,537	27.3	9,865	11.4

Source: Criminal Affairs Bureau, National Police Agency

to enlist new young members, a situation which they have probably never experienced before. Table 18 shows the number of gang members according to age brackets and percentage of each age bracket against the total after 1966. Because the subjects of the statistics became different after 1986, the factors until 1985 are examined. Those in their 20s were 73,259 in 1966, 49.8 percent against the total, but decreased to 39,614, 36.0 percent, in 1976. The number decreased to 22,594, 24.2 percent against the total, in 1985.

Instead, those in their 40s or older increased from 21,185, 14.4 percent against the total, in 1966 to 27,523, 25.1 percent, in 1976 and to 34,295, 36.7 percent, in 1985, showing the aging of gangsters.

The tendency also prevails among new criminal offenders among gangsters committed to prisons in the last decade.

Those in their 20s occupied about 43 percent among those who were imprisoned for violence, violations of the Law for Punishment of Acts of Violence, etc., assembling with dangerous weapons, bodily injuries, homicide and intimidation in 1977.

In 1987, however, those in their 20s decreased to 29 percent among the total. Instead, those aged 40 or older who occupied about 13 percent of the entire new prisoners on these charges in 1977 increased to about 29 percent in 1987.

As discussed in earlier chapters, although juvenile delinquency frequently occurs in the current society in general, young adults rather stay away from crimes. Instead, an increased number of middle-aged and older people commit crimes. Even in the gangland, gangsters are steadily aging since young people try to stay away from gangs. In the past it was said that the supply of gangland members would never be cut. However, each organization is now suffering from the shortage of new young members.

Table 17 shows changes in the number of gangs and their members between 1958 and 1987. According to the table, the number of gangs was 2,487 organizations with 103,955 members in 1980. However, the number of organizations decreased to 2,226 with 93,514 members in 1985. These figures are about a half or even more from the corresponding figures in 1963. After 1986, the number of organizations gradually increased but the number of members decreased to 86,287 in 1987. As a whole, the number of gangsters has been decreasing as a recent tendency.

However, the number of organizations under the NPA-designated seven major syndicates was increasing. It was 1,005 in 1980 with 32,343 members. In 1985, the number of organizations increased to 1,055 and that of the members to 33,771. The number of sub-organizations under the three major syndicates decreased from 771 in 1980 to 722 in 1985. However, their members slightly

Table 19 Violent Intervention in Civil Disputes Reported to the Police, by Type of Dispute (1981～1988)

Year	Total	Collection of Loan	Money Debt	Discounting of Bills	Bankrupcy	Lease of Real Property	Settlement of Traffic Accidents	Sale of Goods	Others
1981	9,665	1,298	1,253	806	447	1,140	1,150	972	2,559
1982	11,327	1,634	1,626	797	443	1,243	1,393	1,306	2,835
1983	12,091	1,769	1,727	905	438	1,258	1,481	1,524	2,989
1984	12,309	1,602	1,819	1,033	610	1,210	1,901	1,228	3,406
1985	15,150	1,957	2,172	1,233	681	1,555	2,230	1,479	3,838
1986	18,707	2,392	2,721	1,278	872	1,993	2,578	1,768	5,105
1987	20,180	2,372	2,803	1,164	761	2,681	2,653	1,852	5,894
1988	20,308	2,180	2,865	1,185	587	2,477	2,644	2,006	6,364

Source: Criminal Affairs Bureau, National Police Agency

increased from 22,761 of 1980 to 23,198 in 1985. Ichiwa-kai affiliated gangs spun out from Yamaguchi-gumi immediately before the 1985 survey and those in Ichiwa-kai were not included in the three major syndicates. We should take into account, however, that they are included in the members of the NPA-designated eight major syndicates.

According to Table 14, the number of gang members cleared by police on Penal Code and special law violations decreased drastically after 1985. Especially, the number of Penal Code offenders has decreased remarkably. According to Table 15, the number of violent crimes and heinous crimes decreased remarkably after 1985. The number of special law violators has also decreased but the number of Stimulant Drug Control Law violations is still high even after 1985, and the number of Anti-Prostitution Law violators has been increasing. These crimes frequently take place probably because trafficking of stimulant drugs and illegal activities concerning prostitution are major money sources for the gang organizations.

These criminal offences of gangsters in general, however, became less typical to gang organizations. As one possible reason, criminal activities of the gang syndicates went further underground. Also, diversification of their revenue sources, such as running companies, have further progressed along with the economic expansion during this period as the background.

Table 19 shows the changes in the number of consultations received by

Table 20 Number and Percentage of Weapons Seized from Bōryokudan Members (1952～1988)

Year	Total		Handguns		Other firearms		Japanese swords	
	Number	Percentage	Number	Percentage	Number	Percentage	Number	Percentage
1952	329	100.0	17	5.2	…	…	48	14.6
1953	1,779	100.0	57	3.2	…	…	131	6.4
1954	4,171	100.0	81	1.9	40	1.0	445	10.7
1955	6,628	100.0	82	1.2	103	1.6	454	6.8
1956	9,192	100.0	132	1.4	188	2.0	735	8.0
1957	6,054	100.0	125	2.1	96	1.6	496	8.2
1958	6,723	100.0	158	2.4	125	1.9	635	9.4
1959	5,100	100.0	162	3.2	86	1.7	604	11.8
1960	5,805	100.0	191	3.3	134	2.3	723	12.5
1961	5,463	100.0	209	3.8	262	4.8	944	17.3
1962	5,662	100.0	226	4.0	290	5.1	967	17.1
1963	5,885	100.0	330	5.6	264	4.5	938	15.9
1964	7,758	100.0	552	7.1	374	4.8	1,358	17.5
1965	6,335	100.0	765	12.1	248	3.9	1,310	20.7
1966	5,589	100.0	402	7.2	219	3.9	1,132	20.3
1967	4,032	100.0	150	3.7	158	3.9	913	22.6
1968	4,827	100.0	122	2.5	188	3.9	1,054	21.8
1969	5,261	100.0	135	2.6	120	2.3	1,090	20.7
1970	5,652	100.0	166	2.9	158	2.8	1,155	20.4
1971	6,592	100.0	428	6.5	244	3.7	1,271	19.3
1972	6,976	100.0	778	11.2	284	4.1	1,185	17.0
1973	7,564	100.0	936	12.4	203	2.7	1,202	15.9
1974	8,410	100.0	1,054	12.5	268	3.2	1,022	12.2
1975	8,821	100.0	1,330	15.1	230	2.6	1,023	11.6
1976	9,547	100.0	1,437	15.1	271	2.8	1,102	11.5
1977	8,835	100.0	1,306	14.8	291	3.3	1,036	11.7
1978	7,824	100.0	1,021	13.0	259	3.3	1,031	13.2
1979	5,961	100.0	907	15.2	124	2.1	669	11.2
1980	6,858	100.0	932	13.6	135	2.0	648	9.4
1981	7,450	100.0	1,027	13.8	158	2.1	712	9.6
1982	7,114	100.0	1,131	15.9	136	1.9	563	7.9
1983	7,039	100.0	1,089	15.5	139	2.0	511	7.3
1984	7,161	100.0	1,729	24.1	135	1.9	478	6.7
1985	6,964	100.0	1,767	25.4	152	2.2	358	5.1
1986	4,846	100.0	1,551	32.0	117	2.4	344	7.1
1987	4,555	100.0	1,540	33.8	101	2.2	361	7.9
1988	3,396	100.0	1,255	37.0	77	2.3	225	6.6

Japanese knives		Jack-knives		Other swords		Others	
Number	Percentage	Number	Percentage	Number	Percentage	Number	Percentage
55	16.7	...	...	...	...	209	63.5
377	21.2	...	...	...	...	1,214	68.2
863	20.7	...	...	...	...	2,742	65.7
1,091	16.5	...	...	...	...	4,898	73.9
1,519	16.5	...	...	...	...	6,618	72.0
954	15.8	...	...	...	...	4,383	72.4
1,102	16.4	...	...	...	...	4,703	70.0
872	17.1	...	...	...	...	3,376	66.2
1,003	17.3	...	...	...	...	3,754	64.7
682	12.5	134	2.5	779	14.3	2,453	44.9
739	13.1	119	2.1	1,049	18.5	2,272	40.1
866	14.7	178	3.0	1,364	23.2	1,945	33.1
1,046	13.5	134	1.7	1,442	18.6	2,852	36.8
888	14.0	109	1.7	1,447	22.8	1,568	24.8
796	14.2	52	0.9	1,682	30.1	1,306	23.4
604	15.0	29	0.7	522	12.9	1,656	41.1
560	11.6	106	2.2	1,002	20.8	1,795	37.2
693	13.2	22	0.4	1,102	20.9	2,099	39.9
731	12.9	16	0.3	1,219	21.6	2,207	39.0
660	10.0	31	0.5	1,324	20.1	2,634	40.0
564	8.1	26	0.4	1,242	17.8	2,897	41.5
581	7.7	16	0.2	1,375	18.2	3,251	43.0
473	5.6	31	0.4	1,378	16.4	4,184	49.8
562	6.4	38	0.4	1,506	17.1	4,132	46.8
505	5.3	31	0.3	1,459	15.3	4,742	49.7
498	5.6	40	0.5	1,543	17.5	4,121	46.6
440	5.6	22	0.3	1,482	18.9	3,563	45.5
381	6.4	15	0.3	1,270	21.3	2,595	43.5
400	5.8	24	0.3	1,335	19.5	3,384	49.3
410	5.5	17	0.2	1,584	21.3	3,542	47.5
265	3.7	8	0.1	1,305	18.3	3,706	52.1
262	3.7	21	0.3	1,085	15.4	3,932	55.9
225	3.1	31	0.4	1,136	15.9	3,427	47.9
149	2.1	17	0.2	980	14.1	3,541	50.8
115	2.4	19	0.4	775	16.0	1,925	39.7
102	2.2	15	0.3	622	13.7	1,814	39.8
90	2.2	19	0.6	540	15.9	1,190	35.0

Source: National Police Agency

the police from citizens on gangster-involved civil disputes as these arising from the loaning of money, tenancy of real estate and amicable settlement in compensation for traffic accidents. Although gangs' meddling in these civil disputes are not new, the statistics suggest that gangsters are now living closely with the general public and are utilizing the civil troubles positively as major money sources during the period under review. This may be regarded as one of the diversified revenue sources of gangs. Also, activities as sokaiya professional shareholders' meeting racketeers and involvement in real estate racketeering and stock speculation operations are also regarded as activities seeking for the diversified money sources. Considering the situation, it is safe to conclude that the diversification and modernization of gangster syndicate management have been drastically progressing.

Another thing we have to note is the progress of armament of gang organizations with guns and other weapons. Table 20 shows the fluctuation in the number of weapons seized from gang syndicates and members. The table shows the marked changes of weapons at gangsters use, from swords and daggers to guns, in step with the changing times. In terms of guns, the number seized and its percentage against the total weapons seized increased since around 1970. Especially, the numbers increased in early 1980s. In recent years, the number of guns occupies about one-third of the all weapons seized. The progress of the armament is the top secret of each syndicate and thus we have to count a large dark figure in those crimes related to weapons. The armament number must be further progressing in reality. Thus, there is concern that the proliferation of high-powered weapons will further progress as gang syndicates have to supplement declining strength due to the difficulties in recruiting successors and the aging of the members.

Finally, we have to point out "internationalization" as one of the important trends of gang syndicates in recent years. Data on internationalization are not necessarily sufficient but we can make light of the following points judging from the recent trend in their crimes.

Crimes involving drugs and weapons, such as violations of the Stimulant Drug Control Law and the Firearms and Swords Control Law, are committed on the international stage in many cases. Considering the situation that these crimes have been frequently taking place, we have to assume that the cooperation between Japanese gangs and foreign criminal syndicates has been considerably progressing. Gambling tours to other countries and tours to obtain drivers' licenses are mostly done in cooperation between Japanese and foreign local gangs, we assume.

In recent years, the violations of regulations on businesses affecting public morals and illegal employment of foreign workers are becoming a social problem. Since the cases are illegal, domestic and foreign criminal organizations are usually involved in their entry into the country, residence and employment. It is worried that Japanese gangs will strengthen ties with foreign syndicates through these activities.

Overseas activities of Japanese gangs, in addition to the above-mentioned activities, so far include operating nightclubs, bars and souvenir shops, introduction of gambling spots and prostitutes to Japanese tourists and sale of pornographic films. Because of the limitation in their language ability, their areas of activity are limited to countries where many Japanese travel. However, as the occasions for strengthening the ties with foreign syndicates increase at home and abroad, "internationalization" of gang syndicates is expected to further progress for the Japanese gangs.

Chapter III. TREATMENT OF OFFENDERS

Section 1. Prosecution and Trials

1. OUTLINE

(1) Organization of Courts and Public Prosecutors Offices

A. Prewar Systems

The prewar organization of courts and public prosecutors offices was established by the Court Organization Law, which was promulgated in February 1890 and came into effect on Nov. 1 of the same year, and other laws. Ordinary courts were divided into four categories–the Great Court of Judicature (Daishinin), Courts of Appeals (kosoin), District Court (chiho saibansho) and Local Courts (ku saibansho). In 1926, the Great Courts of Judicature was located in Tokyo, and there were seven courts of appeals, in Tokyo, Osaka, Nagoya, Hiroshima, Nagasaki, Miyagi and Sapporo; 51 district courts, in Hakodate, Asahikawa, Kushiro and Karafuto (Sakhalin) in addition to the capitals of all prefectures; and 281 local courts. Under the Court Organization Law, a Public Prosecutors Office (kenjikyoku) was attached to each court, except for the Civil District Court.

(In August 1945, the Nagasaki Court of Appeals was moved and renamed the Fukuoka Court of Appeals, and the Takamatsu Court of Appeals was newly established. In May 1935, the Tokyo District Court was abolished, and the Tokyo Civil District Court and the Tokyo Criminal District Court were set up.)

The Great Court of Judicature was headed by the President of the Great Court of Judicature, a Court of Appeal, by the Chief Judge of the Court of Appeals, and a District Court, by the President of the District Court and other judges were assinged to these courts.

The Public Prosecutors Office of the Great Court of Judicature was headed by the Prosecutor General, a Public Prosecutors Office of the Court of Appeals, by the Superintendent Prosecutor of the Court of Appeals and a Public Prosecutors Office of the District Court, by the Chief Prosecutor of the District Court and other public prosecutors were assigned to these public prosecutors offices.

As of 1926, the subject matter jurisdiction over criminal cases was as stated below: first, the Great Court of Judicature had the power to render final judgements over (1) jokoku appeals from the judgments of the courts of appeals and from the judgments rendered by the district courts as the courts of second instance, (2) kokoku appeals, stipulated by the law, from the rulings (kettei) or orders (meirei) rendered by the district courts as the courts of the second instance (3) kokoku appeals, stiplulated by law, from the rulings or orders rendered by the court of appeals and (4) kokoku appeals from the rulings by which the district courts or local courts had dismissed jokoku appeals.

In addition, the Great Court of Judicature had special jurisdiction, as court of both the first and final instance at the same time, over preliminary inquiry proceedings and trials of offences committed against Imperial family members, except defamation of the Imperial family, and over offences of insurrection and offences which were committed by Imperial family members and which might deserve imprisonment without labour or heavier punishment.

Second, a court of appeals had jurisdiction over (1) koso appeals from first-instance judgments of district courts and (2) kokoku appeals, stipulated by law, from rulings or orders rendered by district courts as courts of first instance (except for those belonging to the power of the Great Court of Judicature).

Third, a district court, (1) as court of first instance, had jurisdiction over criminal cases that did not belong to the exclusive jurisdiction of a local court or the special jurisdiction of the Great Court of Judicature, and, (2) as court of second instance, over koso appeals from judgments by local courts and over kokoku appeals, stipulated by law, from rulings or orders rendered by local courts (except for those belonging to the jurisdiction of the Great Court of Judicature).

Fourth, a local court had jurisdiction over offences which did not undergo preliminary inquiry proceedings and which were punishable by penal detention or minor fines or by determinate terms of imprisonment with or without labour (excluding offences punishable by imprisonment with or without labour for less than one year of minimum penality) or by fines.

Public prosecutors were required to perform their duties independently from courts, and it was made clear that each public prosecutor had the characteristic of a fullfledged office in the prosecutorial setup in performing the role of a prosecutor.

B. Postwar Systems

The postwar organization of courts and public prosecutors offices is provided by the Court Organization Law and the Public Prosecutors Office Law, both of which were promulgated in April 1947 and came into effect on May 3 of the same year, and other laws. These laws abolished the public prosecutors offices (kenjikyoku) that had until then been attached to the courts and newly established separate public prosecutors offices (kensatsucho).

The Supreme Court was located in Tokyo, and as lower courts, a total of eight High Courts were set up in Tokyo, Osaka, Nagoya, Hiroshima, Fukuoka, Sendai, Sapporo and Takamatsu. A total of 49 District Courts were established–in Hakodate, Asahikawa and Kushiro in addition to all prefectural capitals. (The Naha District Court was set up in May 1972). Also, 557 Summary Courts were set up. In January 1949, 49 Family Courts were established–one in each city where a district court was situated–to deal with family affairs as well as juvenile delinquency cases. (The Naha Family Court was set up in May 1972).

As for public prosecutors offices, the Supreme Public Prosecutors Office, High Public Prosecutors Offices, District Public Prosecutors Offices and Local Public Prosecutors Offices were established corresponding to the Surpeme Court, High Courts, District Courts and Summary Courts, respectively.

A Supreme Court Chief Justice and Supreme Court Justices were appointed to the Supreme Court, a High Court Chief Judge and judges to each high court, judges and assistant judges to each district court and family court, and summary court judges at each summary court.

A Prosecutor General, a Deputy Prosecutor General and public prosecutors were appointed to the Supreme Public Prosecutors Office, a Superintendent Prosecutor and public prosecutors were appointed to each High Public Prosecutors Office, a Chief Prosecutor and public prosecutors to each District Public Prosecutors Office, and a public prosecutor and assistant public prosecutors to each Local Public Prosecutors Office.

The subject matter jurisdiction over criminal cases of each category of court is as follows:

The Supreme Court has jurisdiction over jokoku appeals and over kokoku appeals specially provided by the Code of Criminal Procedure.

A High Court has jurisdiction over koso appeals from first-instance judgments by district courts, judgments by family courts and judgments by summary courts in criminal cases, over kokoku appeals from rulings and orders rendered by district courts and family courts, and rulings and orders rendered by summary courts on criminal cases (excluding what belongs to the jurisdiction of the Supreme Court).

In addition, a High Court has jurisdiction over first instances of cases in which the court has first-instance jurisdiction, including insurrections.

A District Court has jurisdiction over first instances of cases concerning offences other than those punishable only by penalties lighter than fines (excluding those insurrections and other offences over which a High Court has first-instance jurisdiction).

A Family Court has jurisdiction over hearings and dispositions of juvenile deliquency cases provided for under the Juvenile Law and over first-instance trials of criminal cases involving adult offenders who committed the offences affecting the welfare of children.

A Summary Court has first-instance jurisdiction over (1) cases concerning offences punishable only by penalties of fines and lighter than fines, (2) offences for which fines are provided as an alternative penalty, and (3) offences of habitual gambling, offences of running a gambling house, theft, attempted theft, embezzlement and offences involving stolen property, etc. (excluding cases coming under the exclusive jurisdiction of a Family Court).

(2) Criminal Proceedings

A. Prewar Systems

The prewar criminal proceedings were provided by the so-called old Code of Criminal Procedure, which was promulgated in May 1922 and enforced on Jan. 1, 1924, the Jury Law, which was promulgated in April 1923 (coming partially into effect on June 1, 1927 and completely on Oct. 1, 1928), and the Summary Proceedings for Police Infractions promulgated in September 1885.

The systems that existed before the war but ceased to be practised after the war were the preliminary inquiry proceedings system, the jury system and the system of prompt dispositions in accordance with the Summary Proceedings for Police Infractions.

The first volume (general provisions) of the old Code of Criminal Procedure provided for jurisdiction of courts; causes and procedure for disqualifying of a judge or court clerk by challenges of parties on trial or by the initiation of a judge or clerk; competency to stand trial; right to counsel and assistance; judgments; judicial documents; serving of writs, etc.; period of time; summonses of defendants; arrest and detention; questioning of defendants; seizure and search; inspection; questioning of witnesses; expert testimony; interpreting, and costs of proceedings.

The second volume (first instance) provided for criminal investigation, prosecution, preliminary inquiry proceedings by examining judges and public trials.

The third and succeeding volumes provided for appeals, the proceedings belonging to the exclusive jurisdiction of the Great Court of Judicature, retrials, extraordinary appeals, summary order proceedings without hearing, the execution of sentences, etc., and private action by the victims of crimes.

The old Code of Criminal Procedure of 1922 provided that the institution of public action should be prerequisite to the commencement of court trials (the principle of no trial without prior prosecution) and abolished exceptions existing in the preceding Code of Criminal Procedure, promulgated in October 1890 (enforced on November 1, 1890) in which a person who committed an offence in the presence of a judge in court could be tried by the judge immediately in court and in which in the course of a trial it appeared that the defendant had committed another subordinate offence, the judge could try the defendant on a new subordinate charge without further prosecution.

The old Code of Criminal Procedure of 1922 also put in a statutory form the principle of discretionary prosecution, which had conventionally been practised in place of instituting a public prosecution, and approved also the withdrawal of a public prosecution and the abandonment or withdrawal of an appeal. While expanding the scope in which the investigating authorities were able to exercise their compulsive power, the old Code of Criminal Procedure made it possible for a defendant to hire a defense counsel after information had been filed even during a preliminary inquiry proceeding as well as in a public trial.

Under the preliminary inquiry proceeding that the old Code of Criminal Procedure provided for, an examining judge conducted a relevant investigation to determine whether the case of a particular defendant should be put on trial or not. Because no examining judge was assigned to a Local Court, a case under exclusive jurisdiction of a Local Court was directly referred to public trial without going through the preliminary inquiry proceeding.

Public prosecutors, in instituting a public prosecution of a case belonging to the jurisdiction of a District Court, were able to either directly request a public trial or ask for a preliminary inquiry proceeding. In principle, a preliminary inquiry proceeding was held upon the request of the public prosecutors. When requested, an examining judge conducted seizure, search and inspection of premises, etc., questioned witnesses who were deemed difficult to summon for a public trial and questioned the defendant. Finally, after hearing the statement of the public prosecutor and the defense of the defendant, the examining judge made a decision either to refer the case to trial in court, if a prima facie case for the prosecution had been established, or, if not, to dismiss the case with prejudice. Also, under certain other specified conditions, the examining judge entered rulings of lack of jurisdiction, dismissal without prejudice of public prosecution or dismissal with prejudice of the case examined.

The jury system provided by the Jury Law referred to the system of a so-called trial jury. It was introduced in the public trial of criminal courts of the first instance. There, the twelve jurors, after the questioning the defendant by the presiding judge and others, examination of evidence, statement of public prosecutor and statements of defense counsel and defendant had been completed, made deliberations on the existence or non-existence of those facts constituting the crimes charged and returned their verdict to the presiding judge. The jury system adopted the majority verdict principle. The court had the power to order retrial of a case by another jury when it perceived that the verdict of the jury was improper.

Special cases involving offences under exclusive jurisdiction of the Great Court of Judicature were excluded from the jury system. The system was applied to those cases belonging to the jurisdiction of a District Court involving such offences as those punishable by death, imprisonment for life with or without labour (called a guaranteed jury) and punishable by long-term imprisonment with or without labour for three years or more upon the request of the defendant (called a requested jury). In either event, the jury system was applied in actuality to cases in which the defendant had not admitted the prosecution's charges.

The defendant was not allowed to make a koso appeal of a judgment that a District Court had passed on a case after accepting a jury's verdict, but he was able to lodge a jokoku appeal for other reasons than errors of fact.

The Jury Law fully came into effect on Oct. 1, 1928, and was suspended on April 1, 1943. In cases in which a jury trial was guaranteed by law (guaranteed jury), there were many defendants who admitted the prosecution's charges against them or waived a trial by jury, and in those cases in which a request from the defendant was a prerequisite to a jury trial (requested jury), only an extremely small number of defendants requested a jury. According to the Annual Report on Criminal Statistics, throughout the period (of 14 years and six months) when the jury system was in effect, the numbers of defendants tried by juries classified by final results were: 403 who were sentenced; 94 who were found not guilty; 88 who were subjected to trials in which the public prosecution was dismissed; and 26 who were subjected to another jury.

Dispositions provided by the Summary Proceedings for Police Infractions were those that the chief of a police station or a police substation or a civil servant acting as his deputy promptly imposed on offences against police regulations (offences punishable by penal detention or minor fines). In such prompt dispositions, a sentence was immediately passed after hearing the defendant's statement and examining evidence; or without summoning the defendant, or when the defendant did not appear after he was summoned, a sentence in written form was immediately served to the defendant himself or his address.

When the defendant directly received a sentence in a prompt disposition, he was able to request a formal trial within three days, and when the defendant was served a sentence in written form, he was able to do so within five days. When such a request was made, a formal trial was held at a Local Court.

B. Wartime Legislation

During the war, in March 1941, the National Defense and Security Law (enforced on May 10, 1941) and the Maintenance of Public Order Law (enforced on May 15, 1941, a complete revision of the Maintenance of Public Order Law promulgated in April 1925) were successively promulgated. Each of the two laws provided for its own special criminal procedure-the former concerning such crimes as leakage of state secrets, and the latter concerning such crimes as the act of forming an association for the purpose of changing the so-called national basic structure or the act of knowingly participating in such a group.

Both laws enabled public prosecutors to detain the suspects to conduct compulsory investigations prior to instituting prosecution, such as search and seizure and inspection of premises, etc. Also, it was provided that a defence counsel should be appointed from among those designated by the Justice Minister beforehand and that the defendant should not be able to make a koso appeal from a first instance judgment and was able only to make a direct jokoku appeal to the Great Court of Judicature when he had sufficient grounds to do so.

Under the Maintenance of Public Order Law, moreover, a preventive detention system was newly established for those who had committed the crimes specified in the first chapter of the law (such crimes as the act of forming an association for the purpose of changing the national basic structure or the act of knowingly participating in such a group) and who had been sentenced for the crimes.

The Special Wartime Criminal Law, which was promulgated in February 1942 (enforced on March 21, 1942) provided for the limitation of the number of defence counsels and the simplification of judgment in writing as part of criminal procedure during the war. A partial revision of the law was promulgated in October 1943 (enforced on Nov. 15, 1943) to stipulate exceptional summary order procedure without a hearing, which permitted summary imposition of imprisonment with or without labour for one year or less and penal detention except that for theft and similar crimes, summary imposition of imprisonment with labour for three years or less was permissible.

The wartime exception to the Court Organization Law was promulgated in February 1942 (implemented on March 21, 1942) to provide that koso appeals should not be filed against first-instance judgements covering offences against public security and order and offences of robbery and theft, but that jokoku appeals might be filed when there are sufficient grounds.

The partial revision of the same law was promulgated in October 1943 (implemented on Nov. 15, 1943) and provided that local courts should have subject matter jurisdiction over offences punishable by imprisonment with or without labour for definite terms of one year or more, if the cases did not go through preliminary inquiry proceedings under examining judges The same partial revision also adopted a two-instance system that did not allow a koso appeal in any case.

C. Postwar Systems

After the war, from 1945 to 1947, the Maintenance of Public Order Law, the National Security Law, the Special Wartime Criminal Law, the wartime exception to the Court Organization Law, the Summary Proceedings for Police Infractions and other related laws and ordinances were successively abolished.

(a) Enactment of the New Code of Criminal Procedure, etc.

After the postwar Constitution of Japan was promulgated on Nov. 3, 1946 (implemented on May 3, 1947), the Law Concerning Emergency Measures on the Code of Criminal Procedure in Accordance with the Enforcement of the Constitution of Japan was promulgated on April 19, 1947 (implemented on May 3, 1947). The new law provided for the right of a suspect under arrest to choose a defence counsel and established the system of a court-appointed lawyer for a defendant. It also provided that a warrant issued by a judge should be necessary to conduct a compulsory investigation aimed at collecting demonstrative evidence and securing physical custody and that a suspect may refuse to testify against himself, and limited the admissibility and probative value of evidence and abolished the preliminary inquiry proceedings under examining judges. The law thus stipulated temporary measures on the old Code of Criminal Procedure.

The current Code of Criminal Procedure was promulgated in July 1948 (implemented on Jan. 1, 1949), greatly changing the criminal proceedings. In keeping with the spirit of the Constitution, the new law revised the old Code of Criminal Procedure. Based on the fundamental idea to ascertain the real truth of the fact in a case and to secure the protection of fundamental human rights of suspects and defendants at the same time, the new law introduced much of the Anglo-American legal principles and practises on the European Continental ideology and procedures (The old Code had been patterned after Continental laws for almost 70 years).

The major points of the revisions consisted of (1) a requiring that an indictment should not be accompanied by documents or evidnece when filed at court of trial, (2) abolishing the preliminary inquiry proceeding under the examining judges, (3) strengthening the principle of trial in court in connection with hearing proceedings and rules of evidence, (4) introducing the rules of evidence restricting the admissibility and probative value of evidence as well as the hearsay evidence rule, (5) requiring, in general, that a warrant of a judge should be obtained as the pre-requisite of the compulsory investigation to be carried out by the police and public prosecutors, (6) upholding the rights of a suspect and defendant to refuse to make statements against their will and permitting a suspect under arrest and detention to appoint a defence counsel, (7) establishing the system of a court-appointed defence counsel for a defendant, (8) securing for those detained the right to demand from the detaining judge the disclosure of the grounds for detention, (9) changing the fundamental character of koso appeals from the old system of so-called trial de novo (retrail of whole case) to that of reviewing of errors in the judgements of lower courts, and (10) restricting the grounds for jokoku appeals to the Supreme Court so that error in law in itself does not constitute sufficient reason for jokoku appeal.

(b) Amendments of the Code of Criminal Procedure, etc.

Subsequent amendments of the new Code of Criminal Procedure were as follows:

An amendment was made in December 1948 (implemented on Jan. 1, 1949) to partially revise the procedure of summary order without a hearing requiring a written consent of the defendant to start with the proceeding, and two amendments were made in May 1949 (implemented on May 28, 1949) one resulting from the establishment of family courts, and the other to newly provide for regulations on such matters as collection of fingerprints from suspects under arrest.

In July 1952, an amendment of the Code of Criminal Procedure was made (implemented on July 21, 1952) in accordance with the enforcement of the Anti-Subversive Activities Law, and another amendment was made in the same month (implemented on Aug. 1, 1952) to read "homu sosai" (Attorney General) as "homu daijin" (the Minister of Justice). (The Office of Attorney General had been established after the war in place of the Justice Ministry but reorganized again as the present Justice Ministry.)

Including some changes in wording, a partial revision of the Code of Criminal Procedure was made in August 1953 (and was put into effect on Nov. 5, 1953).

The main points of revision included the following:

Offences punishable by imprisonment with or without labour for a minimum penalty of less than one year were added to those offences for which no limit should be set to the number of renewals of a period of detention, and those for which no bail of right should be approved.

Added to the cases in which no bail of right should be approved were cases in which there was reason enough to suspect that the defendant would do acts to harm or threaten his victims. Added to the cases in which bail should be canceled were cases in which the defendant did acts to harm or attempted to harm or threaten his victims.

A poor defendant was exempted from paying the costs of trial; the wording in which the investigating authorities should inform a suspect of his right to refuse his testimony was changed; proceedings for a trial were stipulated for defendants under detention who violently resisted custodial officers in refusing to appear; a simplified public trial procedure (in which rules of evidence may be applied more flexibly) was established for a defendant who would not dispute charges against him; and the scope of examination of facts was expanded (for example, the fact of victim compensation made after the judgement of the first instance court) for a trial of a koso appeal.

Also in August 1953, a partial revision of the Code of Criminal Procedure was made in accordance with the partial revision of the Penal Code in which the suspension of execution of sentence became permissable for a second time for those defendants who had been under the suspension of execution of sentence. (This revision came into effect on Dec. 1, 1953.)

After that, an amendment was made concerning the territorial jurisdiction of courts in April 1954 (and was brought into effect on July 1, 1954), and an amendment was made in June 1954 in accordance with the enforcement of the Police Law (and was put into effect on July 1, 1954).

A partial revision of the Code of Criminal Procedure was made in April 1958 (and was put into effect on May 20, 1958) to add cases in which it was feared that the defendant would do harm to relatives of his victims to cases in which bail of right should not be approved or bail should be canceled.

The same revision also provided for proceedings to order the defendant to leave the courtroom or other place where testimony was taken when it was believed that a witness (summoned on a fixed date for a public trial or on dates other than that fixed for public trial) could not give sufficient testimony because of the pressure of appearing in front of the defendant.

An amendment of the Code of Criminal Procedure concerning fees for expert examinations by an expert witness was made in April 1971 (and was put into effect on July 1, 1971), and amendments were made in May 1976 (and put into effect on July 1, 1976) to revise provisions concerning the costs of trial and to establish provisions for indemnifying trial costs when a judgment of not guilty was finalized.

An amendment was made in March 1979 (and was put into effect on Oct. 1, 1980) in accordance with the enforcement of the Law for Execution of Civil Judgements, and another amendment was made in May 1986 (and was put into effect on April 1, 1987) in accordance with the enforcement of the law on special measures concerning the handling of legal business by foreign lawyers.

In December 1988, an amendment was made in accordance with the enforcement of the law concerning the holidays of courts (and the amendment was put into effect on Jan. 1, 1989).

(c) Proceedings to Confiscate Property Owned by Third Parties in Criminal Cases

In confiscating property owned by some person other than the defendant (a third party), a system became necessary as part of the proceedings of a criminal case to secure prior notification, a chance for explanation, and defence and ex post facto relief for the third party, aimed at protecting the third party, or the owner. For that purpose, the law on stopgap measures concerning the confiscation of property owned by a third party in criminal cases was promulgated in July 1963 (and was put into effect on Aug. 1, 1963) to stipulate the proceedings in which a person who owns property likely to be confiscated can participate in the criminal trial proceedings as a third party.

(d) System for Summary Procedure of Traffic Cases

The number of so-called traffic cases increased, and an ordinary trial procedure delayed the handling of such cases. Moreover, the contents of traffic cases were simple, and their situations were typical. Therefore, a special method was devised to handle such cases.

In February 1954, the so-called on-the-spot summary order procedure without hearing was adopted in Tokyo in which the three parties consisting of the police officer, the public prosecutor, and the judge sit in the same building or neighboring buildings to complete their respective procedures of referral, indictment and trial–like an assembly line. Later, similar procedures were adopted throughout the country.

The Law Concerning Summary Trial Procedure for Traffic Violation Cases was promulgated in May 1954 (and was put into effect on Nov. 1, 1954), so that a summary court was able to impose a fine of 50,000 yen or less or a minor fine in a speedy trial to be held before a public trial if the defendant did not object. (The fine of 50,000 yen or less was changed to 200,000 yen or less effective from July 1, 1972, as a result of the partial revision, promulgated in June 1972, of the Law of Temporary Measures Concerning Fine, etc.)

The so-called traffic ticket system, in which records of traffic cases were made into simple form, was adopted in January 1963 (and was implemented throughout the country in 1966), and a revision of the Road Traffic Law was promulgated in August 1967 (and was brought into effect on July 1, 1968) to adopt the traffic infraction notification system.

Under this notification system, when the driver of an automobile committed a certain low-danger violation (traffic infraction), he would be exempt from public prosecution if he paid a non-penal fine after being notified of the amount to be paid, except if the driver belonged to a certain category, including those who did not have driver's licences.

At first, juveniles were excluded, but an amendment of the Road Traffic Law was promulgated in May 1970 (and was brought into effect on Aug. 20, 1970) which applied the system to juveniles. Later, an amendment of the law was promulgated in May 1986 (and was put into effect on April 1, 1987) to expand the range of application of the traffic infraction notification system.

(3) The System of Suspension of Prosecution

A de facto system of suspension of prosecution began in 1885, but this was partly because of the criminal policy that trials should be avoided in insignificant cases lacking the necessity of punishment, and partly, in terms of government finances, because prison-related expenses should be curtailed, because they had increased with the increasing number of prisoners.

The system of suspension of prosecution was given legal grounds for the first time with the old Code of Criminal Procedure that was promulgated in May 1922 (and put into effect on Jan. 1, 1924). The system was inherited by the current Code of Criminal Procedure.

Article 279 of the old Code of Criminal Procedure provided that public prosecution of an offender might not be carried out if prosecution was not necessary due to the character, age or circumstances of the offender, and because of the circumstances surrounding the offence and the situation after the offence.

Article 248 of the current Code of Criminal Procedure has similar provisions, and the system of suspension of prosecution in Japan has remained unchanged since before the war.

(4) The System of Suspension of Execution of Sentences

The system of suspended execution of sentences was first adopted with the promulgation in April 1905 (and enforcement on April 1, 1905) of the Law Concerning the Suspension of Execution of Sentences.

According to the law, when a qualified person was sentenced to imprisonment without labour for one year or less, depending on circumstances, the execution of the sentence might be suspended within a period ranging from two years to five years from the day his sentence was finalized. The qualified person was one who previously had not been sentenced to imprisonment without labour or heavier punishment, or one who previously had been sentenced to imprisonment without labour or heavier punishment but who had not been sentenced to imprisonment without labour or heavier punishment within 10 years (a period of disqualification due to a previous criminal record) of the day of completion of the punishment, or the day the execution of the sentence was excused.

The existing Penal Code, which was promulgated in April 1907 (and was put into effect on Oct. 1, 1908), also provided for the suspension of execution of sentences, and its conditions for such suspension were almost the same as the previous ones, except that the period of disqualification due to a previous criminal record was changed to seven years and that the Penal Code stipulated that a person sentenced to imprisonment with or without labour for two years or less might have his sentence suspended within a period ranging from one year to five years from the day his sentence was finalized.

A partial revision of the Penal Code was promulgated in October 1947 (and was put into effect on Nov. 15, 1947) to allow the suspension of execution for imprisonment with or without labour for three years or less or for fines of 5,000 yen or less. (The stipulation concerning fines of 5,000 yen or less was changed to fines of 50,000 yen or less from Feb. 1, 1949, by the Law of Temporary Measures Concerning Fines, etc., promulgated in December 1948, and was changed to fines of 200,000 yen or less from July 1, 1972, by a partial revision of the same law promulgated in June 1972.)

Another partial revision of the Penal Code was promulgated in August 1953 (and was put into effect on Dec. 1, 1953) to shorten the period of disqualification due to a previous criminal record from seven to five years and also to allow a person under the suspension of execution of sentence to be given a second suspension of execution of sentence with probation, provided that the sentence to be imposed was imprisonment with or without labour for one year or less.

Another partial revision of the Penal Code was promulgated in April 1954 (and was put into effect on July 1, 1954) so that a person who was given a suspended execution of sentence for the first time might be placed under probation at the discretion of courts.

(5) Summary Order Procedure without Hearing

The summary order procedure was approved for the first time by the Criminal Summary Order Procedure Law promulgated in April 1913 (and put into effect June 1, 1913), which provided that a local court, at the request of a public prosecutor, might impose a fine or a minor fine on a defendant in a criminal case belonging to its jurisdiction with a summary order before a public trial, if the defendant did not object. (The defendant who received the summary order was able to apply within seven days for a formal trial.)

After that, the old Criminal Procedure Code was promulgated in May 1922 (and was put into effect on Jan. 1, 1924) to similarly provide that fines or minor fines may be imposed with a summary order.

A partial revision of the Special Wartime Criminal Law was promulgated in October 1943 (and was put into effect on Nov. 13, 1943) so that it became possible to impose, with a summary order, imprisonment with or without labour for one year or less (imprisonment with labour for three years or less for theft, etc.) or penal detention.

But the law was abolished in January 1946, making it impossible to impose imprisonment with or without labour or penal detention with a summary order.

The exisiting Code of Criminal Procedure, promulgated in July 1948 (and put into effect on Jan. 1, 1949), provided that a summary court may impose fines of 5,000 yen or less or minor fines with a summary order. After that, the maximum sum of fines that might be imposed with summary orders was increased to 50,000 yen by the Law of Temporary Measures Concerning Fine, etc., promulgated in December 1948 (and carried into effect on Feb. 1, 1949), and again a partial revision of the law was promulgated in June 1972 (and was carried into effect on July 1972) to further increase the sum to 200,000 yen.

2. PROSECUTION

(1) Changes in the Number of Suspects Received by Public Prosecutors Offices

A. Total Number of Newly Received Suspects

Attached Table 4 shows changes in the total number of suspects newly received by the public prosecutors offices (which were called kenjikyoku–Prosecution Bureau–before 1946) in the Showa era, and their breakdown into Penal Code offences excluding professional negligence (from 1975 thereafter, excluding traffic professional negligence), professional negligence, offences against special laws excluding the Road Traffic Law, violations of Road Traffic Law, etc. (Because no data are available on the number of newly received suspects for 1948 and the years before, the number of newly received cases is shown for those years. No data are available for 1945, and no data except those on the total number are available for the period from 1926 to 1930 and for 1944.)

The total number of cases received by the public prosecutors office continued to increase from about 370,000 in the first year of Showa (1926) to more than 500,000 annually from 1933 to 1935, but the number gradually decreased after that and remained between about 350,000 and 390,000 from 1939 to 1944. As a result of the confusion immediately after the war, the number of such cases also sharply increased to about 500,000 in 1946, about 1.1 million in 1947 and about 1.62 million in 1948, and the number of such suspects stayed at the high level of about 1.63 million to 1.66 million between 1949 and 1951.

Then in 1952, the number of suspects dropped to about 1.43 million, but it again showed an upward trend due to an increase in the number of traffic-related offences. It exceeded 2 million in 1954 and topped 3 million in 1960, and it recorded about 5.92 million in 1965.

Partly due to a decrease in the number of road traffic offences resulting from the introduction of the traffic infractions notification system in 1968, the number of suspects received by the public prosecutors offices fell to about 4.05 million the same year and plunged to about 2.7 million in 1969.

However, the number took an upward turn again in 1971 due to the increase in traffic-related suspects received and then showed fluctuations until it registered about 3.24 million in 1986. Partly because the public prosecutors offices received fewer road traffic violators after the scope of application of the traffic infractions notification system was expanded in 1987, the total number of suspects received sharply dropped to about 2.56 million that year and to about 2.3 million in 1988.

B. Penal Code Offenders and Special Law Offenders

Looking at the trends in Penal Code offences, excluding professional negligence, received by the public prosecutors office in the prewar years, the cases involving such Penal Code offences increased from about 320,000 in 1931 to about 390,000 in 1934 and then dropped to about 220,000 in 1941 and to about 190,000 in 1942 and 1943.

After the war, the number of such cases increased from 290,000 in 1946, and the number of such offenders received was between about 590,000 and 630,000 from 1949 to 1951. From 1952, the number of such suspects showed a downward trend, with some fluctuations, and it fell to about 500,000 in 1964 and to about 360,000 in 1974. While showing fluctuations, the number increased from 1975 until it reached about 400,000 in 1982. After that, it continued to decrease again and fell to 345,273 in 1988.

Looking at the trends in special law offences, excluding traffic offences, received by the public prosecutors office in prewar years, the number of cases involving such special law offences was 85,728 in 1931 and remained between 100,000 and 120,000 from 1933 to 1937 and then dropped to between 80,000 and 90,000. As a result of an increase in violations of laws and ordinances aimed at controlling the economy, including the National General Mobilization Law, however, the number of such cases started increasing in 1940 and rose to 161,132 in 1943.

After the war, there were about 200,000 such cases in 1946, and the number then sharply increased in accordance with a rise in violations of economic control laws and ordinances, including the Staple Food Control Law. The number of such cases reached about 970,000 in 1948, and the number of such offenders registered about 860,000 in 1949.

But the number of such offenders started decreasing in 1950 and plummeted to about 180,000 in 1956. After that, the number was between 100,000 to 110,000 most of the time, though the figure went up to the range of between 180,000 and 280,000 in 1959, 1963, 1967, 1979 and 1983 as a result of an increase of election law violators. The number was 110,562 in 1988, a slight drop from

Table 21 Number of Penal Code Offenders by Prosecution and Non-prosecution, etc.

Year	Total	Prosecution (A)	Formal trial (B)	$\frac{B}{A}$ (%)	Summary Proceed-ings (C)	$\frac{C}{A}$ (%)
1931	281,758	56,800	29,789	52.4	27,011	47.6
1936	315,285	69,003	37,336	54.1	31,667	45.9
1941	199,681	56,772	28,495	50.2	28,277	49.8
1946	349,450	159,386	109,547	68.7	49,839	31.3
1951	621,819	166,482	115,716	69.5	50,766	30.5
1956	625,058	236,245	123,547	52.3	112,698	47.7
1961	665,340	291,327	112,500	38.6	178,827	61.4
1966	855,799	420,216	104,178	24.8	316,038	75.2
1971	1,066,824	571,263	91,501	16.0	479,762	84.0
1976	851,792	442,586	102,698	23.2	339,888	76.8
1981	887,451	437,286	91,235	20.9	346,051	79.1
1986	924,928	473,005	82,911	17.5	390,094	82.5
1988	936,784	322,708	71,912	22.3	250,796	77.7

Sources: Annual Report of Criminal Statistics and Annual Report of Statistics on Prosecution

the previous year.

C. Professional Negligence and Road Traffic Offences

Before the war, the number of offences from professional or gross negligence received by the public prosecutors offices gradually increased from 13,958 in 1931, and the number was between 19,000 and 20,000 from 1935 to 1937. Then the number decreased until it registered 6,982 in 1943.

After the war, the number of such cases gradually increased from 4,450 in 1946. The number of such offenders topped 20,000 in 1952 and continued to rise further. It exceeded 100,000 in 1959, 300,000 in 1966 and 500,000 in 1968 until it remained at a high level between about 640,000 and 680,000 from 1969 to 1972. The number then decreased and registered about 460,000 in 1977, but it began to rise again in 1978 and reached about 585,841 in 1988.

Before the war, the number of cases involving road traffic offences newly received by public prosecutors offices fluctuated between about 9,900 and about

Non-prosecution			Referral to family court	Prosecution rate	Suspension rate
	Suspension	Others			
224,958	155,698	69,260	–	20.2	73.3
246,282	193,888	52,394	–	21.9	73.8
142,909	116,769	26,140	–	28.4	67.3
190,064	167,450	22,614	–	45.6	51.2
324,179	246,899	77,280	131,158	33.9	59.7
282,686	215,153	67,533	106,127	45.5	47.7
210,917	166,067	44,850	163,096	58.0	36.3
228,486	181,928	46,558	207,097	64.8	30.2
312,380	249,311	63,069	183,181	64.6	30.4
245,709	195,482	50,227	163,497	64.3	30.6
212,340	165,468	46,872	237,825	67.3	27.5
207,266	164,528	42,738	244,657	69.5	25.8
361,970	319,125	42,845	252,106	47.1	49.7

15,500 a year from 1931 to 1938, and then decreased to 1,512 in 1943.

After the war, the number of such cases sharply increased from 2,686 in 1946 and exceeded the 200,000 mark in 1948, when the Road Traffic Control Law came into effect. From 1964 to 1967, the number of traffic violators received by the public prosecutors offices ranged from about 4.5 million to 5 million, but the number took a sharp downward turn in 1968, when the traffic infractions notification system was put into effect. It decreased to about 1.47 million the following year, 1969.

The number of such traffic violators assumed an upward trend again in 1970, and the number fluctuated between about 2.19 million and 2.32 million from 1983 to 1986. In 1987, when the scope of application of the traffic infractions notification system was expanded, however, the number went down to about 1.5 million. It further decreased to about 1.26 million in 1988.

(2) Disposition of Suspects

A. Penal Code Offences

Table 21 shows changes in the number of Penal Code offenders as a

Table 22 Number of Penal Code Offenders Other Than

Year	Total	Prosecution (A)	Formal trial (B)	B/A (%)	Summary proceedings (C)	C/A (%)
1931	269,817	51,799	29,681	57.3	22,118	42.7
1936	298,580	62,375	37,211	59.7	25,164	40.3
1941	190,149	53,275	28,419	53.3	24,856	46.7
1946	345,960	158,108	109,429	69.2	48,679	30.8
1951	607,064	159,908	115,314	72.1	44,594	27.9
1956	557,544	194,168	122,619	63.2	71,549	36.8
1961	517,337	191,927	108,698	56.6	83,229	43.4
1966	493,722	187,635	94,672	50.5	92,963	49.5
1971	386,208	147,693	76,474	51.8	71,219	48.2
1976	375,735	148,825	92,209	62.0	56,616	38.0
1981	395,804	122,332	81,539	66.7	40,793	33.3
1986	353,642	100,041	72,309	72.3	27,732	27.7
1988	345,185	87,116	63,179	72.5	23,937	27.5

Sources: Annual Report of Criminal Statistics and
Annual Report of Statistics on Prosecution

whole, the number of those prosecuted, the number of those who were not prosecuted, the prosecution rate, the prosecution suspension rate, etc. The figures are those for every five years from 1931 and for 1988. The statistics before 1941 are in terms of cases.

Table 22 shows similar changes concerning Penal Code offenders excluding professional negligence (excluding traffic professional negligence for figures for 1976 and thereafter). Before the war, the prosecution rate of Penal Code offenders as a whole increased from 20.2 percent in 1931 to 28.4 percent in 1941.

After the war, the rate in 1946 registered 45.6 percent, considerably higher than the rates seen before the war. Although it dropped to 33.9 percent in 1951, the rate then increased again and fluctuated between 64.3 percent and 69.5 percent from 1966 to 1986. But it dropped again to 47.1 percent in 1988.

Until 1956, the prosecution rate of Penal Code offenders was almost the same as the prosecution rate of Penal Code offenders excluding professional

Professional Negligence, by Prosecution and Non-prosecution, etc.

Non-prosecution	Suspension	Others	Referral to family court	Prosecution rate	Suspension rate
218,018	152,980	65,038	—	19.2	74.7
236,205	188,448	47,757	—	20.9	75.1
136,874	113,180	23,694	—	28.0	68.0
187,852	166,224	21,628	—	45.7	51.3
317,136	243,119	74,017	130,020	33.5	60.3
265,123	204,146	60,977	98,253	42.3	51.3
184,630	150,368	34,262	140,780	51.0	43.9
149,251	117,759	31,492	156,836	55.7	38.6
128,825	102,299	26,526	109,690	53.4	40.9
108,953	85,241	23,712	117,957	57.7	36.4
88,471	69,039	19,432	185,001	58.0	36.1
68,151	53,433	14,718	185,450	59.5	34.8
69,426	53,013	16,413	188,643	55.7	37.8

negligence, which will be stated later. But from 1961 to 1986, during which the number of professional negligence offenders increased remarkably, the rate for Penal Code offenders as a whole was higher by about 7-11 percentage points than the rate for those excluding professional negligence. However, the former was about about 9 percentage points lower than the latter in 1988.

The fall in the overall rate in 1988 was caused by a decrease in the rate for professional negligence offenders.

Before the war, the rate of those prosecuted for formal trial proceedings (hereafter referred to as "formal trial prosecution rate") among the total prosecuted for all Penal Code offences was 52.4 percent in 1931, 54.1 percent in 1936 and 50.2 percent in 1941.

For some time after the war, the formal trial prosecution rate was higher than before the war, registering 68.7 percent in 1946 and 69.5 percent in 1951, but the rate started dropping in 1956 and fluctuated between 16.0 percent and 24.8 percent from 1966 to 1988.

Table 23 Number of Special Law Offenders by Prosecution and Non-prosecution, etc.

Year	Total	Prosecution (A)	Formal trial (B)	$\frac{B}{A}$ (%)	Summary proceed-ings (C)	$\frac{C}{A}$ (%)
1931	75,197	38,910	1,170	3.0	37,740	97.0
1936	102,635	48,580	3,721	7.7	44,859	92.3
1941	123,690	63,172	1,954	3.1	61,218	96.9
1946	169,384	99,187	11,016	11.1	88,171	88.9
1951	968,399	405,548	28,394	7.0	377,154	93.0
1956	1,863,523	1,248,610	13,204	1.1	1,235,406	98.9
1961	3,129,150	2,355,721	13,745	0.6	2,341,976	99.4
1966	4,818,351	3,894,898	15,644	0.4	3,879,254	99.6
1971	1,716,860	1,336,681	16,205	1.2	1,320,476	98.8
1976	2,417,273	2,086,543	36,405	1.7	2,050,138	98.3
1981	2,188,735	1,823,971	49,584	2.7	1,774,387	97.3
1986	2,384,494	1,955,536	47,076	2.4	1,908,460	97.6
1988	1,411,387	1,106,369	39,738	3.6	1,066,631	96.4

Sources: Annual Report of Criminal Statistics and
Annual Report of Statistics on Prosecution

If the formal trial prosecution rate for all Penal Code offenders is compared with the rate for such offenders excluding professional negligence, the former was extremely low from 1961 onward. This is because the rate of those prosecuted for summary proceedings (hereafter referred to as "summary prosecution rate") among the total prosecuted was considerably high for professional negligence offences.

As we have seen, in the disposition of all Penal Code offenders before the war, the prosecution rate was low, and prosecution was often suspended. But the prosecution rate and the formal trial prosecution rate rose temporarily during the period of confusion immediately after the war, when crime occurred frequently.

After that, offences of professional negligence began to occur frequently in 1956 and thereafter, and most of such offenders were disposed of by the prosecution for summary proceedings, so that the prosecution rate continued

Non-prosecution	Suspension	Others	Referral to family court	Prosecution rate	Suspension rate
36,287	24,026	12,261	—	51.7	38.2
54,055	40,919	13,136	—	47.3	45.7
60,518	51,641	8,877	—	51.1	45.0
70,197	55,178	15,019	—	58.6	35.7
526,921	480,342	46,579	35,930	43.5	54.2
461,835	409,343	52,492	153,078	73.0	24.7
373,950	344,782	29,168	399,479	86.3	12.8
359,978	343,805	16,173	563,475	91.5	8.1
137,523	121,785	15,738	242,656	90.7	8.4
99,022	86,039	12,983	231,708	95.5	4.0
77,423	67,463	9,960	287,341	95.9	3.6
93,304	82,995	10,309	335,654	95.4	4.1
87,475	78,350	9,125	217,543	92.7	6.6

increasing sharply. In 1988, however, the prosecution rate for Penal Code offenders as a whole decreased because the prosecution rate for professional negligence offenders went down.

Now, for Penal Code offenders exluding professional negligence, the prewar prosecution rate increased from 19.2 percent in 1931 to 28.0 percent in 1941, while the prosecution suspension rate, which was 74.7 percent in 1931 and 75.1 percent in 1936, decreased to 68.0 percent in 1941.

The 1941 rise in the prosecution rate was partly because a large number of Penal Code offenders were prosecuted on various charges, but particularly because the prosecution rate for gambling and illegal lottery, which weighed most heavily in Penal Code offences along with theft and fraud, increased suddenly that year (from 69.8 percent in 1936 to 83.7 percent in 1941).

This fact indicates that a policy was taken to strictly deal with these types of offences in order to maintain domestic social order and to prevent any trends that would be harmful to the war effort, such as laziness and waste.

After the war, the prosecution rate for Penal Code offenders excluding

Table 24 Number of Special Law Offenders other than Road Traffic Violations, by Prosecution and Non-prosecution, etc.

Year	Total	Prosecution (A)	Formal trial (B)	$\frac{B}{A}$ (%)	Summary Proceed-ings (C)	$\frac{C}{A}$ (%)
1931	64,460	31,681	1,159	3.7	30,522	96.3
1936	89,866	42,005	3,712	8.8	38,293	91.2
1941	120,752	61,743	1,952	3.2	59,791	96.8
1946	167,022	98,223	11,001	11.2	87,222	88.8
1951	600,289	182,847	28,099	15.4	154,748	84.6
1956	202,344	75,464	12,555	16.6	62,909	83.4
1961	181,253	89,720	12,525	14.0	77,195	86.0
1966	154,939	81,664	10,443	12.8	71,221	87.2
1971	165,347	88,579	11,510	13.0	77,069	87.0
1976	143,468	96,499	24,775	25.7	71,724	74.3
1981	141,056	104,821	36,551	34.9	68,270	65.1
1986	137,667	88,857	35,487	39.9	53,370	60.1
1988	110,553	65,151	30,005	46.1	35,146	53.9

Sources: Annual Report of Criminal Statistics and
Annual Report of Statistics on Prosecution

professional negligence was 45.7 percent in 1946, a figure considerably higher than prewar rates. The rate decreased temporarily after that, but it took an upward turn again and increased from 51.0 percent in 1961 to 59.5 percent in 1986. The rate dropped to 55.7 percent in 1988, however.

The sudden rise in the prosecution rate in 1946 is believed to have been caused by measures taken to cope with a sharp increase in crimes during the period of confusion immediately after the war.

Looking at changes in the formal trial prosecution rate for Penal Code offenders excluding those resulting from professional negligence, the rate was 69.2 percent in 1946, 72.1 percent in 1951 and 63.2 percent in 1956, all higher than prewar rates. The rate dropped to less than 60 percent in 1966 and 1971, but then it assumed an upward trend, increasing from 62.0 percent in 1976 to 72.5 percent in 1988.

Non-prosecution	Suspension	Others	Referral to family court	Prosecution rate	Suspension rate
32,779	21,280	11,499	–	49.1	40.2
47,861	35,143	12,718	–	46.7	45.6
59,009	50,186	8,823	–	51.1	44.8
68,799	53,817	14,982	–	58.8	35.4
397,412	357,293	40,119	20,030	31.5	66.1
117,031	77,486	39,545	9,849	39.2	50.7
77,808	61,799	16,009	13,725	53.6	40.8
60,256	52,223	8,033	13,019	57.5	39.0
69,042	59,863	9,179	7,726	56.2	40.3
41,095	35,282	5,813	5,874	70.1	26.8
28,256	23,812	4,444	7,979	78.8	18.5
24,874	21,210	3,664	23,936	78.1	19.3
20,126	16,441	3,685	25,276	76.4	20.2

On the other hand, the summary prosecution rate for offenders in the same category continued to decrease after jumping from 30.8 percent in 1946 to 49.5 percent in 1966. It fell to 27.5 percent in 1988.

As for the prosecution suspension rate after the war, the rate was 51.3 percent in 1946, considerably lower than prewar figures. Although it rose to 60.3 percent in 1951, the rate then continued to decrease until hitting 34.8 percent in 1986. In 1988, the rate went up slightly to 37.8 percent.

It is believed that the prosecution rate maintained an upward trend from 1956 to 1966 because of an increase in offences involving assault and bodily injury and an increase in the number of summary prosecutions for these offences.

The increase in the prosecution rate from 1976 to 1986 is believed to have been caused partly by the fact that the number of formal trial prosecutions for violent crimes rose during this period.

As we have seen, up until the period of confusion immediately after the

Table 25 Number of Professional Negligence Offenders for Prosecution and Non-prosecution, etc.

Year	Total	Prosecution (A)	Formal trial (B)	$\frac{B}{A}$ (%)	Summary proceedings (C)	$\frac{C}{A}$ (%)
1931	11,941	5,001	108	2.2	4,893	97.8
1936	16,705	6,628	125	1.9	6,503	98.1
1941	9,532	3,497	76	2.2	3,421	97.8
1946	3,490	1,278	118	9.2	1,160	90.8
1951	14,755	6,574	402	6.1	6,172	93.9
1956	67,514	42,077	928	2.2	41,149	97.8
1961	148,003	99,400	3,802	3.8	95,598	96.2
1966	362,077	232,581	9,506	4.1	223,075	95.9
1971	680,616	423,570	15,027	3.5	408,543	96.5
1976	476,057	293,761	10,489	3.6	283,272	96.4
1981	491,647	314,954	9,696	3.1	305,258	96.9
1986	571,286	372,964	10,602	2.8	362,362	97.2
1988	591,599	235,592	8,733	3.7	226,859	96.3

Sources: Annual Report of Criminal Statistics and
Annual Report of Statistics on Prosecution

war, the situation of disposition of Penal Code offences excluding professional negligence was almost the same as the situation of disposition of Penal Code offences as a whole. After that, from 1961, the prosecution rate in this category continued to be at a level between 50 percent and 60 percent, which was lower than the prosecution rate for Penal Code offences as a whole. But this trend was reversed in 1988.

When prosecution in this category is divided between summary prosecution and formal trial prosecution, the number of the former was nearly half the total from 1961 to 1971, but it began to decrease in 1976, with the number of the latter increasing.

B. Special Law Offenders

Table 23 shows developments in the number of special law offenders as a whole, the number of those who were not prosecuted, the prosecution rate, the number of those whose prosecution was suspended, etc., every five years

Non-prosecution	Suspension	Others	Referral to family court	Prosecution rate	Suspension rate
6,940	2,718	4,222	–	41.9	35.2
10,077	5,440	4,637	–	39.7	45.1
6,035	3,589	2,446	–	36.7	50.6
2,212	1,226	986	–	36.6	49.0
7,043	3,780	3,263	1,138	48.3	36.5
17,563	11,007	6,556	7,874	70.6	20.7
26,287	15,699	10,588	22,316	79.1	13.6
79,235	64,169	15,066	50,261	74.6	21.6
183,555	147,012	36,543	73,491	69.8	25.8
136,756	110,241	26,515	45,540	68.2	27.3
123,869	96,429	27,440	52,824	71.8	23.4
139,115	111,095	28,020	59,207	72.8	23.0
292,544	266,112	26,432	63,463	44.6	53.0

from 1931 and in 1988. Table 24 shows similar developments in special law offenders excluding road traffic violators.

If the prosecution rate for special Law offenders as a whole is observed, the rate fluctuated between 47.3 percent and 51.7 pecent before the war, and after the war, it rose to 58.6 percent in 1946, higher than prewar figures. The rate dropped temporarily in 1951, but it soared to over 95 percent from 1976 to 1986 and then fell to 92.7 percent in 1988.

The upward trend in the prosecution rate beginning in 1956 was caused by a rise in the number of Road Traffic Law violations, whose prosecution rate was high.

The formal trial prosecution rate for special law offenders was only between 3.0 percent and 7.7 percent from 1931 to 1941. After the war, the rate increased to 11.1 percent in 1946, considerably higher than prewar figures. But the rate dropped to 7.0 percent in 1951 and remained below 2 percent–below 1 percent from 1956 onward-when the number of road traffic violations increased.

Table 26 Number and Rate of Road Traffic Law Violators, by Prosecution and Non-prosecution, etc.

Year	Total	Prosecution (A)	Prosecution for Formal Trial (B)	B/A (%)	Prosecution for Summary proceedings (C)	C/A (%)
1931	10,737	7,229	11	0.2	7,218	99.8
1936	12,769	6,575	9	0.1	6,566	99.9
1941	2,938	1,429	2	0.1	1,427	99.9
1946	2,362	964	15	1.6	949	98.4
1951	368,110	222,701	295	0.1	222,406	99.9
1956	1,661,179	1,173,146	649	0.1	1,172,497	99.9
1961	2,947,897	2,266,001	1,220	0.1	2,264,781	99.9
1966	4,663,412	3,813,234	5,201	0.1	3,808,033	99.9
1971	1,551,513	1,248,102	4,965	0.4	1,243,407	99.6
1976	2,273,805	1,990,044	11,630	0.6	1,978,414	99.4
1981	2,047,679	1,719,150	13,033	0.8	1,706,117	99.2
1986	2,246,827	1,866,679	11,589	0.6	1,855,090	99.4
1988	1,300,834	1,041,218	9,733	0.9	1,031,485	99.1

But it increased to 2-3 percent in 1981 and rose further to 3.6 percent in 1988.

As we have seen, in treating special law offences as a whole–although the prosecution rate was high compared with the rate for Penal Code offences–prosecutions for formal trial proceedings were few, and most prosecuted offenders were dealt with through summary order procedure without a hearing.

The formal trial prosecution rate in this category rose somewhat during the period of confusion immediately after the war, but after 1956, most special law offenders, including road traffic violators, whose number sharply increased, were disposed of by prosecution of summary proceedings and the prosecution rate increased from about 70 percent to over 90 percent from 1956.

When the disposition of special law offenders excluding road traffic violators is examined, the prosecution rate after the war fluctuated between 46.7 percent and 51.1 percent from 1931 to 1941, and the formal trial prosecution rate remained between 3.2 percent and 8.8 percent.

After the war, the prosecution rate was 58.8 percent in 1946, higher than

Non-Prosecution	Suspension of Prosecution	Others	Referral to Family Court	Rate of Prosecution	Rate of Suspension of Prosecution
3,508	2,746	762	–	67.3	27.5
6,194	5,776	418	–	51.5	46.8
1,509	1,455	54	–	48.6	50.5
1,398	1,361	37	–	40.8	58.5
129,509	123,049	6,460	15,900	63.2	35.6
344,804	331,857	12,947	143,229	77.3	22.1
296,142	282,983	13,159	385,754	88.4	11.1
299,722	291,582	8,140	550,456	92.7	7.1
68,481	61,922	6,559	234,930	94.8	4.7
57,927	50,757	7,170	225,834	97.2	2.5
49,167	43,651	5,516	279,362	97.2	2.5
68,430	61,785	6,645	311,718	96.5	3.2
67,349	61,909	5,440	192,267	93.9	5.6

Sources: Annual Report of Criminal Statistics,
Annual Report of Statistics on Prosecut on, etc.

prewar figures. The rate temporarily dropped in 1951, and then rose from 39.2 percent in 1956 to 78.8 percent in 1981. The rate again started falling in 1986, and registered 76.4 percent in 1988.

The formal prosecution rate fluctuated between 11.2 percent and 16.6 percent from 1946 to 1971, and increased from 25.7 percent in 1976 to 46.1 percent in 1988.

The increase in the prosecution rate and the formal prosecution rate in 1946 were caused by the fact that the number of violations of economic control laws and ordinances, including the Staple Food Control Law and the Price Control Ordinance, increased, raising the prosecution rate and the formal trial prosecution rate for such violations.

In 1951, the prosecution rate dropped, though the formeal trial prosecution rate rose. This indicates that violations of the economic control laws and ordinances calmed down during this period, that the number of prosecutions for

Table 27 Percentage of Prosecution and Non-prosecution, by Type of Offence

Year	Theft		Fraud		Embezzle-ment		Homicide		Robbery		Assault	
	Prose-cution	Suspen-sion of Prose-cution	Prose-cution	Suspen-sion of Prose-cution	Prose-cution	Suspen-sion of Prose-cution	Prose-cution	Suspen-sion of Prose-cution	Prose-cution	Suspen-sion of Prose-cution	Prose-cution	Suspen-sion of Prose-cution
1931	18.9	79.2	7.5	86.9	5.4	92.9	54.8	17.2	65.7	11.9	10.0	61.0
1936	19.6	79.0	9.5	86.6	7.0	91.8	53.8	22.5	78.1	9.5	10.5	57.3
1941	21.1	77.0	14.7	80.5	10.5	88.2	52.0	17.2	79.1	10.6	9.2	67.0
1946	38.1	60.1	46.6	48.9	26.0	71.4	68.5	10.3	88.1	5.0	11.9	66.4
1951	35.1	62.2	21.9	68.8	21.2	74.2	59.0	16.9	71.7	10.4	41.8	55.6
1956	40.5	56.8	27.1	62.6	23.8	70.0	66.8	13.3	74.7	7.4	57.6	40.6
1961	44.4	54.0	34.1	57.0	29.9	64.1	69.0	11.4	79.9	8.0	63.0	36.1
1966	45.9	51.2	35.7	54.7	32.8	60.1	68.4	11.2	79.8	6.4	64.3	35.0
1971	42.3	54.5	37.1	52.3	28.2	64.8	64.1	9.7	71.4	8.1	59.9	39.6
1976	49.5	48.2	51.4	38.8	31.2	63.5	61.3	7.6	77.7	6.1	68.3	30.7
1981	51.8	46.4	57.4	32.4	24.8	71.8	38.8	6.4	79.8	8.1	68.2	31.1
1986	54.5	43.5	60.7	31.7	26.6	70.5	58.1	4.9	73.8	8.8	72.1	27.1
1988	51.1	46.2	61.6	30.3	22.1	75.7	22.2	6.1	71.9	7.7	63.3	35.7

summary order proceedings decreased as a result of the fact that controls were relaxed as a whole, but that prosecution for formal trials were used with considerable frequency for particularly vicious cases.

From 1961 to 1971, an increase in the number of prosecutions for summary proceedings pushed up the prosecution rate to above the 50 percent mark, presumably because there were a large number of violations of the Firearms and Swords Control Law, the Law to Control Business Affecting Public Morals, the Anti-Prostitution Law and similar laws, many of which were treated with prosecution for summary proceedings.

The rise in the prosecution rate as a result of a sharp increase in the formal trial prosecution rate from 1976 to 1988 is believed to have been caused by the fact that many violations of the Stimulant Drugs Control Law, whose number started rising in the first half of the 1970s, were prosecuted for formal trial proceedings because a 1973 partial revision of the law eliminated fines from main punishment provisions.

Bodily injury		Extortion		Rape		Indecent assault		Arson		Stimulant drugs	
Prose-cution	Suspension of Prose-cution	Prose-cution	Suspension of Prose-cution	Prose-cution	Suspension of Prose-cution	Prose-cution	Suspension of Prose-cution	Prose-cution	Suspension of Prose-cution	Prose-cution	Suspension of Prose-cution
30.4	67.0	24.5	64.5	19.9	23.0	46.0	30.3	57.0	13.8	–	–
32.6	66.0	26.4	65.0	28.2	20.8	29.5	44.0	62.4	10.5	–	–
32.9	65.9	26.6	68.0	39.6	17.6	36.0	45.0	49.8	13.2	–	–
40.0	56.9	54.2	41.7	41.1	10.9	21.1	23.8	63.5	7.5	–	–
48.1	48.7	25.7	67.3	28.1	21.2	27.4	41.7	50.0	23.1	48.7	45.0
63.9	33.0	39.3	52.3	34.9	18.5	25.8	25.8	57.7	20.6	56.4	23.1
73.8	24.3	53.7	40.6	50.6	23.6	32.4	31.3	60.9	21.9	83.8	11.0
77.6	20.5	55.1	38.3	57.9	18.4	33.8	32.9	57.7	21.6	78.6	18.3
76.0	21.9	54.2	39.0	53.8	23.2	33.7	28.2	52.6	28.4	81.1	15.0
80.1	16.8	65.2	27.9	55.2	21.1	40.7	17.5	60.7	14.9	79.7	14.2
81.5	15.6	63.8	28.6	58.0	15.9	41.9	17.9	55.9	23.8	89.3	6.2
82.7	14.1	68.2	26.1	62.4	13.9	50.0	12.4	60.3	15.5	89.5	5.2
77.7	19.4	62.9	29.8	63.8	16.1	49.2	13.0	59.2	16.8	87.5	5.9

Sources: Annual Report of Criminal Statistics and
Annual Report of Statistics on Prosecution

As we have seen, in disposition of special law offenders excluding road traffic violators before the war, the prosecution rate fluctuated around 50 percent, but most of the prosecutions were for summary procedure without a hearing.

In 1946, after the war, the number of prosecutions for formal trial proceedings and the prosecution rate went up slightly, but the prosecution rate fell in 1951 and 1956. The prosecution rate rose from 1961 to 1971, for the number of prosecutions for summary proceedings increased. From 1976 onward, the prosecution rate increased, for the number of prosecutions for formal trial proceedings rapidly increased, while the number of prosecutions for summary order proceedings decreased.

C. Professional Negligence Causing Death or Bodily Injury and Road Traffic Violations

Table 25 shows trends in professional or gross negligence causing death or bodily injury–hereinafter referred to as "professional negligence" –every five years from 1931 and in 1988 (from 1976 onward traffic professional negligence), which are classified into the number of those who were prosecuted, the number of those who were not prosecuted, the prosecution rate, the suspension of prosecution rate, etc. (for the year 1941 and before, based on cases). Table 26 shows similar developments in road traffic violations.

In the disposition of professional negligence before the war, the prosecution rate decreased from 41.9 percent in 1931 to 36.7 percent in 1941, but the formal trial prosecution rate remained at around 2 percent, and the suspension of prosecution increased from 35.2 percent in 1931 to 50.6 percent in 1941.

After the war, the prosecution rate in 1946 was not very different from prewar figures, but it suddenly started rising in 1951 and went up to 79.1 percent in 1961. After that, the rate dropped down to 68.2 percent in 1976, and then increased again until hitting 72.8 percent in 1986. The rate was 44.6 percent in 1988.

The formal trial prosecution rate was first considerably higher than prewar figures–at 9.2 percent in 1946 and 6.1 percent in 1951–but from 1956 to 1988, the rate fluctuated between 2.2 percent and 4.1 percent.

The suspension of prosecution rate was 49.0 percent in 1946, similar to prewar figures, but it dropped from 36.5 percent in 1951 to 13.6 percent in 1961. Then from 1966 to 1986, the rate remained between 20 percent and 29 percent, and it jumped to 53.0 percent in 1988. Thus, in treating professional negligence cases before the war, the prosecution rate was comparatively low, with suspension of prosecution frequently used.

After the war, the prosecution rate gradually increased, eventually registering high figures, while the suspension of prosecution rate continued to decrease. In 1988, however, the prosecution rate decreased considerably while the suspension of prosecution rate went up markedly.

A breakdown of the prosecutions shows that more than 90 percent of them have always been carried out for summary order proceedings.

The prosecution rate increased rapidly after the war because traffic professional negligence in connection with the driving of automobiles rose in number, and prosecution for summary order proceedings were frequently carried out to deal with such offences.

In 1988, the prosecution rate decreased considerably while the suspension of prosecution rate went up sharply, apparently because the public prosecutors offices had changed their policy to dispose of professional negligence cases.

When the prewar disposition of road traffic violations is examined, the prosecution rate decreased from 67.3 percent in 1931 to 48.6 percent in 1941, and during that period, the formal trial prosecution rate was extremely low, between 0.1 and 0.2 percent. But the suspension of prosecution rate rose from

27.5 percent in 1931 to 50.5 percent in 1941.

After the war, the prosecution rate was 40.8 percent in 1946, lower than prewar figures, but the rate then increased from 63.2 percent in 1951 to exceed the 90 percent mark in 1966, and recorded 97.2 percent both in 1976 and 1981. After that, the rate fell somewhat, registering 93.9 percent in 1988.

The formal trial prosecution rate was 1.6 percent in 1946, slightly higher than prewar figures, but it remained at 0.1 percent between 1951 and 1966. The rate took an upward turn in 1971 and rose to 0.9 percent in 1988. As such, in treating road traffic violations before the war, the prosecution rate showed a downward trend while the suspension of prosecution rate showed an upward trend.

After the war, the prosecution rate rose rapidly in accordance with an increase in road traffic violations, while the suspension of prosecution rate decreased. From 1966 onward, the prosecution rate stayed above the 90 percent mark, and most of the prosecutions were for summary order procedure without a hearing.

D. Dispositions by Category of Major Offence

Table 27 shows development in the disposition of main offences by category of offence and breakdown of dispositions: prosecution rate and suspension of prosecution rate every five years from 1931 and in 1988.

(a) Theft, Fraud and Embezzlement

Looking at the prewar disposition of theft, fraud and embezzlement cases, we learn that the prosecution rates for all these crimes increased between 1931 and 1941 from 18.9 percent to 21.1 percent for theft, from 7.5 percent to 14.7 percent for fraud, and from 5.4 percent to 10.5 percent for embezzlement.

After the war, the prosecution rate for theft was 38.1 percent in 1946, considerably higher than prewar figures. After dropping somewhat to 35.1 percent in 1951, the rate continued to increase until it registered 54.5 percent in 1986. In 1988, it fell slightly to 51.1 percent.

The prosecution rate for fraud in 1946 was 46.6 percent, substantially higher than prewar figures. After dropping to 21.9 percent in 1951, the rate continued rising and recorded 61.6 percent in 1988.

The prosecution rate for embezzlement was 26.0 percent in 1946, considerably higher than prewar figures. The rate fell to 21.1 percent in 1951 and then continued to increase until it registered 32.8 percent in 1966. After that, the rate zigzagged, dropping to 22.1 percent in 1988.

For each of the three crimes–theft, fraud and embezzlement–the prosecution rate jumped in 1946 in response to the rapid increase in crimes during the period of confusion immediately after the war. The rate for embezzlement started decreasing in 1981, presumably because of an increase in such lighter offences as misappropriation of unattended articles. Thus, the prosecution rates were low in the disposition of theft, fraud and embezzlement before the war, with suspension of prosecution frequently utilized. After the war, however, the prosecution rates went up while the suspension of prosecution rates went down. The postwar rises in the prosecution rates were particularly remarkable for theft and fraud.

(b) Homicide and Robbery

The prosecution rate for homicide fluctuated between 52.0 percent and 54.8 percent from 1931 to 1941, before the war.

After the war, the rate remained between 58.1 percent and 69.0 percent, except for 38.8 percent registered in 1981 and 22.2 percent in 1988. In 1981 and 1988, the rate dropped because there were many more non-prosecution cases than cases of suspension of prosecution. In 1988, one prisoner filed a number of complaints or accusations, one after another, against many correctional officers for attempted murder, but the charges did not include any facts to constitute homicide or any other offences.

The suspension of prosecution rate fluctuated between 17.2 percent and 22.5 percent from 1931 and 1941, before the war. After the war, the rate fluctuated between 10.3 percent and 16.9 percent from 1946 to 1966, and it varied between 4.9 percent and 9.7 percent from 1971 onward.

The prosecution rate for robbery ranged between 65.7 percent and 79.1 percent from 1931 to 1941, before the war. After the war, the rate registered 88.1 percent in 1946, considerably higher than prewar figures, and it has been at about the 70 percent level since 1951, except for 1961, 1966 and 1981, when the rate was as high as 79 percent. The prosecution rate was high in 1946 because many robbery cases occurred in the period of confusion immediately following the war and because strict measures were taken to cope with this trend.

The suspension of prosecution rate for robbery ranged between 9.5 percent to 11.9 percent from 1931 to 1941, before the war. After the war, the rate in 1946 was a comparatively low 5.0 percent, and the rate in 1951 was a comparatively high 10.4 percent. The rate then ranged between 6.1 percent and 8.8 percent from 1956 to 1988.

As we have seen, in the disposition of homicide and robbery throughout the prewar and postwar periods, the prosecution rates were high while the suspension of prosecution rates were low. A comparison of these rates between the prewar and postwar periods does not show such major differences as seen in some other offences.

(c) Assault, Bodily Injury and Extortion

The prosecution rate for assault ranged between 9.2 percent and 10.5

percent before the war. In 1946, after the war, the rate increased somewhat to 11.9 percent, then shot up to 41.8 percent in 1951. After that, the rate rose, while undergoing some ups and downs, to 72.1 percent in 1986. But it fell to 63.3 percent in 1988.

The prosecution rate for bodily injury ranged between 30.4 percent and 32.9 percent from 1931 to 1941 before the war. In 1946, after the war, the rate was 40.0 percent, higher than prewar figures, and then it went up from 48.1 percent in 1951 to 82.7 percent in 1986. In 1988, the rate dropped to 77.7 percent.

The prosecution rate for extortion ranged between 24.5 percent and 26.6 percent from 1931 to 1941, before the war. In 1946, after the war, the rate sharply increased to 54.2 percent, but it dropped to 25.7 percent in 1951. It increased from 39.3 percent in 1956 to 68.2 percent in 1987 and fell to 62.9 percent in 1988.

The prosecution rates for assault, bodily injury and extortion rose in 1946 because a stringent disposition policy was taken to cope with an increase in the number of these crimes immediately after the war. The 1951 rise in the prosecution rate for assault was believed to have occurred partly because assault was excluded from offences subject to prosecution only upon complaint. The rise may also be attributable to an attempt to cope with an increase in this type of offence.

Table 28 shows developments in the formal trial prosecution rates and the summary order request rates for assault, bodily injury and Stimulant Drugs Control Law violations.

The summary prosecution rate remained somewhere between 80 percent and just below 100 percent throughout the prewar and postwar periods for assault, and between 70 percent and 90 percent for bodily injury.

The formal trial prosecution rate for assualt was comparatively high in 1946 and 1951, at 33.3 percent and 12.4 percent, respectively, and the rate for bodily injury was comparatively high in the same two years, at 35.8 percent and 20.5 percent, respectively. From 1976 to 1988, the formal trial prosecution rate for assault rose from 8.2 percent to 12.4 percent, and the rate for bodily injury increased from 21.7 percent to 30.2 percent.

As we have seen, in the treatment of assault and bodily injury, the prosecution rates were low and the suspension of prosecution rates were high before the war. After the war, however, the prosecution rates continued increasing and the suspension of prosecution rates gradually declined. In 1988, the prosecution rate considerably fell and the suspension of prosecution rate rose.

If the prosecutions are classified into formal trial prosecution and sum-

Table 28 Rate of Prosecution for Formal Trial and Summary Proceeding, by Assault, Bodily injury and Stimulant Drugs (1931~1988)

Year	Assault		Bodily injury		Stimulant drugs	
	Rate of Prosecution for Formal Trial	Rate of Prosecution for Summary Proceedings	Rate of Prosecution for Formal Trial	Rate of Prosecution for Summary Proceedings	Rate of Prosecution for Formal Trial	Rate of Prosecution for Summary Proceedings
1931	3.9	96.1	14.4	85.6	–	–
1936	4.0	96.0	16.5	83.5	–	–
1941	8.8	91.2	14.6	85.4	–	–
1946	33.3	66.7	35.8	64.2	–	–
1951	12.4	87.6	20.5	79.5	40.2	59.8
1956	6.2	93.8	13.6	86.4	42.0	58.0
1961	5.1	94.9	15.0	85.0	68.6	31.4
1966	4.6	95.4	13.1	86.9	71.5	28.5
1971	4.4	95.6	15.0	85.0	71.7	28.3
1976	8.2	91.8	21.7	78.3	99.9	0.1
1981	7.0	93.0	23.8	76.2	100.0	0.0
1986	8.8	91.2	27.7	72.3	100.0	–
1988	12.4	87.6	30.2	69.8	100.0	–

Sources: Annual Report of Criminal Statistics, and
Annual Report of Statistics on Prosecution

mary prosecution, most of the prosecutions for both assault and bodily injury were for summary order procedure without a hearing request, but the formal trial prosecution rates started increasing in 1976.

For extortion, the prosecution rate was less than 30 percent and the suspension of prosecution rate was more than 50 percent before the war. After the war, however, the the prosecution rate steadily increased until it exceeded the 60 percent mark, and the suspension of prosecution rate decreased to below 30 percent.

(d) Rape and Indecent Assault

The prosecution rate for rape ranged between 19.9 percent and 39.6 percent from 1931 to 1941. The rate increased considerably to 41.1 percent in 1946, after the war, and then temporarily dropped in 1951, but it began to increase again and reached 57.9 percent in 1966. The rate then fell again but started increasing in 1981 and rose to 63.8 percent in 1988.

The prosecution rate for indecent assault ranged between 29.5 percent and 46.0 percent from 1931 to 1941. After the war, in 1946, the rate was 21.1 percent, lower than prewar figures. After that, the rate started increasing in 1951, when it stood at 27.4 percent, and reached 50.0 percent in 1986. In 1988, the rate decreased somewhat to 49.2 percent.

To sum up, the prosecution rate for rape was comparatively low before the war, with a considerably high rate of suspension of prosecution, but the prosecution rate gradually went up after the war, with the suspension of prosecution rate decreasing. The prosecution rate for indecent assault after the war remained almost unchanged from prewar figures until 1971, but it started increasing in 1976.

(e) Arson

The prosecution rate of those who were charged with arson ranged from 49.8 percent to 62.4 percent between 1931 and 1941. After registering 63.5 percent in 1946, it moved downward for a period of time and then hovered between 50 and 60 percent in recent years. It is clear now that, unlike other types of offences, there were no major changes in the prosecution rate of arsonists between the two periods preceding and following the war.

(f) Offences in Violation of the Stimulant Drugs Control Law

After registering 48.7 percent in 1951, the prosecution rate of those who violated the Stimulant Drugs Control Law continued an upward trend to reach 89.5 percent in 1986, and then dropped slightly to 87.5 percent in 1988. By category of prosecution, the rate of offenders who were brought up for formal trial proceedings increased from 40.2 percent in 1951 to nearly 100 percent in the years following 1976.

The increase in the rate of those brought up for formal trial proceedings and the drop in those handled through summary proceedings in the years since 1976 is primarily due to a partial revision of the Stimulant Drugs Control Law in 1973, which deleted the penalty of fines from among punishments applicable to major offences provided under the law.

As such, dispositions by public prosecutors showed that at the beginning of the enforcement of the law, almost half of those offenders were given suspended prosecution. However gradually the rate of suspended prosecution decreased and the rate of prosecution increased. Also, as for the category of prosecution, at the beginning almost over half of the prosecutions were for summary proceedings but the prosecution for formal public trial proceedings increased rapidly and after 1976 almost all cases were disposed of by prosecution for formal public trial proceedings, and the dispositions of suspension of

Fig.24 Percentage of Disposal Period of Cases by the Public Prosecutors Office (1926～1988)

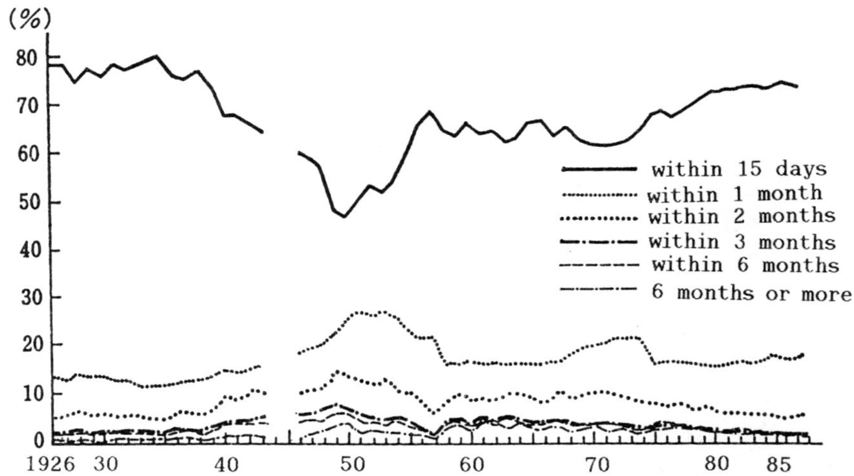

Sources: Annual Report of Criminal Statistics and Annual Report of Statistics on Prosecution

prosecution also went down to a negligible figure in the same period.

As mentioned above, the prosecution rate remained low while the rate of suspended prosecutions was high in the prewar years, in almost all category of offences, when compared with the postwar period. On the other hand, the prosecution rate went up markedly in almost all types of offences following the war, which consequently brought down the rate of suspended prosecution.

Such a rise in the prosecution rate for those offences for which fines are provided by statute is explainable with an increase in the number of prosecutions for summary proceedings, as well as with an increase in recent years in the rate of prosecution through formal trial proceedings, while the rise for other offences occurred as a matter of course due to a rise in the rate of prosecution through formal trial proceedings.

Yet the prosecution rate for those offences involving professional negligence dropped markedly while the rate of suspended prosecution went up sharply in 1988. Both have probably much to do with the revision of the guideline on prosecution concerning these offences.

With some variations among different categories of offences, the prosecution rate went down while the rate of suspended prosecution went up in 1988.

(3) Time Taken for Disposing Cases at the Public Prosecutors Office

Fig. 24 shows the changes in percentages for time taken for disposing

Table 29 Length of Preliminary Examination by Investigating Judges (1926~1940)

Year	Total	within 15 days	within 1 month	within 2 months	within 3 months	within 6 months	six months or over
1926	100.0 (3,876)	9.4	25.0	30.9	13.9	15.0	5.9
1927	100.0 (4,027)	10.3	24.5	30.1	13.8	14.5	6.8
1928	100.0 (4,039)	9.1	23.9	32.2	15.5	15.0	4.3
1929	100.0 (3,678)	8.0	20.4	29.1	16.8	17.6	7.9
1930	100.0 (4,957)	6.4	15.6	30.4	18.9	21.9	6.8
1931	100.0 (4,935)	6.2	16.5	27.9	19.0	21.7	8.5
1932	100.0 (5,102)	7.9	17.3	28.4	17.2	20.1	9.1
1933	100.0 (5,601)	5.9	15.0	25.4	17.0	25.2	11.6
1934	100.0 (5,889)	6.1	14.8	22.8	15.1	20.0	21.2
1935	100.0 (5,540)	7.3	16.4	24.1	15.1	17.2	19.9
1936	100.0 (5,906)	6.3	17.0	25.2	16.2	22.5	12.8
1937	100.0 (4,824)	6.9	19.0	25.7	15.6	18.4	14.4
1938	100.0 (3,881)	6.8	17.6	28.1	14.7	16.6	16.1
1939	100.0 (3,358)	7.3	19.0	32.0	15.2	16.3	10.2
1940	100.0 (3,048)	4.8	16.3	26.8	18.9	18.5	14.6

Source: Annual Report of Criminal Statistics

cases at the public prosecutors office in the Showa era.

The percentage of those cases which were disposed of within 15 days hovered from 73.9 to 79.9 percent to the total disposition at the office between 1926 and 1939. The corresponding figure ranged from 64.0 percent and 57.6 percent between 1940 and 1943. Meanwhile, the ratio of those cases which took more than six months to reach a final disposition hovered from a mere 0.3 percent to 1.1 percent between 1926 and 1943.

The dispositions at the public prosecutors office for the prewar years include those cases against which preliminary inquiry proceedings by examining judges were requested by public prosecutors. As the investigation was virtually conducted during the proceedings, the time spent for preliminary inquiry is reckoned to constitute part of the whole investigation period for disposing the case. Therefore, the time taken for such preliminary inquiry shall also be examined hereafter.

Table 30 Rate of Custody (All Offences)

Year	1961	1966	1971	1976	1981	1986	1988
Suspects arrested / not arrested							
Suspects disposed of by the Public Prosecutors (A)	709,678	678,789	554,471	518,277	533,927	488,937	453,401
Suspects arrested and referred to the Prosecutor by the Police,etc. (B)	203,079	171,067	129,487	109,781	112,558	109,354	100,280
Suspects arrested by the Public Prosecutors (C)	2,072	1,020	661	659	247	405	295
Suspects arrested but immediately released by the Police,etc.	27,000	20,181	14,345	10,859	7,836	5,829	6,874
Suspects not arrested	477,527	486,521	410,008	396,978	413,286	373,349	345,952
Rate of Arrest (B+C)/A	28.9	25.4	23.5	21.3	21.1	22.4	22.2
Request for Detention							
Granted (D)	148,695	113,057	87,822	85,380	90,957	92,318	85,808
Denied (E)	1,412	1,922	2,108	809	367	138	115
Rate of Detention D/(D+E)	99.1	98.3	97.7	99.1	99.6	99.9	99.9
Rate of Request (D+E)/(B+C)	73.2	66.8	69.1	78.0	81.0	84.2	85.4

Note: Suspects of road traffic violation are excluded.

Source: Annual Report of Statistics on Prosecution

Table 29 shows the changes in the percentage of time taken for making preliminary inquiry proceedings at courts of first instance between 1926 and 1940.

The percentage of those cases which spent 15 days or less for making preliminary inquiry ranged from 4.8 percent to 10.3 percent of the total, while that of those cases which took more than one month but less than two months showed the highest figure ranging from 22.8 percent and 32.2 percent. The ratio of those cases which took more than six months for preliminary inquiry ranged between 4.3 percent and 21.2 percent of the total, showing figures higher than the counterparts of those cases disposed of at the public prosecutors office.

In the postwar years, the percentage of those cases which were disposed of by the public prosecutors office within 15 days moved from 60.0 percent in 1946 to 46.3 percent in 1950. In the following years, however, the figure moved up to total 67.9 percent in 1957, then hovered within a range of 60.7 percent and

Table 31 Rate of Custody (Penal Code Offences)

Year	1961	1966	1971	1976	1981	1986	1988
Suspects arrested / not arrested							
Suspects disposed of by the Public Prosecutors (A)	526,166	500,563	391,189	379,062	397,915	354,871	346,286
Suspects arrested and referred to the Prosecutor by the Police,etc. (B)	172,224	151,401	112,617	89,598	83,731	77,307	71,481
Suspects arrested by the Public Prosecutors (C)	1,637	856	515	519	192	223	194
Suspects arrested but immediately released by the Police,etc.	20,428	17,717	12,425	9,274	6,212	4,824	5,875
Suspects not arrested	331,877	330,589	265,632	279,671	307,780	272,517	268,736
Rate of Arrest (B+C)/A	33.0	30.4	28.9	23.8	21 1	21.8	20.7
Request for Detention							
Granted (D)	133,073	103,649	78,188	69,752	67,104	65,126	61,246
Denied (E)	1,103	1,629	1,719	560	292	109	96
Rate of Detention D/(D+E)	99.2	98.5	97.8	99.1	99 6	99.8	99.8
Rate of Request (D+E)/(B+C)	77.2	69.1	70.6	78.1	80 3	84.1	85.6

Source: Annual Report of Statistics on Prosecution

66.2 percent over the 1958-1974 period. The figure, while showing yearly fluctuations, continued its upward trend to total 74.7 percent in 1988.

The percentage of those cases which took more than six months for the prosecutors office to reach its disposition moved from 0.9 percent in 1946 to 3.5 percent in 1950, then moved downward to total 0.7 percent in 1957. The corresponding figure, however, hovered within a range of 1.9 percent and 3.6 percent over the 1958-1980 period, then in and after 1981 moved downward to stand at 1.2 percent in 1988.

The period between 1946 and 1950 was the one when a number of crimes occurred in the treacherous years following World War II, with an increase in the number of offences disposed of by the public prosecutors office pushing up the number of those cases which took a long time for the office to reach its disposition.

(4) Arrest and Detention of Suspects under Investigation

Tabel 32 Rate of Custody (Special Law Offences)

Year	1961	1966	1971	1976	1981	1986	1988
Suspects arrested / not arrested Suspects disposed of by the Public Prosecutors (A)	183,512	178,226	163,282	139,215	136,012	134,066	107,115
Suspects arrested and referred to the Prosecutor by the Police,etc. (B)	30,855	19,666	16,870	20,183	28,827	32,047	28,799
Suspects arrested by the Public Prosecutors (C)	435	164	146	140	55	182	101
Suspects arrested but immediately released by the Police,etc.	6,572	2,464	1,890	1,585	1,624	1,005	999
Suspects not arrested	145,650	155,932	144,376	117,307	105,506	100,832	77,216
Rate of Arrest (B+C)/A	17.1	11.1	10.4	14.6	21.2	24.0	27.0
Request for Detention							
Granted (D)	15,622	9,408	9,634	15,628	23,853	27,192	24,562
Denied (E)	309	293	389	149	75	29	19
Rate of Detention D/(D+E)	98.1	97.0	96.1	99.1	99.7	99.9	99.9
Rate of Request (D+E)/(B+C)	50.9	48.9	58.9	77.6	82.8	84.5	85.1

Note: Suspects of road traffic violation are excluded.

Source: Annual Report of Statistics on Prosecution

A. The Rate of Arrest and Detention as a Whole

Table 30 shows the number of those arrestees and detainees whose cases were disposed of by the public prosecutors office in every five years starting in 1961 up to 1986 and in 1988, excluding those involved in offences of professional negligence (or the traffic professional negligence in the years in and after 1976) and road traffic offenders.

Let's turn to the percentage of those suspects who were either arrested and referred as arrested by police or arrested by public prosecutors against the total number of those disposed of by the prosecutors office (hereafter cited as "rate of arrest"). After registering 28.9 percent in 1961, it gradually went down to total 21.1 percent in 1981. It hovered at the level of 22 percent in both 1986 and 1988. That is to say, some 20 percent of crime investigations were carried out under the situation where suspects were under arrest (called as "investigation under arrest"), while the remaining 80 percent were conducted

Table 33 Rate of Custody (Theft)

Year	1961	1966	1971	1976	1981	1986	1988
Suspects arrested / not arrested							
Suspects disposed of by the Public Prosecutors (A)	209,489	199,274	166,345	187,056	221,600	208,430	203,907
Suspects arrested and referred to the Prosecutor by the Police,etc. (B)	71,683	56,925	38,074	30,708	30,412	31,280	27,913
Suspects arrested by the Public Prosecutors (C)	378	130	88	115	15	27	32
Suspects arrested but immediately released by the Police,etc.	6,906	5,456	4,502	3 263	2,317	2,100	2,295
Suspects not arrested	130,522	136,763	123,681	152 970	188,856	175,023	173,667
Rate of Arrest (B+C)/A	34.4	28.6	22.9	16.5	13.7	15.0	13.7
Request for Detention							
Granted (D)	55,787	41,670	28,098	25.396	25,366	26,528	23,615
Denied (E)	285	371	337	185	92	37	36
Rate of Detention D/(D+E)	99.5	99.1	98.8	99.3	99.6	99.9	99.8
Rate of Request (D+E)/(B+C)	77.8	73.7	74.5	83.0	83.7	84.9	84.6

Source: Annual Report of Statistics on Prosecution

under the situation where the suspects continued to live at large in the community (called as "investigation under freely left at home"). It may well be said that the ideal of voluntary investigation has been adhered to till the present day in the course of crime investigation.

Of the arrested cases, the percentage of those detentions requested by the prosecutors office (hereafter cited as "rate of detention requested") stood at 73.2 percent in 1961, but fell down to 66.8 percent in 1966. The figure, however, steadily moved upward in 1971 to reach 85.4 percent in 1988.

The decline in the rate of arrest tends to bring up the rate of detention requested.

Of the cases which the public prosecutors requested for detention, the rate of those cases which won judge's consent (hereafter cited as "rate of detention granted") ranged between 97.7 percent to 99.9 percent.

B. The Rate of Arrest and Detention among Penal Code Offenders or Special Law Offenders

Table 34 Rate of Custody (Homicide)

Year	1961	1966	1971	1976	1981	1986	1988
Suspects arrested / not arrested Suspects disposed of by the Public Prosecutors (A)	3,079	2,600	2,288	2,408	2,904	2,074	4,037
Suspects arrested and referred to the Prosecutor by the Police,etc. (B)	2,136	1,713	1,394	1,380	1,192	1,276	983
Suspects arrested by the Public Prosecutors (C)	13	10	8	6	1	2	-
Suspects arrested but immediately released by the Police,etc.	17	18	15	11	16	18	20
Suspects not arrested	913	859	871	1,011	1,695	778	3,034
Rate of Arrest (B+C)/A	69.8	66.3	61.3	57.6	41.1	61.6	24.3
Request for Detention							
Granted (D)	2,075	1,649	1,364	1,368	1,181	1,265	977
Denied (E)	2	4	4	3	-	1	-
Rate of Detention D/(D+E)	99.9	99.8	99.7	99.8	100.0	99.9	100.0
Rate of Request (D+E)/(B+C)	96.6	95.9	97.6	98.9	99.0	99.1	99.4

Source: Annual Report of Statistics on Prosecution

Table 31 shows the rate of arrest and detention among Penal Code offenders, excluding those involved in professional negligence (or traffic professional negligence in the years later than 1976), while Table 32 shows the corresponding rate for special law offenders, excluding Road Traffic Law violators, both of which were registered in every five years starting in 1961 up to 1986 and in 1988.

The rate of arrest of those Penal Code offenders, excluding professional negligence offenders, moved down steadily from 33.0 percent in 1961 to 20.7 percent in 1988.

The rate of arrest for those special law offenders, excluding road traffic law violators, moved down from 17.1 percent in 1961 to 10.4 percent in 1971. It then turned upward in following years, to total 27.0 percent in 1988. The rise in the rate of arrest for those special law offenders, excluding road traffic law violators, is considered to have much to do with the increase in the number of the Stimulant Drugs Control Law violators, and the ensuing rise in the rate of

Table 35 Rate of Custody (Bodily injury)

Year	1961	1966	1971	1976	1981	1986	1988
Suspects arrested / not arrested							
Suspects disposed of by the Public Prosecutors (A)	93,100	83,743	62,831	45,903	39,519	31,555	30,280
Suspects arrested and referred to the Prosecutor by the Police,etc. (B)	28,533	23,901	18,184	15,035	14,382	12,466	12,062
Suspects arrested by the Public Prosecutors (C)	277	102	53	57	5	28	25
Suspects arrested but immediately released by the Police,etc.	5,105	4,104	2,733	1,684	1,117	659	812
Suspects not arrested	59,185	55,636	41,861	29,127	24,C15	18,402	17,381
Rate of Arrest (B+C)/A	30.9	28.7	29.0	32.9	36.4	39.6	39.9
Request for Detention							
Granted (D)	19,845	12,789	9,892	10,238	10,435	9,745	9,849
Denied (E)	269	301	272	120	57	18	14
Rate of Detention D/(D+E)	98.7	97.7	97.3	98.8	99.5	99.8	99.9
Rate of Request (D+E)/(B+C)	69.8	54.5	55.7	68.6	72.9	78.1	81.6

Source: Annual Report of Statistics on Prosecution

arrest for those offenders.

The rate of detention requested for those Penal Code offenders, excluding professional negligence offenders, stood at 77.2 percent in 1961, while the corresponding figure for those special law offenders, excluding road traffic law violators, totaled 50.9 percent in the same year. Both figures moved upward in following years, with the former reaching 85.6 percent and the latter totaling 85.1 percent in 1988.

The rate of detention granted for those Penal Code offenders, excluding professional negligence offenders, moved within the range of 97.8 percent to 99.8 percent, while the corresponding figure for those special law offenders, excluding Road Traffic Law offenders, ranged between 96.1 percent and 99.9 percent.

C. The Rate of Arrest or Detention by Category of Offence

Table 33 shows the number of arrestees and detainees who were suspected of theft, registered in every five years starting in 1961 up to 1986 and in 1988.

Table 36 Rate of Custody (Rape)

Year	1961	1966	1971	1976	1981	1986	1988
Suspects arrested / not arrested							
Suspects disposed of by the Public Prosecutors (A)	9,074	9,444	6,797	4,082	3,133	1,872	1,779
Suspects arrested and referred to the Prosecutor by the Police,etc. (B)	5,597	6,018	4,594	2,540	2,036	1,321	1,256
Suspects arrested by the Public Prosecutors (C)	73	33	25	13	-	3	2
Suspects arrested but immediately released by the Police,etc.	104	109	73	41	24	8	3
Suspects not arrested	3,300	3,284	2,106	1,488	1,073	.540	.518
Rate of Arrest (B+C)/A	62.5	64.1	68.0	62.5	65.0	70.7	70.7
Request for Detention							
Granted (D)	5,032	5,087	4,001	2,365	1,848	1,248	1,202
Denied (E)	8	20	34	3	3	1	-
Rate of Detention D/(D+E)	99.8	99.6	99.2	99.9	99.8	99.9	100.0
Rate of Request (D+E)/(B+C)	88.9	84.4	87.4	92.8	90.9	94.3	95.5

Source: Annual Report of Statistics on Prosecution

The rate of arrest on suspicion of theft declined steadily, with the 34.4 percent in 1961 down to 13.7 percent in 1988. The rate of detention requested moved from 77.8 percent in 1961 down to 73.7 percent in 1966, then went up to 84.6 percent in 1988.

Table 34 shows the number of those arrestees and detainees who were suspected of homicide, registered in every five years starting in 1961 up to 1986 and in 1988.

While the rate of arrest hovered on the level of 60 percent between 1961 and 1971, it stood at 57.6 percent in 1976, then 41.1 percent in 1981. It stood at 61.6 percent in 1986, then dipped down to as low as 24.3 percent in 1988. This figure can be explained, as mentioned earlier, by the fact that there were many cases in which the acts alleged to constitute crimes in the complaints or accusations of victims or otherwise did not constitute on their mere face any crime at all. The rate of detention requested moved between 95.9 percent to 99.4 percent.

Table 37 Rate of Custody(Stimulant drugs)

Year	1961	1966	1971	1976	1981	1986	1988
Suspects arrested / not arrested							
Suspects disposed of by the Public Prosecutors (A)	532	822	3,096	17,506	34.388	28,896	26,145
Suspects arrested and referred to the Prosecutor by the Police,etc. (B)	278	381	1,472	7,687	16,944	16,889	15,834
Suspects arrested by the Public Prosecutors (C)	5	1	4	42	18	34	15
Suspects arrested but immediately released by the Police,etc.	14	12	30	109	152	79	115
Suspects not arrested	235	428	1,590	9,668	17,274	11,894	10,181
Rate of Arrest (B+C)/A	53.2	46.5	47.7	44.2	49.3	58.6	60.6
Request for Detention							
Granted (D)	275	352	1,372	7,549	16,326	16,604	15,638
Denied (E)	3	-	9	26	25	10	6
Rate of Detention D/(D+E)	98.9	100.0	99.3	99.7	99.8	99.9	100.0
Rate of Request (D+E)/(B+C)	98.2	92.1	93.6	98.0	96.4	98.2	98.7

Source: Annual Report of Statistics on Prosecution

Table 35 shows the number of those arrestees and detainees on suspicion of bodily injury, registered in every five years starting in 1961 up to 1986 and in 1988. The rate of arrest on suspicion of bodily injury moved slightly down to 28.7 percent in 1966 from 30.9 percent in 1961. It then moved up to total 39.9 percent in 1988. The rate of detention requested moved from 69.8 percent in 1961 down to 54.5 percent in 1966. It then moved upward to 81.6 percent in 1988.

Table 36 shows the number of those arrestees and detainees on suspicion of rape, registered in every five years starting in 1961 up to 1986 and in 1988. The rate of arrest on suspicion of rape ranged between 62.5 percent and 70.7 percent. The rate of detention requested moved from 88.9 percent in 1961 down to 84.4 percent in 1966. It then moved upward to total 95.5 percent in 1988.

Table 37 shows the number of those arrestees and detainees on suspicion of violating the Stimulant Drugs Control Law, registered in every five years starting in 1961 up to 1986 and in 1988. The rate of arrest for those suspects,

Table 38 Number of Persons Adjudicated in Courts of First Instance, by Category of Trial

Year	Total	Formal trial		Summary proceedings	
		Persons	Percent	Persons	Percent
1926	153,073	37,463	24.5	115,610	75.5
1931	151,960	44,594	29.3	107,366	70.7
1936	188,930	61,995	32.8	126,935	67.2
1941	121,019	37,520	31.0	83,499	69.0
1946	…	…	…	…	…
1951	567,811	145,128	25.6	422,683	74.4
1956	1,445,528	120,739	8.4	1,324,789	91.6
1961	2,548,425	97,421	3.8	2,451,004	96.2
1966	4,284,032	92,525	2.2	4,191,507	97.8
1971	1,878,234	76,045	4.0	1,802,189	96.0
1976	2,418,111	80,587	3.3	2,337,524	96.7
1981	2,198,489	79,745	3.6	2,118,744	96.4
1986	2,373,787	77,182	3.3	2,296,605	96.7
1987	1,704,088	75,277	4.4	1,628,811	95.6

Sources: Annual Report of Criminal Statistics,
Annual Report of Judicial Statistics, etc.

after registering 53.2 percent in 1961, remained on the 40 percent level between 1966 to 1981, but moved upward to total 60.6 percent in 1988. The rate of detention requested hovered between 92.1 percent and 98.7 percent, while the rate of detention granted ranged between 98.9 percent to 100.0 percent.

3. *TRIAL*

(1) Persons Finally Adjudicated in Courts of First Instance

Appendix Table 7 shows the number of persons finally adjudicated at district courts or summary courts as court of first instance by category of sentence in Showa Era.

Before World War II, the number of persons finally adjudicated at district courts or summary courts as court of first instance sharply increased from 1933 through 1937, reaching a peak of 191,002 persons in 1936. Though it decreased in 1938 and 1939, it started to increase again in 1940 and reached a new peak of 206,014 persons in 1943.

After World War II, the number went up and down on the 500,000- and 600-,000-level from 1948 through 1952. Then it gradually increased and exceeded 1 million in 1954. It started to increase sharply around 1960 and reached 4,623,128 in 1965, setting the worst record ever.

However, the number developed a tendency to reduce after the traffic offence ticketing system was introduced and the number of road traffic offence cases decreased. Though it dropped to 1,650,666 in 1969, it started to increase again around 1974 and reached 2,655,279 in 1977. Since then the number went up and down. It reached 2,374,301 in 1986 and drastically dropped to 1,704,497 in 1987.

Table 38 shows the number of persons finally adjudicated in every five years from 1926 through 1986 and in 1987 by category of normal first instance, and summary order procedure without any hearing and speedy trial procedure for traffic violations.

Normal first instance accounted for 24.5 percent to 32.8 percent of the total from 1926 through 1951. Summary order procedure without any hearing and speedy trial procedure for traffic violations accounted for 67.2 percent to 75.5 percent in the same period.

However, it changed completely after 1956, and summary order procedure without any hearing and speedy trail procedure for traffic violations accounted for over 90 percent, going up and down around 96 percent. On the other hand, normal first instance accounted for only 2.2 percent to 8.4 percent. Percentage of summary order and speedy trial procedures increased after 1951 because the number of traffic violations soared with advance of motorization, as seen in crime trends.

Appendix Table 5 shows the number of persons convicted (which was got by withdrawing the number of people acquitted and others from the total number) among those finally adjudicated at court of the first instance.

According to that, before World War II, the number of criminal law offenders stayed high from 1934 through 1936 with a peak of 117,104 in 1934. Their number started to increase again in 1940 and reached a peak of 122,988 in 1943.

The number of special law violators also remained high from 1940 to 1943 with a peak of 85,662 in 1942 when the great number of Economic Control Law violations was reported. Also the special law violators accounted for 32 percent to 38.4 percent of persons convicted at court of first instance, showing a relatively high percentage, from 1931 through 1933. Their percentage dropped a little and moved around 31.6 percent or 34.2 percent from 1934 through 1936 when the number of criminal law violators increased. Though the percentage further dropped to the 27-percent level in 1938 and 1939, it started to increase since 1940 when the number of speical law violators was increasing, and reached 46.5 percent in 1942.

After World War II, the number of criminal law violators recorded 228,223 persons in 1948, exceeding the pre-war peak by far. Though it was gradually reducing toward early 1950s, it started to rise again around 1954, and fluctauted at the 160,000-level in late 1950s. After that, it continued to go down with a little fluctuation. It went below 100,000 in late 1970s and dropped to 61,519 in 1987.

Special law violators numbered 321,495 in 1948 and kept exceeding 100,000 unitl 1955. However, their number started to decrease as the number of Economic Control Law violations dropped. It went up relatively high sometimes, exceeding 90,000 in 1959 and 1961, and 80,000 in 1963, 1967, 1983 and 1984. However, the number usually fluctuated around the 50,000- or 70,000-level. In 1987, it was 66,379 persons.

Percentage of speical law violators among persons convicted at court of first instance also remained relatively high, fluctuating between 55.5 percent and 62.1 percent from 1948 through 1951, and between 47.7 percent and 50 percent from 1952 and 1955. After that, the number reduced or did not increase from late 1950s to early 1970s. However, since 1975, the number went up due to an increase of Stimulant Drugs Control Law violations and other offences. It reached 47.8 percent in 1979, 45.4 percent in 1980, 42.4 percent in 1981, and remained at the 50-percent level since 1983. In 1987, it was 51.9 percent.

As to details on the total number of persons convicted at court of first instance and trends by category of offence, see Chapter II, Section 2 and 3.

(2) Situations of Punishment

Appendix Table 7 shows situations of punishment at court of first instance in Showa era by category of offence. Both before and after World War II, the most often imposed punishment is fine, followed by imprisonment with forced labour for a fixed term, minor fine, and imprisonment without forced labour in that order.

Fig. 25 shows changes in the number of persons who were sentenced fine, imprisonment with forced labour, minor fine or imprisonment without forced labour at court of first instance. It proves that fine is the most imposed punishment.

Capital punishment, lifetime imprisonment with or without forced labour were used only exceptionally, and penal detention was used only in the small number of cases.

Fig.25 Number of Offenders Convicted in Courts of First Instance, by Type of Punishment (1926~1987)

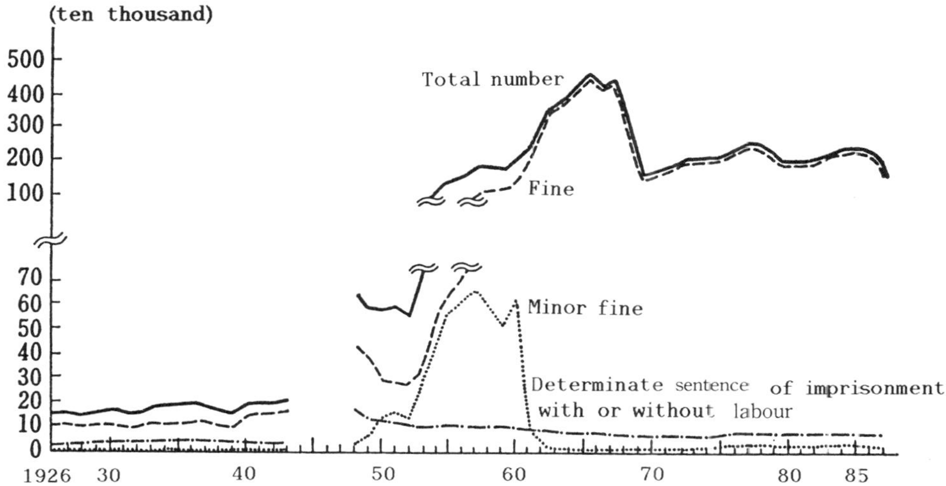

Sources: Annual Report of Criminal Statistics, Annual Report of Statistics on Prosecution, etc.

Before World War II, some 500 to 1,000 persons were found innocent annually from 1926 to 1932. Their number later reduced, flucutating at the 300 level. Though it increased a little from 1936 to 1938, it dropped again after 1939. It was 243 in 1943.

The post World War II period started with large figures, such as 2,944 in 1949, 2,617 in 1950 and 2,539 in 1951. But it gradually went down and settled at the 400 level in late 1950s. It further dropped to the 200 level in late 1970s and to the 100 level in early 1980s. It was 99 in 1987.

Table 39 shows percentage of persons acquitted among those finally adjudicated at court of first instance (the acquittal rate) in every five years from 1926 through 1986 and in 1987. The acquital rate in the post-war period has been lower than that in the pre-war period except 1951. Especially since 1981, it has been less than 0.01 percent.

Changes in the number of persons finally adjudicated by category of sentence will be discussed in the following based on Appendix Table 7.

A. Capital Punishment, and Lifetime Imprisonment with or without Labour

Before World War II, the annual number of persons sentenced capital punishment fluctuated between about 20 and 37 from 1926 through 1938. It decreased from 1939 to 1942, fluctuating between 12 and 16. However, it

Table 39 Acquittal Rate of Persons Adjudicated in Courts of First Instance

Year	Acquittal rate	Year	Acquittal rate
1926	0.5167	1961	0.0167
1931	0.3280	1966	0.0105
1936	0.2775	1971	0.0240
1941	0.1399	1976	0.0126
1946	…	1981	0.0096
1951	0.4247	1986	0.0048
1956	0.0498	1987	0.0058

Sources: Annual Report of Criminal Statistics,
Annual Report of Judicial Statistics, etc.

reached 30 in 1943.

After World War II, the number increased with 116 persons sentenced to death in 1948, 55 in 1949, 62 in 1950 and 44 in 1951. Though it later decreased, the number fluctuated between 12 and 37 until around 1960. Since around 1970, it went down below 10. Only six persons were sentenced to death in 1987. Before World War II, the annual number of persons sentenced lifetime imprisonment with or without forced labour fluctuated between 35 and 72 from 1926 through 1938. Though the number went down since 1939 and settled at the 30 level, it rose to 39 in 1943. After World War II, the number remained at the 100 level until 1952 with a peak of 153 in 1950. Though it started to reduce later, the number fluctuated between some 80 and 100 until around 1960. It later dropped further and became less than 50 since around 1970 with exception of 51 persons in 1977. It fluctuated between 24 and 45 until 1986. However, it increased to 65 in 1987.

Fig. 26 shows the number of persons sentenced capital punishment or lifetime imprisonment with forced labour totaled by every five years from 1928 through 1987. The number of persons sentenced capital punishment or lifetime imprisonment with forced labour remained high during a period of confusions right after World War II, and a following period until late 1960s. Especially the number of persons sentenced lifetime imprisonment with forced labour far exceeded the figures before World War II. It can be attributed to the huge number of criminal cases happened during a period of confusions after the war,

Fig.26 Number of Offenders Sentenced to Capital Punishment and Life Imprisonment with Labour in Courts of First Instance, by Total of Five Years

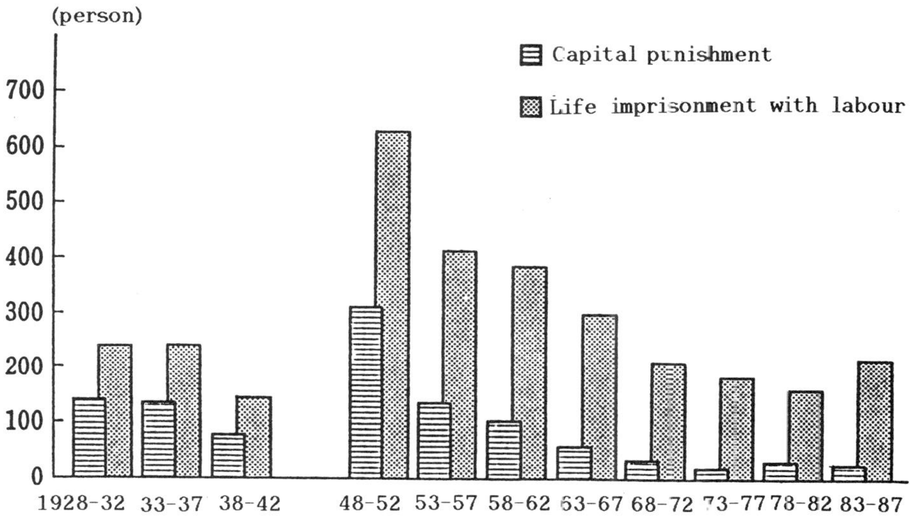

Sources: Annual Report of Criminal Statistics, Annual Report of Statistics on Prosecution, etc.

and the large number of felonies reported in a following period toward late 1960s.

Table 40 shows changes in the number of persons given capital punishment or life imprisonment with labour from 1926 through 1986 by five-year intervals and in 1987 by category of offence.

Both before and after World War II, most of persons given capital punishment committed either homicide, or robbery resulting in death. Most of those sentenced to life with labour committed murder, or robbery resulting in death or injury, or robbery and rape (rape committed by the robber on the spot).

B. Imprisonment for a Determinate Term with or without Labour

Before the war, the number of persons given imprisonment with labour for a determinate term fluctuated mostly at the 30,000 level from 1926 through 1932, and from 1938 through 1943. However, the number was rather high and fluctuated at the 40,000 level from 1933 through 1937 when the number of crimes reached its peak before World War II.

After the war, the number reached a record 172,838 in 1948 and remained at the 100,000 level until 1952. Though it later dropped a little, it fluctuated between 90,000 and 100,000 levels until 1959, and between 60,000 and 80,000 levels from 1960 through 1968. Although it dropped to the 50,000 level from 1969

Table 40 Number of Persons Sentenced to Capital Punishment and Life Imprisonment with Labour in Courts of First Instance

① Capital punishment

Year	Total	High Treason	Homicide	Robbery resulting in death	Arson
1926	25	2	8	15	—
1931	29	—	7	22	—
1936	19	—	5	14	—
1941	12	…	…	…	…
1946	…	…	…	…	…
1951	45	—	6	39	—
1956	24	—	2	22	—
1961	29	—	5	24	—
1966	14	—	6	8	—
1971	4	—	—	4	—
1976	4	—	3	1	—
1981	2	—	1	1	—
1986	5	—	2	3	—
1987	6	—	3	2	1

through 1971, it started to increase again around 1975, and fluctuated at the 70,000 level. The number was 67,877 persons in 1987.

Before the war, imprisonment without labour for a determinate term was seldom sentenced. The number of persons was generally very small with the exception of 1930, 1935 and 1937 when it exceeded 1,000. Even after the war, it remained as small as that before the war until 1955.

However, it gradually increased later and exceeded 10,000 in 1971 and 1972. The number started to decrease again in late 1970s and fluctuated at the 5,000 level. It was 5,306 in 1987.

The number of persons given imprisonment for a determinate term without labour started to skyrocket in the late 1950s because the number of people charged for causing death or injury from negligence related to traffic professional negligence had increased. The number gradually dropped since 1973 after reaching its peak in 1971 and 1972.

A partial revision of Penal Code effective in June 1968 added imprisonment with labour to statutory punishments for causing death or bodily injury resulting from gross negligence or professional negligence (included are those with driver's licences and drive a car in daily life). These are referred to as professional negligence offences. The revision gradually increased the number of people given imprisonment with labour, while it reduced the number of those

② Life imprisonment with labour

Year	Total	Homicide	Robbery resulting in death, Robbery and rape	Rape	Indecent assault	Arson	Kidnapping
1926	49	28	11	2	1	7	—
1931	54	21	28	3	—	2	—
1936	37	15	22	—	—	—	—
1941	32	…	…	…	…	…	…
1946	…	…	…	…	…	…	…
1951	108	29	76	2	—	1	—
1956	83	18	63	—	1	1	—
1961	69	17	51	1	—	—	—
1966	74	27	44	2	—	—	1
1971	38	11	26	—	—	1	—
1976	36	11	22	1	—	2	—
1981	34	8	25	—	—	1	—
1986	36	8	28	—	—	—	—
1987	65	17	46	—	—	2	—

Sources: Annual Report of Criminal Statistics,
Annual Report of Judicial Statistics, etc.

given imprisonment without it.

For example, among 5,306 persons given imprisonment without labour for determinate terms in 1987, 5,289 persons were convicted of professional negligence offences, 10 were offenders of the Public Official Election Law, and four violated the Road Traffic Law.

Table 41 shows changes in the component ratio of persons given imprisonment with or without labour for determinate terms among those found guilty by courts of first instance by length of their terms. The statistics were taken in five-year intervals from 1926 through 1986 and in 1987. In analyzing by length of their terms, it is statistically impossible to differentiate those sentenced to imprisonment with labour from those without labour. It is also impossible to carry out smaller divisions of prison terms in the area of between 3 to 10 years partly because the division of prison terms in the prewar and postwar eras is different.

The component ratio of persons given imprisonment with or without labour for three years or more fluctuated mostly between the 10-percent and

Table 41 Percentage of Persons Sentenced to Imprisonment with or without Labour among Those Convicted in Courts of First Instance, by Length of Term

Year	Total(Persons)	Over 10 years	Over 5 years	From 3 years to 5 years inclusive	of which; over 3 years	2 years or more	of which; over 2 years	1 year or more	6 months or more	Under 6 months
1926	100.0(28,981)	0.9	4.3	7.2	…	10.0	2.2	25.2	31.6	20.8
1931	100.0(35,219)	0.7	4.1	7.3	…	10.7	2.6	27.5	33.7	16.1
1936	100.0(47,974)	0.4	3.1	6.6	…	10.1	2.1	26.2	31.7	21.9
1941	100.0(33,785)	…	…	…	…	…	…	…	…	…
1946	…	…	…	…	…	…	…	…	…	…
1951	100.0(118,229)	0.1	1.3	5 8	2.3	8.4	…	43.2	32.6	8.6
1956	100.0(102,275)	0.2	1.0	5 0	2.0	7.4	…	45.4	33.7	7.3
1961	100.0(83,249)	0.1	1.1	6 5	2.5	8.1	…	42.1	33.2	8.8
1966	100.0(78,814)	0.1	1.2	6 9	2.9	8.5	…	41.0	33.9	8.3
1971	100.0(69,467)	0.1	0.9	6 1	2.4	7.4	…	36.5	38.3	10.7
1976	100.0(75,498)	0.1	0.9	5 8	2.5	7.6	…	34.0	37.6	13.9
1981	100.0(76,219)	0.2	0.8	5 5	2.5	7.0	…	36.0	38.4	12.1
1986	100.0(74,856)	0.2	1.0	5 6	2.7	9.0	…	44.9	29.0	10.2
1987	100.0(73,183)	0.2	1.1	5 6	2.7	9.5	…	47.4	27.1	9.2

Note : Figures in parentheses show the number of the convicted
Sources: Annual Report of Criminal Statistics,
Annual Report of Judicial Statistics, etc.

12-percent levels before World War II. However, after the war, it fluctuated at the 6-percent to 8-percent levels. After 1976, the percentage remained at the 6-percent level. Prison terms ranging from two to three years averaged 10 percent before the war, and registered 7 to 9 after the war. A slight upturn is seen lately.

Both before and after the war, the length of a prison term most often given is in the category of "six months or longer but less than two years." These sentences accounted for 56-percent or 61-percent levels before the war but increased to 71-percent or 79-percent levels after the war. In that category, persons given imprisonment in the category of "six months or more but less than one year" accounted for about a 30-percent level before and after the war.

Table 42 Number of Persons Sentenced to Fine or Minor Fine in Courts of First Instance

Year	Persons convicted (A)	Of whom; persons fined or minor-fined (B)	Of whom; fined (C)	$\frac{C}{A}$ (%)	$\frac{C}{B}$ (%)	Of whom; minor-fined (D)	$\frac{D}{A}$ (%)	$\frac{D}{B}$ (%)
1926	151,825	122,378	103,742	68.3	84.8	18,636	12.3	15.2
1931	151,248	115,911	95,202	62.9	82.1	20,709	13.7	17.9
1936	188,203	140,104	116,345	61.8	83.0	23,759	12.6	17.0
1941	196,254	162,420	154,513	78.7	95.1	7,907	4.0	4.9
1946	…	…	…	…	…	..	…	…
1951	566,617	447,963	284,733	50.3	63.6	163,230	28.8	36.4
1956	1,441,705	1,339,213	724,513	50.3	54.1	614,700	42.6	45.9
1961	2,545,191	2,461,724	2,375,085	93.3	96.5	36,639	3.4	3.5
1966	4,281,922	4,202,762	4,197,963	98.0	99.9	4,799	0.1	0.1
1971	1,876,464	1,806,877	1,804,088	96.1	99.8	2,789	0.1	0.2
1976	2,457,332	2,381,702	2,357,125	95.9	99.0	24,577	1.0	1.0
1981	2,197,953	2,121,832	2,095,147	95.3	98.7	26,685	1.2	1.3
1986	2,373,533	2,298,514	2,272,034	95.7	98.8	26,480	1.1	1.2
1987	1,703,898	1,630,511	1,608,336	94.4	98.6	22,175	1.3	1.4

Sources: Annual Report of Criminal Statistics,
Annual Report of Judicial Statistics, etc.

Though imprisonment in a category of "one year or longer but less than two years" was only at the 20-percent level before the war, it rose to the 30-percent or 40-percent levels after the war.

The component ratio of persons given imprisonment with labour for less than six months was relatively high before the war, such as 20.8 percent in 1926 and 21.9 percent in 1936. After the war, however, it dropped and fluctuated at the 8-percent or 13-percent levels. The ratio of short prison terms was probably reduced gradually as its negative effects were taken into consideration.

When we examine the length of prison terms, the prewar era was marked by the extensive distribution of prison terms, including both long and short ones. But prison terms given in the postwar era were marked by the absence of both long and short terms, shorter than six months. This was offset by an increase in the number of prison terms of longer than one year but shorter than two years.

C. Fines and Minor Fines

Table 42 shows changes in the component ratio of persons given fines or minor fines among those found guilty by courts of first instance by five-year intervals from 1926 through 1986 and in 1987. Also with Appendix Table 7, how monetary punishment (fines and minor fines) was used in Japan will be discussed in the following text.

Before World War II, the component ratio of persons given monetary punishment among those found guilty by courts of first instance was 80.6 percent in 1926 but dropped to the 70-percent level in 1931 and 1936. It rose to 82.8 percent in 1941. After the war, it fluctuated at 90 percent or higher since 1956, and recorded 98.2 percent in 1966. However, it later dropped a little, and was 95.7 percent in 1987.

In monetary punishment, minor fines accounted for 15 percent or 17 percent until 1936, but it plummetted to 4.9 percent in 1941. After the war, it accounted for 36.4 percent in 1951 and for 45.9 percent in 1956. However, it began plummetting since 1961 and accounted for only 0.1 percent in 1966. Though it later recovered slightly, it was just 1.4 percent in 1987. The changes will be examined in detail below.

Before the war, the number of those given fines went up and down until 1939, fluctuating approximately between 90,000 and 110,000 persons. But it skyrocketed after 1940 and recorded 165,085 persons in 1943. The sharp increase after 1940 is attributed to an increase of violators of economic control laws and ordinances before and during the war.

After the war, it started with high figures such as 436,273 persons in 1948 and as 379,651 persons in 1949 due to violations of economic control law and ordinances. However, as the number of those violations were reduced, the number of persons given fines also decreased and reached the 270,000 level in 1952. But it started to increase gradually in early 1950s, and skyrocketed in the late 1950s. It reached 4,535,134 persons in 1965, and fluctuated at the 4-million level until 1967 due to a sharp increase of incidents related to traffic.

As introduction of the traffic infraction ticketing system (traffic infraction notification system) cases to be dealt with through prosecution and court judgments reduced the number of Road Traffic Law violations, the number of persons given fines drastically dropped and reached 1,578,585 persons in 1969. But it again started to increase gradually from 1965 and reached 2,272,034 in 1986. However, it decreased to 1,608,336 in 1987 due to wider application of the traffic offence ticketing system and ensuing reduction of the cases dealt with by the courts.

Before the war, the number of persons given minor fines fluctuated approximately between the 18,000 and 25,000 levels until 1937 except 1928. However, it gradually declined in 1938 and 1939, and started to plummet in 1940. It was 3,047 in 1943. The number of persons given fines increased, and that of those given minor fines decreased probably because the number of violations against economic control laws and ordinances went up, and that of minor traffic offences went down since 1940. However, there was a huge number of persons given minor fines under the Summary Proceedings for Police Infractions before the war. If this is included, minor fines could be the most used sentence in monetary punishment.

After the war, the number of persons given minor fines skyrocketed around 1950, and fluctuated between the 500,000 and 600,000 levels in the late 1950s. It reached 660,282 persons in 1957, and 610,544 persons in 1960. But it suddenly started to decrease after 1961 and became 2,789 in 1971. It gradually increased again after 1973, and numbered 22,175 persons in 1987.

The number of persons given minor fines increased after World War II because of the sharp increase of Road Traffic Control Law offenders. It sharply decreased after 1961 since the new Road Traffic Law put in force in December 1960 strenghtened punishments and began to give punitive fines to violators whereas minor fines had been previously given.

The number started to rise gradually again after 1973 probably because a revision of the Law for Temporary Measures Concerning Fines, Etc., which was put in force July 1972, raised the ceiling amount of minor fines to "less than 4,000 yen," and minor fines started to be used again as punishment for minor Road Traffic Law violations. Among those given minor fines in 1987, 19,433 were Road Traffic Law offenders, 2,316 were Minor Offence Law violators, and 302 were also given minor fines for violations of the Law to Prevent Drunken Conduct Causing Public Nuisance.

Changes in use of monetary punishment, especially minor fines, in the Showa era shows a great difference before and after World War II. Minor fines came to be used less and less often probably because their statutory upper limit, less than 4,000 yen, is still too low, though it was raised in 1972.

Through enforcemnt of the Law for Temporary Measures Concerning Fines, Etc. and its revisions, the maximum level of monetary punishment has been raised by 200 times compared to one stipulated when the present Penal Code was enacted. Nevertheless, it can be said that present minor fines have become unable to give financial pain monetary punishment must at least have for offenders due to a declining value of currency, and other reasons. The same thing can be said with application of fines for those offences in which a maximum level of the fine is set relatively low.

Table 43 Rate of Persons Fined in Courts of First Instance, by Type of Offence and Amount of Fine (1973, 1987)

Offence	Rate of persons sentenced to small amount of fine			Rate of persons sentenced to maximum or similar amount of fine		
	Amount	1973	1987	Amount	1973	1987
House-breaking (10,000 yen)	Less than 10,000 yen	54.6	3.1	10,000 yen	45.4	96.9
Harbouring criminals (40,000 yen)	Less than 20,000 yen	44.4	1.4	40,000 yen	7.8	52.7
Bodily injury (100,000 yen)	20,000 yen or less	54.3	1.7	60,000 yen or more	9.3	54.9
	Less than 40,000 yen	75.5	11.1	80,000 yen or more	4.9	36.1
	Less than 50,000 yen	80.1	16.3	…	…	…
Professional negligence causing death or bodily injury (200,000 yen)	20,000 yen or less	19.3	0.7	100,000 yen or more	9.0	29.7
	Less than 50,000 yen	67.3	23.1	200,000 yen	0.4	2.0
Distribution of obscene literature (1,000,000 yen)	Less than 50,000 yen	49.8	5.2	…	…	…
	Less than 100,000 yen	80.8	31.5	…	…	…

Note : Figures in parentheses show the maximum amount of fine.
Source : Criminal Affairs Bureau, Research and Training Institute, Ministry of Justice

Table 43 shows component ratios of fines concerning house breaking, harboring criminals, bodily injury, professional negligence causing death or injury, and distribution of obscene literature in 1973 and 1987, both immediately after revisions of the Law for Temporary Measures Concerning Fines, Etc. The figures were taken from computerized records of convictions stored in the computer of the Justice Ministry.

The table indicates that fines less than a certain level disappeared or drastically decreased, and rates of fines concentrated around the maximum ceiling concerning violations for which fines are limited to 200,000 yen or less. Those phenomena are not observed in offences for which the limit of fines exceeds 200,000 yen. Concentration of the fines' level around 200,000 yen seems to be related to the upper limit of a fine for summary order procedure without hearing which are set at a maximum of 200,000 yen. Fines exceeding 200,000 yen are, in fact, rarely given.

D. Penal Detention

Before World War II, the number of persons sentenced to penal detention was 392 in 1926 and 265 in 1927. It gradually decreased and fluctuated between five and 20 from 1939 through 1943. However, before the war, over 100,000 persons were placed under penal detention a year by the chiefs of police stations

Table 44 Number and Percentage of Persons Sentenced for Homicide in Courts of First Instance, by Type of Punishment and Term of Imprisonment

Year	Total	Death	Life imprisonment with labour	Determinate term imprisonment with or without labour	Percentage of persons sentenced to determinate-term imprisonment with labour, by term							Rate of suspended execution of Sentence
					Over 10 years	Over 5 years	3 years or more	Over 3 years	2 years or more	Over 2 years	Under 2 years	
1926	930	8	28	894	14.1	20.6	18.0	...	28.5	1.9	18.8	26.7
1931	860	7	21	832	15.6	16.2	19.1	...	36.8	1.1	12.3	30.0
1936	906	5	15	887	9.5	21.1	20.5	...	35.9	2.8	13.0	27.5
1941	603	...	...	...	...	...	...	...	...	...	...	...
1946	...	...	...	...	...	...	...	...	...	...	...	...
1951	1,018	6	29	983	6.2	23.1	44.8	15.3	18.3	...	7.6	34.9
1956	1,295	2	18	1,275	4.8	25.9	43.2	...	18.5	...	7.5	35.2
1961	1,403	5	17	1,379	5.4	28.6	46.1	17.0	13.3	...	6.5	30.5
1966	1,201	6	27	1,168	7.0	31.2	46.3	19.1	11.6	...	3.9	27.6
1971	1,036	—	11	1,025	6.0	31.9	46.3	18.6	12.2	...	3.6	29.4
1976	1,164	3	11	1,150	6.9	27.6	50.3	20.1	13.0	...	2.2	30.8
1981	888	1	8	879	10.0	31.1	46.0	19.0	11.0	...	1.8	25.2
1986	978	2	8	968	13.3	35.1	42.6	18.1	8.3	...	0.7	21.3
1987	908	3	17	888	13.5	36.9	41.1	18.6	8.0	...	0.5	19.9

Sources: Annual Report of Criminal Statistics,
Annual Report of Judicial Statistics, etc.

or their deputies under the Summary Proceedings for Police Infractions. If they are also counted, penal detention becomes the most used form of imprisonment before the war.

After the war, though 1,633 persons in 1948 and 536 persons in 1949 were put under penal detention, the number gradually decreased. Though it was below 100 persons since around 1965, the number gradually increased recently. It was 133 in 1987. All of them were offenders of the Minor Offence Law.

(3) Forms of Punishment by Offences

Changes in forms of punishment are discussed in the following concerning

Table 45 Number and Percentage of Persons Sentenced for Robbery in Courts of First Instance, by Type of Punishment and Term of Imprisonment

Year	Total	Death	Life imprisonment with labour	Determinate-term imprisonment with labour	Percentage of persons sentenced to determinate-term imprisonment with labour, by term							Rate of suspended execution of Sentence
					Over 10 years	Over 5 years	3 years or more	Over 3 years	2 years or more	Over 2 years	Under 2 years	
1926	490	15	11	464	9.9	49.6	23.7	...	11.6	9.1	5.2	3.0
1931	707	22	28	657	6.8	53.3	25.9	...	10.8	7.3	3.1	2.4
1936	784	14	22	748	9.4	47.3	31.3	...	9.9	6.4	2.1	2.0
1941	404	...	...	...	...	...	...	...	...	...	...	...
1946	...	...	...	...	...	...	...	...	...	...	...	...
1951	3,437	39	76	3,322	2.4	30.2	55.1	37.4	9.7	...	2.6	13.8
1956	2,473	22	63	2,388	3.6	21.9	60.5	39.2	11.2	...	2.8	15.8
1961	1,669	24	51	1,594	1.8	21.9	63.9	43.7	10.5	...	1.9	16.9
1966	1,427	8	44	1,375	2.0	27.6	59.8	42.8	8.8	...	1.8	14.3
1971	921	4	26	891	1.8	20.7	64.8	41.2	10.8	...	2.0	18.9
1976	873	1	22	850	2.8	22.1	62.2	41.9	11.2	...	1.6	17.1
1981	807	1	25	781	2.3	23.6	64.3	42.1	8.6	...	1.3	18.4
1986	686	3	28	655	2.0	22.6	67.6	50.2	7.2	...	0.6	13.9
1987	715	2	46	667	3.6	28.0	60.4	42.3	7.3	...	0.6	13.9

Sources: Annual Report of Criminal Statistics,
Annual Report of Judicial Statistics, etc.

homicide, robbery, bodily injury, theft and rape.

A. Homicide

Table 44 shows changes in forms of punishment concerning homicide by five-year intervals from 1926 through 1986 and in 1987. The number of persons given capital punishment or life imprisonment decreased after the war compared to that before the war. Though the number decreased remarkably after 1971, three persons were given capital punishment, and 17 persons were sentenced life imprisonment in 1987, showing an increase from the previous year.

As for imprisonment for a determinate term, the component ratio of persons given imprisonment for five years or more fluctuated between 30.6

percent and 34.7 percent before the war. After the war, it was 29.3 percent in 1951 but later rose to 38.2 percent in 1966. The ratio further increased after 1981 and reached 50.4 percent in 1987. On the contrary, the component ratio of persons given imprisonment for less than three years fluctuated between 47.3 percent and 49.1 percent before the war. After the war, though it was at the 20 percent level in 1951 and 1956, the number dropped after 1961 and fluctuated at the 10-percent level. In 1987, it was 8.5 percent.

The ratio of suspended execution of sentences fluctuated between 26.7 percent and 30 percent before the war, while it fluctuated between 27.6 percent and 35.2 percent from 1951 through 1976 after the war. However, it decreased after 1981 and was 19.9 percent in 1987.

B. Robbery

Table 45 shows the changes in punishments meted out by courts of first instance against those offenders found guilty on the charge of robbery at intervals of five years between 1926 and 1986 and in 1987. The percentage of those who were sentenced to death or life imprisonment, when computed with the total number of those convicted, was higher in the prewar period than in the postwar period. After World War II, those sentenced to capital punishment or life imprisonment decreased after 1971 but those sentenced to life increased in 1987.

There are no specific differences before and after World War II in determinate-term imprisonment with labour. However, it is noteworthy that imprisonment of five years or more remained on the 20-percent level until 1986, except for 1951, but increased to 31.6 percent in 1987.

The rate of those with suspended execution of sentences was very low, ranging between 2.0 and 3.0 percent in the prewar period, but it rose to between 13.8 and 18.9 percent after the war. It was 13.9 percent in 1987.

C. Bodily Injury

Table 46 shows the changes in punishments given by courts of first instance against those offenders found guilty on charges of bodily injuries at intervals of five years from 1926 through 1986 and in 1987. It lists the rate of those sentenced to imprisonment with determinate-terms and the rate of those sentenced to fines and those sentenced to minor fines. The rates are hereafter respectively called "imprisonment rate," "fine rate" and "minor fine rate." The imprisonment rate ranged from 23.3 percent to 25.0 percent, while the fine rate hovered between 66.1 percent and 67.2 percent and the minor fine rate between 7.8 percent and 10.6 percent in 1926 and 1931.

In 1936, the imprisonment rate dropped to 15.2 percent, whereas the fine rate and the minor fine rate increased to 71.9 percent and 12.9 percent, respectively. Minor fines have been rarely meted out after the war. Between

Table 46 Number and Percentage of Persons Sentenced for Bodily Injury in Courts of First Instance, by Type of Punishment and Term of Imprisonment

Year	Total (A)	Determinate-term imprisonment with labour (B)	Rate of imprisonment with labour $\frac{B}{A}$ (%)	Percentage of persons sentenced to with labour, by term			
				3 years or more	Over 3 years	2 years or more	Over 2 years
1926	8,557	2,137	25.0	10.6	…	8.3	1.1
1931	8,310	1,939	23.3	11.9	…	7.7	1.2
1936	10,064	1,533	15.2	11.7	…	10.6	0.6
1941	…	…	…	…	…	…	…
1946	…	…	…	…	…	…	…
1951	22,065	3,771	17.1	10.7	5.5	8.2	…
1956	48,198	5,542	11.5	8.3	3.9	5.6	…
1961	51,537	6,658	12.9	6.3	3.0	3.3	…
1966	49,513	5,639	11.4	5.4	2.1	5.7	…
1971	39,055	4,917	12.6	5.8	2.0	5.4	…
1976	29,518	5,582	18.9	5.1	1.8	6.7	…
1981	21,962	4,418	20.1	5.8	2.5	6.1	…
1986	16,067	3,904	24.3	6.8	2.8	9.3	…
1987	15,162	4,077	26.9	5.7	2.5	7.7	…

1956 and 1971 the imprisonment rate moved between 11.4 percent and 12.9 percent. During the same period, the fine rate was hovering between 87.1 percent and 88.6 percent. However, the imprisonment rate increased after 1976 and reached 26.9 percent in 1987. The increase of the imprisonment rate in and after 1976 could be seen as a movement shifting back to prison sentences from the sentencing of fines. The reason for the phenomenon might be explained by the fact that, as demonstrated by the concentration of sentencing on the upper limit of fines provided by statutes (as mentioned earlier), in not a few cases, the ceiling provided for fines was thought to be too low to meet the offence committed.

As for the term of determinate sentence of impirsonment with labour, the rate of those sentenced to three years in prison or more ranged from 10.6 percent to 11.9 percent in the prewar period. After the war. the rate was 10.7

Determinate-term imprisonment			Fine (C)	Rate of fine $\frac{C}{A}$ (%)	Minor Fine (D)	Rate of minor fine $\frac{D}{A}$ (%)	Rate of suspended execution of sentence
1 year or more	6 months or more	under 6 months					
10.2	27.1	43.8	5,749	67.2	671	7.8	13.4
10.7	23.6	46.2	5,491	66.1	880	10.6	19.0
4.6	24.8	48.2	7,236	71.9	1,294	12.9	19.0
…	…	…	…	…	…	…	…
…	…	…	…	…	…	…	…
21.6	39.1	20.4	18,060	81.8	234	1.1	44.9
18.9	42.0	25.3	42,453	88.2	203	0.4	46.8
19.9	47.2	22.2	44,875	87.1	4	0.0	51.4
25.7	48.9	14.3	43,871	88.6	3	0.0	51.2
27.2	48.4	13.2	34,137	87.4	—	—	54.7
29.8	47.9	10.4	23,933	81.1	2	0.0	55.8
32.3	47.4	8.3	17,544	79.9	—	—	50.5
35.6	42.8	5.5	12,162	75.7	1	0.0	49.6
36.9	44.8	4.9	11,084	73.1	1	0.0	52.2

Sources: Annual Report of Criminal Statistics,
Annual Report of Judicial Statistics, etc.

percent in 1951. However, the rate gradually decreased. It was 5.1 percent in 1976. The rate then increased slightly but again decreased to 5.7 percent in 1987. The rate of those sentenced to two years or more but less than three years was higher in the prewar days than in the postwar period. Before the war, the execution of sentences could be suspended in cases where prison terms were shorter than two years. Taking this into account, the court of law was quite stern in meting out punishments before the war.

The rate of suspended execution sentences was lower before the war, between 13.4 percent and 19.0 percent, but increased to the 44.9-55.8 percent level after the war.

D. Theft

Table 47 shows changes in determinate-term sentences given to those

Table 47 Number and Percentage of Persons Sentenced for Theft in Courts of First Instance, by Term of Imprisonment

Year	Total	Percentage of persons sentenced to determinate-term imprisonment with labour, by term							Rate of suspended execution of sentence
		3 years or more	over 3 years	2 years or more	over 2 years	1 year or more	6 months or more	under 6 months	
1926	11,686	14.1	…	12.8	10.0	34.7	33.9	4.5	6.1
1931	16,317	12.3	…	12.8	9.4	37.8	34.4	2.7	5.0
1936	20,574	12.2	…	13.8	3.3	40.1	32.0	1.9	6.8
1941	15,881	…	…	…	…	…	…	…	…
1946	…	…	…	…	…	…	…	…	…
1951	59,834	4.9	1.4	9.7	…	55.7	28.3	1.3	40.3
1956	55,126	2.7	0.8	8.0	…	56.2	32.0	1.1	43.7
1961	36,208	3.8	1.3	9.0	…	57.1	29.4	0.7	46.1
1966	28,627	4.9	2.1	9.7	…	58.4	26.2	0.7	48.9
1971	20,277	4.7	2.0	9.0	…	57.9	27.7	0.7	53.4
1976	19,524	6.0	2.6	9.1	…	52.5	31.7	0.7	53.6
1981	17,735	7.3	3.3	9.4	…	50.1	32.5	0.7	52.0
1986	17,224	7.4	3.6	11.2	…	54.0	27.0	0.3	51.9
1987	16,442	7.6	3.8	11.8	…	55.7	24.5	0.3	51.0

Sources: Annual Report of Criminal Statistics,
Annual Report of Judicial Statistics, etc.

offenders found guilty on charges of theft at courts of first instance from 1926 through 1986 and in 1987 at intervals of five years.

The ratio of imprisonment for three years or longer stayed between 12.2 and 14.1 percent in the prewar period. After the war, however, the rate drastically decreased. It was between 2.7 and 4.9 percent between 1951 and 1971. The rate started climbing in and after 1976 reaching 7.6 percent in 1987. Similar percentage rates were seen in prison terms for two years and more but shorter than three years. However the difference between the prewar rates and postwar rates was relatively small. It was 13.8 percent in 1936 and 11.8 percent in 1987.

The difference is much smaller in the case of prison terms of less than six months. There is also no major difference in the rate of prison terms of six

Table 48 Number and Percentage of Persons Sentenced for Rape in Courts of First Instance, by Term of Imprisonment

Year	Total	Life imprisonment with labour	Determinate-term imprisonment with labour	Percentage of persons sentenced to determinate-term imprisonment with labour, by term							Rate of suspended execution of sentence
				Over 5 years	3 years to 5 years	Over 3 years	2 years or more	Over 2 years	1 year or more	under 1 year	
1926	173	2	171	10.5	45.0	···	26.3	3.5	18.1	0.0	5.3
1931	154	3	151	13.2	42.4	···	29.8	4.6	14.6	0.0	4.0
1936	269	—	269	11.2	46.8	···	29.4	1.5	12.6	0.0	9.3
1941	···	···	···	···	···	···	···	···	···	···	···
1946	···	···	···	···	···	···	···	···	···	···	···
1951	582	2	580	4.3	31.7	19.8	31.4	···	29.1	3.4	33.0
1956	856	—	856	1.6	50.9	14.8	37.5	···	9.7	0.2	38.7
1961	2,101	1	2,100	1.6	52.6	13.0	36.8	···	8.8	0.3	43.2
1966	2,634	2	2,632	2.7	56.2	17.5	34.5	···	6.6	0.0	12.2
1971	2,444	—	2,444	1.4	51.8	16.4	39.6	···	7.1	0.2	12.3
1976	1,506	1	1,505	2.9	47.3	16.2	43.4	···	6.2	0.2	23.5
1981	970	—	970	3.0	51.5	14.8	39.3	···	6.1	0.1	22.9
1986	702	—	702	5.6	54.7	22.9	35.3	···	4.4	0.0	29.3
1987	661	—	661	5.6	53.3	21.3	36.9	···	4.2	0.0	26.8

Sources: Annual Report of Criminal Statistics,
Annual Report of Judicial Statistics, etc.

months or more but less than one year. However, the rate of imprisonment of more than one year but shorter than two years was between 34.7 percent and 40.1 percent in the prewar period but it increased in the postwar period to the 50.1-58.4 percent range. In general, prewar sentences were stricter than those in the postwar period.

The rate of suspended execution of sentences was low at 5.0 to 6.8 percent in the prewar period but increased in the postwar period, starting with 40.3 percent in 1951. It continued to increase and reached 53.6 percent in 1976. The rate slightly declined thereafter, and the rate in 1987 was 51.0 percent.

E. Rape

Table 48 shows the change in punishment given by courts of first instance to rape offenders at intervals of five years between 1926 and 1986 and in 1987.

Table 49 Number of Persons Granted Suspension of Execution of Imprisonment with or without Labour in Courts of First Instance, by Type of Suspension, and Number of Persons whose Suspension of Execution of Sentence was Revoked

Year	Total	Suspension (A)	Simple suspension	Suspension with probationary supervision (B)	$\frac{B}{A}$ (%)	Rate of suspension	Revocation (C)	$\frac{C}{A}$ (%)
1926	28,981	3,745	–	–	–	12.9	259	6.9
1931	35,219	4,817	–	–	–	13.7	508	10.5
1936	47,974	6,049	–	–	–	12.6	668	11.0
1941	33,785	…	…	…	…	…	637	…
1946	…	…	…	…	…	…	984	…
1951	118,229	54,272	…	…	…	45.9	10,107	18.6
1956	102,275	48,969	42,047	6,922	14.1	47.7	8,974	18.3
1961	83,249	43,142	35,075	8,067	18.7	51.8	5,860	13.6
1966	78,814	42,142	34,130	8,012	19.0	53.4	4,702	11.2
1971	69,467	40,361	33,910	6,451	16.0	58.1	3,324	8.2
1976	75,498	45,892	37,654	8,238	18.0	60.7	4,631	10.1
1981	76,219	44,269	36,052	8,217	18.6	58.0	6,288	14.3
1986	74,856	42,589	36,347	6,242	14.7	56.8	5,884	13.9
1987	73,183	42,062	35,609	6,453	15.3	57.4	5,488	13.1

Sources: Annual Report of Criminal Statistics,
Annual Report of Judicial Statistics, etc.

The rate of imprisonment of three years or longer was between 55.5 and 58.0 percent in the prewar period. The rate was between 50.2 and 60.3 percent in the postwar period except in 1951. However, the rates in 1966, 1986 and 1987 were 58.9, 60.3 and 58.9 percent, respectively, rising above the prewar rates.

The rate of suspended execution of sentences was low between 4.0 percent and 9.3 percent in the prewar period. The rate has been far higher in the postwar period. It topped 30 percent between 1951 and 1961. However, it declined sharply after 1966 to the 12-percent level in 1966 and 1971. The rate increased again thereafter and 1987 the rate was 26.8 percent. The sharp decrease of the suspended execution of sentences between 1966 and 1971 is attributed to strict punishments given to offenders of sex-related crimes which frequently took place in the period.

Table 50 Number of Persons Granted Suspension of Execution of Fine or Imprisonment with or without Labour in Courts of First Instance, by Type of Suspension, and Number of Persons Whose Suspension of Execution of Sentence Was Revoked

① Determinate-term imprisonment with labour

Year	Total	Suspension (A)	Simple suspension	Suspension with probationary supervision (B)	$\frac{B}{A}$ (%)	Rate of suspension	Revocation (C)	$\frac{C}{A}$ (%)
1926	28,835	3,717	…	…	…	12.9	…	…
1931	34,563	4,714	…	…	…	13.6	…	…
1936	44,933	5,855	…	…	…	13.0	…	…
1941	33,568	…	…	…	…	…	…	…
1946	…	…	…	…	…	…	…	…
1951	117,746	53,939	…	…	…	45.8	10,105	18.7
1956	101,339	48,188	41,277	6,911	14.3	47.6	8,965	18.6
1961	80,385	41,015	33,026	7,989	19.5	51.0	5,848	14.3
1966	71,434	36,990	29,295	7,695	20.8	51.8	4,656	12.6
1971	59,131	33,123	27,053	6,070	18.3	56.0	3,246	9.8
1976	69,535	40,966	33,024	7,942	19.4	58.9	4,573	11.2
1981	71,228	39,772	31,805	7,967	20.0	55.8	6,233	15.7
1986	69,535	37,670	31,570	6,100	16.2	54.2	5,844	15.5
1987	67,877	37,177	30,923	6,254	16.8	54.8	5,457	14.7

(4) Suspension of Execution of Sentences

Table 49 shows changes in both the number and percentage of those who were given suspended execution of sentences out of all offenders sentenced to determinate terms of imprisonment with or without labour at courts of first instance at intervals of five years between 1926 and 1986 and in 1987. The suspended execution of sentence rate was between 12.6 percent and 13.7 percent in the prewar period but it was on the 40-percent level in 1951 and 1956 in the postwar period. After 1961 the rate drastically increased. It was 60.7 percent in 1976.

The rate slightly decreased then but it was still high in 1987 at 57.4 percent. This may be explained by the development of current thought to utilize more widely the treatment in community as exemplified by the partial amend-

② Determinate-term imprisonment without labour

Year	Total	Suspension (A)	Simple suspension	Suspension with probationary supervision (B)	$\frac{B}{A}$ (%)	Rate of suspension	Revocation (C)	$\frac{C}{A}$ (%)
1926	146	28	…	…	…	19.2	…	…
1931	613	103	…	…	…	16.8	…	…
1936	3,029	194	…	…	…	6.4	…	…
1941	217	…	…	…	…	…	…	…
1946	…	…	…	…	…	…	…	…
1951	483	333	…	…	…	68.9	2	0.6
1956	936	781	770	11	1.4	83.4	9	1.2
1961	2,864	2,127	2,049	78	3.7	74.3	12	0.6
1966	7,380	5,152	4,835	317	6.2	69.8	46	0.9
1971	10,336	7,238	6,857	381	5.3	70.0	78	1.1
1976	5,963	4,926	4,630	296	6.0	82.6	58	1.2
1981	4,991	4,497	4,247	250	5.6	90.1	55	1.2
1986	5,321	4,919	4,777	142	2.9	92.4	40	0.8
1987	5,306	4,885	4,686	199	4.1	92.1	31	0.6

ment to the Penal Code in 1947 by which courts were given the power to grant under specified conditions suspension of execution of sentences of up to three years imprisonment instead of the previous two years. Out of those given suspended execution of sentences, 14.1 to 19.0 percent were given probational supervision, except in 1961, 1966, 1976 and 1981 when the rate went above 18 percent.

Those given suspended execution of sentences and those whose suspended execution of sentences were cancelled in a specific year do not overlap necessarily and thus the rate of the latter against the former cannot be exactly a cancellation rate of the suspension of execution of sentence. However, it is still useful to see a general tendency of the cancellation rate of the suspension of execution of sentence. It was high in the 18-percent level in 1951 and 1956. After 1961 the rate declined and reached 8.2 percent in 1971. The rate then slightly increased, rising to 13.1 percent in 1987.

Table 50 shows the number of those given suspended execution of sentences by category of determinate term imprisonment with labour, determinate

③ Fine

Year	Total	Suspension (A)	Simple suspension	Suspension with probationary supervision	Rate of suspension	Revocation (B)	$\frac{B}{A}$ (%)
1926	103,742	–	–	–	–	–	–
1931	95,202	–	–	–	–	–	–
1936	116,345	–	–	–	–	–	–
1941	154,513	...	...	...	...	...	...
1946	...	...	...	...	...	...	...
1951	284,733	4,795		...	1.7	26	0.5
1956	724,513	1,281	1,281	–	0.2	6	0.5
1961	2,375,085	410	409	1	0.0	–	–
1966	4,197,963	380	374	6	0.0	1	0.3
1971	1,804,088	129	129	–	0.0	1	0.8
1976	2,357,125	87	87	–	0.0	–	–
1981	2,095,147	48	48	–	0.0	–	–
1986	2,272,034	21	21	–	0.0	–	–
1987	1,608,336	12	12	–	0.0	–	–

Sources : Annual Report of Criminal Statistics,
Annual Report of Judicial Statistics, etc.

term imprisonment without labour and fines, at courts of first instance at intervals of five years between 1926 and 1986 and in 1987.

As for those granted suspension of execution of sentence among the total sentenced to imprisonment with labour, the ratio showed a similar tendency with that shown in Table 49 concerning the suspension of execution ratio among the entire total sentenced to imprisonment with labour and without labour because the number of those sentenced to imprisonment without labour was negligible in number. Those who were given suspension of execution of fines were also very small in number.

The rate of those granted suspended execution of sentence among those given determinate term imprisonment without labour was high in the prewar period, registering 19.2 percent in 1926 and 16.8 percent in 1931, exceeding the suspended execution rate among those given determinate term imprisonment with labour. However, the suspended execution rate among those given imprisonment without labour decreased to 6.4 percent in 1936, reflecting the increase

Table 51 Percentage for Length of Time for Trials in Courts of First Instance

Year	Total	1 month or less	3 months or less	6 months or less	1 year or less	2 years or less	Over 2 years
1926	100.0(28,889)	76.1	20.4	2.6		0.9	
1931	100.0(34,639)	74.3	21.8	2.7		1.3	
1936	100.0(46,254)	79.0	16.8	3.4		0.9	
1941	...	...	...	...		...	
1946	...	...	...	...		...	
1951	100.0(147,068)	27.8	42.4	14.8	7.9	4.6	2.6
1956	100.0(124,179)	25.1	45.7	13.4	8.2	4.7	2.9
1961	100.0(101,778)	18.2	49.7	17.6	7.9	4.0	2.5
1966	100.0(96,094)	13.7	49.6	21.0	9.0	3.3	3.3
1971	100.0(78,932)	8.2	41.9	28.3	14.0	4.8	2.8
1976	100.0(82,992)	7.2	52.9	25.0	9.1	2.8	3.0
1981	100.0(81,393)	7.9	62.2	20.6	5.7	1.8	1.7
1986	100.0(78,602)	6.5	67.1	19.4	4.7	1.3	0.9
1987	100.0(76,483)	6.0	67.0	19.9	4.9	1.4	0.8

Sources: National Police Agency, Annual Report of Criminal Statistics, etc.

in the total number of those sentenced to imprisonment without labour. As such, the rate became smaller than the counterpart in those given imprisonment with labour for determinate periods.

The sharp increase of those given imprisonment without labour for determinate terms and the decline in the suspended execution rate in 1936 is attributed to a sharp increase of violators of election laws, including the House of Representatives Election Law.

In the postwar period, the suspended execution rate for determinate-term imprisonment without labour was relatively high in 1956 at 83.4 percent. With the total increase of determinate–term imprisonment sentences without labour between 1961 and 1971, however, the rate decreased to between 74.3 and 70.0 percent. It increased after 1976 and has been at the high percentage rates of 80 to 90 percent since then. Looking at the cancellation rate, it was remarkably low in the case of imprisonment without labour compared with the counterpart of imprisonment with labour. This is rather natural considering the fact that the

Table 52 Number and Rate of Those under Custody or on Bail at Time of Adjudication in Courts of First Instance

Year	Total number of persons adjudicated (A)	Total number of persons detained (B)	Length of detention			Number of persons released on bail (C)	$\frac{B}{A}$ (%)	$\frac{C}{B}$ (%)
			1 month or less	3 months or less	Over 3 months			
1926	153,087	30,513 (100.0)	25,285 (82.9)	4,518 (14.8)	710 (2.3)	2,749	19.9	9.0
1931	152,049	33,594 (100.0)	23,758 (70.5)	7,712 (23.0)	2,124 (6.3)	2,682	22.1	8.0
1936	188,967	46,692 (100.0)	37,090 (79.4)	8,128 (17.4)	1,474 (3.2)	5,843	24.7	12.5
1941	196,831	32,325 (100.0)	23,523 (72.8)	7,490 (23.2)	1,312 (4.1)	3,872	16.4	12.0
1946	237,309	97,464 (100.0)	65,410 (67.1)	28,555 (29.3)	3,499 (3.6)	15,689	41.1	16.1
1951	147,068	96,511 (100.0)	37,009 (38.3)	49,460 (51.2)	10,042 (10.4)	30,593	65.6	31.7
1956	124,179	93,140 (100.0)	40,761 (43.8)	42,455 (45.6)	9,924 (10.7)	21,874	75.0	23.5
1961	101,778	76,007 (100.0)	29,197 (38.4)	36,749 (48.3)	10,061 (13.2)	22,707	74.7	29.9
1966	96,094	68,203 (100.0)	25,797 (37.8)	32,426 (47.5)	9,980 (14.6)	23,386	71.0	34.3
1971	78,932	52,327 (100.0)	20,497 (39.2)	23,071 (44.1)	8,759 (16.7)	22,886	66.3	43.7
1976	82,992	58,888 (100.0)	21,388 (36.3)	28,331 (48.1)	9,169 (15.6)	23,528	71.0	40.0
1981	81,393	60,454 (100.0)	17,534 (29.0)	34,161 (56.5)	8,759 (14.5)	17,740	74.3	29.3
1986	78,602	58,892 (100.0)	12,502 (21.2)	36,748 (62.4)	9,642 (16.4)	12,323	74.9	20.9
1987	76,483	57,557 (100.0)	12,561 (21.8)	35,635 (61.9)	9,361 (16.3)	12,641	75.3	22.0

Sources: Annual Report of Criminal Statistics,
Annual Report of Judicial Statistics, etc.

majority of postwar offenders who were given determinate–term imprisonment sentences without labour were tried in traffic professional negligence cases.

The decline in the suspended execution rate between 1961 and 1971 is believed to have resulted from strict measures against those offenders involved in serious traffic professional negligence. The rise of the suspended execution rate thereafter is attributed to the fact that imprisonment sentences with labour, rather than imprisonment sentences without labour, came to be applied to offenders of a malignant nature. (See 3-(2)-B of this chapter.)

(5) Duration of Trial

Table 51 shows the changes in the duration of trials at courts of first instance (from the time a prosecution is instituted in a case to its disposition at a court of first instance), at five-year intervals between 1926 and 1985, and in 1987.

Before World War II, a large majority of cases were adjudicated within a month and the percentage of trials which lasted for three months or longer was extremely low.

After the war, however, more than 80 percent of the cases were disposed of by courts of the first instance within six months, except in 1971. The percentage of lengthy trial cases, those lasting six months or longer, fluctuated between 14.4 percent and 15.8 percent from 1951 to 1966, before rising to 21.6 percent in 1971. But it then declined and dipped to 7.1 percent in 1987.

Compared with the prewar period, the duration of trials became longer after the war, probably due to the following reasons. The Code of Criminal Procedure, which was implemented in January 1949, proclaimed a basic idea of putting emphasis on hearings in public trials, the entering of pleas and arguments and direct examinations.

Hearings in public trials under the present Code require more time in examining evidence compared with the prewar period as restrictions on the admissibility of evidence, particularly in the written form of statements made out of court necessitate the introduction of direct testimony of witnesses in court hearings. In 1971, the percentage of lengthy trials shot up because of the prolonged trials of the so-called radical student activists, who were involved in violent incidents reported in great numbers in those days.

(6) Detention and Release on Bail

Table 52 shows the changes in the ratio of those who were detained pending trial (detention ratio) among the total number of defendants adjudicated by courts of the first instance (excluding those involved in criminal cases of adults against juveniles, which come under the jurisdiction of family courts) and

Table 53 Number and Rate of Those under Custody or on Bail at Time of Adjudication by Investigating Judges

Year	Total number of persons adjudicated (A)	Total number of persons detained (B)	Length of detention			Number of persons released on bail (C)	B/A (%)	C/3 (%)
			1 month or less	3 months or less	Over 3 months			
1926	6,746	6,186 (100.0)	1,775 (28.7)	3,143 (50.8)	1,268 (20.5)	2,413	91.7	39.0
1931	8,070	7,665 (100.0)	1,990 (26.0)	3,162 (41.3)	2,513 (32.8)	2,892	95.0	37.7
1936	10,246	9,531 (100.0)	2,148 (22.5)	4,563 (47.9)	2,820 (29.6)	5,055	93.0	53.0
1941	4,025	3,759 (100.0)	604 (16.1)	1,449 (38.5)	1,706 (45.4)	1,071	93.4	28.5
1946	7,088	6,574 (100.0)	621 (9.4)	3,200 (48.7)	2,753 (41.9)	1 566	2.7	25.3

Sources: Annual Report of Criminal Statistics and Summary of Criminal Statistics

those who were released on bail among those detained (bail ratio).

On examining the detention ratio and bail ratio in the Showa era at five-year intervals, and comparing the trends between the prewar period and the postwar period, we first notice that the detention ratio declined substantially after the war.

It reached a peak of 24.7 percent in 1936. This corresponds to the period when the number of criminal cases hit a record high. An increase in the number of cases involving persons without fixed abode and cases in which it was feared that evidence might be destroyed (henceforth referred to as "cases with reasons to detain the defendants") can also be attributed to the sudden surge in the detention ratio in that year. Excluding 1946, the year right after the war, there were no substantial changes in the detention ratio in the postwar period, which fluctuated around the 70-percent mark except for 1951 and 1971 when it dropped to the 60-percent mark.

It was 41 percent in 1946. Considering the fact that criminal cases were still dealt with under the old Code of Criminal Procedure, it was a remarkable increase compared with the percentage in the prewar period and reveals that there were a great number of cases in which there were reasons to detain defendants in those days.

Before the war, detention for a period of up to a month made up 70 percent to 80 percent of all cases, much shorter than that in the postwar period.

Table 54 Number of Accuseds Adjudicated in Appellate Courts and Rate of Koso and Jokoku Appeal

Year	Koso Appeal								Rate of Koso Appeal	Rate of Jokoku Appeal
	Total	Original adjudication overruled	Freshly adjudicated	of which; Not guilty	Order of retrial etc.	Appeal dismissed	Withdrawal	Others		
1926	6,429 (100.0)	…	5,405 (84.1)	237	…	4 (0.1)	941 (14.6)	79 (1.2)	24.6	38.2
1931	5,663 (100.0)	…	4,720 (83.3)	153	…	–	908 (16.0)	35 (0.6)	17.3	38.1
1936	9,194 (100.0)	…	7,971 (86.7)	135	…	–	1,185 (12.9)	38 (0.4)	20.3	44.7
1941	7,117 (100.0)	…	6,044 (84.9)	…	…	2 (0.0)	961 (13.5)	110 (1.5)	21.1	33.9
1946	9,507 (100.0)	…	7,993 (84.1)	93	…	…	1,064 (11.2)	450 (4.7)	…	…
1951	41,598 (100.0)	22,088	21,040 (50.6)	1,139	1,048	13,460 (32.4)	5,167 (12.4)	883 (2.1)	…	…
1956	18,285 (100.0)	4,772	4,590 (25.1)	127	182	11,127 (60.9)	2,320 (12.7)	66 (0.4)	15.7	43.2
1961	12,466 (100.0)	3,130	3,041 (24.4)	93	89	7,321 (58.7)	1,979 (15.9)	36 (0.3)	14.4	39.0
1966	12,502 (100.0)	3,348	3,258 (26.1)	57	90	7,401 (59.2)	1,690 (13.5)	63 (0.5)	13.0	39.6
1971	9,640 (100.0)	2,567	2,504 (26.0)	71	63	5,949 (61.7)	1,075 (11.2)	49 (0.5)	13.0	39.2
1976	8,459 (100.0)	2,049	2,005 (23.7)	52	44	5,266 (62.3)	1,115 (13.2)	29 (0.3)	10.8	36.5
1981	7,643 (100.0)	1,531	1,497 (19.6)	41	34	4,997 (65.4)	1,101 (14.4)	14 (0.2)	9.8	34.9
1986	6,139 (100.0)	1,027	1,019 (16.6)	23	8	3,972 (64.7)	1,120 (18.2)	20 (0.3)	8.8	34.6
1987	6,189 (100.0)	1,055	1,040 (16.8)	18	15	4,099 (66.2)	1,020 (16.5)	15 (0.2)	8.4	33.3

Sources: Annual Report of Criminal Statistics,
Annual Report of Judicial Statistics, etc.

The prewar investigation and trial process was conducted on the principle of "long investigation and short trial." This was partly due to the enforcement of "preliminary inquiry proceedings by examining judges," which apparently made the average detention period short in those days.

Table 53 shows the changes in the number of detainees, their detention periods and others at the end of preliminary inquiry proceedings. In sharp contrast with detention periods pending public trial, the percentage of those who were detained less than one month was low, while the percentage of those who were detained for three months or longer was high.

Looking at the changes in duration of detention in the postwar period, the percentage of detentions which lasted for three months or longer exceeded the 10-percent mark since 1951 and reached 16.7 percent in 1971. Since then it declined until 1981 but inched up to the 16-percent mark after 1986 and reached 16.3 percent in 1987. Conversely, the percentage of detention periods which lasted one month or shorter has been declining since 1976, as the detention period pending trial has been getting longer.

The bail ratio was lower in the prewar period, compared with that in the postwar period, reaching 31.7 percent in 1951 but dipping to 23.5 percent in 1956. Since then, it started to climb again and topped the 40-percent mark in 1971 and 1976 before dipping to 22.0 percent in 1987. One of the main reasons attributable to the recent drop in the bail ratio is an increase in the number of recidivists, etc., among the defendants. Meanwhile, high percentages marked in both 1971 and 1976 can be interpreted as a result of an increase in defendants with no previous criminal records, such as those involved in radical student activities. A relatively high bail ratio marked in 1951 can be attributed to an increase, during the social turmoil shortly after the war, in number of first-time offenders who had no prior criminal record. In 1956, the detention ratio was as high as 75 percent, while the bail ratio was as low as 23.5 percent. However, we should not overlook the fact that crimes involving underworld criminal organizations increased in those days. (See Chapter II-5)

(7) Trial at Appellate Court

Table 54 shows the changes in the percentage of "koso" appeals filed at high courts against judgments by courts of the first instance and the ratio of "jokoku" appeals to the Supreme Court against High Court judgments at five-year intervals between 1926 and 1985, as well as in 1987.

Before the war, the percentage of koso appeals topped the 20-percent mark, except in 1931, being higher than the postwar koso appeal ratio. After the war, the percentage fluctuated at a relatively high level of between 13.0 percent and 15.7 percent from 1956 through 1971. But it started declining after 1976 and dipped to 8.4 percent in 1987.

The total number of defendants adjudicated by courts of koso appeal reached a record high of 9,194 in 1936. It is to be recalled that this surge coincided with the period when crimes became rampant in the prewar era. After the war, it started to decline gradually from 18,285 persons in 1956 and fell to nearly half at 9,640 in 1971. Since then, it declined further and dipped to 6,189 in 1987.

The percentage of withdrawal of koso appeals fluctuated between 12 percent and 16 percent before the war. It continued to fluctuate around the same level even after the war, but increased to 18.2 percent in 1986, remaining at

16.5 percent in 1987.

The percentage of dismissals of koso appeals was extremely low before the war when trial in courts of koso appeal was trial de novo, viz., retrial of the whole case, and not a process of reviewing the judgments of courts of the first instance. Conversely, the percentage of making a new judgment after reversing a lower court judgment was extremely high in the prewar period, compared with that in the postwar period due to the same reason. (Refer to Article 401 of the old Code of Criminal Procedure)

In the postwar period, the percentage of dismissals of koso appeals fluctuated between 58 percent and 66 percent except in 1951, when it dropped to 32.4 percent (13,460 persons). It accounted for 66.2 percent (4,099 persons) in 1987. Also, the percentage of making a new judgment after the reversal of a lower court's judgment has been on the downward trend after the war, from 25.1 percent (4,590 persons) recorded in 1956 to 16.8 percent (1,040 persons) in 1987.

Those who were pronounced not guilty in new judgments rendered by courts of koso appeals after reversing the judgments of courts of the first instance amounted to 127 persons in 1956, and a relatively high figure was also registered in 1971. But it has been declining more or less since and dipped to 18 persons in 1987.

The rate of jokoku appeals taken from the judgments made by koso appellate courts fluctuates between the lower 30 percent and lower 40 percent in both the prewar and postwar periods and there has been no substantial change. The figure, however, started to decline since 1976 and dipped to 33.3 percent in 1987.

Section 2. Correction

1. OUTLINE

A review of the history of Japan's prison administration from the Meiji era to the Showa era shows that the Meiji era was a period when steps were taken toward modernisation of prison administration, as reflected by the enactment of Prison Rules and its Illustration in 1872, an amendment to the Prison Rules in 1889 and the passage of the Prison Law in 1908.

In the Taisho era, the term "kangoku" for prison was renamed "keimusho" (penal institution) on the grounds that the word kangoku gave a gloomy and oppressive impression.

In some prisons, the system of progressive treatment of prisoners started tentatively (for example, at the Toyotama Prison in 1915).

In 1921, the prison health officer system was introduced. In 1922, the seven juvenile prisons (equivalent to reformatories) were established. Thus, efforts were made to enhance the atmosphere of humanitarianism and reformism.

The Showa era saw an unfortunate in-between war period. However, clearly shown in the movement between 1933 when the Progressive Stage System for the Treatment of Prisoners was decreed, and 1972 when the advanced classification system for convicted prisoners was effected, the Showa era was a time of blooming results brought forth by continuous efforts to realise more humanitarian, more socialised and more scientific treatment of prisoners in line with the prevailing ideas in international criminology on preventing repeated offences and on helping prisoners to reintegrate into society.

Improvements in prison administration from 1926 to 1935 saw the parole examination system enacted in 1931 and rules for the administration of juvenile reformatories and the progressive stage system for the treatment of prisoners effected in 1933. In this way, the idea of "penalty for reformation," aiming at the reformation and resocialisation of prisoners undergoing the execution of penalties, was materialised and the concepts and methods for penalty for reformation were established to some extent to improve the treatment of prisoners from a humanitarian and scientific standpoint.

From 1935 to 1945, Japan waged an all-out struggle in the Sino-Japan War and World War II, and prisoners were sent to various places not only in Japan but also abroad to engage in construction of air bases, shipbuilding and production of aircraft and munitions.

Toward the end of the war, out of a total of 151 prisons, including branches, 26 were completely destroyed and 13 were heavily damaged by U.S. bombing raids. Okinawa Prison sustained particularly heavy damage as the prefecture was turned into a battlefield. Hiroshima Prison and the Urakami branch of Nagasaki Prison were also heavily damaged by atomic bombs. At Hiroshima Prison, five officers and 12 inmates were killed instantly and more than 600 others, comprising both officers and prisoners, were injured. Many of the seriously injured died later. At the Urakami branch prison in Nagasaki, 18 officers, including the warden, 35 members of their families and 81 prisoners were killed instantly.

On May 15, 1941, the Tokyo Preventive Detention House was set up at Toyotama Prison following the revision of the Public Peace Preservation Law, and 162 persons, including five women, accused of harboring "dangerous thoughts" were detained as of the end of May 1944.

The period between the end of the war in 1945 and the signing of the San Francisco Peace Treaty in 1952 was a time of change from postwar chaos, typified by overcrowded prisons and extreme shortages of goods, to the restoration of order. At first mass escapes in groups, mob violence and riots broke out frequently. At the same time, a number of prisoners were sent to Hokkaido in 1948 to ease the overcrowding and to help increase food production, besides engaging in land renovation and development. Others were sent to the Tohoku district in 1951 to engage in the construction of hydraulic power stations.

In 1946, the prison administration authorities lost no time in issuing the new principles of prison administration (consisting of principles of respect for basic human rights, of rehabilitation of prisoners and their restoration to society, and of self-sufficiency in prison life) in an effort to project the ideal image of prison administration. At the same time, the prison administrators improved the treatment of prisoners in various fields. In 1948, they promulgated the Guidelines for Prisoners' Diagnosis and Classification and laid the basic ground for scientific classification of prisoners.

After postwar instability ended around 1953, the rapid increase in the number of prisoners ceased, security and order inside the prisons was restored, and prison administration or treatment in correctional institutions made great strides in tune with Japan's economic development.

As a first step in improving prison administration in this period, the volunteer prison visitor system was established in 1953, introducing the counseling services of a wide circle of knowledgeable citizens to the treatment in prisons. This became part of the "socialisation of prison administration."

In 1957, the Classification Center was set up inside Nakano Prison to start full-scale correctional treatment, based on scientific classification. In 1969, Ichihara Prison was established as an open institution to receive an increasing number of traffic violators sentenced to imprisonment without labour. In 1972, the Rule for the Classification of Prisoners was implemented, and this paved the way for scientific classification aimed at individualised treatment based on the ideas of modern criminology. This method has since been substantially established in the treatment of inmates in correctional institutions.

Thus reviewing the changes in prison administration in the Showa era, it is apparent that this was a period when treatment of prisoners progressed amid the admixture of a "humanitarian approach" aimed at an improved treatment environment (improvements in treatment, etc.), a "socialising approach" which sought to reintegrate prisoners into society through a wide understanding and help on the part of the community (public participation), and a "scientific approach" which aimed at correction and rehabilitation based on knowledge of behavioral science (diagnostic classification, etc.).

On the other hand, the current Prison Law has undergone no substantial revisions since its enactment in 1908 and therefore it is quite inadequate to match the changes and advances in ideas on correction. In an effort for modernisation of correctional practices, incorporation of international standards and establishment of statutory bases for correctional practices, the Justice Ministry, viz., the Justice Minister, asked the Legislative Council to study a total amendment of the Prison Law in 1976. The council made its recommendations in 1980. Subsequently, after further deliberations, the ministry submitted a Penal Institution Bill to the 108th Diet session in April 1987. Debate on the bill was launched but continued without completion of the legislation before the end of the Showa era. The task has been carried over into the Heisei era.

2. HUMANITARIAN AND SOCIALISING APPROACH TO PRISON ADMINISTRATION

The humanitarian approach that even prisoners should be treated with respect for human dignity underlies Japan's modern prison administration. On the other hand, from the viewpoint of helping discharged prisoners return to society smoothly, there is another school of thought, viz., the so-called socialising approach in prison administration. There, emphasis in prison treatment has been put on diminishing the difference in living environments between prisons and the community at large as far as practically possible and maintaining and strengthening the prisoner's ties with the outside world. The former idea emanates from modern humanitarianism and the latter stems from reflection on the traditional idea that prisoners should be segregated from society and be kept strictly confined.

These two approaches crossing and influencing each other led the prison administration in the Showa era in a movement to improve the living conditions of prisoners in terms of quarters, food and clothing and to mitigate the segregation of prisoners from society to a reasonable extent by utilising the resources in the community, like the aids from outside volunteer citizens.

The first clear step toward humanitarian treatment of prisoners was enactment of the Rule for the Progressive Stage Treatment of Prisoners in 1933. This was a virtual revision of the Prison Law with a rather strong custodial flavour and introduced humane correctional treatment measures into prison administration. It was an epochal event.

In 1946, amid lingering postwar turmoil, the justice authorities acted to issue an instruction on the basic policy concerning implementation of the Prison Law. The instruction said, "As prisoners do not lose their proper rights concerning life, person and property although they are deprived of liberty, it is required to respect their rights without prejudice and without neglecting care."

Successive reformations in prisoners' treatment followed, as mentioned below:

1) The colour of the prison uniform was changed from red clay to drab green (1947);

2) The prison chaplain system in which religionists were appointed as public officials to serve as chaplains in prisons was abolished in consideration of the Constitutional principle of separation of religion and state, and volunteer religionists from the private sector were registered at each prison instead (1947);

3) The disciplinary punishment of prisoners through maximum solitary confinement in dark cells was virtually abolished (1947);

4) The requirement that prison officials be present during an interview between a prisoner and a lawyer was waived (1948), and

5) The working hours of prisoners were fixed at eight hours a day and 48 hours a week (1953).

The Standard Minimum Rules for the Treatment of Prisoners, adopted at the first United Nations Congress on the Prevention of Crimes and Treatment of Offenders held in 1955, set forth a general principle in correctional treatment calling for humane, educational and therapeutic treatment of prisoners as well as maintenance of security and order in penal institutions. It has since served as an important guideline to accelerate the reformation of the prison administration of Japan.

In 1966, the Rule to Enforce the Prison Law was greatly revised in order to further improve prison administration. The revisions included: 1) shortening the maximum period of solitary cell confinement; 2) relaxing the ban against chatting among prisoners; 3) lifting the ban on laying tatami mats in the cells; 4) lifting the prohibition on reading general daily newspapers and giving permission under specified conditions; 5) abolishing rules specifying the colours of prisoners' clothings and beddings; and 6) permission to grow hair. Thus, life in prison was improved in various ways. Moreover, the work hours were reduced on April 1, 1973 from 48 hours to 44 hours a week in line with the spread of the five-day week system in outside society and from March 20, 1986, a four-week total of 168 hours, equivalent to a biweekly five-day work week system, was adopted.

Reviewing the socialisation trend in the treatment of prisoners, we can take note of the following institutional revisions: 1) the system of private-sector chaplains effected in 1947; and 2) the volunteer prison visitors system created in 1953 to enlist the cooperation of volunteer citizens. Moreover, lecturers and instructors are often invited from outside to help in all scenes of prisoner treatment such as prison industry, vocational training, academic education, intake orientation, living guidance and various club activities. High school correspondence courses and several other kinds of correspondence courses are actively conducted. Recently, "Correctional Exhibitions" consisting mainly of exhibitions and spot sales of products made by prisoners have been held around the country as part of publicity activities to gain the understanding and support of society toward the correctional administration.

3. SCIENTIFIC TREND IN PRISON ADMINISTRATION

In order to prevent a repetition of crimes by prisoners and help them in their resocialisation, it is necessary to scientifically diagnose individual prisoners on their characters and personalities, probe into the reasons for their crimes and provide them individualised treatment to meet their specific needs.

It is said that the introduction of scientism to prison administration in this country started with psychological observation by psychiatrists at Ichigaya Prison in 1927. Later in 1931 the Rule for Examination of Release on Parole was enacted. It referred to heredity, health conditions, mental conditions (intelligence, emotion and will) and other factors as matters to be examined.

The Rule for the Progressive Stage Treatment of Prisoners established in 1933 stipulated that prisoners' personalities and their physical and mental conditions be examined based on the required knowledge such as medicine, psychology, pedagogy and sociology. Thus the new system allowed outsiders to take part in prison administration to promote scientism in the treatment of prisoners.

During the period of the Japan-China War and the subsequent World War II, personal observation of prisoners began to be conducted on select prisoners having higher working ability in response to an increase in the volume of labor outside the prisons for munitions production. In 1944 the guideline for wartime prisoner personality observation was established, making additional progress in the application of scientific knowledge for the treatment of prisoners.

In the postwar age scientism was more positively introduced into prison administration.

In 1946 the Kitakata Prison (currently Jyoto Medical Prison) was created as a facility to receive prisoners suffering from mental disorders. This was the first specialised prison in Japan. In 1947, the Committee on Correctional Science, consisting of medical, psychological and pedagogical experts, came into existence in an effort to promote correctional science. In 1948, the inmate classification examination guideline was set to institutionalise the scentific classification for the fist time. This stipulated detailed criteria on the degree of difficulty in the correction of prisoners, their criminality, prison terms, health conditions, ages and sex and served as the basis for the subsequent progress of the classification system.

In 1957, the Nakano Prison began to serve as a classification center to help promote classified treatment and also as a model facility for classified treatment.

In 1961, the Toyohashi Branch Prison adopted for the first time the open treatment system which had been developing on the concept of individualisation of treatment, following a rapid increase in the number of inmates sentenced to prison without labor as traffic violators since about 1960. Similar facilities have come into existence one after another.

In the meantime the Justice Ministry devised its own such personality diagnosis test as the Justice Ministry-style Sentence Completion Test (MJSCT) (1965) and Justice Ministry-style Personality Inventory (MJPI) (1967) to enhance scientific measurement.

After these steps, in 1972 the Rule for the Classification of Prisoners was enforced with a view to implementing scientific examination and subsequent proper accommodation and treatment of inmates. This rule stipulates important matters in the classification for admission, classification for treatment and classified treatment. It also designates the key facilities in eight blocs as classification centers. Thus the contents of the previous system have been completely renewed and scientific treatment aimed at helping rehabilitation by individualising treatment under the unified national standard has been promoted and institutionalised.

4. *CHANGES IN THE PRISON ADMINISTRATION ORGANIZATION*

The unification of the prison organization started with the promulgation of the Directive on Prison Organization and Personnel in 1903. In 1922 the prison system was completely altered as was seen in the fact that the name of "kangoku" for prison was changed into "keimusho" and the new system went into the Showa era which started in 1926. In the early Showa era 47 prisons, including Kosuge Prison, were located across the country, the juvenile prisons, including the Odawara Juvenile Prison, numbered 8, the prison branches numbered 42, including the Hachioji branch, and offshoot branches numbered 62, including the Yokaichiba subbranch.

The prison officers consisted of wardens, deputy wardens, captains, interpreters, health officers, assistant health officers, chaplains, teachers, technical instructors, assistant technical instructors, prison guards and women prisoner captains, numbering 7,749 in total.

In 1929 the offshoot branches were upgraded to the prison branches and captains were assigned there with a view to improving treatment and clerical works.

The Tokyo Detention House came into existence in 1937 as the first independent detention house for unconvicted prisoners awaiting trials. After that time until 1941 the Nagoya, Kyoto, Osaka and Kobe detention houses were established.

In 1946 the prison officers' titles were categorized into Justice Ministry Administrative Officer, Justice Ministry Technical Officer and Justice Ministry Instructor. In 1947 chaplains as Justice Ministry Instructors were transformed into Justice Ministry Administrative Officers as the task of chaplains was entrusted to the hands of religionist from the private sector. In 1948 the Directive on Prison Organization and Personnel was abolished and the Order for Prisons and Detention Houses was promulgated to formalize the locations and names of individual prisons and detention houses.

In 1949 the Rule for the Organization of Prisons, Juvenile Prisons and Detention Houses, which was the first formal internal rule after the war in terms of prison administration, was established, and the nine sections, including the documentary affairs section, were set up in the prisons and other organizations. The prison branches were divided into the prison branches (Yokosuka Prison branch and 13 others) and the detention house branches (Kumagaya detention house branch and 84 others) in accordance with the purposes of confinement.

In 1952 the rules for organization were revised and the hierarchy of the division-section system was adopted for the interior organization. The Toyotama Prison and 13 other major prisons were newly installed with classification offices. Some other important revisions after that time were as follows:

(1) 1957: The Toyotama Prison, seized by the U.S. Forces, was returned to the Japanese government and the Nakano Prison was newly created.

(2) 1969: The Ichihara Prison was newly established as a concentration prison for the confinement of those sentenced to imprisonment without labour for traffic violations.

(3) 1971: The Kosuge Prison and the Utsunomiya Prison were abolished and the Kurobane Prison and the Okazaki Medical Prison were established.

(4) 1972: The Okinawa Prison was returned to Japan in accordance with the reversion of Okinawa.

(5) 1983: The Nakano Prison was abolished and the Tsukigata Prison was established.

The current prison and other related organizations fall under the control and guidance of the Justice Ministry's Correction Bureau and the eight-bloc Regional Correction Headquarters located in parallel with the jurisdiction of the high courts and high public prosecutor's office and bear part of the task of the Correction Bureau and put under their guidance and contol the prisons and other correction facilities in their territories.

As of the end of December, 1988, the 15 major prisons and one major juvenile prison had five divisions (General Affairs Division, Security and Industry Division, Education Division, Medical Division and Classification Division) under the wardens. The standard-sized prisons numbering 43 and juvenile prisons numbering eight are provided with two divisions (General Affairs Division and Security and Industry Division) and one to three sections under the direct control of the wardens. The organizations of these facilities, however, are slightly different in accordance with the size and the ages and physical conditions of the inmates-whether they are adults or juveniles or whether they need medical treatment, etc. The two major detention houses have four divisions (general affairs, security, classification and medical divisions) and one section under the direct control of wardens. The five standard-sized detention houses have two divisions (general affairs and security divisions) and two sections under the direct supervision of wardens. In accordance with the progress of classification treatment, it became necessary to create facilities having a proper setup for effective implementation of correction and as a result the facilities having organization different from the ordinary facilities have been established. (Such as Ichihara Prison, Hachioji Medical Prison, Kawagoe Juvenile Prison).

As of the end of December 1988, the prisons number 58, the juvenile prisons 9, detention houses 7, prison branches 9 and detention house offshoots 108, and the upper limit of officers is set at 16,995.

5. CHANGE IN THE SITUATION OF ADMISSION IN PRISONS

Herein the continuous situation of accommodations in terms of prison administration from 1926 to 1988 is surveyed based on available data chiefly by means of annual prison administration statistics and an annual report of statistics on correction.

(1) Changes in the Numbers of New Prisoners and New Female Prisoners and Females' Ratio

Fig. 27 shows a shift in the numbers of new prisoners (prisoners newly admitted to prisons in each respective year after they had been given the sentence of imprisonment with or without labour or penal detention and these penalties had become final) and female prisoners and females' ratio (the ratio of female prisoners to the total new prisoners).

The new prisoners numbered 29,583 in 1926. Their number began to rise after 1930 and began to fall after reaching a prewar peak of 42,094 in 1934 and went down to the prewar low of 27,387 in 1942. Their number took an upward trend again in 1943, reached the 60,000 level in 1946 shortly after World War II and registered the Showa era record of 70,727 in the postwar confusion year of

Fig.27 Number of Newly Admitted Prisoners (1926~1988)

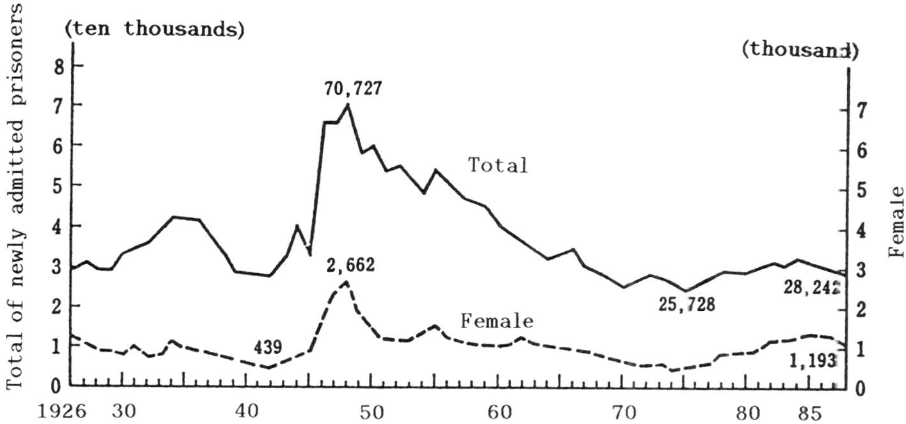

Sources: Annual Report of Statistics on Prison Administration and Annual Report of Statistics on Correction

1948.

After that year, their number followed a general downward course in accordance with the subsiding of social confusion and the upsurge in economic growth and went down to the Showa era record low of 25,728 in 1974. But after that year the number of new prisoners began to rise because of an increase in the inmates convicted of the use of stimulant drugs and reached another peak of 32,060 in 1984. Since then number of these offenders is decreasing slightly.

The number of new prisoners in 1988 was smaller than that in 1926 by 1,341. Considering the fact that the population in 1926, which was 60,741,000, doubled to 122,783,000 in 1988, the ratio of new prisoners to the population in 1988 is 47 with that in 1926 as 100, a decrease by more than half.

In regard to the number of new female prisoners, they numbered more than 700 from 1926 to 1938, and exceeded 1,000 in 1926, 1927 and 1934. After that their number continued to decrease and went down to the Showa era record low of 439 in 1942.

In 1946 immediately after the end of the war, the number of new female prisoners began to skyrocket and reached the Showa era record of 2,662 in 1948. After slight ups and downs their number continued to decrease in general and reached a postwar low of 467 in 1974. In and after 1975 they generally continued to increase and reached a peak of 1,363 in 1985, and after that they have continued to slightly decrease.

The number of new female prisoners was large in the early Showa era because many prostitutes were sentenced to penal detention by the Ordinance for the Punishment of Police Infractions which could cover prostitution.

Fig.28 Number of Average Daily Inmates in Prisons and Rate per Population (1926～1987)

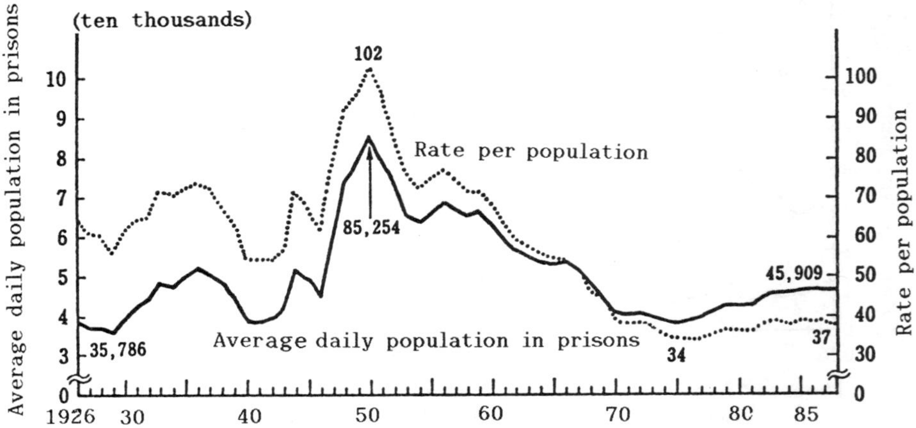

Note: "Rate per population" means average daily population in prisons per 100,000 civilians.
Sources: Annual Report of Statistics on Prison Administration and Annual Report of Statistics on Correction

(Female inmates under penal detention represented 59.5 percent of the total new female prisoners in 1926.)

The record high number of female prisoners in 1948 was due to the increase in the number of thefts against the background of economic plight. The increases in their numbers after 1975 was mainly due to the rise in the number of violators of the Stimulant Drug Control Law.

The females'ratio was mostly in the 2 percent range but topped the 4 percent level in 1926 and in the five years from 1984 to 1988.

(2) Changes of Average Daily Admission of Prisoners and Its Ratio to Population

Fig. 28 and Table 8 in the Appendix show an average daily incarceration of convicted prisoners from 1926 to 1988 and its ratio to 100,000 people.

The average daily incarceration of convicted prisoners in 1926 numbered 39,529, and began to increase in and after 1931 to amount to 51,407 in 1936. They began to decrease and went down to 38,428 in 1941. But they rose to 51,639 in 1944. After a rise and fall for several years, they began to rapidly soar in 1947 and reached the Showa era record high of 85,254 in 1950. They generally were on the downward trend in and after 1951 and reached a record low of 37,850 in 1975. But after that year they began to increase and numbered 45,909 in 1988.

Fig.29 Percentage of Newly Admitted Prisoners by Major Offence (1926~1988)

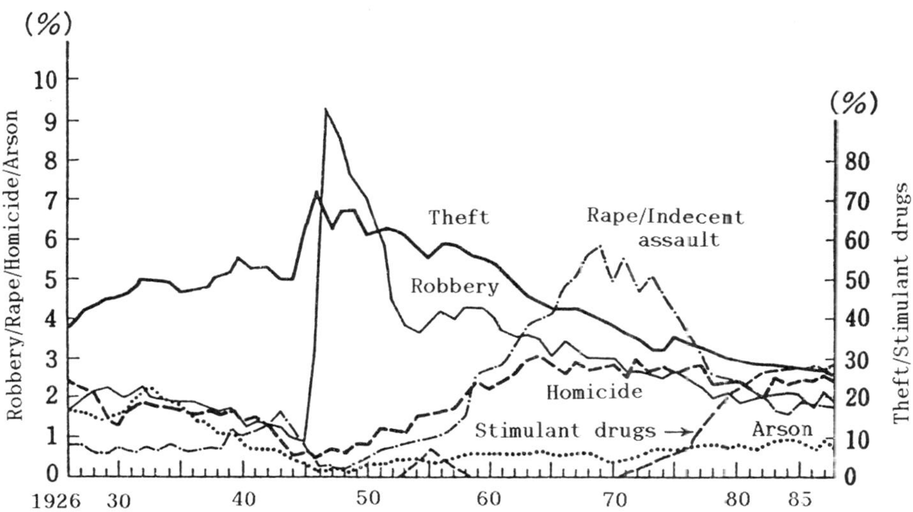

Sources: Annual Report of Statistics on Prison Administration and Annual Report of Statistics on Correction

With regard to their ratio to the 100,000 population, the prewar high record was 73 for 1936 and the low record was 54 from 1940 through 1942. In the postwar era 102 for 1950 was the highest and 34 for 1975 to 1977 was the lowest. It was 37 for 1988. The ratio for 1988 is 57 with the figure for 1926 as 100.

(3) Changes in Percentage of Newly Admitted Prisoners by Offence

Fig. 29 shows a shift of percentage of newly admitted prisoners by offence in and after 1926.

Thefts, which represented 37.3 percent of the total newly admitted criminals in 1926, gradually increased and reached the 50-percent mark in 1938 and the 60-percent level in 1945 before they registered a record high of 71.8 percent in 1946. They went down to the 50-percent mark in 1954, to the 40-percent mark in 1962, to the 30-percent mark in 1969 and to the 20-percent mark in 1979. Their percentage for 1988 was 25.4.

Robberies stayed at about 2 percent until 1939 and dropped to about 1 percent during the war, but sharply rose to 3.1 percent in 1946 and registered a record high of 9.3 percent in 1947. Then they began to gradually fall and stayed at the 2-percent mark after 1978.

Murders registered the 2-percent level from 1926 to 1928 and then dropped

Fig.30 Number of Newly Admitted Prisoners by Type of Punishment (1926~1988)

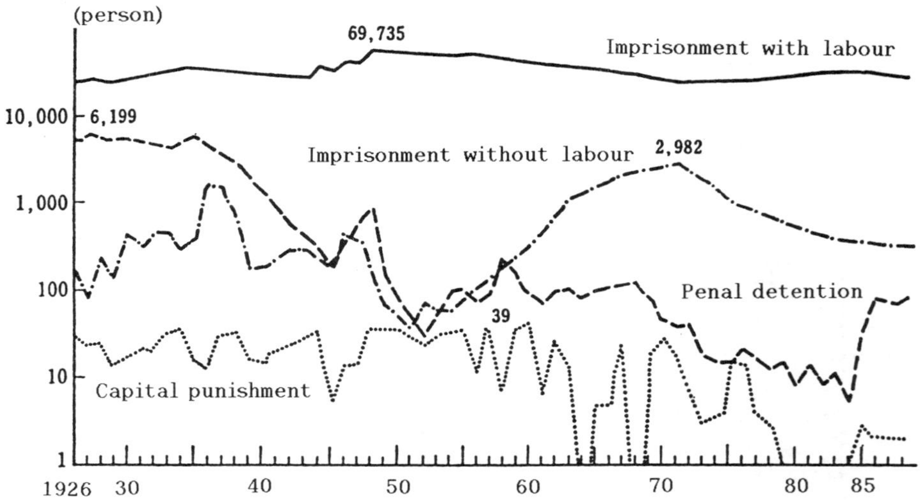

Note: The logarithnic scale is applied in this figure.
Sources: Annual Report of Statistics on Prison Administration and Annual Report of Statistics on Correction

to stay at about the 1.5-percent level. They significantly fell to less than 1 percent from 1943 to 1950 and rose to the 1-percent level in 1951 and to the 2-percent level in 1958. Since then they have remained at the 2-percent mark.

Showing a trend similar to that of murders, arsons stayed at the 1-percent or 2-percent mark until 1939 but began to gradually drop in 1940 and reached the lowest record of 0.1 percent in 1946 and 1948. They slightly increased after that but never exceeded the 1-percent mark. They were 0.8 percent in 1988.

Rapes and indecent assaults stayed below the 1-percent mark until 1954 except for the period from 1939 to 1944 when they remained at the 1-percent level, and began to gradually increase in 1955 and reached the peak of 5.8 percent in 1969. Since then they have continued to decrease and registered 1.8 percent in 1988.

Violations of the Stimulant Drug Control Law represented 6.4 percent in 1955 and then remarkably dropped. But they began to rise in 1972 and registered 27.1 percent in 1985, exceeding thefts and placing first. Since then they are on the upswing.

Gambling and lotteries stayed from the 3-percent to the 9-percent mark in the prewar period and drastically decreased after the war. Recently they have

Fig.31 Percentage of Newly Admitted Prisoners, by Term of Imprisonment with Labour (1926~1988)

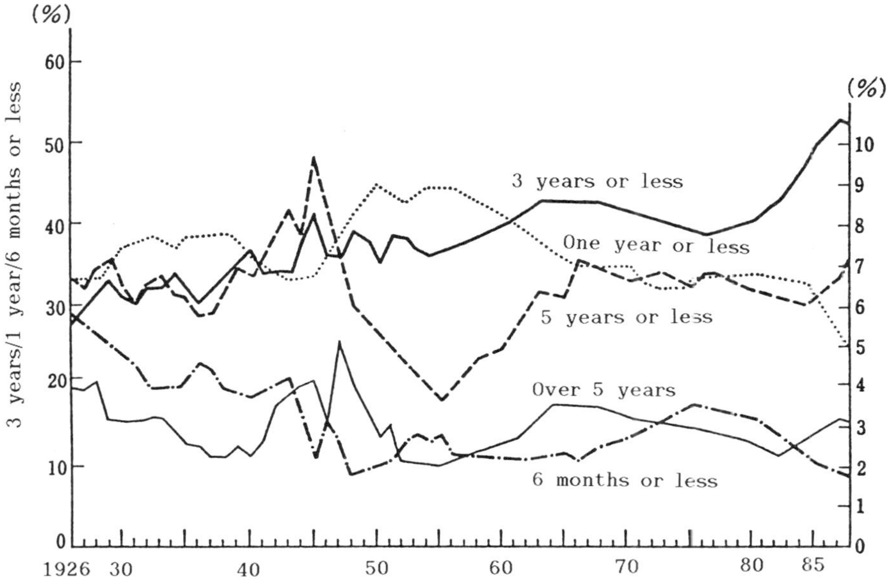

Sources: Annual Report of Statistics on Prison Administration and Annual Report of Statistics on Correction

stayed below 1 percent. On the contrary, the percentage of bodily injuries and extortions is larger in the postwar period than in prewar times.

As mentioned above, thefts sharply increased in the wartime period and the period just after the war when goods were in short supply, murders and arsons drastically decreased during those periods and robberies rose only in the period of postwar confusion. The percentage of arsons was comparatively high in the early Showa era and rapes and indecent assaults began to increase in 1955 with the peak in 1971. The rate of the violation of the Stimulant Drug Control Law has placed first after exceeding that of thefts in 1985. These are noteworthy features in the Showa period.

(4) Change in the Number of Newly Admitted Prisoners by Penalty and in the Rate of Newly Admitted Prisoners by Prison Term

Fig. 30 and Fig. 31 shows the change in the number of newly admitted prisoners by penal type (death sentence, imprisonment with labour, imprisonment without labour and penal detention) and the rates of the prisoners with labour by prison term.

By penal type, the number of prisoners given the sentence of imprisonment without labour, chiefly covering offences of advocating rebellious thought, stayed at the less than 700 mark until 1948, except for 1936 which registered 1,755 and 1937 which recorded 1,438, and dropped to the two-digit level from 1949 to 1955. But with the advent of the age of motorisation the number of prisoners given the sentence of imprisonment without labour, largely traffic violators charged with professional negligence resulting in death and injuries began to rise in 1956 and reached a peak of 2,982 in 1971. Then it moved downward and registered 349 in 1988.

As for the number of those given the sentence of penal detention, it registered 5,871 persons or as high as 19.8 percent of the total prisoners in 1926, mostly violations of the Ordinance for the Punishment of Police Infractions. Similarly, a large portion of those sentenced to penal detention was violators of the ordinance in the early Showa era. Then the number gradually decreased and went down to the three-digit level in 1941 and to the two-digit level in 1950, which persisted in the following years.

As for death penalty, the years when more than 30 death-row prisoners were executed were 1934 in the prewar period and 1948, 1949, 1950, 1954, 1955, 1957, 1959 and 1960 in the postwar period. The number has dropped to the single-digit level since 1977.

Analysis of the length of imprisonment with labour of newly admitted prisoners in the 1926-1974 period shows that those serving life terms comprised 0.2 percent of all newly admitted inmates during that time except for a period from 1936 to 1942 when such "lifers" comprised 0.1 percent of the total. It went down to the 0.1 percent mark in 1973 and has stayed at that level.

Newly admitted prisoners serving terms of over six months but below one year made up 30-to-40 percent of the total in the 1926-1960 period, accounting for the majority of prisoners during those years. Next came those serving prison terms of over one year but under three years, and those imprisoned for less than six months. After 1961, those serving prison terms of over one year but under three years comprised the majority at 40-to-50 percent of the total, followed by those imprisoned for over six months but under one year, and those serving terms of less than six months.

Those serving short prison terms of less than six months comprised about 20 percent of the total in the prewar period and the percentage was somewhere between 10 percent and 15 percent after World War II, except between 1972 and 1980, when it fluctuated between 15 percent and 20 percent. Those serving relatively long prison terms exceeding five years made up more than 4 percent of the total in 1926, 1928, 1944, 1945, 1947 and 1948, and ranged from 2 percent to 3 percent in almost all other years.

Fig.32 Percentage of Newly Admitted Prisoners by Frequency of Imprisonment (1926~1988)

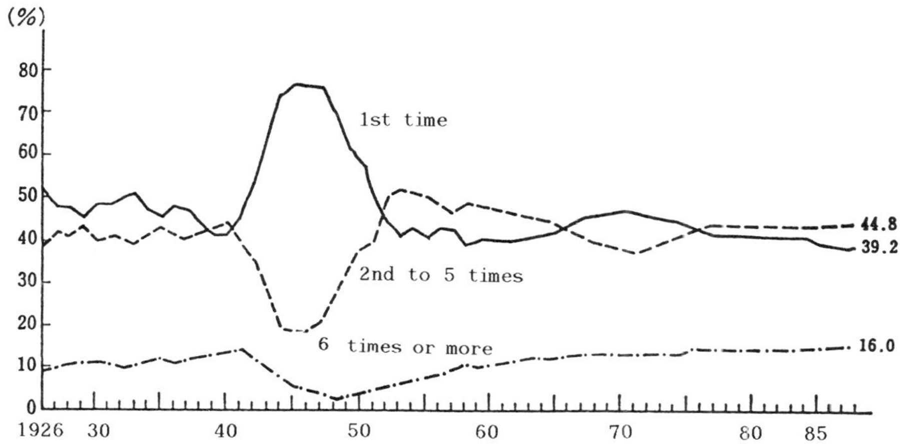

Sources: Annual Report of Statistics on Prison Administration and Annual Report of Statistics on Correction

(5) Change in Percentage of Newly Admitted Prisoners by Frequency of Admission

Fig. 32 shows the change in the percentage of newly admitted prisoners by frequency of admission to prisons since 1926. Those who were imprisoned for the first time comprised 40-to-50 percent of newly admitted inmates in the 1926-1942 period, but sharply increased in 1943 and reached a record high of 76.8 percent in 1946. This rate began to decrease in 1948 and went down to 41.3 percent in 1953. It then leveled off with slight ups and downs and registered 39.2 percent in 1988.

The rate of those imprisoned from two to five times leveled off at about 40 percent of newly admitted inmates in the 1926-1940 period and began to decrease to reach a record low of 17.7 percent in 1945. After that it took an upturn and reached 51.7 percent in 1953 but then fell to 37.9 percent in 1971. It rose slightly after that but has stayed at about 44 percent since 1977.

Those imprisoned six times or more rose from 9.0 percent in 1926 to 13.9 percent in 1941 but decreased remarkably during and shortly after the war and reached a record low of 2.6 percent in 1948. It then began to rise, exceeding 10 percent in 1958 and registering 16.0 percent in 1988.

Fig. 33 shows the results of a survey of 2,122 prisoners as of August 1, 1987, who had been imprisoned more than 10 times and were still serving their prison terms. It is designed to show the years in which those prisoners were first

Fig.33 Number of Recidivists Imprisoned Ten Times or more, by the Year of the First Imprisonment (1926~1977)

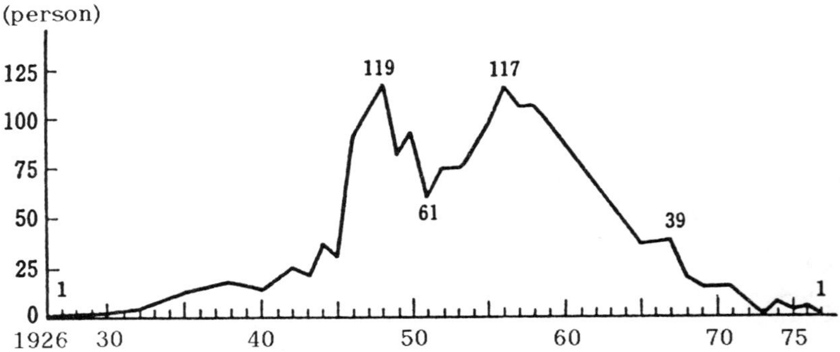

Note: **Subjects are 2,122 prisoners.**
Source: Research and Training Institute Ministry of Justice

Fig.34 Percentage of Newly Admitted Prisoners by age Group (1926~1988)

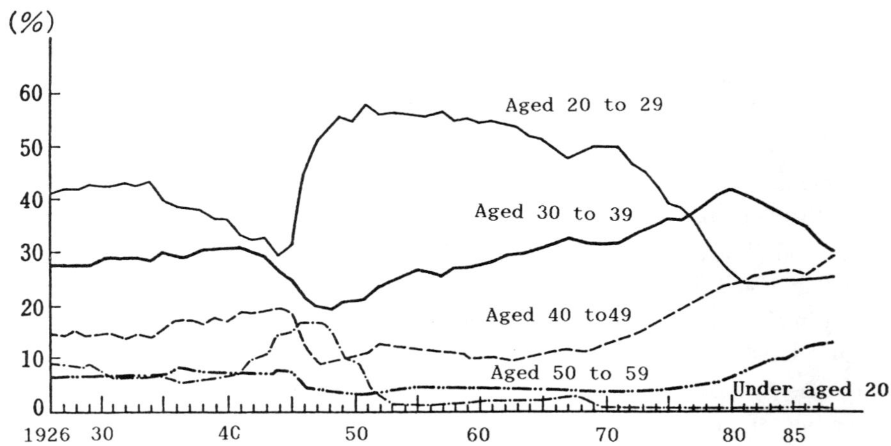

Sources: Annual Report of Statistics on Prison Administration and Annual Report of Statistics on Correction

imprisoned.

The oldest inmate was imprisoned in 1926 for the first time. The newest one was imprisoned in 1977. Fig. 33 shows two remarkable peaks in 1948 and 1956, coinciding with the period of postwar chaos and an economic depression after the Korean War. In particular, 394 (18.6 percent of the total) were imprisoned for the first time from 1946 to 1950, and it is noteworthy that there are a number of people who committed first crimes during the period of postwar turmoil and have not yet rehabilitated themselves and have been serving prison terms even after more than 40 years.

(6) Change in Percentage of Newly Admitted Prisoners by Age

Fig. 34 shows the changes in the percentage of newly admitted prisoners by age in and after 1926. The percentage of those below 20 went below 10 percent from 1926 to 1942 but exceeded 10 percent in 1943 to reach a record high of 16.7 percent in 1947. It rapidly decreased in 1951 when the age at which the Juvenile Law was applied was raised from below 18 to below 20 and tumbled down to the 1.0-percent mark in 1953. Although there was a slight increase after that, it went below 1.0 percent in 1972 and was as small as 0.3 percent in 1988.

As far as those in their 20s were concerned, their percentage exceeded 40 percent from 1926 to 1934 and then began to decrease, reaching 29.7 percent in 1944. But it began to rise greatly after the war and reached a peak of 57.6 percent in 1951. It stayed above 50 percent for most years but went below 50 percent in 1966 and fell drastically in and after 1972, went below 40 percent in 1975 and registered 35.3 percent in 1977, yielding the first position to those in their 30s (37.0 percent). The rate of those in their 20s went down further to 24.1 percent below that of those in their 40s (25.7 percent) in 1982 and has leveled off since then.

As for those in their 30s, their percentage was on the uptrend, with 19.0 percent in 1948 being the lowest, and reached a record high of 41.4 percent in 1980. It has been on the downward trend since then but showed 29.3 percent in 1988, registering the highest percentage among all the age brackets.

Those in their 40s hit their lowest overall mark in 1947 (9.2 percent), those in their 50s in 1948 (3.2 percent) and those in their 60s in 1948 and 1950 (0.8 percent). Their percentage showed slight ups and downs until around 1970 but began to move upward in 1973 and registered 28.8 percent for those in their 40s, 13.1 percent for those in their 50s and 2.9 percent for those aged 60 or older in 1988. These results clearly show the aging of the newly admitted prisoners.

A notable fact is that the newly admitted prisoners below 20 and in their 20s sharply increased from 1946 to 1951, accounting for more than 60 percent of all newly admitted prisoners. This signified the influence of the postwar confusion on the young people.

(7) Change in the Rate of Newly Admitted Prisoners by Degree of Living Standard

Table 55 shows the change in the rate of newly admitted prisoners by degree of living standard. Those whose living standard was "low" represented

Table 55 Percentage of Newly Admitted Prisoners, by Living Standard

Year	Total	Good	Average	Bad	Unaccounted
1926	100.0(23,683)	0.7	4.8	94.4	0.2
1930	100.0(27,410)	0.7	3.2	96.0	0.1
1935	100.0(35,561)	0.3	2.4	97.2	0.1
1940	100.0(27,808)	0.5	3.7	95.5	0.3
1946	100.0(65,766)	0.4	4.9	91.0	3.7
1950	100.0(60,040)	0.5	5.8	93.6	0.2
1955	100.0(54,035)	0.4	5.1	94.3	0.2
1960	100.0(41,008)	0.1	10.8	88.4	0.7
1965	100.0(33,935)	0.1	13.6	85.7	0.6
1970	100.0(25,890)	0.4	48.5	48.6	2.5
1975	100.0(26,175)	0.5	48.2	47.1	4.2
1980	100.0(28,374)	0.6	42.7	50.9	5.8
1985	100.0(31,656)	0.5	39.0	54.1	6.4

Note : Figures in the parentheses show actual number.
Sources: Annual Report of Statistics on Prison Administration and Annual Report of Statistics on Correction

more than 90 percent from 1926 to 1955, but then sharply dropped from 47 percent to 54 percent after 1970.

Those with living standards classified as "middle" were between the 2-percent and 5-percent mark until 1955, but then rapidly increased and stayed between 39 percent and 48 percent in and after 1970. These facts show that most prisoners in the prewar period and the postwar period until 1955 were poverty-level individuals. The facts also show that just less than half of the prisoners in recent years have not always committed crimes because of poverty, and that changes have been observable in their criminal motives. It is also notable that the rate of those with "high" living standards accounted for less than 1 percent in both the prewar and postwar periods.

(8) Change in the Rate of Newly Admitted Prisoners by Degree of Education

Table 56 shows the change in the rate of newly admitted prisoners by

Table 56 Percentage of Newly Admitted Prisoners, by Education Background

Year	Total	University	High-school	Elementary school	Drop out of elementary school	Uneducation	Unaccounted
1926	100.0(23,683)	0.6	4.5	67.7	22.1	5.0	0.1
1930	100.0(27,410)	0.5	5.1	68.2	21.5	4.5	0.1
1935	100.0(35,561)	0.6	5.6	73.7	17.3	2.8	0.0
1940	100.0(27,803)	0.5	5.1	75.3	16.3	2.6	0.1
1946	100.0(65,766)	0.5	4.0	78.3	12.2	4.8	…
1950	100.0(60,040)	1.7	11.2	74.6	7.8	4.7	…
1955	100.0(54,035)	1.1	6.4	81.4	7.7	3.5	…
1960	100.0(41,008)	1.0	9.8	81.9	5.5	1.8	0.1
1965	100.0(33,935)	1.0	11.7	82.1	3.8	1.3	0.1
1970	100.0(25,890)	1.5	13.0	81.7	3.1	0.7	0.1
1975	100.0(26,175)	1.4	13.1	82.1	2.6	0.6	0.1
1980	100.0(28,374)	1.4	14.1	81.6	2.1	0.4	0.4
1985	100.0(31,656)	1.6	16.0	80.6	1.5	0.3	0.1

Note : Figures in the parentheses show actual number.
Sources: Annual Report of Statistics on Prison Administration and Annual Report of Statistics on Correction

educational background in and after 1926.

Those who dropped out of elementary school represented 22.1 percent and those who had never attended school 5.0 percent in 1926, but their rates went down later. The elementary school dropouts accounted for 12.2 percent in 1946, and those who had never attended school accounted for 4.8 percent. In 1965, the figures were 3.8 percent for the former and 1.3 percent for the latter. In 1985, the figures were 1.5 percent and 0.3 percent.

On the other hand, those who had graduated from high school (including those from middle school under the old education system) accounted for about 5 percent in the prewar period and stayed below 10 percent up until 1960. The rate began to increase after 1965, and it registered 16.0 percent in 1985.

The figures for those who had graduated from university (including high school under the old education system) stayed between 0.5 percent and 0.6

Table 57 Cumulative Rate of Recidivist Prisoners by Duration of Time Spend between Last Release from Prison and Re-commitment of Crime

Year of reception	Under 3 months	Under 6 months	Under 1 year	Under 2 years	Under 3 years	Under 4 years	Under 5 years	5 years or more
1925	21.6	33.5	47.9	61.3	69.9	75.3	80.1	100.0(11,517)
1930	25.9	39.9	54.4	69.2	76.6	81.7	85.1	100.0(14,241)
1935	33.8	47.4	63.0	76.4	81.9	85.1	87.1	100.0(19,298)
1940	31.6	46.1	60.8	74.5	81.5	85.7	88.0	100.0(15,962)
1945	29.4	42.2	57.8	71.7	78.7	83.6	86.8	100.0(5,490)
1950	26.8	43.8	65.2	84.1	90.8	94.0	95.5	100.0(24,701)
1955	21.9	36.3	54.2	73.1	84.7	90.7	93.8	100.0(29,772)
1960	25.1	41.3	61.2	78.8	86.8	91.2	93.5	100.0(23,988)
1965	22.6	36.8	54.7	73.1	82.5	88.3	92.1	100.0(18,811)
1970	16.1	29.7	48.5	67.9	79.2	85.8	90.0	100.0(13,395)
1975	14.9	26.6	44.6	63.3	74.1	80.6	85.3	100.0(14,703)
1980	13.8	26.4	46.3	65.7	75.6	81.5	85.1	100.0(16,320)
1985	13.4	25.5	45.5	66.3	77.0	83.1	87.1	100.0(18,857)

Note : Figures in the parentheses show actual number.
Sources: Annual Report of Statistics on Prison Administration and Annual Report of Statistics on Correction

percent in the prewar period, and stabilized around the 1-percent mark in the postwar period, registering 1.6 percent in 1985. Thus the degree of educational background of new prisoners became higher throughout the Showa era.

(9) Repetition of Crimes by Ex-Convicts

Table 57 shows how soon ex-convicts repeat their crimes. For instance, in 1985, 18,857 ex-convicts were admitted to prisons throughout Japan for repeating offences. Of them 13.4 percent were found to have committed their offences within three months after serving their previous prison terms. The table examines the changes in every five years from 1926 through 1985 over eight periods ranging from up to three months to more than five years. The table shows that the rate of ex-convicts repeating their offences within three months since their release from prison was relatively high with about 30 percent during the last war-from 1935 through 1945. Starting in 1965, however, it went down, falling to the 13-percent level in and after 1980. Similar trends prevails in the section covering a period of up to one year. The rate tended to fall in years close to 1985-46.3 percent in 1980 to 45.5 percent in 1985. Generally speaking this trend also prevails in the last half of the period under review-from 1926 through 1985.

In this way those who committed repeat offences after short intervals are becoming fewer in the latter half of the Showa era than in the first half of the same period.

(10) Changes in the Rate of Prisoners by Type of Release

Appendix Table 9 shows the change of the rate of prisoners by type of release in and after 1926. Those released on parole accounted for the low figure of 5.7 percent in 1926, and exceeded 10 percent in 1933 to register 10.1 percent. Their rates rapidly increased in accordance with an increase in the number of those working in shipbuilding and other war industries amid the expansion of the scale of the war, and registered 30.9 percent in 1944.

Shortly after the war, the number of those released on parole further increased in consideration of the overcrowded condition of prisons to rise to a record high of 79.7 percent in 1949. After that the rate went down to 60 percent in 1952 and 50 percent in 1964, reaching a postwar low of 50.8 percent in 1982. Later, their rate also increased and stayed between 55 percent and 57 percent in the past four years because of a more active and flexible approach to parole on the part of the authorities in charge under the Justice Ministry.

As for escape, escapees numbered from three to 31 until 1942, but rapidly increased in number in 1943 and reached a record high of 541 in 1945. After that, the number decreased and stayed at the two-digit level from 1951 on, and at the one-digit level from 1971. In 1982 and 1988 there were no escapes, signifying that the situation of security in terms of prison administration is very stable.

As for death, 424 prisoners died in 1926, at which point the number began to increase, exceeeding the 1,000 mark in 1942 to reach 1,048. In 1945, the number of those who died, including those killed in air raids, was 7,284, accounting for 15.0 percent of the total number of inmates. Their number later decreased drastically, falling to the three-digit level in 1948 and to the two-digit level in 1968. In 1988 they numbered 94, equivalent to 0.2 percent of the daily average number of inmates.

In recent years, the fact that the number of deaths has decreased despite aging among the inmates signifies that levels of nutrition are high, and hygine and medical care are in a very good condition.

Reviewing the shift in the situation of admission in the Showa era, the following points are noted as future potential problems in correction and rehabilitation: 1) The number of prisoners aged 40 or older have tended to increase since 1973; 2) The percentage of inmates convicted of violation of the Stimulant Drug Control Law has been higher than all others since 1985; and 3) The ratio of repeat offenders to newly admitted prisoners has been about 60 percent since 1983. The ratio of six-time-or more frequent-offenders to newly admitted prisoners has increased slightly but gradually.

6. WOMEN'S GUIDANCE HOME

(1) Enactment of the Anti-Prostitution Law and Establishment of the Women's Guidance Home

Controls on prostitution in Japan started with the enactment of the Regulations to Control Licensed Prostitute in 1900. The regulations admitted state-regulated prostitution by stating, "Those who are not registered as licensed prostitutes cannot perform prostitution." The Ordinance for the Punishment of Police Infractions, enacted in 1908, punished those who performed clandestine prostitution or those who arranged prostitution or accommodated prostitutes. Thus, unlicensed prostitution was prohibited and this system continued until the end of the war.

After the war, in response to the "memorandum on the abolition of so-called licensed prostitution in Japan," issued on January 21, 1946, by the General Headquarters of the Allied Powers, the Japanese government on February 2 in the same year abolished the Regulations to Control Licensed Prostitute and banned licensed prostitution.

On January 15, 1947, the government promulgated the "Imperial Ordinance on the Punishment of Those Who Compel Women to Perform Prostitution." This ordinance stipulated penalties on the act of persuading women taking advantage of their perplexity to perform prostitution without resorting to violence or intimidation or entering into a contract with a woman to obligate her to engage in acts of prostitution under similar circumstances.

In the meantime, the Ordinance for the Punishment of Police Infractions was abolished in 1948, when the Minor Offence Law was put into effect. After that, there was no law to impose penalties on simple acts of prostitution. This situation led to the approval of areas which had been designated in the past as licensed prostitution areas, as so-called "red-light districts" or gay quarters. As a result, it became difficult to perform effective regulation on prosititution.

With the situation as it was, public opinion mounted, demanding the maintenance of sex morals and public morals, and the protection of women. After discussions on comprehensive countermeasures against prostitution, the government on April 1, 1957 nullified the Imperial Ordinance on the Punishment of Those who Compel Women to Perform Prostitution, and instead, the Anti-Prostitution Law was enacted. (Regulations concerning criminal punish-

Table 58 Percentage of Violations of Anti-Prostitution Law, by Type of Offence

Year	Total	Solicitation & similar acts	Arrangement & similar acts	Contracts for prostitution	Offering of places	Employment for prostitution	Others
1959	100.0(19,600)	72.2	13.3	1.1	8.9	4.2	0.3
1960	100.0(17,045)	73.2	12.3	1.0	9.1	4.2	0.2
1965	100.0(11,385)	67.9	14.2	0.9	8.9	7.5	0.6
1970	100.0(6,711)	60.3	18.6	1.8	12.5	6.0	0.8
1975	100.0(2,983)	52.8	26.1	2.9	13.0	5.2	1.0
1980	100.0(2,205)	39.9	22.9	3.2	23.2	9.1	1.6
1985	100.0(3,617)	18.6	45.5	16.2	11.2	7.7	0.8
1988	100.0(2,921)	11.6	53.7	16.0	15.5	2.4	0.9

Source: National Police Agency

ment under this law came into effect on April 1, 1958).

The new law was Japan's first epoch-making and comprehensive counter-prostitution law. It clarifies the illegality and antisocial character of prosititution and prohibits women from performing prostitution and men from becoming their partners. In order to preempt prostitution, it imposes penalties on various acts which may promote prostitution, such as arrangement for prostitution, and apparent acts aimed at soliciting or waiting for customers in the presence of the public and annoying the public.

On March 25, 1958 the Anti-Prostitution Law was partly revised (the revision came into effect on April 1 the same year). The revision made it possible to place women aged 20 or older under guidance if they are indicted and convicted of soliciting or awaiting men in public, and when the court suspends the execution of their sentence of imprisonment.

At the same time the Women's Guidance Home Law was legislated and the Women's Guidance Home was established as a facility to accommodate the women placed under guidance for rehabilitation. At first, homes of this kind were set up in Tokyo, Osaka and Fukuoka (three other branches were also established). As of the end of 1988, the only home of this kind is in Tokyo.

(2) Change in the Violation of the Anti-Prostitution Law and Accommodation at Women's Guidance Home

Table 58 shows the rates of the violations of the Anti-Prostitution Law by type in 1959, 1960, every five years after 1965 and 1988. (The figures until 1960 mean those cleared by the police and those after 1965 mean those referred to prosecutors).

The year 1959 was first with a total of 19,600, and then the number declined, registering 2,205 in 1980. Later, it rose slightly and registered 2,921

Fig.35 Number of Inmates Newly Admitted to Women's Guidance Homes (1958~1988)

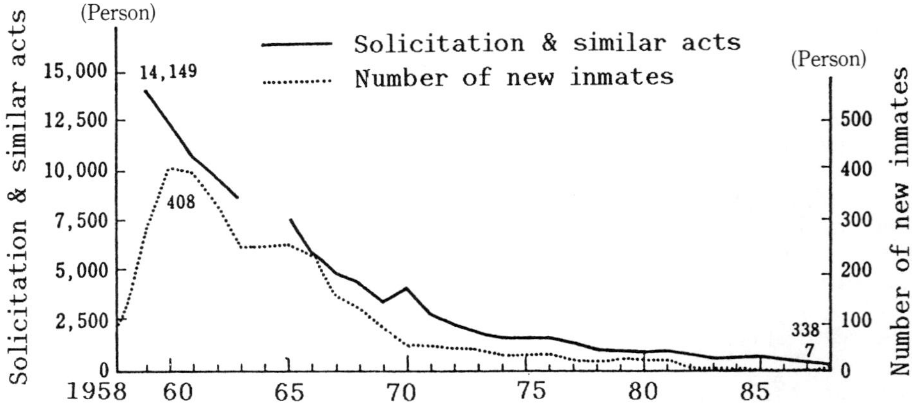

Sources: National Police Agency and Annual Report of Statistics on Correction

in 1988.

By type, those charged with solicitation and similar acts represented the largest percentage in 1960 at 73.2 percent, but the figure declined continuously to register 11.6 percent in 1988. With regard to charges other than solicitation and similar acts, arrangement and similar acts accounted for 13.3 percent in 1959 and 53.7 percent in 1988, and "contracts for prostitution" represented 1.1 percent in 1959 and 16.0 percent in 1988, both of which showed an upward trend.

As for cases of "offer of places," they accounted for 8.9 percent in 1959 and rose to 23.2 percent in 1980. After a slight decline, they represented a 15.5 percent in 1988.

A decline in the number of those referred to prosecutors and a change in the rates of types indicate that the tricks used for prostitution have become so elusive that investigations into it have become difficult. At the same time, these facts indicate that the major type of prostitution has been shifting from "street prostitution," exemplified by solicitation on the streets, to other forms.

Fig. 35 shows the shift in the number of those newly admitted to the Women's Guidance Home and in the number of those charged with solicitation and other similar acts. (The figures until 1960 are numbers of those cleared by the police and the figures in and after 1961 are numbers of those referred to prosecutors).

The number of those newly admitted to the Women's Guidance Home reached a peak with 408 in 1960, and later decreased to less than 10 annually,

Table 59 Percentage of Inmates Newly Admitted to Women's Guidance Homes, by Age Group, I.Q., Physical and Mental Conditions, Education Backgrounds and Frequency of Admission

Subjects	1958 1959	1960 1964	1965 1969	1970 1974	1975 1979	1980 1988
Age group	100.0	100.0	100.0	100.0	100.0	100.0
	(187.0)	(326.2)	(168.6)	(40.8)	(23.0)	(7.7)
20 29 years	51.9	48.5	36.3	22.5	14.8	11.6
30 39 years	33.2	35.1	39.7	36.8	37.4	36.2
40 49 years	12.8	13.8	18.5	33.3	32.2	29.0
50 years & over	2.1	2.6	4.9	7.4	15.7	23.2
Intelligence quotient	100.0	100.0	100.0	100.0	100.0	100.0
	(181.5)	(322.2)	(163.2)	(39.6)	(22.0)	(7.7)
69 & under	58.1	50.3	62.6	52.5	47.3	39.1
70 79	19.6	21.6	18.8	22.2	25.5	23.2
80 89	12.7	15.9	11.4	14.6	10.9	17.4
90 & over	9.6	12.2	7.2	10.6	16.4	20.3
Physical & mental conditions	100.0	100.0	100.0	100.0	100.0	100.0
	(82.5)	(332.6)	(138.4)	(45.6)	(21.2)	(7.7)
Being ill	6.7	16.4	24.6	25.4	42.5	46.4
Weak mindedness	37.6	36.0	31.5	29.8	24.5	17.4
Abnormal character	4.2	5.2	5.1	13.6	2.8	1.4
Normal	51.5	42.5	38.7	31.1	30.2	34.8
Education backgrounds	100.0	100.0	100.0	100.0	100.0	100.0
	(139.0)	(326.0)	(168.6)	(40.8)	(22.4)	(7.7)
Not entered school	5.8	4.3	2.8	5.4	5.4	0.0
Graduated from or dropped out of primary school	46.0	37.5	37.0	28.4	17.9	18.8
Graduated from or dropped out of middle-school	40.3	49.6	48.6	57.8	67.9	73.9
Graduated from or dropped out of high school	7.9	8.6	11.5	8.3	8.9	7.2
Frequency of admission	100.0	100.0	100.0	100.0	100.0	100.0
	(187.0)	(326.2)	(168.6)	(40.8)	(22.4)	(7.7)
1 time	88.5	64.4	58.4	59.8	62.5	47.8
2 times	11.2	23.4	23.5	24.0	13.4	20.3
3 times	0.3	8.6	11.0	10.3	13.4	10.1
4 times	–	2.6	4.5	3.9	5.4	11.6
5 times & over	–	1.0	2.6	2.0	5.4	10.1

Sources: Annual Report of Statistics of Justice Ministry and
Annual Report of Statistics on Correction

particularly after 1980. In the meantime those charged with solicitation and similar acts peaked with 14,149 in 1959 and later generally declined, registering 338 in 1988. It is known that the number of those admitted to the Women's Guidance Home is much lower than the number of those charged with solicitation and similar acts.

Table 59 shows the percentage of those newly admitted to the Women's

Guidance Home in terms of several factors. The segmentation of the term was the years 1958 and 1959 for their annual average, and every five years in and after 1960 until 1979 for their annual average, and nine years from 1980 until 1988 for their annual average.

By age, the rate of those in their 20s continued to decrease from 51.9 percent for 1958 and 1959, and went down to 11.6 percent for 1980 to 1988. The rate of those aged in their 40s and 50s rose from 14.9 percent for 1958 and 1959 to 52.2 percent for 1980 to 1988. Thus the aging of those admitted to the Women's Guidance Home is a trend.

By intelligence quotient, the rate of those having comparatively low IQs of 79 or less slightly declined from 77.7 percent for 1958 and 1959 to 62.3 percent for 1980 to 1988. But those with lower IQs still comprised a high percentage.

By mental condition, the rate of those classified loosely as "normal mind" represented 51.5 percent for 1958 and 1959, and later decreased to stabilize at the 30-percent mark in recent years.

By the need for treatment for illness (mostly social diseases), their rate accounted for 6.7 percent for 1958 and 1959 but increased to the 40-percent mark in and after the 1975-1979 period. Thus, many of the inmates have some mental or physical problems.

By education, most of the inmates have an educational background of middle school or less.

By frequency of admission, the number of first-time inmates was the largest, accounting for about 50-60 percent from 1960 to 1964. But later, the rate of three-time, or more, inmates increased, registered to 31.8 percent for the period from 1980 to 1988. Besides, there are a number of inmates who are in the predicament of having no guarantors when they are released and therefore have to return to rehabilitation homes.

Section 3. Rehabilitation of Offenders

1. ESTABLISHMENT OF REHABILITATION SERVICE PROGRAMMES

(1) Rehabilitation Services in Early Showa Era

Rehabilitation services for offenders around 1930 consisted of two areas, one was the protection of juvenile offenders and the other was aid to discharged offenders, such as those discharged from prison, those whose prosecution or execution of sentence has been suspended, and so forth.

Rehabilitation services in both fields had been conducted mostly by volunteer groups since the Meiji era and the national government did not go further than facilitating their activities by providing subsidies for prisoner aid services.

Legal provisions regulating rehabilitation services for juvenile offenders under the old Juvenile Law had been introduced to as few as five prefectures in 1923. Another 20 years had to elapse before the rehabilitation service was administered nationwide.

The Ministry of Justice established the Rehabilitation Section in the Minister's Secretariat in October 1920 to conduct research on planning and administering rehabilitation services for juvenile offenders in preparation for juvenile law revision. It was the first such body designed mainly to cope with rehabilitation work.

In May 1922, the Prison Bureau transferred the matters under its jurisdiction assigned under the name of "Ex-Prisoners' Aids" to the Rehabilitation Section and the matters were renamed "Rehabilitation Service for the Discharged." Also placed under the jurisdiction of the Section were those matters concerned with the disposition and treatment of juvenile delinquents. These two matters or services combined became known as the judicial rehabilitation service.

The Juvenile Tribunal (separated from court of justice, it conducted inquiry and disposition of those juvenile offenders who were granted suspension of prosecution and referred to the Tribunal at the discretion of the public prosecutor) instituted in 1923 under the old Juvenile Law, had two functions at the same time. One was to determine and pronounce proper protective treatment measures for those juveniles and the other was to administer or execute those measures pronounced.

The Tokyo and Osaka juvenile tribunals were staffed with 45 government officials in 1927. These officials included judges of the juvenile tribunals and juvenile probation officers. There was the system of entrusting volunteers versed in education or religion with the work of juvenile probation officers and these volunteers were called commissioned juvenile probation workers. Juvenile probation officers mainly worked on preparing case reports for submission to the enquiry proceedings of the Tribunal, while the "probationary supervision by the probation officers," one of the dispositions under the old Juvenile Law, was left to, actually entrusted to, the commissioned juvenile probation workers.

(2) Development of Judicial Rehabilitation Service System

The judicial rehabilitation service system saw remarkable expansion after 1935.

The Law for Supervision of Political Offenders was proclaimed in May 1936 and took effect that November. The law required a person who had violated the Maintenance of Public Order Law to be placed under probationary supervision after a decision to that effect had been made by the Committee for Examination and Observation of Political Offenders. Eighty-six officials were stationed at 22 probation supervision offices for political offenders established across the nation.

The Judicial Rehabilitation Service Law was enacted in March 1939 and took effect that September. The law required private organizations to obtain a government permit to carry out rehabilitation services over offenders who were under suspension of prosecution or execution of sentence or discharged from prison on completion of the term of their sentences and so forth. The law also stipulated the supervisory power of the officials concerned, financial assistance and tax exemption for such businesses. At the same time, volunteer judicial rehabilitation workers were nominated to help in rehabilitation services for offenders.

Offices to administer those affairs concerning the guidance and instruction of the volunteer judicial rehabilitation workers were set up in seven locations around the nation in November 1940.

Meanwhile, the provisions for rehabilitation service for juvenile offenders under the old Juvenile Law were applied in only five prefectures in 1923 when the law was put into effect. The provisions were gradually introduced in stages to additional prefectures in 1934, 1936, 1938 and 1941 and finally applied throughout the nation in 1942.

Rehabilitation systems were much improved while the nation was under wartime conditions when fostering capable citizens was an important national objective. According to Article 2 of the Judicial Rehabilitation Service Law, the purpose of rehabilitation was to give a second chance to offenders to carry out what they were born to do as a Japanese national. From around 1941, the year when the Pacific War broke out, organizations engaged in supervising and rehabilitating juvenile offenders began to give them military training in the same way as was done in schools. After 1943, when the tide of war turned against Japan, the training programmes became shorter and more intensive.

(3) Transformation into Modern Rehabilitation

In October 1945, shortly after the war ended, the Maintenance of Public Order Law, the Law for Supervision of Political Offenders and the probation supervision offices for political offenders were abolished by the Imperial Ordinance concerning Orders to be issued in consequence of the Acceptance of the Potsdam Declaration. Meanwhile, the military courts of the occupation forces had a concurrent jurisdiction over Japanese nationals who violated those regulations which prohibited such acts as obstructing the aims of the occupation. There were not a few Japanese who were put on probation and the work of probationary supervision was left to Japanese authorities, including the volunteer judicial rehabilitation workers.

This was accompanied by work to revise laws concerned with judicial rehabilitation services, followed by the establishment of additional juvenile tribunals and their branches in 1946, 1947 and 1949. Thus Japan's postwar rehabilitation service actually commenced in the field of juvenile probation.

Among modern revisions of laws and acts stands out the new Juvenile Law, a totally revised version of the 1923 Juvenile Law. It was enforced in January 1949, and was followed by the Offenders Prevention and Rehabilitation Law, proclaimed on May 31, 1949 and enforced on July 1 that year.

The Offenders Prevention and Rehabilitation Law aimed to promote the reformation and rehabilitation of offenders, ensure the proper granting of pardons and establish a fair and adequate system for the administration of paroles and related matters and encourage crime prevention activities, thus protecting society and promoting the welfare of the public and individuals. It clarified the purpose of the rehabilitative treatment in the light of the ideal of the new Constitution and defined the probationary supervision system for parolees and juvenile delinquents.

At the same time as the enforcement of the Offenders Prevention and Rehabilitation Law, the National Offenders Rehabilitation Commission, an extra-ministerial office under the umbrella of the Justice Ministry, was formed to exercise central control over the reformation-rehabilitation service.

For the practical operation of the service, the District Juvenile Offenders Rehabilitation Board and the District Adult Offenders Rehabilitation Board were set up in every city where a high court was located. In addition, to perform the administrative affairs of the Juvenile and Adult Offenders Rehabilitation Board, Juvenile Probation Offices and Adult Probation Offices were established in every city where a district court was located. Both the National Offenders Rehabilitation Board and the District Offenders Rehabilitation Board for juveniles and adults were administrative organs whose decisions were based on consultations.

When the Offenders Prevention and Rehabilitation Law was enforced in July 1949, the Probation-Parole Supervision Office was still operated with the cooperation of the rehabilitation service associations and volunteer rehabilitation workers under the prewar Rehabilitation Service Law. When the Law for Aftercare of Discharged Offenders and the Volunteer Probation Officer Law took effect in May 1950, however, the Rehabilitation Service Law was abolished.

The Law for Aftercare of Discharged Offenders provided for up to six months emergency assistance for those not subject to probationary supervision and excluded from aftercare service under the Offenders Prevention and Rehabilitation Law but who asked for assistance upon completion of their prison terms. Similar assistance was made available upon request to those released under suspended prosecution or suspended execution of sentence. The law further defined the licensing and supervision of the activities of Rehabilitation Aid Associations.

The Volunteer Probation Officer Law provided for volunteer probation officers whose function was to engage in probationary supervision, to enlighten public opinion in order to facilitate the reentry of offenders into society, and to organize and participate in community movements for crime prevention.

The enforcement of the Offenders Prevention and Rehabilitation Law, the Law for Aftercare of Discharged Offenders and the Volunteer Probation Officer Law established the foundation for the current reformation-rehabilitation service systems.

In August 1952, the National Offenders Rehabilitation Commission was replaced by the Rehabilitation Bureau, an intra-ministerial office of the Justice Ministry. At the same time, the District Juvenile Offenders Rehabilitation Board and the District Adult Offenders Rehabilitation Board were integrated into the District Offenders Rehabilitation Board, which, in turn, is empowered to examine and judge on parole applications. As a result of these changes, the Probation-Parole Supervision Office is no longer a part of the Board, engaging in its administrative affairs, but has become a regional administrative branch for probationary supervision and so forth.

A law enforced in December 1953 partially revised the Penal Code and amended the provisions for suspending the execution of sentences. It eased the conditions for suspending the execution of sentences and enabled defendants under suspended execution of sentence to receive the privilege for a second time, provided, however, that the defendant this time is to be placed under probationary supervision without fail.

An amendment of the Penal Code, enforced in July 1954, paved the way for those given a suspended execution of sentence for the first time to be placed at the same time under probationary supervision at the discretion of the court. To administer appropriate supervision of such probationers, the Law for Probationary Supervision of Persons under Suspended Execution of Sentences was enacted and enforced in July 1954. The law focused the supervision of probationers on guidance and assistance and established a probationary supervision system that allowed more relaxed conditions to be observed under supervision than those for parolees and others.

The partially revised Anti-Prostitution Law, enacted in March 1958 and enforced the following month, established a new system of guidance treatment in the Women's Guidance Home. Under the system, those prostitutes granted parole from the Women's Guidance Home were also placed under probationary supervision.

Though no additional legislative measures were taken to broaden the probationary supervision system, it was administered in a flexible manner, including short-term probationary supervision for juvenile traffic violators and other diversified and advanced treatment programmes. (See Division 3 of this section.)

When Okinawa was returned to Japan in May 1972, a Probation and Parole Supervision Office was set up in Naha, bringing the total number of such offices to 50 throughout Japan. A council composed of three members of the Kyushu District Offenders Rehabilitation Board was also sitting in Naha City to expedite the examination of parole applications and related matters.

Branches of the Probation and Parole Supervision Offices were set up in Hachioji, Sakai and Kitakyushu in 1970 to facilitate efficient rehabilitation service. Small offices stationed by a probation officer also began to be established in smaller cities in 1963. At present, such offices are located in 27 cities, including one in Odawara City in Kanagawa-ken.

(4) Establishment of Volunteer Probation Officers' System

Under the probationary supervision system, which formed the nucleus of the rehabilitation service system of Japan, volunteer probation officers are regarded as administrative agents to help offenders with rehabilitation. They are appointed by the Justice Minister and treated as part-time, non-paid government officials. In principle, however, they are volunteers selected from the public and the number was limited to 52,500. The Japanese rehabilitation service system is characterized by the participation of a wide variety of people, including these volunteer officers, members of the women's rehabilitation aid societies and the BBS.

Groups involved in rehabilitation service in local communities asked the people in the area to assist them in supervision and guidance of released offenders from the mid-Meiji era, or around the end of the previous century. The volunteers were given various titles, such as protection officers, local officers and visiting officers.

For example, the Fukudenkai society in Fukui-ken, which was formed in 1913, established branch offices across the prefecture and appointed "local officers" at every branch office. The well-organized set-up was later used as a model when the system of volunteer judicial rehabilitation worker was introduced.

Currently the rehabilitation service is administered with the help of volunteer probation officers appointed by the Justice Minister. A similar system to mobilise volunteers with special experience or expertise under the nomination of ministers in charge and other heads of governmental services had been established by law. The system of commissioned juvenile probation officer appointed by the Justice Minister under the old Juvenile Law of 1923 was the first such step to mobilize volunteer workers on the job to help in the rehabilitation of offenders and delinquents.

This system of commissioned juvenile probation officer, however, was introduced not so much because the government appreciated the activities of local rehabilitation service groups, but rather because such a system of "commissioned officer" was generally utilised by government offices in those days. The Law for the Supervision of Political Offenders, which was enforced in 1936, also employed a similar system of commissioned probation officer for the same reason.

The volunteer judicial rehabilitation worker system, which was introduced after the Judicial Rehabilitation Service Law was enacted in 1939, reflected to some extent the achievements gained by the activities of local rehabilitation service groups. The districts where the volunteer judicial rehabilitation workers were stationed almost corresponded to the jurisdictions of police stations in the area. The service term of the volunteer judicial rehabilitation workers was fixed at three years and 14,000 such workers were appointed by the Justice Minister under the Judicial Rehabilitation Service Law in 1939. Since then, their number continued to increase to reach 35,000 in 1944.

The system of commissioned probation officers, created to deal with political offenders, was abolished shortly after the war. In addition, the aforementioned system of "commissioned officer" was entirely abolished in 1948.

As a result, the commissioned juvenile probation officer was renamed an investigator for the Juvenile Tribunal and again renamed a volunteer juvenile probation officer in the same year. The post was finally given the name of volunteer judicial rehabilitation worker under the Offenders Prevention and Rehabilitation Law enforced in 1949.

The Volunteer Probation Officer Law, which was proclaimed and enforced in 1950, renamed the volunteer judicial rehabilitation worker as a volunteer probation officer and stipulated the conditions of the office, including procedures for recommendation and appointment, regulations for service and the number of officers to be employed, and set the term of service at two years.

As the District Offenders Rehabilitation Boards and Probation Offices had been separately set up for adults and for juveniles, the volunteer probation officers, in line with the separation of these offices, were named separately for adults and juveniles. The overall reorganization of the Justice Ministry and the revision of the Volunteer Probation Officers Law removed the dual supervision system in 1952 and the two types of volunteer probation officers–for adults and for juveniles–came to be called simply a volunteer probation officer.

(5) Crime Prevention Activities

After World War II, crime prevention activites was added as one of the most important programmes in the rehabilitation system.

In the 1949 Offenders Prevention and Rehabilitation Law, the crime prevention programmes were part of the rehabilitation service which aimed to prevent repeated crimes by offenders, and thus were applied only to a limited area. In July 1952, however, the law was revised not only to strengthen the probationary supervision service but also to focus the crime prevention programmes on a more direct effort to prevent occurrance of crimes.

One of the programmes systematically organized in an effort to prevent crimes is the "movement for a brighter society," which has held meetings in July every year nationwide under the sponsorship of the Ministry of Justice. Relevant groups, both private and official, participate in the movement, working at the executive committees set up in the central government and municipalities across the nation. The one held in July 1989 marked the 39th of this annual event.

Prior to the establishment of the movement, there were two similar activities which laid the foundation for it. One was the "Protection Day" commenced in 1925 and the other was the "Juvenile Protection Day" initiated in 1928.

The "Protection Day" was set up in the commemoration of the amnesty decree issued at the time of the funeral of the Emperor Meiji, as the decree triggered a boom in the rehabilitation business for released inmates across the nation. The 13th of September, the day the imperial proclamation of the amnesty was issued, was seen as an opportunity to promote the idea of rehabilitation service nationwide.

The 17th of April, the day the old Juvenile Law was proclaimed, was established as the "Juvenile Protection Day" and the rehabilitation of juvenile offenders was promoted on the day.

The two special days were renamed "Judicial Probation Day" and "Juvenile Probation Day," respectively, in 1937 and continued until after World War II.

A one-month programme of the "movement for the enhancement of the correctional rehabilitation service" was held in April 1949. It was followed by the correctional rehabilitation service campaign in July 1950, commemorating the enforcement of the Offenders Prevention and Rehabilitation Law in the same month of the previous year. They resulted in the first "movement for a brighter society," held in 1951.

While the "Protection Day" and "Juvenile Protection Day" campaigns were conducted mostly by those who were working for rehabilitation service groups and aimed at the promotion of the idea of rehabilitation of offenders, the "movement for a brighter society" intended to involve the whole nation in crime prevention activities.

Supported by an executive committee consisting of many related organizations, the movement has been developed as a crime prevention programme based on the idea of rehabilitation of offenders. It's goal is to gain the understanding of the entire population of the rehabilitation of offenders and prevention of crimes to create a crime-free, brighter society through the cooperation of the people.

At the same time, efforts to develop the crime prevention programme on a daily basis, centering on the above-mentioned movement, are still being continued by the people working in the rehabilitation service.

2. RELEASE ON PAROLE

Now we will discuss and examine conditional release from prison, one of our parole systems. The release on parole from Juvenile Training School will be explained in Chapter IV-2-6.

The current Penal Code enacted in 1907 stipulates that the conditional release from prison shall be granted by the administrative authorities to the offenders who, having been sentenced to imprisonment, show genuine repentence and reformation after serving the designated term in prison.

The authorities mentioned here mean the Justice Minister under the 1907 Criminal Code and the Attorney-General from February 1948. The Offenders Prevention and Rehabilitation Law enforced in July 1949, however, established District Juvenile Offenders Rehabilitation Boards and District Adult Offenders Rehabilitation Boards as the authorities to grant release on parole. The boards are the predecessors of the current District Offenders Rehabilitation Boards.

The Prison Law enacted in 1908 and other laws determined that the offenders released on parole from prison be placed under police surveillance. The released offenders were required to report to local police stations when going on a trip and returning home. Police permission was necessary to change their addresses. They were also required to report to the police station every month.

However, after reconsideration of the practices under the system, the old Juvenile Law enacted in 1922 provided that juvenile offenders released on parole

Fig.36 Number of Parolees and Prisoners (1926~1988)

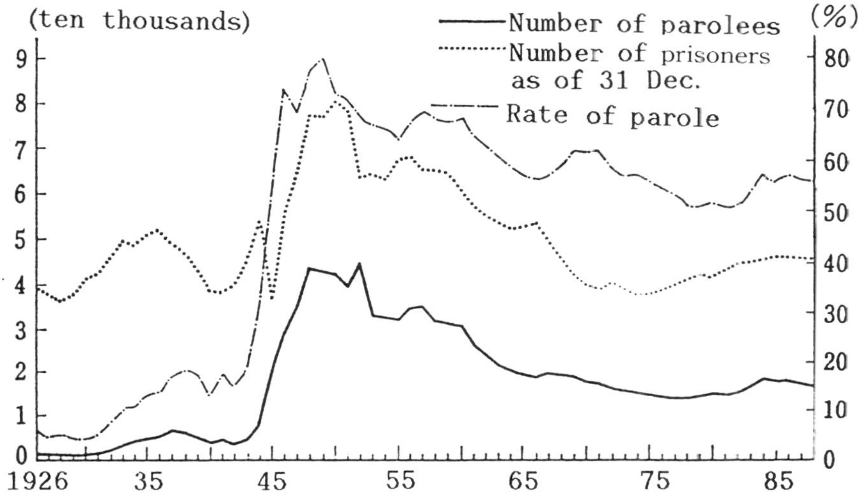

Sources:Annual Report of Statistics on Prison Administration and Annual Report of Statistics on Correction

from prison to be placed under the supervision of juvenile probation officers.

The Offenders Prevention and Rehabilitation Law enforced in July 1949 required all the offenders released on parole from prison to be put under supervision of the probationary supervision service organizations. Accordingly, the police surveillance system was abolished by law.

The operation of the conditional release from prison during the Showa era is shown in the Fig. 36 (See Table 9 in the Appendix) by the number of those released and the ratio of parolees to the total number of those released from prisons both by termination of prison terms and by release on parole. The ratio from 1926 to 1931 remained as low as around five percent. In those days whether an offender could obtain conditional release from prison or not was actually decided almost by the impression of the wardens of the prison toward the prisoner.

In an effort to coordinate the actual practices and to facilitate and activate appropriate application of the system, the Ministry of Justice issued instructions: Rule for Examination of Release on Parole and set up concrete guidelines in May 1931. As a result, the release rate showed signs of increase from 1933 to 1943, though fluctuating between 10 percent and 19 percent.

It exceeded the 30 percent mark in 1944 and surpassed 55 percent in 1945 to register a jump to 74.0 percent in 1946. The rapid increase during these three years was attributable to the positive application of the system. It came from an effort to keep less offenders in prison for shorter periods due to the extremely bad sanitary conditions, shortage of food supplies and dire necessity to cut expenses in the last stage of the World War II and in the postwar chaos.

The percentage reached as high as 79.7 percent in 1949, when the Offenders Prevention and Rehabilitation Law was enforced. Also in the period between 1947 and 1951 the percentage exceeded the 70 percent mark. This was due to the fact that in those days prison administration facilities were overburdened with too many prisoners, and it became necessary to increse the number of prisoners released. Between 1952 and 1960 also, when the number of the prisoners as of the year-end exceeded 60,000, the release percentage was as high as between 65 percent and 70 percent. The officials of related organizations were positive about releasing offenders in those days, trying to promote the newly initiated rehabilitation service system.

After the confused post-war period, when the number of prisoners decreased with the decrease of crimes committed by adult offenders in the early 1960s, the release rate gradually decreased and hit the record low of 50.8 percent in 1982 since the Offenders Prevention and Rehabilitation Law was established. In March 1984, the Ministry of Justice set forth fresh guidelines for appropriate and positive application of release on parole. The release rate consequnetly exceeded the 55 percent mark every year until 1988.

The rejection rate of applications made by the wardens of prisons in every five years is as follows; 5.2 percent in 1950-54, 5.7 percent in 1955-59, 11.0 percent in 1960-64, 13.4 percent in 1965-69, 10.9 percent in 1970-74, 11.2 percent in 1975-79, and 6.8 percent in 1980-84. The figure for the three-year period from 1985-88 was 5.0 percent. These figures of the parole application rejection rate show a positive stance until around 1960, followed by a policy of discretion until around 1980 and a shift in policy toward the positive use of the system after that year.

3. *PROBATIONARY SUPERVISION*

As mentioned in 1-(3) of this section, the rehabilitation service system in Japan made a fresh start with the enforcement of the Offenders Prevention and Rehabilitation Law in July 1949. The system was operated by volunteer workers during the Meiji and Taisho eras and by the juvenile protection and rehabilitation service (See Chapter IV-2) and judicial rehabilitation service during the earlier Showa era.

Here we examine the changes of cases placed under the probationary supervision in the new rehabilitation service system and the development of the treatment under the probationary supervision system.

Fig.37 Number of Probationers and Parolees (1949～1988)

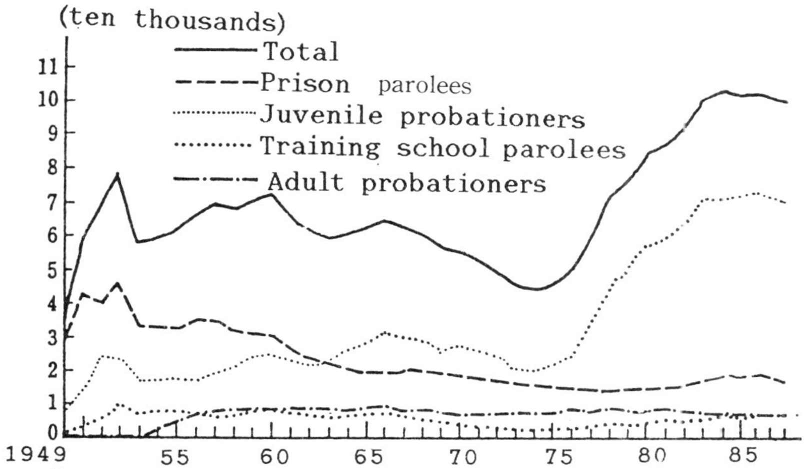

Sources: Annual Report of Judicial Statistics and Annual Report of Statistics on Rehabilitation

(1) Changes in the Number of Offenders Placed under Probationary Supervision

Fig. 37 shows changes in the number of offenders who were newly placed under probationary supervision and parole supervision (hereafter, probationary supervison) classified by the type of subjects (probationers or parolees) during the period between 1949 and 1988. (See Table 10 in the Appendix)

In 1950, the next year after the enforcement of the Offenders Prevention and Rehabilitation Law, 59,739 people were admitted to probationary supervision. In 1952, as many as 77,999 people were placed under probationary supervision, partly because of the proliferation of prison-parolees due to the overcrowded conditions of prisons in those days and also because of the increase of juvenile offenders put on probation and juvenile parolees released from the Juvenile Training Schools resulting from a drastic increase of juvenile delinquency. The number of the newly placed under probationary supervision, however, once decreased to 58,237 in 1953 as the number of prison-parolees decreased.

The number of the newly placed again rose to reach 71,720 in 1960, the highest in a 10-year period starting in 1955. This was due to the fact that the number of offenders who got suspended execution of sentences with probation increased after 1954 and that of juvenile offenders put on probation also increased after 1957. After that, although there was some fluctuation, the number of the newly placed registered the lowest figure of 44,310 in 1974 due to

Table 60 Percentage of Prison Parolees Newly Received by Type of Offence

Year	Total	Penal Code Offences	Homicide	Robbery	Assault Bodily injury	Extortion	Theft	Fraud
1956	100.0 (34,821)	94.5	1.6	5.7	5.0	3.2	56.3	11.7
1960	100.0 (30,824)	96.9	2.2	5.7	5.1	4.3	58.9	10.2
1965	100.0 (19,430)	96.1	3.5	6.2	7.2	5.9	47.5	9.2
1970	100.0 (17,861)	97.3	4.0	4.6	5.7	4.1	40.6	7.5
1975	100.0 (14,933)	90.7	5.7	4.1	6.3	4.0	34.7	6.5
1980	100.0 (15,206)	75.1	3.1	3.2	5.6	3.3	33.4	7.1
1985	100.0 (17,795)	65.5	2.5	2.8	4.3	2.4	31.0	7.1
1988	100.0 (16,540)	63.9	2.9	2.3	4.1	3.1	31.6	6.1

the decrease of prison-parolees and of juveniles released from the Juvenile Training School after 1968.

After 1975, the newly placed under probationary supervison again increased due to the rise of the juvenile probationers and in 1983 reached 100,019, surpassing the 100,000 mark for the first time. In 1988, however, the figure fell a little short of the 100,000 mark to 95,736. The increase after 1977 was brought about mainly by the introduction of the short-term probationary supervision system for traffic offenders in April 1977. In the following year, 20,000 people were placed in the newly established probationary supervision programme and the number of new probationers under the programme continued to rise to register 45,565 in 1987.

The amendment of the Road Traffic Law enacted April 1, 1987, increased applications of the Traffic Infraction Notification system and more minor traffic violation cases were excluded from the judicial process. It thus decreased the number of new probationers to 44,099 in 1988.

As mentioned above, the changes of the number of those newly placed under probationary supervision reflect the crime trends as well as the dispositions and treatments to cope with them.

(2) Probationary Supervision of the Released on Parole from Prison

Table 60 shows the ratio of offences committed by new parolees from prisons in 1956, every five years between 1960 and 1985, and in 1988.

The ratio of theft had always been high but gradually decreased from

Rape	Violent acts	Professional negligence	Others	Special Law offences	Stimulant drugs	Poisonous Substances	Road traffic violations	Others
1.0	…	…	10.1	5.5	2.9	…	0.1	2.5
2.0	0.4	…	8.0	3.1	0.3	…	0.1	2.7
4.7	1.2	…	10.7	3.9	0.3	…	0.7	2.9
6.6	1.7	15.3	7.0	2.7	0.3	…	0.7	1.7
6.5	1.4	15.1	7.0	9.3	2.6	…	4.2	2.5
3.2	1.1	8.4	6.1	24.9	17.1	0.1	5.4	2.3
1.8	0.7	7.0	5.3	34.5	28.1	0.3	4.3	1.8
1.7	0.6	6.6	4.9	36.1	28.9	0.7	4.1	0.5

Source: Annual Report of Statistics on Rehabilitation

56.3 percent in 1956 to 31.6 percent in 1988. The figure for professional negligence remained a little above 15 percent in 1970 and 1975, but afterward went down, reaching 6.6 percent in 1988. The figure for fraud also decreased from over 10 percent in 1956 and 1960 to 6.1 percent in 1988. The ratio of robbery decreased from 5.7 percent in 1956 and 1960 to 2.3 percent in 1988.

In contrast, the ratio of the Stimulant Drugs Control Law offenders, having remained below 1 percent from 1960 until 1970, showed a steep increase after 1980, with figures showing 28.1 percent in 1985 and 28.9 percent in 1988. These figures were approximately the same as those for theft.

The parolees from prisons are placed under probationary supervision during their provisional release. Fig. 38 shows the ratio of parolees by the term of probationary supervision every five years from 1966 to 1986 and in 1988. The ratio of up to one month duration of probationary supervision drastically decreased from some 30 percent in 1966 and 1971 to 16.9 percent in 1981 and 2.6 percent in 1988. The ratio of more than three months and up to six months, in contrast, increased from 15.7 percent in 1966 to 22.4 percent in 1981 and 30.4 percent in 1988. The ratio of for more than six months up to a year remained around 10 percent between 1966 and 1981 but rose to 17.9 percent in 1986 and 19.3 percent in 1988.

These figures reflect the effort which has been made since 1984 to release offenders earlier from prison on parole and to place them under probationary supervision for a longer duration.

Fig. 39 shows the ratio of prison-parolees at the time of the termination

Fig.38 Percentage of the Parole Term of Parolees

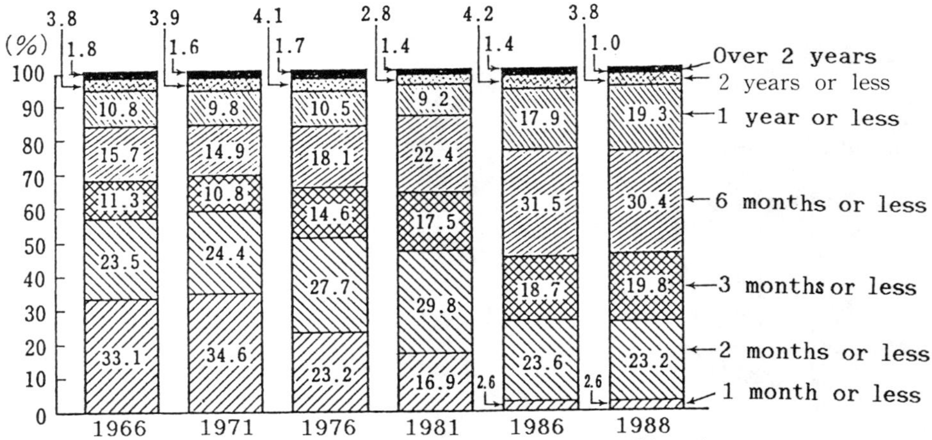

Source:Annual Report of Statistics on Rehabilitation

Fig.39 Percentage of Prison Parolees, by Result of Supervision (1956～1988)

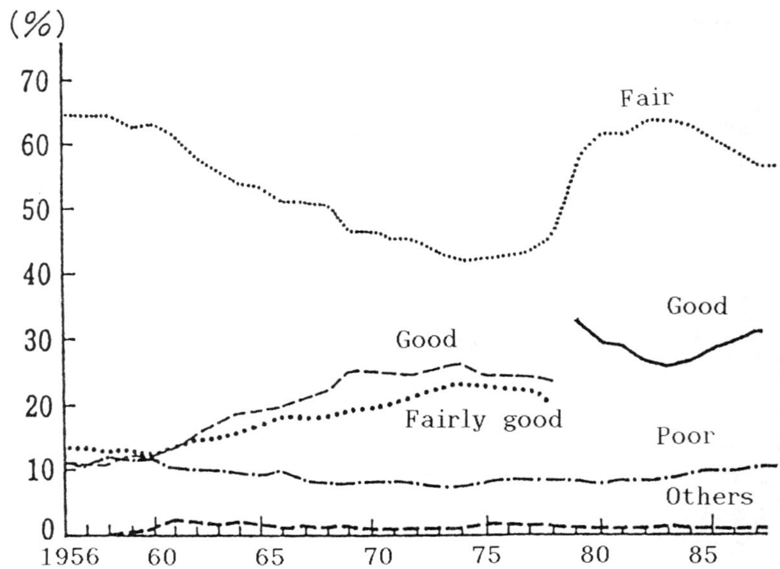

Note:The standard of evaluation for probationary supervision was changed from four grades (good, fairly good, fair, poor) to three grades (good, fair, poor) from 1978.

Source: Annual Report of Statistics on Rehabilitation

Fig.40 Number of Prison Parolees by Reason of Termination (1945～1988)

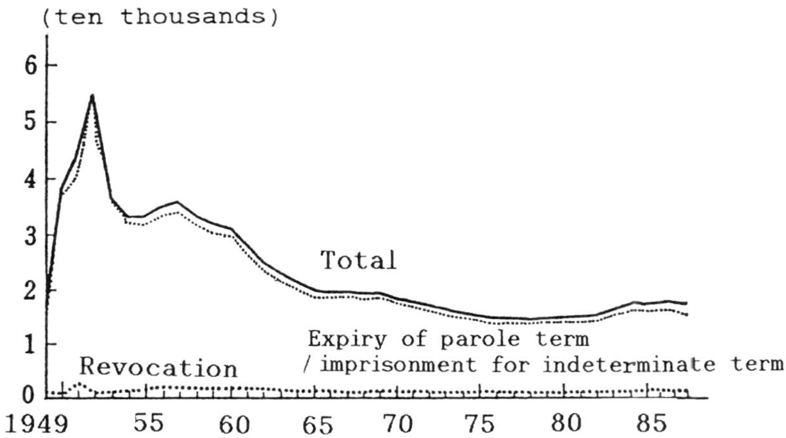

Sources: Annual Report of Judicial Statistics and Annual Report of Statistics on Rehabilitation

of the probationary supervision by grading of their attitude during probationary supervision.

The ratio of those terminated as graded average remained above 60 percent from 1956 to 1961 and decreased gradually to 46.2 percent in 1978, while the rate for those graded good or fair rose from a little above 20 percent from 1956 to 1962 to 49.7 percent in 1974.

Since 1979, when the grading was changed from four ranks into three-bad, average and good, the ratio of those graded average again drastically increased to 56.9 percent and those graded good decreased to 31.2 percent in 1988. Meanwhile, the ratio of those graded bad remained around 10 percent all through the period.

Fig. 40 shows the trend of the number of prison-parolees who completed their terms and that of those had their release cancelled during the period between 1949 and 1988.

The ratio of those who completed their release terms to that of the entire prison-prolees always exceeded the 90 percent mark, while the ratio of those who had their release cancelled increased from 1 percent in 1952 to around 4 percent from the late 1950s to late 1960s. It began to rise again in 1983, when the number of prolees increased, to reach 8.6 percent in 1988.

Table 61 shows the comparison of re-institutionalization between parolees and releasees on completiong prison terms every five years from 1960 to 1985 and in 1986.

Table 61 Comparison of Re-institutionalization between Parolees and Releasees on Completion of the Prison Term

Year	Parole			
	Parolees	Subjects Re-institutionalized		
		1st year	2nd year	3rd year
1960	30,751	2,139(7.0)	5,383(17.5)	2,596(8.4)
1965	19,432	1,042(5.4)	2,846(14.6)	1,483(7.6)
1970	17,855	694(3.9)	1,958(11.0)	1,331(7.5)
1975	14,933	544(3.6)	1,799(12.0)	1,182(7.9)
1980	15,202	572(3.8)	2,270(14.9)	1,658(10.9)
1985	17,795	632(3.6)	2,590(14.6)	1,810(10.2)
1986	18,130	630(3.5)	2,559(14.1)	1,796(9.9)

Percentages of parolees and that of releasees on completion of prison terms were 7.0 percent and 14.5 percent in 1960, 3.9 percent and 10.4 percent in 1970, 3.8 percent and 12.0 percent in 1980, and 3.5 percent and 12.3 percent in 1986, respectively. As shown by these figures, the rate of the former always fell less than half of the latter.

The percentage of those returned to prison within three years after release from prisons remained around 30 percent for parolees while the rate was as high as 50 percent for those released from prisons after completing their prison terms. The comparisons above show parolees always made a better record. Both groups showed the highest rate of returning to prisons in the second year after the release from prisons.

(3) Offenders with Suspended Execution of Sentences and Probationary Supervision

Fig. 37 shows the trend in the number of newly received probationers and parolees by status from 1949 to 1988. (See Table 10 in the Appendix)

Of them, the number of probationers with suspended execution of sentences increased year by year to 8,282 in 1958 from 2,385 in 1954, when the system of the suspended execution of sentences with probationary supervision was established. It lingered around 8,000 for a while and began to decrease to 7,779 in 1967 and went further down to 6,771 in 1971. It again showed a sign of increase in 1972 and reached 8,501 in 1978. Though in fluctuation after 1979, it

Release on completion			
Releasees	Subjects Re-institutionalized		
	1st year	2nd year	3rd year
14,088	2,039(14.5)	3,479(24.7)	1,281(9.1)
14,453	1,804(12.5)	3,446(23.8)	1,235(8.5)
11,015	1,145(10.4)	2,162(19.6)	1,236(11.2)
11,736	1,290(11.0)	2,786(23.7)	1,501(12.8)
14,140	1,695(12.0)	3,714(26.3)	1,868(13.2)
14,143	1,877(13.3)	3,473(24.6)	1,792(12.7)
13,687	1,686(12.3)	3,303(24.1)	1,684(12.3)

Note Figures in parentheses show percentage.
Source: Annual Report of Statistics on Correction

gradually decreased to 6,076 in 1988.

Table 62 shows the rate of the offenders with suspended sentences with probation by offence every five years from 1955 to 1985 and in 1988. Among the offenders of the Penal Code, the rate for theft has been the highest though it decreased from 57.2 percent in 1955 to 31.3 percent in 1988.

The figure for bodily injury and assault also decreased from 11.0 percent in 1970 to hit a low of 5.3 percent in 1985 but rose a little to reach 6.0 percent in 1988. The figure for professional negligence remained around 8 to 10 percent after 1970.

As for the figures for special law offenders, the rate of the offenders of the Stimulant Drugs Control Law always exceeded 20 percent after 1980, followed by that of the Road Traffic Law offenders surpassing 10 percent.

Those who are placed under the suspension of execution of sentence with probation can be provisionally discharged from probationary supervision by the decision of the District Offenders Rehabilitation Board (DORB). And the decision can be overturned again by the DORB when it judges to do so based on the conduct of the discharged.

Table 63 shows the number of the offenders who got provisional discharge from probationary supervision after being placed under the suspension of execution of sentence with probation and that of those who had their discharge

Table 62 Percentage of Adult Probationers, by Type of Offence

Year	Total	Penal Code offences	Homicide	Robbery	Assault Bodily injury	Extortion	Theft	Fraud
1955	100.0 (4,361)	90.9	0.2	1.2	4.6	4.3	57.2	11.6
1960	100.0 (8,525)	92.8	0.5	1.9	9.3	9.7	49.0	8.2
1965	100.0 (8,350)	90.3	0.5	1.3	10.5	10.8	38.5	7.6
1970	100.0 (6,908)	92.7	0.7	1.4	11.0	8.5	35.7	5.5
1975	100.0 (7,048)	78.2	0.7	0.9	8.9	5.2	36.6	4.5
1980	100.0 (8,058)	61.4	0.5	0.5	5.7	3.0	29.6	3.7
1985	100.0 (7,180)	63.1	0.6	0.7	5.3	3.3	31.5	4.9
1988	100.0 (6,076)	63.1	0.4	0.5	6.0	3.7	31.3	3.6

Year	Rape	Violent acts	Professional negligence	Others	Special Law offences	Stimulant drugs	Poisonous substances	Road-traffic violations	Others
1955	0.6	…	…	2.4	9.1	5.3	…	0.1	3.7
1960	4.0	0.9	…	9.4	7.2	0.1	…	0.6	6.4
1965	4.0	3.8	…	13.2	9.7	0.4	…	1.7	7.6
1970	6.5	2.8	10.3	10.4	7.3	0.5	…	2.0	4.8
1975	3.1	2.1	8.0	8.3	21.8	7.3	…	10.1	4.4
1980	2.1	1.5	8.4	6.5	38.6	21.5	0.1	14.4	2.7
1985	1.0	0.7	8.6	6.4	36.9	21.8	1.3	11.5	2.4
1988	0.8	0.9	9.8	5.3	36.9	20.1	1.9	11.8	3.1

Sources: Annual Report of Judicial Statistics,
Annual Report of Statistics on Rehabilitation

cancelled afterwards every five years from 1955 to 1985 and in 1988.

The number of the former rose gradually from 370 in 1960 to 1,741 in 1985, but decreased in 1988 to 1,376. Meanwhile, the number of those who were

Table 63 Number of Adult Probationers, by Provisional Discharge and Its Cancellation

Year	Number of the Provisional Discharged	Number of Cancellation of the Provisional Discharged	Number of Probationers at end of the year (A)	The Provisional Discharged at end of the year	
				Number (B)	$\frac{B}{A}$ (%)
1955	11	0	6,012	10	0.2
1960	370	6	22,483	339	1.5
1965	480	9	23,649	502	2.1
1970	827	11	22,233	813	3.7
1975	968	20	21,555	1,025	4.8
1980	1,721	95	23,368	2,220	9.5
1985	1,741	133	21,430	2,489	11.6
1988	1,376	114	18,447	1,926	10.4

Source: Annual Report of Statistics on Rehabilitation

under provisional discharge at the end of the year was 2,220 in 1980 and remained on the 2,000 level until it fell short of the 2,000 mark to 1,926 in 1988.

The number of those who had their provisional discharge cancelled was roughly proportional to the number of those who obtained provisional discharge but remained relatively small, 114 in 1988.

Fig. 41 shows the changes in number of those who terminated their term of suspended execution and probationary supervision classified by reason of termination from 1959 to 1988.

The revision of the Penal Code in 1953 and 1954 established the system of suspension of execution of sentence with probation for adult offenders and expanded the scope of the application of the system. It thus brought an increase in the number of the offenders who were accommodated by the system. The number of such offenders ranged between 7,000 and 8,000 after 1960.

The number of those who finished the probation term was 1,114 in 1957 and increased to 2,263 in the following year. It soared to over 5,000 between 1961 and 1987. The 1988 figure showed a little decrease to 4,864.

The revocation of the suspensions of executions of sentences soared to 1,314 or 84.2 percent in 1956 and remained above 2,000 from the following year. But it decreased a little to just over 1,000 in 1968 and again surpassed 2,000 in 1976, when the rate of cancellation once more reached 30 percent. The rate has

Fig.41 Number of Adult Probationers by Reason of Termination (1949~1988)

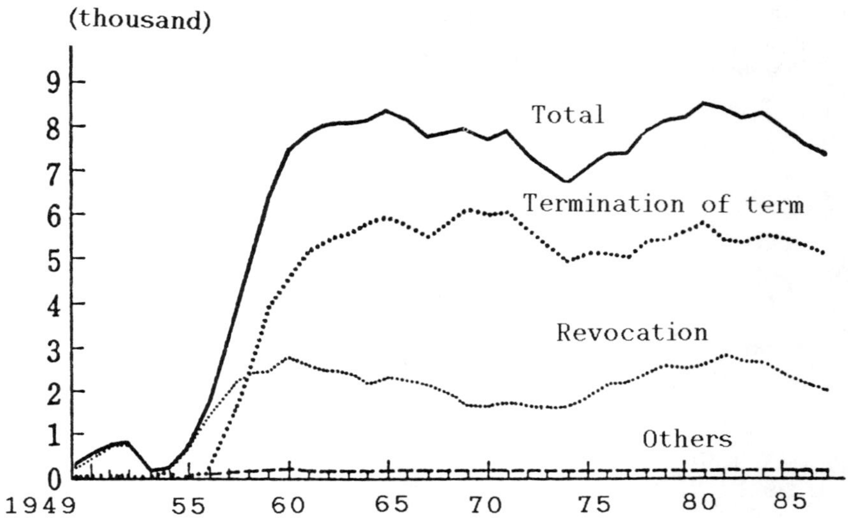

Sources:Annual Report of Judicial Statistics and Annual Report of Statistics on Rehabilitation

been at the same level since then.

When an offender who obtained suspension of execution of sentence with probation violates conditions for the privilege and the circumstances are seriously unfavorable to him, the suspension of execution of sentence granted to him may be revoked by courts at the request of public prosecutors. The number of such people, however, has not been large with 220 registered in 1980 as the largest number so far. It was around 100 in recent years.

(4) Treatment of the Offenders Placed under Probationary Supervision

The probationary supervision system of Japan is characterized by the way it is administered. Probation officers and volunteer probation offices cooperate in carrying out the probationary supervision. In practice, however, the roles of the two kinds of officers were not clearly defined. In the first decade starting in 1949, the year the system was introduced, they tried various ways to find the appropriate administration of the system.

In November 1960, the Ministry of Justice issued an administrative note calling for the tightening of the probationary supervision with the worsening of the crimes committed by juveniles. Probation offices around the nation, on receiving the note, began strenghthening the supervision of those who were prone to commit another dreadful crime and started concentrated supervision focused on such persons (focused supervision).

In the course of these developments, the probationary supervision system gradually began to work well. Probation officers came to take more important roles and their expertise was valued more. Moves became more active to distinguish the roles of professional probation officers from volunteer probation officers.

From 1961 to 1963, an experiment on the roles to be played by probation officers and volunteer probation officers in their treatment of offenders was undertaken. In this experiment, probation officers treated 50 probationary supervision cases (included here No. 1 to No. 4 probationary supervision: No. 1 for juvenile probationers, No. 2 for parolees from Juvenile Training Schools, No. 3 for parolees from prisons and No. 4 for those granted suspension of execution of sentences with probation.) by themselves and 150 in cooperation with volunteer officers in order to find out the most effective treatment methods.

The experiment prompted introduction of the "outset supervision" system at the Tokyo, Osaka and Nagoya offices in April 1965. In the new system, probation officers take up by themselves the supervision during the first two months and list problems of particular offenders. The data were to be used as reference in determining future treatment.

The idea was further promoted by setting up direct supervision teams of professional probation officers at probation offices in Tokyo and Osaka in April 1974. The system, at first, was applied to offenders under 23 years of age in limited areas with an emphasis on intensive treatment and development on treatment skills for these. The system is now applied to both adult and juvenile offenders nationwide.

In an attempt to improve the probationary supervision, a system to classify the ways of probationary supervision by the degree of involvement of the professional probation officers was introduced in September 1967. With the three classifications-A, B, and C-more effective supervision was expected. In October 1971, based on the achievements, another system was introduced. It classified offenders into A and B, depending on how difficult they were to treat.

For Group A involving difficult cases, professional probation officers participate more systematically and actively in the treatment of offenders and communications between probation officers and volunteer probation officers was further strengthened by exchanging information and opinions. Though the system was initially applied only to urban areas within the jurisdiction of the offices concerned, it was later expanded to cover the jurisdictional areas.

Later the research on the classification progressed further. In January

1986, classification tables were subdivided into three categories consisting of No. 1 and No. 2 (juveniles), No. 3 (prison parolees) and No. 4 (suspended execution with probation). Moreover, items in these tables were reduced to half and differential emphasis was placed on each item for evaluation. These changes are still observed today.

In order to effectively carry out the classification system, a probation officer regularly visits city, town and village offices. Under what is called a "stationing system," he stays a day at these municipalities monthly where he meets offenders and their parents and confers with voluntary probation officers.

The Probation Office also classifies offenders into several categories depending on the crimes they committed and social background and so forth, such as those related to gangs, hot-rodders, thinner sniffing, those sentenced to life but out of prison on parole, those suffering from mental disorders, in-school assault offenders and stimulant drug abusers, and effective treatment measures to meet the different needs of the clients have been carried out. And group counseling and other guidance in groups is given at probation offices nationwide to those charged with drug abuses like thinner sniffing.

With the increase of traffic violations and juvenile delinquency, more effective probationary supervision was sought. In April 1965, the Ministry of Justice worked out a guidline in handling juvenile offenders under probationary supervision for violations of the Road Traffic Law. Under the guideline, they are treated differently from those under other charges. It is aimed at fostering the spirit to observe the law and to drive safely. It is characteristic that they are treated in groups, in addition to individual treatment.

Since 1975, several probation offices have tried out a group counseling in panel discussion formula. After 1975, several probation offices edited handbooks on safe driving for juvenile traffic offenders and through interviews and counseling, and making use of these handbooks, achieved remarkable records.

Noteworthy in connection with probationary supervision work involving traffic offenders is a special short-term programme introduced in April 1977. The programme is given to juvenile offenders whose violation is not chronic, based on the advice of the family court. Under the system, these offenders serve probationary supervision in groups for a short period, for three to four months, under probation officers or specifically nomiated volunteer probation officers specialized in traffic affairs. The number of these offenders is increasing year after year, with more than 40,000 being recruited yearly in the programme over the past five years.

Another noteworthy treatment of juvenile offenders involves probationary observation for juvenile parolees released from short-term juvenile training schools, which was introduced in May 1977. Under the treatment designed to be completed within six months after release on parole, probation officers maintain close contact with offenders and their families in the initial stage. Special consideration is given to help ensure smooth socialization of such juveniles.

In October 1966, a pre-parole investigation was put into effect. Under the system, probation officers from the District Rehabilitation Board visit correctional institutions before an application for parole is submitted.

The officers interview inmates and consult with officers of correctional institutions so that their return to society, following parole, will be made smoothly and adequately. In this process, they prepare for parole examination. These efforts are also designed to deepen the organic link between correctional treatment in institutions and reformative rehabilitative services to be followed thereafter.

The system was revised in September 1984, whereby probation officers from District Rehabilitation Boards, on top of the pre-parole investigation, are stationed at correctional institutions. There they give advice to and consult with inmates and adjust the family and other environments where the inmates would return following discharge.

Treatment of long-term inmates in connection with their release on parole was introduced in April 1979. This system applies to those sentenced to life or eight years or more in prison. Called the "halfway house treatment system," it enables long-term inmates to settle down at a rehabilitation aid hostels for a certain period, if and when they agree to such measures. Besides aid to help find jobs, living guidance and other training to get used to society are given by workers of the rehabilitation aid society.

The period of stay was shortened to one month from three months after the system was revised in June 1986. All long-term inmates are made as a principle subject to the system under the revised measures.

Turning to juvenile delinquents, those in the younger age group, including middle school students, tend to commit crimes. Taking this observation into account, the Ministry of Justice issued an administrative note urging closer probationary supervision for youths in March 1983. This was followed by another note issued in December 1985 calling for more intensive probationary supervision for those sentenced to life and discharged on parole. This note was issued in order to prevent a repetition of vicious crimes.

4. REHABILITATION AID SOCIETY

(1) Outline

A rehabilitation aid society is a private organization which undertakes rehabilitation services with a license issued by the Justice Minister. There are two kinds, one being direct and the other indirect. The direct service, which is more common, actively engages in services, including providing accommodations. The indirect service limits itself to extending subsidies or assuming such work as liaison and providing other minor aid.

Subject to the protective service of the society include (1) those who are given urgent aftercare service under the Law for Urgent Aftercare of Discharged Offenders like those discharged from prison after completion of their prison terms, (2) those under probationary supervision and entrusted by the chiefs of probation offices, and (3) those whose continuing aftercare service was found necessary although the term of aftercare service provided for in the Law had already elapsed. Accommodations, food, and assistance in job placement are among the services being offered by the society.

(2) Changes in Rehabilitation Aid Society

Meizen Kimbara pioneered in introducing a private rehabilitation center in Japan, founding a "company to protect persons discharged from prison" in Shizuoka-ken in 1888.

In the following years, the number of private organizations to help rehabilitate discharged prisoners (prisoners aid associations) and juvenile offenders (juvenile protection and rehabilitation service associations) increased, numbering 800 in 1927. (This number includes branches of such facilities and those indirect societies explained above.) This followed: 1) abolition of a system to allow an ex-prisoner having no kith or kin to live in special facilities within prison; 2) discharge of prisoners as a result of amnesty on several occasions during the Meiji and Taisho eras; and 3) a government policy shift encouraging the establishment of prisoners aid associations.

However, these associations were run by volunteers in cooperation with local governments. The central government limited itself to extending subsidies in operating such facilities.

After May 1936, when the Law for Supervision of Political Offenders was enacted, societies to look after political offenders were set up one after another. In Novemver the same year, the rules for funds to operate prisoners aid services was replaced by the rules for funds to operate judicial rehabilitation services.

The Judicial Rehabilitatoin Service Law was subsequently enforced in September 1939, requiring rehabilitation service organizations (for those with suspended sentences, those discharged, juvenile delinquents and political offenders) to obtain licenses issued by the Justice Minister. Under the law, rehabilitation service societies, then numbering more than 1,000, were integrated into 692 licensed bodies.

Fig.42 Number of Rehabilitation Aid Societies

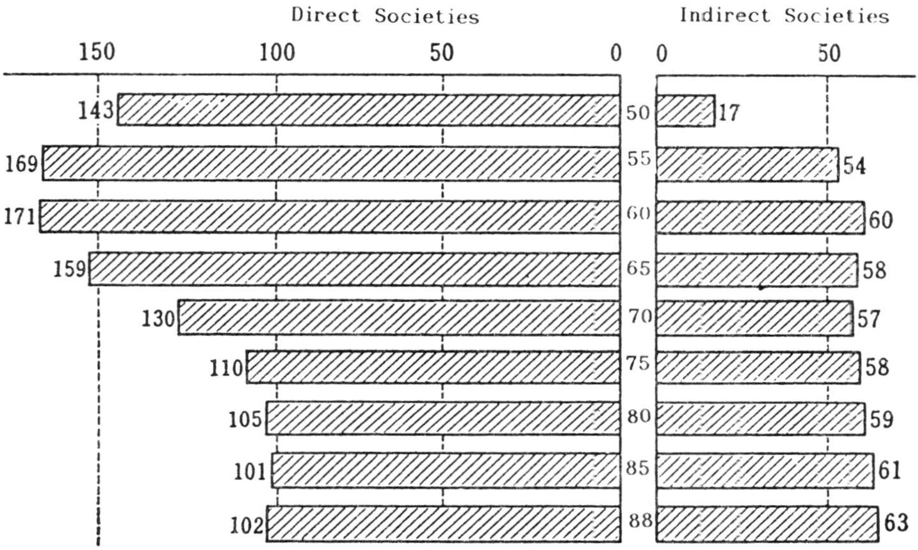

Note : The Function of the Indirect Society is to do financial support to the direct society and to coordinate among the direct society and so on.
Source:Rehabilitation Bureau, Ministry of Justice

In December of the same year, the Judicial Rehabilitation Society (a juridical foundation and the predecessor of the current Japan Rehabilitation Association) was brought into being. It unified three major rehabilitation societies-the Hoseikai, Shotokukai and Japan Juvenile Rehabilitation Society-to undertake the rehabilitation services for released inmates and political offenders.

In 1942, protective, rehabilitative treatment measures imposed by the Juvenile Tribunal began to be implemented nationwide, encouraging the establishment of juvenile rehabilitation societies. With the nation totally involved in the war, however, they were increasingly faced with difficulties in running their facilities.

In October 1945, following the end of World War II, those with suspended sentences and parolees could not make their living in the postwar economic chaos. Under the circumstances, judicial guidance offices were set up at judicial rehabilitation societies to protect them. In March 1949, the juvenile rehabilitation societies were abolished and transformed into Juvenile Training Schools and child welfare homes.

Fig.43 Number of Persons Entrusted to Rehabilitation Aid Societies (1961～1988)

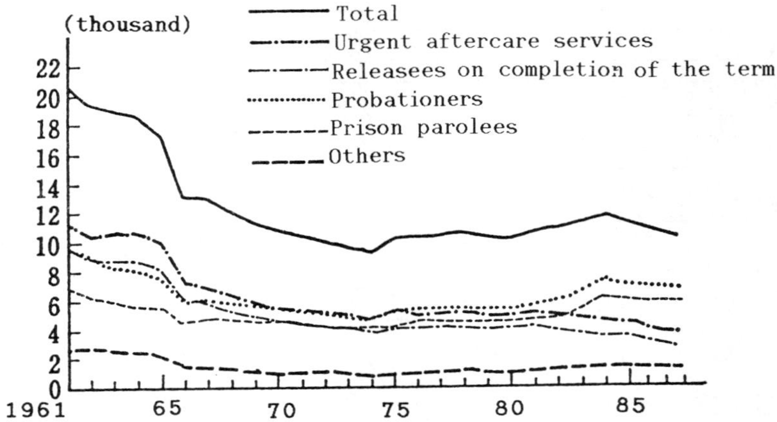

Source: Annual Report of Statistics on Rehabilitation

In May 1950, the Judicial Rehabilitation Service Law was abolished and the Law for Urgent Aftercare of Discharged Offenders was enforced. As a result, the judicial rehabilitation societies which had been formed before the war were reorganized into rehabilitation aid societies licensed by the Justice Minister.

The old judicial rehabilitation societies numbered as many as 600 before the war. However, many of the organizations ceased to exist or were forced to close during or after the war, as a result of bombing, economic difficulties, or modification or abolishment of various laws and systems. Newly licensed rehabilitation aid societies under the Law for Urgent Aftercare of Discharged Offenders totaled only 143.

Fig. 42 shows the changes in the number of rehabilitation aid societies every five years between 1950 and 1985 and in 1988. Many organizations directly providing rehabilitation service were formed or discontinued in the early 1950s and their number remained between 160 and 170 in the late 1950s.

With the economic recovery of the nation from the late 1950s through the 1960s, however, the number of those who were referred to rehabilitation services dropped and not a few of rehabilitation aid societies were forced to close due to financial difficulties.

The shrinkage was halted in 10 years from 1975 but only 102 bodies had survived as of the end of December 1988. (Of them, 100 facilities of 98 organizations were in active service.)

Table 64 Number of Inmates in Rehabilitation Aids Societies

Fiscal year	Number of societies as of 31 March	Capacity of accom-modation as of 31 March	Total capacity of accommodation for the year (A)	Real number of inmates for the year	Total number of accommodation for the year (B)	Number of inmates referred from POs (C)	Number of inmates not referred from POs	Rate of accommo-dation $\frac{B}{A}$ (%)	Rate of referral $\frac{C}{B}$ (%)
1958	150	3,921	1,425,204	30,440	1,058,447	567,421	491,026	74.3	53.6
1960	158	4,122	1,495,443	36,698	1,138,923	646,830	492,093	76.2	56.8
1965	137	3,721	1,425,557	13,915	848,504	616,175	232,329	59.5	72.6
1970	121	3,589	1,230,433	12,896	611,232	478,515	132,717	49.7	78.3
1975	103	2,972	1,076,939	11,754	530,301	418,344	111,957	49.2	78.9
1980	100	2,645	978,302	11,314	526,076	443,175	82,901	53.8	84.2
1985	98	2,470	913,872	12,066	545,037	476,459	68,578	59.6	87.4
1987	98	2,433	893,520	11,002	542,662	482,550	60,112	60.7	88.9

Source: Rehabilitation Bureau, Ministry of Justice

(3) Changes in Treatment

Fig. 43 shows the changes in the number of offenders who were entrusted to the rehabilitation aid societies from 1961 to 1988 by the type of treatment. In 1961, over 20,000 offenders were referred to rehabilitation aid societies but the number gradually went down to below 10,000 in 1973. After 1975, the number slightly increased but hovered somewhere between 10,000 and 11,000.

Viewed from the type of treatment, the number of offenders placed under the urgent aftercare service was the largest between 1961 and 1969 but was surpassed by that of those put under probationary supervision in 1976 and the gap between the two has widened since that time.

Table 64 gives a rough sketch on the situation of the rehabilitation aid societies in 1958, in every five years between 1960 and 1985 and in 1987.

In 1960, there were 158 rehabilitation aid societies with accommodation totaling 36,698 persons in real numbers, handling a total of 1,138,923 people in accumulation. The rate of accomodation was as high as 76.2 percent of the total capacity of accommodation.

With rehabilitation aid societies decreasing in number, offenders accepted by those societies also decreased. In 1980, rehabilitation aid societies numbered 100 with accommodation in real numbers totaling 11,314 offenders, dealing with 526,076. In 1987, there were 98 rehabilitation societies with accommodation of 11,002 offenders in real numbers, handling 542,662 in that year.

A comparison of the figures of 1960 with those of 1987 shows a reduction to one third in terms of the accommodation in real numbers and a half in the number of accommodations accumulated. In looking at the figures of 1987 in more detail, it becomes clear that the number of those receiving accommodation on a voluntary and continuous basis-after the term of service provided for under the Law had already elapsed-decreased more than the counterpart receiving the accommodation service on the basis of the entrustment by the chiefs of probation offices. (Accordingly, the duration of accommodation per person decreased and naturally the number of accommodations accumulated decreased more than the decrease of accommodations in real numbers.)

Rehabilitation aid societies are run by private volunteers. Depending on the economic situation of the times, they were often not able to recruit the staff necessary to run the installations in terms of number and quality.

Though many of the existing rehabilitation aid societies are not always in good financial condition, their role in assisting released offenders in rehabilitation is significant as almost one-fifth of those released from prison seek to settle down at such rehabilitation aid societies.

Meanwhile, it is becoming an increasingly difficult problem in operating rehabilitation aid societies to obtain the understanding and cooperation of the residents of the community where the rehabilitation aid society is located.

5. *PARDON*

(1) Outline

There are two types of pardons. One is amnesty, etc. by Cabinet Order which is given uniformly to offenders by the type of offence or sentence, and the other is individual pardon which is given to specific offenders who meet certain criteria.

The former consists of three categories. One is amnesty, another is commutation of punishment, and yet another is restoration of rights.

The latter consists of four categories. One is pardon, the second is commutation of punishment, the third is exemption of execution of sentence (reprieve), and the fourth is restoration of rights. Individual pardon is granted after giving careful consideration to the conduct of the individual offender and taking into account public reactions.

Individual pardon is given on two occasions. One is given on a day-to-day basis in the exercise of adequate criminal policies and the other is given on the occasion of granting amnesty, etc. by Cabinet Order to supplement the latter, known as the pardon on special standards.

Table 65 Amnesty, etc., by Order and Special Standard Pardons in the Showa Era

Date of Promulgation	Causes of Pardon	Amnesty by Order	Special Standard Pardon	Commutation of Sentence by Order	Special Standard Commutation of Sentence	Special Standard Exemption of Execution of Sentence	Restoration of Civil Rights by Order	Special Standard Restoration of Civil Rights
1927. 2. 7	The Taisho Imperial Mourning	Imperial Order No.11 Subjects 137,669	Cabinet Directions Subjects 1,457	Imperial Order No.12 Subjects 46,138	Cabinet Directions Subjects 163		Imperial Order No.13 Subjects Unavailable	
1928.11.10	Coronation of the Showa Emperor		Cabinet Directions Subjects 16,923	Imperial Order No.270 Subjects 48,653	Cabinet Directions Subjects 480		Imperial Order No.271 Subjects 10,517	
1934. 2.11	Birthday of the Crown Prince			Imperial Order No.19 Subjects 71,735			Imperial Order No.20 Subjects Unavailable	
1938. 2.11	Fifties' Anniversary of the Meiji Constitution			Imperial Order No.76 Subjects 1,299	Cabinet Directions Subjects Unavailable		Imperial Order No.77 Subjects Unavailable	Cabinet Directions Subjects Unavailable
1940. 2.11	Celebration of the 2,600 Year Reign of the Emperor			Imperial Order No.45 Subjects 74,858	Cabinet Directions Subjects 33		Imperial Order No.46 Subjects 213,598	Cabinet Directions Subjects 7,532
1942. 2.18	The First Victory of World War II		Cabinet Directions Subjects 15,916				Imperial Order No.94 Subjects Unavailable	
1945.10.17	The End of World War II	Imperial Order No.579 Subjects 264,403	Cabinet Directions Subjects 346	Imperial Order No.580 Subjects 50,019	Cabinet Directions Subjects 2		Imperial Order No.581 Subjects 109,374	Cabinet Directions Subjects 381
1946.11. 3	Promulgation of the New Constitution	Imperial Order No.511 Subjects 44,623	Cabinet Directions Subjects 1,500	Imperial Order No.512 Subjects 84,776	Cabinet Directions Subjects 80		Imperial Order No.513 Subjects 38,855	Cabinet Directions Subjects 40

The pardons function:

1) To correct apparently inappropriate aftermath inevitable to the uniform application of statutes;

2) To correct court sentences in response to later and big changes in situation; and

3) To change court sentences or to restore civil rights, as part of criminal policy, in response to the good conduct of offenders after the sentence became final.

Date of Promulgation	Causes of Pardon	Amnesty by Order	Special Standard Pardon	Commutation of Sentence by Order	Special Standard Commutation of Sentence	Special Standard Exemption of Execution of Sentence	Restoration of Civil Rights dy Order	Special Standard Restoration of Civil Rights
1947.11. 3	Supplement of the Cabinet Order concerning Commutation of Sentence on the Occasion of the End of World War II and Promulgation of New Constitution			Cabinet Order No.118 Subjects 4,750				
1952. 4.28	Promulgation of the Peace Treaty	Cabinet Order No.117 Subjects 444,208	Cabinet Directions Subjects 1,623	Cabinet Order No.118 Subjects 277,814	Cabinet Directions Subjects 356	Cabinet Directions Subjects 128	Cabinet Order No.119 Subjects 282,470	Cabinet Directions Subjects 29
1952.11.10	The Official Investiture of the Crown Prince		Cabinet Directions Subjects 2,063		Cabinet Directions Subjects 1,391			Cabinet Directions Subjects 24
1956.12.19	Acceptance in the United Nations	Cabinet Order No.355 Subjects 69,627	Cabinet Directions Subjects 337		Cabinet Directions Subjects 84	Cabinet Directions Subjects 224		Cabinet Directions Subjects 1,510
1959. 4.10	The Marriage of the Crown Prince		Cabinet Directions Subjects 1,211		Cabinet Directions Subjects 286	Cabinet Directions Subjects 931	Cabinet Order No.113 Subjects 45,797	Cabinet Directions Subjects 513
1968.11. 1	Anniversary of the Meiji 100 Years		Cabinet Directions Subjects 3,250		Cabinet Directions Subjects 259	Cabinet Directions Subjects 119	Cabinet Order No.315 Subjects 148,732	Cabinet Directions Subjects 458
1972. 5.15	Reversion of Okinawa		Cabinet Directions Subjects 2,011		Cabinet Directions Subjects 72	Cabinet Directions Subjects 40	Cabinet Order No.196 Subjects 32,329	Cabinet Directions Subjects 51

Source: Annual Report of Justice Ministry

At any rate, pardons bear grave consequences as they are granted with the administrative authority overriding the right of punishment of the state.

(2) Changes in the System of Pardons

The history of pardons dates back as far as to the Nara era. It was granted on either congratulatory or funeral occasions of the Imperial household or the shogunate government. The Imperial Japanese Constitution, which was promulgated in February 1889, stipulated pardons belonged to the supreme power of the Emperor, ruling that the Emperor grants amnesty, pardons, commutation of punishment and restoration of civil rights. Under the old Constitution, the core of the pardons consisted of the Imperial Order (so-called general amnesty, etc.) and pardons on special standards. Pardons on a day-to-day basis were granted only on limited occasions.

Under the new Constitution enacted in May 1947, the Cabinet has the power to grant pardons, attested by the Emperor.

In the same year, the Amnesty Order (The 23rd Imperial Order of the first year of the Taisho era) was abolished. It was replaced with the Amnesty Law and an ordinance to implement the law was enforced. Under the new rules, individuals concerned were allowed to apply for pardon extensively, a point of the new criminal policies.

In May 1949, partial revisions of the the Amnesty Law and the related ordinance were effected in order to incorporate the views of the general public and specialists in carrying out pardon and the National Offenders Rehabilitation Committee (a predecessor of the current National Offenders Rehabilitation Commission) was inaugurated to study the problem.

(3) Amnesty, etc. in Showa Era

Table 65 shows the general amnesty, etc. and special standard pardons practiced in the Showa era. In recent years, there has been a deliberate attitude in granting pardons because they actually modify court decisions with the administrative authority.

Pardons were granted on the occasion of the Emperor Showa's death. A Cabinet Order to grant amnesty was the first since December 1956, when Japan was admitted to the United Nations and a Cabinet Order to restore rights was the first since May 1972, when Okinawa was returned to Japan.

(4) Pardons on a Day-to-Day Basis

Table 11 in the Appendix shows changes in the number of those individual cases disposed of by the National Offenders Rehabilitation Commission between 1949 and 1988. In the 10 years from 1955, the figure ranged between 100 and 200, and after small changes in the said figures, it totaled 929 in 1969 (of whom 852 were given a favorable decision of the Commission; adequate to be granted pardon, etc. and referred to the Cabinet), and 692 in 1973 (of whom 414 were given a favorable decision of the Commission and referred to the Cabinet).

In the past 10 years, the number of cases where pardon or commutation of punishment were granted have been extremely small and most cases were limited to the restoration of rights or reprieve. Cases judged by the Commission as having no reason to grant pardons have slightly increased.

Chapter Ⅳ. Juvenile Delinquency and Treatment of Juvenile Delinquents

Section 1. *Trends in Juvenile Delinquency*

1. SURVEY OF JUVENILE DELINQUENCY

There are fundamental differences between juvenile laws before and after World War II. Under the old law, a juvenile was a person under 18 years of age, while the current law stipulates that a juvenile is a person under 20 years of age. This section will regard those under 20 years of age as juveniles and examine the trends of juvenile delinquency in the Showa era by relying on available statistics based on the number of juvenile offenders cleared by the police.

Only limited prewar statistics on juvenile offenders are available in records compiled by the police since 1936 and they include law-breaking children under 14 years of age who were exempted from criminal responsibility. Therefore, statistics on juvenile Penal Code offenders mentioned in this section will include the number of law-breaking children unless described otherwise.

Table 12 in the Appendix shows the annual number of juvenile Penal Code offenders cleared by the police in and after 1936 and their ratios to each 1,000 persons between 14 and 19 years of age in the population (See Fig. 2). The figures are compared with the counterpart number of adult offenders. (Statistics on adult offenders before 1940 are not available.)

According to the Table, the number of juvenile Penal Code offenders cleared in 1936 was 46,550 (the ratio to 1,000 juveniles in the population was 3.2—hereafter listed as (3.2:1,000). The number increased to 53,048 (3.4: 1,000) in 1940 and to 61,366 in 1943 (the latter ratio to the juvenile population is not available because there are no population statistics from 1941 to 1943). In 1944, the number further increased to 75,314 (4.6:1,000). After a decline in 1945 to 54,787 (3.3:1,000), it rebounded to 111,790 (6.7:1,000) in 1946 in the immediate postwar period. In 1951, it climbed to 166,433 (9.5:1,000), the first peak of juvenile delinquency in postwar Japan. The number declined until 1954 but from 1955 the figure turned upward. In 1964, the second peak was reached at 238,830 (11.9:1,000). Since then the figure showed a gently declining trend until 1976 when it reached 194,024 (12.1:1,000). From 1977, the number turned upward and in 1981 it exceeded the 300,000 mark. In 1983, it reached 317,438 (17.1:1,000), marking a postwar high and the third peak of juvenile delinquency. From 1984, the number declined, but rose in 1988 to 292,902 (15.3: 1,000), an increase of 3,706 from the previous year.

Table 66 Number and Rate of Juvenile and Adult Penal Code Offenders Cleared by the Police, Excluding Traffic Professional Negligence (1966～1988)

Year	Juveniles		Adults		Percentage of juveniles
	Number	Rate per 1,000 juveniles	Number	Rate per 1,000 adults	
1966	182,255	9.0	285,296	4.5	39.0
1967	160,377	8.3	273,218	4.2	37.0
1968	147,354	8.0	276,706	4.2	34.7
1969	138,677	7.8	270,514	4.0	33.9
1970	148,022	8.7	267,555	3.8	35.6
1971	141,197	8.6	254,865	3.6	35.7
1972	136,980	8.4	247,937	3.4	35.6
1973	146,957	9.1	249,527	3.4	37.1
1974	151,631	9.4	247,856	3.3	38.0
1975	152,382	9.4	247,335	3.2	38.1
1976	150,164	9.3	243,732	3.1	38.1
1977	154,536	9.4	243,945	3.1	38.8
1978	177,719	10.7	244,941	3.1	42.0
1979	184,839	10.9	224,968	2.8	45.1
1980	219,956	12.8	226,040	2.8	49.3
1981	252,808	14.3	233,260	2.8	52.0
1982	257,856	14.3	250,033	3.0	50.8
1983	261,634	14.1	241,922	2.9	52.0
1984	248,540	13.2	253,952	3.0	49.5
1985	250,132	13.1	238,133	2.8	51.2
1986	235,176	12.1	214,513	2.5	52.3
1987	227,978	11.8	217,570	2.5	51.2
1988	231,210	12.1	205,002	2.3	53.0

Note: Juveniles mean aged from 10 to 19, and adults aged 20 or more,
Sources: National Police Agency and Management and Coordination Agency

As seen above, prior to the end of the war, the number of juvenile Penal Code offenders peaked in 1944. However, the number was rather small. After World War II, there have been three peaks—the first in 1951, the second in 1964 and the third in 1983.

Behind the 1944 peak lay depression and poverty, which pervaded society as a whole under wartime pressure. After 1945, the postwar rise in the number of juvenile delinquencies was due largely to social disorder, economic hardships, family breakups and other chaotic conditions in the aftermath of the war. On the other hand, the delinquency peak in the decade from 1955 through 1965 was due to drastic social changes and frictions stemming from rapid industrialisation and urbanisation as Japan began to achieve high economic growth. Also, large numbers of wartime children were reaching their high teens.

After 1975, increases in juvenile delinquencies were largely due to the changing circumstances of an affluent society, increasing diversity of values among the people, declining attention paid to caring for and educating children on the part of families and local communities, and more opportunities for juveniles to commit crimes.

The number of adult Penal Code offenders in 1941, on the other hand, was 281,708 (ratio cannot be calculated because no population statistics for that year are available). Since then the figure gradually decreased with only occasional rises. In 1945, it reached 187,858 (5.0 per 1,000 in the adult population—hereafter listed as (5.0:1,000). However, the figure in 1946 saw a quantum jump to 333,694 (8.4:1,000) and in 1948 exceeded the 400,000 mark. After peaking in 1950 at 458,297 (10.1:1,000), it leveled off at around the 400,000 mark. It turned upward in 1963 and exceeded the 500,000 mark in 1965. In 1970, it recorded a postwar high of 883,254 (12.6:1,000). After registering gradual decreases, it leveled off below the 700,000 mark between 1974 and 1982. From 1983, it turned upward, and the 1988 figure was 733,886 (8.3:1,000).

Meanwhile, juveniles accounted for 15.8 percent of the total number of Penal Code offenders cleared by the police in 1941. After that, the ratio stayed at around 20-30 percent. In 1988, the ratio was 28.5 percent.

Hitherto, the statistical survey has been based on the number of offenders involved in all Penal Code offences cleared by the police. However, the increase in the number since the early part of 1960s was due largely to an increase in the offence of criminal negligence involving car drivers. It would be pertinent, therefore, to look at the trends of juvenile delinquency here on the basis of the juvenile offenders involved in Penal Code offences other than the offence of professional or gross negligence causing death or bodily injury (provided in Article 211 of the Penal Code—hereafter cited as "non-traffic Penal Code offences"). Table 66 shows the number of juvenile offenders involved in non-traffic Penal Code offences cleared by the police (hereafter cited as "juvenile non-traffic Penal Code offender"), its ratio to the juvenile general population and the percentage of juveniles among the total number of non-traffic Penal Code offenders since the year 1966. The reason for taking up the year 1966 as a starting point is that the statistics of the National Police Agency have been reshaped and refined on the basis of non-traffic Penal Code offences.

In that year (1966), the number of juvenile non-traffic Penal Code offenders was 182,255, or 9.0 per 1,000 juveniles in the population. It gradually decreased until 1972 when it registered 136,980 (8.4:1,000). It turned upward in 1973, and exceeded the 200,000 mark in 1980. In 1983, it rose to 261,634 (14.1: 1,000), marking the highest record since 1966. It gradually decreased with occasional rises and in 1988, it was 231,210 (12.1:1,000).

Meanwhile, the number of adults involved in non-traffic Penal Code offences cleared by the police (hereafter cited as "adult non-traffic Penal Code offenders") was 285,296 or 4.5 per 1,000 adults in the population. It then declined with occasional rises until 1988 when it was 205,002 (2.3:1,000).

Now, looking at the percentage of juveniles among the total number of non-traffic Penal Code offenders, it was 39.0 percent in 1966 and it kept rising to exceed the 50 percent mark in 1981 and 53.0 percent in 1988.

As mentioned earlier, juveniles accounted for 15.8 percent of the total number of Penal Code offenders cleared by the police in 1941 and 24.2 percent in 1944. However, as the number of offenders involved in traffic negligence offences cleared by the police was small in the prewar period, the ratio of juveniles to the total number of non-traffic Penal Code offenders should be almost the same as the figure just mentioned above. The ratio of juveniles to the total number of non-traffic Penal Code offenders in the prewar period was, as mentioned above, about 16 percent in 1941 and about 24 percent in 1944, while in the postwar period it was 39.0 percent in 1966 and 53.0 percent in 1988. It means that the ratio of juvenile delinquents to the total number of Penal Code offenders has been rising sharply in the postwar period, particularly in recent years.

2. GENERAL TRENDS IN JUVENILE DELINQUENCY

(1) Juvenile Penal Code Offences

A. Trend by Age Bracket

The general trend of juvenile delinquency by age bracket differs considerably depending on whether or not the statistics include traffic professional negligence offences. Fig. 44 shows the ratios of juvenile Penal Code offenders cleared by the police (hereafter cited as "juvenile Penal Code offenders") per 1,000 juveniles classified by age bracket (based on the age at the time the

Fig. 44 Rate of Juvenile Penal Code Offenders Cleared by the Police per 1,000 Population, by Age Bracket(1954-1988)

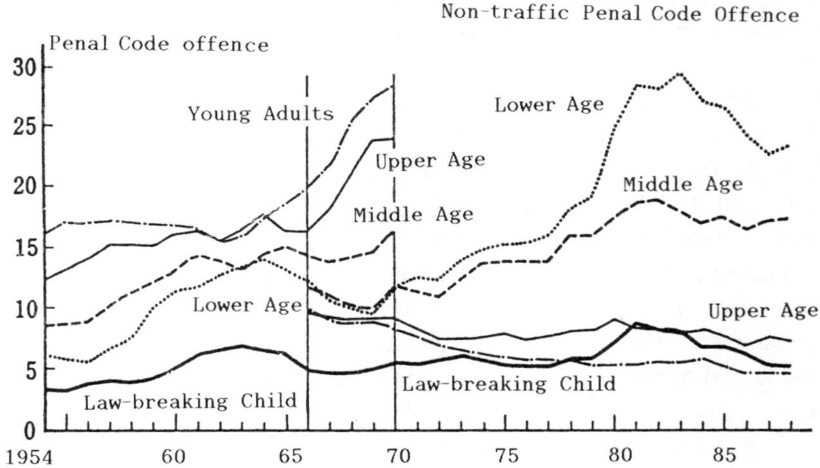

Note:1 "Young adult" means aged 20-24, "upper age" 18-19, "middle age" 16-17 , "lower age" 14-15 and "law-breaking child" 10-13 years old.
2 The number of traffic professional negligence cases is excluded from 1966 to 1988.

Sources: National Police Agency and Management and Coordination Agency

offence was committed) —hereafter cited as "the ratio of juvenile Penal Code offenders" —from 1954 (statistics on juvenile delinquents by age bracket were not kept in and before 1953) in comparison with the young adult (between not less than 20 and less than 25 years of age) counterparts (in that age bracket).

Statistics by age bracket on juveniles are available both with or without the number of those involved in traffic professional negligence between 1966 and 1970. However, those statistics in and before 1965 include only those involved in traffic professional negligence while those after 1971 exclude them. Hereafter, based on the data available, the trends in the ratio of juvenile and young adult Penal Code offenders per 1,000 juveniles and young adults, respectively, shall be examined.

As for the lower age group (between not less than 14 and less than 16 years of age), the ratio of juvenile Penal Code offenders was 6.1 (20,687 in number) in 1954. The ratio increased year by year and peaked at 14.0 (65,883 in number) in 1964. The ratio dropped in and after 1965, but rebounded since the early 1970s.

Now, looking at it based on non-traffic Penal Code offences, the comparable ratio decreased from 12.1 in 1966 to 9.1 in 1969. The ratio turned upward in 1970 and leveled off in 1972. However, it jumped considerably from 1973 and recorded a postwar high of 29.5 (110,437 in number) in 1983. After that, the ratio began to decline, but rose slightly from the previous year to 23.4 (96,023 in number) in 1988.

As for the middle age group (between not less than 16 and less than 18 years of age), the ratio of juvenile Penal Code offenders was 8.5 (29,780 in number) in 1954 and it increased to 14.5 (69,451 in number) in 1964 and to 15.0 (73,297 in number) in 1965. Based on non-traffic Penal Code offences, the comparable ratio was 11.6 (54,162 in number) in 1966. After that it decreased until 1969, but turned upward in 1970 and then leveled off or increased slightly after 1971. The ratio peaked in 1982 at 18.9 (61,350 in number), but fell to 17.4 (69,826 in number) in 1988.

As for the upper age group (between not less than 18 and less than 20 years of age), the ratio of juvenile Penal Code offenders was 12.3 (43,875 in number) in 1954. After that, the ratio increased year by year, reaching 18.0 (87,533 in number) in 1967 and 23.7 (101,216 in number) in 1969.

Based on non-traffic Penal Code offences, the comparable ratio was 9.8 (46,405 in number) in 1966. Since then it decreased or leveled off. In 1988, the ratio was 7.3 (27,907 in number). The figures indicate that the upper age group accounted for a rather small proportion of the population in that age bracket.

As for law-breaking child offenders (under 14 years of age) who were investigated by the police in 1954, the ratio was 3.3 per 1,000 persons in the age bracket between not less than 10 and less than 14 years of age, and the actual number was 26,071. In 1957, the ratio was 4.0 (30,204 in number), 6.2 (57,572 in number) in 1961, and 6.9 (55,366 in number) in 1963, showing gradual increases over the years. Since 1963, however, the ratio has been on the decline. Based on non-traffic Penal Code offences, the comparable ratio was on the rise between 1966 and 1981. In 1966, the ratio was 5.0 (34,006 in number) and 8.9 (67,906 in number) in 1981. Since 1982, however, the ratio has fallen, reaching 5.3 (38,004 in number) in 1988.

As for young adults between not less than 20 and less than 25 years of age, the ratio of young adult Penal Code offenders cleared by the police (hereafter cited as "young adult Penal Code offenders") per 1,000 people in that age bracket increased drastically from 1954. However, it was largely due to an increase in the number of traffic professional negligence offences. In 1966, the ratio of young adult Penal Code offenders was 19.8 while the comparable figure based on non-traffic Penal Code offences was 9.8. In 1970, the ratios were 28.7 and 8.2, respectively. Since 1966, the number of young adults cleared by the police for non-traffic Penal Code offences saw a decline. As such, in

Fig.45 Percentage of Juvenile Penal Code Offenders Cleared, by Offence

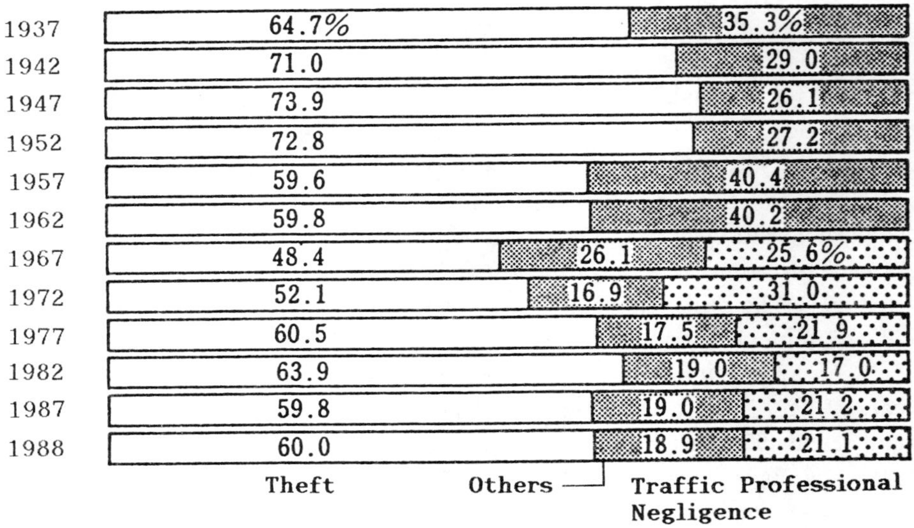

Source: National Police Agency

1988, 39,332 young adults, or 4.6 per 1,000 people in that age bracket, were cleared by the police. It may be said that the crime trends have been stabilised in the young adult age group, too, except traffic professional negligence offences.

As stated above, the number of juvenile delinquents peaked in 1983. However, the number of juvenile delinquents is still high and it is to be particularly noted that their average age has been falling since 1978.

B. Trend of Juvenile Delinquency by Type of Offences

Fig. 45 classifies the types of offences committed by juveniles into theft and other crimes and gives their percentages to the total for every five years since 1937. From 1967 on, juvenile offences have been classified every five years into theft, traffic professional negligence, and others. (See Table 13 in the Appendix).

Before the war, theft always topped the list of juvenile offences followed by many property-related crimes such as fraud and embezzlement. After the war, theft also topped the list. In the late 1940s, the number of thefts and armed robberies increased and from the late 1950s to the late 1960s the number of violent offences as well as sexual offences increased. From the early 1960s, cases of traffic professional negligence registered quantum jumps and from 1975 cases of embezzlement and theft increased tremendously.

Fig.46 Percentage of Juvenile Theft Offenders, by Modus Operandi (1966～1988)

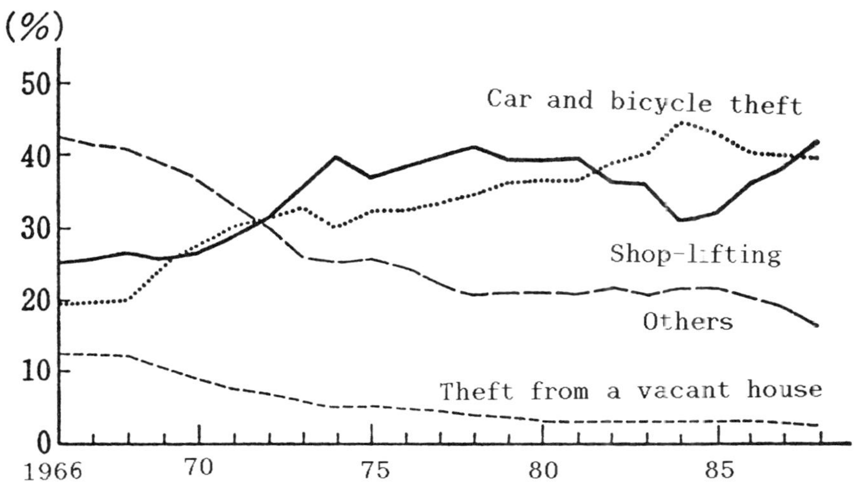

Source: National Police Agency

(a) Theft and Embezzlement

Theft is the most frequent offence committed by juveniles. According to Table 13 in the Appendix, 29,750 juveniles were cleared by the police on charges of theft in 1936. From 1937 to the end of the war, the figure ranged from 30,000 to 50,000 per year. After the war, the number jumped considerably, reaching 87,825 cases in 1946 and 127,122 cases in 1951. After declining for a while, the figure turned upward from 1959, reaching 136,027 cases in 1963. It dipped after 1965 and recorded a postwar low of 96,032 cases in 1969. It then rebounded, with 103,451 cases in 1972 and 202,028 in 1983 before it began to decline, reaching 175,734 cases in 1988.

As shown in Fig. 45, the percentage of theft cases to the total number of Penal Code offenders came to 64.7 percent in 1937 and 71.0 percent in 1942. After that the percentage increased gradually. In the decade from 1945 to 1954, it stood at over 70 percent. However, after 1955, it dropped to around 50 percent. In 1967, it recorded a postwar low of 48.4 percent, but then rebounded and hit 63.9 percent in 1982. The 1988 figure was 60.0 percent.

Fig. 46 shows the percentages of juvenile theft offenders by modus operandi since 1966. A breakdown of prewar theft statistics is not available. In the past 20 years, however, burglaries such as stealing or breaking into houses decreased considerably while shoplifting and car and bicycle thefts increased. The latter is due to the spread of supermarkets and the growth in numbers of cars and bicycles that provided more temptations for juveniles to commit such thefts.

Juvenile offenders involved in embezzlement cases totaled 2,000 to 3,000 in the late 1930s. After that, the figure dropped and reached a low of 603 in 1945. It then rebounded to over 3,000 in the early 1950s. It declined from 1955, but rose again in the early 1970s. It exceeded the 10,000-mark in 1980 and doubled to 20,000 in 1984. The 1988 total was 24,616.

In 1988, 99.9 percent of embezzlement cases involved misappropriation of unattended or neglected articles such as bicycles parked in front of train stations.

Juvenile offenders involved in fraud cases totaled 3,297 in 1936. The figure fell for a while but jumped to 6,368 in 1950. It then declined and came to around 400 or 500 after 1975. But it increased to over 600 in 1983 and rose to 1,036 in 1988.

(b) Violent Crimes

Detailed statistics on juvenile offenders in assault and battery, bodily injury, extortion and intimidation are not available between 1936 and 1950. Statistics on violent offences (that includes assault and battery, bodily injury extortion and intimidation), however, are available from 1949. Cases totaled 14,203 in 1949 and leveled off until around 1954. The figure jumped from 1955 and totaled 23,107 in 1956, 30,590 in 1957, 38,977 in 1958 and a record high 47,030 in 1964. Since then the figure has declined with only occasional rises. The 1988 figure was 21,182. Behind the increases from 1955 onward were instability and frictions resulting from social changes, such as rapid urbanisation and industrialisation, as well as other environmental changes producing unrest among youths, causing them to vent their frustrations through aggressiveness.

(c) Heinous Crimes

There were small numbers of juvenile offenders involved in heinous crimes such as homicide, robbery, etc., in both prewar and postwar periods. However, their numbers comparatively increased from 1945 to 1965 in the social confusion after the war. From 1965, the figure was on the decline.

Less than 200 juveniles a year were cleared by the police in connection with homicide cases between 1936 and 1945. From 1946 to 1970, the figure was about 200 to over 400. In 1951 and 1961, the figure was a record high of 448. From the early 1970s, the figure was on the decline and dipped below the 100 mark in 1975. It stayed at the 70-90 level and was 82 in 1988.

Juveniles cleared by the police in connection with robberies totaled 311 in 1936. The number stayed at around 300 to over 400 before the end of the war. In 1946, the number leaped to 2,903 and to 3,878 in 1948. From 1955, the number stayed at around the 2,000 mark and from 1965 it was on the decline. In 1971, the figure dipped below the 1,000 mark and was 869. After that, the figure was on the decline with occasional rises. In 1988, 569 juveniles were cleared by the police on suspicion of robbery charges.

(d) Sex Crimes

A total of 197 juveniles were cleared by the police in connection with rape cases in 1936. Before the end of the war, the figure stayed at around 200 to over 300. In 1948, after the war, however, the figure made a quantum jump. In 1949, 1,176 juveniles were cleared by the police and 4,649 youngsters in 1958. After that the figure was on the decline with occasional rises. In 1977, the figure dipped below the 1,000-mark and was 509 in 1988.

Juveniles cleared by the police on indecent assault charges totaled 76 in 1936. From 1942, the figure increased to around 300 and over 400. After the war in 1947, the figure decreased to 163, but rebounded to over 1,000 in 1958. Until around 1970, the figure stayed at over 1,000. In 1966, it recorded a postwar high with 1,772. In 1972, the figure dipped the 1,000 mark to 966. After that the figure was on the decline with occasional rises. In 1988, it totaled 593.

Increases in sex crimes from 1958 on can be attributed to law revisions, effective in May 1958, that excluded rape and indecent assault committed by two or more persons from crimes indictable upon a complaint. They can also be attributed to the general social tendency toward loosening moralistic sexual mores.

(e) Delinquency of Girls

In general, there is a considerably fewer number of girls than boys cleared by the police. The fact can be explained by physical and psychological characteristics of girls, as well as their social status, roles and other factors. However, because of the differences from boys, a special notice should be given to the delinquency of girls.

There are no statistics on girl delinquents before World War II. After the old Juvenile Law was put into effect in Jan. 1, 1923, Juvenile Tribunals were established. (Initially they were established in Tokyo and Osaka, which covered Tokyo, Kanagawa-ken, Osaka-fu, Kyoto-fu and Hyogo-ken. Later, the tribunals gradually increased, expanding the number of prefectures covered by the offices.) (Refer to Chapter Ⅳ-2-1-(1)) There were prewar statistics on girls under 18 years of age who violated the Penal Code and were dealt with by the Juvenile Tribunals which could give some sense of what the delinquency of girls was like before the war.

According to the statistics, the female juvenile Penal Code offenders who were arrested by the police totaled 594 in 1934, accounting for 8.7 percent of the total number of juveniles dealt with by the tribunals. After that the figure

Fig.47 Number and Rate of Female juvenile Penal Code Offenders Cleared by the Police (1950~1988)

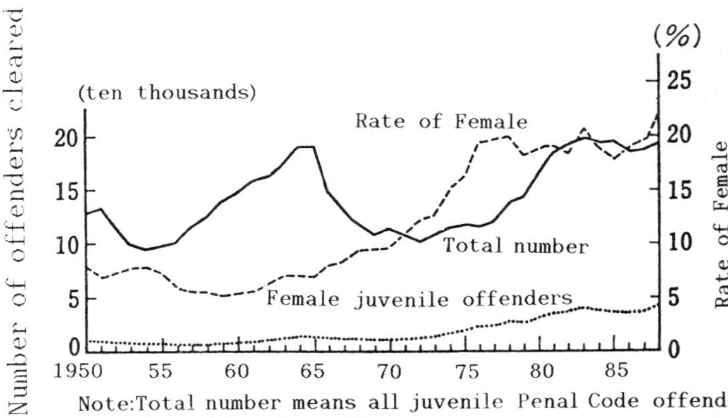

Note:Total number means all juvenile Penal Code offenders cleared by the police.
Source: National Police Agency

stayed at around 600 to over 700. In 1942, when the protective, rehabilitative measures for juvenile delinquents were made applicable nationwide under the old Juvenile Law, female juvenile delinquents totaled 2,239, accounting for 9.5 percent of the total. In 1945, the number decreased to 1,581, or 9.5 percent of the total. After that it turned upward, totaled 3,241 in 1947 and 4,041 in 1948.

Fig. 47 shows the number of girls cleared by the police on suspicion of Penal Code offences and girls' percentage in the total number of juvenile cleared by the police from 1950 when statistics on girl delinquents became available. (However, the figures do not include child offenders under 14 years of age.) In 1950, 10,239 female juvenile offenders were cleared by the police, accounting for 7.9 percent of the total. In 1951, however, the figure dipped below the 10,000 mark and after that it stayed from 6,000 to over 9,000. In 1956, it slacked to 6,114, a record low. After that, it turned upward and totaled 13,397 in 1964, accounting for a low 7.0 percent of the total. From the early 1970s, however, female juvenile delinquency became conspicuous and the figure exceeded the 10 percent mark. Since statistics from 1966 do not include traffic professional negligence, the following figures cannot automatically be compared with those in the decade from 1945 and 1954. From 1965, however, the figure stood at around the 10,000 mark. In 1974, the figure was 17,286, or 14.9 percent of the total, and exceeded the 30,000 mark in 1980 and the 40,000 mark in 1983. In 1988, the figure was an all-time high 43,162, accounting for 22.3 percent of the total. For the past few years, the ratio of females increased at a higher rate than that of males.

By type of offence, theft is the most frequent crimes among girls in any given years. In 1988, female juvenile offenders cleared by the police on suspicion of property offences, including theft, fraud and embezzlement, totaled 40,227, accounting for 93.2 percent of the total number of female juvenile Penal Code offenders cleared by the police. In recent years, however, the number of offences such as bodily injury, extortion, or assault and battery has been increasing, although their numbers were rather small. In 1988, 1,255 female offenders were cleared by the police on charges of bodily injury, 666 on extortion, and 385 on assault and battery, indicating that girls were becoming increasingly violent. Behind the increases in the number of girl delinquencts, it is believed, are changes in the values to which they attach importance and expansion and shifts of their societal behavioral patterns.

(2) Special Law Offences by Juveniles

Based on documents filed by juvenile tribunals, this part will examine juvenile special law offenders before the war. As described above, before 1942, when these tribunals were established nationwide, they handled juveniles under 18 years of age in limited areas. However, the documents might be able to reveal approximate features of the juvenile offenders of special laws at the time.

In 1934, 340 juvenile offenders of special laws were handled at these tribunals. By type of offence, offenders of the Automobile Traffic Control Ordinance topped the list with 173 youngsters, or 50.9 percent of the total number of juvenile offenders of special laws. It is followed by offenders of the Guns and Explosives Control Law with 57 (16.8 percent), Railroad Business Law violaters with four and Violent Act Control Law offenders with four. In 1935, special law offenders totaled 408. By type of offences, Automobile Traffic Control Ordinance offenders topped the list with 206 (50.5 percent), followed by Guns and Explosives Control Law offenders with 92 (22.5 percent), Publication Law offenders with 26 (6.4 percent). In 1936, special law offenders totaled 488 and the ratio of each type of offences remained about the same. In 1942, the total number of special law offenders leaped to 5,249. By type of offences, offenders of Ordinance for the Punishment of Police Infractions topped the list with 3,838 (73.1 percent). In 1943 and 1944, the figure was 2,605 and 2,397, respectively. The decreases in the figure resulted from a drastic drop in the number of offenders of the Ordinance for Punishment of Police Infractions, which surged in 1942.

Table 67 indicates the trend in the number of juvenile offenders referred to the public prosecutors offices by type except traffic violations from 1956 on, when a breakdown of statistics on juvenile special law offenders became available on police statistics. First, we will examine postwar trends of total

Table 67 Number of Juvenile Special Law Offenders Referred to Public Prosecutors Offices (1956～1988)

Year	Total	Fire arms and swords	Narcotics	Cannabis	Stimulant drugs	Poisonous substances	Others
1956	9,046	3,343	28	2	308	2	5,363
1957	11,696	4,756	18	–	28	4	6,890
1958	10,655	5,179	38	–	5	–	5,433
1959	12,482	6,032	71	–	16	1	6,362
1960	15,915	8,079	124	–	32	–	7,680
1961	14,325	8,011	90	1	19	2	6,202
1962	16,108	8,849	133	1	21	5	7,099
1963	18,967	10,129	91	–	66	–	8,681
1964	17,155	9,646	28	1	38	3	7,439
1965	16,328	8,389	18	6	28	14	7,873
1966	15,012	7,721	14	1	33	2	7,241
1967	11,795	5,362	11	14	15	1	6,392
1968	10,590	3,804	1	37	13	–	6,735
1969	9,532	3,031	3	28	11	–	6,459
1970	9,515	2,532	11	78	30	2	6,862
1971	8,078	1,764	10	100	30	1	6,173
1972	8,613	1,469	43	112	75	1,243	5,671
1973	11,791	1,045	84	152	152	4,117	6,241
1974	13,400	963	44	139	128	6,562	5,564
1975	16,106	843	17	173	259	10,125	4,689
1976	23,332	619	5	151	454	17,368	4,735
1977	23,403	536	3	153	816	17,315	4,580
1978	29,900	541	8	179	1,423	23,117	4,632
1979	30,500	443	–	159	1,663	23,107	5,128
1980	36,033	405	15	135	2,031	27,677	5,770
1981	35,040	470	2	90	2,575	26,130	5,773
1982	39,016	453	17	108	2,750	29,254	6,434
1983	39,062	424	4	89	2,667	29,127	6,751
1984	37,538	417	12	98	2,552	27,655	6,804
1985	33,877	407	2	72	2,062	25,370	5,964
1986	29,571	511	2	88	1,708	22,326	4,936
1987	29,137	523	1	124	1,502	22,381	4,606
1988	30,258	525	1	131	1,273	24,656	3,672

Source: National Police Agency

juvenile special law offenders referred to the public prosecutors offices. In 1956, the figure was 9,046, and was on the rise until the early 1960s. After it peaked in 1963 at 18,967, it was on the decline. In 1971, the figure was a record low with 8,078. It turned upward in 1972 and exceeded the 20,000 mark in 1976. In 1983, it reached to 39,062, a record high since 1956. After that it decreased gradually and in 1988 it totaled 30,258.

As we will discuss later, increases in the figure in the decade from 1955 to 1964 resulted largely from increases in the number of offenders of the Firearms and Swords Control Law. Increases in the number in the decade from 1975 to 1984 were largely due to increases in the number of offenders of drug-related laws.

By type of offence, the number of offenders of the Firearms and Swords Control Law topped the list in the decade from 1955 to 1964. In 1963, it totaled 10,129, accounting for 53.4 percent of the total number of juveniles who violated special laws except traffic laws. After that, it declined rapidly, and from 1977 it stood at between 400 and just over 500. In 1988, it was 525.

Besides them, steep increases in the number of offenders of drug-related laws were noteworthy. Looking at the juvenile offenders of the Stimulant Drugs Control Law, the number was 308 in 1956. After that, it decreased and stood at between 5 and 66, but it turned upward from the early 1970s. It was 152 in 1973; 259 in 1975; 1,423 in 1978; 2,031 in 1980, making steep increases. After it peaked in 1982 with 2,750, it turned downward. In 1988, it totaled 1,273.

As for the offenders of Poisonous and Injurious Substances Control Law, the number rapidly increased from 1973. The increase was due to revisions of the law, effective August 1972, that penalized not only the abusive use of paint thinner and other organic solvents but also the sale of the substances with the knowledge of their being provided for abusive use. Before the law revisions, juveniles who were found sniffing paint thinner were only given guidance by the police. The figure exceeded the 10,000 mark in 1975, the 20,000 mark in 1978. After it peaked in 1982 with 29,254, it turned downward. In 1988, it totaled 24,656, accounting for 81.5 percent of the total number of juveniles arrested on special law offences excluding the traffic law violators. That indicates the abuse of drugs remains a major problem among juvenile special law offenders.

As many people started using cars and motorcycles as means of transportation, there were many more opportunities for juveniles to drive during the course of their daily lives. Driving is not only a means of transportation to enhance the mobility of juveniles but also a way to get rid of frustration, because driving at high speed can be satisfying and thrilling to juveniles.

The number of juvenile traffic law violators became conspicuously high from around 1955. Fig. 48 shows the trend of the number of juvenile road traffic

Fig.48 Number of Juvenile Traffic Violators Cleared by the Police and Referred to Public Prosecutors Offices (1956~1988)

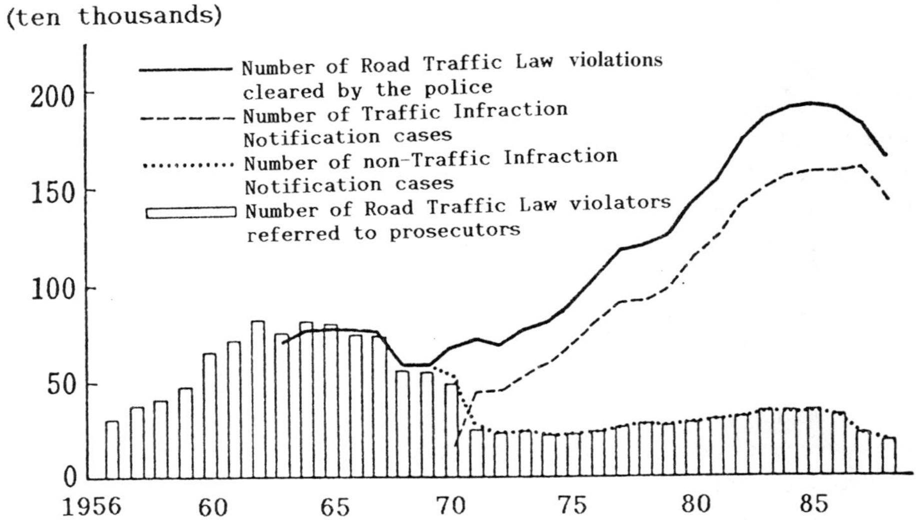

Source: National Police Agency

offenders referred to public prosecutors offices from 1956 on, and the number of Juvenile Road Traffic Law offenders cleared by the police since 1963. In 1956, a total of 308,172 juvenile road traffic offenders were referred to the public prosecutors offices. After that the figure rapidly increased. It exceeded the 600,000 mark in 1960 and the 800,000 mark in 1962. After that it fluctuated between 500,000 and more than 800,000. In 1971, however, it dropped to about 250,000. The sharp drop was due to revisions in the Road Traffic Law, effective August 1970, that included juveniles under the coverage of the traffic infraction notification system. From 1972, the annual number of juvenile road traffic offenders stood at between 200,000 and more than 300,000. In 1988, it totaled 199,297.

Juvenile Road Traffic Law offenders cleared by the police totaled 696,702 in 1963. After fluctuations, it turned upward from 1970. It exceeded the 1,000,000 mark in 1976, the 1,500,000 mark in 1981 and the 1,900,000 mark in 1984. After it recorded a postwar high in 1985 with 1,938,980, it was on the decline. In 1988, it totaled 1,660,131. Of the 1988 total, 1,460,856 juveniles, or 88.0 percent, were processed through the traffic infraction notification system (ticket system). By type of Road Traffic Law Offenders in 1988, speeding

Table 68 Number of Pre-delinquent Juveniles Adjudicated in Family Courts, by Type of Delinquency (1969～1987)

Year	Total	Female	Run away from home	Bad friendship	Promiscuity	Leaving school	Unwholesome amusement	Nocturnal habits	Others
1969	5,842	2,449	1,632	391	1,245	72	518	54	1,930
1970	4,961	1,970	1,170	361	977	77	296	48	2,032
1971	5,099	1,963	1,105	405	1,068	52	281	46	2,142
1972	3,679	1,530	863	328	869	60	149	24	1,386
1973	2,426	1,296	848	257	680	54	46	15	526
1974	2,172	1,117	785	278	544	59	51	28	427
1975	2,513	1,207	957	326	524	87	100	23	496
1976	2,560	1,310	984	298	543	84	71	58	522
1977	2,625	1,564	1,119	334	548	73	83	31	437
1978	2,973	1,780	1,253	341	665	62	86	39	527
1979	2,928	1,809	1,337	343	553	109	65	48	473
1980	3,275	1,879	1,466	420	554	105	95	53	582
1981	3,018	1,769	1,434	414	424	115	68	27	536
1982	3,131	1,731	1,450	365	393	163	82	74	604
1983	3,418	1,825	1,493	449	405	188	87	85	711
1984	3,137	1,747	1,497	371	341	166	79	59	624
1985	2,818	1,671	1,476	371	278	121	60	74	438
1986	2,438	1,457	1,202	330	279	129	29	48	421
1987	2,475	1,497	1,240	347	300	104	27	64	393

Source: Annual Report of Judicial Statistics

Table 69 Composition of Guardians of Juvenile Delinquents

Year	Real Parents	Real father Real mother			Real mother and step father Real father and step mother	Step-Parents	Other Guardians	No-guardians
			Father only	Mother only				
1955	45.1	34.6	16.8	17.8	5.9	0.8	13.6	···
1960	47.1	37.1	19.3	17.8	4.3	0.7	9.7	1.1
1965	73.3	18.2	4.3	13.8	4.8	1.1	2.3	0.4
1970	74.2	17.3	4.3	13.0	5.3	1.0	2.0	0.3
1975	76.3	15.6	4.3	11.3	5.3	0.8	1.8	0.2
1980	75.8	16.6	···	···	5.2	0.7	1.5	0.1
1985	71.4	21.0	···	···	5.2	0.7	1.6	0.1
1990	69.7	22.7	···	···	5.3	0.6	1.6	0.1

Source: Annual Report of Judicial Statistics

accounted for 38.6 percent of the total, failure to carry the driver's license with them for 8.8 percent, failure to stop at a stop sign for 8.1 percent, parking violations for 8.0 percent, loading people into the car beyond the car's capacity for 7.7 percent, driving without a license for 6.0 percent, or driving a car in an inadequate maintenance of automobile for 5.2 percent.

(3) Juveniles Feared to Commit Crime in the Future

The police gave guidance to those juveniles who were found smoking, drinking, fighting or engaging in other conduct considered harmful to the moral nature of themselves and others. Among them, those considered to be in a state of pre-delinquency were referred to family courts or child guidance centers. According to police statistics compiled in 1952, pre-delinquent juveniles and misbehaved juveniles totaled 268,666. Of them, 7,658, or 2.9 percent of the total were sent to family courts. According to judicial statistics, the number of pre-delinquent juveniles processed at family courts from 1952 to 1968 stood at around 5,000 to over 7,000 a year.

Table 68 shows the trend of the number of pre-delinguent juveniles adjudicated in family courts by type of delinquent acts from 1969 on. According to the Table, 5,842 were processed by family courts in 1969. After that, it fluctuated and then decreased. In 1973, it stood at over 2,000 and increased to

Table 70 Living Standard of Guardians of Juvenile Delinquents

Year	Wealthy	Ordinary	Poverty	In need of assistance
1955	0.8	29.8	59.5	9.9
1960	0.8	34.9	58.3	6.0
1965	2.3	71.9	22.9	2.9
1970	2.7	76.0	18.4	2.9
1975	2.9	82.8	11.5	2.8
1980	2.7	83.9	10.1	3.3
1985	2.0	83.5	10.5	4.0
1987	2.0	84.1	10.2	3.7

Source: Annual Report of Judicial Statistics

over 3,000 in the early 1980s, but decreased to just over 2,000 in 1985. In 1987, a total of 2,475 juveniles were processed.

By type of delinquency, runaway, association with other delinquents, promiscuity, absenteeism and pleasure-seeking at night were most frequent. The ratio of girls in the total number of pre-delinquent juveniles increased year by year. In 1969, their percentage was 41.9 percent, 48.0 percent in 1975 and 60.5 percent in 1987.

(4) Backgrounds of Juvenile Delinquency

A. Family

Family provides the environment where children learn about social relations for the first time. With their family, children learn how to adapt themselves in a society by being nurtured, protected and disciplined through communication with other family members. Therefore, if there is something wrong with family functions toward children, it is likely to adversely affect the character-building of children, prompting juveniles to violate laws.

This part will examine the backgrounds of juvenile delinquency by discussing the financial situation and other conditions of juveniles' guardians, which reportedly have profound effects on the educative and protective roles of families.

There are no prewar statistics available on the conditions of families which produced juvenile delinquents. Table 69 shows the family composition of juvenile delinquents who were handled by family courts for offences other than traffic violations every five years from 1955 to 1987. According to the table, 45.1 percent of those juveniles had both real parents in 1955 and 47.1 percent in 1960. In 1965, the percentage jumped to 73.3 and stayed at around 70 since then, indicating those juvenile delinquents without one or both real parents were on the decline. From the early 1980s, the percentage of such juvenile delinquents with only one real parent due to divorce, separation or death was slightly on the rise. In 1985 the percentage was 21.0 and 22.7 in 1987.

Table 70 shows the financial situations of guardians of juvenile delinquents in every five-year period from 1955 through 1987. In 1955, 30.6 percent of the guardians fell in the categories of average and wealthy while 69.4 percent fell in the categories of poverty or in need of financial assistance. In 1965, however, their percentages reversed, at 74.2 percent and 25.8 percent, and in 1975, the percentages were 85.7 percent and 14.3 percent. By 1987, they were 86.1 percent and 13.9 percent, marking considerable increases in percentage of juvenile delinquents from wealthy and average families.

(B) Schools

Schools provide juveniles with an important environment, along with families. From 1974, more than 90 percent of juveniles went on to high schools, making schooling more closely linked to the lives of juveniles.

There are no prewar statistics on the status of juvenile delinquents regarding whether they were working or attending school, so we will examine the situation after the war.

In 1955, 121,753 juveniles were cleared by the police on suspicion of Penal Code offences, including traffic professional negligence. Of them, students totaled 46,279, or 38.0 percent of the total, working youths 45,116, or 37.1 percent, and unemployed youngsters 30,358, or 24.9 percent. In 1965, of the 234,959 juveniles cleared by the police, 129,224 (55.0 percent) were students, 78,748 (33.5 percent) working youths and 26,987 (11.5 percent) unemployed youngsters.

Fig. 49 shows the levels of school attended by juveniles who were cleared by the police on suspicion of Penal Code offences other than traffic professional negligence in 1966, 1970, 1975, 1985 and 1988. Middle school students accounted for 30.1 percent of the total juveniles cleared by the police with 54,897 in 1966 but their percentage jumped to 43.0 percent with 99,407 in 1988. High school students accounted for 15.9 percent of the total with 28,948 in 1966 and their percentage jumped to 30.6 percent with 70,638 in 1988. The percentage of working youths, on the other hand, decreased from 28.9 percent (52,707 persons) in 1966 to 9.1 percent (21,042 persons) in 1988. The percentage of unemployed youths also dropped from 13.6 percent (24,853 persons) in 1966 to

Fig.49 Percentage of Juvenile Penal Code Offenders Excluding Traffic Professional Negligence Cleared, by Status

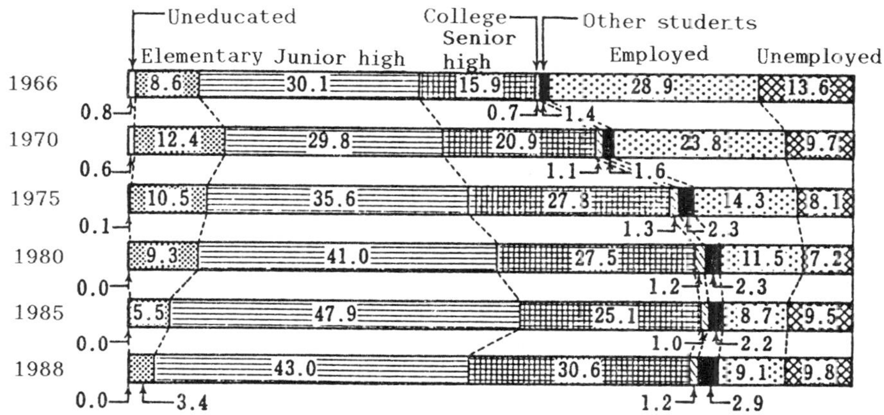

Source: National Police Agency

9.8 percent (22,680 persons) in 1988. The figures indicate that the percentage of students in the total number of juveniles cleared by the police has been on the rise.

Following is a summary of juvenile delinquency in the Showa era. The number of juveniles cleared by the police before World War II was rather small. Their number and percentage per 1,000 in the juvenile population were lower than the number of adults cleared by the police and their ratio per 1,000 in the adult population. After the war, the number of juvenile delinquents drastically increased. Their percentage per 1,000 in the juvenile population has always exceeded that of adults per 1,000 in the adult population since 1958. From 1966 there were a great number of juveniles involved in Penal Code offences excluding traffic professional negligence. Even after it peaked in 1983, there were a considerable number of juvenile delinquents. It makes a vivid contrast to the number of adult Penal Code offenders who have been gradually decreasing. Juveniles accounted for more than 50 percent of the total people cleared by the police almost every year since 1981.

By age bracket, the number of juveniles in the lower age group of 14- and 15-year-olds who were cleared by the police made steep rises, while that of juveniles in the upper age group between of 18- and 19-year-olds leveled off or was slighly on the decline.

By type of offences, theft cases increased in the decade from 1935 to 1944 due largely to financial difficulties and theft, and armed robbery cases increased in the decade from 1945 to 1954 due largely to social confusion and poverty after the war. From 1955 to the early 1970s, the number of violent crimes and sex crimes made quantum jumps. They can be attributed to the development of the means of transportation as the economy expanded and conflicts resulting from industrialization and urbanization in addition to the climate for free sex. From 1975 to the present, shoplifting at supermarkets and embezzlement of lost articles, such as misappropriation of a bicycle unattended in front of train stations, have been on the rise in the affluent society, indicating that trifle crimes by juveniles have become a fact of life. In addition, the number of juveniles cleared by the police on suspicion of abusing paint thinner, other organic solvents and stimulant drugs increased. From the early 1970s, girls involved in Penal Code offences, especially drug-related violations, were on the rise.

As to the environments surrounding juvenile delinquents such as family, there were many juvenile delinquents who came from poor families, without both or either one of their real parents, in the confusion after the war. There were no prewar statistics on the financial situation or composition of families that produced juvenile delinquents. From 1965, however, juvenile delinquents came more from average families without financial difficulties and with both parents. In addition, students became increasingly involved with crimes.

Section 2. Treatment of Juvenile Delinquents

1. OUTLINE

(1) Treatment of Juvenile Delinquents under the Old Juvenile Law

Until 1948, delinquent juveniles were treated in accordance with the Juvenile Law, which was enacted in April 1922 and put into effect in January 1923. (Herewith, this old Juvenile Law will be referred to as the old Juvenile Law.)

This period may be said to be the time in which efforts were made to implement the modern idea for the treatment of juveniles through expanding gradually the criminal policy newly codified by the Juvenile Law by enlarging its scope of application to the nationwide level.

Since the early Meiji era, Japan tried to treat delinquent juveniles, separatly from adult offenders.

Under the old Penal Code of 1880, those juveniles under 12 years of age were treated as incapable of criminal acts because of their young age. As for those between 12 and 15, their dispositions were divided into two categories: First, if the juveniles committed an offence while having no ability to distinguish right from wrong, they were exempted from criminal responsibility, but according to the circumstances of each case, they could be detained in a House of Correction, the maximum term being reached at the age of 20. Second, if they had the ability to distinguish right from wrong when they committed the offence, they could not be exempted from criminal liability but they should be be given a reduction of punishment instead.

The 1881 prison rules provided the system under which delinquent juveniles aged between 8 and 20, who were uncontrollable and delinquent, could be admitted to the House of Corrections upon the request of their parents.

However, as a matter of fact the treatment in the House was not much different from the treatment of ordinary inmates serving their prison sentences.

Alarmed by the situation, a private Reform School was established in Tokyo in 1885 and other similar schools were opened at various places later.

In 1900, the Child Reform Law was enacted, and the first public Reform School opened in the same year. It was established to admit those juveniles between 8 and 15 years of age and their term of admission was until they reached 20, provided that those juveniles were found by the Prefectural Governors to be lacking appropriate parents or guardians and were living a bad life or keeping bad company, or were temporarily admitted awaiting the approval of courts to refer them to the House of Corrections.

The present Penal Code enacted in 1908 raised the age of criminal incapacity from less than 12 to less than 14 and stipulated those under 14 years who committed criminal acts were exempted from punishment. The Code also abolished the disposition of referral to the House of Corrections.

Accordingly, in the same year, the Child Reform Law was amended to the effect that the upper age limit to admit to the Reform School was lifted from less than 16 to less than 18 and the prerequisite conditions for admission were also amended as follows: when Prefectural Governors decided that admission to the School was necessary: 1) On the ground that the juveniles did or were feared to do delinquent acts and no adequate person existed to exercise parental authority over them; or 2) on application of parents or guardians.

Also, in 1917, the National Reform School Ordinance was enacted and it provided that the national Reform School should accommodate from among those juveniles qualified to be admitted to the general Reform School those who were 14 years and older and who had a particularly advanced tendency to live a bad life in society.

The old Juvenile Law, which was introduced in 1923 after these series of changes, developed for the first time in Japan a legal system for juvenile delinquents. It separated the treatment and criminal prosecution for juveniles from adults.

The main pillars of the old Juvenile Law were:

1) The application of the law was limited to those who were under 18 years old;

2) It provided protective rehabilitation service for juvenile delinquents who violated or were likely to violate criminal laws;

3) It established Juvenile Tribunals to examine and decide on those cases referred for protective rehabilitative measures;

4) The protective rehabilitative measures consisted of nine different treatments including:

–entrusting juvenile delinquents to temples, churches and other protective rehabilitative organizations or appropriate individuals,

–placing juvenile delinquents under probationary supervision of Juvenile Probation Officers,

–referring them to Reform Schools or Reformatory Schools.

5) It provided exceptions for juveniles in the disposition of punishment such as banning in principle the imposition of capital punishment and life imprisonment for juveniles under 16 years old at the time of the offence committed. It also established an indeterminate sentence system for juvenile offenders;

6) Those juveniles who were given suspended execution of sentences or granted release on parole were to be placed under the probationary supervision of Juvenile Probation Officers.

The old Juvenile Law marked a milestone in Japan's history of the treatment of juvenile delinquents. Yet, at its starting point, only two Juvenile Tribunals were established, one in Tokyo and the other in Osaka.

Also, the protective rehabilitation service provided under the Law came into operation in only five metropolitan prefectures, including Tokyo, Kanagawa, Osaka, Kyoto and Hyogo.

Gradually, the protective rehabilitation service expanded its operational areas as Juvenile Tribunals were set up in Nagoya in 1934 and in Fukuoka in 1938. However, it was not until 1942 that the service was finally fully operated nationwide.

Simultaneously, with the enactment of the old Juvenile Law, the Reformatory School Law, which provided for the institution designed to accommodate juvenile delinquents referred to it from the Juvenile Tribunals, was enacted.

In 1923, the first Reformatory Schools were established in Tokyo and Osaka. In 1928, the branch offices of Reformatory Schools were established in the neighborhood of Juvenile Tribunals to accommodate those Juveniles temporarily entrusted to it by Juvenile Tribunals, etc. (These offices became the forerunners of the present Juvenile Classification Homes.)

The old Juvenile Law enacted for the first time a probationary supervision system for juvenile deliquents and it was applied most actively among the disposition of protective, rehabilitative measures.

The probationary supervision by juvenile probation officers accounted for 25 percent of all dispositions of protective, rehabilitative measures given by Juvenile Tribunals between 1926 and 1930.

Another noteworthy aspect in the pre-war juvenile delinquent treatment was that various private social resources were utilized to help rehabilitation of juvenile delinquents.

Referral to the private organizations for juvenile protection and rehabilitation occupied almost 20 percent of all disposition of protective rehabilitative measures.

Furthermore, special protective organizations for girls and minors with mental and physical handicaps were also established.

These private institutions played vital roles in treating delinquent girls and minors who needed medical attention, because there was no reformatory schools designed for girls and those who needed medical care.

The old Juvenile Law also stipulated that the juvenile prisoners who were given prison sentences instead of protective, rehabilitative measures were to be treated separately from ordinary prisoners and in 1922, specific prisons which accommodated prisoners under 18 years of age were specified by names and locations and as such these juvenile prisons were established.

Even after the enforcement of the old Juvenile Law, treatment was carried out under the Child Reform Law for those children who were under 14 years of age and exempted from criminal responsibility as well as for those juvenile delinquents who lived in areas where the protective, rehabilitative service was not yet available.

Following the enactment of the Child Education and Training Law in 1934, the Child Reform Law was abolished and Reform Schools were renamed Child Education and Training Homes. Previously, in 1922, the Child Reform Law was amended in accordance with the enforcement of the old Juvenile Law and the upper age limit of children to be covered by the new law was lowered to less than 14 years of age with the exception that the previous age limit of under 18 years was applicable when the parents and others who had parental authoritiy over the juveniles so requested. However, this exception was abolished by the enactment of the Child Education and Training Law and the abolishment of the Child Reform Law in 1934.

Also, under the provision of the Child Education and Training Law, it was made possible to set up an organ to engage in scientific examination of children and Child Behaviour Clinics were gradually established in the Child Education and Training Homes. These Clinics were succeeded by the Child

Guidance Centers established after the war under the Child Welfare Law.

In the early Showa period, a severe depression hit the farming communities. Plagued with famine and malnutrition, the buying and selling of women and children as well as child abuse became serious social problems.

In 1933, the Law to Prevent Child Abuse was introduced, giving the prefectural governors the authority to take appropriate measures such as to admonish those who were responsible for the care and protection of children whenever the children under their care committed or were feared likely to commit offences due to maltreatment or gross negligence of care on their side.

Since the early 1940s, delinquency was spreading among the working youth and juveniles who were mobilized as wartime production forces. Emergency Measures to Guide Working Youth and Juveniles (cabinet resolution) was issued and a short and intensive training program was introduced in Reformatory Schools and private organizations for juvenile protection and rehabilitation. As such, the effects of the wartime social order had a bearing upon the operation of the juvenile protection and rehabilitation service, too.

(2) Enactment of the Present Juvenile Law

After the war, in the late 1940s and early 1950s, fundamental changes were brought about in the old laws and ordinances. The treatment system for juvenile delinquents also went through wide scale reformation.

First, in December 1947, the Child Welfare Law was enacted and the treatment of those children under 14 years and those maltreated children who had been under the coverage of either the Law for Child Education and Training or the Law to Prevent Child Abuse were covered by an overall treatment scheme aimed at the healthy and sound growth and welfare of all children.

Accordingly, the Child Education and Training Home was renamed the Education and Training Home and considered as one of the child welfare facilities, and both the Law for Child Education and Training and the Law to Prevent Child Abuse were abolished.

In July 1948, the present Juvenile Law was enacted after a complete revision of the old Juvenile Law. The major revisions in the new law which came into effect in January 1949 included:

1) The maximum age of the application of the new Law was moved up to less than 20 years from the previous less than 18 years (effective as of January 1951);

2) A Family Court system was introduced as a judicial organ to decide whether to refer delinquent juveniles to criminal prosecution proceedings or put them in either one or another of the rehabilitation programs or to release them. The rehabilitation programs were subdivided into the following three cate-

gories, viz, first, probationary supervision of probation officers; second, referral to Education and Training Homes or Homes for Dependent Children; and third, commitment to Juvenile Training Schools;

3) Family Courts are bestowed with subject matter jurisdiction over criminal cases involving the adult offenders who committed such offences which seriously affected the welfare of children;

4) Juveniles are given the right of kokoku appeals to the High Court from the decisions of the Family Court placing them on a rehabilitation programs;

5) Criminal prosecution can only be initiated against those juvenile delinquents over 16 years of age at the time of disposition of the Family Courts. The lower age limit to impose capital punishment or life imprisonment was moved up to less than 18 years from the previous less than 16.

Along with the Juvenile Law, the Juvenile Training School Law was introduced and the Reformatory School Law was abolished.

Juvenile Training Schools are classified into primary, middle, special and medical schools.

Private organizations for juvenile protection and rehabilitation which had served as private correctional insititutions under the old Juvenile Law were closed in March 1949.

Of 165 such organizations, 32 became Juvenile Training Schools, 28 social welfare institutes and the remaining 109 organizations were closed down. The Juvenile Protective Guidance Center was newly established to accommodate juveniles referred to it by the decision of the courts to put juveniles under protective detention. The Juvenile Classification Home was attached to it to diagnose and classify the juveniles sent to the center. Juvenile Classification Homes and Juvenile Protective Guidance Centers were combined into Juvenile Protective Classification Centers in 1950 and renamed Juvenile Classificaiton Homes in 1952.

Introduction of Juvenile Classification Homes and the Family Court Investigator system, which stressed the importance of scientific inquiry of a case prior to the hearing and disposition of the family court judges, is another noteworthy feature in the present Juvenile Law.

New legislation covering probationary supervision was enacted slightly after the introduction of the Juvenile Law. In July 1949, the Offenders Prevention and Rehabilitation Law came into force. Probationary supervision by Juvenile Probation Officers under the old Juvenile Law was replaced by that of Probation Offices.

Juvenile delinquents were placed under probationary supervision in the following cases: -when the family courts put them on probationary supervision by their decisions; -when they were released on parole from Juvenile Training

Schools and juvenile prisons; and -when they were given and still under suspended execution of sentences of imprisonment with or without labour provided they were under 18 years of age at the time of the sentencing in court.

The Penal Code was amended twice in 1953 and 1954 and probationary supervision was expanded to juvenile offenders of 18 years of age or older provided that they were given suspension of execution of prison sentences.

(3) Progress in the Treatment System of Juvenile Delinquents

Systems to implement the current Juvenile Law were perfected in years from 1945 through 1955. However, this was accompanied by a sharp rise in the number of juvenile delinquents. Accordingly, numerous steps were taken to enrich and strengthen the treatment measures for juvenile delinquents.

From the mid-1950s and early 1960s, the overcrowding of Juvenile Training Schools became a serious problem. Despite this problem, efforts were made to promote treatment under the classification system by way of specializing and professionalizing the Juvenile Training Schools according to the treatment categtories such as academic education, vocational training and medical care.

At the same time, practical applications and research were undertaken repeatedly in order to systematize treatment under living guidance and group counseling programs.

At the Juvenile Classification Home, new classification methods were enthusiastically tried out. For more accurate classification of juvenile delinquents, the Justice Ministry-style tests were developed.

In the 1965-75 period, the average daily population in Juvenile Training Schools started to level off. In the mid-1970s, it decreased to a record low. Meanwhile, more flexible and effective treatment to meet the individual needs of each juvenile was required in response to the changing and diversified forms of juvenile delinquency.

In 1977, new measures were implemented to improve the operation of Juvenile Training Schools, by dividing treatment at the facilities into two categories: one a short-term treatment program and the other a long-term treatment program.

In the field of probationary supervision, a new system was introduced in 1971 to classify juvenile delinquents according to the difficulties in their treatment.

Also, direct treatment by professional probation officers was enhanced to provide more intensive guidance and supervision. Furthermore, as the number of juvenile delinquents put on probation for road traffic violations began to soar, a traffic short-term probationary supervision system was started for such juveniles nationwide in 1977.

In 1977, the Justice Ministry's Legislative Council recommended to the Justice Minister that the Juvenile Law be amended. The main pillars of the recommendation were:

1) Improvement of the proceedings of hearings and decision-making at Family Courts with the view toward strengthening the protection of the rights of juveniles under the proceedings and at the same time, expanding the participation of public prosecutors in the proceedings;

2) The upper age group of juveniles, 18 and older, shall be treated, to a certain degree, differently from middle and lower age groups of juveniles;

3) Within certain limitations, investigative agencies should be allowed to drop minor cases involving juvenile offenders;

4) Protective rehabilitation measures should be more diversified and should be made more flexible.

More than 40 years have passed since the present Juvenile Law was introduced. The social background as well as trends in juvenile delinquency have greatly changed since the law was first introduced.

Up to the present time, reforms in the administration and executive ingenuity have managed to cope with the changing situations of juvenile delinquency and demands of current thought. It seems, however, that more thought should be given continuously as to whether revisions of the present laws are needed or not, taking into consideration the trends in juvenile delinquency, particularly to fill the gaps or rectify defects likely to exist in the present legislation, including such problems as introducing further protection of procedural due process into juvenile court procceedings.

2. PROSECUTION AND TRIALS OF JUVENILE DELINQUENTS

(1) History of Prosecution of Juvenile Delinquents

A. Prosecution of Juvenile Delinquents under the Old and Current Juvenile Law

The roles of public prosecutors in the investigation and disposition of cases involving juvenile delinquents differ greatly before and after World War II.

Under the old Juvenile Law enacted in 1923, those who were under 18 years old were defined as juveniles, while the present Juvenile Law calls those who under 20 years old juveniles.

Under the old system, the Juvenile Tribunal had the power to place those juveniles who had violated or were prone to violate criminal laws under protective rehabilitation service programs.

However, those juveniles mentioned below could not be dealt by at the

Juvenile Tribunal and were excluded from rehabilitation service programs.

These juveniles included: 1) those who were in military service or civilian employees of the military; 2) those who had committed those crimes such as treason, to be subjected to the special jurisdiction of the Great Court of Judicature; and 3) those who were under criminal proceedings in criminal courts.

As for those juveniles who committed an offence punishable by the death penality, imprisonment with or without labour for life or for less than three years of minimum penalty and those juvenile offenders who were 16 years and older at the time when the public prosecutor made the disposition of the case, the public prosecutor first decided whether to institute prosecution in those juvenile cases. And the Juvenile Tribunal could try such juvenile cases when: 1) the prosecutor referred the case to the Tribunal after suspending prosecution and with the opinion that the juvenile should be put on protective, rehabilitative treatment measures; or 2) the criminal court after hearing the juvenile cases transferred them to the Tribunal with the opinion that the juveniles could better be dealt with under the protective, rehabilitative programs.

Now, let us review the role of the public prosecutor in juvenile cases in general under the old Juvenile Law.

Juvenile delinquents cleared by the police were all referred to the public prosecutors offices except for minor cases handled by the police under the Summary Proceedings for Police Infractions.

The public prosecutor disposed of juvenile cases either (1) by instituting prosecution when the case was considered to deserve prosecution and punishment or (2) by suspending prosecution in consideration of the circumstances of the case or (3) by referring the case to the Juvenile Tribunal when protective, rehabilitative treatment measures were most appropriate for the juvenile suspect.

In 1926, 12,394 juveniles were dealt with by dispostions of non-prosecution for minor offences or by suspension of prosecution, while 15,974 juveniles were received by Juvenile Tribunals for protective rehabilitative treatment measures. This figure shows that suspension of prosecution, etc., in juvenile cases accounted for a large part of the dispositions by public prosecutors in those days. Incidently, public prosecutors had the right to appeal against the decisions made by the criminal courts to transfer those juvenile cases prosecuted by public prosecutors to Juvenile Tribunals for protective, rehabilitative treatment measures.

These statistics demonstrate that the prosecution dropped charges against a large number of juvenile delinquents in those days.

When a court of law decided to put the juvenile delinquents on rehabilitation programs, the prosecution could appeal the family court decision.

The 1949 Juvenile Law defines those who are under 20 years of age as juveniles. Juvenile offenders were first referred to the family court. The family court was empowered first to decide whether to refer them to the prosecutor or to put them on protective rehabilitative treatment.

Under the present system, juvenile cases involving offences punishable by fines or lesser penalties are directly referred to the family court by the police and those cases involving offences punishable by imprisonment or heavier penalties are first referred to the public prosecutors.

The public prosecutor, after the investigation is over, has to refer the case to the family courts provided that a prima facie case has been made against the juvenile or otherwise, there are reasons to refer the case to the disposition of the Family Courts on the ground that the juvenile is prone to commit another offence in the future.

Public prosecutors are given the power to institute prosecution only when family courts, after thorough examination, refer the case back to public prosecutors on the ground that the case deserves criminal prosecution considering the gravity of the offence, the criminal circumstances under which the offence was committed and so forth. However, family courts cannot refer back to the prosecutors such cases that involve offences punishable only by fines or lesser penalities or juveniles younger than 16 years of age at the time of the referral back to the prosecutors.

Under the present system, public prosecutors have to, in principle, institute prosecution against the juvenile offenders who were referred back from the family court for criminal prosecution provided that the prosecutors believe that there is sufficient cause for believing the juvenile has committed the offence. Also, public prosecutors are not given the power to appeal against the family courts decisions on their side.

Such being the case, public prosecutors' power over juvenile cases is considerably diminished in comparison with the power given under the old Juvenile Law.

B. Trends in Number of Juvenile Offenders Received by the Public Prosecutors Office

Table 71 shows the changes at five-year intervals in the ratio of juveniles among total offenders (total suspects) newly received by the Public Prosecutors Office between 1950 and 1985 as well as in 1988. (No such statistics are available before 1949. All the data presented in this chapter start with 1926 or the earliest date after that year when such statistical data became available.)

The table shows that the ratio of juveniles among total offenders newly received by the Public Prosecutors Office dipped to a record low of 9.5 percent

Table 71 Rate of Juveniles among Total Offenders Newly Received by Public Prosecutors Offices

Year	Total	Total excluding traffic cases	Penal Code Offences	Penal Code offences excluding profes-sional negli-gence	Special law offences excluding traffic offence	Profes-sional negli-gence	Road traffic violations
1950	12.1	…	20.1	…	…	…	…
1955	9.5	…	16.6	…	…	…	…
1960	17.0	…	24.3	…	8.9	…	15.8
1965	13.4	…	25.7	…	7.5	…	11.7
1970	22.5	22.9	18.2	28.5	6.8	11.9	27.3
1975	12.7	22.6	19.5	31.0	3.3	10.0	10.6
1980	16.9	32.5	25.5	44.0	5.1	10.9	14.1
1985	17.7	42.0	26.9	50.6	18.6	10.4	14.1
1988	20.4	47.1	27.2	36.2	23.0	11.0	15.2

Source: Annual Report of Statistics on Prosecution

in 1955. Except for 1970, when the figure shot up to 22.5 percent, it fluctuated between 12.1 percent and 17.7 percent until 1985, but went up to 20.4 percent in 1988.

Next, looking at the ratio of juveniles among the total number of newly received offenders, excluding therefrom cases of professional or gross negligence causing death or bodily injuries (hereafter "professional negligence") and violations of the Road Traffic Law (hereafter "road-traffic violation"), the figures came to 22.9 percent in 1970, 32.5 percent in 1980 and 47.1 percent in 1988. The ratio continues to rise rather sharply.

As for Penal Code offenders newly received, excluding professional negligence, juveniles accounted for 28.5 percent of all such offenders in 1970. It increased to 44.0 percent in 1980 and reached 50.6 percent in 1985, before dropping to 36.2 percent in 1988.

Among special law offenders newly received, excluding road-traffic violators, juveniles made up 8.9 percent in 1960, but the ratio dropped to 6.8 percent in 1970 and inched down to 5.1 percent in 1980.

But the ratio jumped to 18.6 percent in 1985 and to 23.0 percent in 1988

Table 72 Rate of Juvenile Offenders Newly Received by Prosecutors Offices, by Major Offence and Age Group

Category		1950	1955	1960	1965	1970	1975	1980	1985	1988
Total	Total	100.0	100.0	100.0	100.0	100.0	100.0	100.0	100.0	100.0
	lower	15.2	12.0	12.4	13.6	10.9	16.3	18.8	19.7	23.0
	middle	31.0	31.0	36.9	42.6	36.5	37.9	35.8	36.1	36.1
	upper	53.8	57.0	50.7	43.8	52.6	45.8	45.3	44.2	40.9
Penal Code offence	Total	100.0	100.0	100.0	100.0	100.0	100.0	100.0	100.0	100.0
	lower	20.4	19.8	22.6	27.4	29.3	36.1	42.4	46.1	43.3
	middle	35.5	30.4	34.5	38.7	35.6	38.6	36.9	36.9	39.1
	upper	44.1	49.9	42.9	33.9	35.1	25.3	20.8	17.0	17.6
Theft	Total	100.0	100.0	100.0	100.0	100.0	100.0	100.0	100.0	100.0
	lower	26.0	27.9	34.2	41.7	35.3	39.1	45.4	46.8	44.5
	middle	37.2	31.0	33.3	36.7	35.1	39.1	37.3	37.9	40.2
	upper	36.8	41.1	32.5	21.6	29.6	21.8	17.3	15.3	15.2
Assault/ Violent acts	Total	100.0	100.0	100.0	100.0	100.0	100.0	100.0	100.0	100.0
	lower	9.5	7.1	14.9	21.8	16.3	26.1	30.6	50.7	46.4
	middle	31.6	28.3	34.3	38.2	35.3	36.3	36.3	28.1	29.8
	upper	58.9	64.7	50.8	39.9	48.4	37.6	33.1	21.2	23.8
Extortion	Total	100.0	100.0	100.0	100.0	100.0	100.0	100.0	100.0	100.0
	lower	12.4	8.4	19.7	25.7	22.8	36.7	40.5	50.1	46.2
	middle	35.4	37.5	43.5	46.9	44.5	40.4	37.2	34.0	36.1
	upper	52.2	54.1	36.8	27.4	32.7	22.8	22.4	15.9	17.6
Rape/ indecent assault	Total	100.0	100.0	100.0	100.0	100.0	100.0	100.0	100.0	100.0
	lower	11.0	11.8	14.3	18.3	14.0	15.8	19.9	30.6	20.8
	middle	42.2	38.9	43.0	45.2	32.6	34.0	34.4	33.8	35.6
	upper	46.8	49.2	42.6	36.5	53.4	50.2	45.7	35.6	43.5
Robbery	Total	100.0	100.0	100.0	100.0	100.0	100.0	100.0	100.0	100.0
	lower	8.3	6.7	11.8	15.2	10.3	13.1	15.1	27.5	26.3
	middle	36.4	32.4	38.3	44.8	39.1	32.9	41.3	36.4	37.4
	upper	55.3	60.9	49.9	40.0	50.5	54.0	43.5	36.1	36.3
Special law offence	Total	100.0	100.0	100.0	100.0	100.0	100.0	100.0	100.0	100.0
	lower	5.4	6.2	17.6	19.6	19.8	16.2	8.4	20.5	21.5
	middle	22.6	31.5	37.6	41.6	38.5	33.2	32.7	44.2	44.1
	upper	72.0	62.3	44.8	38.8	41.7	50.6	59.0	35.3	34.4
Stimulant drugs	Total	—	100.0	100.0	100.0	100.0	100.0	100.0	100.0	100.0
	lower	—	4.1	—	—	—	5.7	3.7	4.2	3.4
	middle	—	19.5	17.1	31.0	11.5	27.9	28.9	29.0	24.8
	upper	—	76.4	82.9	69.0	88.5	66.4	67.4	66.8	71.7
Traffic offence										
Professional negligence	Total	…	…	…	…	100.0	100.0	100.0	100.0	100.0
	lower	…	…	…	…	1.1	0.9	0.9	0.8	0.7
	middle	…	…	…	…	23.6	26.1	21.1	18.8	14.1
	upper	…	…	…	…	75.3	72.9	77.9	81.0	85.3
Road traffic violation	Total	…	…	100.0	100.0	100.0	100.0	100.0	100.0	100.0
	lower	…	…	8.3	8.6	7.3	8.5	8.3	7.6	10.7
	middle	…	…	37.8	44.0	39.3	40.3	38.1	38.0	39.4
	upper	…	…	53.9	47.4	53.4	51.3	53.6	54.3	49.9

Note: "Lower" means aged 14・15, "middle" aged 16・17 and "upper" aged 18・19

Source: Annual Report of Statistics on Prosecution

due to a sudden rise in the number of juvenile offenders newly received for violation of the Poisonous and Hazardous Substance Control Law.

Meanwhile, the ratio of juveniles among total offenders newly received for professional negligence hovered between 10 percent and 11 percent between 1970 and 1988, while the ratio of juveniles among total road-traffic violators fluctuated between 10.6 percent and 15.8 percent, except for 1970 when the figure shot up to 27.3 percent. In both cases, there is no significant change in the percentage of juvenile offenders among total offenders newly received by the Public Prosecutors Office.

Table 72 shows the changes at five-year intervals in the percentages of juvenile offenders newly received by the Public Prosecutors Office by type of major offences and age groups between 1970 and 1985 and in 1988. The total number of juvenile offenders newly received by the Public Prosecutors Office reached 197,685 in 1950, but has since increased gradually. It reached a record high of 793,318 in 1965. Afterwards, the number declined in 1970 and 1975, when the number dropped to 384,553, nearly half the 1965 figure. The number started to increase in 1980 and 1985, when it reached 598,248. But it dropped to 470,167 in 1988.

By type of offences, the number of juvenile offenders newly received by the public prosecutors office for theft varied from 60,000 to 90,000 between 1950 and 1975. But the number increased to the 120,000 mark in 1980 and the 130,000 mark in 1985. It reached 139,546 in 1988, second only to the record 142,338 set in 1983.

By age group, the lower age group (14 to under 16) increased dramatically from 21,781 in 1950 to 62,124 in 1988. Proportionally, the upper age group (18 to under 20) dropped to 15.2 percent in 1988 from 36.8 percent in 1950, while the lower age group rose to 44.5 percent in 1988 from 26.0 percent in 1950.

The number of juvenile offenders newly received by the Public Prosecutors Office for physical violence such as bodily injuries, assault and aggravated assault under the Law for the Punishment of Acts of Violence, etc., hovered around the 10,000 mark in 1950 and 1955. It shot up to the 30,000 mark in 1960 and 1965, before it started to decline to the 20,000 level in 1970. (A record high was set in 1964 at 32,804). It dropped to slightly more than 20,000 in 1970 and has hovered around the 10,000 mark since 1975.

A breakdown of such violent acts committed by different age groups shows the upper age group accounted for 64.7 percent (9,726 persons) in 1955; 50.8 percent (104,372) in 1960, but its share dropped dramatically to 21.2 percent (3,568) in 1985 and 23.8 percent (3,349) in 1988.

Meanwhile, the lower age group accounted for 1,067 (7.1 percent) in 1955, 4,216 (14.9 percent) in 1960, then jumped to 8,511 (50.7 percent) in 1985 and 6,534 (46.4 percent) in 1988.

The number of juveniles involved in extortion fluctuated between 4,000 and 5,000 in 1950 and 1955, but soared to the 13,000-14,000 mark in 1960 and 1965. (A record high of 15,317 cases was set in 1963). It started to fall under the 7,000 mark after 1965 and dipped to 5,571 in 1988. By different age groups, the upper age group accounted for more than 50 percent of all extortions committed by juveniles in 1950 and in 1955, while the middle age group (16 to under 18) made up more than 40 percent between 1960 and 1975 and since 1980, the lower age group accounted for more than 40 percent of extortions, each age group showing the highest percentage of each respective period.

Along with the passage of time, the main core of juvenile delinquents has gradually shifted from the upper age group to the middle age group and then to the lower age group.

The number of juvenile delinquents involved in rape and indecent assault totaled 1,791 in 1950, 2,634 in 1955, and hit the 5,000 mark in both 1960 and 1965, reaching a record high of 5,652 in 1966. Since then, it has started to decline and has hovered around the 1,000 mark in both 1980 and 1985. In 1988, it decreased to 960.

The number of juveniles involved in robbery fluctuated at around the 2,000 mark between 1950 and 1965 (reaching a record high of 2,622 in 1970), but fell substantially to 1,102 in 1970, 563 in 1985 and 593 in 1988.

A breakdown by age group of juvenile delinquents involved in rape, indecent assault and robbery shows the upper age group accounted for more than 40 percent of such offences until 1980, while the lower age group never accounted for more than 20 percent. This showed that older juveniles were more prone to commit such crimes.

However, in recent years, the lower age group's involvement in rape and indecent assault cases increased to 30.6 percent in 1985 and 20.8 percent in 1988, while in robbery cases it has risen to 27.5 percent in 1985 and 26.3 percent in 1988. The statistics show that the age of those involved in such crimes is becoming lower and lower.

Meanwhile, juvenile offenders against the Stimulant Drugs Control Law totaled 1,859 in 1955 but dropped to less than 35 persons in 1960, 1965 and 1970. It went up again to 265 in 1975 and jumped to the 2,000 mark in 1980 and 1985, before dipping to 1,306 in 1988. (It hit a record high of 3,076 cases in 1982). The figure fluctuates wildly from year to year but juveniles in the upper age group have accounted for about two-thirds of the Stimulant Drug Control Law offenders every year.

The number of juveniles newly received for professional negligence and road-traffic violations remains extremely high, accounting for more than 60 percent of all juvenile offenders newly received by the Public Prosecutors Office. As stated at the beginning of this chapter, the trend in overall number of offenders newly received by the Public Prosecutors Offices since 1970 on seems to have been in accordance with the changes in the total number of traffic offenders newly received.

Among juvenile traffic offenders newly received, the number of those involved in professional negligence dropped dramatically to 46,953 in 1975 from 81,159 in 1970. However, it started to climb again and topped the 50,000 mark in 1980 and 1985, before reaching 64,206 in 1988. (It hit a record high in 1969 with 81,728).

The number of juvenile road-traffic violators newly received increased to a record 577,598 in 1965 from 407,392 in 1960. The number started to decline after the traffic violation notification system was applied to juveniles in 1970. It decreased below the 400,000 mark in 1970 and dropped to the 200,000 mark in 1975 and 1980. It went up to 327,120 in 1985 but declined again when the traffic violation notification system was expanded in 1987. It reached 191,355 in 1988.

By age group, the upper age group accounts for more than 70 percent of professional negligence cases and nearly 50 percent of road-traffic violations.

Although the average age of juvenile offenders is becoming lower and lower in other offences, the upper age group has steadily increased in number in professional negligence cases between 1980 and 1988.

(2) Historical Transition in Juvenile Trials

A. Juvenile Tribunal

Juvenile trial refers to the proceeding of hearings and decisions to decide on the treatment and disposition for juvenile offenders involved in crimes. Juvenile proceedings are different from the trial proceedings for ordinary criminal cases. The juvenile trial system started with the enactment of the old Juvenile Law which was succeeded by the current Juvenile Law.

In line with the enactment of the old Juvenile Law in 1923, the Juvenile Tribunal was established as Japan's first institution to conduct juvenile trials.

The Juvenile Tribunal was an administrative organ under the supervision of the Justice Minister to conduct trials of the juvenile cases referred to it concerning disposition for protective, rehabilitative measures. Its function also included the implementation of protective, rehabilitative measures as well as the supervision of implementation of such measures. Judges of the Juvenile Tribunal, juvenile probation officers and secretaries were assigned to work at Juvenile Tribunals.

Judges of the Juvenile Tribunal were not judicial officers but administrative officers in their official capacity. However, the law allowed a judge to be assigned concurrently to the post and as a matter of fact, mainly those who had experience as a judge or public prosecutor were assigned to judge Juvenile Tribunals.

Juvenile Probation Officers were assigned the task to help the judge of the Tribunal in providing the information necessary for hearings and decisions and also engaging in probationary supervision. They carried out investigation of the juveniles to prepare materials for the hearing and in addition, they engaged in probationary supervision on juveniles who were put on "probationary supervision by Juvenile Probation Officer" by the Juvenile Tribunal as one of the protective, rehabilitative measures.

Juvenile Tribunals were first established in Tokyo and Osaka and set up in Nagoya in 1934, in Fukuoka in 1938, Hiroshima in 1941, and Sendai and Sapporo in 1942. In an effort to cope with a sharp rise in juvenile delinquency after World War II, Juvenile Tribunals were established in Shizuoka, Nagano, Kyoto, Kanazawa, Matsue, Takamatsu, and Kumamoto and Akita in 1946 and in Maebashi, Kobe and Asahikawa in 1947.

Under the old Juvenile Law, juveniles under 18 years of age who had either violated or were prone to violate criminal laws were made the subject of protective measures. Juvenile Tribunals could accept the cases involving juveniles who were not less than 14 and less than 18 years of age as protective cases under its jurisdiction when the cases were referred to by public prosecutors or by a court of law.

In addition, the Juvenile Tribunal could accept those cases as protective cases when it acknowledged the juvenile in need of protective, rehabilitative measures and when it received reports from ordinary citizens who acknowledged a juvenile in need of protective, rehabilitative measures.

Children under 14 years of age could not be tried at the Juvenile Tribunal, except those who were referred to it by prefectural governors.

Of all cases accepted at the Juvenile Tribunal in 1926, 7,072 were referred to it by public prosecutors (accounting for 44.3 percent of the total juveniles accepted by the Juvenile Tribunal that year); seven were referred to it by courts of law (0.0 percent); 95 were referred to it by prefectural governors (0.6 percent); 8,597 were handled based on the acknowledgement by Juvenile Tribunals themselves (53.8 percent) and 170 (1.1 percent) were taken up based on reports from ordinary citizens.

Fig. 50 and Appendix Table 14 show the changes in numbers of juvenile delinquents who were involved in juvenile cases handled by Juvenile Tribunals between 1926 and 1948.

The total number of juvenile delinquents handled at Juvenile Tribunals

Fig.50 Number of Juvenile Offenders Adjudicated by Juvenile Tribunals (1926~1948)

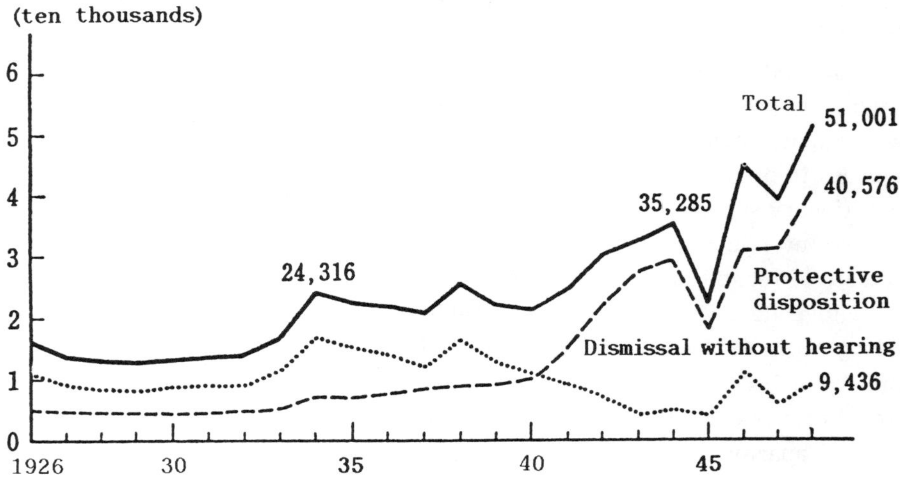

Source: Synopsis of Justice Ministry

increased, as more and more Juvenile Tribunals were established nationwide. The number of juvenile delinquents disposed of at the Juvenile Tribunals totaled 16,000 in 1926, and this number climbed to the 20,000 mark after 1934.

In 1942 when the protective, rehabilitative measures were implemented nationwide, it increased to 30,452 and reached a record high of 51,001 in 1948 since the first tribunal was opened in Japan.

By types of treatment prescribed for the juvenile delinquents disposed of at Juvenile Tribunals, more than 64 percent of all cases disposed of at the tribunal were dismissed without hearings between 1926 and 1935, while 30 to 35 percent were placed on protective measures. Until 1940, more than half of the juvenile cases disposed of at the Juvenile Tribunals were dismissed without hearings.

However, this trend reversed after 1941 when more than 60 percent of the juvenile offenders were placed on protective, rehabilitative measures. The figure rose to more than 80 percent between 1943 and 1945.

In those days, protective, rehabilitative measures included the following nine categories:

1) To admonish juvenile delinquents;

2) To instruct school principals to admonish juvenile delinquents for their anti-social behavior;

3) To obligate juvenile delinquents to pledge to correct their anti-social

Fig.51 Number of Protective Disposition by Juvenile Tribunals (1926~1948)

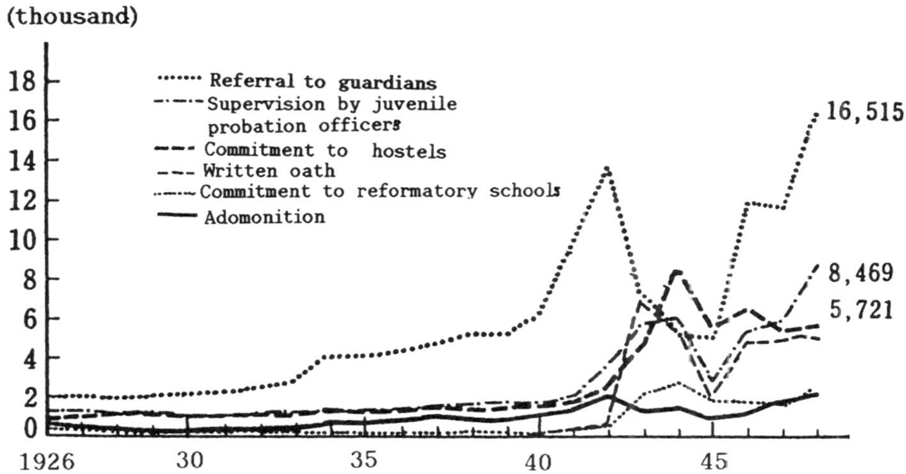

Source: Synopsis of Justice Ministry

behavior in written oaths;

4) To put juvenile delinquents under the care of their parents or guardians with specific conditions;

5) To entrust juvenile delinquents to temples, churches and other organizations for juvenile protection and rehabilitation or appropriate individuals;

6) To place juvenile delinquents under probationary supervision by juvenile probation officers;

7) To put them in reform schools (which were later renamed Child Education and Training Homes (see I-1 of this section);

8) To put juvenile delinquents in Reformatory Schools;

9) To hospitalize juvenile delinquents or entrust them to hospitals.

Fig. 51 and Appendix Table 14 show the changes in numbers of juvenile delinquents disposed of by Juvenile Tribunals by types of treatments they received.

In 1926, 1,957 persons (40.1 percent of the total of juvenile delinquents disposed of by Juvenile Tribunals with protective rehabilitative measures in that year) were placed under the care of their parents or guardians, but the number increased to 13,576 in 1942 (60.7 percent). Those who received admonishment accounted for 514 persons (10.5 percent) in 1926, and 1,954 persons (8.8 percent) in 1942, while those who had to pledge to reform themselves in written oaths amounted to 233 persons (4.8 percent) in 1926 and 550 (2.5 percent) in 1942.

These statistics show that more than half of juvenile delinquents received these temporary treatments in both 1926 and 1942.

Among the treatments designed to provide continuing protective, rehabilitative measures to juvenile delinquents, 1,223 persons (25 percent) were placed under the probationary supervision of juvenile probation officers in 1926 and 3,512 (15.7 percent) in 1942. Those who were entrusted to the care of organizations for juvenile protection and rehabilitation were 875 (17.9 percent) in 1926 and 2,411 (10.8 percent) in 1942. The number of juvenile delinquents put in Reformatory Schools accounted for 77 (1.6 percent) in 1926 and 357 (1.6 percent) in 1942.

The influence of World War II began to affect the implementation of protective, rehabilitative measures designed to reform juvenile delinquents and after 1943, the number of those juvenile delinquents increased who were either sent to Reformatory Schools or placed under the care of organizations for juvenile protection and rehabilitation to receive short and strict training programmes. In 1944, 2,733 (9.3 percent) were referred to Reformatory Schools, while 8,565 persons (29.1 percent) were placed under the care of organizations for juvenile protection and rehabilitation.

B. Family Court

The current Juvenile Law enforced in 1949, succeeded the system of non-accusatory form of proceedings like the hearing and decision procedure adopted by the old Juvenile Law. However, the power to conduct the hearing and disposition on juvenile cases was transferred to the court of law. The old Juvenile Tribunal was abolished and the new Family Court was established.

In line with this change, the organ to decide on protective, rehabilitative measures and the organ to actually implement such measures were separated. The current Juvenile Law stipulates that the family courts, in principle, only hand down the decisions on protective, rehabilitative measures, and actual implementation of such measures are left to administrative organs.

The old Juvenile Law allowed the Juvenile Tribunal to either cancel or change the protective, rehabilitative measures whenever it deemed it proper. But the current Juvenile Law states that the family courts can never change or cancel decisions on such measures once the decision is made, except in very exceptional cases.

The old Juvenile Law, on the other hand, never allowed juveniles to file a complaint against the prescribed protective, rehabilitative measures. But the current law allows juveniles to take kokoku appeals to a high court from the decision of the family court on the ground that error in law, error in fact or grossly unfair and inadequate dispositions merit the reversal of the decisions rendered by the family court.

Fig.52 Number of Juvenile Delinquents Received by Family Courts (1949~1987)

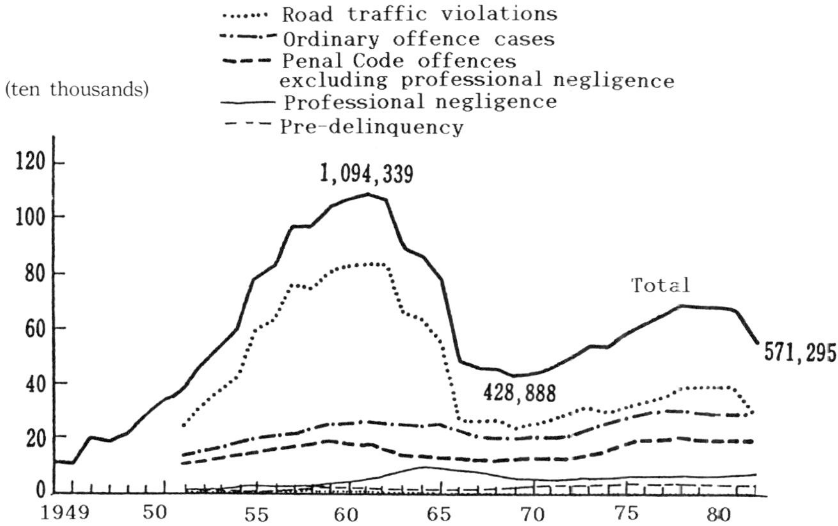

Source: Annual Report of Justice Statistics

The Juvenile probation officer system, which was established under the Juvenile Tribunal, was succeeded under the present Juvenile Law by the family court investigator system under the family court.

The title of juvenile probation officer was used when the family court system was first started, but it was changed to juvenile investigator in 1950 and changed again in 1954 to the present family court investigator.

The main function of a family court investigator consists of helping judges by conducting needed social investigation of the pending case, and preparing for the hearing and disposition of the judge. Also, it is stipulated that a family court investigator has the role of performing the supervision and observation of juveniles waiting the final disposition of the family courts judge. (Family court investigators are commonly called family court probation officers.)

C. Trends in Juvenile Cases Received by Family Courts

Fig. 52 shows the changes in number of juveniles received by family courts between 1949-the year when the family court system was established-and 1987. (The number of juveniles received by types of offences is shown after 1956.)

The total number of juveniles received by family courts hovered around the 100,000 mark in 1949 and 1950 but increased to 198,183 in 1951. The number

Fig.53 Number of Ordinary Juvenile Delinquents Adjudicated at Family Courts (1951～1987)

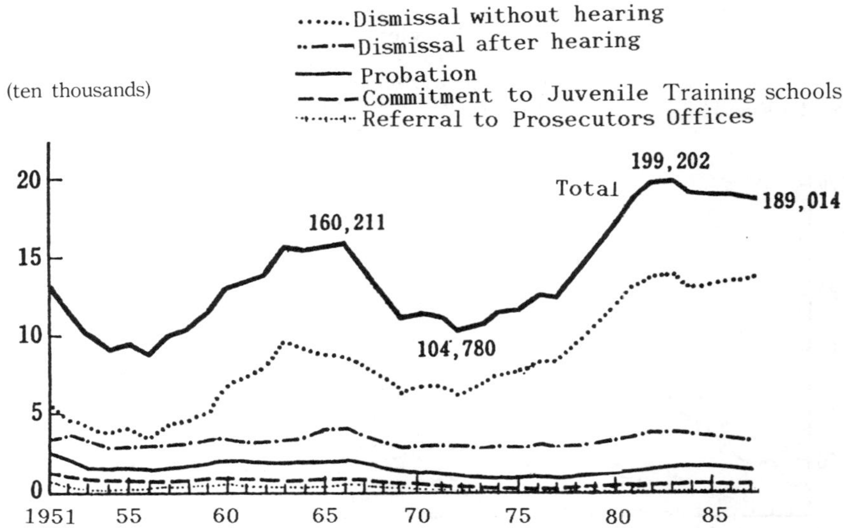

Note: Numbers of pre-delinquent and traffic professional negligence cases are excluded.
Source: Annual Report of Judicial Statistics

continued to rise after 1953 and peaked in 1966 at 1,094,339.

Since then, it started to decline sharply and dropped to 455,128 in 1972 and fluctuated between the 420,000 and 460,000 mark until 1976. But it started to increase again slowly after 1977 and reached 684,830 in 1983. Afterward, it declined with small fluctuations and reached 571,295 in 1987.

Such variation in the number of juveniles received by family courts has been in accordance with increases or decreases in the number of juvenile traffic offenders, who have made up nearly half of total juvenile offenders received by family courts.

·The number of juveniles received by family courts for ordinary offences (including pre-delinquency but excluding violations of the Road Traffic Law) increased to 252,143 in 1966 from 133,885 in 1956. It started to dip after 1967 with small fluctuations and dropped to 196,637 in 1974. It began climbing again after 1975 and totalled 302,856 in 1983 and has been hovering around the 290,000 mark since 1984.

D. Trends in Disposition by Family Courts

Fig. 53 and Appendix Table 15 show the changes in number of juveniles who were adjudicated by family courts between 1951 and 1987 for involvement in ordinary offences, however excluding here traffic professional negligence and also pre-delinquency (hereafter cited as "those juveniles adjudicated").

The total number of those juveniles adjudicated declined to 90,558 in 1956 from 134,946 in 1951. But it started to increase after 1957 and reached 160,211 in 1966. Declining again after 1967, it dipped to 104,780 in 1972, then rose once more from 1973 to reach 199,202 in 1983. Since then it has been fluctuating around the 190,000 mark.

By category of disposition, juveniles dismissed without a hearing made up the biggest percentage among those juveniles adjudicated. Until 1960, nearly 40 percent of all those juveniles adjudicated were dismissed without a hearing, which increased to the 50-percent mark up until 1970 and to the 60-percent level up until 1980, since then reaching 70 percent.

When the number of juveniles dismissed after a hearing are added, the percentage of combined total juveniles who were either dismissed without a hearing or dismissed after a hearing has steadily increased from 65.7 percent recorded in 1951, with small fluctuations. Since 1973, nearly 90 percent of all those juveniles adjudicated by family courts have been either dismissed without a hearing or after a hearing.

Meanwhile, among the dispositions composed of continuing protection and guidance, probationary supervision is the largest. But the percentage of juveniles placed under probation among all those juveniles adjudicated declined to 6.9 percent in 1974 from 18.8 percent in 1951 and has been fluctuating between 7 percent and 8 percent since then.

The number of juveniles committed to juvenile training schools is the second largest, although the percentage among all those juveniles adjudicated declined to 1.5 percent in 1974 from 9.0 percent in 1951 and has been hovering around 2 percent since then.

The number of juveniles referred to public prosecutors is slowly declining. The percentage among all those juveniles adjudicated dropped to 0.6 percent in 1977 from 5.6 percent in 1951 with small fluctuations and has since been hovering below the 1.0-percent level.

Taking up the dispositions in which the greatest variations in number can be seen comparing 1951 with 1986, dismissal without a hearing marked a 2.5-fold increase to 136,277 in 1987 from 53,739 in 1951, while commitment to juvenile training schools declined to 4,493 in 1987, a third of the 12,132 recorded in 1951. Likewise, referral to public prosecutors declined to 859 in 1987, a fifth of the 7,582 recorded in 1951.

Table 73 shows the changes in number of juveniles who were adjudicated by family courts for traffic professional negligence (hereafter called "juvenile negligent drivers adjudicated") in 1952, the figures being for every five years between 1955 and 1985 and in 1987.

Table 73 Number of Juvenile Professional Negligence Drivers Adjudicated by Family Courts

Year	Total	Referral to prosecutors		Commitment to training school	Probation	Commitment to child education and training home, etc.	Referral to governor/Child guidance center	Dismissal after hearing	Dismissal without hearing
		Criminal disposition	Over 20 yrs						
1951	1,189 (100.0)	201 (16.9)	33 (2.8)	—	24 (2.0)	3 (0.3)	—	483 (40.6)	445 (37.4)
1955	4,546 (100.0)	962 (21.2)	78 (1.7)	—	106 (2.3)	—	—	2,051 (45.1)	1,349 (29.7)
1960	19,365 (100.0)	7,679 (39.7)	383 (2.0)	4 (0.0)	781 (4.0)	—	—	6,267 (32.4)	4,251 (22.0)
1965	36,942 (100.0)	13,785 (38.2)	381 (1.1)	15 (0.0)	1,683 (4.7)	—	—	15,461 (42.9)	4,717 (13.1)
1970	77,831 (100.0)	21,663 (27.8)	1,192 (1.5)	36 (0.0)	4,934 (6.3)	1 (0.0)	—	40,978 (52.6)	9,027 (11.6)
1975	45,851 (100.0)	7,599 (16.6)	946 (2.1)	69 (0.2)	3,776 (8.2)	—	—	29,836 (65.1)	3,625 (7.9)
1980	49,394 (100.0)	5,410 (11.0)	1,204 (2.4)	188 (0.4)	12,036 (24.4)	—	—	26,357 (53.4)	4,199 (8.5)
1985	55,526 (100.0)	6,038 (10.9)	2,283 (4.1)	155 (0.3)	14,283 (25.7)	—	—	27,466 (49.5)	5,301 (9.5)
1987	63,385 (100.0)	5,569 (8.8)	2,593 (4.1)	113 (0.2)	17,339 (27.4)	—	—	32,170 (50.8)	5,601 (8.8)

Source: Annual Report of Judicial Statistics

The total number of juvenile negligent drivers adjudicated sharply increased in just more than a decade from 1955 and peaked in 1970 at 77,831. It declined to 45,851 in 1975 but began to rise again in 1980 and 1985 and reached 63,385 in 1987.

By type of disposition, juveniles referred to public prosecutors accounted for 41.7 percent of all juvenile negligent drivers adjudicated in 1960, but it declined to 12.9 percent in 1987.

The number of juveniles committed to juvenile training schools increased sharply between 1975 and 1980 but it accounted for only 0.4 percent of all juvenile negligent drivers adjudicated in 1980, when the number set a record high. Since then the ratio started to decline and dipped to 0.2 percent in 1987.

Until 1975, less than 10 percent of total juvenile negligent drivers adjudicated were placed under probationary supervision.

The number started to increase sharply, however, when the new system

Table 74 Number of Juvenile Road Traffic Violators Adjudicated by Family Courts

Year	Total	Referral to prosecutors		Commitment to training school	Probation	Commitment to child education and training home, etc.	Referral to governor/Child guidance center	Dismissal after hearing	Dismissal without hearing
		Criminal disposition	Over 20 yrs						
1951	31,112 (100.0)	756 (2.4)	…	14 (0.0)	100 (0.3)	–	1 (0.0)	1,273 (4.1)	28,968 (93.1)
1955	190,498 (100.0)	7,752 (4.1)	714 (0.4)	4 (0.0)	755 (0.4)	11 (0.0)	2 (0.0)	28,136 (14.8)	153,124 (80.4)
1960	519,908 (100.0)	53,230 (10.2)	3,854 (0.7)	11 (0.0)	3,430 (0.7)	–	5 (0.0)	62,890 (12.1)	396,488 (76.3)
1965	757,548 (100.0)	120,542 (15.9)	3,226 (0.4)	19 (0.0)	6,356 (0.8)	–	–	157,008 (20.7)	470,397 (62.1)
1970	506,751 (100.0)	54,947 (10.8)	2,678 (0.5)	35 (0.0)	9,675 (1.9)	–	–	179,767 (35.5)	259,649 (51.2)
1975	206,399 (100.0)	38,924 (18.9)	2,978 (1.4)	48 (0.0)	8,789 (4.3)	–	–	123,103 (59.6)	32,557 (15.8)
1980	260,591 (100.0)	35,310 (13.5)	4,335 (1.7)	205 (0.1)	29,996 (11.5)	–	1 (0.0)	143,087 (54.9)	47,657 (18.3)
1985	339,633 (100.0)	56,722 (16.7)	8,819 (2.6)	317 (0.1)	41,845 (12.3)	1 (0.0)	3 (0.0)	168,976 (49.8)	62,950 (18.5)
1987	264,766 (100.0)	36,462 (13.8)	7,034 (2.7)	310 (0.1)	39,126 (14.8)	4 (0.0)	–	133,442 (50.4)	48,388 (18.3)

Source: Annual Report of Judicial Statistics

of short-term probationary supervision for traffic offenders was introduced in 1977. The percentage reached 24.4 percent in 1980 and 27.4 percent in 1982.

The percentage of juveniles dismissed without a hearing declined to 7.9 percent in 1975 from 29.7 percent in 1955 and has remained less than 10 percent since then. Meanwhile, the percentage of juveniles dismissed after a hearing came to more than 40 percent, except for 1960 when the rate dropped to 32.4 percent.

Since 1970, it was more than 50 percent of total juvenile negligent drivers adjudicated, with the only exception in 1985. The combined total of those juveniles who were either dismissed without a hearing or dismissed after a hearing has been fluctuating between 56.0 percent and 74.8 percent of all juvenile negligent drivers adjudicated.

Table 74 shows the changes in juvenile violators of the Road Traffic Law adjudicated by family courts (hereafter called "juvenile traffic law violators

Table 75 Number of Pre-Delinquent Juveniles Adjudicated by Family Courts

Year	Total	Commitment to training school	Probation	Commitment to child education and training home, etc.	Referral to governor/Child guidance center	Dismissal after hearing	Dismissal without hearing
1951	5,096 (100.0)	1,113 (21.8)	710 (13.9)	187 (3.7)	201 (3.9)	998 (19.6)	1,887 (37.0)
1955	6,995 (100.0)	1,069 (15.3)	977 (14.0)	70 (1.0)	126 (1.8)	1,693 (24.2)	3,060 (43.7)
1960	5,921 (100.0)	815 (13.8)	999 (16.9)	80 (1.4)	169 (2.9)	1,329 (22.4)	2,529 (42.7)
1965	7,153 (100.0)	737 (10.3)	1,196 (16.7)	104 (1.5)	170 (2.4)	1,840 (25.7)	3,106 (43.4)
1970	5,409 (100.0)	300 (5.5)	855 (15.8)	92 (1.7)	107 (2.0)	1,527 (28.2)	2,528 (46.7)
1975	2,662 (100.0)	222 (8.3)	497 (18.7)	70 (2.6)	39 (1.5)	819 (30.8)	1,015 (38.1)
1980	3,437 (100.0)	489 (14.2)	905 (26.3)	105 (3.1)	77 (2.2)	1,022 (29.7)	839 (24.4)
1985	2,920 (100.0)	454 (15.5)	986 (33.8)	140 (4.8)	108 (3.7)	744 (25.5)	488 (16.7)
1987	2,558 (100.0)	378 (14.8)	808 (31.6)	103 (4.0)	88 (3.4)	693 (27.1)	488 (19.1)

Source: Annual Report of Judicial Statistics

adjudicated") in 1951, every five years between 1955 and 1985, and in 1987.

The total number of juvenile traffic law violators adjudicated peaked much earlier than that of juvenile negligent drivers adjudicated. It reached 757,548 in 1965 and peaked in 1966 at 790,084. It started to decline sharply after 1975 and dipped to 206,339 in 1975, but began to rise again and reached 339,633 in 1985 before falling to 264,766 in 1987.

By type of disposition, those who were referred to public prosecutors fluctuated around the 10-percent level between 1960 and 1987, except for 1975 when it increased to 20.3 percent.

Those who were committed to juvenile training schools comprised less than 0.1 percent, although the number of juvenile traffic law violators has been steadily increasing since 1980.

Like juvenile negligent drivers adjudicated, the number of juvenile traffic

Table 76 Number of Ordinary Juveniles Adjudicated at Family Courts, by Frequency of Previous Disposition

Category	1955	1960	1965	1970	1975	1980	1985	1987
Total	131,512 (100.0)	158,902 (100.0)	202,158 (100.0)	115,274 (100.0)	118,024 (100.0)	174,249 (100.0)	192,461 (100.0)	189,974 (100.0)
No-disposition	91,415 (69.5)	103,928 (65.4)	154,222 (76.3)	90,009 (78.1)	93,787 (79.5)	133,228 (76.5)	143,302 (74.5)	143,399 (75.5)
Previous disposition	40,097 (30.5)	54,974 (34.6)	47,936 (23.7)	25,265 (21.9)	24,237 (20.5)	41,021 (23.5)	49,159 (25.5)	46,575 (24.5)
1 time	21,443 (16.3)	27,612 (17.4)	28,162 (13.9)	15,127 (13.1)	15,860 (13.4)	25,749 (14.8)	29,332 (15.2)	27,767 (14.6)
2 times	9,395 (7.1)	12,635 (8.0)	10,578 (5.2)	5,352 (4.6)	5,019 (4.3)	8,926 (5.1)	11,181 (5.8)	10,379 (5.5)
Over 3 times	9,259 (7.0)	14,727 (9.3)	9,196 (4.5)	4,786 (4.2)	3,358 (2.8)	6,346 (3.6)	8,646 (4.5)	8,429 (4.4)

Source: Annual Report of Judicial Statistics

law violators adjudicated who were placed under probation has been on the rise after the introduction of the new system of short-term probationary supervision for traffic offenders. The total, which accounted for less than 5 percent until 1975, increased to 11.5 percent in 1980 and to 14.8 percent in 1987.

The combined percentage of juveniles dismissed without a hearing together with those dismissed after a hearing exceeded 70 percent until 1980, but dipped to 68 percent in 1985 and 1987.

Table 75 shows changes in the number of juveniles adjudicated by family courts for pre-delinquent acts in 1951, every five years between 1955 and 1985, and in 1987.

The total number fluctuated between the 5,000 and 7,000 mark until 1970, but it started to decline after 1975 to the 2,000 and 3,000 level before dropping to 2,558 in 1987.

By type of disposition, those who were committed to juvenile training schools fluctuated between 10 percent and 15 percent, except for 1951 when the figure reached 21.8 percent, and in 1970 and 1975 when it dropped to less than 10 percent.

The number of juveniles placed under probationary supervision hovered around 10 percent until 1975, but it started rising after 1980, going up to 33.8 percent in 1985 before dipping to 31.6 percent in 1987.

Those who were committed to child education and training homes and homes for dependent children accounted for 3.7 percent in 1951 and hovered

Table 77 Number of Juveniles Referred Back from Family Courts to Public Prosecutors Offices

Year	Total number	Prosecution			Non-prosecution	Referral to family courts again	Rate of road traffic offences
		Total	Formal trial	Summary proceedings:			
1961	73,113	71,312	3,071 (4.3)	68,241	1,687	114	95.4
1965	122,612	120,366	3,005 (2.5)	117,361	1,882	364	97.8
1970	67,877	66,363	2,326 (3.5)	64,037	1,351	163	97.6
1975	38,581	38,067	1,061 (2.8)	37,006	444	70	98.5
1980	32,491	32,054	1,178 (3.6)	30,876	375	62	98.3
1985	52,776	51,685	1,013 (2.0)	50,672	1,027	64	98.0
1988	25,018	24,448	812 (3.3)	23,636	472	98	98.1

Source: Annual Report of Statistics on Prosecution

around 1 percent between 1955 and 1970. After 1975 it started to increase, reaching 4.8 percent in 1985 and 4.0 percent in 1987.

The combined percentage of juveniles dismissed without a hearing together with those dismissed after a hearing came to 56.6 percent in 1951 and exceeded 60 percent between 1955 and 1975. But it dipped under the 60-percent mark in 1980 and declined to 46.2 percent in 1987.

Table 76 shows the changes in number of juveniles newly adjudicated by family courts for ordinary offences excluding, since 1970, traffic professional negligence (hereafter "newly adjudicated juveniles") by frequency of previous disposition at five-year intervals between 1955 and 1985, and in 1987.

The percentage of those who were previously adjudicated by family courts against the overall total of newly adjudicated juveniles stood out in 1955 and 1960 at 30.5 percent and 34.6 percent, respectively. After 1965, it fluctuated between 20.5 percent and 25.5 percent and came to 24.5 percent in 1987.

Among those previously adjudicated by family courts, the percentage of those who were adjudicated once to the overall total of newly adjudicated juveniles fluctuated between 13.1 percent and 17.4 percent, while those adjudicated twice fluctuated between 4.3 percent and 8.0 percent. Those adjudicated three times or more stood out in 1955 and 1960 at 7.0 percent and 9.3 percent respectively, but dropped to less than 5.0 percent after 1965. The high percentage shown in 1955 and in 1960 for those juveniles with records of one or more, particularly with more than three previous dispositions by family courts

Table 78 Number of Juvenile Penal Code Offenders Found Guilty at Courts of First Instance

Year	Total	Sex		Age group			Rate of juveniles
		Boy	Girl	Under 16	Under 18	Under 20	
1926	3,265	3,100	165	143	760	2,362	3.1
1930	2,893	2,798	95	110	602	2,181	2.9
1935	3,280	3,180	100	179	670	2,431	2.7
1940	3,030	2,957	73	158	584	2,288	2.7
1945	17,436	17,100	336	785	5,128	11,523	2.7
1950	7,577	7,420	157	42	1,276	6,259	7.2
1955	1,818	1,791	27	5	251	1,562	1.9
1960	2,965	2,937	28	1	459	2,505	3.5
1965	2,745	2,708	37	12	537	2,196	3.7
1970	2,541	2,517	24	4	254	2,283	4.0
1975	1,199	1,175	24	—	93	1,106	2.2
1980	1,193	1,169	24	5	76	1,112	2.4
1985	1,243	1,211	32	—	61	1,182	2.5
1987	1,173	1,139	34	1	73	1,099	2.5

Sources: Annual Report of Criminal Statistics, Annual Report of Judicial Statistics, etc.

illustrates the difficulties of rehabilitating juveniles who went astray in the postwar social chaos in the late 1940s and the early 1950s.

(3) Changes in Juvenile Criminal Trials

Under the current Juvenile Law, protective, rehabilitative measures can be applied to juveniles who are under 20 years of age. But the old Juvenile Law defined only those under 18 years of age as juveniles. As a result, up until 1951, when the upper age limit of a juvenile was lifted to less than 20 years, after its transition period following the 1949 enactment of the current Juvenile Law, the protective, rehabilitative measures could not be applied to those 18 years of age and older, and instead, they were subjected to criminal dispositions.

Also, the current Juvenile Law stipulates that family courts cannot refer juveniles under 16 years of age, at the time of referral, to the public prosecutors for criminal prosecution. But under the old Juvenile Law, criminal penalities were sometimes given to those who were between 14 and 16 years of age.

Table 77 shows the changes in disposition by public prosecutors offices of juvenile offenders who were referred back from family courts which had ruled that those juvenile offenders deserved criminal dispositions in 1961 and at five-year intervals between 1965 and 1985 as well as in 1988. Total number of juveniles prosecuted by public prosecutors offices was 71,312 in 1961 and which increased to 120,366 in 1965. After 1970, it started to decline and dipped to 32,054 in 1980 but rose again to 51,685 in 1985, before it decreased once again to 24,488 in 1988. Of all juveniles prosecuted, more than 95 percent were for summary order proceedings without hearing (or summary hearing in court). The ratio of juvenile offenders prosecuted for formal trial proceedings hovered around the 3 percent level except for 1961 when it stood up at 4.3 percent and in 1985 when it dropped to 2.0 percent.

A large majority of cases which were referred back from family courts to public prosecutors offices were traffic-related cases, viz, traffic professional negligence and road traffic offences. The ratio of traffic-related offenders to all juvenile offenders referred back and disposed of by prosecutors offices accounted for 97.6 percent in 1970, 98.0 percent in 1985 and 98.1 percent in 1988.

Table 78 shows the changes in the number of juveniles (less than 20 years of age at the time of committing the offence charged) prosecuted in formal trial proceedings and found guilty on Penal Code offences at the courts of first instance and the ratio of such juveniles to the total number of those found guilty on Penal Code offences at such courts, at five-year intervals between 1926 and 1985 and in 1987. When such statistics were not available in the fifth year, the data of the following year is listed.

First of all, the overall number of such juveniles did not change much between 1926 and 1940, recording 3,265 and 3,030 respectively in these years. But it soared to 17,436 in 1946 one year after the end of World War II, although it shrunk to 7,577 in 1951. Overall fluctuation shows that the number of juveniles stood out in this period, demonstrating that the increase in crimes amidst the social confusion in Japan immediately after the war had involved many juveniles and as a result, many juveniles were left to be criminally disposed of.

The fluctuation in the number of such juveniles started to change in 1951, when juveniles were newly defined as those aged under 20 years. Although it is not included on the table, the number dropped to 2,305 in 1952 and fluctuated between 1,000 and 2,000 after 1955. Since 1975, it has been hovering around 1,200 mark.

Secondly, the ratio of such juveniles hovered around 2 to 3 percent throughout the Showa era without significent change, except for 1951 when it

Table 79 Number of Juveniles Found Guilty at Courts of First Instance

Year	Total	Death	Life imprison-ment	Determinate term imprisonment				Fine	Refer-ral to family courts
				Indeter-minate term	Deter-minate term	of which, Suspen-sion of execution	Probation		
1957	1,524	1	9	946	513	506 (34.9)	231 (45.7)	55	…
1960	2,150	—	8	1,180	819	812 (40.6)	358 (44.1)	143	24
1965	2,125	1	7	876	1,074	953 (48.9)	393 (41.2)	167	19
1970	1,276	—	1	426	815	802 (64.6)	284 (35.4)	34	12
1975	607	—	—	175	418	411 (69.3)	106 (25.8)	14	11
1980	712	—	—	139	527	526 (79.0)	152 (28.9)	46	7
1985	611	—	—	125	477	470 (78.1)	147 (31.3)	9	4
1987	637	—	3	147	476	472 (75.8)	123 (26.1)	11	8

Source: Annual Report of Judicial Statistics

stood out at 7.2 percent.

However, by type of offences, the percentage of negligence offences causing bodily injuries, mostly professional or gross negligence resulting in death or injuries, increased in the latter half of the Showa era, accounting for 23.6 percent in 1965, 48.8 percent in 1975 and 57.9 percent in 1987.

Table 79 shows the changes in the category of sentences given to juveniles (under 20 years of age at the time of sentencing) found guilty in courts of first instance at five-year intervals between 1960 and 1987 as well as in 1957. The total number of such juveniles was 1,524 in 1957 but it exceeded the 2,000 mark in 1960 and 1965. But it declined to 1,276 in 1970 and has been hovering between 600 and 700 after 1975.

By category of penalties, capital punishment was never handed down except for one juvenile in 1969. Life imprisonment sentences were 5.6 in number on a yearly average until 1969. After 1970 the yearly average dropped to 0.6. The decline in the number of capital punishment and life imprisonment sentences is connected to a drop in heinous crimes committed by juveniles by the year 1970. At the same time, it reflects a general tendancy toward leniency in sentencing.

As for determinate term imprisonment with or without labour, suspension of the execution of such sentences accounted for less than 40 percent until

1965, but it has been gradually increasing since then, topping 60 percent in 1975 and 70 percent in 1980.

3. JUVENILE CLASSIFICATION HOMES

(1) Transitional Changes in Juvenile Classification System and Treatment in Juvenile Classification Homes

The Juvenile Classification Home was established in 1949 as an institution attached to the Juvenile Protective Guidance Center, a facility established under the jurisdiction of the Attorney General's Office (the present Justice Ministry).

In line with a partial amendment of the Juvenile Law and the Juvenile Training School Law, the Juvenile Protective Guidance Center and the Juvenile Classification Home were combined into the Juvenile Protective Classification Center in 1950, which was renamed again the Juvenile Classifcation Home in 1952—the system which continues to the present day.

The Juvenile Classification Home was, in principle, established in the same localities where the main offices of family courts were situated. The number of juvenile classification homes has increased in line with the establishment of branch homes, promotion of branch homes into homes as well as the establishment of the Naha Juvenile Classification Home, following the reversion of Okinawa to Japan.

As of May, 1989, there were 51 juvenile classification homes and two branch homes nationwide.

Since its establishment, the internal organization of a juvenile classification home consisted of four sections; 1) general affairs; 2) observation and treatment; 3) classification; and 4) medical care, under the supervision of a director. (Small-scale insitutions, however, sometimes do not have the medical section.) A deputy director may be assigned under a director, depending on the size of the instituion.

In April, 1988, a part of the regulations concerning the organization of Juvenile Training Schools and Juvenile Classification Homes was amended. After the amendment, the section for observation and treatment and the section for classification were combined into a classification center. At the same time, a specialist staff system was introduced and the newly created classification center was put under the supervision of a head classification specialist. A number of senior classification specialists and specialists were assigned under the head classification specialist.

This specialist system was created based on the understanding that highly specialized knowledge of behavioral science in psychology, education and sociology is vital to observation and treatment as well as for classification of juvenile delinquents. The specialist system is a working-level organizational system which was developed to enable qualified staff members to engage in classification of personalities as a group.

The Juvenile Classification Home, which was started after the war as a juvenile correctional institution under overcrowded conditions, had to face the need for enormous efforts to establish the organizational structure, like facilities and equipment, recruitment and deployment of personnel and the operational standards of the system, etc.

At that time, it was urgently required to develop the functions of the Juvenile Classification Home which had the mission to introduce scientific principles in the treatment of juvenile delinquents.

It had to recruit doctors and experts who had specialized knowledge in behavioral science to classify juvenile delinquents. At the same time, the rules, regulations and formularies relating to juvenile classification homes were drafted and subsequently adopted.

In 1951 when the assignment of qualified staff members to existing institutions was completed, the diagnostic classification service system for ordinary juveniles was established in order to contribute to the healthy and sound development of youths in society as a whole.

Until about 1970 following the establishment of the Juvenile Classification Home, institutional buildings and the quality of staff members were steadily improved. Clinical knowledge and techniques were actively borrowed from Europe and the United States and were implemented in Japan in the field of classification techniques, in particular.

Also, a big breakthrough was made in improving the quality of staff members, with the start of systematic training.

However, on a nationwide basis, wide discrepancies in administration, observation and treatment as well as classification remained among the institutions.

In 1965, standardization of classification procedures started in an effort to solve the aforementioned problems. Standardization has the purpose of rationalizing the administration of the Juvenile Classification Homes and upgrading the functions of the classification, observation and treatment. Standardization is the process to correct the imbalance in the operations among institutions and establish operational formulae adaptable to the size of each institution.

Standardization includes the efforts to secure an adequate environment to prepare juveniles to attend the diagnostic classification process and the hearings in family courts without fear, by effectively combining in an organic unity the functions of classification, observation and treatment.

In 1966 and 1969, the results of the standardized administration program were examined at juvenile classification homes run on a trial basis. Later, in 1971, the Juvenile Classification Homes Standardization Subcommittee (which was integrated into a working committee to improve classification services in 1975) was established within the Justice Ministry's Correction Bureau to standardize the overall administration of the Juvenile Classification Home.

The major achievements during this period included: -the establishment of construction standards for juvenile classification homes; -the planning of programs to improve the homes; -the development of various psychological tests which started in 1967; and -the publication of the "Juvenile Classification Case Book," which was first issued in 1974.

Responding to a strong public call to provide special classification for juvenile traffic offenders, the "Traffic Offender Classification Handbook," referring to various tests related to diagnostic classification of traffic offenders, was published in 1973. The handbook has been used for standardized classification of juvenile traffic offenders, who have started to make up a large percentage of overall juvenile offenders received for classification by Juvenile Classification Homes.

Around 1975, the number of juveniles admitted to the Juvenile Classification Home declined. But the type of offences and personalities of juvenile delinquents had become diversified, which prompted the further improvement in classification precision. Research and discussions on classification methods have been conducted very actively since then.

In line with the administrative reform of the Juvenile Training School which was carried out in 1977, the need to forge a strong connection among such institutions involved in treatment of juvenile delinquents, including the Juvenile Training School, were stressed.

As further sophisticated and diversified diagnostic classification was required in order to provide effective treatment guides for each individual juvenile, the organic unity of treatment, observation and diagnostic classification was attempted and so called "exploratory treatment" (diagnostic treatment) and a specialist staff system were introduced.

In 1986, the format of a classification result notification form was completely reversed. It was designed to standardize the classification report to be submitted to family courts. It was also required to write in the report the reasons why the findings in the report were reached in order to clarify the grounds to support the conclusions of the classification report in an effort to standardize the classification result notification methods.

The classification process is now rapidly being computerized.

As we have stated so far, the Juvenile Classification Home was a newly established institution after the war to conduct scientific treatment of juvenile delinquents as called for by the current Juvenile Law.

Throughout its process of development, the home has been emphasizing the importance of application of the knowledge in human behavioral science as a part of the overall criminal policy.

Diagnostic classification experts, gathering at Juvenile Classification Homes, were formed into groups of professionals. Not only did they perform meritoriously in these Homes but also some of them, being assigned to prisons and Juvenile Training Schools and expanding their specialist knowledge and techniques, contributed greatly to promote the scientific approach in the post-war treatment of inmates in the entire range of correctional institutions by way of establishing the treatment system under classification and introducing various treatment techniques.

In cooperation with the Research and Training Institute of the Ministry of Justice, specialists belonging to the Juvenile Classification Home have made wide-range contribution in the study of criminology and delinquency through their study of the delinquncy prediction, categorization of juvenile delinquents and the study of special characteristics of various juvenile delinquents.

(2) Trends in Newly Admitted Inmates in Juvenile Classification Homes

Fig. 54 and Appendix Table 16 show the changes in number of newly admitted inmates in the Juvenile Classification Home, since the institution's establishment in 1949.

The Table shows that number of new inmates admitted in juvenile classification homes totaled 16,094 in 1949. Since then, it started to increase and reached a record high of 40,820 in 1951, before it began to decline gradually and dipped to 29,332 in 1956. But it began to rise again and hovered on a plateau between 1959 and 1966. Since then, it declined slowly, touching the low of 10,410 in 1974. But again, it began to increase and reached to 22,593 in 1984, before it dipped back to 19,372 in 1988.

The number of juveniles newly admitted in juvenile classification homes fluctuates almost in parallel to the fluctuation of the number of juveniles cleared by police.

The percentage of girls in the total number of juveniles who were newly admitted in juvenile classification homes dipped to a record low in 1960 with 8.5 percent and hovered around 10 percent until 1972. But it topped the 10-percent mark every year after 1973. Since then, it increased and accounted for about 15 percent in the recent five years. The level reached 15.4 percent in 1988.

Appendix Table 16 shows that the average daily population of juvenile classification homes fluctuated around the 2,000 mark since 1949 until 1967. But

Fig.54 Number of Juveniles Committed to Juvenile Classification Homes (1949～1988)

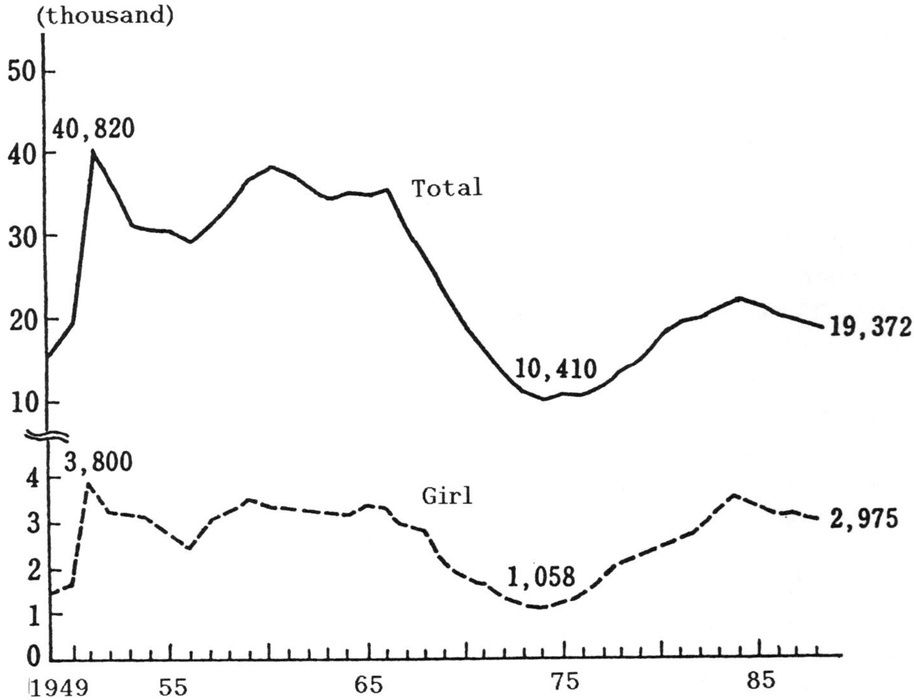

Sources: Annual Report of Statistics on Juvenile Correction, Annual Report of Statistics on Correction, etc.

it began to decrease to below 1,000, touching a low of 593 in 1974. Since then, it started to increase again and reached 1,386 in 1984. It began to decline gradually again, however, dipping to 1,195 in 1988.

Appendix Table 16 also shows the ratio of juveniles who were newly admitted to juvenile classification homes against the total juvenile population (the ratio of the juveniles who were newly admitted in juvenile classification homes among every 10,000 juveniles).

According to the Table, the ratio stood out in 1951 and 1960, reaching 39.0 and 35.7 respectively. After 1961, it started to decline and hit the record low of 10.8 in 1974. But it started to rise again and reached around 21 in 1983 and 1984, before dropping to 16.2 in 1988.

Fig. 55 shows the trends in the component ratio of age group of new inmates, by sex, at the five-year intervals between 1955 and 1985 and in 1988.

Among boys, the component ratio of the age group is set at the following

Fig.55 Percentage of Newly Admitted Juveniles, by Age Group

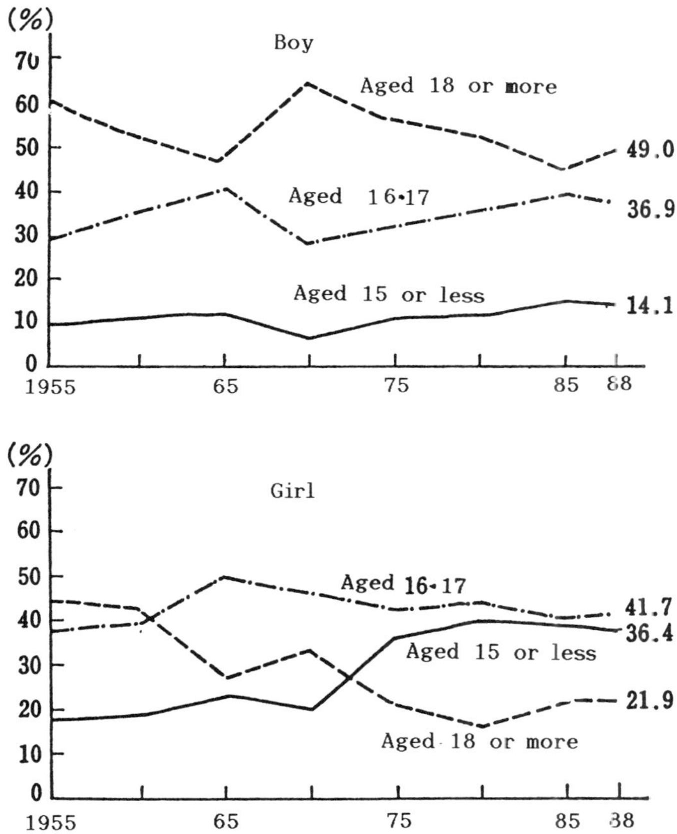

Sources: Annual Report of Statistics on Juvenile Correction, Annual Report of Statistics on Correction, etc.

order in any given year: the upper age group; the middle age group; and the lower age group.

While the component ratio of the upper age group continued to dip between 1960 and 1965, the ratio of the middle age group and the lower age group increased. After 1965, the ratio of the upper age group increased and reached a record high of 64.7 percent in 1970. During the same period, the ratio of the middle age group and the lower age group both declined to the record low of 28.8 percent and 6.4 percent respectively.

Since then, the component ratio of the upper age group continued to decline until 1985, while the ratio of the middle age group and the lower age

Table 80 Rate of Inmates Newly Admitted to Juvenile Classification Homes, by Type of Delinquency

Type of delinquency	1955	1960	1965	1970	1975	1980	1985	1987
Total	100.0 (31,021)	100.0 (37,171)	100.0 (36,936)	100.0 (21,332)	100.0 (11,894)	100.0 (18,320)	100.0 (22,531)	100.0 (20,786)
Penal Code offences	82.9	87.8	86.3	86.6	83.5	72.1	70.9	72.3
Homicide	0.5	0.7	0.8	0.7	0.6	0.1	0.4	0.4
Robbery	3.1	4.4	4.1	3.8	3.7	2.5	1.5	1.9
Bodily injury	6.3	8.7	8.9	7.9	7.3	8.4	9.0	9.7
Assault	1.5	2.7	1.9	0.9	0.9	0.6	0.6	0.4
Extortion	4.2	11.6	11.5	8.3	7.9	4.5	5.9	6.3
Theft	52.7	44.2	42.3	47.0	46.6	37.3	42.0	43.2
Fraud, embezzlement	6.0	2.5	1.6	1.1	0.9	0.6	0.8	0.9
Rape, indecent assault	4.0	7.1	8.3	8.2	7.2	4.2	2.8	2.7
Arson	0.3	0.3	0.2	0.3	0.4	0.4	0.3	0.3
Violent acts	…	…	2.9	2.5	2.8	5.7	2.2	1.8
Professional negligence	1.3	2.4	0.9	2.1	2.2	2.9	2.0	1.9
Others	2.9	3.2	2.9	3.8	3.0	4.9	3.4	2.9
Special Law offences	6.2	4.8	4.3	3.1	4.6	14.7	16.0	15.2
Firearms and swords	0.9	1.1	1.8	1.1	0.6	0.2	0.2	0.3
Stimulant drugs	2.8	0.0	0.0	0.1	0.8	6.4	6.9	5.6
Poisonous substances	…	…	…	…	1.9	6.2	6.8	7.0
Prostitution	0.5	1.8	1.3	0.6	0.2	0.1	0.2	0.2
Others	2.0	1.9	1.2	1.3	1.0	1.7	1.9	2.2
Pre-delinquency	10.9	7.4	9.4	10.3	11.9	13.2	13.1	12.5

Source: Annual Report of Judicial Statistics
Note : Excluding traffic offenders

group increased.

In 1988, the component ratio of the upper age group inched up again to 49.0 percent, while the ratio of the middle age group and the lower age group dipped to 36.9 percent and 14.1 percent respectively.

In girls, the component ratio of the age group was set as the following order until 1960: the upper age group; the middle age group and the lower age group.

However the order changed to the middle age group, the upper age group and the lower age group order in 1965 and 1970.

After 1975, the order was changed to: the middle age group; the lower age group; the upper age group.

The ratio of the upper age group declined to 21.9 percent in 1988, while the percentage of the middle age group and the lower age group accounted for 41.7 percent and 36.4 percent respectively.

The age of the new inmates is getting younger in both sexes, in girls in particular, although this tendency is not so apparent as shown in the component ratio of the age group of the juveniles cleared by police.

Table 80 shows the number of inmates newly admitted to juvenile classification homes, by type of offence, at the five-year intervals between 1955 and 1985 and in 1987.

The percentage of Penal Code offenders accounted for 80 percent until 1975, but it has dropped to 70 percent since then.

Among the Penal Code offenders, the percentage for larceny was the highest in any given years. It always exceeded the 40 percent mark, except for 1980 when it dropped to 37.3 percent.

The percentage for bodily injury was the second highest with 6.3 percent in 1955. But between 1960 and 1975, the percentage for extortion become the second highest, fluctuating between 11.6 percent and 7.9 percent.

After 1980, the percentage for injury and assault became the second highest again, and topped the 9 percent mark in 1985.

Extortion declined to 4.5 percent in 1980 but it inched up to 5.9 percent in 1985 and 6.3 percent in 1987, becoming the third common offence.

Meanwhile, the special law offences hovered between 3.1 percent and 6.2 percent between 1955 and 1975. After 1980, it started to rise and fluctuated between 14.7 percent and 16.0 percent between 1980 and 1987 due to a sharp increases in violations of the Poisonous and Hazardous Substances Control Law and the Stimulant Drugs Control Law, although violations of the Anti-Prostitution Law declined after 1980.

The percentage of inmates for pre-delinqunc y acts declined to 7.4 percent in 1960 from 10.9 percent in 1955 but it increased again and reached 13.2 percent

Table 81 Component Ratio of Recommendations to Family Courts by Juvenile Classification Homes

Recommendation	1950	1955	1960	1965	1970	1975	1980	1985	1988
Total	100.0 (5,825)	100.0 (27,675)	100.0 (35,598)	100.0 (35,836)	100.0 (20,990)	100.0 (12,701)	100.0 (18,161)	100.0 (21,965)	100.0 (19,207)
Protective measures unnecessary	4.1	2.4	1.0	1.0	2.7	1.7	0.3	0.2	0.6
Uninstitutional treatment	32.6	34.9	39.6	55.6	58.9	59.4	51.9	43.4	45.8
Institutional treatment	58.1	52.5	50.5	35.4	27.3	30.8	45.9	48.1	45.6
Primary J.T.S.	11.8	5.4	5.4	4.8	2.3	3.8	5.0	7.1	6.4
Middle J.T.S.	29.9	34.7	35.7	22.7	19.0	21.8	35.5	35.6	33.7
Special J.T.S.	5.1	8.0	6.0	4.4	3.4	2.6	2.4	2.1	2.1
Medical J.T.S.	4.8	3.2	2.3	2.3	1.6	1.5	1.2	1.4	1.3
Child education & training home, etc.	6.5	1.2	1.2	1.2	1.0	1.3	1.8	1.9	2.2
Protective measures inadequate	1.5	1.4	2.9	4.2	6.3	4.7	1.7	1.9	1.7
Other	3.8	8.8	6.0	3.8	4.8	3.3	0.2	6.4	6.2

Sources: Annual Report of Statistics on Juvenile Correction,
Annual Report of Statistics on Correction

in 1980, before dipping to 12.5 percent in 1988.

Table 81 shows the trend in the component ratio of recommendation of the Juvenile Classification Homes sent to the family courts and listed at the five-year intervals between 1950 and 1985 and in 1988.

As the maximum age for the application of the Juvenile Law was moved up to 19 years of age in 1951, here we will examine the data in and after 1955 for their continuity.

Until 1960, the percentage of those recommendations to confine the juveniles to institutions under rehabilitative protective measures was the highest, accounting for more than 50 percent. But between 1965 and 1980, the percentage of such recommendations to let the juveniles stay at their homes under rehabilitative protective measures became the highest, accounting for more than 50 percent.

In 1985, the percentage of such recommendations for confinement accounted for 48.1 percent, exceeding the percentage of recommendations to let the juveniles stay at their homes, which accounted for 43.4 percent in that year.

Table 82 Component Ratio of Adjudications at Family Courts on Dispositional Recommendation from Juvenile Classification Homes

Category	1950	1955	1960	1965	1970	1975	1980	1985	1988
Total	100.0 (5,825)	100.0 (27,675)	100.0 (35,598)	100.0 (35,836)	100.0 (20,990)	100.0 (12,701)	100.0 (18 161)	100.0 (21,965)	100.0 (19,207)
Dismissal without or after hearing	9.7	12.3	10.4	8.7	9.8	9.5	7.2	5.7	5.5
Probation	27.5	22.0	26.8	29.6	31.2	31.3	39.9	38.3	41.3
Commitment to institutions	38.9	29.6	25.1	22.3	19.4	20.9	26.8	29.0	27.1
Primary J.T.S.	8.5	3.5	3.4	2.9	1.6	2.2	2.9	3.8	3.3
Middle J.T.S.	18.8	16.9	15.3	13.4	12.9	14.0	19.9	21.0	19.5
Special J.T.S.	4.7	5.8	3.9	3.2	2.7	2.3	1.7	1.5	1.4
Medical J.T.S.	3.3	2.5	1.8	1.9	1.4	1.2	1.0	1.1	1.0
Child education & training home, etc.	3.5	0.9	0.7	0.9	0.9	1.2	1.3	1.5	1.8
Referral to prosecutors	3.9	4.2	5.0	4.8	5.7	4.2	2.2	2.5	2.3
Referral to the governor/child care center	…	0.5	0.4	0.3	0.3	0.2	0.2	0.5	0.4
Other disposition	…	1.3	1.8	2.2	0.7	0.8	0.2	0.0	0.0
Tentative probation	…	21.9	23.8	22.6	19.6	20.8	18.2	15.9	15.9
Other	20.1	8.2	6.6	9.3	13.2	12.3	5.1	8.0	7.5

Sources: Annual Report of Statistics on Juvenile Correction,
Annual Report of Statistics on Correction

In 1988, the percentage of juveniles classified into each of these two recommendations categories accounted for almost same at 45 percent.

Of the juveniles who were recommended to be confined to institutions for protection and rehabilitation, the percentage of juveniles who were recommended to be consigned to Middle Juvenile Training School was the highest all the time, topping 30 percent, except between 1965 and 1975, when it fluctuated around 20 percent.

Table 82 shows the trend in the component ratio of adjudications made by the family courts on those juveniles whose recommendations for dispositions were referred to from Juvenile Classification Homes in the five-year intervals between 1950 and 1985 and in 1988. Again we examine the data after 1955 for the same reason stated earlier in this section.

The percentage of cases dismissed without hearing and dismissed after hearing by family courts declined to 5.5 percent in 1988 from 12.3 percent in 1955. The percentage of the cases placed on probationary observation under family courts accounted for 23.8 percent in 1960. But it again declined to 15.9 percent in 1985 and 1988.

On the other hand, the percentage of juveniles placed under the supervision of probation officers steadily increased from 22.0 percent marked in 1960. It climbed up to 41.3 percent in 1988, after fluctuating on the 20 percent level until 1965 and hovered around the 30 percent mark after 1970.

The percentage of the juveniles confined to institutions for rehabilitative protective measures peaked at 29.6 percent in 1955, but it declined to a record low of 19.4 percent in 1970. After 1975, it started to increase, and reached 29.0 percent in 1985, but dipped to 27.1 percent in 1988.

Apart from the classification of the juveniles in custody by order of the family court, the Juvenile Classification Home also provides the following diagnostic classification services: classification of juveniles at large at the request of family courts, classification of juveniles referred from correctional institutions, Probation Offices, and Public Prosecutors Offices, all affiliated with the Justice Ministry, and classification of the ordinary juveniles requested by families and schools.

Trends in the percentage of juveniles received for classification by the Juvenile Classification Home, by types of the aforementioned categories of classification, are shown in Table 83.

The table shows that the total number of juveniles received by the Juvenile Classification Home continued to rise and peaked at 80,418 in 1965. But the number started to decline and dipped to 40,168 in 1975. Since then it hovered around the 40,000 mark and reached 49,835 in 1988.

By categories of classification, family court-related classification topped 90 percent until 1955 after the establishment of the Juvenile Classification Home.

The percentage of the ordinary classification increased after 1960, and the percentage of Justice Ministry-related classification started to rise in 1975, reaching 39.1 percent and 15.0 percent in 1988.

After about 1960s, the number of juvenile traffic offenders started to increase. In line with this upward trend, the number of traffic classifications also increased.

The statistics of the Justice Ministry's Correction Bureau show that the total number of juvenile traffic offenders who were required to be classified, while in custody or at large, by family courts as well as those who were received for classification by the Juvenile Classification Homes at the request of the organs affiliated with the Justice Ministry totaled 4,276 in 1965 and increased

Table 83 Percentage of Juveniles Received at Juvenile Classification Homes, by Category of Clients

Category	1950	1955	1960	1965	1970	1975	1980	1985	1988
Total	100.0 (8,643)	100.0 (34,618)	100.0 (67,652)	100.0 (80,418)	100.0 (66,490)	100.0 (40,168)	100.0 (45,373)	100.0 (44,786)	100.0 (49,835)
Family courts	93.4	93.9	62.8	54.0	46.7	44.6	47.9	55.7	45.9
Commitment to institutions	…	91.9	60.4	47.4	32.9	30.8	44.1	54.0	42.5
Staying at the home	…	1.8	2.4	6.3	13.8	13.7	3.7	1.8	3.4
Others	…	0.2	0.0	0.3	0.0	0.0	0.0	0.0	0.0
Justice Ministry	2.0	0.5	1.7	6.1	4.1	11.3	21.8	14.9	15.0
Correction	…	…	…	3.9	3.3	6.4	4.8	3.1	2.1
Probation office	…	…	…	0.3	0.4	4.6	16.5	11.2	12.5
Prosecutors offices	…	…	…	1.8	0.5	0.3	0.5	0.6	0.3
Outside agencies or individuals	4.6	5.7	35.5	39.9	49.2	44.1	30.3	29.4	39.1

Sources: Annual Report of Statistics on Juvenile Correction,
Annual Report of Statistics on Correction, etc.

to 11,472 in 1988.

4. JUVENILE TRAINING SCHOOL

(1) Changes in Treatment

A. Establishment of Reformatory School (Juvenile Training School) and Its Treatment

The Reformatory School Law was proclaimed on April 17 in 1922 (implemented on Jan. 1, 1923) and two reformatory schools were established, one in Tokyo and the other in Osaka for the first time in Japan.

In line with the expansion of the areas where the protective rehabilitation program for juvenile delinquents were implemented, the number of reformatory schools also increased.

When the protective rehabilitation program for juvenile delinquents was implemented nationwide in 1942, there were a total of seven reformatory schools nationwide, in Tokyo, Osaka, Nagoya, Fukuoka, Hiroshima, Sendai and Sapporo. (These institutions were classified as "reformatory schools" by the law, but actually the term "training school" was used in the name of such a institution, like Tama Training School and Naniwa Training School.)

The Reformatory School Law stipulated that reformatory schools were national institutions to admit juveniles who fell in the following categories: -Those who were referred to reformatory schools by the Juvenile Tribunals as a kind of the protective rehabilitative measures, and; -Those who were permitted for commitment to reformatory schools in accordance to Article 882 of the old Civil Code. (Request filed by the party who held the parental power over the juveniles.)

The maximum age of inmates committed to reformatory schools was set at 23.

Juveniles referred to reformatory schools could be released on parole when the purpose of the commitment was achieved, with the permit from the Juvenile Tribunal.

When the inmates had spent six months in reformatory school, they could also be released on parole with specific conditions.

Although the law stated that reformatory schools ought to be created to admit juvenile delinquents separated by their sex, but in those days, there were only the institutions to accommodate boy delinquents. The reformatory schools for girl delinquents were not created until 1948.

Treatment for inmates were cheifly aimed at improving their character by educating them under a strict discipline as well as giving them practical vocational training essential for living in society.

In order to educate the inmates, curricula, selection of academic subjects taught at reformatory schools as well as the text books and reading materials were decided based on the educational standards for middle schools and technical schools or lower level. (Refer to the Regulations on the Treatment at Reformatory School implemented in 1923)

Not many records and materials are left to-date to tell us the details of treatment conducted at reformatory schools in those days. However, remaining records tell us that academic classes were formed based on the intelligence and study ability of the inmates. Staff members with teacher's certificates taught the class according to each subject.

Vocational technique teachings were given on the following subjects: agriculture, horticulture, woodwork and printing. The products created by the inmates were exhibited to the public and even auctioned.

Living guidance at dormitories where the inmates lived was considered as the main pillar of the rehabilitation education.

There, supplementing the life under strict discipline, autonomous activities were performed among the juveniles themselves such as the selection of the head and other posts of the dormitory and assignment of their part in daily life.

The duration of commitment to reformatory school was fairly long in those days and each inmate spent an average of two years.

The Reformatory School was organized with four sections under the supervision of the superintendent: General Section; First Section (concentrated on the academic and vocational education); Second Section (concentrated on maintenance of law and order in the institution, living guidance and matters related to the release of the inmates); and Third Section (concentrated on medical care and and general hygiene.)

B. Wartime Treatment

In 1943, the dispositional standards for protective, rehabilitative measures were changed in line with the Urgent Policies to Guide Working Youth (Cabinet Determination) and it became possible to refer mildly delinquent juveniles to Reformatory Schools. There, these juveniles were put through a short-term intensive training program for two months in order to let them work in private munitions plants after the completion of such training. As a result, those juveniles who were in advanced stages of delinquency and were not suitable for such short-term training programs were admitted to Sendai Reformatory School. The emphasis of the treatment in the short-term intensive training program was placed on mental and physical training, such as moral and spiritual instruction and military drills.

C. Development of Postwar Treatment

(a) Enactment of the Current Juvenile Training School Law

The short-term intensive training program was abolished when the war ended and conventional treatment courses were revived. However, Reformatory Schools were overcrowded in those days due to a sharp increase of juvenile delinquents. A number of Reformatory Schools were established-one in 1946, four in 1947 and eight in 1948.

Efforts were made to create a modern treatment system for the new era under the very difficult circumstances presented by shortages of food and materials.

On July 15 in 1948, together with the enactment of the present Juvenile Law, the current Juvenile Training School Law was proclaimed (implemented on Jan. 1, 1949).

Compared with the Reformatory School Law, the treatment outlined by the Juvenile Training School Law is characterized by the following:

1) It defines the Juvenile Training School as an institution to provide correctional education, thus clarifying its educational traits in the law itself. The law has also stipulated the contents of the education program as academic education, and guidance in vocational skills, as well as adequate training and medical care;

2) It established four different types of juvenile training schools, clearly adopting the allocation system under classification, namely, primary, middle, special and medical, depending on the age, sex and the degree of advancement of delinquent tendency, as well as the mental and physical condition, of the inmates.

3) As a part of the academic education, it specifically guarantees that the Juvenile Training School provides elementary- and middle-school-level education for those who have not yet completed their compulsory education;

4) It has introduced the progressive grade treatment system to treat the inmates differently in accordance with their improvement.

The organization of the Juvenile Training School was also altered and under the supervision of the superintendent, each institution consists of four sections; general affairs section, education section (which actually is involved in the education of inmates), classification and rehabilitation section (which is involved in the matters related to admission, parole and discharge, as well as classification and investigation) and medical care section. Deputy superintendents are assigned to assist the superintendents.

Like the Juvenile Classification home, a specialized staff system was introduced in April 1988, in an effort to create an environment where the specialist staff, which has advanced knowledge and experience in education, psychology and sociology, etc., can engage in education activities as a group.

For this purpose, the education section and the classification and rehabilitation section were combined into the education center, and a plural number of senior and other specialists were assigned to work under head specialist.

(b) Improvement and Perfection of Education Courses

In 1949, when the Juvenile Training School Law was implemented, 20 institutions which were originally created as Reformatory Schools became Juvenile Training Schools, based on the new law. In addition, eight new Schools were created.

By about 1955, as the number of inmates continued to increase, 28 new Schools had been established, bringing the total number of Juvenile Training Schools nationwide to 56. (As of December 31, 1988, after a number of Schools were closed and a number of others opened, there were 54 Schools nationwide.)

However, a majority of such Schools were diverted from the facilities of juvenile protective rehabilitation societies and former military facilities. As a result, facility equipments was insufficient. Besides the problem of overcrowdedness, difficulties in school management and administration continued throughout the decade from 1955 to 1964.

Under such circumstances, however, administrative circulars concerning guidance in vocational skills, education by correspondence classes, audio-vidual education and guidance through interviews by volunteers, have been issued since the early 1950s.

Also, various new experiments were carried out, including educational experiments concerning academic education and vocational training.

In 1958, another administrative circular concerning living guidance was issued. It defined living guidance as the activity that constitutes the foundation of correctional education at juvenile training schools. It added that living guidance is aimed at further developing the inmates' personalities and the improvement of their way of thinking and attitude toward society, based on the understanding of each inmate's individuality and through day-to-day guidance based on drill simulations derived from realistic life situations.

In the early 1960s, an experiment was conducted at each School which placed special emphasis on specific treatment, such as academic education, education of vocational skills and physical training, in order to make the institutional treatment more effective.

Vocational training, such as woodworking, metal working, welding and electrical work, was provided at juvenile training schools. Vocational training courses at juvenile training schools were approved as public job training one after another, based on the Vocational Training Law, since 1963 (after 1985, based on the Human Resources Development Law). Certificates verifying completion of human resources development courses have been given to the inmates by the Director General of the Labor Ministry's Job Training Bureau (after 1985, by the Human Resources Development Bureau Director-General), which has become a great motivation in the resocialization of juveniles.

During the decade from 1965 to 1974, the number of inmates started to decline and the problem of overcrowdedness was finally solved. Subsequently, the treatment in juvenile training schools has been further improved and so-called individualized treatment has been provided to inmates in accordance with the type of delinquent tendencies, character of the individuals, and environmental problems.

At the same time, in an effort to cope with the sharp increase in juvenile traffic offenders, an experiment was made to provide them with short-term intensive treatment.

Furthermore, since around 1970, another experiment was made to provide relatively short-term treatment to juveniles whose delinquent tendencies were not so advanced.

(c) New Development in the Treatment of Juvenile Training School

In 1977, another administrative circular concerning " the administration of the Juvenile Training School" was issued. This was a major reform in the post-war juvenile training school system, which was designed to: -Provide more diversified treatment programs suited for individual inmates; -Make the duration of confinement more flexible; -Make each school specialized in specific treatments; -Effectively combine the treatment at Schools with probation programs after parole release, and; -Further strengthen communication and cooperation with related organs and outer communities.

This reform was carried out after re-examining such tendencies as the duration of confinement to juvenile training schools, which tend to be fixed at about one year, and the uniformities found in the treatment provided in schools.

After the reform, a new categorization of treatments was established according to the tendency of delinquency, individual personality and the rehabilitative treatmtent needs of inmates, in an effort to further and secure the individualised, differential treatment of inmates.

Treatment was basically divided into the Short-Term Program and the Long-Term Program. The newly formulated short-term program was subdivided into the two categories of General Short-Term Treatment and Short-Term Treatment for Traffic Offenders.

The Long-Term Program was divided into the following five new treatment courses: 1) Living Guidance Course; 2) Vocational Training Course; 3) Academic Education Course; 4) Special Education Course; and 5) Medical-Care course.

As for the contents and methods of treatment, the circular requires that a basic treatment scheme shall be formulated in each treatment program at each School and also that correctional education curricula shall be divided in three stages, viz., education at admission, mid-term education and education in preparation for release. The contents and methods of education shall be formulated under the progressive stage system so as to be most suitable for each stage.

In addition, it requires that an individualized treatment scheme shall be planned for each individual and that individualized educational objects to be achieved by each individual inmate shall be established, and the contents and methods of education needed for attaining such objectives shall be systematically deployed.

In 1980, a new series of administrative notes were issued, concerning "the formulation and operation of educational curricula at the Juvenile Training School" and "the standard for academic evaluation at the Juvenile Training School." As the standards to formulate the educational curricula and the standards to accurately evaluate the education results on each inmate were shown and the basic framework of the correctional education at juvenile training schools were established and improved.

The Justice Ministry compiled "the Educational Guidebook by Tech-

Fig.56 Number of Juveniles Committed to Reformatory Schools and Training Schools and Committal Rate by Juvenile Tribunals and Family Courts (1923～1987)

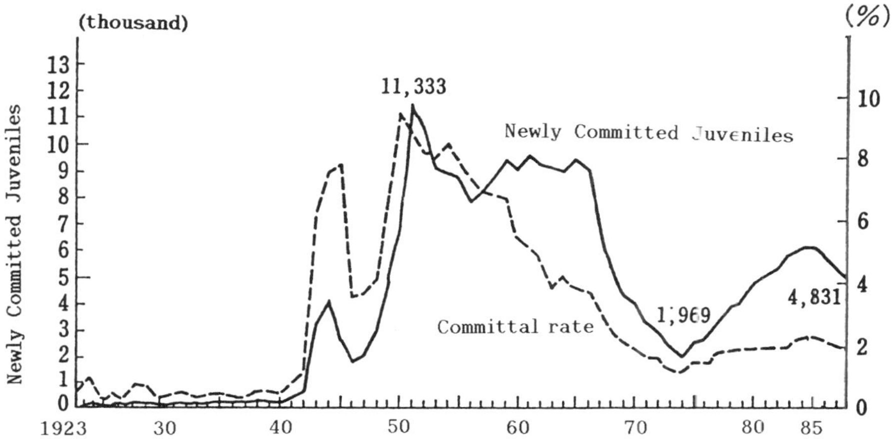

Sources: Annual Report of Statistics on Juvenile Correction, Annual Report of Statistics on Correction, etc.

niques" (Part 1 and Part 2) in 1981 and 1982. Various efforts have been made to introduce and to spread the use of such new therapeutic treatment techniques as psycho-dramas, counseling, training for self-governing and analysis through communications, in addition to the teaching through composition, self-reflection, reading, participating in gatherings and fulfilling given roles in everyday activities at schools.

Teaching of juveniles by categories of their problems is also introduced in an effort to remove their delinquent tendency by working directly toward such problematic behaviors as drug abuse and automobile-related delinquency.

At some juvenile training schools, middle-school students who are consigned to juvenile training schools and are put on the General Short-Term Treatment Course, are allowed to return to their home before the expiration of their confinement terms and attend the schools that they were originally enrolled on a trial bases, in an effort to smooth out the process of their return to school after discharge.

Various efforts have been made to make the process of resocialization easier for them, through close communications with related organizations.

(2) Trends in Juveniles Committed to Juvenile Training Schools

A. Changes in the Number of Juveniles Committed to Juvenile Training Schools

Fig. 56 shows the changes in the number of final dispositions involving juveniles newly committed to Reformatory Schools or Juvenile Training Schools and their ratio to the total number of juveniles processed by juvenile tribunals or family courts (that ratio hereinafter called "the commitment rate").

First we will examine the number of juveniles who were newly committed to Reformatory Schools under the old Juvenile Law. In 1942 when Reformatory Schools were established nationwide, only 607 juveniles were committed. From 1943 to 1945, the number rose steeply due to the introduction of an intensive short-term training program. In 1944, the figure reached 4,144. Then it climbed from 1,862 in 1946 to 6,868 in 1950, due to an increase in the number of homeless juveniles committed to the institutions after the war.

The current Juvenile Law, which raised the age limit to juveniles who were under 20 years of age, was enacted in 1951. In that year, the number of juveniles newly committed to Reformatory Schools and Juvenile Training Schools recorded an all-time high of 11,333. Between 1954 and 1966, it decreased slightly, hovering between 7,000 to more than 8,000. From 1967 the number dropped drastically, recording a postwar low of 1,969 in 1974. From 1975, however, it began to increase, reaching a total of 6,062 in 1984. After that it began to decline again, dropping to 4,831 in 1988.

The commitment rate stood at less than 1 percent before 1942. It is believed that only severe delinquent cases were committed to the institutions at that time. From 1951 to 1955 the rate averaged about 8 percent. After that it decreased considerably, to 1.2 percent in 1974. Then it rose again, standing at more than 2 percent until 1988.

B. Trend in Characteristics of Juveniles Newly Committed to Juvenile Training Schools or Reformatory Schools

There is a scarcity of statistics that reveal the characteristics of juveniles committed to Juvenile Reformatory Schools while the Reformatory School Law was still effective. Based on available statistics, we can assume that more than half of the juveniles were 16 or 17 years of age and that most of them had committed theft. It may also be assumed that a considerable number of juveniles in Juvenile Reformatory Schools had not finished their compulsory education. Much less than half of them had both natural parents, and many of them had been in unhappy circumstances.

After the Juvenile Training School Law was enacted in 1949, sufficient official documents were available to track various statistics. We will examine the characteristics of juveniles committed to Juvenile Training Schools based on these official documents.

Fig. 57 shows separate graphs, by sex, that indicate the percentage of juveniles, by age bracket, who were newly committed to the institutions from 1949 to 1988.

Fig.57 Number of Juveniles Newly Committed to Juvenile Training Schools by Age Group (1949~1988)

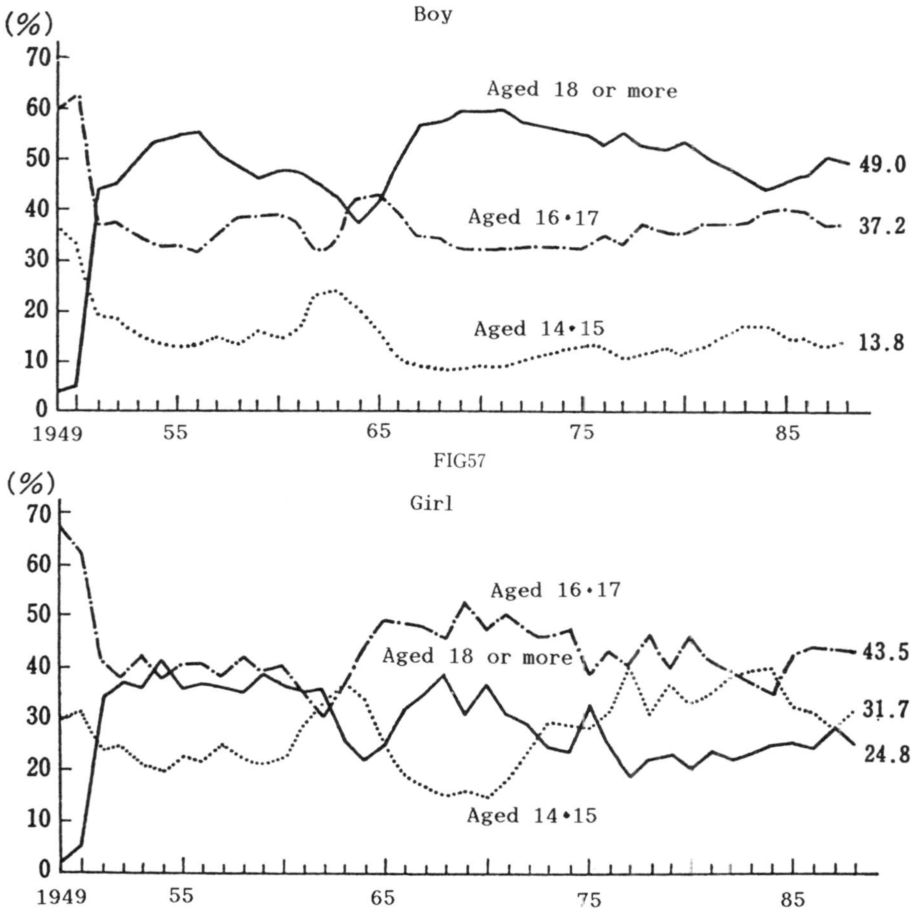

Sources: Annual Report of Statistics on Juvenile Correction, Annual Report of Statistics on Correction, etc.

After 1951, the percentage of boys over 18 years of age, at about 50 percent, was the highest. This was except for the years 1964 and 1965, when the percentage of those between 16 and 17 years of age was higher. After reached 59.3 percent in 1971, it gradually decreased. In 1988, the percentage was 49.0 percent.

The percentage of 16 and 17 year olds was the second highest, at about 30 percent, except in 1964 and 1965, when it exceeded 40 percent.

The percentage of those who were 14 and 15 years old hovered from 10 percent to over 20 percent between 1945 and 1965. After that it dipped to below

Table 84 Percentage of Inmates Newly Admitted to Juvenile Training Schools, by Type of Offence

Offence	1950	1955	1960	1965	1970	1975	1980	1985	1988
Male Total	100.0 (6,142)	100.0 (7,805)	100.0 (8,166)	100.0 (7,140)	100.0 (3,658)	100.0 (2,364)	100.0 (4,201)	100.0 (5,276)	100.0 (4,254)
Homicide	0.2	0.4	0.8	0.8	0.8	0.9	0.2	0.5	0.4
Robbery	3.7	5.0	6.5	6.4	7.0	5.7	4.3	2.3	2.9
Bodily injury	1.7	3.0	6.4	7.5	6.0	5.3	7.5	8.6	9.8
Assault, unlawful assembly with weapons	…	…	…	1.7	1.1	0.9	0.7	0.5	0.4
Extortion	3.1	3.9	13.1	11.8	8.0	8.4	3.8	5.3	4.9
Theft	77.4	64.1	53.2	48.6	52.4	52.1	44.5	48.0	48.0
Fraud	3.1	4.3	1.7	1.3	0.8	0.8	0.4	0.3	0.3
Rape, indecent assault	1.4	3.1	7.2	11.1	12.1	8.5	6.4	4.7	5.3
Arson	0.4	0.5	0.6	0.5	0.7	0.8	0.9	0.7	0.6
House breaking	0.6	0.6	0.4	0.6	0.7	0.7	0.5	0.6	0.9
Professional negligence	…	…	…	0.1	0.9	3.1	4.8	3.3	2.6
Violent acts	…	…	…	1.6	1.1	0.7	2.5	1.3	1.1
Stimulant drugs	…	…	…	0.0	0.1	0.8	6.0	5.9	4.0
Poisonous substances	…	…	…	…	…	…	5.2	3.9	5.4
Road traffic violations	…	…	…	0.2	1.0	2.7	4.9	7.5	7.2
Pre-delinquency	5.2	9.5	5.8	4.8	4.6	5.3	4.7	4.1	3.9
Others	3.2	5.5	4.2	3.1	2.7	3.4	2.8	2.4	2.1
Female Total	100.0 (726)	100.0 (799)	100.0 (826)	100.0 (734)	100.0 (307)	100.0 (185)	100.0 (519)	100.0 (753)	100.0 (577)
Homicide	…	0.5	0.1	0.5	1.3	3.2	0.2	0.8	0.5
Robbery	…	0.4	1.1	1.1	0.3	0.5	1.5	1.3	1.0
Bodily injury	0.1	…	0.7	0.4	0.7	0.5	3.3	6.8	7.6
Theft	64.2	45.2	39.6	34.6	35.8	36.8	19.5	18.1	17.2
Fraud	7.2	7.6	4.6	2.6	2.9	2.2	0.2	0.3	0.2
Stimulant drugs	…	…	…	…	…	2.2	16.4	28.4	21.8
Poisonous substances	…	…	…	…	…	…	4.0	5.6	8.5
Prostitution	…	…	…	10.9	5.9	2.7	1.0	0.7	0.2
Pre-delinquency	16.1	37.3	32.7	44.4	44.6	45.4	46.6	31.5	34.0
Others	12.4	9.0	21.2	5.4	8.5	6.5	7.3	6.6	9.0

Sources: Annual Report of Statistics on Juvenile Correction,
Annual Report of Statistics on Correction, etc.

10 percent in about 1970. From the early 1970s the percentage rose slightly and hovered between 10 percent to more than 20 percent.

The percentage of girls in each age bracket has fluctuated over the years. The percentage of 16- and 17-year-old girls was higher than those in the other two age brackets, except in 1954, 1962, 1963, 1983 and 1984. From 1945 to around 1960, the percentage stood at about 40 percent; after that it fluctuated between 40 percent and 50 percent.

The percentage of 14- and 15-year-old girls varied from 10 percent to more than 20 percent until 1975, except in 1963 when it came close to 40 percent. After that it rose, exceeding 40 percent in 1984. Then it gradually dropped, falling to 31.7 percent in 1988.

The percentage of girls who were over 18 years old remained at more than 30 percent until the early 1970s, except between 1963 and 1965 when it was over 20 percent but below 30 percent. After that it declined, to remain between 20 percent and 29 percent.

Table 84 indicates, in percentages, the types of offences the juveniles were charged with and classified under, by sex, for every fifth year between 1950 and 1988.

For boys, theft topped the list of offences in any given year. In 1950, theft accounted for 77.4 percent. After that, though there were occasional increases, the percentage generally decreased. In 1980 it dipped to below 50 percent and in 1988 dropped to 48 percent. Fraud accounted for 4.3 percent in 1955, decreasing to 0.3 percent in 1988.

Offences for professional negligence and traffic violations increased considerably in 1975, the combined percentage remaining at about 10 percent after 1980. The percentage for violation of the Stimulant Drugs Control Law and Poisonous and Injurious Substances Control Law increased notably, accounting for about 10 percent in and after 1980.

Armed robbery, extortion, rape and indecent assault showed similar tendencies over the years. Their percentages rose in 1960, 1965 and 1970. Armed robbery accounted for 7 percent in 1970, extortion for 13.1 percent in 1960, and rape and indecent attack together for 12.1 percent in 1970, while their percentages were low in 1950 and 1955 and after 1975.

For girls, the percentages for theft and fraud dropped conspicuously, as it did for boys. In 1950, the percentages for theft and fraud were 64.2 percent and 7.2 percent, respectively. In 1988, the percentages were 17.2 percent and 0.2 percent, respectively.

Girls committed to Juvenile Training Schools for violation of the Anti-Prostitution Law accounted for 10.9 percent in 1965, but dropped to 0.2 percent in 1988.

Table 85 Percentage of Inmates Newly Admitted to Juvenile Training Schools, by Previous Disposition, Education Backgrounds and Guardians

Subjects	1950	1955	1960	1965	1970	1975	1980	1985	1988
Male Total	100.0 (6,142)	100.0 (7,805)	100.0 (8,166)	100.0 (7,140)	100.0 (3,658)	100.0 (2,364)	100.0 (4,201)	100.0 (5,276)	100.0 (4,254)
Previous disposition									
Commitment to juvenile training school	17.5	24.8	21.9	21.0	17.6	13.7	17.3	22.0	24.1
Commitment to child education & training home, etc.	…	…	…	11.2	11.8	12.6	6.5	7.8	7.8
Probation	…	…	…	45.8	49.1	50.6	56.8	62.5	63.6
Education backgrounds									
Not finished compulsory education	79.0	37.5	16.4	8.3	2.6	2.5	0.7	0.4	0.0
Attending middle school	5.7	4.8	8.1	10.4	6.6	8.3	8.0	10.4	10.0
Graduated from middle school	12.0	46.8	64.2	66.1	68.2	56.7	51.4	59.0	62.4
Attending or dropped out of high school	3.1	9.9	10.8	14.5	21.0	30.3	36.9	28.1	25.6
Graduated from high school	0.2	0.9	0.6	0.6	1.5	2.1	3.0	2.1	1.5
Guardians									
Real parents	37.2	41.1	48.3	57.2	61.5	58.8	63.7	51.3	48.9
Real father only	15.4	15.4	10.3	14.3	13.3	16.0	11.3	12.3	13.8
Real mother only	18.4	19.9	20.0	21.1	20.3	19.4	15.4	18.6	20.3
Others & unknown	29.1	23.6	21.4	7.4	4.9	5.9	4.6	17.7	16.9
Female Total	100.0 (726)	100.0 (799)	100.0 (826)	100.0 (734)	100.0 (307)	100.0 (185)	100.0 (519)	100.0 (753)	100.0 (577)
Previous disposition									
Commitment to juvenile training school	7.0	12.1	16.9	13.9	11.7	7.6	9.4	15.3	14.2
Commitment to child education & training home, etc.	…	…	…	10.9	4.9	10.3	4.4	6.4	8.0
Probation	…	…	…	27.0	31.9	26.5	31.2	42.9	44.5
Education backgrounds									
Not finished compulsory education	84.7	41.7	21.2	10.4	3.6	0.5	1.0	0.9	0.2
Attending middle school	4.3	9.8	13.0	14.7	9.4	21.6	23.9	24.4	23.2
Graduated from middle school	9.0	41.7	59.6	67.7	69.7	49.2	43.2	55.1	53.6
Attending or dropped out of high school	1.9	6.1	5.8	6.9	16.6	25.9	31.4	18.5	21.3
Graduated from high school	0.1	0.8	0.4	0.3	0.7	2.7	0.6	1.1	0.9
Guardians									
Real parents	32.4	36.8	37.4	52.6	51.5	57.8	62.8	38.2	39.2
Real father only	14.9	11.5	11.4	17.3	17.6	17.3	10.8	13.4	12.3
Real mother only	22.3	18.5	22.2	20.6	19.5	19.5	20.4	25.0	26.5
Others & unknown	30.4	33.2	29.1	9.5	11.4	5.4	6.0	23.4	22.0

Sources : Annual Report of Statistics on Juvenile Correction,
Annual Report of Statistics on Correction, etc.

On the other hand, the percentage of pre-delinquent girls committed to Juvenile Training Schools increased, recording, from 1965, the greatest increase over all other types of crimes. From 1965 to 1980 it exceeded 40 percent, decreasing slightly in 1985. The percentage was 34 percent in 1988.

Other offences that increased over the years included bodily injury and drug-related offences. The percentage of girls committed to Juvenile Training Schools for bodily injury offences was 0.1 percent in 1950. This figure jumped to 7.6 percent in 1988. Those committed for offences of the Stimulant Drugs Control Law and Poisonous and Injurious Substances Control Law increased drastically from 1980. Combined, they exceeded 30 percent in and after 1985.

The percentage of Stimulant Drugs Control Law offences remained the second highest, following that of for predelinquency.

Table 85 shows the previous dispositions of protective rehabilitative measures, educational backgrounds and family composition of juveniles newly committed to Juvenile Training Schools every fifth year from 1950 and 1988. Most of those, both boys and girls, that had been previously recorded had previous histories of having been put on probation. That percentage, in general, increased over the years. In 1988, it was 63.6 percent for boys and 44.5 percent for girls. The percentages of those who had previously been committed to Juvenile Training Schools gradually decreased until 1975 to about 10 percent for boys and less than 10 percent for girls. After that the percentages increased, reaching 24.1 percent for boys and 14.2 percent for girls in 1988.

Regarding their educational backgrounds, in 1950, 79.0 percent of the boys and 84.7 percent of the girls had not completed their compulsory education. After that the percentages decreased dramatically, to 0.0 percent for boys and 0.2 percent for girls in 1988.

The percentage of those who had graduated from middle schools increased, as opposed to those who had not completed their compulsory education. In 1970, 68.2 percent of the boys and 69.7 percent of the girls had graduated from middle schools, reaching the highest percentages for this category, respectively. Decreasing after 1975, the percentages rebounded to 62.4 percent for boys and 53.6 percent for girls in 1988.

The percentages of those who attended, dropped out of or graduated from high schools or institutions of higher learning rose over the years for both boys and girls. In 1980, the combined percentages were 39.9 percent for boys and 32.0 percent for girls. After that the percentages decreased to 27.1 percent for boys and 22.2 percent for girls in 1988. Considering the fact that more than 90 percent of all students in Japan went on to high school in and after 1974, the educational backgrounds of juveniles committed to Juvenile Training Schools were much lower.

Regarding parents and guardians, the percentages of both boys and girls who had both real parents increased over the years. In 1980 it was 68.7 percent for boys and 62.8 percent for girls. After that it decreased to 48.9 percent for boys and 39.2 percent for girls in 1988. Meanwhile, 29.1 percent of the boys and 30.4 percent of the girls in 1950 had guardians who were not their real parents or were unknown. The percentages decreased to 4.6 percent for boys in 1980 and 5.4 percent for girls in 1975. Then they increased to 16.9 percent for boys and 22.0 percent for girls in 1988, indicating that many juveniles had unusual family situations.

5. *JUVENILE PRISONS*

(1) Changes in the Treatment of Juvenile Inmates

A. The Establishment of Juvenile Prisons

From the Meiji period, juveniles who committed crimes were treated differently from adults. The Prison Rules enacted in 1881 said that juvenile offenders of over 8 years old but under 20 years old should be committed to the place of discipline and cure separate from the prison quarters designated for adult offenders, according to the circumstances of their crimes.

In 1902, the Kawagoe branch of Urawa Prison was designated as a correction facility for those convicted juvenile offenders under 16 years of age or those who were found to be in need of discipline and cure. After that, similar facilities for underage inmates were established.

The Prison Law enacted in 1908 said that "those under 18 years of age who are sentenced to imprisonment with labour for more than two months should be committed to juvenile prison or specified areas at a prison that is separate from other areas."

When the old Juvenile Law was enacted in 1922, the locations and names of specifically established prisons for juveniles were made public. Juvenile prisons were established in seven places, including Odawara and Kawagoe. Later, new juvenile prisons were added and some were abolished. As of the end of 1988, there were nine juvenile prisons located in Kawagoe, Mito, Matsumoto, Himeji, Nara, Iwakuni, Saga, Morioka and Hakodate.

Under the old Juvenile Law, juveniles were able to remain in juvenile prisons after they turned 18 years old and until they reached 23 years old.

B. Prewar Education

Those who were imprisoned with labour had to work during their prison terms. Article 24 of the Prison Law said that "imposition of prison labour to those under 18 years of age shall be made by taking into consideration the need, among other things, for helping expand their cultural level." And Article 30 of the law stipulated that juvenile convicts under 18 years of age should be reeducated. Juvenile convicts, therefore, were given special consideration because it was felt they were educable. They were required to take educational classes, aside from engaging in prison industries, that focused on correcting and improving their characters.

Until the beginning of the Showa era, there was no uniform eudcation program at juvenile prisons. The contents of education courses were decided individually by each institution. They used textbooks designated by the state and mainly taught a curriculum to fulfill compulsory education requirements. Classes were geared to the academic abilities of the attendees, and vocational training was also provided for. In 1929, the need for uniform education led to the compilation of Japanese language and mathematics textbooks for juvenile inmates across the nation.

A Circular for Juvenile Inmates Education was issued in 1933, and academic education at juvenile prisons was standardized. According to the circular, the curriculum would be divided into two programs-general and vocational-for juvenile inmates. In the two-year general academic program, juveniles were divided into six grades, approximating those of primary school. A one-year vocational program to teach agricultural and industrial skills was provided for those who had graduated from primary school programs or who had equivalent educational backgrounds. The two programs also placed importance on physical and military training to increase the physical strength of the inmates, as well as programs that would be of practical use in their actual lives. Inmates in the general program studied 18 hours a week and those in the vocational program 12 hours a week.

When wartime efforts strengthened in 1941, a Circular to Juvenile Prisons for Physical Drills for Inmates was adopted and the Circular for Juvenile Inmates Education was totally revised. The former step was taken to deal with an increasing number of juvenile inmates who had finished their compulsory school education and to give education equivalent to what was taught at the youths' schools.

The latter was designed to provide those who had not finished their compulsory school education with general academic education as was taught at primary schools.

The former circular was designed to train inmates both physically and mentally, as well as to cultivate their moral characters, therefore training the juvenile inmates to be ideal "Japanese subjects." Youth drill centers, which had the equivalent status of the youths' schools, were established in juvenile prisons for the purpose. Furthermore, as the war situation worsened, juvenile inmates were organized into "Service Teams for Shipbuilding," mobilized to help build ships as part of the effort to support military production.

C. Development of Education in Juvenile Prisons after the War

In 1949, shortly after the war, the current Juvenile Law was enacted, raising the upper age limit to under 20 years of age. The law allowed juvenile inmates to stay in juvenile prisons from when they were 20 years old until they were 26 years old.

Education until now for juvenile inmates after the war differs from prewar education in areas, including those of academic education, vocational training and guidance for living. The prisons provide juvenile inmates who have not completed their compulsory education with an academic education, gives supplementary lessons to those with low academic ratings and provides correspondent courses for those who wish to receive a high school education through taking such courses.

A branch school of a local public middle school was established on Matsumoto Juvenile Prison premises in 1955 to provide qualified inmates, selected on nationwide basis, with a compulsory education. From 1975, qualified juvenile and young adult inmates at Nara Juvenile Prison were allowed to take correspondence courses of local high schools, and from 1976 Matsumoto and Morioka Juvenile prisons adopted the program, which aimed at upgrading the inmates' academic education.

After General Instruction for Vocational Training of Prisoners was issued in 1926, vocational training centering on carpentry and woodcraft was provided to adult inmates. From 1930, similar vocational training was provided to juvenile inmates, but this training was not the major part of juvenile treatment.

From the early 1950s, training in barber and car mechanic skills and other occupations was actively adopted focusing on juvenile prisons. Since then facilities for vocational training have gradually improved and the number of vocational training courses have increased. In 1956 Rules for Vocational Training of Prisoners was promulgated, making the status of vocational training in prisons clearer and helping prisons conduct more effective, organized and systematic training.

Vocational training was initially provided for prisoners under 40 years of age. But after 1980, it was extended to high middle-aged and older prisoners and special consideration was given to those under 26 years of age with the purpose of providing young adult and juvenile prisoners with more opportunities for vocational training.

As for vocational training in juvenile prisons, as of December 31, 1988, four juvenile prisons-Kawagoe, Nara, Saga and Hakodate-were authorized by the Minister of Labour as "general vocational training institutes," where intensive vocational training is provided for those qualified trainees who are recruited on a nationwide basis. Trainees who have completed vocational training programs in these juvenile prisons are given certificates issued by the Director General of the Human Resources Development Bureau of the Labour Ministry. Training in welding, machinery operation, sheet metal processing, carpentry, plastering and a variety of other skills are being provided at these prisons. Other juvenile prisons also provide a variety of vocational training, such as operating construction machinery and boilers, auto driving, etc.

Although living guidance was provided at juvenile prisons before World War II, it was adopted more enthusiastically at these institutions after the war, with the aim of cultivating healthy, sound minds and bodies, and independent law-abiding spirits in addition to teaching knowledge and attitudes necessary for living a healthy and sound life in society. Living guidance is conducted in the daily routine through counseling, lectures, gatherings and burden sharing as well as in leisure, physical, cultural and other activities.

According to the Rules for Classification of Prisoners, juvenile prisoners fall into J-class. They are further divided into A-class and B-class. A-class is for those who do not have advanced criminal tendencies and B-class is for those who have advanced criminal tendencies. Young adult prisoners under 26 years of age fall into Y-class and then are divided into A-class and B-class. Since it became difficult for juvenile prisons to provide group education for only J-class inmates due to a drop in the number of juvenile prisoners, as a matter of practice J-class juveniles and Y-class young adults are grouped together in juvenile prisons with the view of providing effective correctional education.

As of December 31, 1988, five juvenile prisons (Kawagoe, Nara, Iwakuni, Saga and Hakodate) confined JA- and YA-class inmates and three juvenile prisons (Matsumoto, Himeji and Morioka) accommodated JB- and YB-class convicts. Only one prison in Mito accommodated YB-class convicts.

(2) Trends in Juvenile Convicts Admmitted to Juvenile Prisons

Fig. 58 shows the number of juveniles newly admitted to juvenile prisons each year in the Showa period and in addition the ratio of those under 18 years of age in the total number of juveniles admitted to juvenile prisons from 1951 on. (From 1926 to 1950, the number included only those under 18 years of age when they were newly admitted to juvenile prisons. From 1951 to 1975 the number included only those under 20 years of age when they were newly admitted to juvenile prisons. After 1976 the figure included those under 20 years of age when they were given prison sentences.)

From 1926 to 1941, the number of newly admitted juvenile prisoners fluctuated between 500 and 700. From 1942, however, the number jumped and recorded a postwar high in 1946 at 4,104. Until 1948 the figure remained over

Fig.58 Number of New Juvenile Prisoners and Percentage of Prisoners under 18 Years of Age (1926~1988)

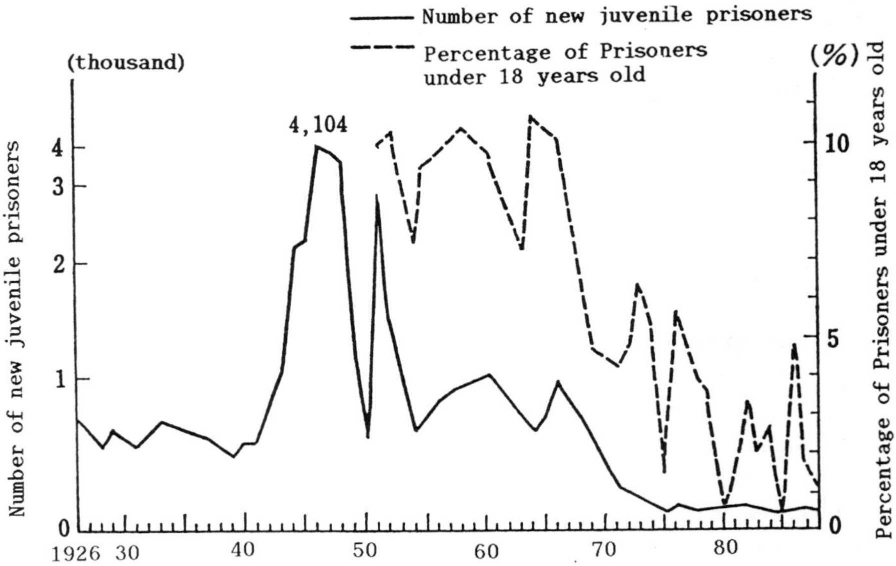

Sources: Annual Report of Statistics on Prison Administration and Annual Report of Statistics on Correction

3,000. After that, the figure decreased considerably and was 622 in 1950. In 1951 the number of newly admitted juvenile prisoners increased to more than 3,000 largely because a law revision raised the age limit of juveniles covered by the Juvenile Law to under 20 years of age. After that it decreased and stayed between 600 and 1,000 from 1954 into the late 1960s. Then the figure further declined to around 100 and was 99 in 1988.

Meanwhile, the ratio of those under 18 years of age in the total number of juveniles admitted to juvenile prisons stayed at about 10 percent between 1951 and the late 1960s. Then the ratio decreased and stayed at about 5 percent until around 1975. Then it dipped below the 5 percent mark with some exceptions, indicating that the ratio of convicts under 18 years of age was on the decline.

Fig. 59 shows the ratio by type of offences committed by juveniles who were newly admitted to juvenile prisons each year in the Showa period. It shows that theft accounted for over 70 percent between 1926 and 1948 except 1944 and 1947. After that its ratio decreased and stayed at around 10 percent to 20 percent from the early 1970s. Its ratio was 20.2 percent in 1988.

Professional negligence accounted for 0.8 percent of the total in 1960. But its ratio gradually increased and had been the highest among other types of

Fig.59 Percentage of New Juvenile Prisoners, by Major Crime (1926~1988)

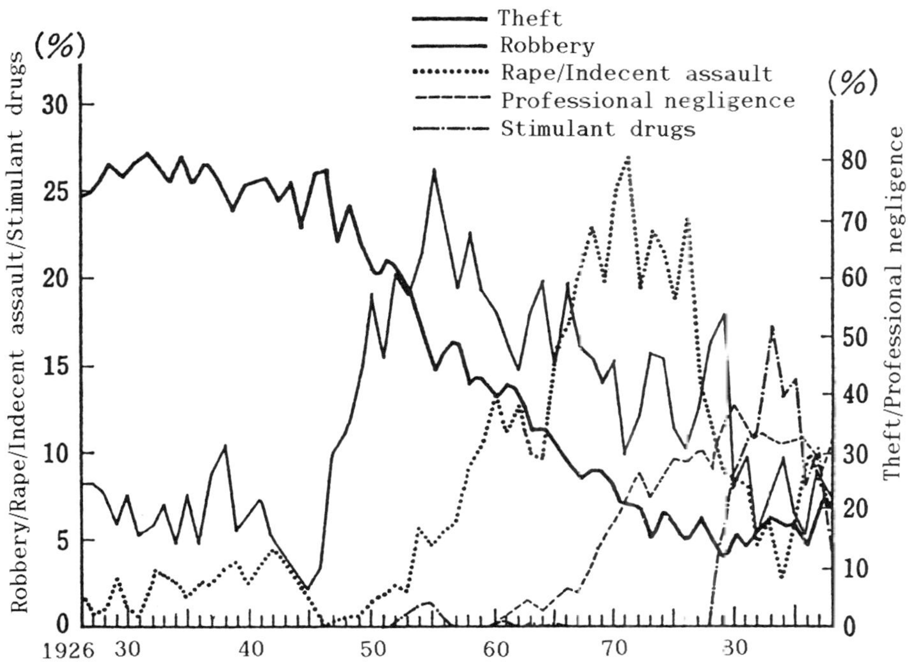

Sources: Annual Report of Statistics on Prison Administration and Annual Report of Statistics on Correction

crime at around 30 percent after the early 1970s. In 1988 the ratio was 34.3 percent.

Stimulant Drugs Control Law violations accounted for 4.8 percnet in 1979. Its ratio increased after that and stayed at over 10 percent from 1981. It was, however, decreased to 4.0 percent in 1988.

Robbery accounted for less than 10 percent between 1926 and 1947 except 1938. From 1948 to 1979, the ratio stayed at between 10 percent and slightly over 20 percent. Especially from 1952 to 1958, its ratio stayed at over 20 percent. But from 1980 the ratio was on the decline once again and dipped below the 10 percent mark. In 1988 the ratio was 7.1 percent.

Rape and indecent assaults accounted for less than 10 percent between 1926 and 1958 and for more than 10 percent until 1978. They account for more than 20 percent between 1967 and 1976 in general. From 1979, the ratio was on the decline and dipped below the 10-percent mark. It was 6.1 percent in 1988.

Table 86 Rate of Newly Admitted Juvenile Prisoners, by Term of the Sentence

Year	Total	Life & Over 10 years	10 years or less	5 years or less	3 years or less	2 years or less	1 year or less	6 months or less
1926	100.0(714)	0.3	8.8	35.9	44.9	7.6	1.7	0.8
1930	100.0(616)	0.5	4.7	24.2	60.2	10.1	0.3	—
1935	100.0(654)	0.9	4.7	18.3	65.0	9.8	0.8	0.5
1940	100.0(567)	0.2	2.8	14.5	70.2	9.5	2.3	0.5
1945	100.0(2,259)	0.1	2.9	19.7	52.6	17.0	6.9	0.8
1950	100.0(622)	1.0	9.5	14.6	29.7	22.3	19.1	3.7
1955	100.0(747)	2.3	16.1	24.2	29.5	19.1	6.8	2.0
1960	100.0(024)	1.0	14.2	24.0	25.3	30.4	3.9	1.3
1965	100.0(738)	1.8	17.6	22.5	19.8	29.4	7.3	1.6
1970	100.0(338)	0.3	13.6	27.2	17.8	23.1	15.7	2.4
1975	100.0(134)	0.7	11.9	21.6	12.7	31.3	18.7	3.0
1980	100.0(141)	—	3.5	16.3	13.5	41.8	22.7	2.1
1985	100.0(129)	0.8	9.3	8.5	10.9	45.0	22.5	3.1
1988	100.0(99)	2.0	12.1	4.0	16.2	55.6	9.1	1.0

Sources: Annual Report of Statistics on Prison Administration and Annual Report of Statistics on Correction

Table 86 shows the ratio of newly admitted juvenile prisoners by term of imprisonment in every fifth year from 1926 to 1988. They were classified into seven categories according to their prison terms. In case of indeterminate sentences, the maximum term was used for calculating percentages.

Those who were sentenced to relatively short prison terms-in the categories of over six months but under one year and over one year but under two years-were on the rise since 1926 with some fluctuations. Juveniles in the two categories combined accounted for 9.3 percent in 1926; over 10 percent from 1930; over 20 percent after 1945; over 50 percent from 1975 and 64.7 percent in 1988.

On the other hand, those sentenced to comparatively long prison terms-in the categories of over two years but under three years and over three years but under five years-were on the decline. From 1926 to 1940, those in the two categories combined accounted for over 80 percent, but after that it turned

Table 87 Rate of Newly Admitted Juvenile Prisoners, by Type of Previous Protective Disposition

Year	Total	Commitment to juvenile training school	Commitment to child education and training home, etc.	Probation	No record
1966	100.0 (1,045)	48.5 (507)	1.8 (19)	6.3 (66)	43.3 (453)
1970	100.0 (403)	38.0 (153)	1.2 (5)	8 2 (33)	52.6 (212)
1975	100.0 (173)	21.4 (37)	2.9 (5)	5.2 (9)	70.5 (122)
1980	100.0 (141)	27.7 (39)	1.4 (2)	5.7 (8)	65.2 (92)
1985	100.0 (129)	42.6 (55)	1.6 (2)	11.6 (15)	44.2 (57)
1988	100.0 (99)	47.5 (47)	—	9.1 (9)	43.4 (43)

Source: Annual Report of Statistics on Correction

downward. From 1950 to 1970 except 1955, they accounted for over 40 percent. After that their percentage dropped and was 20.2 percent in 1988.

Table 87 shows the ratio of newly admitted juvenile prisoners, who had previously received protective rehabilitative measures, by the type of protective rehabilitative measures in 1966, 1970, 1975, 1980, 1985 and 1988. In any given year, most juvenile prisoners either had previously been sent to juvenile training schools or had received no protective rehabilitative measures. Those who had been sent to juvenile training schools accounted for 48.5 percent in 1966 and after that the figure decreased and was 21.4 percent in 1975. Then it turned upward and was 47.5 percent in 1988. Those who had received no protective rehabilitative measures accounted for 43.3 percent in 1966. After that their percentage increased and was 70.5 percent in 1975. Then it turned downward and was 43.4 percent in 1988.

Although a Table has not been prepared, we will further look into the other characteristics of juvenile prisoners. Those who had graduated from middle schools only or had not finished middle school compulsory education accounted for 84.8 percent in 1966 and 57.6 percent in 1988, indicating gradual decreases. Those who were attending, had dropped out of or graduated from high schools accounted for 15.2 percent in 1966 and 42.4 percent in 1988, indicating increases in the number of juvenile prisoners who had studied at higher schools. Juvenile prisoners who were members of "Boryokudan" gangs accounted for over 10 percent from 1966, exceeded the 20 percent mark in around 1980 and was 23.2 percent in 1988.

6. REHABILITATION OF JUVENILE DELINQUENTS

In the early Showa era "probationary supervision by juvenile prbation officers" were carried out as a non-institutinal treatment of juvenile delinquents (under 18 years of age).

Those who were put under such probationary supervison included: 1) those juveniles put under such supervison by juvenile tribunals; 2) those juveniles conditionally released from reformatory schools; 3) those juveniles conditionally released from prisons while they were still under 18 years of age; and 4) those juveniles who were sentenced to suspensions of execution of prison sentences. The probationary supervision for those released from reformatory schools was based on the Reformatory School Law and others on the old Juvenile Law.

After the new Juvenile Law and Offenders Prevention and Rehabilitation Law were enacted in 1949, introducing a new probation system, however, the four categories for probation remained with some changes. Under the new laws, not only juveniles but also adults conditionally released from prisons are subject to supervision by probation officers. After a revision in the Penal Code in 1953, a sentencing judge has now the power to put on probation not only those juveniles under 18 years of age but also over 18 years and adults, who have been sentenced to prison terms with a stay of execution.

Since we already touched on the changes in the probation system and development in policies of Justice Ministry's Rehabilitation Bureau regarding probation treatment in Chapter III-3, we will touch mainly on the situation involving probation of juvenile.

(1) Juveniles Put on Probation

As we stated before, provisions for protective, rehabilitative treatment under the old Juvenile Law gradually expanded to cover juveniles nationwide in 1942.

If we examine the trend of juveniles under 18 years of age who were put on probationary supervision by juvenile probation officers by the decision of juvenile tribunals over the years based on Table 14 in the Appendix, about 1,000 to over 1,200 juveniles were put on probation between 1926 and 1936. From 1937 their number was on the rise, exceeding the 3,000 mark in 1942 and reaching over 6,000 in 1944. In 1945 when the war ended, the number halved but after

Table 88 Number of Juvenile Probationers under Short-Term Supervision for Violation of Road Traffic Law (1977～1988)

Year	Reception	Expiry	
			Early discharge
1977	12,471	6,143	6,101
1978	23,963	21,868	21,696
1979	28,472	27,403	27,153
1980	30,638	29,367	29,041
1981	33,083	32,369	31,991
1982	35,642	33,689	33,328
1983	41,772	40,182	39,710
1984	42,924	42,533	41,535
1985	44,361	43,228	42,799
1986	45,499	45,311	44,855
1987	45,565	47,230	46,841
1988	44,099	43,351	43,149

Source: Annual Report of Statistics on Rehabilitation

that it increased and reached the highest figure under the old Juvenile Law in 1948 with 8,469.

Fig. 37 and Table 10 in the Appendix show the number of juveniles put on probation each year after the current Juvenile Law was enacted in 1949 (the figure shows those under 18 years of age in 1949 and 1950 and those under 20 years of age after 1951). After their number registered 23,612 in 1951, it was on the decline for a while. But it surged upward and reached a second peak in 1966 with 30,647. After that it declined again and was 19,942 in 1974. The number rapidly increased from 1977, exceeded the 50,000 mark in 1979 and surpassed the 70,000 mark in 1983. It was 68,367 in 1988.

Rapid increases in the total number of juveniles put on probation were largely due to increases in the number of those put on traffic short-term probationary supervision which was introduced in 1977 and centers on group treatment. The number of juveniles put on traffic short-term probationary supervision each year is indicated in Table 88. It shows that their number stayed at over 40,000 from 1983. If we subtract those put on traffic short-term probationary supervision from the total number, the figure was 28,613 in 1983

Fig.60 Number of Juvenile Probationers, by Reason of Termination (1949~1988)

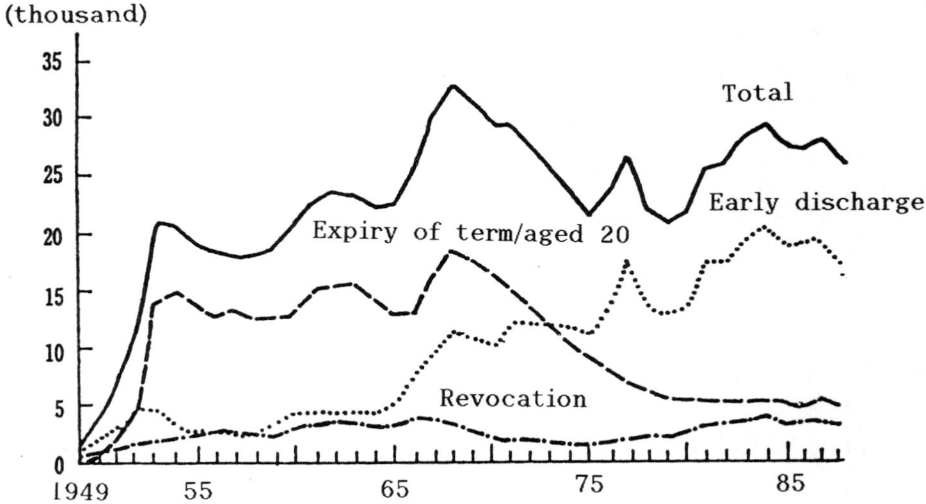

Source: Annual Report of Statistics on Rehabilitation

and then decreased to 24,268 in 1988.

Fig. 60 shows the trend in the number of juvenile probationers who terminated their probation term, after being classified by the grounds for termination.

The revocation of probation on the grounds of committing a new offence registered the highest in 1966 at 3,947 (15.7 percent of all those who terminated probation terms in that year). Since then their number decreased and bottomed out in 1974 at 1,360. After that it was on the rise and exceeded the 3,000 mark in the early 1980s. It was 3,377 in 1988, accounting for 13.0 percent of the total number.

The number of those whose termination of probation granted by the decision to terminate earlier on the grounds of outstanding performance on the part of the probationers has exceeded since 1973 the termination on the grounds of expiration of probation periods. It indicated that the probation of juveniles had been carried out more effectively and that there have been more juveniles whose probation was terminated early due to increase in the number of traffic short-term probationary supevisions. In 1988, the number of juveniles who were released from probation because of their good behavior was 17,992, accounting for 69.2 percent of the total number of juveniles who finished their probation periods that year. Those who finished their probation periods because their probation periods expired was 4,515, accounting for 17.4 percent of the total.

Fig.61 Number of Average Daily Inmates of Training School, Juvenile Parolees and Rate of Parole (1926~1988)

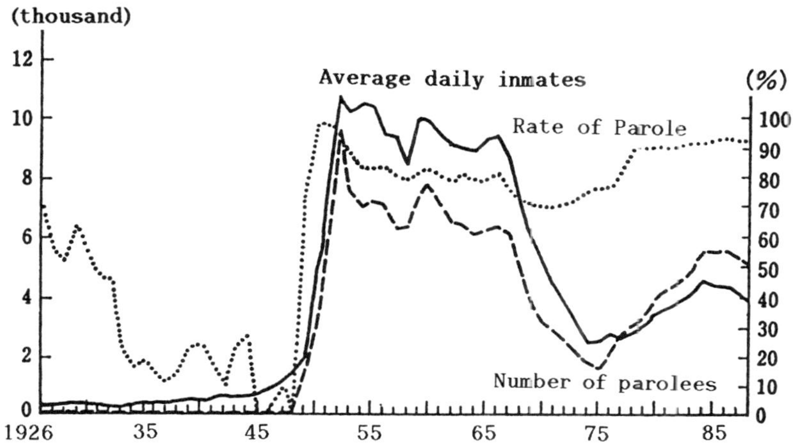

Sources: Annual Report of Statistics on Juvenile Correction, Annual Statistics on Correction, etc.

(2) Juvenile Training School Parolees

Under the Reformatory School Law, the head of a Reformatory School was able to provisionally release juveniles (grant a release on parole) with permission from a Juvenile Tribunal when the juveniles spent more than six months in the School after being committed there by the Tribunal. He was also able to release irrevocably juveniles (absolute release) with permission from Juvenile Tribunals if he determined that the purposes of the custody of the juvenile had been fulfilled.

Fig. 61 shows the trend in the ratio of juveniles released on parole in the total number of juveniles released on parole and given absolute release in the Showa era. Their ratio under the Reformatory School Law fluctuated between 50 percent and 70 percent from 1926 to 1930, around the 40 percent mark in 1931 and 1932, and stayed at between 10 percent and 27 percent from 1933 to 1944. When the war ended in 1945, 131 were irrevocably released because their performances were satisfactory and nobody was released on parole. As we stated above, juveniles released from the school because of their satisfactory performance outnumbered those provisionally released on parole from the schools from 1931.

After the Offenders Prevention and Rehabilitation Law was enacted in 1949, the District Juvenile Offenders Rehabilitation Board, the predecessor of the Regional Offenders Rehabilitation Board, was established as a parole board, and the probation system was improved. In addition, the management

Fig.62 Number of Juvenile Training School Parolees, by Reason of Termination (1949~1988)

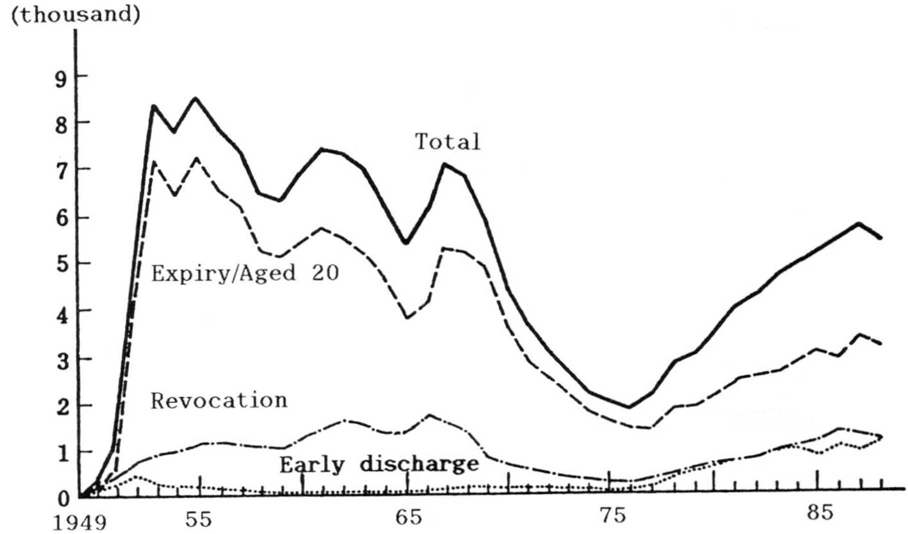

Source: Annual Report of Statistics on Rehabilitation

of juvenile training schools was carried out from that year based on the current Juvenile Law. Those laws made it a principle to release juveniles on parole. After those laws were enacted, the ratio of release on parole stayed at over 80 percent between 1950 and 1966 and over 70 percent between 1967 and 1976. When short-term treatment programs were introduced at juvenile training schools in 1977, the ratio was 84.0 percent. After 1978, the ratio constantly exceeded the 90 percent mark from 1978.

Fig. 62 and Table 31 in the Appendix show changes in the grounds on which juvenile training school parolees finished their probationary supervision period from 1949.

According to the Figure, the number of those parolees whose probationary supervision was terminated because their probationary supervision periods expired and those who reached the age limit was highest in any given year from 1949. The number fluctuated as did the total number of juvenile parolees who finished their probationary supervision periods. The number of parolees who were granted absolute release from schools while under probationary supervision because of their good performance was on the rise from 1977. This reflects the fact that the Reginal Offenders Rehabilitation Board (Parole Board) has the policy to give early grants of absolute release to those parolees who have been released on parole from the short-term treatment programs in the juvenile

Table 89 Number of Juvenile Probationers and Parolees Supervised by Juvenile Probation Officers(1928~1947)

Year	1928	29	30	31	32	33	34	35	36	37	38	39
Parolees	6	4	–	3	2	3	3	–	–	1	–	3
Probationers	38	32	29	35	46	51	92	73	62	66	62	61

Year	40	41	42	43	44	45	46	47
Parolees	6	5	5	7	7	95	624	1,065
Probationers	76	107	133	160	154	169	298	448

Sources: Synopses of Justice Ministry and Attorney General Agency

Table 90 Number of Juvenile Probationers and Parolees (1960~1988)

Year	1960	61	62	63	64	65	66	67	68	69	70	71	72	73	74
Parolees	101	120	90	98	83	75	94	98	98	83	52	41	36	44	33
Probationers	429	449	456	379	338	421	466	469	402	312	284	235	191	162	156

Year	75	76	77	78	79	80	81	82	83	84	85	86	87	88
Parolees	34	18	17	22	20	18	14	19	24	17	15	15	14	12
Probationers	110	124	105	126	107	146	130	180	149	150	142	120	124	127

Source: Annual Report of Statistics on Rehabilitation

training schools. The ratio of absolute release in the total number of parolees whose probationary supervision was terminated was constantly over 16 percent after 1978. The ratio registered its highest in 1983 with 21.2 percent and dropped to 18.6 percent in 1988. The ratio of those who were put back into juvenile training schools or had their probation cancelled because of bad performance increased gradually from 1953 when it registered 10.8 percent of the total. Their ratio peaked in 1966 at 28.3 percent, turned downward to record 13.0 percent in 1974, and increased to 22 percent in 1988.

(3) Juvenile Prison Parolees

Since the Meiji Era, parolees were subjected to surveillance of police stations. However, since 1923 under the old Juvenile Law, juvenile parolees were placed under the supervision of juvenile probation officers in place of police surveillance.

Parole was approved by the Justice Minister (after February, 1948, by the Attorney-General) based on the applications of the prison warden. The applications were generally submitted after the Standing Committee of Prison Officers made a thorough examination of each case.

In addition, in case of juveniles, the examination for parole proposals was made once every month at a Council composed of judge, public prosecutor and juvenile prison wardens since July 1931. However, this Council was abolished in June, 1944, in order to simplify the parole recommendation processing system. Since then, parole applications were examined at a Standing Committee of prison officers.

The Offenders Prevention and Rehabilitation Law was enacted in 1949 and the authority to approve or to reject parole applications was shifted to the District Juvenile Rehabilitation Board (presently District Offenders Rehabilitation Board) from the Attorney General. At the same time, parolees, both adults and juveniles, were placed under the supervision of probation officers.

Table 89 shows the number of juvenile parolees (under 18 years of age) who were placed under the supervision of juvenile probation officers between 1928 and 1947 in accordance with the old Juvenile Law.

Between 1928 and 1944, the total number remained in a single digit, fluctuating between zero and seven. However, it went up to 95 in 1945 and jumped to 624 in 1946 and soared to 1,065 in 1947.

After the Offenders Prevention and Rehabilation Law was implemented, no statistics are available on the number of juvenile parolees who were put under the supervision of probation offices between 1949 and 1959.

Table 90 shows the changes in the number of juvenile parolees (under 20 years of age) between 1960 and 1988. The number of juvenile parolees totaled 101 persons in 1960, (accounting for 0.3 percent of the total number of parolees); 75 in 1965 (0.4 percent); 34 in 1975 (0.2 percent); 15 in 1985 (0.1 percent) and 12 (0.1 percent) in 1988.

(4) Juvenile Offenders under the Suspended Execution of Sentence with Probationary Supervision

Juvenile offenders (under 18 years of age) suspended from execution of sentence were subjected to the supervision of juvenile probation officers under the old Juvenile Law. Under the Offenders Prevention and Rehabilation Law enacted in 1949, they also became the subject of probationary supervision.

Table 89 shows the number of juvenile offenders (under 18 years of age) who were subjected to the supervision of juvenile probation officers under the old Juvenile Law after they were suspended from execution of sentence between 1928 and 1947.

Before 1940, it dipped to a record low in 1930 at 29 and hit a peak in 1934 at 92. But it topped the 100 mark in 1941 and increased sharply to 298 in 1946 and 448 in 1947.

Next, we will examine the trends in the number of juvenile offenders who were suspended from execution of sentence with probationary supervision between 1949, the year when the Offenders Prevention and Rehabilitation Law was implemented, and 1988.

Between 1949 and 1952, only the juvenile offenders under 18 years of age were subjected to probationary supervision after they were suspended from execution of sentence. In 1949, it totaled 1,257 but declined to 173 in 1952 (refer to Table 10 in the Appendix).

In line with the partial amendment of the Penal Code in December, 1953, adult offenders who were suspended from execution of sentence could also be placed on probationary supervision. Accordingly, statistics on the specific number of juveniles among the total number of those who were suspended from execution of sentence with probationary supervision became unavailable between 1953 and 1959.

Table 90 shows the number of juvenile offenders (under 20 years of age) who were suspended from the execution of sentence with probationary supervision between 1960 and 1988. It marked 429 in 1960 (accounting for 5.0 percent of the total number of offenders who were suspended from prosecution with probationary supervision); 421 (5.0 percent) in 1965; 110 (1.5 percent) in 1975; 142 (2.0 percent) in 1985 and 127 (2.1 percent) in 1988. After 1972, it has been fluctuating between 100 and 200.

Chapter V. CONCLUSION

Section 1. Characteristic Features of the Showa Era

The 60-plus years of the Showa era (1926-1989) were filled with events and upheavals unprecedented in the nation's history. Parliamentary government declined early in the era, pushing the nation along the path toward a totalitarian state, eventually leading to the Manchurian Incident, the war with China and finally into World War II.

In the decades after World War II, Japan, as a peace-loving, democratic nation, transformed itself into an economic superpower and won an international status commensurate with its economic muscle, thanks to the strenuous efforts of its hardworking citizens.

The country's economy in the early Showa era was based chiefly on such primary industries as agriculture and fisheries or small and medium-sized secondary industries such as spinning and textiles, which were then followed by the emergence of heavy and chemical industries, boosting the war machine.

Rising from the ashes of devastation after the war, the country succeeded in promoting such heavy industries as steel, shipbuilding and power generation, then in fostering such industries as automobiles, home electric appliances and petrochemicals. In recent years, the nation's economy has been transformed into industries based on advanced technology, including computers and electronics, and other information-intensive businesses.

As a result of such developments, the per capita gross national product (GNP), which came to only about $120 (a mere 15 percent of the United States) in the early Showa era, grew to $19,664 in 1987, surpassing the U.S. figure of $18,570, while the GNP for the nation as a whole has become the second largest among the Western democracies, next only to the United States.

Meanwhile, the average life expectancy for both sexes, which hovered around 45 years in the early Showa era, rose above 50 years in 1947, then grew to 75.5 years for men and 81.3 years for women in 1988, making the Japanese the world's leaders in longevity.

As noted earlier, the Showa era saw the nation swing from one extreme to another, swayed by war and peace, totalitarianism and democracy, poverty and affluence. How can this era be characterized in terms of crime patterns or the treatment of offenders in such treacherous times?

Section 2. Crime Trends

1. PENAL CODE OFFENCES

(1) Trends in the Number of Penal Code Offences

The number of Penal Code offences reported to the police, excluding professional negligence offences (hereafter cited as "professional negligence"), totaled about 710,000 in 1926, then peaked off in 1934 at about 1,550,000. The number reached a record low during World War II, but rose gradually after the war to around 1,600,000 in 1948. The figure remained almost the same or declined somewhat in the following years.

After registering a postwar low of 1,190,000 in 1973, it jumped upward since the mid-1970s, hitting the Showa era's record high of about 1,640,000 offences in 1988.

The high figure in 1934 was due to a rapid rise in offences in all categories, including crimes related to property, primarily due to economic hardships and social unrest in and around that year. The rise in 1948, on the other hand, was due to a sharp increase in such offences as robbery, larceny and fraud, chiefly due to social upheaval and economic chaos shortly after the war.

The high figure in 1988 stemmed from an increase in relatively light cases of thefts or embezzlement (i.e., misappropriation) of lost or unattended properties, due to the increasing opportunities to commit offences, being related to the rapid spread of supermarkets as well as the number of bicycles parked carelessly on the streets.

While the number of Penal Code offences, excluding professional negligence, has been rising throughout the era, the nation's population increased from 60.74 million in 1926 to 122.78 million in 1988.

If the reported Penal Code offences, excluding professional negligence, are viewed against a ratio of one per 100,000 people, the ratios come to 1,171 in 1926, 1,422 in 1929, 2,282 in 1933 (a prewar high), then down to 984 in 1945 (a record low).

After the war, it registered a postwar high of 2,000 per 100,000 people in 1948 and a record low of 1,091 in 1973. The ratio for 1988 came to 1,337, showing no major changes from the early Showa years.

The percentage of juvenile and child offenders among the total number of offenders cleared by the police was approximately 16 percent in 1941, but rose to about 49 percent in 1988.

While the number of adult offenders cleared by the police kept declining steadily since 1956, the corresponding figure for juvenile and child offenders kept climbing until 1983, with only some yearly fluctuations. After turning downward in the following years, the number rebounded in 1987 and 1988.

Although no records are available on the percentage of female offenders involved in non-traffic Penal Code offences cleared by the police in the prewar years, a marked increase was registered after the war, starting from some 10 percent of the nation's total offenders in 1945 to about 21 percent in 1988.

Hitherto, the trends in reported offences have been taken up. In addition, the number of those who were adjudicated and convicted (mostly drawing prison sentences) on charges of Penal Code offences, other than professional negligence, through formal proceedings at courts of the first instance shall be analysed here, in order to see a changing crime picture of the Showa era from the angle of seriousness of crimes: which periods of the era saw more of serious crimes than others.

The number of those convicted as such reached a prewar low of 84,000 in 1928, and a prewar high of about 123,000 in 1943. The corresponding figures for the postwar years were a high of 228,000 in 1948 and a low of about 62,000 in 1987.

While there were no great differences in the prewar and postwar highs of the number of Penal Code offenders cleared by the police, the postwar high of the number of those convicted was much higher than that in the prewar years, reflecting the serious crime situation shortly after World War II.

The number of those convicted continued its downturn since 1949 to register the Showa era's record low in 1987. It has now become clear that the high incidence of non-traffic Penal Code offences reported in recent years stemmed from offences committed by juveniles and children, as well as such relatively light offences as those not warranting indictment. (See Chapter II-2-1)

(2) Trends in Types of Offences

Let us look in more detail at the number of reported non-traffic Penal Code offences by category of offence. Showing no major changes throughout the Showa era were arson, negligence in causing fires, and murder. Offences that declined in number in the postwar period were gambling and illegal lotteries, forcible abduction and kidnapping, while those that rose in number in the postwar years were theft, extortion, robbery, assault, bodily injury, rape and indecent assault.

During the chaotic period shortly after the war, cases of theft, particularly housebreaking, and robbery rose markedly. As social stability grew in the following years, the two offences dwindled, while the number of cases of assault, bodily injury, extortion and the like rose from the early 1950s to the mid-1960s, the period which saw the nation achieve rapid economic growth.

In the years after 1975, offences in most categories decreased, although the number of theft and embezzlement cases rose sharply, mostly due to such relatively light offences as shoplifting, bicycle thefts and the like which do not involve housebreaking or misappropriation of lost bicycles, mostly committed by juveniles.

As many of the youths, the age group usually keeping the crime rate high, were sent overseas to fight during World War II, the number of crimes in most categories fell off during that particular period with the exception that rape and gambling increased in the number of cases investigated by the police.

The number of professional negligence, which was low in the prewar period, rose sharply from around 1956, due to the rapid growth of car traffic. It reached a record high of about 650,000 in 1970, showing no signs of abatement in the following years.

As such, the total number of Penal Code offences reported to the police set a record in 1970 (previous highs in 1934 and 1948 were, as mentioned above, based on the number of non-traffic Penal Code offences reported), and it was followed by a record high for the entire Showa era in 1988.

The figure for 1988, however, was chiefly due to an increase in the number of light cases of thefts and embezzlement, and negligent driving cases, while those for homicide, robbery, arson, bodily injury and rape declined, most of which fell lower than their respective record highs in the prewar period, indicating that crime trends in general have recently been stabilized. (See Chapter II-2-2, 3, 4)

(3) Comparison with Other Countries

An international comparison of three major crimes reported–homicide, rape and robbery–among the United States, United Kingdom, West Germany, France and Japan may serve to illustrate the characteristics of crime trends in Japan.

The number of these offences reported per 100,000 people (hereinafter called the "crime rate") in Japan did not show marked differences with those in other countries up until 1960. The homicide rate in Japan exceeded those in West Germany and the United Kingdom, while that for rape ran higher than the rate in the United Kingdom until 1960.

While the incidence of these crimes in Japan remained almost the same, or showed signs of decline in the following years, the corresponding figures for other countries either rose markedly or were steadily increasing.

As a result, each crime rate (the number of each reported crime-homicide, rape and larceny–per 100,000 population) in Japan had become lower than those in other countries both during the latter half of the 1950s and in the mid-1970s, with the gap continuing to widen in recent years. The clearance rate of major offences in Japan has also been much higher than that in the other Western countries.

As mentioned above, the crime rate in major offences in Japan was not low throughout the Showa era when compared with that in other countries. It was driven down in the postwar years, and the gap with the other countries widened. This was chiefly due to general improvement in social stability and the increase in economic well-being, as well as continued strenuous efforts on the part of criminal justice authorities in Japan in the postwar period. (See Chapter II-4)

2. OFFENCES INVOLVING SPECIAL LAWS

The number of special law offenders (up to 1948 the number refers to special law offences) referred to public prosecutors offices, excluding Road Traffic Law violators or violations, (hereafter called "special law offenders" or "special law offences"), rose from around 86,000 in 1931 to a prewar high of some 160,000 in 1943. The two figures accounted for approximately 21 percent and 46 percent, respectively, of the total offences and offenders newly received by public prosecutors offices, excluding those involved in Road Traffic Law violations and professional negligence, during the respective two years.

The number of special law offences amounted to some 970,000 in 1948, then that of the offenders around 860,000 in 1949, but dropped sharply in the 1955-1965 period. The two figures accounted for some 69 percent and some 59 percent of the total offences and offenders, excluding the offences or offenders in Road Traffic Law violations and professional negligence referred to during the respective two years.

The numbers of special law offenders hovered at an annual average of well over 100,000 in the following years, exceeding the 200,000 mark in some years. It then totaled around 110,000 in 1988 (about 24 percent of the total offenders, excluding those involved in Road Traffic Law violations and professional negligence).

It should be noted that most of those offenders who were disposed of by the chiefs of police stations through summary proceedings for violating police infractions in the prewar period were to be classified as special law offenders. Although the number of these offenders topped 1 million on an annual average up until 1936, the figures were never included in the statistics, either of the public prosecutors office or of the court.

By category, the special law offences mainly comprised relatively minor cases such as violations of the codes of police infractions and road traffic regulations and the like up until 1939. They were then followed by a marked increase in violations of the laws and regulations for economic control, such as the National General Mobilization Law, from 1940 onward.

In the postwar years, the number of offences against such economic control laws and regulations as the Staple Food Control Law increased markedly up until 1960. It was first followed by a marked rise in offences against the Anti-Prostitution Law roughly between 1960 and 1965. In the following years, there was a conspicuous increase in violations of both the Firearms and Swords Control Law and the Law Regulating Business Affecting Public Morals, followed by a marked increase in drug-related offences, including those against the Stimulant Drugs Control Law, since around 1970.

The number of Road Traffic Law violations, which was also high in the prewar years, rose sharply since 1949 and reached an estimated total of 4.97 million (some 96.6 percent of the total special law offences, including Road Traffic Law offences) in 1965.

The same figure dropped markedly in the ensuing years, due to the introduction of the notification system administered by the police for traffic infractions, as well as its extended applications in later years. The figure, however, reached an estimated total of 1.26 million (some 91.9 percent of the total special law offences, including Road Traffic Law violations) in 1988. (See Chapter II-3)

As explained earlier, the trends of special law offences reflect much of the actual circumstances of the society and the corresponding policies adopted by the law enforcement authorities for maintaining law and order for a given period.

Section 3. Treatment of Offenders

1. PROSECUTION

(1) Penal Code Offenders

The prewar rate of prosecution for Penal Code offences other than professional negligence went up from 19.2 percent in 1931 to 28.0 percent in 1941. The prewar rate of suspension of prosecution, on the other hand, went down from 74.7 percent in 1931 to 68.0 percent in 1941.

The rate of those offenders involved in Penal Code offences other than professional negligence who were brought to formal trial (namely the ratio of those prosecuted for formal trial proceedings to total number prosecuted, hereafter cited as "rate of formal prosecution") ranged from 53.3 percent to 59.7 percent between 1931 and 1941.

Following the end of World War II, the rate of prosecution rose to 45.7 percent in 1946, much higher than prewar levels. After decreasing slightly for some years, it went up again from 51.0 percent in 1961 to 59.5 percent in 1986, then came down to 55.7 percent in 1988.

The rate of suspended prosecutions was as low as 51.3 percent in 1946, much lower than the prewar level. After rising to 60.3 percent in 1951, it declined steadily to register 34.8 percent in 1986, but rose to 37.8 percent in 1988.

The rate of formal prosecution after the war was much higher than in the prewar years, registering 69.2 percent in 1946 and 72.1 percent in 1951. Although the rate dropped to the 50-percent level in the decade following the mid-1960s, it rose to 62.0 percent in 1976 and to 72.5 percent in 1988.

The rate of prosecution in the prewar period was lower than in the postwar years in most categories of offences, including theft, fraud, extortion, assault, bodily injury, rape, and professional negligence. Most of these cases were then disposed of through the suspension of prosecution. In the postwar years, the prosecution rate rose markedly, thus pushing down the suspended prosecution rate.

The rise in the rate of prosecution in the postwar years was chiefly due to an increase in prosecutions involving summary proceedings without court hearings (hereafter cited as "summary prosecution") on those crimes for which monetary penalties are provided for in the statutes, as well as an increase in the prosecution rate leading to formal trial.

In 1988, however, the prosecution rate dropped, while the rate of suspended prosecution rose in many categories of offences, including professional negligence.

The prosecution rate for homicide, robbery, and arson, however, continued to remain at high levels, while the rate of suspended prosecutions remained low throughout the entire Showa era. Unlike other categories of offences, there were no major changes in either rate of prosecution or suspended prosecution for these three offences between the years preceding and following the war. (See Chapter III-1-2- [2])

(2) Disposition of Special Law Offenders

Between 46.7 percent and 51.1 percent of the special law offenders, excluding Road Traffic Law violators, were prosecuted in the prewar years of 1931-1941. Offenders who were prosecuted for formal trial proceedings comprised only 3.2 percent to 8.8 percent of all special law offenders prosecuted, and most of the prosecutions were for summary proceedings. In the postwar period, the prosecution rate rose to 58.8 percent in 1946, then dropped slightly for some years that followed. After rising to 78.8 percent in 1981, it began to drop again in 1986 to reach 76.4 percent in 1988. The rate of prosecutions for formal trial proceedings ranged from 11.2 percent to 16.6 percent between 1946 and 1971. The rate, however, rose from 25.7 percent in 1976 to 46.1 percent in 1988. The sharp increase in recent years was chiefly due to a marked rise in violators of the Stimulant Drugs Control Law, resulting in increased prosecutions for formal trial proceedings.

By category of offences, the prosecution rate for Road Traffic Law violators fluctuated from 48.6 percent to 67.3 percent between 1931 and 1941 in the prewar period. (The rate of prosecutions for formal trial proceedings among the total prosecutions was 0.1 percent to 0.2 percent in the same period). In the postwar years, the prosecution rate stood at 40.8 percent (formal prosecution rate: 1.6 percent) in 1946, but rose from 63.2 percent (ditto: 0.1 percent) in 1951 to as high as 93.9 percent (ditto: 0.9 percent) in 1988. And the prosecution rate for violators of the Stimulant Drugs Control Law rose from 48.7 percent (ditto: 40.2 percent) in 1951 to 89.5 percent (ditto: 100 percent) in 1986. The rate then inched down to 87.5 percent (ditto: 100 percent) in 1988.

As such, the prosecution rate for special law offenders also increased in postwar years. In particular, the marked increase in formal prosecutions for violations of the Stimulant Drugs Control Law is a characteristic feature of recent Japan.

2. TRIAL

Throughout the Showa era, most offenders tried in courts of the first instance were fined, followed in order by fixed-term imprisonment with forced labour, minor fines and fixed-term imprisonment without labour.

Only a very small number were either sentenced to death, life imprisonment with/without labour, or penal detention (of less than 30 days).

In the postwar years, the acquittal rate (the percentage of acquittals to total final judgements delivered by courts of the first instance) was lower than in the prewar years, excepting a brief period shortly after the war. The acquittal rate has been less than 0.01 percent since 1981. (See Chapter III-1-3-[2])

(1) Sentences of Fines and Minor Fines

The percentage of those who were fined by courts of the first instance ranged from 59.1 percent to 80.1 percent between 1926 and 1943. In the postwar years, it exceeded the 90-percent mark from 1961 onward.

The corresponding figure for those who were given minor fines ranged from 1.5 percent to 14.0 percent between 1926 and 1943. It ranged from 25.8 percent to 42.5 percent between 1951 and 1960 in the postwar period, but nosedived in the following years, ranging from 0.1 percent to 1.3 percent between 1966 and 1987.

Both fines and minor fines were imposed more often in the postwar period than in the prewar years. The number of those punished with minor fines, however, dropped markedly in 1961, but increased slightly since 1973, with the actual number of those receiving minor fines reaching par with that in the prewar period.

A fact to be noted here is that in prewar years, the chiefs of police stations had the power to impose minor fines under the Law for Summary Proceedings on Police Infractions and that in the three years between 1934 and 1936, minor fines were imposed on more than one million persons per year. Taking this into account, minor fines represented the form of punishment most often meted out in the prewar years, much more often than in the postwar years.

As both fines and minor fines lost much of their deterrent effects in line with inflation and rises in the people's income after World War II, the ceilings for the two categories of fines were raised, first by the enactment of the Law on Temporary Measures Concerning Fines, etc., then by a partial amendment of the same law later.

As the deterrent effects of both categories of fines continued to diminish later on, there was a tendency to impose near maximum penalties for offences whose ceilings of statutory penalty had been set at relatively low levels.

Nevertheless, even for those offenders who violated those provisions of law which provided for maximum fines of more than 200,000 yen rarely have fines exceeding that amount been imposed, as the maximum fine has been set at 200,000 yen (under the Criminal Procedure Code) for those defendants who undergo summary proceedings without a hearing.

Punishment through minor fines has also become a rarity in recent years. (See Chapter III-1-3- [2])

(2) Determinate-Term Imprisonment with Labour

The number of defendants sentenced to determinate-term imprisonment with labour in the 1926-1943 period ranged from 30,000 to 40,000 per year, accounting for some 20 percent to 25 percent of the total defendants disposed of by the final and conclusive judgements of courts of the first instance.

After hitting a postwar peak of about 173,000 (about 26 percent of the total) in 1948, there was a gradual decrease in such sentences until the figure dropped to about 68,000 (about 4 percent) in 1987, with some fluctuations in the intervening years.

Determinate-term imprisonment without labour was not imposed so often in the prewar years. However, as traffic offences involving professional negligence increased gradually in the postwar years, the figure exceeded the 10,000 mark (0.5 percent) in both 1971 and 1972, then fell to about 5,300 (0.3 percent) in 1987.

One reason was an increase in sentences of imprisonment with labour for those offenders involved in professional negligence, owing to the fact that the relevant provision of law (Article 211 of the Penal Code) was amended in 1968 and the penalty of determinate-term imprisonment with labour was newly introduced in law.

As to length of imprisonment, either with or without labour, the percentage of those sentenced to imprisonment lasting either more than two years or less than six months was lower in the postwar period than in prewar years.

Although there were no major changes, between the two periods, in the rates of those who were sentenced to imprisonment ranging from six months up to less than one year, the rates of those who were sentenced to more than one year and less than two years was higher in the postwar years.

It may be said, therefore, that the sentencing in practice in the prewar years varied widely from relatively long terms to short ones, but the variations narrowed markedly in the postwar years.

The rate of those who were sentenced to determinate-term imprisonment with or without labour but whose sentences were suspended ranged from 12.6 percent to 13.7 percent in the prewar years, but varied between 40 percent in 1951 and 60.7 percent in 1976.

Although the rate went down slightly in subsequent years, the figure still came to 57.4 percent in 1987, much higher than the prewar level, indicating clearly that more frequent use has been made of rehabilitation within the community in postwar years. (See Chapter III-1-3- [2])

(3) Death Sentence and Life Imprisonment with or without Labour

The number of those who were sentenced to death ranged between 12 and 37 a year in the prewar period. It reached 116 in 1948, then ranged from 44 to 62 between 1949 and 1951.

In the following years, however, the number fell to the prewar level of 12 to 37 by the mid-1960s, and even further to less than 10 since around 1970, registering only 6 in 1987.

By category of offences committed, those who were sentenced to death were convicted either of homicide or of robbery resulting in death, in both the prewar and postwar periods.

The number of those who were sentenced to life imprisonment with or without labour ranged between 22 and 72 a year from 1926 to 1943. After totaling 151 in 1948, it ranged from 80 to 100 persons per year in the following years. Although the rates remained below the level of 50 per year since 1965, they climbed to 65 in 1987, coming close to the prewar level.

Most of the offenders sentenced to life imprisonment with labour were convicted of homicide, robbery resulting in death, followed by robbery-rape, both in the prewar and postwar years. (See Chapter III-1-3- [2])

(4) Penal Detention

The number of persons sentenced to penal detention, which came to less than 400 a year in the prewar years, reached about 1,600 in 1948. However, the number dropped gradually to total some 130 in 1987.

In the postwar period, the number of those who were sentenced to penal detention by courts of the first instance was, in the early years, higher than those of prewar years. However, considering the fact that in the prewar years the chiefs of police stations imposed penal detention on more than 100,000 persons per year under the Summary Proceedings on Police Infractions, penal detention was the most common form of punishment employed in the prewar period. (See Chapter III-1-3- [2])

(5) Trends in Sentencing by Category of Offence

Of those who were convicted of homicide, the number of those who were sentenced either to death or to life imprisonment with labour became lower in the postwar period compared with that in the prewar years. The figure has steadily declined in particular since 1971, although it marked a year-to-year increase in 1987. The prison term for those who were sentenced to determinate-term imprisonment with labour has become longer in the postwar period.

Of those convicted of robbery, fewer were sentenced either to death or to life imprisonment with labour in the postwar years. Although there were no major changes in the length of imprisonment for those sentenced to determinate-term imprisonment with labour between the prewar and postwar periods, the suspended sentence rate was higher in the postwar years.

As to those convicted of causing bodily injury, imposition of minor fines has been applied less often in the postwar years.

Fines were in more frequent use and the rate of sentencing to imprisonment with labour has declined in much of the postwar period. However, it has been rising since 1976 and is now as high as the prewar figures, and the term for those sentenced to determinate-term imprisonment with labour has become shorter in postwar years compared with that in the prewar period. The suspended sentence rate has also gone up in the postwar years.

The same can be said of those convicted of larceny, both in terms of length of imprisonment and the rate of suspended sentences.

Of those convicted of rape, the tendency of sentencing has become slightly severer and the number of those sentenced to long-term imprisonment with labour increased slightly in the postwar period; however, the suspended sentence rates have gone up in the same period. (See Chapter III-1-3- [3])

3. CORRECTION

(1) Changes in Convict Numbers

The number of prisoners newly sentenced and admitted to penal institutions totaled around 30,000 in 1926, but fell to around 28,000 in 1988. As the total population has almost doubled over these years, the 1988 figure in proportion to the total population has been virtually halved when compared with that in 1926.

Broken down by category of crimes committed by newly admitted prisoners, the number for larceny has increased gradually since the early Showa era. However, the figure went up markedly during the wartime years and shortly after World War II when shortages of food and other daily necessities were acute across the country.

The number for either homicide or arson has dropped markedly during the same periods, while that for robbery rose greatly during the chaotic period after the war.

The number for either rape or indecent assault rose from around 1955 up until 1969. That for violating the Stimulant Drugs Control Law has become the highest, replacing larceny, since 1985.

Regarding the types of penalty imposed on the newly admitted prisoners, the prewar years were characterized by high frequency in the use of penal detention imposed under summary proceedings for police infractions, accounting for around 11 percent to 20 percent of the total between 1926 to 1935. The penalty of penal detention became rare in the postwar years.

In terms of length of imprisonment, about 20 percent were sentenced for less than six months in the prewar period. In recent years, the rate of those imprisoned for less than six months has hovered around 10 percent.

Between 1926 to 1960, those sentenced to prison terms of more than six months and up to one year made up the largest number, accounting for about 30 percent to 40 percent of the total. Since 1961, those sentenced for longer than one year and up to three years have increased gradually, accounting for about 40 percent to 50 percent of the total imprisoned, also the largest number in this period. This means that short-term prison sentences have decreased in the postwar years. (See Chapter III-2-5- [1] [3] [4])

(2) Changes in Characteristics of Those Newly Imprisoned

A. By Age and Sex

The number of newly admitted prisoners increased markedly during the period shortly after World War II, mostly due to an increase in the number of prisoners under 30 years of age. The percentage of those who fall into this group is much higher in the total number of those who were sentenced to imprisonment during this period, compared to the prewar years.

The percentage of this age group, however, declined slightly, while the number of those older than 40 has been increasing since 1973.

The number of females newly admitted to prison was more than 1,000, yearly on the average in the early Showa era, with more than half of them imprisoned under Penal Detention (less than 30 days) imposed by chiefs of police stations to reduce the incidence of prostitution.

The average number of females imprisoned shortly after the war topped 2,600 per year. Most of these women were sentenced on charges of theft, primarily due to economic hardships during that period.

Although the number went down gradually, it has hovered around 1,200 in recent years, primarily due to an increase in the number of the women who violated the Stimulant Drugs Control Law. (See Chapter III-2-5- [1] [6])

B. Changes in Frequency of Imprisonment

The proportion of those serving a prison sentence for the first time (hereafter cited as "first-time prisoners") among the total number of newly admitted prisoners (hereafter called "newly admitted") hovered around 40 percent to 50 percent between 1926 and 1942. After registering a record high of 76.8 percent in 1946, the number of first-time prisoners went down in following years. It remained at around the same level for some time and stood at 39.2 percent in 1988.

The number of those who had already served prison sentences for the sixth time or more among the newly admitted went from 9.0 percent in 1926 to 13.9 percent in 1941. Although the number dropped markedly during the war and shortly after the war, it continued its upward trend, accounting for 16.0 percent of the newly admitted in 1988. (See Chapter III-2-5- [5])

C. Changes in Living Standards and Level of Education of Prisoners

The living standards of most of those who were newly imprisoned in the prewar period fell into the category of "below average" while they lived in society. Those with "below-average" living standards, however, accounted for slightly higher than half the newly admitted in recent years.

As for the level of education, those imprisoned who had either not completed their primary-school education or had no school education at all accounted for 27.1 percent of the newly admitted in 1926.

The number in this category, however, dropped steadily in following years, and accounted for only 1.8 percent of the newly admitted in 1985.

The proportion of those who were readmitted to prisons to serve a sentence imposed for those offences committed within less than three months after being released from prison remained high during the war-time years.

The ratio, however, went down after 1965, indicating a downward trend of those who committed an offence punishable by imprisonment within a relatively short period of time following their release from prison.

The number of those who escaped from prison or died during their imprisonment went up markedly at around the end of the war.

The corresponding figure, however, was reduced remarkably since around 1965, showing stability in terms of discipline and order among prisoners as well as general improvement in terms of supplies, health-care and medical services inside the prisons in recent years. (See Chapter III-2-5- [7] [8])

(3) Treatment within Prison

The trends in prison administration in the Showa era were characterized by a process of transformation from the old to the new, in step with modern society. The process started with the introduction of the Rule for the Progressive Stage Treatment of Prisoners in 1933 and ended with the Rule for the Classification of Prisoners in 1972.

Underlying ideas behind the changes included a shift toward more "humanitarian treatment" with a stress on improving the overall conditions for the betterment of treatment of prisoners, and toward "socialization" which emphasized the soliciting of a broad range of understanding and assistance from society (public participation), by adopting measures to help prisoners in their struggle for social rehabilitations.

There also was a trend to place more stress on "scientific approaches," that included working out better ways to rehabilitate prisoners through scientific analysis of their behavioural patterns, exemplified by treatment under the classification system.

All these concepts, which converged with time, have been promoted throughout the period.

Thus, in line with the modern philosophy of criminology the groundswork was layed for the treatment of prisoners based on the scientific classification system that stressed differential treatment for individual prisoners with the aim of helping them to reform and in their social rehabilitation.

The groundwork was completed by the end of the Showa era. (See Chapter III-2-1, 2, 3)

(4) Women's Guidance Home

The Anti-Prostitution Law, which was comprehensive legislation against prostitution, was enacted in 1957, with those statutes stipulating penal punishment coming into effect in 1958.

In 1958, the Women's Guidance Home Law was put into effect, leading to the establishment in the same year of Women's Guidance Homes to accommodate those women who were sentenced to suspension of execution of prison sentence and placed under guidance and to give them needed guidance and correction for their social rehabilitation.

Although the number of those newly admitted to such homes topped 400 per year shortly after their establishment, admittance dropped gradually to only a few yearly, from around 1980. (See Chapter III-2-6)

4. *REHABILITATION SERVICES*

(1) Changes in Institutions

Rehabilitation services in the six decades of the Showa era underwent great changes. These changes are roughly divided into two periods, with the first preceding 1949 and the other following that year when the current Offenders Prevention and Rehabilitation Law came into effect.

Rehabilitation services in 1926 followed two basic principles. One was aimed at giving aid to those who were released from incarceration, viz, those who were discharged from prison, and those who were released under suspended prosecution, or under suspended execution of sentence. The other was aimed at protecting and reforming juvenile offenders. The practical application of these principles was delegated mostly to voluntary organizations or other groups in the private sector.

While the national government had only administered and offered subsidies to these voluntary prisoners' aid organizations or groups at that time, these organizations gradually began to take on the color of governmental services in accordance to the enactments of the Law for the Supervision of Political Offenders in 1936 and the Judicial Rehabilitation Service Law in 1939.

Under the latter law, the services related to prisoners' aid–carried out at the discretion of the private sector–came to be regulated with an official licencing system. This put into effect stricter regulations over the related services, while offering financial back-up through public subsidies.

The law also helped build a nation-wide network of rehabilitation services, with a large number of volunteer judicial rehabilitation workers implementing the services.

However, the Law for the Supervision of Political Offenders, which stipulated the system of probationary supervision of those who violated the

Maintenance of the Public Order Law, was abolished when the war ended. The probationary supervision offices for political offenders also had been dismantled by that time.

By the enactment of the new Offenders Prevention and Rehabilitation Law in 1949, a new probationary supervision system was introduced. Unlike past systems it was based on principles followed in the probation and parole system in the United States aiming at helping offenders achieve social rehabilitation through self-help efforts.

In the same vein, the national government established in 1949 the National Offenders Rehabilitation Board (which was replaced by the Justice Ministry's Rehabilitation Bureau in 1952), the District Juvenile and Adult Offenders Rehabilitation Board (which was then replaced by the ministry's Regional Offenders Rehabilitation Regional Parole Board), and the probation offices for the juveniles and adults (which came to be called probation offices in the same year).

The modernization of the nation's rehabilitation services was completed by the enactment of the Law for Aftercare of Discharged Offenders, and of the Volunteer Probation Officer Law, both in 1950. (See Chapter III-3-1)

(2) Release on Parole

The enactment of the new Offenders Rehabilitation Law in 1949 led to great changes in the nation's parole system.

Prior to the law's enactment, parolees, except for juveniles aged below 18 who were placed under the "probationary supervision of juvenile probation officers" in accordance with the old Juvenile Law, came under the supervision of police authorities.

With the enactment of the new law, however, supervision by police authorities was ended, putting both adults and juveniles under the supervision of the Justice Ministry's probation offices.

In the years prior to 1944, the number of parolees who were under 18 years of age and placed under probationary supervision in accordance with the old Juvenile Law had never risen above seven per year. The figure, however, rose sharply after 1945, topping 1,000 in 1947.

In the years following the enactment of the new Offenders Rehabilitation Law in 1949, which covered adult offenders as well, the number of those who were discharged from penal institutions and placed under the supervision of probation offices rose quickly and totaled about 45,000 in 1952.

After declining gradually to about 14,000 in 1978, the number of parolees accepted by the nation's probation offices rose sharply to reach some 19,000 in 1984. The number, however, has been on the decline since 1987.

The percentage of parolees against the total number of prisoners discharged from penal institutions hovered around 5 percent between 1926 and 1931. It was on an upward trend, fluctuating within a 10-19 percent range between 1933 to 1943, and then reached as high as 74.0 percent in 1946.

Even after the 1949 enactment of the Offenders Prevention and Rehabilitation Law, the percentage remained over 70 percent until 1951.

Although the figure never dipped below 65 percent until 1960, it went down gradually in following years, chiefly due to an overall decline in the number of convicted prisoners, registering as low as 50.8 percent in 1982.

After the Justice Ministry adopted new policies in March 1984 to carry out release on parole in an appropriate and positive manner, the ratio of parolees from penal institutions surpassed 55 percent per year in the years up to 1988. (See Chapter III-3-2)

(3) Suspended Execution of Sentence with Probation

After the enactment of the old Juvenile Law, probationary supervision was extended only to those under 18 in age who had been given suspended sentences.

With a partial amendment of the Penal Code in December 1953, those who were given suspension of execution of sentence for the second time were placed under probationary supervision without fail. Then with yet another amendment in 1954 of the Penal Code and enactment in the same year of the Law for Probationary Supervision of Persons under Suspension of Execution of Sentences, probation was granted by discretion of the courts even to those who were given suspended execution of sentences for the first time. The age limit of under 18 years old was also abolished at that time.

Juveniles under 18 years of age who were placed under the "supervision of a juvenile probation officer" in accordance with the old Juvenile Law had been generally increasing in prewar years, standing at 38 in 1928, then exceeding 50 in 1933, and rising to over 100 in 1941.

Under the old provision (repealed by an amendment of the Penal Code in 1953) in the Offenders Prevention and Rehabilitation Law enacted in 1949, the number of those under 18 years of age, who had been given suspension of execution of sentence and came under probationary supervision, went down from around 1,300 in 1949 to around 90 in 1953.

With the introduction of suspended execution of sentences with probation, the number of those who were given a suspended execution of sentence with probation moved within a range of 6,900 to 8,600 per year between 1956 and 1985. The number, however, has been on the decline since 1986, dropping to around 6,000 in 1988. (See Chapter III-3-3- [3])

(4) Trends in Probationers and Parolees Newly Received by Probation Offices

The total number of those probationers and parolees received by probation offices reached about 78,000 in 1952 following the adoption of the new Offenders Prevention and Rehabilitation Law a few years earlier. (Probationers and parolees include hereafter juvenile offenders placed on probation, juvenile parolees from juvenile prisons and juvenile training schools, adult parolees from prisons, those who were given suspended execution of sentences with probation and parolees from women's guidance homes.)

Since parolees from prisons, juvenile prisons and juvenile training schools declined in number in following years, the total number decreased to about 44,000 in 1974.

Due to a rise in juvenile delinquency in general and intensive use of probation on juvenile traffic law violators, as well as the diversification in treatment of probationers, including the introduction of a short-term treatment of probationers, since around 1977, the total number received by probation offices exceeded 100,000 in 1983. The figure stood at around 96,000 in 1988. (See Chapter III-3-3- [1] [2] [3])

(5) Rehabilitation Aid Societies

Looking at the history of Rehabilitation Aid Societies which worked in providing homes and in helping those discharged persons in need, aiming at their rehabilitation, there existed in 1927 more than 800 such societies engaged in prisoners' aid services and rehabilitation services for juveniles.

When those groups which were set up to help political offenders were added, at times the number of these back-up organizations reached more than 1,000.

Partly due to the social upheavals following the end of the war, and partly due to revisions of relevant legislation, the Aid Societies which were approved anew under the Law for Urgent Aftercare of Discharged Offenders in 1950 numbered only 143.

Although a number of Aid Societies were newly established by around 1960, which brought the total up to 172 at one time, the number of these societies, excluding those which temporarily suspended their operations, totaled, as of the end of 1988, 100 hostels of 102 societies. The low figure is often blamed on the fact that these societies tend to suffer from financial difficulties as well as manpower shortages. (See Chapter III-3-4)

(6) Characteristics of the Probation and Parole Supervision System

The probation and parole supervision system is characterized in Japan by the fact that a small number of official probation officers and a great number of volunteer probation officers–some 49,000 in all–work together successfully.

An array of treatments have been devised and made available for probationers and parolees who come under probationary supervision, such as differential treatment under the classification system according to individual needs and the system of stationing of official probation officers at designated places at regular intervals to meet with and advise clients, volunteer probation officers, etc.

In addition, the following treatment measures are practiced: traffic group counseling for juvenile traffic offenders under probationary supervision, preparole investigation into the social environment of the prisoners in order to help them return smoothly to society, and care in prisoners aid hostels utilizing these as halfway houses for those released from prison after serving long terms. (See Chapter III-3-3- [4])

(7) Pardons

Last year, a Cabinet order to grant amnesty, commutation of punishment and restoration of civil rights was issued (decided by the Cabinet and attested by the new Emperor) following the demise of the late Emperor. The number totaled 15 for the Showa era as a whole with six given in the prewar period, under Imperial Order, since the power to grant pardons was the right of the Emperor, and nine in the postwar years.

To be noted is the fact that Cabinet or Imperial orders have been issued in commemoration or in memory of major events either for the Imperial family or for the nation as a whole.

As amnesty, pardons, commutation of punishment, etc. granted by the administrative power of the Cabinet, abolishing the punishment or remitting the sentence imposed, etc., tend to reduce or circumvent the power of legislative and judicial authority, they have been granted less often in recent years.

Turning to day-to-day dispensation by the National Offenders Rehabilitation Commission of individual cases where pardons, commutation of sentence, restoration of civil rights, etc. were applied for, the number of these dispositions ranged between 100 to 200 a year in the 10-year period following 1955.

Although the figure showed an increasing trend after 1965 and rose to 929 persons in 1969, (852 of whom were given the decision: adequate to be granted pardon, etc. and referred to the Cabinet) the number dropped to 172 in 1988 (111 of whom were given the decision: adequate to be granted exemption of execution of sentence with 14 persons, and restoration of civil rights for 97 persons). (See Chapter III-3-5)

Section 4. Juvenile Delinquency

1. GENERAL TRENDS IN JUVENILE DELINQUENCY

The percentage of juvenile Penal Code offenders cleared by the police stood at nearly 16 percent against the total number of Penal Code offenders cleared in 1941, and about 24 percent in 1944.

The percentage of juvenile offenders among the total non-traffic Penal Code offenders cleared by police, however, rose sharply following the end of the war. Although the number peaked in 1983 at 261,634 in number, the percentage accounted for more than 50 percent of the total in the years following 1981. This showed that cases of juvenile delinquency were limited in number before the war but increased dramatically after the war.

Looking back at juvenile Penal Code offenders by type of offence in the Showa era, there was a marked rise in larceny in the 10 years following the mid-1930s, primarily due to economic hardships of the times. This was followed by rapid rises in the number of both larceny and robbery cases in the latter half of 1940s, chiefly due to social upheavals and economic difficulties shortly after the war.

The number of juvenile offenders involved either in traffic-related professional negligence cases, in violent crimes, or in sex-related offences increased rapidly between the mid-1950s and early 1970s, partly attributable to ever-spreading motorization and a variety of social conflicts stemming from industrialization and urbanization of society, and partly due to a decline in sexual morality among the public during that period.

There has been a marked rise, since the mid-1970s, in the number of juveniles who were involved either in larceny, like shoplifting and stealing of bicycles, or in embezzlement, mostly, misappropriation of lost property, like the unauthorized use of unattended bicycles. This reflects a general growth in crime opportunities coming within reach of juveniles, because of the affluence of society during these years.

Regarding special law offences, there has been a marked increase in the number of juveniles involved in the violation of the Poisonous and Hazardous Substances Control Law or of the Stimulant Drugs Control Law in recent years.

By age group, the number of juveniles in the lower age group (aged between 14 and 15) went up markedly, while the number in the upper age group (aged between 18 and 19) either leveled off or dwindled in the postwar years.

To be noted is the rapid rise in the number of girl offenders since early 1970s, particularly among those who were involved in violation of drugs-related laws.

Although it is not known clearly what type of school education or living environment at home juvenile delinquents experienced in the prewar years, it can be said that during the period shortly after the war, many delinquents came from families in which no real parents were living together and family members were forced to suffer economic hardships.

Since the mid-1960s, however, there was a rise in the number of juvenile offenders who were reared by families enjoying average living standards and were cared for by both parents.

Also noteworthy was the increase of full-time students among the total of juvenile offenders and conversely the decrease of those not enrolled as students, whether they were employed or not, in the same period.

Among those "hard-core" juvenile offenders who were admitted to juvenile training schools, however, a growing number were found to have been deprived of a good family life in recent years. More than half of them were found to have been under the guardianship of someone other than their real parents. (See Chapter IV-1)

2. TREATMENT OF JUVENILE DELINQUENTS

(1) Prosecution and Trial of Juvenile Delinquents

The official functions of the public prosecutors office in its dealing with juvenile delinquency differ greatly in the prewar years and after the war.

Under the old juvenile-related legislation, including the old Juvenile Law, the public prosecutor had the power to decide first, whether or not to prosecute a juvenile offender referred to him or her by the police. When and after giving non-prosecution dispositions, the public prosecutor again had the discretionary power to choose from among those not prosecuted, those who needed protective, rehabilitation measures and refer them to the Juvenile Tribunals for disposition.

Under the current Juvenile Law, however, the family courts first decide whether the juvenile offenders referred to the courts shall be treated under protective rehabilitative measures or be tried by criminal courts and sentenced to penal punishment. The public prosecutor is given the power to institute public prosecution only against those juvenile offenders who were, as such, retransferred by the family court on the ground that to impose penal punishment on them was appropriate in their cases. The prosecutor then is obliged, as a rule, to prosecute these juveniles in these cases.

Under the old Juvenile Law, those under 18 years of age were considered juveniles, but those juvenile offenders of 14 year of age or older could be subject to criminal proceedings.

Under the current Juvenile Law, however, those under 20 years of age are considered juveniles, and only those juveniles who have committed an offence punishable by imprisonment without labour or a heavier penalty, and who were 16 years or older at the time of disposition, are sent back to public prosecutors office for possible prosecution.

Under the old Juvenile Law, the Juvenile Tribunal was an administrative organ whose functions included deciding appropriate protective, rehabilitative measures for juvenile offenders, as well as carrying out and supervising such measures.

Under the current Juvenile Law, the Family Court is the judicial organ which adjudicates on the fact and law of the case and decides on appropriate dispositions, including protective, rehabilitative measures for juvenile offenders, while the measures are executed by an administrative organ. (See Chapter IV-2-1, 2- [1] [2])

(2) Juvenile Tribunal and the Family Court

The articles stipulating protective, rehabilitative measures for juvenile offenders were put into effect only in a limited area of jurisdiction shortly after the old law was enacted. However, these areas were gradually expanded and the articles became effective across the country in 1942. In line with this expansion, the number of Juvenile Tribunals also increased in Japan.

According to data compiled by the Juvenile Tribunal the dispositions of dismissal without a hearing accounted for more than 64 percent of the total dispositions, with the remaining 30-35 percent given protective, rehabilitative measures, in the period between 1926 and 1935.

In the following years, however, the number of protective, rehabilitative measures increased. While dismissal without hearing accounted for less than 20 percent of the total, protective, rehabilitative measures accounted for more than 80 percent between 1943 and 1945.

Also high in number were those juveniles prosecuted in criminal courts by public prosecutors, or those given suspended prosecution without referral to the Juvenile Tribunals.

Of the total juvenile cases, excluding traffic-related professional negligence violations of the Road Traffic Law and pre-delinquency disposed of by the Family Courts after the war, the percentage of dismissals without a hearing or dismissals after a hearing went up steadily from 65.7 percent in 1951 to nearly 90 percent in the years after 1973.

Meanwhile, among the total dispositions, the rate of probation went down from 18.8 percent in 1951 to 7.5 percent in 1987, commitment to juvenile prisons dropped from 9.0 percent in 1951 to the 2-percent level in 1987, and referral to public prosecutors for possible prosecution declined from 5.6 percent in 1951 to 0.5 percent in 1987, with each category showing some fluctuations in the periods.

It is clear that the number of juveniles dismissed without a hearing or dismissal after a hearing was much higher in the postwar years than in the prewar years, although there were major differences in the legal systgem in the two periods.

Most juvenile cases adjudicated in the postwar period were given protective, rehabilitative measures, including probation, with the number brought before criminal proceedings accounting for only a small percentage of the total. (See Chapter IV-2-2- [2])

(3) Trials of Juvenile Delinquents

Of the juveniles whom the Family Court decided to transfer to the Public Prosecutors Office for possible prosecution, most were involved in traffic professinal negligence offences or road-traffic violations (98.1 percent of the total in 1988).

Moreover, most of these juveniles were prosecuted by summary proceedings (over 95 percent of those prosecuted in the same year), while the percentage of those who were tried under formal trial proceedings has hovered around 3 percent since 1965.

The number of juveniles, caught at the time of committing offences, convicted in courts of the first instance through formal proceedings stood around 3,000 per annum in the prewar years. In 1946, the total was around 17,000. Most of these were charged with criminal offences committed shortly after the war. In the following years, however, the number decreased gradually to total 1,000 to 2,000 per year since 1955. (See Chapter IV-2-2- [3])

(4) Juvenile Classification Homes

Juvenile classification homes were established for the first time in 1949 with the aim of keeping juvenile delinquents in custody as well as diagnosing and classifying them by their conduct, personal history, temperament and other factors, thus improving and expanding the nation's diagnostic classification services related to juvenile delinquencies.

The number of those newly admitted to juvenile classification homes rose from about 16,000 in 1949 to a record high of nearly 41,000 in 1951. After fluctuating almost in line with the number of juvenile offenders cleared by the police in following years, the number totaled about 19,000 in 1988.

The Juvenile Classification Home stressed the importance of taking a scientific approach with juvenile offenders on the basis of behavioural science in line with the new Juvenile Law.

At the same time, diagnostic classification experts, centering on these homes, were formed into a group of professionals, thus contributing greatly to the establishment of the treatment system on classification programs as well as promoting the scientific approach in the treatment of inmates at the Juvenile Classification Home, the Juvenile Training School, and at other penal institutions. (See Chapter IV-2-3)

(5) Reformatory Schools and Juvenile Training Schools

With the enactment of the Reformatory School Law in 1923, two reformatory schools were established in Tokyo and Osaka.

As provisions of the old Juvenile Law, concerning protective rehabilitative treatment measures, came to be applied more widely in the following years, the number of reformatory schools went up accordingly.

By 1942 when the provisions came into effect nation-wide, the reformatory schools numbered seven.

The number of juveniles admitted newly by the reformatory schools stood at 607 in 1942, but the number rose sharply to nearly 4,100 in 1944, chiefly due to the introduction of the short and strict training program.

Following the war, the number increased from about 1,900 in 1946 to about 3,000 in 1948.

With the enactment of the Juvenile Training School Law in 1949, reformatory schools were transformed into juvenile training schools.

Under the new Juvenile Law, upper age limit of a juvenile was raised to less than 20 years in 1951, while the number of juveniles who were admitted newly by juvenile training schools totaled about 11,000 in the same year.

In the following years, this figure went down, dropping to a record low of about 2,000 in 1974. It rose again after 1975, and then went down once more after 1985 to total about 4,800 in 1988.

As mentioned previously, the number of juveniles who were newly admitted to juvenile training schools showed a marked increase after the war, but declined in recent years to a level as low as the number admitted to reformatory schools in 1944.

There was a marked difference of treatment between the old reformatory schools and the current juvenile training schools. In the past treatment given at the reformatory schools was chiefly aimed at improving the character of inmates by educating them under strict discipline as well as by giving them practical vocational training essential for living in society.

At one time during the late wartime years, a short and strict training program was introduced under which juvenile delinquents, including those who were considered minor offenders, were admitted to the schools. After a short-term training period, they were then sent to work in munitions plants.

After the war, efforts were made to improve and expand the treatment for inmates, by placing special emphasis on such areas as academic lessons, vocational guidance, and counseling on daily life, all in step with the new Juvenile Law.

In 1977, drastic measures were taken in the treatment of inmates, by emphasizing individualized treatment, with flexibility according to the term of admission, and providing for the availability of different and unique treatment programs at each school.

As for the length of penal treatment in schools, both the short-term and long-term admissions came to be adopted. The former was further divided into two types, namely non-traffic short-term treatment and traffic short-term treatment. The latter covered five different categories of treatment: counseling on day-to-day life; vocational training; academic lessons; special education and medical care.

In addition, development and expansion of innovative treatment technology has taken place in the substance, techniques and evaluation of the treatment measures.

At the same time, a standardized yardstick for implementing the educational curriculum was adopted, thus enhancing the overall level of correctional education. (See Chapter IV-2-4)

(6) Juvenile Prisons

The number of juveniles newly admitted to juvenile prisons remained below 1,000 per year in most of the prewar years. Although the number rose above 3,000 at one time after the war, it has moved downward since about 1950 to reach about 100 annually in recent years. This indicates that the number of juveniles who are given prison sentences has become very small in recent years.

By category of offence, more than 70 percent of the juveniles, who were imprisoned from 1926 until the mid-1940s, were involved in theft. The percentage of those involved in theft declined in following years, dropping to as low as about 20 percent of the total juveniles imprisoned in recent years.

In contrast, the number of those involved in professional negligence increased markedly since about 1960, accounting for about 30 percent of the total in recent years, and registering some 34 percent in 1988.

As for treatment measures, the education as treatment given to inmates during the prewar years consisted of academic classes centering on the compulsory primary education level and vocational training to provide knowledge and skills in such fields as agriculture and manufacturing.

In the postwar years, however, the treatment measures aimed at helping the inmates achieve smooth rehabilitation to return to society have been actively undertaken, with special emphasis being placed on academic education, vocational training and guidance on living. (See Chapter IV-2-5)

(7) Probationary Supervision of Juvenile Offenders

The number of juveniles who were sentenced by juvenile tribunals to "probationary supervision by juvenile probation officers" increased from about 1,000 in 1926 to nearly 6,000 in 1944, and then registered a high of about 8,500 in 1948 after the war.

The number of juveniles who were placed under the probationary supervision following the enactment of the current Juvenile Law in 1949 stood at about 24,000 in 1951. Although the number declined for some years, it went up again to total about 30,000 in 1966.

The figure slid down again to total only about 20,000 in 1974, but it rose markedly since 1977 when the traffic short-term probationary supervision came into place. Thus, it surpassed annually the 50,000 level since 1979, and totaled over 70,000 yearly for most of the years following 1983.

The number of those released on parole from Reformatory Schools never topped 100 with the year 1947 registering a hitherto high of 83 under the Reformatory School Law which was effective until 1948.

Following the enforcement of both the Juvenile Training School Law and the Offenders Prevention and Rehabilitation Law, the number of those released on parole from Juvenile Training Schools totaled nearly 9,700 in 1952, and then gradually decreased to about 1,600 in 1975.

The figure rose to about 5,600 in 1985, chiefly due to the introduction of the short-term treatment program at Juvenile Training Schools. The total was about 4,800 in 1988.

As mentioned previously, under the old Juvenile Law the probationary supervision system was applied to those parolees who were under 18 years of age when released from prisons as well as those juveniles who were given the suspension of the execution of sentences and who were 18 years of age at the time of sentencing.

Following the postwar amendments of laws, however, the probationary suspension system came to be applied to adult offenders as well. Thus, the system which was originally designed to provide protective rehabilitative measures for juvenile offenders grew into a system that constitutes one of the nation's general criminal policies covering adult offenders as well.

After the war, the number of those juveniles placed by the family courts under probationary supervision went up markedly, particularly after the traffic short-term probationary supervision system–stressing group treatment–came into use in 1977.

The percentage of juveniles among the total number of parolees released from prisons has recently accounted for less than 0.1 percent, while the ratio of juveniles among the total number of those who were given suspended execution of sentences with probationary supervision has come to account for a mere 2 percent, in recent years.

This is chiefly due to the wide application of protective, rehabilitative measures, including protective rehabilitative treatment, to juvenile offenders, thus reducing the number of juveniles prosecuted for criminal punishment. (See Chapter IV-2-6)

Section 5. *Conclusion*

While using an array of statistical data and references, following the same pattern of the past issues of the "White Papers on Crime," this book took a general overview of crime trends, changes and characteristic features in the treatment of offenders, and changes in the criminal laws and in the nation's criminal and judicial systems in the Showa era.

The book, however, has illustrated only the basic changes in crime patterns and criminal policies in Japan in the past era and also it has failed to depict major crime incidents that have occurred, due chiefly to limited space.

Again, those questions that have arisen in the course of the analysis have to be clarified by future research.

Yet, it is meaningful to consider in a general way both the crime patterns and criminal policies in this country in the eventful Showa era, since this may provide invaluable references for the establishment and implementation of appropriate measures against crime in the future.

In this respect, the book was aimed at illustrating how the nation transformed itself, through many hardships, into a country which has come to be praised as one of the world's safest today.

By illustrating the characteristics and major trends of criminal policies in the past era, the book intended to offer some meaningful hints for further development of the nation's criminal policies, thus contributing to a more stable and peaceful new Heisei era.

In line with the general changes that took place in our society, the crime patterns and criminal policies in the past era went through disturbing periods in the gloomy prewar years and in the years immediately after the war. In contrast, there were brighter years toward the end of the Showa era.

With the backdrop of major social upheavals in the prewar era, which started with an economic depression and ensuing political turmoil and which was followed by the Manchurian Incident and the war with China, the nation saw its crime rate go up sharply.

As mentioned previously, an array of proper measures in criminal policy were taken, as was demonstrated by the fact that more suspended prosecutions were given in the prewar years than in the postwar years.

On the other hand, investigation and punishment against political offenders under the Maintenance of Public Order Law, the strengthening of national control under the National General Mobilization Law and frequent imposition of penal detention and minor fines for minor police infractions under the Summary Proceedings for Police Infractions, and preventive detention for political offenders represent so to speak the dark side of the criminal policy of the time.

Shortly after the war, when the nation was undergoing terrible economic hardships and social turmoil, an unprecedentedly high rate of crimes of a serious nature occurred, along with crimes related to property, which brought about stringent dispositions and harsher punishment against those offenders on the part of the criminal justice agencies.

Thanks to improvements in social stability and in the administration of the criminal justice system, the number of Penal Code offenders decreased in later years, while the number of people who violated drug-related laws fluctuated over the years.

The number of offenders involved in traffic-related professional negligence offences and Road Traffic Law violators increased after the mid-1960s. The number of Stimulant Drugs Control Law offenders went up after about 1970.

Also increasing in number since the mid-1970s were offenders who were charged with such minor crimes as shoplifting, stealing bicycles and misappropriation of neglected bicycles. The number of juvenile delinquents has been on a steady rise throughout the postwar period.

Throughout these years, law enforcement authorities, including the police, in Japan maintained a clearance rate of crimes much higher than in any other advanced country. Prosecutions by the public prosecutors office and the sentencing by the court have been made in a manner appropriate to and in line with the changing pattern of each crime, thereby reducing the crime rate as well as preventing the rate from rising further.

At the same time, legislation and revisions of relevant laws have been made, as shown by the partial revisions of such laws as the Stimulant Drugs Control Law, the Road Traffic Law, and the Penal Code, all aimed at dealing more effectively with changing crime trends.

The enactment of the Code of Criminal Procedure, the Juvenile Law and the Offenders Prevention and Rehabilitation Law in the postwar years made an epoch in history. These laws were drafted on the basis of reflection on old laws and their implementation in the prewar years. They were aimed at carrying out criminal investigation, public trials, and treatment of offenders, keeping a proper balance between crime control and the protection of the basic human rights of the suspects.

Also, treatment in the community has been expanded by way of the adequate treatment for juvenile delinquents relying mainly on the protective, rehabilitative treatment measures in society as well as more frequent use of monetary punishment and suspension of execution of sentence. Treatment in correctinal institutions, too, has become more humanized, more scientific and more socialized and as such has been contributing to prevent the recurrence of crimes.

In addition to the overall improvement in such factors as the social environment, comprehensive countermeasures in criminal policy mentioned above contributed to help Japan become one of the safest countries in the world.

Although law and order in Japan is regarded as good when compared with other countries, there remain many problems which have to be solved in the future.

One of the problems is how to prevent and deal with the crimes committed by Boryokudan (organized groups prone to commit violent and unlawful acts) and their members.

Among Penal Code offenders arrested in 1988, the percentage of the Boryokudan offenders was high in certain offences, including 25 percent for homicide, 19 percent for robbery, 23 percent for bodily injury, and 64 percent for intimidation. This has had a major influence on the overall crime situation in Japan.

Their crimes also include violations of drug-related laws, and smuggling of firearms into the country, as well as unlawful acts involving civil disputes, and illicit activities carried out under the guise of legitimate corporate activities.

Meanwhile, juvenile delinquency has been on the rise in recent years, with the number of juvenile offenders accounting for more than half the total Penal Code offenders cleared by the police, excluding those involved in professional negligence. Although small in number, cases of juvenile offences of the most atrocious nature, including homicide, have occurred in recent years.

The number of Stimulant Drugs Control Law offenders still remains high, while drugs smuggled into the country constitute one of the major sources of operational funds for the Boryokudan. There were a number of terrible crimes committed by drug-addicts, as well.

Also, crimes of an international nature committed by foreigners here in Japan or invovling Japanese nationals overseas occurred quite frequently.

The international crimes included not only criminals who violated drugs-related laws, or those who were suspected of international terrorism, but also those who were involved in offences of an outrageous nature, or in intellectual crimes.

With the continuing progress in means of transportation and telecommunications, as well as growing interaction with foreign nationals, crimes of an international nature are expected to rise in number.

Therefore, it will become even more important to strengthen international cooperation in terms of criminal investigation and the extradition of criminals, as well as international action in terms of crime prevention, with the United Nations and other international organizations.

As terrorist attacks have recently been escalating, both in terms of their viciousness and tactics, and consequently have had a stronger impact on the society, more effectrive control and more stringent investigation and punishment are hoped for in the future.

Monetary punishment, particularly fines, have been used most often in the postwar years. However, because of the rise of prices and people's incomes over the years, the real effect of the fines mandated by the current law has been weakening.

Problems concerning the merits of monetary punishments, including those of appropriate maximum level of fines mandated by the Penal Code and others, remain to be solved in the future.

As a result of the growing number of Boryokudan members and offenders with multiple previous convictions, as well as offenders of advanced age, being imprisoned in recent years, it seems that more appropriate treatment measures need to be developed to discourage these offenders not to repeat crimes or where appropriate, other criminal justice agencies than prisons shall be involved in their dispositions and treatment.

As to protective rehabilitative treatment, probationary supervision conducted through collaboration between volunteer probation officers and professional probation officers, there appears to be an urgent need to sustain a sufficient number of appropriate volunteer probation officers under the circumstances of the weakening of human ties in the local community, as well as to work out ways for the appropriate sharing of roles between professional officers and volunteer workers.

In the Showa era, overall revisions in the Penal Code and the Prison Law could not be completed. Both laws date back to the Meiji era. The latter law needs to be revised so that it can deal more effectively with rapid changes that have been taking place in society as well as in crime patterns.

The revision is also needed in order to bring the law further in line with the present-day actual situation in the treatment of offenders and penal theories and treatment theory.

Further study should be continued toward the overall revision of the former law, and at the same time partial revisions should be made in a timely manner as the special need arises in society.

The Juvenile Law also requires study, particularly on the need to revise those provisions concerning the general improvement and expansion of the procedural due process, such as the protection of the rights of juveniles under the proceedings of courts by taking into account the actual situation in juvenile delinquency and changing basic ideas of the care and protection for juveniles.

No matter how drastically the people's views toward law and order change, an important question for the society as a whole is whether the general public will retain enough law-abiding spirit and whether the people will continue to extend their support and cooperation to the police and other agencies in criminal justice in the future.

As society becomes affluent, the process of urbanization and the growth of the information society are accelerated. These developments change the roles and functions of the family and community life as a whole.

The transformations will then greatly influence the nature of juvenile crimes and delinquency.

As crimes already have occurred indicative of these changes, new countermeasures to properly deal with such situations are needed. Also, it is indispensable for society to retain stable economic strength in order to contain crimes under a peaceful and safe society in the future.

However, many of problems related to crime trends and criminal policies to deal with crime have been left over from the Showa era for the Heisei era to solve.

Some measures that were taken in the prewar years should be carefully reflected upon for the future. Viewing as a whole the criminal policies taken in the postwar years, it seems that they deserve high esteem for their effectiveness in dealing with an array of problems that occurred in the period, particularly in the turbulent years shortly after the war, and thus helping the nation become one of the safest countries in the world.

Despite the dramatic social changes in the postwar years, due chiefly to the rapid process of industrialization and urbanization across the country, Japan has maintained a relatively stable and secure society, in contrast to other countries in the West which have often been plagued with high crime rates due to industrialization and urbanization. Why has this been possible?

Major underlying factors as generally mentioned are Japan's highly law-abiding citizens, excellent economic performance, low unemployment rate, high educational standards, the web of informal social control at work in local communities, the geographical condition of the country as "an island nation", the highly cooperative spirit of its citizens toward the criminal justice administration, strict control by the law enforcement authorities on firearms, swords, and drugs, efficient investigations by police demonstrated by a high crime clearance rate, as well as just and effective functions of the criminal justice agencies in our country.

It can be said that the combination of these factors worked to build the general stability of the crime situation and security of our society in the later period of the Showa era. But these positive factors could be weakened in these times of change. Even Japan's geographical condition as "an island nation" has been losing its significance due to the rapid process of internationalization in so many areas.

As the new era of Heisei begins, further efforts are needed to strengthen and expand preventive factors or measures against crimes, as well as to control and eliminate the contributory factors or root-causes of crime in society as a whole, by giving full attention and reflection on the crime trends and criminal policies implemented in the Showa era.

Meanwhile, all agencies in the criminal justice system should commit themselves anew, in collaboration with citizens, to the challenge of maintaining a stable and secure society with a low crime rate, through realization of more effective criminal policies, in the years ahead.

Table 1 Number of Penal Code Offences Reported to and Offenders Cleared by the Police, Clearance Rate and Crime Rate (1926 - 1988)

Year	All Penal Code Offences			Penal Code Offences other than Traffic violations			Population (unit = 1,000)
	Offences reported	Offenders cleared	Clearance rate	Offences reported	Offenders cleared	Crime rate	
1926	716,286	396,863	94.2	710,981	…	1,171	60,741
1927	748,133	413,454	92.2	741,628	…	1,203	61,659
1928	786,146	…	93.3	777,980	…	1,243	62,595
1929	912,245	…	94.0	902,634	…	1,422	63,461
1930	1,049,986	…	97.7	1,039,118	…	1,612	64,450
1931	1,181,705	…	96.2	1,169,770	…	1,787	65,458
1932	1,298,397	…	96.1	1,285,972	…	1,936	66,434
1933	1,552,039	…	96.8	1,538,788	…	2,282	67,432
1934	1,566,435	…	97.8	1,550,645	…	2,270	68,309
1935	1,528,188	…	95.9	1,511,722	…	2,183	69,254
1936	1,306,902	…	92.8	1,291,141	…	1,841	70,114
1937	1,221,697	…	89.6	1,205,246	…	1,706	70,630
1938	1,243,636	…	90.3	1,230,078	…	1,732	71,013
1939	1,027,845	…	86.9	1,016,462	…	1,424	71,380
1940	1,026,955	…	84.0	1,017,273	…	1,414	71,933
1941	922,526	334,417	83.6	914,432	326,165	1,276	71,680
1942	890,331	299,395	77.6	883,286	292,299	1,220	72,385
1943	979,336	346,709	80.5	973,528	340,559	1,336	72,883
1944	905,836	310,951	78.3	900,899	305,939	1,243	73,064
1945	711,596	242,645	66.4	708,809	239,865	984	71,998
1946	1,387,080	445,484	57.9	1,384,222	442,579	1,883	73,114
1947	1,386,020	459,339	50.3	1,382,210	455,097	1,770	78,101
1948	1,603,265	550,540	50.6	1,599,968	546,991	2,000	80,003
1949	1,603,048	585,328	57.8	1,597,891	579,897	1,954	81,773
1950	1,469,662	616,723	68.0	1,461,044	607,769	1,756	83,200
1951	1,399,184	619,035	69.6	1,387,289	606,686	1,641	84,541
1952	1,395,197	575,852	68.1	1,377,273	557,521	1,605	85,808
1953	1,344,482	547,550	71.0	1,317,141	519,707	1,514	86,981
1954	1,360,405	539,789	70.0	1,324,333	496,412	1,501	88,239
1955	1,478,202	558,857	68.4	1,435,652	501,429	1,608	89,276
1956	1,410,441	527,950	63.7	1,354,102	470,522	1,502	90,172
1957	1,426,029	544,557	63.8	1,354,429	471,600	1,490	90,928
1958	1,440,259	545,272	62.8	1,353,930	457,212	1,475	91,767
1959	1,483,258	557,073	62.4	1,382,792	454,898	1,493	92,641
1960	1,495,888	561,464	64.1	1,378,817	442,527	1,476	93,419
1961	1,530,464	581,314	66.6	1,400,915	451,586	1,486	94,287
1962	1,522,480	569,866	67.2	1,387,784	430,153	1,455	95,181
1963	1,557,803	606,649	67.1	1,374,476	425,473	1,433	96,156
1964	1,609,741	678,522	68.8	1,385,358	449,842	1,426	97,182
1965	1,602,430	706,827	66.7	1,343,625	440,563	1,367	98,275

Year	All Penal Code Offences			Penal Code Offences other than Traffic violations			Population (unit = 1,000)
	Offences reported	Offenders cleared	Clearance rate	Offences reported	Offenders cleared	Crime rate	
1966	1,590,681	740,055	66.1	1,293,877	433,545	1,306	99,036
1967	1,603,471	802,578	67.2	1,219,840	402,738	1,217	100,196
1968	1,742,479	923,491	69.2	1,234,198	393,831	1,218	101,331
1969	1,848,740	999,981	68.7	1,253,950	377,826	1,223	102,536
1970	1,932,401	1,073,470	70.5	1,279,787	380,850	1,234	103,720
1971	1,875,383	1,026,299	70.5	1,244,168	361,972	1,183	105,145
1972	1,818,088	976,706	71.2	1,223,546	348,788	1,137	107,595
1973	1,728,741	931,329	70.9	1,190,549	357,738	1,091	109,104
1974	1,671,965	852,372	69.2	1,211,005	363,309	1,095	110,573
1975	1,673,755	830,176	68.9	1,234,307	364,117	1,103	111,940
1976	1,691,247	830,717	70.2	1,247,631	359,360	1,103	113,094
1977	1,705,034	822,319	68.0	1,268,430	363,144	1,111	114,165
1978	1,776,843	843,538	68.6	1,336,922	381,742	1,161	115,190
1979	1,738,452	840,333	69.9	1,289,405	368,126	1,110	116,155
1980	1,812,798	869,844	69.9	1,357,461	392,113	1,160	117,060
1981	1,925,836	904,643	69.2	1,463,228	418,162	1,241	117,902
1982	2,005,319	944,051	69.4	1,528,799	441,963	1,288	118,728
1983	2,039,209	963,554	70.0	1,540,717	438,705	1,289	119,536
1984	2,080,323	961,363	71.8	1,588,693	446,617	1,321	120,305
1985	2,121,444	970,369	72.9	1,607,697	432,250	1,328	121,049
1986	2,124,272	967,997	68.0	1,581,411	399,886	1,300	121,672
1987	2,132,617	983,931	73.5	1,577,954	404,762	1,291	122,264
1988	2,207,380	988,784	70.1	1,641,310	398,208	1,337	122,783

Notes : 1. Clearance rate $= \dfrac{\text{Number of offences cleared}}{\text{Number of offences reported}} \times 100$

2. Crime rate means the number of reported offences per 100,000 population.

Sources: National Police Agency, Statistics Bureau of Management and Coordination Agency, etc.

Table 2 Number of Penal Code Offencers

Year	Total	Theft	Fraud	Embezzle-ment	Homicide	Robbery	Assault
1926	716,286	364,441	133,472	84,241	2,516	1,659	1,601
1927	748,133	383,640	136,934	91,840	2,495	1,906	1,646
1928	786,146	408,217	145,525	104,815	2,350	2,066	1,478
1929	912,245	462,658	182,446	123,090	2,064	2,412	1,462
1930	1,049,986	540,310	209,930	153,222	2,315	2,282	1,553
1931	1,181,705	584,542	250,979	171,277	2,415	2,198	1,655
1932	1,298,397	667,132	253,587	199,965	2,700	2,435	1,461
1933	1,552,039	704,913	388,666	265,357	2,713	2,156	1,653
1934	1,566,435	724,986	334,830	282,595	2,594	2,126	1,498
1935	1,528,188	674,893	371,317	250,960	2,484	2,215	1,553
1936	1,306,902	648,860	240,305	211,625	2,491	1,975	1,282
1937	1,221,697	633,534	217,444	190,665	2,226	1,790	1,051
1938	1,243,636	634,341	244,057	185,208	1,957	1,461	873
1939	1,027,845	554,237	157,285	144,291	1,692	1,279	732
1940	1,026,955	573,225	181,177	114,314	1,513	1,232	586
1941	922,526	544,143	111,629	97,415	1,424	1,148	525
1942	890,331	587,616	82,695	91,467	1,175	1,390	405
1943	979,336	649,367	94,663	75,885	1,112	1,210	333
1944	905,836	660,842	67,195	51,017	933	1,258	205
1945	711,596	561,537	33,574	39,115	919	1,474	207
1946	1,387,080	1,155,392	84,101	31,397	1,791	9,120	410
1947	1,386,020	1,141,294	90,279	34,801	1,938	9,186	720
1948	1,603,265	1,246,445	133,666	47,087	2,495	10,854	5,796
1949	1,603,048	1,165,605	161,047	60,296	2,716	6,780	11,851
1950	1,469,662	982,341	187,528	65,616	2,892	7,821	19,730
1951	1,399,184	995,641	139,254	48,834	2,865	6,124	19,101
1952	1,395,197	986,987	140,143	47,071	2,871	6,140	22,656
1953	1,344,482	931,791	141,000	46,329	2,944	5,296	25,105
1954	1,360,405	948,587	128,772	42,940	3,081	5,753	27,533
1955	1,478,202	1,056,974	124,633	37,527	3,066	5,878	30,808
1956	1,410,441	1,007,649	101,558	31,445	2,617	5,285	36,039
1957	1,426,029	1,005,101	100,767	31,143	2,524	5,029	38,038
1958	1,440,259	990,602	98,174	26,362	2,683	5,442	45,797
1959	1,483,258	1,027,992	89,457	24,241	2,683	5,192	46,784
1960	1,495,888	1,038,418	82,886	22,144	2,648	5,198	44,250
1961	1,530,464	1,051,874	82,357	21,614	2,619	4,491	45,650
1962	1,522,480	1,055,237	77,637	18,743	2,348	4,142	43,167
1963	1,557,803	1,066,044	70,569	15,682	2,283	4,021	44,687
1964	1,609,741	1,057,531	75,891	16,734	2,366	3,926	46,965
1965	1,602,430	1,027,473	78,609	14,922	2,288	3,886	44,103

Reported, by Major Offence (1926～1988)

Bodily injury	Extortion	Rape	Indecent assault	House breaking	Arson	Fire caused by negligence	Gambling lottery	Bribery	Kidnapping
23,051	4,296	…	…	4,874	2,297	12,624	34,246	521	1,497
23,448	3,826	…	…	4,858	2,144	11,934	32,903	592	1,239
22,946	4,441	…	…	4,993	2,109	11,657	26,754	763	1,247
22,846	5,077	…	…	5,600	2,235	12,731	29,185	735	1,376
24,358	6,884	…	…	7,404	2,355	11,859	28,647	526	1,286
24,510	10,647	…	…	7,532	2,612	12,337	31,187	861	1,190
24,571	14,693	…	…	9,406	2,609	12,291	28,917	585	1,178
26,200	12,849	1,586	1,768	10,007	2,495	12,431	35,294	1,664	1,326
28,860	14,868	1,498	1,257	9,640	2,388	14,077	53,594	3,885	1,417
29,290	32,173	1,598	1,186	10,390	2,262	12,843	47,521	3,089	1,254
27,556	34,329	1,548	1,257	10,445	1,918	11,820	44,221	4,471	1,079
25,592	9,586	1,286	1,063	9,448	1,598	10,907	39,656	2,469	898
23,115	8,712	1,223	1,015	9,495	1,491	11,373	44,029	2,365	806
21,651	7,866	1,134	815	11,083	1,312	11,707	63,396	1,774	690
18,221	7,608	1,018	974	8,696	1,238	12,642	50,661	2,128	648
17,114	6,360	1,159	1,164	8,833	1,064	9,872	59,844	2,722	555
13,414	5,373	1,589	1,238	12,027	1,068	10,033	39,155	3,299	341
11,196	5,246	1,624	1,076	15,976	1,113	10,158	63,817	6,166	239
7,885	5,677	1,318	653	14,407	1,011	8,246	43,419	3,273	131
4,493	3,319	650	285	6,949	553	6,711	29,438	2,343	23
7,927	11,205	611	217	2,559	697	8,424	29,533	1,403	100
11,865	15,283	863	237	2,640	807	9,333	28,149	2,489	62
21,434	25,691	1,936	656	4,283	940	8,694	20,301	4,119	143
32,627	29,550	2,732	984	7,719	1,395	8,837	14,970	8,941	360
42,769	32,740	3,558	1,190	10,076	1,905	9,124	9,545	5,363	457
43,890	19,891	3,268	1,021	9,614	1,707	9,926	6,981	3,035	531
48,396	20,586	3,735	978	9,946	1,797	9,443	4,449	2,609	526
52,525	18,777	3,517	1,225	10,080	1,846	10,704	3,332	2,044	411
58,545	25,538	4,148	1,915	9,759	1,902	9,977	2,568	2,090	365
65,978	28,419	4,046	1,835	10,141	1,922	9,550	2,098	1,291	414
66,883	27,736	3,749	1,658	9,044	1,607	8,729	1,924	1,032	325
70,023	28,269	4,121	1,881	9,066	1,520	8,547	1,823	1,318	253
73,985	38,684	5,988	2,234	9,727	1,720	7,859	1,527	816	150
73,014	41,599	6,140	2,338	9,367	1,662	7,430	1,374	584	124
68,304	41,060	6,342	2,510	9,224	1,743	8,189	1,371	1,005	166
68,321	45,306	6,487	2,955	9,088	1,757	8,639	1,840	1,671	186
63,918	45,034	6,125	3,087	9,287	1,567	8,631	1,792	1,356	229
59,730	42,032	6,239	4,195	9,357	1,493	7,706	1,790	1,303	334
61,282	40,892	6,857	4,293	10,312	1,597	7,716	3,072	2,149	256
58,702	35,287	6,648	4,710	9,750	1,457	8,157	4,751	1,820	250

Year	Total	Theft	Fraud	Embezzlement	Homicide	Robbery	Assault
1966	1,590,681	1,001,412	70,226	13,180	2,198	3,558	41,132
1967	1,603,471	954,549	61,379	10,287	2,111	3,009	38,136
1968	1,742,479	975,347	60,706	9,657	2,195	2,988	36,268
1969	1,848,740	1,008,013	58,662	9,001	2,098	2,724	33,134
1970	1,932,401	1,039,118	58,340	9,362	1,986	2,689	32,028
1971	1,875,383	1,026,094	51,386	8,008	1,941	2,439	28,936
1972	1,818,088	1,006,675	57,658	9,349	2,060	2,500	26,754
1973	1,728,741	973,876	55,473	10,172	2,048	2,000	27,079
1974	1,671,965	1,013,153	49,764	9,493	1,912	2,140	24,228
1975	1,673,755	1,037,942	53,647	10,575	2,098	2,300	21,944
1976	1,691,247	1,049,748	59,462	11,670	2,111	2,095	20,560
1977	1,705,034	1,073,393	56,120	13,891	2,031	2,095	19,931
1978	1,776,943	1,136,648	64,866	15,781	1,862	1,932	18,135
1979	1,738,452	1,107,477	54,642	16,532	1,853	2,043	15,466
1980	1,812,798	1,165,609	58,958	21,391	1,684	2,208	15,301
1981	1,925,836	1,257,354	63,710	25,900	1,754	2,325	15,851
1982	2,005,319	1,313,901	66,472	29,595	1,764	2,251	14,836
1983	2,039,209	1,335,258	59,463	30,705	1,745	2,317	13,975
1984	2,080,323	1,365,705	72,455	36,615	1,762	2,188	13,615
1985	2,121,444	1,381,237	74,424	41,567	1,780	1,815	12,171
1986	2,124,272	1,375,096	64,788	37,436	1,676	1,949	10,808
1987	2,132,617	1,364,796	69,844	42,580	1,584	1,874	9,970
1988	2,207,380	1,422,355	65,125	45,678	1,441	1,771	10,004

Bodily injury	Extortion	Rape	Indecent assault	House breaking	Arson	Fire caused by negligence	Gambling lottery	Bribery	Kidnapping
59,080	27,454	6,583	3,268	9,950	1,421	6,829	5,092	1,672	272
59,234	21,361	6,393	3,416	10,378	1,323	6,984	3,815	1,054	266
57,822	19,030	6,136	3,604	10,692	1,415	6,790	3,860	2,063	266
54,392	18,204	5,682	3,609	10,351	1,304	6,014	3,448	1,801	343
50,836	18,775	5,161	3,299	10,355	1,587	5,819	4,199	1,276	351
46,090	17,406	4,862	3,374	10,087	1,676	4,958	3,800	709	288
43,194	16,053	4,677	3,139	9,622	1,612	4,554	4,318	1,141	286
43,385	14,652	4,179	3,233	9,949	1,576	4,947	4,377	1,243	281
37,687	13,852	3,956	2,954	9,841	1,729	4,530	4,411	742	196
34,136	14,255	3,704	2,841	10,018	1,600	4,206	3,945	1,060	182
32,536	11,497	3,239	2,694	10,537	1,891	4,514	3,201	1,034	171
32,479	10,964	2,945	2,992	11,079	2,155	4,286	3,035	765	153
28,938	9,895	2,897	2,994	11,002	2,004	4,217	2,574	898	189
26,431	8,843	2,810	2,829	12,180	2,127	3,079	1,944	507	130
26,264	8,830	2,610	2,825	12,017	2,014	2,867	2,062	807	139
25,778	10,048	2,638	2,735	12,650	1,994	2,754	1,957	765	122
25,202	11,647	2,399	2,645	12,529	2,291	2,399	3,026	794	113
23,803	11,992	1,970	2,464	12,279	2,102	1,534	2,968	515	76
23,540	12,408	1,926	2,369	12,564	1,980	1,622	2,325	475	82
22,302	12,679	1,802	2,645	12,675	2,028	1,358	1,396	460	98
21,171	12,904	1,750	2,291	12,564	1,776	1,102	1,739	342	113
21,046	11,855	1,823	2,404	11,776	1,814	933	2,122	328	106
21,516	12,136	1,741	2,867	12,065	1,629	1,036	1,970	311	112

Sources: Home Office and National Police Agency

Table 3 Number of Penal Code Offenders Adjudicated at

Year	All Penal Code Offences	Penal Code Offences excluding Professional Negligence	Theft	Fraud	Embezzlement	Homicide	Robbery	Assault
1926	104,671	102,056	11,686	4,110	2,330	930	490	201
1927	106,340	103,371	13,802	4,065	2,105	961	630	160
1928	87,776	84,465	12,774	3,678	1,934	816	642	142
1929	96,801	92,502	13,959	4,140	2,024	573	676	116
1930	98,261	93,680	16,508	4,537	2,020	754	748	186
1931	99,483	94,572	16,317	4,703	2,259	875	713	166
1932	94,258	89,369	18,343	4,990	2,168	931	862	128
1933	108,421	103,278	20,087	5,561	2,633	953	817	150
1934	123,200	117,104	21,843	5,910	3,011	1,053	804	164
1935	122,603	116,192	19,936	6,101	3,169	924	802	119
1936	121,766	114,995	20,574	6,356	2,919	910	785	118
1937	111,441	104,589	19,652	6,099	2,699	882	711	90
1938	111,135	104,840	19,250	5,764	2,787	760	631	73
1939	105,189	99,797	16,277	4,826	2,139	634	463	57
1940	112,259	108,216	17,547	4,306	2,107	586	425	47
1941	116,005	112,703	15,881	3,947	2,133	603	404	…
1942	101,060	98,371	15,625	3,891	2,028	523	348	…
1943	125,470	122,988	17,440	3,859	2,114	435	364	…
1944	…	…	…	…	…	…	…	…
1945	…	…	…	…	…	…	…	…
1946	…	…	…	…	…	…	…	…
1947	…	…	…	…	…	…	…	…
1948	230,553	228,223	99,632	11,811	5,646	1,194	9,233	1,187
1949	172,624	169,733	72,540	10,461	5,481	953	5,182	2,749
1950	169,904	165,728	64,990	12,391	7,077	1,164	4,920	5,334
1951	158,495	152,022	61,859	11,485	7,150	1,157	3,525	5,918
1952	153,507	144,409	56,726	11,461	6,743	958	2,615	7,145
1953	150,288	134,750	47,415	11,174	6,633	1,011	2,144	8,124
1954	159,581	137,402	46,173	11,187	5,829	1,160	2,032	9,058
1955	186,137	156,230	52,692	11,764	5,355	1,403	2,546	11,518
1956	208,108	166,753	55,126	10,532	4,908	1,295	2,473	14,685
1957	218,435	167,096	51,474	9,711	4,428	1,261	2,208	16,709
1958	225,464	166,564	45,896	9,813	3,864	1,474	2,486	17,833
1959	237,005	163,773	43,987	9,166	3,694	1,581	2,330	18,577
1960	243,057	158,391	40,350	8,396	3,590	1,404	1,901	18,265
1961	249,916	154,821	36,208	7,315	3,165	1,403	1,669	18,389
1962	263,715	153,077	32,248	7,272	2,885	1,387	1,520	18,163
1963	271,399	145,526	29,121	6,630	2,486	1,431	1,492	19,679
1964	311,568	149,594	26,898	6,196	2,336	1,271	1,326	20,433
1965	357,977	155,780	27,972	6,594	2,458	1,272	1,350	20,673

Courts of First Instance, by Major Offence (1926～1987)

Bodily injury	Extortion	Rape	Indecent assault	House breaking	Arson	Fire caused by negligence	Gambling lottery	Bribery	Kidnapping
8,557	798	173	43	1,230	582	3,171	62,318	277	202
8,469	698	179	41	1,190	608	2,724	62,116	322	136
7,554	672	143	30	1,053	528	2,357	47,221	418	96
7,532	680	162	39	1,171	515	2,653	53,122	397	140
8,341	960	185	32	1,411	609	2,248	49,692	358	167
8,323	1,126	154	40	1,293	825	2,187	48,989	438	151
8,814	1,448	223	38	1,620	955	1,840	40,837	343	120
9,681	1,531	240	41	1,510	876	1,942	50,710	578	130
10,391	1,577	279	53	1,512	943	2,374	59,965	1,136	192
10,153	2,998	236	64	1,352	875	1,895	60,374	1,492	198
10,064	1,643	269	62	1,517	716	1,694	60,713	1,296	221
9,320	1,166	261	65	1,440	611	1,613	54,636	919	232
8,147	851	239	65	1,849	518	1,642	57,513	637	232
7,967	730	234	59	2,076	372	1,646	57,906	588	208
6,325	643	240	44	1,576	320	2,207	67,767	696	178
…	548	…	…	1,555	312	1,533	74,364	…	182
…	468	…	…	1,783	284	1,773	61,312	…	143
…	499	…	…	2,289	265	2,090	82,595	…	90
…	…	…	…	…	…	…	…	…	…
…	…	…	…	…	…	…	…	…	…
…	…	…	…	…	…	…	…	…	…
…	…	…	…	…	…	…	…	…	…
11,120	5,561	314	86	1,789	226	2,307	62,907	1,957	22
14,058	3,822	440	54	1,893	277	1,963	36,553	2,286	26
20,741	4,241	600	81	2,043	349	1,972	26,654	1,740	53
21,856	2,724	601	119	2,347	381	2,270	17,747	1,317	91
25,630	2,699	602	99	2,088	398	2,287	12,097	1,178	118
29,295	2,428	527	143	1,791	416	2,641	9,066	1,152	101
35,034	2,846	666	165	2,007	457	2,813	6,534	1,265	115
43,710	3,505	835	160	2,229	458	2,923	4,935	836	117
48,198	4,096	856	146	2,103	459	3,186	5,000	914	120
51,315	4,097	928	183	2,250	453	3,271	4,660	824	88
53,950	4,966	1,644	197	2,488	490	2,957	4,675	650	50
52,740	5,420	2,153	199	2,420	501	2,899	3,860	738	31
51,235	5,407	2,382	253	2,394	471	3,231	3,913	802	53
51,537	5,768	2,101	271	2,378	436	3,670	4,548	593	57
51,913	5,820	2,196	307	2,382	401	3,894	5,238	752	68
49,322	5,622	2,314	308	2,405	401	3,567	5,095	761	107
50,233	5,542	2,221	300	2,642	371	3,570	8,773	957	74
48,561	5,242	2,426	365	2,586	367	3,589	2,516	228	117

(Table 3)

Year	All Penal Code Offences	Penal Code Offences excluding Professional Negligence	Theft	Fraud	Embezzlement	Homicide	Robbery	Assault
1966	388,632	159,557	28,627	6,477	2,403	1,201	1,427	20,398
1967	425,040	143,585	25,175	5,378	1,946	1,121	1,088	19,255
1968	529,721	142,702	24,095	5,212	1,837	1,134	1,064	18,025
1969	572,046	133,361	22,665	4,726	1,579	1,015	1,005	16,707
1970	582,035	127,669	21,489	4,444	1,338	1,004	959	15,025
1971	545,254	120,193	20,277	4,478	1,314	1,036	921	14,341
1972	534,773	124,896	20,565	4,922	1,521	1,117	951	14,748
1973	481,504	124,066	17,462	4,494	1,290	1,101	841	13,802
1974	414,771	107,162	17,578	3,932	1,165	1,004	804	12,690
1975	385,953	101,761	19,406	4,340	1,048	956	884	11,335
1976	398,514	102,983	19,524	4,837	1,244	1,164	873	11,631
1977	383,636	97,731	18,392	4,560	1,075	1,084	813	11,162
1978	382,829	91,878	18,080	4,842	1,104	1,043	766	9,825
1979	381,280	83,282	17,394	4,418	981	891	733	8,448
1980	284,046	79,758	16,928	4,150	999	944	695	7,626
1981	395,178	79,210	17,735	4,378	1,076	888	807	7,243
1982	401,664	77,638	18,007	4,896	976	891	781	6,273
1983	412,427	75,438	17,516	4,488	848	1,022	763	5,912
1984	413,178	73,646	17,993	5,064	963	978	840	5,943
1985	421,848	69,984	17,830	5,033	958	974	720	5,642
1986	438,309	63,893	17,224	4,234	858	978	686	4,576
1987	352,460	61,519	16,442	4,294	714	908	715	3,960

Bodily injury	Extortion	Rape	Indecent assault	House breaking	Arson	Fire caused by negligence	Gambling lottery	Bribery	Kidnapping
49,513	4,670	2,634	386	2,703	337	3,263	13,288	978	99
48,386	3,818	2,590	413	2,711	345	3,184	9,532	761	113
48,160	3,818	2,733	425	2,518	272	3,403	10,907	1,144	98
44,572	3,728	2,566	414	2,513	283	2,848	10,477	980	89
42,405	3,932	2,391	365	2,430	304	2,888	10,285	748	96
39,055	4,072	2,444	450	2,250	328	2,595	9,293	664	89
39,207	4,345	2,330	407	2,578	404	2,395	11,224	831	89
37,961	3,726	2,141	447	2,524	330	2,314	10,369	708	80
34,069	3,378	1,868	421	2,479	335	2,149	9,753	607	66
29,709	3,389	1,745	391	2,590	352	1,775	8,340	628	71
29,518	3,685	1,506	425	2,783	406	1,709	7,870	779	68
28,864	3,399	1,233	416	2,806	399	1,733	7,176	535	51
26,828	3,231	1,147	371	2,662	450	1,372	6,059	561	41
24,022	3,106	1,062	409	2,479	431	1,248	4,847	595	28
22,916	2,618	1,052	392	2,414	422	1,064	5,377	497	40
21,962	2,809	970	344	2,365	387	968	4,961	599	29
20,266	2,725	916	330	2,152	432	802	6,348	574	32
19,270	2,679	698	303	1,950	467	622	7,515	506	31
19,031	2,798	686	283	1,812	453	586	5,149	467	31
17,539	2,929	706	330	1,818	420	540	3,996	363	47
16,067	2,714	702	311	1,704	408	424	3,507	313	44
15,162	2,892	661	296	1,525	407	326	4,599	329	42

Sources: Annual Report of Criminal Statistics,
Annual Report of Judicial Statistics, etc.

Table 4 Number of Suspects Newly Received by the Public Prosecutors Office (1926~1988)

Year	Total	Penal Code Offences excluding Professional Negligence(A)	Professional Negligence	Special Law Offences excluding Road traffic violations(B)	Road traffic violations	$\frac{B}{A+B}$(%)
1926	370,629	…	…	…	…	…
1927	375,414	…	…	…	…	…
1928	359,252	…	…	…	…	…
1929	396,540	…	…	…	…	…
1930	421,851	…	…	…	…	…
1931	435,417	322,459	13,958	85,728	13,272	21.0
1932	450,736	338,960	14,462	85,484	11,830	20.1
1933	502,551	366,292	15,103	111,253	9,903	23.3
1934	538,979	394,145	17,604	116,158	11,072	22.8
1935	518,734	374,125	19,374	110,413	14,822	22.8
1936	497,716	347,359	19,054	115,801	15,502	25.0
1937	445,378	309,235	19,101	102,730	14,312	24.9
1938	406,882	289,552	16,287	87,864	13,179	23.3
1939	354,124	246,157	13,864	86,246	7,857	25.9
1940	392,059	235,463	11,792	139,039	5,765	37.1
1941	381,688	224,262	9,915	144,130	3,381	39.1
1942	363,131	192,676	8,433	159,770	2,252	45.3
1943	361,055	191,429	6,982	161,132	1,512	45.7
1944	374,289	…	…	…	…	…
1945	…	…	…	…	…	…
1946	496,956	287,705	4,450	202,115	2,686	41.3
1947	1,102,438	309,413	6,954	710,163	75,908	69.7
1948	1,623,010	431,014	9,226	971,676	211,094	69.3
1949	1,658,248	590,273	8,216	860,160	199,599	59.3
1950	1,631,868	631,590	11,619	642,694	345,965	50.4
1951	1,655,182	624,646	15,674	603,992	410,870	49.2
1952	1,433,859	579,377	21,844	445,497	387,141	43.5
1953	1,717,578	543,535	31,354	389,105	753,524	41.7
1954	2,224,064	534,672	42,526	403,515	1,243,351	43.0
1955	2,503,995	558,993	51,647	355,914	1,537,441	38.9
1956	2,444,098	548,784	65,493	178,281	1,651,540	24.5
1957	2,736,364	539,526	80,998	180,731	1,935,109	25.1
1958	2,727,237	527,861	96,787	183,045	1,919,544	25.7
1959	2,804,419	519,850	114,206	229,662	1,940,701	30.6
1960	3,410,317	505,482	130,959	201,913	2,571,963	28.5
1961	3,731,172	510,219	140,840	165,825	2,914,288	24.5
1962	4,956,770	491,126	152,486	185,617	4,127,541	27.4
1963	5,077,642	479,078	200,290	276,179	4,122,095	36.6
1964	5,482,358	504,369	253,423	161,146	4,563,420	24.2
1965	5,922,489	489,600	292,500	175,327	4,965,062	26.4
1966	5,501,484	488,695	353,605	154,516	4,504,668	24.0
1967	5,700,737	444,207	443,560	215,307	4,597,663	32.6
1968	4,049,447	436,540	583,674	171,432	2,857,801	28.2
1969	2,702,454	415,717	674,535	141,582	1,470,620	25.4
1970	2,692,414	409,565	680,336	142,459	1,460,054	25.8

Year	Total	Penal Code Offences excluding Professional Negligence(A)	Professional Negligence	Special Law Offences excluding Road traffic violations(B)	Road traffic violations	$\frac{B}{A+B}$ (%)
1971	2,720,796	388,602	666,875	166,669	1,498,650	30.0
1972	2,897,482	375,053	643,162	141,759	1,737,508	27.4
1973	2,943,086	364,016	586,398	142,620	1,850,052	28.2
1974	2,862,574	359,288	495,756	139,280	1,868,250	27.9
1975	3,026,047	387,476	467,497	167,796	2,003,278	30.2
1976	3,235,092	380,574	471,870	152,581	2,230,067	28.6
1977	3,447,464	374,934	457,217	153,925	2,461,388	29.1
1978	3,294,245	378,230	463,734	144,124	2,308,157	27.6
1979	2,969,317	362,609	473,015	189,637	1,944,056	34.3
1980	2,979,731	379,769	479,675	159,751	1,960,536	29.6
1981	3,015,210	395,847	488,317	139,757	1,991,289	26.1
1982	3,089,841	401,094	501,040	133,904	2,053,803	25.0
1983	3,316,654	388,547	523,930	179,574	2,224,603	31.6
1984	3,369,463	381,588	516,922	160,083	2,310,870	29.6
1985	3,372,119	374,174	539,003	137,770	2,321,172	26.9
1986	3,242,755	353,582	566,156	137,412	2,185,605	28.0
1987	2,562,160	347,810	578,857	135,213	1,500,280	28.0
1988	2,301,329	345,273	585,841	110,562	1,259,653	24.3

Sources: Annual Report of Criminal Statistics and
Annual Report of Statistics on Prosecution

Table 5 Number of Offenders Convicted at Courts of First Instance (1931~1987)

Year	Penal Code Offences excluding Professional Negligence (A)	Special Law Offences excluding Road traffic violations (B)	$\frac{B}{A+B}$ (%)	Year	Penal Code Offences excluding Professional Negligence (A)	Special Law Offences excluding Road traffic violations (B)	$\frac{B}{A+B}$ (%)
1931	94,572	44,422	32.0	1961	154,821	94,391	37.9
1932	89,369	47,570	34.7	1962	153,077	60,796	28.4
1933	103,278	64,412	38.4	1963	145,526	88,950	37.9
1934	117,104	54,078	31.6	1964	149,594	76,229	33.8
1935	116,192	54,518	31.9	1965	155,780	71,898	31.6
1936	114,995	59,877	34.2	1966	159,557	65,410	29.1
1937	104,589	61,210	36.9	1967	143,585	88,102	38.0
1938	104,840	38,739	27.0	1968	142,702	75,402	34.6
1939	99,797	38,669	27.9	1969	133,361	63,783	32.4
1940	108,216	70,258	39.4	1970	127,669	66,717	34.3
1941	112,703	78,325	41.0	1971	120,193	73,301	37.9
1942	98,371	85,662	46.5	1972	124,896	61,072	32.8
1943	122,988	78,553	39.0	1973	124,066	67,287	35.2
1944	…	…	…	1974	107,162	59,962	35.9
1945	…	…	…	1975	101,761	68,398	40.2
1946	…	…	…	1976	102,983	60,006	36.8
1947	…	…	…	1977	97,731	64,695	39.8
1948	228,223	321,495	58.5	1978	91,878	59,891	39.5
1949	169,733	277,899	62.1	1979	83,282	76,279	47.8
1950	165,728	207,230	55.6	1980	79,758	66,360	45.4
1951	152,022	189,873	55.5	1981	79,210	58,291	42.4
1952	144,409	144,624	50.0	1982	77,638	51,199	39.7
1953	134,750	130,685	49.2	1983	75,438	90,939	54.7
1954	137,402	129,567	48.5	1984	73,646	86,350	54.0
1955	156,230	142,432	47.7	1985	69,984	72,366	50.8
1956	166,753	81,051	32.7	1986	63,893	72,334	53.1
1957	167,096	73,053	30.4	1987	61,519	66,379	51.9
1958	166,564	81,729	32.9				
1959	163,773	99,336	37.8				
1960	158,391	84,157	34.7				

Sources: Annual Report of Criminal Statistics,
Annual Report of Judicial Statistics, etc.

Table 6 Number of Offenders Finally Convicted at Courts of First Instance (1931~1987)

Year	Penal Code Offenders excluding Professional Negligence (A)	Special Law Offenders excluding Road traffic violations (B)	$\frac{B}{A+B}$ (%)	Year	Penal Code Offences excluding Professional Negligence (A)	Special Law Offences excluding Road traffic violations (B)	$\frac{B}{A+B}$ (%)
1931	287,406	822,291	74.1	1961	305,186	156,193	33.9
1932	302,449	676,412	69.1	1962	283,039	128,427	31.2
1933	341,682	845,498	71.2	1963	267,049	199,726	42.8
1934	381,725	829,643	68.5	1964	281,715	142,494	33.6
1935	368,562	808,947	68.7	1965	272,704	133,248	32.8
1936	350,543	782,362	69.1	1966	277,316	117,633	29.8
1937	310,900	587,078	65.4	1967	251,917	166,651	39.8
1938	295,388	469,954	61.4	1968	256,221	136,671	34.8
1939	258,985	358,049	59.0	1969	246,944	113,130	31.4
1940	260,102	429,330	62.3	1970	240,444	117,178	32.8
1941	254,205	400,402	61.2	1971	222,491	133,165	37.4
1942	207,995	341,067	62.1	1972	220,770	103,653	31.9
1943	230,541	268,899	53.8	1973	216,909	116,680	35.0
1944	…	…	…	1974	199,188	105,403	34.6
1945	…	…	…	1975	191,934	121,193	38.7
1946	…	…	…	1976	187,481	95,293	33.7
1947	…	…	…	1977	181,811	105,991	36.8
1948	421,699	594,896	58.5	1978	171,881	89,313	34.2
1949	389,240	733,998	65.3	1979	154,999	117,394	43.1
1950	455,361	612,084	57.3	1980	151,444	99,982	39.8
1951	395,139	547,168	58.1	1981	147,696	82,109	35.7
1952	370,166	409,365	52.5	1982	148,010	73,579	33.2
1953	358,759	351,433	49.5	1983	139,142	121,051	46.5
1954	349,012	374,075	51.7	1984	134,647	111,536	45.3
1955	380,530	319,963	45.7	1985	127,759	91,841	41.8
1956	370,896	158,535	29.9	1986	113,867	93,545	44.5
1957	357,213	154,848	30.2	1987	115,730	91,776	44.2
1958	334,240	158,542	32.2	8			
1959	325,021	201,440	38.3	9			
1960	308,033	154,057	33.3	0			

Sources: Annual Report of Criminal Statistics,
Annual Report of Judicial Statistics, etc.

Table 7 Number of Persons Finally Adjudicated at Courts of First Instance, by Category of Punishment (1926~1987)

Year	Total	Capital Punishment	Life imprisonment with or without labour	Imprisonment with labour	Imprisonment without labour	Fine	Penal detention	Minor fine	Probation	Acquittal	Others
1926	153,073	25	49	28,835	146	103,742	392	18,636	3,745	791	457
1927	154,953	32	57	30,586	284	104,322	265	18,156	4,217	932	319
1928	141,585	25	44	27,752	815	95,669	188	15,656	3,835	1,027	409
1929	153,841	21	35	29,514	424	101,427	163	20,142	4,027	587	1,528
1930	165,773	28	40	33,533	1,191	107,386	113	20,901	4,485	697	1,884
1931	153,940	31	57	34,606	613	95,202	78	20,709	4,817	505	2,139
1932	150,472	37	66	37,635	682	88,930	133	19,963	4,238	499	2,527
1933	179,772	26	44	41,061	479	114,590	81	20,786	5,205	339	2,366
1934	184,895	28	72	44,184	286	111,627	44	25,801	5,753	351	2,502
1935	185,861	31	52	44,003	1,751	113,484	69	23,778	6,709	387	2,306
1936	191,002	19	37	44,945	3,029	116,345	69	23,759	6,049	530	2,269
1937	181,769	31	37	40,336	1,471	115,024	36	22,345	5,712	421	2,068
1938	158,217	22	38	37,787	565	99,813	22	17,616	5,995	446	1,908
1939	149,141	15	27	33,448	390	99,622	15	13,727	5,571	219	1,678
1940	186,449	15	22	34,492	269	140,180	16	9,720	5,452	279	1,456
1941	198,066	12	32	33,568	217	154,513	5	7,907	6,091	277	1,535
1942	190,131	16	26	32,309	595	150,705	10	4,581	6,747	263	1,626
1943	206,014	30	39	36,651	169	165,085	20	3,047	8,155	243	730
1944	…	…	…	…	…	…	…	…	…	…	…
1945	…	…	…	…	…	…	…	…	…	…	…
1946	…	…		…	…	…	…	…	…	…	…
1947	…	…		…	…	…	…	…	…	…	…
1948	655,835	116	151	172,838	230	436,273	1,633	29,750	66,914	2,386	12,458
1949	587,240	55	106	131,983	332	379,651	536	62,014	61,401	2,944	9,619
1950	580,990	62	153	125,895	256	285,568	324	137,834	61,116	2,617	28,725
1951	597,844	44	111	117,746	483	284,733	270	163,230	59,067	2,539	29,128
1952	527,743	37	113	106,911	369	273,854	165	136,019	51,863	1,572	8,703
1953	681,448	22	83	94,494	688	329,259	155	252,222	46,100	1,215	3,313
1954	1,027,951	20	76	95,797	732	502,023	140	426,453	47,048	869	1,841
1955	1,328,407	34	92	106,617	970	651,394	136	565,220	51,129	928	3,016
1956	1,447,503	24	83	101,339	936	724,513	110	614,700	50,340	721	5,077
1957	1,710,997	35	83	94,061	900	949,765	141	660,282	46,180	571	5,159
1958	1,737,303	25	87	91,357	1,000	1,060,864	306	581,135	44,123	420	2,109
1959	1,766,742	28	101	90,799	1,403	1,161,129	226	507,852	45,244	464	4,740
1960	2,184,148	12	80	86,396	2,066	1,481,940	113	610,544	45,173	492	2,505
1961	2,548,688	29	69	80,385	2,864	2,375,085	120	86,639	43,552	425	3,072
1962	3,564,892	12	53	76,173	4,332	3,461,124	160	18,712	41,795	513	3,813
1963	3,790,482	12	59	70,999	4,503	3,701,954	154	8,764	39,364	600	3,437
1964	4,144,922	12	75	68,036	5,477	4,060,398	154	6,835	39,512	474	3,461
1965	4,623,128	16	49	72,661	6,667	4,535,314	222	4,965	42,831	410	2,824

Year	Total	Capital Punish-ment	Life imprison-ment with or without labour	Imprison-ment with labour	Imprison-ment without labour	Fine	Penal deten-tion	Minor fine	Proba-tion	Accuit-tal	Others
1966	4,284,968	14	74	71,434	7,380	4,197,963	257	4,799	42,522	448	2,599
1967	4,470,179	6	45	64,126	8,155	4,390,192	229	3,895	40,536	421	3,110
1968	3,069,115	15	48	61,746	9,798	2,989,680	205	3,728	40,550	543	3,352
1969	1,650,666	9	45	57,639	8,719	1,578,585	128	3,193	38,041	483	1,865
1970	1,701,154	9	40	57,347	9,400	1,629,362	71	2,932	38,553	589	1,404
1971	1,878,535	4	38	59,131	10,336	1,804,088	75	2,789	40,490	451	1,623
1972	2,093,032	3	40	63,701	10,436	2,012,050	79	3,827	44,033	425	2,474
1973	2,154,973	4	33	60,500	9,015	2,070,727	59	12,769	41,294	405	1,461
1974	2,147,872	6	24	56,856	7,230	2,061,951	68	18,099	38,956	424	1,214
1975	2,244,419	5	43	63,371	5,877	2,152,506	69	21,024	41,379	347	1,183
1976	2,462,380	4	36	69,535	5,963	2,360,724	89	24,577	45,979	310	1,142
1977	2,655,279	9	51	70,194	5,548	2,551,518	88	26,538	46,069	219	1,114
1978	2,507,041	6	29	72,295	5,258	2,399,845	66	28,401	46,213	24[illegible]	900
1979	2,183,794	7	34	70,950	5,634	2,080,960	51	25,036	46,202	254	868
1980	2,159,766	9	40	70,710	5,770	2,056,065	36	26,078	46,213	187	871
1981	2,198,966	2	34	71,228	4,991	2,095,147	42	26,685	44,317	212	625
1982	2,235,282	11	26	71,845	4,842	2,131,774	40	25,982	43,701	163	599
1983	2,405,857	5	43	72,141	5,068	2,301,509	37	26,285	45,106	141	625
1984	2,498,170	6	38	73,650	5,011	2,388,103	35	30,659	44,974	111	557
1985	2,495,361	9	39	72,245	5,186	2,387,825	86	29,290	44,396	113	568
1986	2,374,301	5	36	69,535	5,321	2,272,034	121	26,480	42,610	115	654
1987	1,704,497	6	65	67,877	5,306	1,608,336	133	22,175	42,074	99	500

Sources: Annual Report of Criminal Statistics,
Annual Report of Judicial Statistics,etc.

Table 8 Number of Average Daily Prisoners and Rate per Population (1926~1988)

Year	Total Population (100,000)	Prisoners	Rate per Population	Year	Total Population (100,000)	Prisoners	Rate per Population
1926	607	39,529	65	1958	918	65,406	71
1927	617	37,633	61	1959	926	66,194	71
1928	626	37,368	60	1960	934	63,329	68
1929	635	35,786	56	1961	943	59,620	63
1930	645	39,030	61	1962	952	56,400	59
1931	655	41,981	64	1963	962	54,897	57
1932	664	43,404	65	1964	972	53,024	55
1933	674	48,062	71	1965	983	52,813	54
1934	683	47,512	70	1966	990	53,736	54
1935	693	49,825	72	1967	1,002	51,928	52
1936	701	51,407	73	1968	1,013	48,094	47
1937	706	50,672	72	1969	1,025	44,438	43
1938	710	48,387	68	1970	1,037	40,917	39
1939	714	44,632	63	1971	1,051	40,039	38
1940	719	38,837	54	1972	1,076	40,509	38
1941	717	38,428	54	1973	1,091	39,949	37
1942	724	39,020	54	1974	1,106	38,598	35
1943	729	41,739	57	1975	1,119	37,850	34
1944	731	51,639	71	1976	1,131	38,469	34
1945	720	48,977	68	1977	1,142	39,225	34
1946	731	44,285	61	1978	1,152	40,795	35
1947	781	61,092	78	1979	1,162	42,041	36
1948	800	73,399	92	1980	1,171	42,142	36
1949	818	78,834	96	1981	1,179	42,580	36
1950	832	85,254	102	1982	1,187	44,214	37
1951	845	80,743	96	1983	1,195	45,304	38
1952	858	72,339	84	1984	1,203	45,035	37
1953	870	65,378	75	1985	1,210	45,805	38
1954	882	63,934	72	1986	1,217	46,107	38
1955	893	66,505	74	1987	1,223	46,076	38
1956	902	68,901	76	1988	1,228	45,909	37
1957	909	67,170	74				

Note : Rate per Population means average daily prisoners per 100,000 population.

Sources: Annual Report of Statistics on Prison Administration, Statistics Bureau, Administration and Coordination Agency, etc.

Year	Releasees	Release by termination of sentence	Parole	Stay of Execution of Sentence	Change of Status	Escape	Death	Others
1966	35,571	15,001(44.2)	18,956(55.8)	182	814	12	106	499
1967	36,380	15,032(43.1)	19,877(56.9)	164	798	9	121	379
1968	34,437	13,723(41.3)	19,523(58.7)	144	651	9	63	324
1969	32,183	11,915(38.3)	19,173(61.7)	144	564	17	90	280
1970	29,835	11,015(38.2)	17,855(61.8)	126	465	13	75	286
1971	29,021	10,639(37.9)	17,462(62.1)	125	393	7	64	331
1972	29,099	11,789(41.8)	16,436(58.2)	118	361	9	57	328
1973	29,160	12,188(43.2)	16,008(56.8)	158	382	4	66	354
1974	28,026	11,655(42.9)	15,536(57.1)	142	345	3	70	275
1975	27,512	11,736(44.0)	14,933(56.0)	109	359	6	83	286
1976	27,926	12,272(45.6)	14,668(54.4)	126	423	6	72	359
1977	28,028	12,709(46.9)	14,381(53.1)	111	408	8	73	338
1978	29,168	13,750(48.9)	14,373(51.1)	98	440	3	68	436
1979	29,594	14,010(48.9)	14,638(51.1)	92	423	3	47	381
1980	30,215	14,140(48.2)	15,202(51.8)	99	365	2	64	343
1981	30,461	14,463(49.0)	15,040(51.0)	103	399	4	63	389
1982	31,361	14,901(49.2)	15,381(50.8)	94	526	—	65	394
1983	32,464	14,561(46.3)	16,885(53.7)	99	554	2	78	285
1984	33,644	13,791(42.4)	18,716(57.6)	96	649	5	78	309
1985	33,033	14,143(44.3)	17,795(55.7)	85	619	4	90	297
1986	32,893	13,687(43.0)	18,130(57.0)	82	615	3	92	284
1987	32,108	13,413(43.2)	17,603(56.8)	77	624	3	89	299
1988	30,828	13,300(44.6)	16,540(55.4)	66	540	—	94	288

Sources: Annual Report of Statistics on Prison Administration,
Annual Report of Statistics on Correction

Table 9 Number of Prisoners, by Cases of Release (1926~1988)

Year	Releasees	Release by termination of sentence	Parole	Stay of Execution of Sentence	Change of Status	Escape	Death	Others
1926	29,570	26,573(94.3)	1,605(5.7)	305	647	15	424	1
1927	32,778	29,610(95.5)	1,411(4.5)	349	712	19	412	265
1928	30,356	27,188(94.9)	1,476(5.1)	281	619	3	396	393
1929	28,216	25,846(95.8)	1,145(4.2)	251	591	11	351	21
1930	29,560	26,976(96.3)	1,050(3.7)	225	856	15	438	—
1931	32,918	29,686(94.7)	1,669(5.3)	219	910	6	428	—
1932	32,215	28,292(92.3)	2,346(7.7)	224	943	8	399	3
1933	35,922	30,623(89.9)	3,453(10.1)	234	1,142	8	461	1
1934	43,179	36,476(89.4)	4,315(10.6)	274	1,359	7	507	241
1935	38,977	31,931(86.7)	4,905(13.3)	243	1,384	20	494	—
1936	40,935	33,377(86.4)	5,272(13.6)	313	1,387	4	582	—
1937	41,626	32,646(82.9)	6,743(17.1)	309	1,281	8	639	—
1938	36,838	28,360(81.5)	6,428(18.5)	277	1,018	16	738	1
1939	31,875	25,161(83.1)	5,122(16.9)	210	710	18	654	—
1940	33,724	27,920(87.3)	4,078(12.7)	189	582	31	717	207
1941	27,536	21,445(82.4)	4,568(17.6)	211	460	23	827	2
1942	26,367	21,014(85.2)	3,652(14.8)	221	400	30	1,048	2
1943	26,991	20,360(81.4)	4,641(18.6)	258	366	62	1,304	—
1944	31,422	18,740(69.1)	8,367(30.9)	582	313	104	3,316	—
1945	48,653	16,189(44.9)	19,895(55.1)	2,317	113	541	7,284	2,314
1946	47,405	10,201(26.0)	28,989(74.0)	3,418	90	391	3,768	548
1947	57,953	15,730(30.8)	35,344(69.2)	3,302	181	505	1,154	1,737
1948	59,094	11,831(21.4)	43,446(78.6)	1,454	154	402	812	995
1949	56,460	10,952(20.3)	43,087(79.7)	884	170	251	604	512
1950	59,675	15,445(26.8)	42,141(73.2)	619	438	152	516	364
1951	56,853	15,653(28.3)	39,625(71.7)	419	367	89	373	327
1952	71,284	21,018(31.8)	44,980(68.2)	407	436	74	263	4,106
1953	50,592	16,547(33.2)	33,223(66.8)	211	…	53	226	332
1954	50,491	16,732(33.9)	32,636(66.1)	347	…	48	240	488
1955	51,588	18,322(36.3)	32,198(63.7)	335	…	32	167	534
1956	52,133	16,523(32.3)	34,705(67.7)	330	…	19	182	374
1957	51,254	15,163(30.2)	35,105(69.8)	380	…	28	215	363
1958	47,549	14,844(31.8)	31,893(68.2)	316	…	17	148	331
1959	47,391	14,949(32.4)	31,180(67.6)	708	…	25	170	359
1960	46,562	14,179(31.6)	30,751(68.4)	1,067	…	27	159	379
1961	42,528	14,484(35.2)	26,679(64.8)	861	…	24	100	380
1962	40,117	14,333(37.1)	24,352(62.9)	175	710	17	139	391
1963	37,883	14,375(39.5)	22,022(60.5)	166	767	30	106	417
1964	36,147	14,224(41.0)	20,437(59.0)	152	780	22	90	441
1965	35,488	14,546(42.8)	19,432(57.2)	152	802	14	96	446

Table 10 Number of Probationers and Parolees Newly Received by Probation Offices (1949∼1988)

Year	Total	Juvenile Probation-ers	Parolees from Train-ing Schools	Parolees from Prisons	Adult Probation-ers	Parolees from Womens Guidance Homes
1949	36,221	6,317	848	27,799	1,257	—
1950	59,739	13,291	3,121	43,106	221	—
1951	69,446	23,612	5,505	40,147	182	—
1952	77,999	22,657	9,704	45,465	173	—
1953	58,237	16,994	7,724	33,427	92	—
1954	59,206	16,702	7,295	32,824	2,385	—
1955	61,265	17,094	7,375	32,435	4,361	—
1956	65,893	17,003	7,161	34,821	6,908	—
1957	68,699	19,253	6,427	35,290	7,729	—
1958	67,592	20,763	6,481	32,046	8,282	20
1959	70,361	23,410	7,256	31,230	8,369	96
1960	71,720	24,408	7,797	30,824	8,525	166
1961	65,319	22,757	7,206	26,708	8,562	86
1962	61,158	21,607	6,598	24,356	8,556	41
1963	59,310	22,569	6,456	22,043	8,216	26
1964	60,513	26,044	6,143	20,432	7,883	11
1965	62,258	28,173	6,301	19,430	8,350	4
1966	64,542	30,647	6,423	18,953	8,513	6
1967	62,950	29,055	6,240	19,871	7,779	5
1968	60,643	28,549	5,016	19,534	7,542	2
1969	56,228	25,999	3,895	19,171	7,161	2
1970	55,320	27,383	3,167	17,861	6,908	1
1971	52,525	25,403	2,888	17,458	6,771	5
1972	50,096	23,900	2,540	16,427	7,228	1
1973	46,088	20,686	2,188	16,024	7,187	3
1974	44,310	19,942	1,812	15,542	7,014	—
1975	44,958	21,384	1,593	14,933	7,048	—
1976	48,791	23,981	2,071	14,671	8,068	—
1977	58,774	33,735	2,763	14,379	7,897	—
1978	70,874	44,934	3,066	14,373	8,501	—
1979	76,226	50,031	3,440	14,625	8,128	2
1980	83,652	56,322	4,063	15,206	8,058	3
1981	86,871	59,214	4,285	15,036	8,336	—
1982	91,711	63,519	4,644	15,385	8,223	—
1983	100,019	70,385	4,945	16,890	7,798	1
1984	102,737	70,758	5,569	18,718	7,692	—
1985	101,971	71,411	5,585	17,795	7,180	—
1986	102,434	72,268	5,580	18,130	6,456	—
1987	100,140	70,747	5,313	17,603	6,477	—
1988	95,736	68,367	4,753	16,540	6,076	—

Sources: Annual Report of Justice Statistics and Annual Report of Statistics on Rehabilitation

Table 11 Number of Pardons on Day-by-Day Basis Dispensed by NORC (1949~1988)

Year	Total Number	Adequacy					Inadequacy					Others
		Total	Pardons	Commutation of sentence	Reprieve	Restoration of civil right	Total	Pardons	Commutation of sentence	Reprieve	Restoration of civil right	
1949	81	49	26	17	2	4	32	1	26	3	2	—
1950	371	255	206	34	6	9	116	14	98	—	4	—
1951	510	405	373	14	9	9	105	5	64	6	30	—
1952	1,306	939	494	354	65	26	367	117	208	38	4	—
1953	4,543	3,613	2,063	1,391	135	24	930	39	861	21	9	—
1954	172	89	9	45	20	15	83	5	58	15	5	—
1955	240	140	12	48	40	40	100	2	85	9	4	—
1956	156	86	4	24	31	27	70	—	59	3	8	—
1957	270	120	17	38	48	17	150	3	136	4	7	—
1958	109	44	—	11	14	19	65	2	48	9	6	—
1959	100	53	5	20	15	13	47	2	34	4	7	—
1960	134	56	18	9	6	23	78	14	58	3	3	—
1961	87	47	9	6	8	24	40	4	23	4	9	—
1962	119	66	6	11	15	34	53	4	27	5	17	—
1963	107	44	1	7	9	27	59	8	37	3	11	4
1964	81	45	1	11	11	22	34	—	19	4	11	2
1965	98	46	1	5	14	26	50	3	19	8	20	2
1966	299	230	1	4	7	218	67	6	50	—	11	2
1967	671	361	4	21	25	311	302	55	114	2	131	8
1968	128	87	7	28	20	32	20	1	12	4	3	21
1969	929	852	410	170	106	166	55	5	42	2	6	22
1970	195	171	35	45	36	55	21	5	7	4	5	3
1971	326	225	33	29	54	109	90	20	31	14	25	11
1972	376	314	133	19	46	116	41	9	18	4	10	21
1973	692	414	105	47	97	165	265	28	186	28	23	13
1974	257	202	26	35	55	86	53	15	20	4	14	2
1975	316	256	16	43	58	139	46	20	8	3	15	14
1976	271	223	4	19	45	155	48	5	16	5	22	—
1977	329	204	—	9	30	165	116	2	29	7	68	9
1978	292	246	5	7	47	187	39	11	12	1	25	7
1979	221	175	—	4	28	143	40	2	23	4	11	6
1980	239	194	2	2	30	160	31	3	8	6	14	14
1981	188	120	—	—	29	91	64	4	9	11	40	4
1982	254	203	2	—	43	158	49	7	13	2	27	2
1983	275	218	—	1	59	158	54	6	14	6	28	3
1984	268	235	—	—	38	197	31	2	5	4	20	2
1985	238	187	—	1	45	141	48	3	1	12	32	3
1986	263	199	1	—	47	151	63	5	19	6	33	1
1987	181	96	1	—	22	73	78	4	6	15	53	7
1988	172	111	—	—	14	97	59	1	—	13	45	2

Sources: Annual Report of Justice Ministry, Annual Report of Statistics on Rehabilitation, etc.

Table 12 Number of Penal Code Offenders Cleared by the Police, and Rate per population by Juveniles and Adults (1936～1988)

Year	Juveniles		Adults		Percent of juveniles
	Number	Rate per 1,000 juveniles	Number	Rate per 1,000 adults	
1936	46,550	3.2	…	…	…
1937	46,046	3.1	…	…	…
1938	48,933	3.2	…	…	…
1939	48,367	3.1	…	…	…
1940	53,048	3.4	…	…	…
1941	52,709	…	281,708	…	15.8
1942	66,588	…	232,807	…	22.2
1943	61,366	…	285,343	…	17.7
1944	75,314	4.6	235,637	6.0	24.2
1945	54,787	3.3	187,858	5.0	22.6
1946	111,790	6.7	333,694	8.4	25.1
1947	104,829	6.1	354,510	8.4	22.8
1948	124,836	7.3	425,704	9.8	22.7
1949	131,916	7.7	453,412	10.2	22.5
1950	158,426	9.2	458,297	10.1	25.7
1951	166,433	9.5	452,602	9.8	26.9
1952	143,247	8.0	432,605	9.1	24.9
1953	126,097	7.0	421,453	8.7	23.0
1954	120,413	6.6	419,376	8.4	22.3
1955	121,753	6.7	437,104	8.6	21.8
1956	127,421	7.1	427,192	8.2	23.0
1957	144,506	7.9	430,255	8.1	25.1
1958	155,373	8.1	420,893	7.8	27.0
1959	176,899	8.8	417,455	7.6	29.8
1960	196,682	9.7	413,565	7.4	32.2
1961	216,456	10.6	422,430	7.4	33.9
1962	220,749	10.8	406,925	6.9	35.2
1963	229,717	11.3	432,298	7.2	34.7
1964	238,830	11.9	488,080	8.0	32.9
1965	234,959	11.7	515,963	8.3	31.3
1966	226,203	11.2	547,866	8.7	29.2
1967	215,477	11.1	617,984	9.5	25.9
1968	218,950	11.8	734,819	11.0	23.0
1969	218,458	12.4	812,952	11.9	21.2
1970	224,943	13.3	883,254	12.6	20.3
1971	214,799	13.0	845,590	11.9	20.3
1972	198,441	12.1	814,394	11.2	19.6
1973	202,297	12.5	767,778	10.4	20.9
1974	198,763	12.3	689,787	9.2	22.4
1975	196,974	12.1	668,802	8.7	22.8

Table 13 Number of Juvenile Penal Code Offenders Cleared by the Police, by Major Offence (1936~1988)

Year	Theft	Fraud	Embezzlement	Assault	Bodily injury	Intimidation	Extortion	Rape	Indecent assault	Homicide	Robbery	Arson
1936	29,750	3,297	3,491	…	2,555	…	…	197	76	153	311	266
1937	29,783	3,006	3,269	…	2,631	…	…	172	79	155	310	272
1938	32,503	2,973	3,207	…	2,596	…	…	211	88	161	302	279
1939	31,409	2,787	2,801	…	3,073	…	…	217	87	123	310	291
1940	35,999	2,361	2,485	…	1,901	…	…	230	188	146	475	263
1941	36,954	2,028	2,111	…	2,997	…	…	255	180	107	436	256
1942	47,267	2,184	4,028	…	3,106	…	…	328	361	126	406	213
1943	45,113	1,552	1,358	…	2,998	…	…	335	439	94	377	204
1944	54,852	1,767	1,148	…	2,968	…	…	294	417	177	442	215
1945	42,818	1,044	,603	…	1,746	…	…	218	308	149	455	92
1946	87,825	3,193	1,132	…	2,874	…	…	258	282	249	2,903	164
1947	77,514	2,999	1,209	…	3,059	…	…	298	163	216	2,851	116
1948	90,066	4,173	2,020		* (1,904) **6,826			584	272	354	3,878	173
1949	94,214	4,470	2,475		14,203			1,176	283	344	2,866	340
1950	111,526	6,368	3,148		19,698			1,538	447	369	2,897	470
1951	127,122	4,886	3,142	3,126	8,653	461	3,635	1,530	347	448	2,197	446
1952	104,344	4,954	3,117	3,243	8,519	459	3,285	1,870	338	393	1,956	530
1953	88,586	4,875	3,155	3,339	7,992	416	2,819	1,535	407	383	1,582	410
1954	81,298	4,310	2,787	3,245	9,195	448	3,041	1,977	459	411	1,830	407
1955	80,626	3,885	2,393	3,784	10,329	485	4,007	2,121	495	345	2,003	328
1956	80,770	3,122	2,005		23,107			2,053	600	324	2,033	321
1957	86,065	3,318	2,095		30,590			2,865	689	313	2,222	334
1958	83,528	2,860	1,723	10,250	15,939	840	11,948	4,649	1,044	366	2,405	412
1959	96,793	2,549	1,655	11,165	16,410	854	14,013	4,599	1,114	422	2,624	445
1960	110,752	2,388	1,655	10,897	16,268	940	14,564	4,407	1,265	438	2,762	605
1961	127,234	2,331	1,482	11,490	17,197	982	14,834	4,224	1,320	448	2,442	694
1962	132,096	1,870	1,242	11,842	16,164	1,031	15,771	3,983	1,473	343	2,307	642
1963	136,027	1,778	1,227	12,793	15,290	1,117	15,829	3,898	1,550	393	2,139	530
1964	135,849	1,781	1,123	13,881	16,669	1,252	15,228	4,242	1,630	361	1,987	535
1965	128,341	1,711	1,145	13,705	15,774	1,141	13,506	4,362	1,759	370	1,998	513
1966	117,938	1,803	1,014	13,652	16,221	1,049	11,014	4,281	1,772	368	1,901	381
1967	104,206	1,487	945	12,011	15,280	786	8,557	3,851	1,698	343	1,500	375
1968	109,266	1,067	839	9,645	12,543	593	6,702	3,294	1,506	286	1,261	390
1969	96,032	833	927	8,518	10,867	448	5,867	2,515	1,371	265	1,198	534
1970	106,359	722	1,107	8,962	10,211	450	6,909	2,212	1,208	198	1,092	469
1971	102,671	629	1,441	7,892	8,500	349	6,860	2,022	1,043	149	869	585
1972	103,451	561	2,062	6,784	7,091	231	6,029	1,818	966	149	790	351
1973	111,529	487	3,079	6,946	7,923	286	5,796	1,526	863	111	705	394
1974	116,863	418	3,252	7,246	7,293	233	5,987	1,499	716	102	677	370
1975	116,849	517	3,770	6,814	7,302	354	6,681	1,341	685	95	732	387

Year	Juveniles		Adults		Percent of juveniles
	Number	Rate per 1,000 juveniles	Number	Rate per 1,000 adults	
1976	194,024	12.1	671,229	8.6	22.4
1977	197,909	12.1	659,747	8.4	23.1
1978	224,095	13.5	660,361	8.3	25.3
1979	233,292	13.8	648,722	8.1	26.4
1980	269,769	15.7	653,958	8.1	29.2
1981	303,915	17.2	668,634	8.1	31.2
1982	310,828	17.2	699,149	8.4	30.8
1983	317,438	17.1	710,957	8.5	30.9
1984	301,252	16.0	715,986	8.4	29.6
1985	304,088	16.0	722,296	8.4	29.6
1986	292,290	15.1	725,510	8.4	28.7
1987	289,196	15.0	735,521	8.4	28.2
1988	292,902	15.3	733,886	8.3	28.5

Note : Rate per 1,000 juveniles means the number of juveniles and child Penal Code offenders per 1,000 juvenile aged 10 through 19, and Rate per 1,000 adults means the number of adults Penal Code offenders per 1,000 adults aged 20 and over.

Sources: National Police Agency and Statistics Bureau, Management and Coordination Agency.

Year	Theft	Fraud	Embezzlement	Assault	Bodily injury	Intimidation	Extortion	Rape	Indecent Assault	Homicide	Robbery	Arson
1976	116,838	520	4,522	6,162	6,940	179	5,314	1,035	623	80	618	393
1977	119,805	471	6,101	6,384	7,357	205	4,527	949	708	77	529	453
1978	140,611	547	7,748	6,724	7,120	245	4,150	946	746	91	522	446
1979	146,469	504	9,533	6,167	7,030	160	3,996	925	709	97	572	510
1980	172,842	556	12,612	7,633	9,068	206	4,830	984	720	49	788	478
1981	197,397	538	15,582	8,918	10,415	202	6,358	1,027	778	60	779	527
1982	198,701	591	17,666	8,409	11,635	171	8,417	878	823	86	806	574
1983	202,028	662	19,624	7,660	11,406	158	8,504	750	756	87	788	389
1984	190,420	744	22,848	6,450	11,594	100	8,192	757	714	76	690	383
1985	191,238	770	22,658	6,062	10,612	193	8,185	681	760	100	572	364
1986	177,766	696	21,042	5,842	10,860	119	9,173	635	640	96	708	343
1987	173,029	828	22,958	4,462	9,977	113	7,357	567	581	79	604	330
1988	175,734	1,036	24,616	3,992	10,154	122	6,914	509	593	82	569	273

Source: National Police Agency

Table 14 Number of Juveniles Adjudicated by Juvenile Tribunals (1923~1948)

Year	Total	Dismissal without hearing	Protective				
			Total	Admonish-ment	admonishment by the Principal	Written oath	hand to parents
1923	10,099	8,384	1,658	120	2	76	513
1924	11,733	8,423	3,271	193	2	180	1,331
1925	14,938	10,729	4,154	296	1	195	1,845
1926	16,000	11,078	4,885	514	1	233	1,957
1927	13,880	9,052	4,803	350	1	217	1,987
1928	13,039	8,405	4,605	334	—	153	1,899
1929	12,989	8,325	4,636	262	—	102	2,006
1930	13,441	8,893	4,528	261	—	78	2,108
1931	13,804	9,127	4,647	336	—	61	2,175
1932	14,151	9,148	4,984	321	—	92	2,352
1933	16,883	11,557	5,306	342	—	91	2,676
1934	24,316	16,900	7,326	600	—	90	4,005
1935	22,521	15,264	7,158	602	—	63	4,051
1936	22,118	14,344	7,682	758	—	79	4,259
1937	20,879	12,178	8,626	950	2	80	4,618
1938	25,803	16,643	9,064	843	1	124	5,105
1939	22,295	13,083	9,110	732	—	118	5,150
1940	21,607	11,281	10,188	933	—	102	6,119
1941	24,817	9,408	15,105	1,116	4	268	9,820
1942	30,452	7,286	22,380	1,964	4	550	13,576
1943	32,670	4,458	27,471	1,219	—	7,204	6,646
1944	35,285	5,133	29,433	1,366	1	5,425	5,238
1945	22,397	3,950	18,133	881	1	1,991	4,965
1946	45,079	11,442	31,306	1,040	4	4,797	11,833
1947	39,410	6,110	31,389	1,740	15	4,909	11,798
1948	51,001	9,436	40,576	2,087	23	5,528	16,515

Rehabilitative Dispositions					Referral to a public prosecutor	Referral to another tribunal
Entrustment to a protective organization	Probation by a juvenile probation officer	Commitment to a reformationary school	Commitment to a house of corrections	Commitment to a hospital		
147	748	7	45	—	28	29
386	1,046	6	127	—	17	22
652	1,129	5	31	—	20	35
875	1,223	4	77	1	6	31
963	1,226	3	55	1	4	21
1,002	1,116	3	98	—	9	20
967	1,213	—	86	—	2	26
954	1,079	—	48	—	3	17
1,000	1,005	1	69	—	7	23
1,101	1,045	—	73	—	1	18
1,176	955	—	66	—	—	20
1,253	1,259	—	119	—	2	88
1,118	1,220	1	102	1	1	98
1,193	1,296	—	96	1	3	89
1,376	1,508	—	92	—	2	73
1,285	1,548	—	158	—	1	95
1,367	1,600	—	143	—	3	99
1,366	1,562	—	106	—	—	138
1,692	1,971	—	233	1	—	304
2,411	3,512	5	357	1	1	785
4,585	5,771	3	2,040	3	—	741
8,565	6,105	—	2,733	—	—	719
5,593	2,926	3	1,773	—	—	314
6,556	5,411	10	1,654	1	4	2,327
5,497	5,897	37	1,490	6	24	1,887
5,721	8,469	94	2,120	19	29	960

Source: Summary of Justice Ministry

Table 15 Number of Ordinal Juvenile Cases Adjudicated by Family Courts (1951~1987)

Year	Total	Referral to prosecutors: Deserved Criminal Disposition	Referral to prosecutors: Over Limited age	Commitment to J.T.S.	Probationary supervision	Commitment to Reformatory school, etc.	Governor or Child Center	Dismissal after hearing	Dismissal without hearing
1951	134,946	7,582	…	12,132	25,414	240	885	34,954	53,739
1952	120,475	4,086	1,154	9,496	21,256	232	757	36,850	46,644
1953	102,990	2,581	1,056	7,915	15,773	208	439	33,194	41,824
1954	94,131	2,157	1,077	7,721	14,788	190	432	29,028	38,738
1955	96,640	2,448	949	7,579	15,268	180	508	29,184	40,524
1956	90,558	2,722	829	6,847	14,402	174	564	29,348	35,672
1957	101,315	3,238	977	7,162	15,748	183	497	30,390	43,120
1958	107,249	3,308	887	7,649	16,314	194	524	31,678	46,695
1959	116,359	4,049	926	8,356	18,404	226	592	32,691	51,115
1960	133,616	4,291	957	8,137	19,127	178	547	33,695	66,684
1961	138,143	3,887	852	7,994	18,993	215	667	32,073	73,462
1962	143,585	3,461	706	7,493	17,569	310	773	32,747	80,526
1963	158,761	3,125	702	6,873	17,193	223	635	33,495	96,515
1964	157,460	2,886	605	7,360	18,331	231	606	35,521	91,920
1965	158,963	3,119	488	7,079	19,262	228	561	39,862	88,364
1966	160,211	3,959	519	7,499	20,135	200	490	40,595	86,814
1967	144,923	3,619	555	6,130	17,411	158	365	35,462	81,223
1968	130,732	3,075	526	4,891	15,584	150	311	32,242	73,953
1969	112,930	2,459	489	3,962	12,790	122	297	27,974	64,837
1970	114,680	2,009	414	3,599	12,168	115	230	28,457	67,688
1971	112,340	1,415	402	2,898	10,993	115	246	28,786	67,485
1972	104,780	1,134	316	2,525	9,427	118	217	28,240	62,803
1973	107,396	1,056	318	1,977	8,100	89	226	27,497	68,133
1974	115,016	842	273	1,756	7,968	111	159	28,636	75,271
1975	118,575	856	257	2,230	8,656	115	168	28,510	77,783
1976	126,803	645	329	2,281	9,353	114	190	30,521	83,370
1977	125,843	501	307	2,697	8,821	117	162	28,646	84,592
1978	139,463	613	322	3,185	10,535	110	117	29,375	95,206
1979	155,787	645	416	3,385	11,334	127	135	31,905	107,840
1980	172,855	829	435	3,894	13,786	143	153	33,546	120,069
1981	188,541	768	453	4,191	14,139	165	160	35,880	132,785
1982	198,441	862	462	4,393	15,362	179	189	38,248	138,746
1983	199,202	1,008	473	4,758	15,171	192	183	38,049	139,368
1984	192,167	993	468	5,145	15,784	209	182	37,787	131,599
1985	191,342	854	490	5,173	15,026	199	175	35,574	133,851
1986	191,625	824	381	4,995	14,991	254	150	34,655	135,375
1987	189,014	859	457	4,493	14,133	209	212	32,374	136,277

Source: Annual Report of Juvenile Statistics

Table 16 Number of Average Daily Inmates in Juvenile Classification Homes and Rate per Population (1949~1988)

Year	Newly admitted inmates				Average Daily Inmates	Rate of Juve-niles
	Total	Boy	Girl	Rate of girls		
1949	16,094	14,599	1,495	9.3	658	15.7
1950	19,486	17,772	1,714	8.8	904	18.8
1951	40,820	37,020	3,800	9.3	2,130	39.0
1952	36,822	33,567	3,255	8.8	2,045	35.2
1953	31,488	28,335	3,153	10.0	1,806	30.5
1954	30,727	27,660	3,067	10.0	1,788	29.4
1955	31,031	28,274	2,757	8.9	1,807	29.3
1956	29,332	26,819	2,513	8.6	1,671	27.2
1957	31,610	28,621	2,989	9.5	1,775	28.9
1958	34,027	30,819	3,208	9.4	1,925	30.3
1959	37,413	33,925	3,488	9.3	2,128	33.2
1960	38,661	35,366	3,295	8.5	2,157	35.7
1961	37,591	34,297	3,294	8.8	2,089	33.4
1962	35,856	32,656	3,200	8.9	1,971	30.5
1963	34,489	31,349	3,140	9.1	1,922	28.0
1964	35,267	32,170	3,097	8.8	1,981	28.0
1965	35,289	31,979	3,310	9.4	2,024	27.3
1966	35,892	32,603	3,289	9.2	2,045	26.8
1967	30,814	27,962	2,852	9.3	1,739	23.9
1968	27,474	24,730	2,744	10.0	1,526	22.6
1969	23,113	21,004	2,109	9.1	1,303	20.3
1970	19,633	17,911	1,722	8.8	1,084	18.4
1971	16,451	14,845	1,606	9.8	902	16.2
1972	13,930	12,579	1,351	9.7	788	14.0
1973	11,235	10,078	1,157	10.3	637	11.5
1974	10,410	9,352	1,058	10.2	593	10.8
1975	11,261	10,026	1,235	11.0	646	11.8
1976	11,264	9,910	1,354	12.0	649	11.9
1977	12,191	10,482	1,709	14.0	700	12.7
1978	14,198	12,178	2,020	14.2	833	14.6
1979	15,486	13,281	2,205	14.2	916	15.7
1980	18,421	16,055	2,366	12.8	1,101	19.0
1981	20,023	17,473	2,550	12.7	1,203	20.0
1982	20,659	17,949	2,710	13.1	1,239	20.1
1983	21,854	18,754	3,100	14.2	1,321	20.8
1984	22,593	19,167	3,426	15.2	1,386	21.0
1985	22,126	18,850	3,276	14.8	1,359	20.2
1986	21,014	17,962	3,052	14.5	1,302	18.2
1987	20,333	17,280	3,053	15.0	1,258	17.3
1988	19,372	16,397	2,975	15.4	1,195	16.2

Note : Rate of juveniles means the number of newly admitted inmates aged from 14 to 19 per 10,000 juveniles.

Sources: Annual Statistics on Juvenile Correction, Annual Statistics on Correction, etc.

LIST OF FIGURES AND TABLES

Chapter II CRIME TRENDS

Section 2. Trends of Penal Code offences

Section 3. *Trends in Special Law Offences*

Section 4. *Comparison of Crime Trends in Foreign Countries*

Section 5. Trends in Crimes by Gang Organizations

Chapter III TREATMENT OF OFFENDERS

Section 1. Prosecution and Trials

Section 2. Correction

Section 3. *Rehabilitation of Offenders*

Chapter IV JUVENILE DELINQUENCY AND TREATMENT OF DELINQUENTS

Section 1. *Trends in Juvenile Delinquency*

Section 2. Treatment of Juvenile Delinquents

List of Tables in the APPENDIX I

BIBLIOGRAPHY

1 "Criminal Justice in Japan" Ministry of Justice (Tokyo 1960)

2 "Juvenile Delinpuency in Japan" Ministry of Justice (Tokyo 1958)

3 "Law of Penal Code" Ministry of Justice (translation)

4 "Law of Penal Code Procedure" Ministry of Justice (translation)

5 "Court Organization Law and Public Prosecutors Office Law" Ministry of Justice (1979) (translation)

6 "Juvenile Law" Ministry of Justice (translation)

7 "Japanese Legal System" Hideo Tanaka (ed.) University of Tokyo Prese

8 "Japanese Criminal Procedure" Shigemitsu Dando, Fred B. Rothman & Co. (1965)

9 "Laws for Correction and Rehabilitation of Offenders" Ministry of Justice

10 "Correctional Institutions in Japan" Correction Bureau, Ministry of Justice (1990)

11 "The Penal Institution Bill" The Japanese Correctional Association (1989)

12 "Community-based Treatment of Offenders in Japan" Rehabilitation Bureau, Ministry of Justice (1990)

13 "Summary of the White Paper on Crime" from 1975 to 1988 Research and Traing Institute, Ministry of Justice

14 "Resource Material Serieses" No.1-No.33 United Nations Asia Far East Institute for Prevention of Crim and Treatment of Offenders (UNAFEI) (1962-1988)

15 "Bulletin of the Criminological Research Department" No.1-No.32 Research and Training Institute, Ministry of Justice

16 "Crime Prevention for Freedom, Justice, Peace and Development" National Statement of Japan for the Seventh United Nations Congress (1985)

17 "Court and Constitution in Japan" John M. Maki University of Tokyo Press. (1962)

18 "A Preparatory Draft for the Revised Penal Code of Japan" B.J.George, Jr. Sweet & Maxwell Limited (1961)

19 "The Constitztion of Japan Its First Twenty Years" Dan Fenno Henderson (ed.) University of Washington Press. (1978)

20 "Conciliation and Japanese Law Tokugawa and Modern" Dan Fenno Henderson (ed.) University of Washington Press.

21 "Law in Japan" Arthur Taylor von Mehren (ed.) Harvard University Press. (1963)

22 "Crim Control in Japan" William Clifford Lexington Books (1976)

23 "Public Administration in Japan" IIAS Tokyo Round Table Organizing Committee c/o Administrative Management Agency (1982)

INDEX

K

L

M

Multiple Problem Youth:
Delinquency, Substance Use, and Mental Health Problems
D.S. Elliott, D. Huizinga and S. Menard

Selective Incapacitation and the Serious Offender:
A Longitudinal Study of Criminal Career Patterns
Rudy A. Haapanen

Deterrence and Juvenile Crime: Results from a National Policy Experiment
Anne L. Schneider

Developments in Crime and Crime Control Research: German Studies on Victims Offenders and the Public
Klaus Sessar and Hans-Jürgen Kerner (Eds.)

Human Development and Criminal Behavior: News Ways of Advancing Knowledge
Michael Tonry, Lloyd E. Ohlin, and David P. Farrington, with contributions by Kenneth Adams, Felton Earls, David C. Rowe, Robert J. Sampson, and Richard E. Tremblay

Urban Crime, Criminals, and Victims: The Swedish Experience in an Anglo-American Comparative Perspective
Per-Olof Wikström

Understanding Crime Incidence Statistics:
Why the UCR Diverges From the NCS
Albert D. Biderman and James P. Lynch

Crime and Criminal Policy in Japan:
Analysis and Evaluation of the Showa Era, 1926–1988
Minoru Shikita and Shinichi Tsuchiya